D1879793

THE PARSI RELIGION

THE PARSI RELIGION

As Contained In The Zand-Avastá And Propounded And Defended By The Zoroastrians Of India And Persia, Unfolded, Refuted, and Contrasted with Christianity

By

John Wilson D.D., M.R.A.S.,

GYAN

Published by

GYAN

Gyan Publishing House
5, Ansari Road
Daryaganj, New Delhi-110002
Phone: 011-47034999, 9811692060
E-mail: books@gyanbooks.com

Distribution Network
gyanbooks.com
India, USA, Canada, UK, Australia, France

© Publisher

All rights reserved. No part of this work may be reproduced, stored, adapted, or transmitted in any form or by any means, electronic, mechanical, photocopying, micro-filming, recording or otherwise, or translated in any language, without the prior written permission of the copyright owner and the publisher.

ISBN : 978-81-212-6258-3 (PB)
First Published, 1843

2nd Impression 2022

Printed at: Gyan Press, Delhi.

The book is sold subject to the condition that it shall not, by way of trade or otherwise, be lent, resold, hired out, or otherwise circulated without the prior publisher's written consent.

THE PARSI RELIGION
Author: John Wilson D.D.

THE PÁRSÍ RELIGION:

AS CONTAINED IN THE

ZAND-AVASTÁ,

AND

PROPOUNDED AND DEFENDED BY THE ZOROASTRIANS OF INDIA AND PERSIA,

UNFOLDED, REFUTED, AND CONTRASTED WITH CHRISTIANITY.

BY JOHN WILSON, D.D., M.R.A.S.,

PRESIDENT OF THE BOMBAY BRANCH OF THE ROYAL ASIATIC SOCIETY, AND MISSIONARY OF THE CHURCH OF SCOTLAND, BOMBAY.

Λογῳ καὶ τὴν ἄγνοιαν ἤλεγξε καὶ τὴν ἀλήθειαν ἔδειξε.

Theodoritus.

The course of argument and fair reason cannot be impeded.

Bombay Government.

1843.

TO THE OFFICE-BEARERS AND MEMBERS

OF THE

BOMBAY BRANCH OF THE ROYAL ASIATIC SOCIETY.

GENTLEMEN,

I beg leave to inscribe to you this volume, in token of my gratitude for the kindness and indulgence extended to me while very imperfectly discharging the duties, and supporting the honours, of your Chair, and for the warm interest which many of you individually have taken in my labours to disseminate useful, but more especially divine, knowledge among the natives of this great country, whose present social and moral condition, as well as past history, it is one of the principal objects of our Society to investigate and unfold.

I am, Gentlemen,

Yours very respectfully,

JOHN WILSON.

Bombay, December, 1842.

PREFACE.

The Religion of the Pársís, notwithstanding the puerilities and absurdities with which it is now associated, is substantially the same, in its general principles, at the present day, that it was in the ages of antiquity. As that of the united hosts of Medes and Persians, who were providentially instrumental in the destruction of the mighty power of Babylon, and the deliverance of the Jews, the favoured depositaries of divine knowledge during the general apostasy of the world from God, — who, in the noon-day splendour of their reign, ruled over the larger portion of the Greater and Lesser Asia—who attempted to crush the infant liberties of Europe in the Grecian States, — who carried their victorious arms to the north of Africa, and usurped for a season the rule of the Pharaohs in the land of Egypt, — who, after having for centuries succumbed to Macedonian and Parthian rule, recovered their freedom, and first set limits to the Roman Empire in the East, — who long formed a barrier to the irruption of the barbarous hordes of Scythians and Huns and Turks, by whom the civilized world was ultimately inundated, — and whose signal achievements and failures, from the very dawn of profane authentic record, have so much employed the pen of the historian, it is not without high interest in the history of the speculations and errors of the human mind. It did not form an element in the greatness of its professors, for, — except in the circumstance that it discarded the use of the works of men's hands, both as the emblems and special residences of the divinity, —it was perhaps inferior in its elements and institutions to the forms of faith professed by at least some of the surrounding nations; but on this very account it merits attention, affording, as it does, an illustration of the almost unbounded scope which the human mind will indolently, or actively, give to the device and practice of vanity, and,— I will add,—folly and impiety, in connexion with its professed intercommunion with the powers of the unseen world. Its internal energy was happily too weak to resist the influence of the Christian teacher in the early ages of the Church ; and it called for, and used, the sword, by the cruel hands of the descendants of Sásán, to oppose the progress of the truth, till such time as it was foiled, and nearly annihilated, by its own weapon, wielded by the Saracen invader. In the solitudes of Yazd and Kirmán, and in the busy scenes of commerce on the Western shores of India, it has still a remnant of adherents, to be reclaimed, it is to be hoped speedily, from the vain traditions received from their fathers, by the still small voice of the Gospel ; and it is worthy of attention by all who have dealings with them, and especially by those who entertain philanthropic desires on their behalf. Much has been done towards its elucidation by our learned countryman Dr. Hyde, who first made it the subject of an elaborate treatise; by Anquetil du Perron, the interpreter of its sacred books; by Mr. William Erskine, who has taken an able survey of its principles as developed both in ancient and modern times, and of the present practices of its votaries in India ; by M. Burnouf, whose philosophical and philological research has done so much to facilitate the knowledge of the Zand, preserved only in its own records; by Professor Bopp, a most accomplished and successful auxiliary in the same undertaking ; and by several other distinguished writers on the Continent of Europe. The labours of these men, however, rather invite than repel the farther investigation which they facilitate, and encourage the attempt to present the result of their research in a practical compass. It is manifestly desirable, that the Pársí system should be exhibited in the light of Christianity ; and it is with a view to *aid* in this attempt, that I have endeavoured to improve the advantages of observation and inquiry which I have enjoyed in connexion with my professional duties in Bombay, and contemplated for some time the publication of a general treatise on the tenets and observances of the Zoroastrians, and that with a particular reference to their own improvement. The *form* which this volume has ultimately assumed, is entirely to be ascribed to the publication of certain works by the Zoroastrians themselves, in explanation and defence of their faith, and in opposition to Christianity, which the benevolence of their well-wishers in distant lands is now pressing on their attention. The circumstances in which the works to which I now refer have appeared, are detailed in our first Chapter ; and it is only the mere mention of them individually which is here required.

I. The first of them, a quarto of 268 pages, bears the following titles : — " TALIM-I-ZURTOOSHT ; or the DOCTRINE OF ZOROASTER in the Guzrattee language, for the instruction of Pársí youths ; together with an ANSWER TO DR. WILSON'S LECTURE ON [THE] VANDIDAD, compiled by a Parsee priest. Bombay 1840." " તાલીમે જરતોસત ઈઆને જરતોસતી ધરમનો ખોલાશો* ગુજરાતી ભાસામો પારશીઓનાં જવાંન છોકરાઓને સમજવાને સારૂં. તે સાથે* ડાકતર વીલસનનો વંદીદાદ ઊપરની મુજાહેમતનો જવાબ* એ બનાવનાર એક જરતોસતી મોબેદ* સને ૧૮૪૦" As here mentioned, the work is in the Gujaráti language, with the exception of some quotations in English, Persian, and Zand, which, however, are uniformly translated into Gujaráti. Its avowed author is Dosabhái Sohrábjí, a respectable munshí, well known to both the Native and European communities of Bombay. He is not as a writer a volunteer, but the hireling, as he confesses, of the Pársí Pancháyat, or Sanhedrim. His exposition of the Zoroastrian faith, owing to his having found it more convenient to disguise than defend the system, is both brief and inaccurate. He seems to have forgotten the proverb,

كه زنگي به شستن نگردد سفيد

" An Ethiopian is not made white by washing." It is too late in the day for any person now to attempt to resolve the Pársí Ahriman, or Evil Principle, into a mere personification of the evil qualities inherent in man; and not till the Yaçna is wholly disused, shall we believe that the Pársís consider fire nothing more than a ***kibláh***, or centre of worship. That very priesthood of which our author is a member, has in its major part discarded his opinions, if we may form a judgment either from public report, or from the work the title of which we now subjoin.

2. بنام ایزد بخشایندهٔ بخشایشگر مهربان --- એ કેતાબ મોઅજે-જાતે જરતોશતી* ઇઆને હજરત જરતોશતનાં બરહક મો-જજાઓ તમામ અવલથી તે આખેરશુધીનાં તથા જરતોશતી દીનનું મુખતેશર બઇઆન* બનાવનાર દશતુર એદલજી દા-રાબજી રશતમજી શંજાંણાં* શને ૧૨૦૯ ઇઅજદજરદી* શને ૧૮૪૦ ઇશવી* The literal rendering is as follows: — " In the name of God the bountiful, the liberal, and the gracious, the Book MAUJAZA'T-I-ZARTOSHTI.* That is to say, the un-

* The correct form, the Dastur should observe, is either *Maujazát-i-Zartusht*, or *Maujazát Zartushti*.

doubted Miracles of Zoroaster, complete from beginning to end, with an exposition of the Zoroastrian Faith. The author [is] Dastur Edaljí Dárábjí Rustamjí Sanjáná. In the year of Yazdejard 1209, and in the year of Christ, 1840." The writer of this work, familiarly known by the name of Edal Dáru, is the chief priest of the *Rasamí*, the larger of the two sects into which the Indian Pársís are divided. It has been composed, he informs us, agreeably to the "orders," and at the expense, "of Jamsetjee Jeejeebhoy", the opulent and liberal Pársí merchant, on whom her Majesty lately conferred the honour of knighthood. It is scarcely of a controversial nature, though it states, in the preface, that it has been composed to aid the followers of the "Good Faith" in their discussions with the *Júd-dín*, or Gentiles, which have for some time been proceeding. Unlike the *Tálim-i-Zartusht*, it speaks without disguise, and in general without perversion; and in many places it is directly opposed to that work. Its exposition of the principles of Zoroastrianism is pretty copious; and from the situation of the writer as the head of the Pársí priesthood, it is viewed by many as authoritative. Its collection of legends respecting Zoroaster, and his immediate followers, is principally according to the *Zartusht-Námah* of Zartusht Bahrám; and truly it contains,

——————"Little else but dreams,
Conjectures, fancies built on nothing firm."

The author being considered a person of peculiar sacredness, has been living for many years almost in a state of seclusion at the principal fire-temple; and he seems, to a considerable extent, to have escaped the untoward march of intellect. It is to his credit that he has preserved his temper throughout his work. It is comprised, I may add, in 127 pages, quarto.

3. The third work, a duodecimo of 347 pages, has two titles. That which is most indicative of its contents, is the second, inserted partly within the figure of the blazing sun :— નેરંગ હા કલમ કસ* શ્રી મુંબઈ દુરબીનનાં કેટલાંએક વરતમાન પતરોમથી એક "કલમ કસને" નાંમે ડાકતર વીલસનને પુછેલા કોઈ બેશુમાર સવાલો ચુટી કાહડીને હેઠલ છાપી પરગટ કીધા છે :—which may be rendered, "THE NIRANG-HA' OF KALAM KAS : a countless number of questions proposed to Dr Wilson in the Durbín newspaper, under the name (signature) of Kalam Kas, are here extracted and published." By some of the respectable Pársís of Bombay, I have been requested not to hold their community responsible for the publication of this book, which they declare to be the production of ignorance and stupidity. I do not see, however, that, in respect of the character ascribed to it, it differs much from its neighbours. But, except when it advances statements, and hints at arguments, not to be found in the other controversialists, I have made few direct references to it. Had the Durbín been a proper organ for religious discussion, I might have replied to the articles which it embodies at the time of their appearance.

4. The fourth work appears in Gujarátí and English :— હાદીએ-ગોમ-રેહાન ઈઆને ગોમરાહ લોકોને રાહબત લાવનારી કેતાબ પાદરી વીલશંનનાં વંદીદાદ ઊપર કરેલાં લેચરના ૨૬ જવાબો* એ કેતાબ એ અસપંદીઆરજી ફરામજી એ બનાવી છે* "THE HADIE-GUM-RAHA'N, or a Guide to those who have lost their way, being a Refutation of the Lecture delivered by the Rev. Dr. John Wilson, D. D. on the Vandidád Sádé of the Pársís. By Aspandiarjee Framjee. 1841." It is written, the author informs us, "at the special request of Shet Jeejeebhoy Dadabhoy, Esq., one of the most distinguished patrons and supporters of the Mazdyasní

religion." It contains a running comment on my Lecture on the Vandidád, the argument of which it not unfrequently misapprehends and misrepresents. Its appeals to the Zand writings are pretty numerous ; but the translations and interpretations made of them are much more inaccurate than those of Anquetil du Perron, on which, nine years ago, when I published the pamphlet on which its animadversions are made, and before I devoted myself seriously to the study of the Zand, I was almost wholly dependent for my knowledge of the sacred books of the Pársís. The author when he finds my arguments insuperable, generally retreats, like Dosabháí, into a parabolical sanctuary, which his imagination has called into being as a dernier place of resort for Zoroaster and his foiled followers. In the ruins of this sanctuary, if I mistake not, he has found a place of sepulture.

In replying to the works now mentioned, under the different divisions of my subject, — intended to embrace the general principles of the Pársí religion, — I have endeavoured to collect together all the information which they contain and all the reasonings which they advance. I have, in this way, I flatter myself, overcome the disadvantages arising from the want of order on their part, as well as imparted a liveliness to the discussion which it could not otherwise have possessed, however methodically pursued. I trust that my opponents will admit that in dealing with their expression of opinion, I have endeavoured to do it ample justice, to give a clear and intelligible statement of it, principally in their own words, and to point out the grounds on which it is made to rest. The Pársí religion, I have set forth, not only as propounded and defended by them and their countrymen in general, but as developed in its own standards, comprised in the Zand-Avastá. The whole of the Vandidád, I have perused in the original Zand, having respect to its legitimate meaning, so far as it can be discovered by such a grammatical analysis as the philological labours of Rask, Burnouf, and Bopp, and a consideration of the analogies to the Sanskrit, which are neither few nor insignificant, have enabled me to make, and by a comparison of the French version with the Gujaráti translation, paraphrase and comment of Frámjí, the father of Aspandiárjí, made under the patronage and direction of the late celebrated Mullá Firuz and other learned Dasturs connected with the sect of the Kadímís, and which latter work embraces the traditional renderings and interpretations of the Pahliví and Persian versions. A similar course, I have pursued with many of the liturgical pieces. My success, notwithstanding the helps which I have enjoyed, has not been equal to my expectations; and, in common with the Pársís themselves I have been unable, in many instances, to penetrate the obscurity which rests upon the pages of the Zand. What I have ventured to advance, however, in the following work, rests, I am persuaded, as far as every matter of the least consequence is concerned, on safe grounds. I have throughout adduced a sufficiency of documentary proof, and made a sufficiency of precise references to the recognized sources of information. In my studies during the last few months, I have enjoyed the kind countenance and companionship and able assistance of Mr. N. L. Westergaard of Copenhagen, the author of the "Radices Linguæ Sanscritæ," a gentleman who has already taken a most advanced place among the philologists of Europe, and who will ere long do more than ample justice to the patronage of his sovereign, His Danish Majesty Christian the Eighth, which has brought him on a literary mission to the East. May I venture in passing, to express the hope that my friend in union with M. Burnouf will soon give to the world a critical edition of the whole of the Zand writings, prepared from the Copenhagen and Paris manuscripts, and those which we are now collecting in India.

The body of the Zand writings, I may here remark, is comprized in the ZAND-AVASTA' or ZAND WORD, which I have never seen in the hands of the Pársís in a collected form. It consists of the VANDIDA'D, which is composed of the Vandidád properly so called, and the two larger liturgical works, the YAÇNA and VISPARD, which are interspersed with it, and recited along with it during the celebration of the most extended service of the Zoroastrians; the KHURDAH-AVASTA', or minor liturgy; the YASTS; and other detached pieces.

The VANDIDA'D, properly so called, consists of the report of an alleged dialogue between Hormazd and Zoroaster. In my sixth chapter, I have presented the reader with a complete analysis of the work; and I need here make no attempt to enumerate its contents.

The YAÇNA or IZASHNE', the Grand Sacrificial Service, is divided into seventy-two sections, or *Hás*. On the first of them, a most able and elaborate comment, forming a large quarto volume, has been published by Professor E. Burnouf, of Paris. Translations of specimens of these Hás will be found in the subsequent pages. The subject of them is the adoration of Hormazd, and the whole creation, animate and inanimate, said to be effected by him.

The VISPARD is similar to the Yaçna in its contents. Its name indicates its dedication to "all the masters," or objects, of purity addressed by the Zoroastrians. It is divided into twenty-seven small sections, or *kardahs*.

The arrangement of the KHURDAH-AVASTA' is attributed by the Pársís to A'darbád Máhrespand, a contemporary of Sháhpur, the successor of Ardeshir Bábegán. In both the manuscript and printed copies of the work which I have examined, I have observed great differences as to the amount of its actual contents. The following are the pieces found in a curious manuscript belonging to myself, evidently written by the

Gabars of Persia. 1. The Benediction, *Ashem Vóhu.* 2. The *Ahunavar*, *Yathá ahu vairyó.* 3. *Avastá-i-nán khurdan*, the *Avastá* for bread-eating. 4. *Avasta-i-kamez kardan*, the *Avastá* for shedding urine. 5. *Yadman Alalunatan*, the washing of hands. 6. *Kustik Açrunatan*, the tying of the Kustí, or Cincture. 7. *Avastá-i-nákhan-chídan*, the Avastá for paring nails. 8. The five *Níáíshes*, or Laudations, — of Khurshíd, the Sun; Meher, the Dawn or Venus; Máh, the moon;* A'tísh, fire; and Arduisur, water. 9. The five *Gahs*, or Offices for the Watches of the day, — Hávan, Rapitan, Osiren, Evesrutem, and Oshen. 10. The *Yasts*, or Sacrificial Services for the Izads,—of Hormazd, Ardebihist, Sarosh Hádokht, and the little Sarosh. 11. The *Nám-Sitáíshné*, or Salutation of the names of Hormazd.* 12. The *Afrigáns*, or Delectations, of Dáhman, Sarosh, the Gahambárs, and Rapitan. In the last printed edition of the Khurdah-Avastá, the following additional pieces are found. The *Nirang*, muttering, for taking the water *Zur*. The *Hoshbám*, or prayer at the Dawn. The *Dawa-Visp-humat*, at the Háwan Gah, the reverencing of all good thoughts, etc. The *Namaskár*, or Salutation, of the four points of the compass. The *Patets*, or Penitential services, — The Pasmání, Irání, and that for departed souls. The *Báj*, or muttering at meals, and the *Báji Parhezwání*; the *Namaskárs*, or Salutations of Lamps, Muktad, the Dakhmas, mountains, water, and vegetation. The prayer for health. Prayer for the true faith. The *Yasts*,—Nirang Hormazd, the great Haftan, the small Haftan, Khurdád, A'wá, Máh, Tashtar, Tír, Gosh, Meher, Nirang Meher, Nirang Sarosh Hádokht and Rátní, Rashné, Farvardín, Behrám, Rám, Dín, Arsasang, Zámiád, Hom the greater and smaller, Nirang Hom, Wanant, Nirang Wannant, Sirozah, Nirang Ardebehist. The *Nirangs* for the

* This piece is in Pahliví and not in Zand.

daily and occasional offices, — that to be repeated after the Níáísh, after the Yasts, and after instructing children, on cutting hair and paring nails, after the completion of the Gahs, by the Nasásáls when carrying corpses. The *Avastá* for the happiness of departed spirits. The *Avastá* for leading the spirits in hell to repentance. The prayer to be repeated by the Dasturs at the time of the Barasnum, or great Penance. The *Nirang* for consecrating *vekrí*, the Pahliví Nirang to be stuck on doors on the twelfth day of the fifth month. The *Bajes* for eating (the greater,) ablutions, sleeping, awakening. The *Satom* to be read for the dead. The *Nirang* to be repeated the third day after the death of a person. An introduction to the Afrigáns. The *Afrigáns*, of Ardá-fravash and of the Gahs. The *Afrins*, or Delectations, of the Gahambár páví, the Gahambár, the Ardá-fravash, the names of the illustrious, Dáhman, Miyazd, Rapitan. The names of the seven *Hamkárs*. The names of the twelve *angels* presiding over the elements. The funeral ceremonies. The *Ahunavar* for those who cannot read the Zand-Avastá. The *A'shírváds*, or Blessings, that of the Paimání Pahlivi, that in the name of the Creator, the Sanskrit, for health of body, and the five *Gahs*, separately. Account of clothing a child with the Sadra. The names of the thirty *days*, twelve *months* and five *Gahs*. Ten *Hás* from the *Izashné*. A few of these pieces are in Pahliví and Sanskrit; and some of them are extracts from the larger liturgy. In a large manuscript in my possession, formed principally of the Rawáyats, or traditions, I observe many additional prayers in the Zand language, to be used on particular occasions of which the Pársís are now ashamed. They refer principally to the different functions and states of the soul and body.

Of the Khurdah-Avastá, several editions, in the Gujarátí character, have been published by the Dasturs. Two of them, noticed in subsequent parts of this work, have Gujarátí translations accompanying them. That last printed has no translation; and the deficiency is not felt by the Pársí laymen, whose devotion consists wholly in the emission of sound. An edition of the Vandidád has been lithographed in its proper character in Bombay, as well as at Paris. The Zand and Pahliví metallic type which I have used in this work, is the first which has been cast in the East. It is the production of the foundry of the American Mission Press, an extensive and well conducted establishment sacred to the diffusion of useful and divine knowledge in India; and at present under the vigilant superintendence of my valued friend and fellow-labourer the Rev. D. O. Allen.

To the Pahliví and Persian writings of the Pársís, which I have frequently quoted and described, it is not necessary for me particularly to refer. Should the Pársís be inclined to extend their discussions with me, I shall not be disinclined to bring to public view their ceremonial, with all its absurdities, as it is unfolded in their Rawáyats, copies of which, I have procured with extreme difficulty. For the translation of the Zartusht-Námah, or legendary life of Zoroaster, inserted in the appendix, and some other curious documents, I am indebted to my friend, Lieut. E. B. Eastwick, whose high attainments in the oriental languages, will, I doubt not, continue to be consecrated to the cause of philanthropy. Mr. Aviet Aganur, one of the respected heads of the Armenian community in Bombay, has furnished me with the translation of a curious passage from Esnik of the fifth century. For chronological purposes, I have given in the appendix, I, an abridgement of a part of Sir William Jones' View of Persian History.

The system of representing Zand letters which I have adopted,* will be learned from the appendix, J.

* I may here mention that the difference in the orthography of many of the Oriental words which I have introduced, is owing to the fact that I have had respectively before me the Zand, Pahliví, Persian, and Gujarátí representations.

I have now to add, that throughout this work I have most anxiously endeavoured to abstain from unnecessarily hurting the feelings of my opponents, and of those who are directly or indirectly responsible for the appearance of their publications. Direct, repeated, and aggravated provocations, I have overlooked ; and palpable injuries I have forgiven. I have spoken plainly, that I might not be misunderstood ; but, I trust, affectionately, under the persuasion that the wrath of man worketh not the righteousness of God. It is not to the Pársís, as a people, but it is to the errors in which they are in a greater or less degree involved, that I have placed myself in an attitude of hostility. The advancement of the cause of *truth*, I can freely say, has been my constant and only aim. If I understand aright the present state of feeling in the native community of Bombay, the day is not far distant when many of the Pársís who now question my motives, will accord to me the persuasion of my disinterested desire to promote their welfare. Had not my regard for their interests in time and eternity, been powerful and effective, this volume would never have seen the light. For the last two years, especially, it has demanded of me an amount of labour by night and by day, such as in ordinary circumstances, I should shrink to attempt to render. When my friends and medical advisers stood around, what appeared to them to be my dying couch, it was my prayer that I might be spared to bring it to a conclusion ; and now when in the providence of God, I have seen the accomplishment of my anxious desire, I commit the fruit of my labour to the divine blessing. May it be extensively instrumental in leading the Pársís to embrace the doctrines of salvation, in quickening the prayers and efforts of Christians on their behalf, and in revealing to the natives of India in general the unreasonableness and sinfulness of polytheism, and the idolatry of nature !

That a great show of answering my statements and reasonings will immediately be made by numbers of the Pársí community, I have not the slightest doubt. The Rahnamá-Zartoshtí, a magazine which has been lately commenced for the defence of Zoroastrianism, and the assault of Christianity,—and most of the feeble reasonings of which have been already anticipated in this volume,—in particular will not be silent. The Pársís, however, are beginning to distinguish between declamation and criticism, between faithful renderings and appropriate statements, and perversions and misrepresentations. In the Chábuk, edited by Naurojí Dárábjí, I have of late seen admirable refutations of its contemporaries, and particularly of the periodical which I have now mentioned; and I hope that its able conductor will prove himself, through the blessing of God, to be not only a bold but successful and consistent Reformer. Though the state of my health compels me to leave India for a season, I shall not overlook what may be advanced in my absence; and others I trust, will be found who will in due time supply my lack of service. From a distant land I hope to forward for publication in India the substance of this work in Gujarátí, for the benefit of those who are ignorant of English. The Pársí community is daily rising in intelligence and enterprize, and under more extended efforts for the diffusion in it of Christian knowledge, and through the operation of the Divine Spirit, we cannot but look for its ultimate, and probably speedy, approach to God through Him who is the Way, the Truth, and the Life.

CONTENTS.

CHAPTER I.

CHAPTER II.

THE PA'RSI' NOTIONS OF THE GODHEAD, AND THE RELATIONS OF ZARVA'NA-AKARANA AND HORMAZD.

CHAPTER III.

THE DOCTRINE OF THE TWO PRINCIPLES, HORMAZD AND AHRIMAN.

CHAPTER IV.

THE WORSHIP OF THE ELEMENTS AND HEAVENLY BODIES, AND OF THE AMSHA'SPANDS AND I'ZADS, WHO ARE SAID TO PRESIDE OVER THEM AND THE OTHER WORKS OF NATURE.

Statement respecting the Polytheism of the Pársís — Their Worship of the Elements and Heavenly Host — Alleged explanation of Gibbon — Testimony of the Greeks and Romans — Testimony of the Fathers and Historians of the Christian Church — Difficulties of Gibbon and confession of Hyde — Testimony of the Musalmáns — Perversion of that of Firdausi by the Pársí controversialists — Notions of the present Pársís on the Worship of the Elements, Angels, and Celestial Bodies — Explanation and attempted vindications of Edal Dáru — Perversions and explanations of Dosabháí, Aspandiárjí, etc. — Comparison of the views of the controversialists with the admissions of the Kadím Táríkh, Sanján Shlokas, Kissah-i-Sanján, the dastur who instructed Mr. Lord, and the Zartusht-Námah — Refutation of the defences and apologies of the controversialists — Fire not the Glory or Substance of God — Impiety and unreasonableness of the worship of Angels said to preside over Fire or any of the other works of God — Errors respecting the number and combination of the Elements — Fire not a superintendent and preserver of man — Dosabháí ashamed of the honours conferred on Fire in the Vandidád — Specimen of these honours — Blasphemous Worship of Fire illustrated by a translation of the A'tish-Behrám Níáísh, etc. — Comment on this form of prayer — Unreasonableness of a legend in the Sháhnámah respecting the discovery of Fire by Hoshang — Explanation of the unquenchable fires of A'zar-Baiján — Worthlessness of the legend of the Sháhnamah respecting the A'tish-burzín-Meher — Theories respecting the origin of the Worship of the Heavenly Host and the Elements — General remarks on the unreasonableness and sinfulness of worshipping any of the inanimate or intelligent Powers of Nature.

CHAPTER V.

THE GENERAL POLYTHEISM OF THE PA'RSI'S.

Origin of the Polytheism of the Pársís — Attempt at classifying and enumerating the principal objects of their worship—Quotations in proof and illustration from the Zand-Avastá — Extract from the Vandidád — Translation of the first Há of the Yaçna, according to Burnouf — New translation of the seventy-first Há of the Yaçna — Comment on the Polytheism of the Pársís — Jumbling together and confusion of the objects of worship — Illustration from a supposed congratulatory address to a Governor of Bombay — The same terms of respect, prayer, praise, supplication, etc. applied to all the different objects of worship — Criticism on the meaning of these terms, as employed in the Zand writings, and used by the Pársís — The service of the inferior objects of worship occupies more space in the Zand-Avastá

CHAPTER VI.

REVIEW OF THE HISTORICAL, DOCTRINAL, AND CEREMONIAL DISCOVERIES AND INSTITUTES OF THE VANDIDA'D, EMBRACING AN ANALYSIS OF THAT WORK, ACCORDING TO THE ORDER OF ITS FARGARDS.

CHAPTER VII.

THE PA'RSI' NOTIONS OF THE RESPONSIBILITY, DEPRAVITY, AND GUILT OF MAN, AND THE MEANS OF HIS SALVATION.

CHAPTER VIII.

THE ALLEGED PROPHETICAL MISSION OF ZOROASTER DISPROVED, AND THE IMPUGNMENT OF THE EXTERNAL AUTHORITY OF THE BOOKS WHICH THE PA'RSIS' RECKON THE STANDARD OF THEIR FAITH AND PRACTICE.

APPENDIX.

INDEX.

THE PÁRSÍ RELIGION.

THE PÁRSÍ RELIGION.

CHAPTER I.

REVIEW OF THE AUTHOR'S FORMER DISCUSSIONS WITH THE PA'RSI'S OF INDIA, AND NOTICE OF THE ORIGIN OF THE LATE PUBLICATIONS IN DEFENCE OF THE ZOROASTRIAN FAITH.

Study of the Pársí Religion — Review published in a Bombay periodical — Correspondence in the Samáchár newspaper on religious inquiry, and the propagation of Christianity — Extracts from pamphlets published by the Editor of the Harkárah and Vartamán, on the same subject — The religion which has not God as its author should be forsaken — Some of the errors of the Pársí faith admitted — Divine Mission of Zoroaster not established by evidence — Motives which lead Christians to seek the conversion of the natives of India — Encouragements to Missionary labour — Allusions to the means of Salvation. Reprobation and defence of the Bundéshné by some of the Pársís — Notice of letters published in the Harkárah and Vartamán — The Bible the standard of the Christian faith — Divine and human natures of Christ — Testimony of the apostles of Christ — Prophecies respecting the Saviour — Claims of the different sects of Christians to be determined by the Bible — Pársí rule of faith destitute of divine authority — Notice of Lectures on the Pársí religion by the author — Publication of a Lecture on the Vandidád — Summary of its contents — Criticisms upon it — Not vindicated by attacks on the Bible — These attacks repelled — Unsuccessful attempt made by the Pársís to vindicate the Vandidád from the charge of recommending the destruction of a child in particular circumstances — Endeavours to diffuse a knowledge of Christianity among the Pársís — Foundation of the General Assembly's Insti-

tution — Conversion of two Pársí youths — Prosecution of the author, on a writ of Habeas Corpus — The liberty of the converts guaranteed — Notice of the " Anti-Conversion Memorial, " and its reception by Government — Effects of the discussions caused by it, and of other proceedings — Publication of various works by the Pársís — The Pársís exhorted to the prosecution of religious Inquiry — Notice of irrelevant matter introduced by the Pársí controversialists into their late publications — Failure of their attempts to disparage the Christian converts — Vanity of their confidence in Voltaire and Gibbon — Gibbon's opinion of Zoroaster — Christianity not answerable for the deceptions practised by the Jesuits — The miraculous powers exercised by the Apostles not needed by their descendants — Plan to be pursued in further discussing the merits of the Pársí religion.

THE references which are made by the Pársí gentlemen to whose works I sit down to reply, to my former discussions with individuals of their tribe, and to the pamphlets to which they gave rise, and the incorrect and unjust assertions which they have frequently ventured to make respecting them, compel me to take a brief, but calm, review of these discussions, and to make such quotations, with additional notes, both from my own communications, and those of my opponents, as will remove any misapprehensions which exist, and exhibit in a proper light the misrepresentations, in which some have indulged. The course which I have thus laid down for my guidance, will sufficiently inform the reader about the circumstances in which the present publication originates; and it will enable me conveniently to notice some of the reasonings of my present opponents, which are not essential to the main arguments which it is my duty to pursue.

When I commenced my missionary operations in Bombay in 1829, I found the Pársís a numerous and very influential portion of its varied community, and well entitled to a large share of the evangelistic efforts which are being made for the instruction and conversion of the natives of India. With a view to qualify myself for advantageously holding intercourse with them, and unfolding to them the truths of divine revelation, I considered it my duty early to embrace such opportunities as might be presented to me of becoming acquainted with their religious tenets and observances, their national history, and the present manners and customs of their society. With this view, I directed my attention to most of the works treating of these subjects which are accessible to the European student in India, and especially to Anquetil du Perron's translation of their sacred books comprised in the Zand-Avastá, and I also sought to profit by the intercourse which I maintained with individuals of their tribe able and willing to give me correct information.

In the numbers for July and August 1831 of the Oriental Christian Spectator, — with the editorship of which I was connected, — I took occasion, when reviewing the "History of Vartan, and the Battle of the Armenians, containing an account of the Religious Wars between the Persians and Armenians, by Elisæus," and translated by Mr. C. F. Neumann*, to give a very brief and general account of the religious works of the Pársís, and the doctrines which they propound. I was not without hope that my observations, simple as they were, would attract the attention of some individuals belonging to the interesting tribe to which they referred; and I was not disappointed. On the 14th of the same month on which my article appeared, a Pársí gentleman addressed himself to the editor of the Samáchár, — a respectable Gujarátí newspaper, — with a view to his obtaining some assistance in forming an opinion of my lucubrations. The magazine, he said, "contains some remarks on the religion of the Pársís, which I think incorrect; but I wish to inquire of *you*, if what is therein asserted concerning our religion, and Zoroaster, and his doctrines, be true. Do the *shets* †, and those skilled in the knowledge of our belief, intend to say nothing [in refutation]? I am astonished that you, Mr. Editor, should have been silent on the subject, and exceedingly regret that you have not translated the remarks into Gujarátí, and pointed out their errors for the benefit of your readers.‡"

* Published by the Oriental Translation Committee.

† This honorary term is applied to all classes of native gentlemen.

‡ Letter signed *Kusti-bandni*, (a wearer of the kustí,) in the Bombay Samáchár, 18th July, 1831.

With characteristic caution, the editor of the paper thus replied:—"I have seen the pamphlet alluded to; but I am not anxious to take on my own shoulders the burden of disputation, leaving this, as it properly falls, to those who are thoroughly acquainted with our faith, and to persons more advanced in years. To the question, whether the statements it contains are true or not, I reply that some of them are correct, and others false; and it would seem that the writer has got his information from former authors, not of our faith, whose word he has trusted. It is, however, the way of the world for one sect to run down another. The missionaries are but Christian padres, and what wonder is it if they should abuse other religions? Moreover, the business of missionaries is to instruct persons of another religion and bring them into their own, and without abusing other religions how can they get on? With regard to translating the remarks about our religion contained in the magazine, as suggested to us, we must declare that we cannot see the use of it, — that we should not regard any of the falsities of infidels, for they are our enemies, — and that if we did so, we might be blamed by believers. We now drop the undertaking; but if it be recommended and thought advisable by the intelligent of our tribe, we shall give it a reconsideration."

Thinking that some explanations were demanded of me, and that good might result, if a peaceful discussion of the matters at issue were encouraged, I thought it my duty to come forward in *propriâ personâ*.

"I am not ashamed to acknowledge", I wrote on the 27th of July, "that I am the author of the review of which you and your correspondent complain. I got the information which it contains from the French translation of the Zand-Avastá, from some English, Armenian, and Latin books in my possession, from my own observation, and from conversation with some of the learned *dasturs*,* and respectable gentlemen of your tribe. You say that some of my statements are true, and others

* The chief-priests of the Pársís are called *dasturs*; those below them, *mobeds*; and the lowest of all, *herbads*.

false. Point out the errors, and show your proofs, for I am ready to correct what may be wrong, and I am willing to get translated into English, and to publish in the Oriental Christian Spectator, whatever you may write in reply. Tell me your whole mind. It is my business, and that of the American missionaries in Bombay, and all the missionaries in India, to teach the Christian religion to those who are ignorant of it, as you correctly remark. The Christians in our native countries, have sent us hither for this very purpose; and in order to set forth the doctrine of Christ to the natives of India, we have left our homes and our beloved friends. We preach in our houses and chapels, in the streets and highways, * in public and private, to Hindús, Pársís, Musalmáns, and Jainas, and to all whom we meet who are ignorant of the way of salvation. We distribute the Scriptures, and other books, in various languages; and we establish schools and educate the young. We believe that the Christian religion is that alone which has truth on its side, and we wish all men to come to Christ and be saved. We seek to do good. We exhort our fellow-men to flee from hell. You say that we reproach the Hindú and Pársí religions; but we declare only what is true respecting them. We reason; but we use no violence. We enter into discussion that truth may appear; and we say to all, *Inquire.*"†

The frank avowal of my connexion with the article to which reference was made, was not without its due effect. "It was out of our power," said the editor in reply, "to refuse to insert his letter, after the gentleman has so unhesitatingly given us his name. Whether it will have the effect of making those persons to whom it refers look anxiously about themselves, and turn over the pages of their shástras with all haste, we do not take upon ourselves to say. If our friend the writer, John Wilson, (may the grace of God be upon him!) is desirous of drawing us into a discussion

* In such places as injurious interruptions are not anticipated.

† Samáchár, 1st August, 1831.

of this character, we plainly say to him what we told the wearer of the *kustí*, that it is not suitable for us to take the controversy on ourselves.... Having said this much, we must add, that if any pandit, religious officer, or intelligent person of one of the castes to which he has referred, should fulfil his wish, we are perfectly indifferent in the matter, and feel neither joy nor sorrow. Should the writer of the letter ask our private opinion on the point, we tell him very willingly, that it is a good work for one to take pains in instructing another of his own caste in his own faith, and to direct him in the right path; but that to trouble himself about another's faith is what he should avoid." This personal judgment was accompanied by the earnest request that the repose of his people might not be disturbed. "Permit us, permit us," he said, "to follow the road on which we have been travelling, for at last all roads meet in one point. There is no Redeemer of any. The finding of a man is according to his acting. We shall not say more than this, but sit in silence. From striking two stones together you will elicit nothing but fire."*

Though I feared that the door was shut against me in this quarter, I thought it right to offer a few explanatory remarks, particularly as I found that our previous correspondence had attracted particular attention in the native community.

"Discussion *conducted with the desire of promoting the interests of truth*," I observed, "is a *good* thing. The spark elicited by striking two stones together, may ignite a lamp, to remove the darkness of a chamber, and it may kindle a flame, which may devour the rubbish which has been long accumulating, and which proves injurious. There is sometimes, moreover, a crust around the diamond of truth which requires to be abraded, before the truth itself can dart forth its splendent rays....

"You seem to think that no attempt should be made by persons of any particular religion to convert those who are devoted to another. I entirely disagree with this sentiment,

* Samáchár, 8th August, 1831.

which supposes that all religions are alike true, and acceptable to God, and beneficial to man. There is only one religion, however, which discovers the glory of God ; and all other religions reproach him. There is only one religion which brings man to knowledge and civilization ; all other religions keep him in darkness and ignorance. But I do not wonder that many persons agree with your opinion. When Christian missionaries first came to Britain, they were after this fashion addressed by our fore-fathers : —' Do not seek to convert us. We will not forsake our own religion. We will continue to worship our idols, and to serve our priests. We will continue to offer human sacrifices to our gods. We will never cease to call upon the name of Thor, who holds the seven planets in his left hand, and a sceptre in his right. We will never cease to worship the sun when he rises and sets, and when we behold his image, as half a man, with the rays of light proceeding from his face, and with a flaming wheel on his breast; and we will never cease to worship the moon and the starry host'. The Christian Missionaries heard all these and many more such things, but they did not in despair abandon their work. They put their trust in God, and declared his word. They used no force, but appealed to reason ; and in the day of God's power, a change began to appear. Our fore-fathers listened to the truth, and it entered into their souls. ' Our fathers have erred,' they said, ' and we will no longer walk in their paths. We will worship Him who made the heavens and the earth. We will confess our sins, and, in the name of Christ, pray for pardon. We will by the help of God follow his commandments.' They thus became Christians; and God blessed both them and their descendants. Will you, Mr. Editor, affirm that the change which they made was bad ? No ! You see the *advantages* which Christianity has conferred upon us as a nation. We are indebted to it for the possession of all that is great and glorious among us ; and it is the source of all our hopes of happiness in the world which is to come. The Christian missionaries were the friends of our fathers, and our benefactors. Those who call upon you, and the Pársís, and Hindús, of Bombay to embrace the true religion, are the *friends* of the natives; and what they offer, in the name of Christ is happiness in time and eternity.

"You say that all roads meet in one point. How do you prove this assertion? If you mean that all souls go to God to be judged after death, I agree with you; and I am sure that you will agree with me in thinking that it is a most important matter, to consider, while we dwell in this body, what we can answer God for our sins, when we depart. Our repentance, though it is necessary, cannot save us, for it cannot clear away the sins which we have committed before repentance; and our good deeds cannot save us, for there is always sin mingled with them, and as they cannot go beyond the demands of the law of God, which requires all that we can do, there can be no merit in them, which can make amends for our past deficiencies.

"Allow me to propose the consideration of a most important question to your learned dasturs, and to all the pandits in Bombay. It will be allowed, that if sinners be saved at all, their salvation must be brought about through the *grace of God*, and if they be saved, it is evident that their salvation must be accomplished so as to give no occasion to the impeachment of the holiness, and justice, and authority of God, who is the universal Sovereign, and who is required, for the preservation of his kingdom, to manifest his hatred of sin. *How*, I ask, *are the mercy of God, and the holiness of God, displayed by the means of salvation in which the Pársis and Musalmáns put their trust?* To the wise of the land, I look for a reply."*

The editor of the Samáchár kept to his resolution of maintaining silence. On publishing my letter, he merely intimated, that his next number would contain an epistle in the Persian and Gujarátí languages by Hájí Muhammad Háshim, in reply to a charge against Muhammad, which I had casually brought, in my first communication to his paper. This promised document, in due time, appeared; and it gave rise to an

* Samáchár, 8th August, 1831.

extensive correspondence on the claims of the Koran, to which I need not here allude.*

The small "spark which had been struck," was not destined immediately to expire. Brief and simple as our discussion had been, it extensively formed the subject of conversation in Bombay. A bold and enterprizing spirit soon stood forth, to uphold the honor of the Pársís. Naurozjí Mobed Dárábjí, a printer who had issued the prospectus of another newspaper, extensively advertised his readiness to receive and print, and circulate *gratuitously* whatever communications, on either side of the question, might be entrusted to his care, till such time as his own periodical, which should afford "a fair field and no favour," could be regularly issued. He kept his promise sacred, and at his own expense published several pamphlets, neatly printed on excellent paper, and in the form of royal quarto.

A Pársí, who assumed the signature of "Nauroz Goosequill,"† was the principal defendant of the Pársí religion. He could not justify, however, what he said in its favour. It has sometimes been with me a matter of doubt, in fact, whether, as regards much which fell from his pen, he was in real earnest. The following are a few of the passages contained in his first article.

"You write that other religions were made by men. In reply to this, it is incumbent on me to inquire, whether, if without men, God himself has ordained any religion, and whether any prophet has established his faith without making books. I also ask you, who made the books of *your* religion? . . . . .

"You write that in the book of the Christians, it is written that the nations do not know the way of salvation; and

* Hájí Muhammad Háshim ultimately addressed to me a considerable pamphlet, a reply to which I have published in Hindustání and Persian, under the title of "*Raddi-i-din-Musalmáni*, or Refutation of Muhammadism," through the Bombay Tract and Book Society.

† It was jocularly hinted to this writer, that he was in danger of earning for himself the character of a *goose*. He consequently, ultimately, changed his signature to that of "*Swan-quill*."

that it has to be *shown* to them, that they may walk according to the commandments of God. The answer to this is, *why* do you take so much trouble, because from the first we place no faith in your shástras, and we reckon the book of Mary's Son, Jesus, as a fable, for it was made by a man with two hands like ourselves, and not by God himself. I am able to detect the faults of your books, as well as you those of ours; and I have no kind of hesitation in so doing, because the defects of each religion having been drawn forth, and compared with reason, what appears good is to be retained, and what bad to be rejected. This is my practice. I do not proclaim, as *you* do, that *my* religion only is holy. We leave you missionaries to speak in this manner. But as when we were quietly sleeping, we were kicked and awakened, there is no reason why we should not speak likewise. One thing was being kicked, and the other was being aroused, from the place wherein we were quietly sleeping.....

"You say, 'we declare the way of righteousness.' But I tell you that we shall not go to heaven by the road of salvation which you point out, for the way to paradise was shown to us by our true prophet Zartusht * before you came. True it is, that without your aid, he was not ignorant of the way to heaven, because he himself went to paradise and returned. Besides, by the *grace* of the merciful God, who made the heavens and the earth, men and brutes, birds and insects, and every thing else, for his own glory, and who can create living flesh from the dead clay of thousands of years, we shall get to heaven.

"Again, you write that the pious people of Scotland and America have sent you hither for the purpose of going about the streets and lanes to proclaim the Gospel to all other tribes, which according to your belief, is right..... The answer to this is, why do you come here for so many thousands of miles to labour? It becomes you to go back to Scotland and America, and after having made Protestants of a number of your own people, to come and make Christians of the Pársís.

* Zartusht is one of the Persian forms of the name of Zoroaster.

Without you, in this way, set your own to rights, no one will believe either you or your religion. Your own not being right, do you pretend to find out the defects of others? It is true that you have come to exercise your calling; there can be no doubt of this. But rest assured, it does not appear to me that even a single Pársí will ever become a Protestant. Do you not know, that for about a hundred years, great trouble has been taken by the Pársís regarding the difference of a month; but one [party] will not yet yield to the other*.....

* The reference here is to the *Kabísah* controversy, which has divided the Pársí community of India into two sects — those of the *Qadímís* and *Rasamís*. The Qadímís, at the head of whom was the learned Mullá Firúz, the author of the George-Námah, form the smaller body, and profess to follow the custom of the ancients, as to the non-admission of an intercalary month to compensate for the time lost by reckoning the religious year merely at 365 days. The Rasamís admit the intercalation, and celebrate their holidays a month later than their rivals.

The following is a statement of the matter, from the preface to the *Dafá-ul Hazl* of Hájí Muhammad Háshim of Isfáhán:—

"The question in dispute is this, whether the intercalation is a religious institution, sanctioned by the practice of the Pársís (the ancient Persians) prior to their last king Yazdijird? or whether another era without intercalation for religious purposes was also sanctioned? That is, whether the intercalary era was an observance instituted by their kings only for the affairs of Government, the collection of revenue, and the equalization of the seasons, or whether it was also employed for purposes connected with religion? The latter the Churigarians wrongfully deny."

"The following," says Mr. Romer in his Illustrations of the Zand and Pahlivi languages (Journal of the Royal Asiatic Society, No. viii, p. 360), "is an amusing example of their love of effect, where they thought something magnificent and high-sounding was attainable. Since the division among the Pársís of India, which arose nearly a century ago, on the subject of computing their year, — the era of Yazdijird — distinguishing names between the parties have been introduced. This era, known at the time in Persia by the name of 'Sál-i-qadim,' was found to differ from that observed by the Indian Pársís by one month, commencing just thirty days earlier according to the names of the months, than the Indo-Persian year. A Pársí had deen deputed to Persia to inquire into the matter; he was a Chúrigar, or bracelet-maker, and appears to have seen reason for following the custom of Persia. On a small number of the community adopting his opinion, and resolving to correct their year and bring it to the Persian standard, it received the name of its introducer's business and was called Chúrigar, as well as Sál-i-qadím, and its observers Chúrígariyáns

Sit down quietly; no Pársí will ever become a Christian.... By embracing your religion, no one will get to paradise. But it is written thus in all religions, and the expounders of law say the same, that if a man observe these three rules, he will unquestionably go to heaven. The first is, to retain power over his anger; the second, to keep his body undefiled from all things; and the third, not to tell lies. Whatever man performs these three things, he is accepted of God. There is no doubt of this. Now tell me, is it not written according to this in your shástra also?....

"Again, you say, the Pársís of Persia, knowing the Christian religion to be true, embraced it; therefore you believe that the

and Qadímís. The great mass of the Pársí population, however, adhered to the existing era, and thence-forward took the names of Rasimiyán and Shaharsáíyán from their year, which was denominated Rasamí, 'customary,' and Shahar-sáí, or 'city-like,' 'common'; and these names continue to prevail among this people, to their separation in many things of social and religious observance and duties.

"During another dispute which began some years ago among the Pársís of India regarding the observance of the Kabísa, or intercalary month, and is not ended yet, some one proposed to substitute for the word 'Shahar-sáí' with its Gujarátí affix, as a corrected reading Sháhansháhi, and thus convert the vulgar into the imperial year, and simple citizens into kings of kings. The thing was considered a joke, and laughed at by the Qadímís and their leader Múllá Fírúz, as passing the reception of the most ignorant; nevertheless the absurd change has been adopted, and among others by the Editor of the lithographed version of the Vendidád, a copy of which was presented to the Asiatic Society; departing from the hitherto unvaried usage, he dates the dedication of his book on the 1st day of the 5th month of the Sháhansháhi year 1200, instead of writing 1st Shaharewar, 1200 Shaharsaí or Rasamí. But this is surpassed by a writer on the Kabísa question, who, professing to follow the authority of the Qissa-i-Sánján, (innocent, I am bound to add, of the egregious anachronism), gravely informs his Pársí readers, that it was the persecution of the Portuguese which compelled their ancestors to quit Diu, an event, we have seen, that occurred about the year of grace 717."

The writer to whom Mr. Romer here refers, is probably the late dastur Aspandiárjí Kámdínjí, of Baroch, the author of the *Kadim Tárikh Párshioní Kasar*. He says of the Pársís at Diva, that ફીરંગીના અમલના સબબથી દીનનો મારગ સારી પઠે ચાલી નહીં સક્યો "on account of the Government of the Firangis, the practice of religion could not proceed in a right manner!"

Pársís of the present generation will likewise embrace this religion, after which I shall make known to you the particular doctrines of my faith. The answer is this,—What are the names of those Pársís, and let me know in what year, in what wilderness, and in what country, they did become Christians. You state that afterwards you will make known the particular matters of your religion, but consider, that when we go to a shop to make purchases, we first of all see the article and then bargain for it. If yours be really the true faith, explain beforehand its particulars; and if it appear in my judgment to be true, most assuredly I shall acknowledge it. Even admitting that the Pársís of Persia embraced Christianity, you are aware that all men are not alike. If a tree grow straight up out of the ground, can you bend it; and if it grow up crooked can you make it straight? Because the Persians believed, shall we believe also? . . . .

"With regard to what you have written in the Oriental Christian Spectator about the Bundéshné, I beg to inform you that this book Bundéshné is not one of our religious books. Nor is it the work of any of our dasturs. Some enemy of our religion probably composed it about a thousand years after our holy prophet Zartusht, because what is written in the Bundéshné is entirely false, and is far removed from our religion and faith. The person who translated this Bundéshné into Gujarátí, according to my judgment, knew nothing whatever of our religion and practice. . . . . Should he wish to argue with me on this point, so long as I live, I shall be ready to meet him. . . . .

"It appears to me most strange, that when men come to the years of discretion, and can understand good and evil, they do not forsake the customs of their childhood. It is not of any consequence, if from the fear of their parents and nurses, they embrace any particular opinions; but when they come to the age of manhood and understand all things, and can reason about all things, it is wonderful that they do not improve their religion in any way whatever, but maintain it without change. It appears, therefore, in my opinion, that though they reach the years of manhood, they still retain the understanding of children."

With the same readiness with which Naurozjí gave publicity to the tract from which these extracts are made, he printed and circulated my reply, * of which a few passages may be here inserted.

"You profess that you have not understood all the article in the Oriental Christian Spectator, which refers to the religion of the Pársís. I shall, therefore, with much pleasure, according to your request, and that of some of the other gentlemen of your tribe, endeavour to get it translated into Gujarátí. I am very desirous that the charges which are brought against your faith should become known: and that you should have an opportunity of fully stating your opinion respecting them. You need be under no restraint on this subject. Speak openly and without fear. Conceal nothing which you believe will defend your sacred books. If you can prove that they came from heaven, and that it is the will of God that you should obey them, you have no reason to be afraid of anything which can be said against them. If, on the other hand, it can be shown that they did *not* come from heaven, as I most firmly believe it can, then you should put no confidence in them. It is not the religion made by *man* about which you should be concerned; but it is the religion sanctioned by *God.* When you perceive, as you say, that 'the greatest pain which can be inflicted on a man is to condemn his religion,' you should diligently inquire whether or not it is worthy of condemnation. It is foolish to be grieved about that which is not profitable; and it is sinful to follow that which is not right. Many things cause pain, which ultimately produce much good. That medicine which is very bitter and nauseous to the taste, is often the means of saving the life. And declaring the evil of a false religion, though it is much disliked by the persons devoted to error, will do much good, if it lead to inquiry and to a search for the true religion. I know a missionary who met a very learned Bráhman,

* It appeared on the 24th September, 1831.

and who told him that the pardon of sin, and the salvation of the soul, cannot be obtained through the Hindú gods. The Bráhman became very angry on this declaration ; and having said to the missionary, ' you have greatly offended me', he returned to his own house. His mind was much distressed at what he heard ; but after reflecting for a long time, he thought that the best way of getting peace, was by inquiring fully into the subject. In the midst of his search, he became convinced, that what the missionary said was true, and he abandoned the religion of his fathers. . . . .

" When I told the editor of the Samáchár, that the Christian religion will assuredly spread over the whole world, I mentioned to him one of the encouragements which we have to prosecute our labours. You inform me that you do not ' believe this prophecy ; ' but it is my belief which influences and directs my conduct, and not yours which influences and directs it. I sec, moreover, that the prophecy is in the course of being fulfilled. The Christian religion, which manifests the glory of God, and promotes the good of men, is increasing its boundaries. God is evidently favouring it. Wherever it is made known, and understood, and wherever its claims to the acceptance of mankind are duly considered, it meets with attention. None have hitherto been able to withstand it. It has begun to spread in India according to its purity ; and the time is coming when the Pársís will enter into it. There are many prophecies in the Christian Scriptures which have already been fulfilled ; and not one of the others which remain will ever fail. If you were fully acquainted with them, you would not be able to scoff at them as you do. The Christian Scriptures contain nothing of the recording of which we have any reason to be ashamed. Many persons have sat down to condemn them, who have been overpowered by their evidence. In no degree, do I fear your exposure of them. Read them from the beginning to the end. If you will call upon me, I shall be happy to give you a complete copy of them in the language which you best understand.

" You seem to call in question my assertion, that the Pársí religion had merely a human origin ; but you have been altogether unsuccessful in proving that it had a divine origin. 'Without man,' you ask, 'what religion did God himself ordain?' This is not the question. God *has* used the instrumentality of man in the establishment of religion; but when men appear, and claim the authority of God on their own behalf, they must show their *credentials*, and they must be consistent in all that they teach. *Every thing* which they reveal must be worthy of God, and free from error of any kind. Now, instead of endeavouring to prove that Zoroaster had a divine commission, and that his doctrines were in every respect pure and holy, you admit that your own religion has defects and faults; and that it is your practice to reject what is bad. You are consequently in a painful situation. Because your religion has faults, it is evident that it did not come from God. Since your 'prophet Zartusht,' in the name of God, teaches what is wrong on several subjects, you can have no certainty of his divine mission; nay, you have the proof that in saying that he came from God, he was an impostor. They who awaken you from the sleep in which you say you were indulging, deserve your best thanks. It is not the time for you to sleep, when you should be awake, and inquiring about the way of salvation.

"It is true that you declare that the way to paradise was shown to you by Zartusht. You say that he himself ascended up thither, and returned. Before venturing your faith on this subject, however, many inquiries should be made by you. You should particularly seek to know what evidence he gave that he had ever left the earth, or was brought into close communion with God. You should ask whether his narrative is consistent with itself and facts which have really occurred. It is manifest to me that he gave no proof of his divine mission; and it is clear that his sentiments are erroneous. He said that he went up into heaven that he might be instructed by God; that he held the very conversation with Hormazd which is to be found in the Avastá; that Hormazd informed him that the whole of this Avastá should be the guide of the faith of mankind till the end of the world; and that it is distinguished by every excellence. If this his narrative, which is to be found in several passages of the books which you esteem true, be correct, it is impossible to account for the loss of by far the greater part of the Avastá, and for the absurdities with which the portions which remain are filled. Can you for a moment believe, that that great Being, who is from eternity, and to whom Zoroaster gives the name of Zaruána, is altogether unmindful of the concerns of the universe? Can you believe that he would sanction the worship of those who are derived from him, and who are inferior to him, and permit them to engross all the reverence, and gratitude, and service, of men? Would God ever recommend the worship of inanimate objects? Would he ever give such trifling orders as are to be found in the Avastá? Would he speak of his being afraid of Ahriman, the prince of devils? Would he ever teach that men can sin when they please, and themselves remove the sin which they commit by the works of their own hands, or by a few insignificant ceremonies? Would he ever seek to amuse mankind by silly and childish descriptions of birds and dogs? Would he ever give false accounts of the rivers and plants of the earth? Consider these questions, and if you are guided by candour, and the love of truth, you will assuredly acknowledge, that the Avastá cannot claim God as its author. Many pages could be filled with the statement of its errors. Do not think that we speak at random on this subject. Since the year 1771, a French translation of your sacred books has been in the hands of Europeans; and we have sufficient means of forming a judgment for ourselves.

"There is an excellent precept of the Saviour, Jesus Christ, with which you seem to have some acquaintance, though you have not quoted it correctly in your letter. It is, 'Thou shalt love thy neighbour as thyself.' The consideration of this command, is one of the reasons why missionaries have been sent from their native countries to Bombay, to proclaim the gospel. True Christians have philanthropic desires of the most extensive kind. They are anxious that, in obedience to the will of Christ, the way of salvation may be made known to all the tribes and nations on the face of the earth. Their own countrymen around them who are not Protestants, are not neglected by them, for, both from books and from ministers, they may receive the instruction which they need; and the inhabitants of India and China, and other idolatrous countries, ought not to be neglected by them. There are many persons in Britain who have no knowledge of mathematics and geography, yet none of your tribe, at the annual meeting of the Native Education Society, stand up and say, 'Gentlemen, you are aware that in Ireland, and England, and Scotland, there are many persons who have no knowledge of the branches of education which you seek to introduce amongst us. Give us then no more aid. Go and instruct your own countrymen.' In like manner, none of you should refuse the gospel, because there are some nominal Christians, who do not walk according to its injunctions. The persons who seek your conversion are your best friends. They ask nothing for themselves. They seek to lead you to reflection, to bring you to the sole worship of the Supreme God, and to induce you to seek the righteousness of the Saviour Jesus Christ, in the room of your own, which has been destroyed by your sins. You declare that you have much to say concerning our deceit. You will find it difficult to prove that we have practised deception of any kind * I assure you that the most respectable gentlemen of your own tribe, are highly displeased with what you have said on this point. You probably spoke in anger; but you should strive never to indulge this passion, except when there may be proper occasion.

"You wish for further information respecting the early spread of Christianity in Persia. On this subject, I would remark that, though it was particularly noticed in Hadiabene, it extended over many of the provinces.† The disciples of Christ, in seeking to fulfil the command of their Lord, used no compulsion and practised no bribery. They

* Dosabhái, and some of the other controversialists whose works are now before me, talk a good deal about the "wiles" and "deceptions" of missionaries. They have not ventured, however, to condescend on any dealings in Bombay, to which they can apply these abusive terms.

† For information on this subject, see the author's Sermon, entitled, *The Doctrine of Jehovah; addressed to the Parsis*, pp. 11—19.

commenced their labours without the protection and favour of man, and they persevered in them amidst the scorn and persecution of many of the Zoroastrian priests and rulers. I am not such a child as to say to you, 'Because many Pársís have become Christians, you ought to become Christians likewise;' but most certainly I say, that it would be well for you, like the Pársís who became Christians, to inquire into the subject, and that you ought not to think it impossible that you and many thousand Pársís should become Christians, when you reflect on what has already taken place. Are you not aware that many of your countrymen, both in Bombay and Surat, entertain great doubts respecting the religion of Zartusht. Those of them who possess most wisdom and information have the least confidence in it. I look on their conversion as being as easy to God, if I may use such an expression, as that of any 'Moghal or Maráthá.' I only lament that hitherto so little has been done for their instruction. They are very enterprising in trade and merchandise, and very diligent in the accumulation of riches. I pray that they may soon think of that which is of infinitely greater importance,—the salvation of their immortal souls.

"On the subject of the Christian religion, you appear to labour under many errors. In the hope of being able to remove some of them, I have appended to this communication a Gujarátí translation (with which I have been furnished through the kindness of a well-wisher of the Pársís) of a letter which has already appeared in the Oriental Christian Spectator, and which was originally addressed to the heathen inhabitants of Persia many hundred years ago.* I invite your candid attention to its statements and reasonings; and I hope that, by the divine blessing, the perusal of it may do you much good. I would remark here, however, that Christianity has existed ever since the fall of man; and that through faith in the coming Redeemer, many persons were saved before he appeared in the world. We desire nothing so much as a full and diligent consideration of the doctrines of our holy

* Extracted from the History of Vartan.

religion. We wish no one to embrace it without inquiry and without conviction. In none of my letters to the editor of the Samáchár, can you find the declaration which you unjustly lay to my charge: — 'Come into the Christian religion, and then we shall tell you the particular matters of it.' I informed the editor of the Samáchár, that I should furnish him with an account of our doctrines; but I never imagined that either you or he, or any other person, could suppose for one moment, that I, or any other Christian minister, could ever make a proposal so absurd as that to which you refer. Jesus Christ acknowledges no disciples who are ignorant of the way of salvation through his atonement, and who do not strive to regulate their conduct by the precepts of holiness. If any of his servants willingly acknowledge any persons as his disciples who do not appear to have the requisitions of the Bible, they are guilty of sin. Hypocrites may find entrance into the Christian Church, for it is sometimes difficult to detect them; but none of the ungodly, till they have been instructed, and till they have exhibited signs of repentance, should ever be reckoned Christians.

"The work of conversion, I readily allow, is exceedingly difficult. It is the work of God; and it transcends the power of man. It is difficult, as you yourself remark, to make a crooked tree straight, and 'men in matters of religion,' if left to themselves, 'retain the understanding of children.' Truth, however, by the grace of God will ultimately prevail. He who formed the human soul can mould it after his own will. By his Holy Spirit, he can lead it to desire salvation, and to love holiness. In the case even of professing Christians, a change of the *heart* is necessary. This is a subject to which, perhaps, you may not have hitherto adverted.

"You speak contemptuously of the persons who have been admitted into the Christian Church in this part of India. Though they have generally had a respectable station in society, and though some of them have been distinguished for their learning, you have not hesitated to speak of them as Kulís. I must tell you, however, that even though they were the poorest and vilest of the earth, I should certainly greatly rejoice over their conversion. The soul of a beggar is as precious as that of a king on his throne. It is immortal; and it will be judged according to the state in which it is found at death. According to the doctrine of the Bible, it will either ascend into heaven, to behold the glory of God, and to engage in his service; or sink into hell, to suffer the punishment of its transgressions.

"It is melancholy to think how people deceive themselves, and suffer themselves to be deceived, respecting the means of salvation. On this most important subject, they very seldom make the slightest inquiry. They become the prey of superstition in millions. They rest their faith on the declaration of trifling books, without ever submitting their claims to reason. They seldom think of the connection which exists between the end and the means by which it is to be obtained. They are like the fools, who think that they can secure the return of light after an eclipse, by taking a dose of medicine. You think, perhaps, that you are much wiser than most of them; for you say that whatever be a man's religion, he will go to heaven, provided he 'retain power over his anger,' 'keep his body undefiled from all things,' and 'abstain from telling lies.' But you must not be offended at me, when I tell you that you are overlooking the great extent of the duty of man, the high and unbending authority and holiness of God, and the very nature of salvation. The commandments of God are exceeding broad. He requires not only purity of the body, but purity of the soul. He requires not only the subduement of anger, and the abstaining from telling lies, but non-indulgence in any kind, or degree of evil, and the constant practice of all that is good. He commands men to love him with the whole soul, and strength, and mind. Sin is committed whenever his precepts are violated. All men are transgressors, and even in their best estate in this world, they daily sin against their Maker. They must be pardoned before they can be saved; and, when God pardons them, he must evince that he is just and pure as well as merciful. Unless he shows that he hates sin, and that it is an evil of the greatest magnitude, he will himself appear as the approver of sin. It is this consideration which declares the value, and points out the glory, of the Christian religion, which shows both the righteousness and the compassion of God. Christ Jesus, in the exercise of his infinite love, suffered in the room of sinners; and His righteousness will be available for all who will ask it, and receive it. Since your own righteousness has been forfeited by your sins; you ought, without delay, but with the greatest humility and earnestness, to betake yourself to the search of a righteousness which God will accept, and for the sake of which he will blot out the sins which you have committed, prepare you for entering into heaven, and confer upon you unspeakable and eternal glory. I pray that you, and many of your country-men, may act in this manner. It is not to wound your feelings merely that I have addressed you, and that I have spoken the truth concerning your religion. In truth, when spoken in a right manner, and on a proper occasion, there is no abuse. As there can be only one true religion, it follows that all others are false.....

"On the subject of the Bundéshné, I say nothing at present. A letter printed at the Akhbár press, has been addressed to you respecting it, by Dastur Edaljí Dárábjí. I shall afterwards advert to it, if it appear necessary."

The letter from which I have now introduced these quotations, did not meet with immediate attention from the person to whom it is addressed, though it attracted considerable notice in the Pársí community. A challenge was given to Naurozjí from another quarter; and it was of such a nature that it could not be overlooked. The dastur, whose name has just been mentioned, and who is the translator into Gujarátí of the Bundéshné, stepped forward to support its claims, and thus curiously defied its impugner to the contest. "Brother Naurozjí, the son of Goosequill, in the strength of what science do you make your assertions, and by the force of what learning do you wish to discuss them as long as you live? If you possess real science, and feel truly strong in knowledge, let not you heart be afraid, neither let any fear come over it. Without hesitation publicly make known your name, that I may see whether you, desirous of determining a genuine book to be a spurious work, are possessed of learning; or that, without learning, you are merely talking big words, and by getting up such letters are seeking your private ends, so that if they pass current you may obtain a livelihood..... Should you make known your name, and there be the strength of learning within you, most certainly I will reply to you, according to the rules of books, and the laws of science, and convince you beyond a doubt. Should it appear to me, on your name becoming known, that there is no learning whatever in the case, then, in this manner knowing you, I will kill the matter. Besides who is he among *your* dasturs that is learned?* Should such a person take up the cudgels in your behalf in this matter, and you will make known his name, openly stating that such a person asserts that the book Bundéshné, is the work of a Jud-dín, and contains nothing but what is foreign to [our] religion, then I will answer him according to the rules of science, and the laws of knowledge. But that a priest should contend with a stone, and a wise man with a fool, I do not consider becoming or consistent..... If you will continue to scrape sand together, and write without effect, I will on no account acknowledge such statements." †

The editor of the Harkárah and Vartamán invited this champion to try the strength of his own learning by handling the padre's letters, ‡ and Goosequill, while he determined to remain *incog*, opined that he ought not to be silent. After much recrimination directed against the dastur, he proceeded without reserve, nay with great boldness, to attack his protegè, the Bundéshné.

" A few of its principles are quoted below," he said, " by which it will be manifest to all readers, that this solitary Adhyáru Edaljí Dárábjí, without dissent, doubt, or hesitation,

* Goosequill is here supposed to be a Quadímí. When Mullá Firúz, who had lately died, was alive, the "strength of learning" was certainly with his sect.

† Circular, dated 14th September, 1831.

‡ Pamphlet, dated 24th September, 1831.

wishes to *intrude* the book Bundéshné, in which such things are written, into the pure Mazdiyasní religion, which descended from heaven, and reached us by means of the exalted Zartusht Asfantamán Anushe-rawán. They are as follows: —

" ' God himself feared and trembled at Satan. — Bears and monkies sprung from the offspring of Jamshíd. — The earth trembled, upon which God infixed the mountains as pins to steady it. — Ahrimán beheld the son of Gaiomard [Kaiomars the first Peshdadian king], upon which, becoming dejected ,he remained with drooping head. A demon then said to Ahriman, Father, arise,why hangest thou thy head, and why art thou dejected ? We are powerful enough, by means of mighty war, to inflict damage on Hormazd and his amsháspands (archangels). — In the Zéré-paránkard (Caspian) sea, God created a white ass, which possessed three feet, and six eyes, and nine mouths, and two ears, and which was the speaker of a certain word. Each of his mouths is as large as a house, his shoulders are of proportionate size, each of his feet falls as heavily on the ground as a thousand feet, and one of his legs is a thousand times as big as a horse's. His two ears are so great that they would reach to the city of Mázandrán. His single voice equals the roaring of the Zéré-paránkard sea, and is as loud as the bellowings of a thousand cows and a thousand asses together. When this ass brays, the demons disappear. When he immerses his head in the sea and shakes his ears, the waves arise on the waters of the Zéré-paránkard sea, and all the females of the sea become pregnant on the braying of the ass, and the pregnancy of the noxious animals in the waters, becomes destroyed. When the ass deposits water in the sea, the water of the seven worlds becomes purified by it. The sea is filled with the water of the ass, and that water goes into hell twice every day. Whenever it is ebb-tide, the water comes back muddy ; but as soon as the ass beholds it, and deposits water, it becomes purified, and were it not for the water of the ass, the waters of the sea would remain polluted. Ahriman cast poison into the sea, and then by the command of God, Tashtar Tír Izad, with the assistance of the ass, took out the water from the Zéré-paránkard sea, and showered rain into it; and by means of the dung and water of the ass, caused the poison to be removed. All the noxious animals died by reason of the rain, and through their poison the waters of the sea became salt, for at first Dádár Hormazd had created them sweet. — Fever departs at the sound of the guitar. — Poison is rendered innocuous by hearing the buzzing of flies. — Dogs fight with the devils. — When men are drowned in the sea, it is a devil of the sea which drowns them, for the water which God has created can never cause the death of any man. The water, indeed, with a view to preserving a man, relieves him twice from the hands of the devil, and raises him to the top, if haply any one may see him and draw him out. — Whenever the fish Karmánik goes down to the bottom of the sea, then the tide flows, and when he rises up again, then it becomes ebb-tide. This fish is as long as a vigorous man could walk between the rising and the setting of the sun. — Dádár Hormazd created trees, and Ahriman, having fought with God, created empoisoned bark upon them. — The *ganámino* (evil) Ahrimán cries, and beats (his breast) in nine different ways. — God created fire, and Ahriman, out of malice, created the smoke within it. Rats, and noxious animals, by reason of their holes, bring Satan up from beneath the earth. — God made 100,000 golden aqueducts, through which he formed the sea. Ahriman cast noxious animals upon the earth, on which God ordered Teshtar Tír Izád to rain a very heavy rain; and he poured down such a heavy one that every drop was big as a cauldron, and through this the earth became divided into seven parts. Formerly the earth was entire. — When there is lightning, it is occasioned by the flashes from the swords of Tashtar Tír Izad and the demons; when there is thunder it springs from the voices of their horses. At the day of judgment, the *darun* * will fight with Satan.'

* Pieces of bread used in a ceremonial way, at the time of prayers, and particularly for the dead. In the fiftieth *gate* of the abridgment of the *Sad-dar*, in the hands of the Pársís, it is thus enjoined, "If a child die between the age of a day and its seventh year, let the *Sarosh Báz* be repeat-

"Now it becomes wise men to take into consideration the above passages, which I have selected from the book Bundéshné, to read, and to investigate them, and to see whether in the pure Mazdiyasní faith such things could be written, that even a sucking child would not credit them. How then shall we term such a book, a book of religion? Moreover, in every page and paragraph of this Bundéshné, there are a thousand matters written with far grosser stupidity than those which have been quoted, by reading and hearing which we ourselves incur damnation; for in the perusal of this book, a thousand blasphemies against the Creator and Preserver of both worlds, appear. . . . For the person who admits that the Bundéshné is a book of religion, there will be no escape from hell before the day of the resurrection, nor will he be released from misery until that final day."*

This was, indeed, a bold assault; and it quite astonished the members of the Pársí community, who had hitherto been accustomed to view the Bundéshné, (or, as Anquetil du Perron writes it, the Boun-dehesch), with great respect, as containing the account of the cosmogony to which they attached their faith, and a tolerably good digest of their religious opinions.†

Little was, or could be, said in favour of the reprobated work; and dastur Edaljí himself remained silent for two years, when in his preface to the Awán Yast,‡ he thus delivered himself: —

ed for its sake, and on the fourth night, let the *darun* (sacred cake) of *Sarosh* be presented." In the fifty-seventh *gate*, persons setting out on a journey are commanded to offer the *safar-darun*, or the darun of the journey.

* Pamphlet dated 3rd Ocrober, 1831. Of the *Din Hadis*, published by Fardunjí the brother of the translator of the Bundéshné, Goosequill observes, that "it is a thousand degrees viler than the Bundéshné, and there are hundreds of observations in it so contradictorily written, that they are utterly at variance with all sense."

† Anquetil supposes the work, which is in Pahliví, to have been composed from original Zand authorities, about the seventh century of the Christian era. Zend-Avesta, tom. iii. p. 337.

‡ Published, with a Gujarátí translation, on the 5th September, 1833.

"The gentleman who, assuming the name of Nauroz Goosequill, has in the Harkárah pamphlet printed reproach about the *Kharé-talátá*, and the fish *Kar*, is informed by his obedient humble servant, that in the Haftan Yast Há of the Izashné, named *Yasmaídhé amsáspantá** there is evidence about the *Kharé talátá* and the fish *Kar*. It is as follows: —

વાશીમચા॰ ઇઆંમ॰ પંચા॰ ઝદુઅરાંમ॰ ઇઅજમેદ* ખરે મચાઇમ॰ અશોનેમ॰ ઇઅજમેદ* ઇઓાઇ॰ હેશતેતે મે દેમ॰ જરીઅંગોહો* વોરોકેશોહે* જરીઓ॰ વોરોકેશેમ ઇઅ જમેદ*

"The meaning of the foregoing *pad* is, 'I worship the *Wasé-panchás-dawarg* fish, which, in Pahliví, is called *Karmání*. I worship the Kharé talátá† which, like a holy being, is in the Zéré-paránkard sea.'‡ Now, gentlemen will observe that the Bundéshné is no made-up book, for this all is the meaning of the Avastá. In the Awán Yast there are several passages to the same purport, as may be seen in their places; and in the other Yasts, and in the Vandidád, Izashné, and other Nusks, there is similar information. Let not gentlemen, then, reckon it [the book] false."

The dastur correctly quotes this passage from the forty-second§ Há of the Izashné,‖ an address used with more than ordinary frequency in the liturgical services of the Pársís; and he also gives us an accurate translation. He

* The words with which the Há commences.

† This passage is in Zand, but in the Gujarátí character, as given by the dastur himself. It will be observed from it, and others afterwards given in the same form, that notwithstanding the similarity of power in the Indian and Zand alphabets, the dasturs are careless in many instances in making it appear in their transferences.

‡ The animal of the three [feet], that is the ass, described in the Bundéshné.

‖ Anquetil du Perron has misapprehended the meaning of this passage. He renders it, Je fais izeschné aux cinq especes d' oiseaux. Je fais izeschné a l'âne pur qui est au milieu du fleuve Voorokesché (Araxe.) Je fais izeschné au fleuve Voorokesché. Zendavesta, tom. i. p. 124.

§ Forty-first of Anquetil.

thus clearly makes the Zand-Avastá reponsible for the monstrous fictions about the ass and fish, as well as the Bundéshné, which his opponent, and others like-minded with himself, have utterly rejected as a religious authority! When Goosequill took his sword into his hand, he did not perceive that it was a two-edged weapon, that with the same movement it would destroy alike what he considered sacred, and what he clearly saw to be absurd. I took care afterwards, in my letters, to show to him, that his own admitted grounds of objection to the book which he condemned, exist in all their strength in the book which he sought to exalt, and to set forth as the result of the inspiration of God. Some of the matters here referred to, will, in subsequent chapters, come under our notice.

The same pamphlet that contained Goosequill's assault on the Bundéshné, set forth an epistle addressed to myself, from a new correspondent who signed himself "Monitor." It contains little of an argumentative character, and is evidently the product of a mind more bent on ignorant objection, than calm and candid inquiry. The following are its most important paragraphs.

"This padre Wilson Saheb affirms his own religion to be true. Now it is known to all, that every one pronounces his own religion to be true; but this padre invites people into the Christian religion, by requesting them to walk in the faith of the Son of God, by which they will find the way of salvation. These missionaries, however, do not consider in their hearts, that in their own country, there are many people of the Christian sect, who, in the conduct and observances of their faith, have many open and concealed variances and differences, on account of which they are continually disputing amongst themselves. If it be necessary to consult about the matters in dispute, then let the book named Martyrology be read, in which lákhs of Protestants are represented as killed in the prime of life. Their customs and observances are so contradictory that they have in consequence given evil names to each other. It becomes them first to set to rights their own religion, and afterwards to set upon that of others.

"But I am desirous that this padre Wilson, or any other missionary, or their companions, will prove by such arguments as can be comprehended, in what manner their prophet Jesus Christ is the Son of God, and how he was born of a virgin; for this Jesus Christ sprung of a family of the Jewish nation, and the people of that ancient nation considering him as a deceiver, by many contrivances, murdered him. The whole particulars of this event are made known in their Bible. But Jesus Christ himself, by his own mouth, declared that he was the 'Son of man.' This padre Wilson Saheb, and the people of his tribe, however, have settled it that he is the Son of God; and, believing upon him, they say that Jesus is the second in the Trinity. The meaning of Trinity is three glories united in one God. The names of the three glorious (essences) in English are, "the Father, the Son, and the Holy Ghost.". . . .

"In the New Testament, in the 17th chapter and 22d verse of Matthew, Jesus Christ makes known before-hand to his own disciples the events which were to happen to himself, as follows:—

"'And while they abode in Galilee, Jesus said unto them, the Son of man shall be betrayed into the hands of men, and they shall kill him, and the third day he shall be raised again, and they were exceeding sorry.'

"Now from this it clearly and openly appears, that Jesus Christ determined himself to be the Son of man; if he were the Son of God, why is it not written in the place, that 'I the Son of God, will be given into the hands of men?' From hence it is proved, that he was the Son of man; and in the same manner it is openly declared in the same book — and in all the other books of the gospel, that he is the Son of man....

"Now there is amazing ignorance in diverse people calling him the 'Son of God.' Many also affirm that he is God himself, but the reason of calling him so, appears to my humble judgment to be, that of this Isá, who is also called Jesus Christ, no book seems to exist, for the New Testament, which is called the Evangile, appears to have been made after the death of Christ by his disciples, whom he had chosen from amongst poor men. In this work, Christ, in several places, calls God his Father. But when he was conversing with his own disciples and others, and instructing them at such times, instead of their God, he called him my Father; from which it may be suspected that these people may term him so likewise. But he called them all customarily the sons of God, that is, his creatures. But another doubt arises about that Testament, because those disciples were very poor people. Many were fishermen, such as we call Kúlis here. Of such he had also made disciples, from which it may be suspected that they were totally ignorant of the art of reading and writing. Nor can I find-out what was the original language of the Gospels, and of the New Testament, or who was their author: and the present English and other translations upon which it is endeavoured to fix [men's] faith—from what language were they [translated], because the language of that city, [Jerusalem] was probably Hebrew? But the Jewish nation was much opposed to the religion of Christ, and bore great enmity to it; and therefore, after much management, they killed Christ, because he set up claims to be a prophet, and to be called the true Messiah. But regarding the coming of the Messiah, the prophets of this ancient nation had given signs, and had pointed out the time; according to their belief many circumstances did not coincide during the life of Jesus, and therefore being suspicious of him, they, as above related, killed him. All the particulars of these matters are related in their New Testament, and in other books. The elements of the Christian religion are all founded upon the Gospels and Testament — There is not a single sentence of Jesus's own [composition], but this book is similar to a book of tales. Now what faith is to be placed in this book?

"To make the matter short — let them be only asked how many Christians have these missionaries made, and how much have they extended their religion. How many years is it now since they are labouring here, — and are persuading the sons of Ghátí Kúlís in every lane and every street. This is not the way to increase their religion, — but it is meanness. It becomes them in the first place to set to rights their own religion, and to bring into one way the numerous Christian people who walk in different paths, — and afterwards to attempt [to convert] others. Otherwise, some will say, 'You are converting people of other religions to Christianity; — to which sect do you invite me, — to the Catholic, or Protestant, or the Lutheran, or the Calvinist, or the Jacobite, or the numerous other divisions into which you are split? And of all these different schisms which is the best, write and let me know." *

Some of the objections contained in this extract have been repeated in the controversial works which are now before me. I therefore insert a translation of the greater part of my reply.

" The faith into which I pray that the Pársís may be brought is that of the *Bible*. This sacred book contains all that is necessary for man to know concerning the character of God, the natural state of man, the means of salvation, the judgment of God, and heaven and hell. The religion of Christ, the Saviour, is to be found in it without any error. If its precepts and doctrines be observed, there will be no putting to death on account of differences of religious sentiment. On the contrary, there will be love and peace among all who really rest on it their belief. There are some persons of the sects which you mention, who, being deprived of the Bible by their corrupted teachers, embrace doctrines, and follow practices, which are entirely opposed to it, and who have no right to the name of Christian. There are others, who, though they differ in opinion on some comparatively unimportant subjects, are agreed on all that is necessary to salvation. The Bible is a proclamation from heaven ; and when it is presented to *you*, it will avail you nothing to refuse to believe it, that others despise it. It will in no respect mislead the humble and diligent inquirer. Its wisdom is that of God, and not that of man. If you wish to know what Christianity is, you must peruse the sacred page.

" Monitor appears to have fallen into several most important mistakes concerning the Saviour. Jesus Christ is un-

* Pamphlet, published 3d October 1831.

doubtedly, in the highest sense, the Son of God. He is one of the glorious persons of the Trinity alluded to by Monitor; and to the Father he stands in the relation of only-begotten Son, not because his being was derived from the Father, for he is from everlasting to everlasting, but because he is of the same nature as the Father, because he is the object of the Father's peculiar love, because he is the manifestation of the Father's glory, and because of other reasons which may be learned from the perusal of the Bible. God sent his Son into the world to save sinners. He became incarnate by the power of the Holy Ghost, through the virgin Mary, as related in the Gospels. On this subject, there is the following account by Luke:—'And in the sixth month the angel Gabriel was sent from God, unto a city of Galilee, named Nazareth, to a virgin espoused to a man whose name was Joseph, of the house of David; and the virgin's name was Mary. And the angel came unto her, and said, 'Hail, thou that art highly favoured, the Lord is with thee: blessed art thou among women.' And when she saw him, she was troubled at his saying, and cast in her mind what manner of salutation this should be. And the angel said unto her, 'Fear not Mary; for thou hast found favour with God. And behold, thou shalt conceive in thy womb, and bring forth a son, and shalt call his name JESUS, [that is, Saviour]. He shall be great, and shall be called the Son of the highest; and the Lord God shall give unto him the throne of his father David: and he shall reign over the house of Jacob for ever, and of his kingdom there shall be no end.' Then said Mary unto the angel, 'How shall this be, seeing I know not a man?' And the angel answered and said unto her, 'The Holy Ghost shall come upon thee; and the power of the Highest shall overshadow thee; therefore also that holy thing which shall be born of thee shall be called the Son of God.'*

"In accordance with this narrative, Jesus appeared on earth as the Son of God, and one with the Father, and he was acknowledged as such, as may be learnt from the following

* Luke i. 26—35.

passages of the New Testament, which Monitor has entirely overlooked; Matthew xiv. 33; xxvi. 63, 64; Mark iii. 11; Luke xxii. 70, 71; John iii. 18; v. 25; x. 36; xi. 4; xix. 7; xx. 31. Rev. ii. 18, &c. He proved himself to be declaring the truth on this, and all other points, by his wonderful works, and by his resurrection from the dead, and ascension into heaven. He was viewed as the Son of God, and even as very God, by his disciples; and all who believe in him look to him in the same characters.* There is nothing in all this

* As more than one of the controversialists to whom I now reply, have ignorantly asserted that the doctrine of the Divinity of Christ is not taught in the Sacred scriptures, I here beg to lay before them a portion of the evidence by which they ought to be convinced of their mistake.

THE DIVINITY OF CHRIST PROVED FROM THE OLD TESTAMENT.

I.—*Several personal manifestations of Christ as God are recorded.* Genesis xvi. 7—13, compared with Malachi iii. 4. and John i. 18; Genesis xviii. Genesis xxi. Genesis xxxi. 11—13; Genesis xlviii. 15; Exodus iii. 1—15; Exodus xxiii 20—23; Isaiah lxiii. 7—9; Zechariah iii. 6—7; or Zechariah xii. 8—II. *The names and titles of God are applied to the Messiah.* Job xix. 25—26; Psalm xlv. 6, 7, compared with Hebrews i. 8; Psalm cx; Isaiah vii. 14. compared with Matthew i. 23, and other passages of the New Testament; Isaiah ix. 6; Isaiah xl. 3, 9, 10, and 21—25, compared with Romans xiv. 11, and Philippians ii. 10, 11. *Divine honours are ascribed to the Messiah.* Psalm ii. 12; compared with Psalm xl. 4, and Jeremiah xvii. 5; Zechariah xiii. 7.

THE DIVINITY OF CHRIST PROVED FROM THE NEW TESTAMENT.

I.—*The names of God are given to Christ.* GOD. John i. 1; John xx. 28; Acts xx. 28; Romans ix. 5; 1 Timothy iii. 16; Titus i. 3; Hebrews i. 8; I John v. 20. LORD. Acts x. 36; Romans x. 12; I Corinthians ii. 8; James ii. 1; I Corinthians xv. 47; Revelation xvii. 14; I Corinthians viii. 6; Luke i. 16, 17, 76, compared with Isaiah xl. 3.—II. *The attributes of God are ascribed to Christ.* ETERNITY. John i. 1; John xvii. 5; Colossians i. 17; Revelation xxii. 13. UNCHANGEABLENESS. Hebrews i. 12; Hebrews xiii. 8. OMNIPRESENCE. John iii. 13; Matthew xviii. 20; Matthew xxviii. 20. OMNISCIENCE. Matthew xi. 27; John vi. 46; John ii. 24, 25; I Corinthians iv. 4, 5; Colossians ii. 3; Revelation ii. 23; compared with Jeremiah xvii. 9, 10. OMNIPOTENCE. Philippians iii. 21; Hebrews i. 3; I Corinthians i. 24; II Peter i. 3. HOLINESS. Acts iii. 14, 15.—III. *The works of God are ascribed to Christ.* CREATION. John i. 3; Colossians i. 16, 17; Hebrews i. 2, 10. GIVING OF LIFE. John i. 4; Acts iii. 15; John x. 18. MIRACULOUS WORKS IN HIS OWN NAME. John x. 37; Matthew viii. 3. SALVATION. Matthew i. 21. II Timothy ii. 10; Hebrews v. 9. JUDGMENT OF THE WORLD. Matthew xxv. 31, 32, &c;

inconsistent with his being the Son of man, for he was the Son of man as born of the virgin Mary.

"Had not Christ Jesus been a divine person, he could never have been the Saviour of mankind. The reason you will learn from what follows. Men lose all their righteousness before God whenever they commit a single sin, for the law of God promises life only to those who perfectly obey it. No *created being* can be their Saviour, for every creature, however great and powerful, is only the servant of God, and can never serve God more than he is bound to do, and never procure any righteousness which he can give to another.

"Some people, like the Pársís, say that God can give to men righteousness, and can deliver them from the punishment of sin, without their having any Saviour; but such persons overlook both the law and character of God. When God gives his commandments to men, he informs them that the consequence of disobedience is punishment, and when his commandments are violated, punishment must be inflicted. God cannot pardon sin without showing that he views it with infinite hatred. Were he to act otherwise, it would not appear to his creatures, in this and other worlds, that he is perfectly holy. They would not perceive the exceeding evil of sin, and they would not respect his authority. Taking these facts into consideration, we see the glory of Christ as a Saviour. He took upon himself the nature of man, and suffered in the room of man. Those who believe in him, and who are made holy by his Spirit, receive eternal salvation.

"Long before Jesus appeared in the world, the Jewish prophets had foretold that he would surrender himself to be put to death by the Jews; and their sayings were fulfilled. He was holy, harmless, undefiled, and separated from sin-

John v. 22, 27; Acts x. 42, Acts xvii. 31; Romans ii. 16; Romans xiv. 10; II Corinthians v. 10; II Timothy iv. 1, 8.—IV. *The honours of God are given to Christ.* Matthew xxviii. 19; John v. 23; John xiv. 13; Acts vii. 59; Acts iii. 66. II Corinthians xiii. 14; Romans ix. 5; Philippians ii. 10; Revelation i. 5, 6; Revelation v. 11, 12, &c.—V. *The relations of God are ascribed to Christ.* John x. 30, 38; John xiv. 9, 11; John xvii. 10; II Corinthians iv. 4. Colossians i. 15, 16; Hebrews i. 3; Colossians ii. 9.

ners. He taught the law of God with authority, and he reproved every kind and degree of iniquity. He was consequently hated by most of the Jews, and though the Romans could find no fault in him, they gave him up to the Jews to be crucified. He did not choose to deliver himself from the hands of his enemies, though he possessed infinite power. He knew that unless he died for sinners, the salvation of men could not be accomplished, and, in the exercise of love to man, he gave his life. He rose, however, from the dead on the third day ; and ascended into heaven.* He wrote none of our Scriptures, but knowing assuredly that his cause was the cause of God, he committed the teaching of his doctrines to his apostles, and by the Holy Ghost, endowed them for the discharge of their duties. Had Christ been an impostor, he himself would probably have composed some book to support his cause, and have sought at once to get the rich and the powerful arrayed on his side. He did not, however, act in this manner. He chose his apostles principally from among fishermen ; and thus gave us occasion to repose in their veracity. We know that their testimony must have been true, for their cause without any worldly recommendations, could not have prevailed, had they been untruthful men. When we see them boldly declaring in Jerusalem, where all the facts of the case were known, that their Master had risen from the grave ; when we see them in no degree afraid of investigation ; when we see the Roman and Jewish rulers threatening them with death, and unable either to deter them from their work, or to produce the body of Jesus ; when we see hundreds and thousands believing in their doctrine, and submitting to great trials on its account ; and when we see them preach with great success in the different countries of the earth, we receive the assurance that God himself was on their side.

* Dosabháí, Kalam Kas, &c. object to the Bible, because Christ did not evince his divine power by coming down from the cross. They must remember, that it was necessary that he should offer himself as a sacrifice for the sins of his people. By rising from the dead, he performed a greater miracle, than if he had saved himself from the cross when alive.

"Many prophecies respecting Christ are to be found in the the Old Testament received by the Jews, and all of them which referred to his incarnation, have been fulfilled in the minutest manner. It was foretold, for example, that the Messiah should be both God and man; that as man he should be born of the family of David, in the village of Bethlehem, and that his mother should be a virgin; that he should be worshipped by wise men; that in his infancy he should be carried into Egypt; that he should be a Prophet; that he should be a Priest; that he should be hated and persecuted; that he should be sold for thirty pieces of silver; that he should be accused by false witnesses; that he should not plead on his trial before his judge; that he should be insulted, buffetted, and spit upon; that he should be crucified; that his hands and feet should be pierced; that he should be patient under his sufferings; that he should die along with malefactors; that he should give his life, not for his own sins, but for the sins of others; that there should be an earthquake at his death; that he should be buried with the rich; that he should rise again from the dead on the third day; and that remission of sins should be preached in his name among all nations. You will perceive from the Gospel that all these events have actually taken place in regard to Christ. It is true that the great body of the Jews did not believe in him, but it is also true that God signally punished them for their unbelief. Their city was destroyed, and great numbers of them were driven from their country. Their descendants, who approve of their ways, are still scattered, as you know, over the face of the whole earth.

"In the Hebrew language, the Old Testament, which was written before the coming of Christ, and which principally treats of his advent as about to take place, is composed. In the Greek language, which was most generally known and spoken at the time of Christ,* is composed the New Testament,

* The Greek language was most extensively diffused throughout Asia, and the North of Africa, in consequence of the conquests of Alexander the Great, and the subjection of numerous countries to the sway of the Greeks.

which principally treats of the Saviour's birth, doctrines, miracles, sufferings, death, resurrection, ascension, and reign. When Monitor has diligently read these books in the Gujaráti or English translation; when he has perceived their glory; and when he has believed on him whom they reveal, he will be at no great loss to determine into what sect of Christians he should enter. When their truths are more widely and boldly proclaimed, and when God is pleased, by his Spirit, to rouse the inhabitants of this city to inquiry, and to incline them to flee from the 'wrath to come,' the converts will be numerous. In the meantime, we must both labour and pray, and be grateful for the success which has been experienced. There is no meanness in addressing those who are inclined to listen to us, in public places. Men are perishing for lack of knowledge; and it is our duty to communicate it to them wherever they can be most advantageously found. We profess to be the servants of him who came down from heaven to save the lost; and it should be our delight to engage in any service, however humble, which has the tendency to promote his praise, and benefit mankind. Did ever any of the Pársís complain because the Honorable Company has appointed vaccinators for the poor, who bring their children to them at the places of public concourse? It is the glory of the Christian religion, that it despises none on account of their rank in society. In this respect, it differs widely from the Hindú and Pársí religions, according to which righteousness can be purchased with money, and according to the first of which, all Shudras are despised.

"It is not my wish, nor that of any other Christian, to condemn any true prophet who existed five hundred years before Christ. All the true prophets, however, rejoiced to speak of the coming of Christ. Zartusht cannot be reckoned among the number of those who have received a commission from God, and yet the Pársís put their trust in him. I am grieved when I consider that they deceive themselves, and that few of them ever inquire about the evidence of Zartusht's mission. The books on which they rely are full of errors and absurdities. Some of these I have already pointed out; and after I have received the letter which Nauroz Goosequill has promised to send to me, I shall point out many more. In the meantime, I recommend Monitor to read and judge for himself. Let truth *prevail.*" *

A few days before this letter was circulated among the Pársís, I had presented to all the subscribers to the Harkárah and Vartamán newspaper, a copy of Matthew's Gospel in Gujarátí, furnished by the Bombay Bible Society. The gift was recommended to the careful attention of the Pársís by the editor of the periodical now mentioned, as well as myself; and there is reason to believe that it was not neglected by many who received it. A considerable number of applications for other portions of the divine word, were soon made by natives; and it became evident that there was no small degree of religious inquiry in the island of Bombay. This was the first desired result of our discussions, from which no beneficial result could be expected without strict attention to the divine testimony.

Before the close of the year in which the correspondence which we have now noticed took place, Nauroz Goosequill favoured me with a long rejoinder to the communication which I had addressed to him. "The second letter of Pársí Nauroz Goosequill addressed to the Rev. John Wilson," it was said in a Bombay periodical, "is exceedingly long, and exceedingly stupid. It contains little which can be called argument; but is filled with expressions of confidence in the faith of Zoroaster, and with vain attempts to rebut the objections which have been brought against it. The writer confesses that he possesses not the least ability to urge his steed upon the disputed field, and the reader must admit that this is the case.

"'The reliance of myself, and the people of my tribe,' he observes, 'is wholly upon the excellent Mazdayasní religion, transmitted to us by means of our prophet Hazrat Zartusht Asfantamán. This religion has long been established and confirmed by a thousand proofs, and by a thousand miracles, and the casting censures upon it, by scurrilous people, will not alter

* Pamplet published on the 26th October, 1841.

it to the degree of a barley-corn ; of this be assured. From our true scriptures which have come down from heaven, you pick out a few insignificant errors. Now, of our true scriptures which have descended from heaven, and which have long been established by a thousand proofs and a thousand miracles, — of these scriptures, I say, if your wish be to have your mind convinced, then it were easy for me, or the people of my tribe having re-established them, to prove them true by a hundred illustrations.'

" There is no attempt made to adduce any of these numerous proofs. ' Whosoever casts aspersions on our pure religion, will not escape from hell-fire till the resurrection, and at the time when infants cry, Zoroaster smiled,' are viewed as declarations amply sufficient to supply their place. No difficulty is felt in accounting for the loss of the greater part of Zoroaster's writings ; and Europeans are said to believe not only in the authenticity, and genuineness, but in the divine origin, of the fragments which remain !

" You yourself allow, it is said, that God propagated a religion by the hands of man. Now all that is necessary for me to do is, to make you acquainted with the witnesses of the assurance of the mission of Zartusht. That true prophet brought a religion from the court of heaven, and pointed out to the peculiar people of God a path, which was revealed in all the Pársí scriptures, of which there was no limit. Had all the voluminous celestial books remained to the present time, — had they not, by the wilfulness of Sikandar Rumí, and Umar Khalíf been destroyed, then you would have found no ground for questioning our scriptures. From them alone, would entire satisfaction have been obtained, and there would have been no necessity for us to speak. Nevertheless, those writings which, by the compassion of the Most High, yet remain, are sufficient to substantiate the truth of those which are lost. Of these there are demonstrative tokens. Concerning our true prophet Zartusht, there is in our own scriptures, indeed, a vast quantity written ; but the evidence respecting him is from the wise men of your race, of whose names few places on earth can be ignorant. They having dived and pried into this matter with close investigation, have established it upon well-founded proofs ; and this is declared in many books.

"In reply to these statements, the following passage occurs in Mr. Wilson's rejoinder. 'Every person must perceive that the Pársís are entirely destitute of an authoritative rule of faith. The books which they esteem sacred are mere fragments of works which are now lost, and being nothing better than scraps, it becomes an object to inquire into the reason of the loss of the original works to which they are said to have belonged. It is easy to say that they were destroyed by Sikandar Rumí*, the Khalíf Umar, and other individuals. This may be very true, but it still remains to be explained, why books pretending to be a revelation from God, and asserting that they should always be in use, should be lost. Zoroaster says that his work was eternal. How comes it to pass, if this were the case, that the twentieth *núsk* is all that remains of the Avastá.† Had Zoroaster said that most of his book was to be lost, we should not have framed an objection to him from the violence of the Greeks and Muhammadans ; but when he says that all the Avastá was to remain, and we perceive that most of it has perished, we are forced to declare that his claims had no ground in truth.'

"It was expedient to undeceive the Pársís in regard to the opinions which Europeans entertain of their sacred books and religion ; and in order to accomplish this object, several extracts were adduced by Mr. Wilson. Reference was particularly made to the opinion of Prideaux, Rollin and others, that 'Zoroaster, with the exception of Muhammad, was the greatest impostor that ever lived' ; and to that of Sir William Jones, who in his satirical letter addressed to Anquetil du Perron observes, 'Ou Zoroastre n'avait pas le sens commun, ou il n'ecrivoit pas le livre que vous lui attribuez.'‡ Some of

* Alexander the Great.

† According to the Pársís, there were originally twenty-one núsks.

‡ "Either Zoroaster had not common sense, or he did not write the book which you attribute to him."

the Pársís were not satisfied by these, and similar statements, and they resorted to private inquiry among their European friends. They were informed that all Christians are bound to believe that their religion is an exclusive system, and that the followers of other systems are deceiving and injuring themselves by neglecting inquiry.

" From the strain of Nauroz's letter, it appears very plain that many of the Pársís believe that the mere report of miracles said to have been performed by Zoroaster, and the insertion of some good doctrines in the Avastá, are sufficient to prove his divine mission, and the heavenly origin of his instructions. In order to exhibit the vanity of this confidence, the following remarks were made in the rejoinder.

" ' The Pársís, like Nauroz Goosequill, are accustomed to tell us that Zartusht was introduced into the world in miraculous circumstances, and that during the course of his life he himself performed a variety of wonderful works. They tell us that an angel was sent to his father, who persuaded him to drink a glass of wine, and that his wife soon afterwards conceived and bare a son. They tell us, like Nauroz Goosequill, that at the time of his birth, when other children cry, Zartusht smiled; that the hands of the persons who sought to kill him, agreeably to the order of the king, were arrested by a divine impulse; that he was exposed to the fury of wild beasts which did him no harm; that when the king wished to drive herds of cattle upon him, one of them stood over him till they had all passed by; that he was thrown into the flames and came out unhurt; and that he was caught up into heaven, and brought down the Zand-Avastá. It would be well if the Pársís in Bombay would seek for the *proofs* of these assertions. They ought not to be believed without certain evidence.

" ' I have asked some persons to state their reasons for believing in these stories; and they have not been a little puzzled. Some of them say that they have heard them from their parents; others that they have read them in books. Are these sufficient reasons for crediting them? Many foolish tales are afloat in the world, and many errors and falsehoods of various kinds are contained in books. An investigation of the strictest kind must be resorted to; and the most diligent search must be made. Who saw the miracles? Who gave testimony respecting them? Who examined the witnesses? Who recorded the evidence? Who can prove that it is uncorrupted? These are inquiries which most undoubtedly ought to be made.

"'It is found that there are no witnesses, and that there is no collateral history for the guidance of the student. The Musalmáns, it is said, have made sad havoc, and only one núsk of the Avastá, and a few other insignificant works, remain. These, we are told, are letters from heaven; and they ought to be received as such. Are they worthy of this character?

"'Though the Pársí scriptures contained many good things, I would not, on that account alone, say that they have come from God. You yourself, Mr. Editor, are able to write clever things, and good things. Thousands in every country are able to do the same. They can lay down good moral precepts; they can give good advice; they can dilate on the arts and sciences; they can describe the different countries of the world, and their various inhabitants and productions; they can frame curious stories; they can compose poetry; they can write philosophical treatises; and they can speculate on the planets, stars, and other worlds far removed from our globe. Are they, on these accounts, to be esteemed prophets, and their writings to be reckoned books from heaven? Most assuredly not. Before, then, you believe in the Pársí scriptures, you should perceive that their excellency transcends the power of men, and that they are worthy of God to bestow. If the wisdom, and holiness, and glory of God, is not to be found in them, you ought to have no faith in them. If they are of little or no importance, and, if they contain any falsehoods, or any errors, it is manifest that they are not from God.'"*

My reply to Nauroz was given in sixteen chapters, which

* Oriental Christian Spectator, May, 1832.

were published in as many numbers of the Gujarátí Harkárah and Vartamán newspaper. The objects which I kept in view throughout, were to impugn the authority of the Vandidád, and point out its numerous errors in theology, and morals, and at the same time to set forth the evidence and excellence of Christianity, in its doctrines, precepts, examples, and scheme of salvation. The charges which I made against the Vandidád I afterwards collected together in a lecture, which I delivered to an audience, composed both of natives and Europeans, on the 19th and 26th June, 1833.* This discourse was preceded by an extended course of lectures on natural religion, and formed part of a general inquiry into the question, Where is a divine revelation to be found? It was published in the circumstances mentioned in the preface.

" The following lecture," it is there remarked, " forms part of a short series of discourses which I have lately delivered on the Pársí religion. It is published in compliance with the expressed wish of a number of respectable individuals who are attached to that faith ;† and it is submitted to their candid consideration, not with the view of wantonly wounding their feelings, but in the hope that it may contribute, in some degree, to lead them to such inquiry as may issue in the rejection of error and embracement of truth. The Pársís of India are superior in many respects to most of their countrymen ; and it is the earnest hope and desire of not a few of their European friends, that they may be among the first who will rigidly examine the claims of the different religious systems, and devote themselves, with their acknowledged intelligence and vigor, to the pursuit and practice of truth. The zeal, and good temper, with which they have entered into religious

* The substance of the lecture, and more than this, I beg the reader to observe, had been published in Gujarátí, the vernacular language of the Pársís, in tho newspaper above-mentioned.

† Aspandiárjí politely says, that "the conclusion, [from my not specifying their names] would be, that Dr. Wilson had been advised by some vagabond Pársís, actuated by no other motive than that of earning some paltry means to fill their hungry bellies" ! !

discussions during the two last years; the decision with which many of them have already renounced the claims of the Bundéshné, and Ardai-Viráf-Námah; the encouragement which they have afforded to the native newspapers, which, under good management, may prove invaluable blessings to the community; the increased readiness which they evince to promote a general education; their gradual inclination to the adoption of what is praiseworthy in European customs; and many other circumstances which could easily be enumerated, tend to strengthen these expectations."

My remarks on the Vandídád, were founded principally on the French translation of Anquetil du Perron, published in 1771. "From his version," I observed, "and with an occasional reference to the Gujarátí translation and original [Zand], which I was enabled to inspect through the assistance of a learned Pársí, I have made an English version, to which I shall appeal. I have a considerable degree of confidence, that, in all essential points, my quotations will be found correct." Since the publication of my lecture, I have been enabled to devote considerable attention to the Zand language, the key to which I obtained in the interlineary Gujarátí Translation and Paraphrase of the late Frámjí Aspandiárjí, in the Commentaire sur le Yaçna of M. Burnouf, and Bopp's Comparative Grammar of the Sanskrit, Zand, and other languages,* and by following out the philological inquiries which the language itself suggests. Though I have found that it is not difficult to improve upon Anquetil's version, I have also seen that for the purpose of ordinary theological discussion it is, generally speaking, sufficiently accurate.

The principal object of my lecture, is to prove that the Vandidád has no claim to be considered a divine revelation. The position which I lay down respecting it, I endeavour to support by the following remarks:—

* Vergleichende Grammatik des Sanskrit, Zend, Griechischen, Lateinischen, Litthauischen, Gothischen and Deutschen von Franz Bopp. Berlin, 1833.

1. There are no proofs of its authenticity, genuineness, or credibility.

2. The Vandidád Sádé is very defective as a rule of faith.

3. The Vandidád robs God of all his glory, inasmuch as it represents the supreme God as inactive, as disregardful of the concerns of the universe, and as having surrendered the administration of affairs to Hormazd.

4. The Vandidád gives a highly irrational account of the origin and operations of natural good and evil.

5. The Vandidád teaches and recognizes the deification of the elements, and other inanimate objects.

6. The Vandidád gives an erroneous view of the natural state of man.

7. The Vandidád contains gross scientific blunders.

8. The Vandidád prescribes an immense number of absurd ceremonies.

9. The Vandidád ascribes an absurd power, or influence, to the ceremonies which it recommends.

10. The Vandidád represents ceremonial observances, as more important than moral observances.

11. The Vandidád contains some passages directly opposed to morality.

12. The Vandidád does not propose a reasonable scheme of salvation.

13. The Vandidád does not give a becoming account of the future state.

The doctrines of the Vandidád on the matters here adverted to, are contrasted throughout with those of the sacred Scriptures.

As it is principally in reply to my lecture that the works which I at present undertake to confute have been prepared, and as the various topics of which it treats must pass in detail before our notice in subsequent parts of this work, I shall not in this place enter into any particular statements respecting them. It is sufficient to allude to the manner in which it was at first received by the Pársí public.

The first criticism upon it appeared in the Jám-i-Jamshíd

newspaper, on the 16th September 1833, under the signature of "A Zoroastrian."* The writer of the article says that he has discovered several errors in the pamphlet, though he does not point them out, and does not profess himself to be able to understand the Vandidád. "It is incumbent on some of the *pious priests,*" he says, "to reply to all the remarks." He seems inclined to put a parabolical interpretation on the words Hormazd and Ahriman, the names of the good and evil Principles of the Pársís. "The honorable prophet Zoroaster," he says, "has declared matters of wisdom, by various secrets (or mysteries,) and signs, and minute circumstances, that by some persons they should be considered as facts, and not fall into the hands of the ignorant, but should be understood in their whole meaning and mystery by the wise." He objects to the Bible, as "absurd and unreasonable," because it contains this statement:—"And the Lord said, I will destroy man whom I have created from the face of the earth; both man and beast, and the creeping thing and the fowls of the air: for it repenteth me that I have made them."† And he speaks of the miracles of Zoroaster as equally authenticated with those of Christ.

The attempt made by this writer to shield the Vandidád from a just criticism, by asserting that it is full of secrets and mysteries, appeared in its proper character to the acute and intelligent editor of the Harkárah and Vartamán. In his paper of the 19th September, he says, "The Jám-i-Jamshíd, backed by its learned *dasturs* and *munshís*, has dared a reply. The correspondent of our contemporary has ventured to assert that 'Mr. W. knows nothing of his subject,' and as a reason adds, that 'the subject is a secret one,' stating, however, that he intends to employ his dasturs to answer what he himself knows nothing of. By whom was this secret dis-

* From much of what follows, the reader will perceive that there is no foundation for the following observation of Aspandiárjí:—"It was after a very long time that the knowledge of this publication, and its contents spread among the Pársís of this place."

† Genesis vi. 7.

closed to *him?* How has *he* proved the Vandidád to be a secret? Has he any heavenly commerce? What is his reason for disclosing a secret? Let these [questions] be answered. He acknowledges his own ignorance of the subject, and in another place, instead of a direct reply, attacks the Bible..... A dastur, we understand, is now preparing a work opposed to Mr. Wilson, and we are happy to see the dasturs coming forward in such a cause; but as we take to ourselves the merit of first calling upon our priests for an explanation of the difference between Hormazd and Ahriman, we request them to give us an answer to *our* question of the secret. The writer of the *Jámi* gives no credit to Mr. Wilson for his pamphlet, because it refers to a secret subject; but who of the dasturs for the last 1100 years, has let us into this secret? If any fortunate man has had a dream lately on the point, we are ready to hear it. 1100 years ago the Vandidád Sádé was regarded by the Pársí priests as a *secret;* but no one during that time has solved it, and whither are we going for a solution! We sincerely hope that the members of the Pancháyat * will take this matter into consideration, not depending on the dasturs, as that confidence, we fear, would only injure our cause. While, too, the missionaries are so active, in proving the errors of our religion, are we to be idle? Our countrymen must not be offended at our notice of their *valued* work, as we believe it is to their advantage we have gone so far. Any reply by pamphlet shall be instantly attended to." †

These reasonable remarks called forth nothing but abuse from the person for whose benefit they were particularly intended. The Zoroastrian, in reply, endeavoured to explain

* Etymologically, this word means the Council-of-Five. The Sanhedrim of the Pársís, however, consists of eighteen members, more or less.

† This article appeared both in English and Gujárati, in both of which languages the Harkárah and Vartamán newspaper was now published. It is much to be regretted that few of the native papers in the vernacular languages pass under the eye of Europeans. Were their editors aware that an intelligent judgment was formed by our countrymen of their lucubrations, they would write in a more decent and respectful tone than that in which they commonly indulge.

them, by alleging that the writer was entirely "under the thumb of the missionaries!"

In a letter which I myself addressed to the Jám-i-Jamshíd, I wrote as follows:—"I am glad to receive from the Zoroastrian the expression of his opinion, that it is incumbent on the priests to reply to all my remarks; and that a learned gentleman is at present engaged in writing a rejoinder..... It appears to me, that the attempt which is made by your correspondent to traduce the Bible, is a strange mode of defending the Vandidád. If you were accused, in a court, of theft and robbery, the judges would think that you were making a very poor defence, were you, instead of vindicating *yourself*, to proceed to accuse some of your *neighbours* of the crimes laid to your charge. The proof of *their* guilt would not establish *your* innocence. The charges made against yourself would still hang over you; and if you could not remove them, by proving that they were unjust, a sentence, agreeable to the amount of evidence brought forward, would be pronounced against you.

"It must not be supposed from these remarks that I am afraid of an investigation of the Bible. I greatly desiderate on its behalf the strictest inquiry. 'The Bible,' I have remarked, 'has sustained the most rigorous investigation by friend and foe; and it has commanded the assent and veneration of men of the greatest intellect and education. It has proved victorious over persecution the most direful, and barbarism and ignorance the grossest and most confirmed, and disseminated civilization and holiness in many a land. Its statements are distinguished by the greatest simplicity, consistency, importance, wisdom and truth. The revelation which it makes of the character of God, comports with the discoveries which he gives of his character and moral government in his works, and is calculated to advance his glory in a manner which the unaided imagination of man cannot conceive. Its discovery of the state of man, explains all the perplexing appearances which force themselves on our attention, and lays the very thoughts and intents of his heart open to our view. It manifests a scheme of salvation, in the appointment of Jesus Christ, the Son of God, to be the surety and substitute of, and sacrifice for sinful man, which accords with both the mercy and justice of God; which is calculated in the highest degree to advance the divine glory; which emphatically illustrates the evil of sin, and deters from its commission; and which effectually secures the pardon and sanctification, by the divine Spirit, of all those who sincerely rest upon it, and harmonize with it in their conduct. It furnishes man with the most powerful motives to obedience, and communicates to him the most glorious hopes. It supports him under the heaviest afflictions and calamities, illumines the darkness of the grave, and makes known to him an immortality of perfect happiness, and unalloyed and unutterable joy.'*

"The objections which the Zoroastrian has endeavoured to bring against the Bible, are easily removed. When Moses says that God 'repented' that he had made man, he does not say that God repented in the exact sense that men repent, for you will find him in his fourth book, (xxiii Chapter, and 19th verse,) writing thus:—'God is not a man that he should lie; neither the Son of man, that he should repent. Hath he said it, and shall he not do it? or hath he spoken, and shall he not make it good.' When it is intimated that God repented that he had made man, proper figurative language is used. We learn nothing more from the statement, than that the conduct of man was so bad that it required a corresponding change in the procedure of God. This change we best understand by the term repentance. We never suppose that the repentance spoken of, is like that of man, any more than we suppose that when the 'hand of God' is spoken of, any thing more is meant than the energy, or power, of God. The literal passages in the Bible inform us how we are to understand the figurative.

"Your correspondent seems to think that the miracles attributed to Zoroaster establish his divine mission as well as those attributed to Jesus Christ establish *his* divine mission. Let him again peruse what I have said on this subject under the first head of my lecture. He will learn from the observa-

* Lecture on the Vandidád, pp. 47, 48.

tions which he will there find, that there is *no evidence* that *any* miracles were ever performed by Zoroaster." *

The reply which the Zoroastrian offered to these remarks, appeared in the Jám-i-Jamshíd of the 14th October. Nothing can be said in favour of either its justice or discretion. The principal points connected with Christianity to which it adverts, will be sufficiently set forth by the allusions which are made to it in my brief rejoinder.

"It appears *wonderful* to the Zoroastrian, that God should have so loved the world as to give his only-begotten Son, that whosoever believeth in him should not perish, but have everlasting life. If he will inquire into the evidences of Christianity, which are neither few nor small, he will find that what is wonderful in this instance is also *true*. If the Zoroastrian will reflect on the nature of sin, he will perceive that it is an infinite evil; that no efforts of his own can of themselves remove that sin which has been already committed; and that if salvation be obtained at all, it must be through the merit of a divine substitute. Christ, he will find on inquiry, delivers from the punishment of sin, and saves from the power of sin, all those who put their trust in his name. Men's works are imperfect, in every case, and in many instances positively sinful, and if the Zoroastrian looks to *his* works for his acquittance, he will find himself miserably disappointed. The danger of trusting in our self-righteousness, I have exposed at length in my lecture."

The Zoroastrian boastingly said, "With regard to the conversion of a Pársí, you cannot even dream of the event, because even a Pársí babe, crying in the cradle, is firmly confident in the venerable Zartusht". "The conversion of a Pársí," I allow, "is a work too difficult for *me* to accomplish. The conversion of any man is a work too difficult for me to accomplish. It is not too difficult, however, for the Spirit of God. It is my part to state the truth of God; and it is God's part to give it his blessing."

Along with the "Zoroastrian," another controversialist, as-

* Jám-i-Jamshíd, 7th October, 1833.

suming the signature of Mahiárí, appeared, to espouse the side of the question to which he was attached. The contents of his communications respecting several matters, were exactly similar to passages in the letters of others, which we have already inserted. We shall confine our notice to arguments which we have not hitherto introduced into these pages.

On the following passage in the Gospel of Matthew, he considered it expedient to furnish a comment. — "And when they were departed, behold, the angel of the Lord appeareth to Joseph in a dream, saying, Arise and take the young child [Christ] and his mother, and flee into Egypt, and be thou there until I bring thee word : for Herod will seek the young child to destroy him. When he arose, he took the young child and his mother by night, and departed into Egypt." "The above quotation proves," he said, "that Jesus Christ is not the Son of God. Had the celebrated Jesus Christ been the Son of God, and had God produced him on the earth to show the right way, a million of kings, similar to Herod, could never, if they had been disposed to kill him, slay him, even with a great force, till he had preached the right way among the people of this world. . . . Was God divested of supernatural power to save Jesus Christ from being destroyed by Herod, that he should have sent his angel to Joseph, and that Joseph, according to the direction of the angel, should have removed Jesus Christ and his mother Mary into Egypt ?. . . Look to what Zartusht Behrám says in the work named *Zartusht-Námah*, or the History of Zoroaster, composed by himself. Zartusht Behrám states as follows : — 'The news of the birth of the celebrated Zartusht, the prophet of the Pársís, became known to Dúránsarún, the emperor, who immediately repaired to the spot where Zartusht was, and ordered his followers to bring Zartusht outside, and unsheathed his sword, with the design of beheading him. When he was going to strike the blow, his hand with the sword became benumbed, and he consequently could not accomplish his fatal design. Then becoming helpless and despondent, he went home dejected, and was attacked with convulsions.' * It is evident from the

* This account agrees only generally with that of Zartusht Behrám.

preceding circumstances, that Zartusht the prophet of the Pársís was a true prophet appointed by God, as he was saved by God from the sword of Dúránsarún the cruel king..... Had Jesus Christ been a real prophet from, and the Son, of God, he would have been likewise delivered from the fear of Herod, so as not to have rendered it necessary that he should be removed from one country to another. Look to Matthew, Chap. ii. 17, 22: — "But when Herod was dead, behold an angel of the Lord appeareth in a dream to Joseph in Egypt, saying, Arise and take the young child and his mother, and go into the land of Israel, for they are dead which sought the young child's life. And he arose and took the young child, and his mother, and came into the land of Israel. But when he heard that Archelaus did reign in Judea in the room of his father Herod, he was afraid to go thither; notwithstanding being warned of God in a dream, he turned aside into the parts of Galilee.' Now observe, there are two highly reprehensible mistakes, in the above statement. First, God could not in spite of Herod, preserve his prophet at a certain station, and consequently made him adjourn from one country to another. Secondly, when God directed his angel to appear to Joseph, the father of Jesus Christ, the carpenter, in a dream, and to order him to take Jesus Christ to the land of Israel, he did not perceive that Herod's son did reign in the room of his father."

The reply given to this representation was the following: "Neither all the kings of the earth, nor all the devils in hell, could have inflicted death on Jesus Christ, [without his will,] till the appointed time had arrived. We must not limit God, however, as to the *means* to be employed in his preservation. He could, no doubt, have preserved Jesus in the land of Judah; but it was his will that he should be conveyed into Egypt, for this, perhaps among other reasons, that the prophecy, 'Out of Egypt have I called my Son,' might be fulfilled. It was his will also, that Jesus for the fulfilment of prophecy, should be conveyed into Galilee. To his will we cannot object; and to the fulfilment of it, through the warning of an angel, [or any other instrumentality,] we cannot object.

"The miracle reported by Zartusht Behrám is entirely *destitute of proof.* Zartusht Behrám lived many hundred years after the time at which it is reported Zoroaster lived. According to the common opinion, he flourished about the 647th year of Yazdajard [A. D. 1277]; and, consequently, his testimony to Zoroaster's reputed miracle is not worth a cowrie.* Matthew was a contemporary of Christ, and he had a personal knowledge of all the matters of his narrative. He published his account of Christ at a time when its truth or falsehood could be investigated. His Gospel, ever since his day, has been in the hands both of the friends and enemies of the Christian cause, and its statements never have been, and never can be, disproved."†

The Mahiárí tried his skill also, by inventing objections to the words of Christ, "Blessed are the peace-makers, for they shall be called the children of God," when contrasted with the declaration, "Think not that I am come to send peace on

* Zartusht Behrám himself gives the date of his work, as here mentioned, near its conclusion. The author says also, at the same place, that he was "*intoxicated*," on the day intervening between that on which he commenced and finished the work.

"In this day of A'zar, I took [this work] in hand. On A'bán was the feast, and we were intoxicated (*mast.*) On the night of Khúr, I wrote it to the end. In this very day I completed it." By his intoxication, we might have supposed, he probably meant a kind of *inspiration*, had not his reference to the feast of A'bán suggested a real debauch. His inspiration, if such be claimed for him, was certainly neither that of truth, nor of the Spirit of truth. An accurate translation of his book, which is in Persian, made by my friend E. B. Eastwick, Esq. is contained in the appendix (A). My Persian copy, from which this translation is made, was written 206 years ago.

In a subsequent letter of Mahiárí, which does not require special notice, he says that the author of the Zartusht-Námah, wrote agreeably to the information contained in a Pahliví book still existing. Let this work, I say, be produced, let its history be given, let its evidence be weighed, and I shall be prepared to furnish a comment upon it. To the authority of the Zartusht-Námah, I advert in a subsequent chapter.

† Letter in Jám-i-Jamshíd, dated 6th Oct. 1833.

earth : I came not to send peace, but a sword. For I am come to set a man at variance against his father, and the daughter against her mother, and the daughter-in-law against her mother-in-law." "These contradictory sayings [of Christ], he observed, "are sufficient to prove him not to have been a prophet."

"Christ," I remarked in reply, "was both a peace-maker, and a peace-breaker. As a peace-maker, he recommended, both by his words and actions, the promotion of peace to all his disciples. As a peace-breaker, he commanded his disciples to adhere to his cause, notwithstanding of whatever disturbance and persecution might arise. He was not, however, a culpable peace-breaker, as you will perceive from the illustration which I am about to give. If you were convinced that Christianity has its foundation in truth, and if you were to signify to your parents, brothers, and sisters, that you were determined to become a Christian, they would probably rise up against you, and persecute you. It would, nevertheless, be your duty to follow the dictates of truth, and to become a Christian. Your friends would say to you, You are a peace-breaker; why should you leave us and create dissension in our family? You would then tell them that it is your duty to obey God rather than man, and that they would be to blame for any disturbances occasioned by you. Christ does not make disturbances; but wicked men make them on account of Christ. It is in *this* sense, that he said, 'Think not I am come to send peace on the earth: I came not to send peace, [the peace of sinful compliance,] but a sword.'"

Missionary operations, according to Mahiárí, are directly contrary to the will of Christ. Jesus said, he observed, "Go not into the way of the Gentiles, and into any city of the Samaritans enter ye not; but go rather unto the lost sheep of the house of Israel . . . . . The celebrated Jesus Christ *forbad* his disciples to go to the men of another religion, that is, to convert them to Christianity."

"It is true," it was answered, "Jesus, in the first instance, commanded his disciples to 'go to the lost sheep of the house of Israel.' It is also true, however, that before his ascension to heaven, he commanded his disciples to "Go and teach *all nations,* baptizing them in the name of the Father, and of the Son, and of the Holy Ghost."*

Besides those contained in the letters from which I have now introduced these extracts, no comments on the Lecture on the Vandidád, worthy of any notice, appeared, so far as I know, till about five years after its publication. In some of the numbers of the Jám-i-Jamshíd for June and July 1838, an attempt was made by a Pársí, signing himself *Farmábardár,* to impugn my translation of a passage, in the 15th fargard of the Vandidád, according to which the followers of Zoroaster are commanded to destroy an illegitimate child. I invited the complainant to disprove my interpretations by a critical analysis of the original Zand, which I had considered my warrant, or to meet me at any place which he might appoint, for the purpose of discussing the merits of the case. For some time he contrived to evade my reasonable request; and when he did at last make the attempt to meet my wishes, he betrayed such an ignorance of the principles of universal grammar, as called down the reprehension of the Pársí newspaper the Chábuk, edited by the gentleman who had formerly conducted the Harkárah and Vartamán, and which showed to me that I could expect little assistance from his critical abilities.

Three of the controversialists whose works are now before me, have thought proper to refer to the passage in the Vandidád which was the subject of this discussion. It grieves me to be obliged to say, that every one of them has acted in the matter, both dishonorably and dishonestly. Dosabhái, when professing to extract the passage, stops short at the very word with which it commences.† Aspandiárjí, while pretending to quote the passage, and its context, has the effrontery to convert four distinct instances of crime into one, by four several times omitting the words *upáiti çatátó ratum vá paradátum vá aparadátãm vá putrámchá ḣĕ dadẖáiti,* with which the statement of each of them commences; and he makes an interpretation of the whole quite unwarranted by the original

* Matthew. xxviii, 19. † Tálím-i-Zartusht, pp. 102, 103.

Zand.* And Kalam-Kas contents himself by quoting one of the refuted letters of *Farmábardár*, published in the Samáchár newspaper,† without making the slighest reference to the comments upon it which I laid before the Pársí community, through the same medium. This is a way of conducting religious discussion, of which, I have no doubt, many of the Pársís in Bombay will be heartily ashamed, the moment that they direct to it the slightest attention.

The passage which I have made the ground of the charge that child-murder, in a particular instance, is recommended in the Vandidád, is the following. I quote from the lithographed copy of that work, edited by Edal Dáru himself.

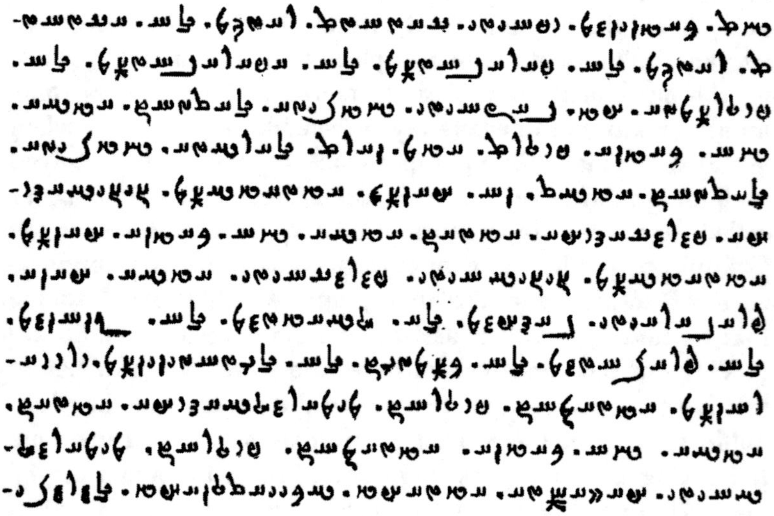

This remarkable passage, in Roman characters, is as follows:—*Yo kaĕninem upáiti çatátó ratum vá açtátó ratum vá paradátãm vá aparadátãm vá puthrãmcha hĕ dadhaiti. Yĕzicha vaochát aĕsa yá kaĕna puthró aĕm naró varsta ; yĕzicha vaochát aĕsó ná hanãm aĕtáĕsãm jijisanguha pereçanguha ; aĕtat aĕsa yá kaĕna hanãm aĕtaĕsãm jijisáiti pereçáiti. Aĕsa*

* Hádí-i-Gum-Rahán, pp. 80, 83.

† Nirang-Há, pp. 327—335.

‡ Vandidád, lithographed, pp. 445, 446.

hana frabaraiti banghem vá kẖsaêtem vá ghanánem vá frazátem [*frazpátem?*] *vá kãmchíd vá vítáchininãm uruaranãm. Aêtamẖát puṯẖrát mimarekhsanguha. Aêtaṯ aêsa ha kaêna aêtamẖáṯ puthráṯ mimarekhsáiti havañta aêtahé skyaothnahê verezĩãn nácha kainicha hanácha.*

I omit the translation of the first sentence, about the meaning of which there is no dispute, because of the indelicacy of the subject to which it refers. The meaning of the rest of the passage, is as follows: —"If she who is the girl, shall say, this son is the production of this man; [and] if the said man say, visit your nurse and ask her [for the poisonous drug]; [and] in this way she who is the girl visits her nurse and asks [her]. The nurse brings *bhang*, or *kshaét, or ghanán,* or *frazát,** or something or other pertaining to the juices of trees. Take the life from this child. If the girl shall take the life from this child, then both the man, and the girl, and the nurse, are alike guilty." I defy all the mobeds in Bombay to prove, how the words *aétamẖáṯ puṯẖráṯ mimarekẖsanguha*, can with propriety be translated otherwise than, "Take the life from this child." The last of them is the second person singular of the imperative of the verb signifying to kill. *Guha* is shown by M. Burnouf to correspond with the Sanskrit स्व, the formative of this part of speech.† All the dasturs make *peresanguha*, an exactly corresponding part of the verb, and used above, express the meaning "ask," and consistency alone will require them to admit the correctness of my version. The verb [Zend script] *mereñchanguha*, of nearly the same meaning, and of the same part of speech, is, in the commencement of the nineteenth fargard, applied to Zoroaster as

* These are certain narcotics, the meaning of which I do not profess to explain. In the Pehlivi and Gujarátí translations, *bhang* is rendered by "hair," a word which is evidently wrong. The Sanskrit भंगा *bhangá*, (Cannabis sativa) so much used in the East, is no doubt what is pointed out. The words which follow are rendered as verbs by the dasturs, but they are evidently nouns in the accusative coupled together by the conjunction *vá*, which, as in Sanskrit, is equivalent to "or." *Kshaêtem* according to the allied Sanskrit radix, probably means "facientem ut intereat." See Westergard's "Radices Linguæ Sanskritæ." p. 28.

† Alphabet Zend, p. cxxvii.

the cry of the devil, and is with the words *asáum Zarathustra*, in connexion with which it is used, translated by Aspandiárjí Frámjí, *Kill the holy Zoroaster*. Anquetil supposes that the dastur, or the magistrate, is to be the instrument of the destruction of the illegitimate child, or abortion, and it is probable that he is right in his conjecture on this point. In this summary of the contents of the fifteenth fargard of the Vandidád, he says with reference to the offending woman, "On doit détruire son fruit, mais il ne faut pas qu'elle le fasse elle-même."* And in his translation, he says, "On les menera devant le Destour, ou devant le Roi, qui frappera, detruira, qui gâtera de quelque maniere qui ce soit avec (du suc) d'arbre, que fera périr l'enfant."† This, as will have been seen, is more the scope of the passage than a literal version.

But I must now proceed to notice matters of another kind. When I perceived that the publication of my pamphlet on the Vandidád had aroused the attention of a goodly portion of the followers of Zoroaster in Bombay, and thus accomplished the principal object for which it was published, I considered it a matter of the greatest importance to direct their attention to the truth of God, as well as to expose the errors of the system to which they are unfortunately devoted; and I had the pleasure of observing the regular attendance of several respectable individuals at a course of lectures on Natural Religion, and the Evidences and Doctrines of Christianity, which I continued to deliver for several years. They often conversed with interest on the subjects which were brought before their notice; but I could not but perceive the disadvantages under which they laboured for want of early Christian education, and could not but regret that few or none of their connexions were attending any Christian schools in Bombay. As soon as there was the prospect of the transference of the Scottish Mission, with which I was connected, to the guidance and support of the General Assembly of the Church, the most suitable body for conducting a missionary enterprize, I determined to make every exertion to have its operations directed to the promotion

* Zend-Avastá, tom. ii. p. lxx. † Zend-Avastá, tom ii, pp. 393, 394.

of the benefit of the Pársís, as well as that of the other tribes of the community. With this view, when founding, toward the close of 1835,* its central educational Institution, in which literature, science, and theology, were to be taught, through the medium of English, both for the general instruction of the natives, and the training of converts for the Christian ministry, I chose, after consulting with different friends, a locality for its situation, which appeared to suit the convenience of the Pársís; and, through the native newpapers, and other channels, I gave them notice of the commencement of its operations. I made no concealment of any of the objects which I had in view; and even if I had attempted it, the effort would have been altogether unsuccessful, for my profession and pursuits were well known throughout the whole of the island and the adjacent country. I was not content, however, to leave my proceedings, and those of my coadjutors, open to the inspection of all who were interested in them; but I gave express intimation through the public journals that, the Christian instruction of all our pupils formed an essential part of our plan. Though I had set myself in opposition to Zoroastrianism, I had never proved unfriendly to any of the Pársís professing their attachment to that system of faith; and they had no reason of complaint against me for the temper in which our discussions had from time to time been carried on. I enjoyed the acquaintance of not a few of their number; and I had the pleasure of soon seeing many of their youth take their places in our different classes. The attendance of Pársís at the Assembly's Institution, for four years after its formation, exceeded that at the central school of the Native Education Society, and the Elphinstone College, from both of which Christianity is systematically excluded. The parents and guardians frequently saw their wards engaged in their particular studies, and heard them catechized from the Bible and other religious books. Printed notices of the different subjects of instruction, were extensively circulated among them on the occasion of our annual examinations, at

* At this time, I was the only Scotch missionary in Bombay.

which many of them did not fail to attend. In our public addresses, when we were favoured with their presence, we most clearly, emphatically, and fully declared all the objects which we had in view. They were particularly noticed in all the reports which from time to time we gave to the public, and in the correspondence which we maintained with our constituents in Scotland. There are special reasons, as will afterwards appear, for my being so particular in these statements.

With the motives which induced the Pársís to send their youth to our seminary, they themselves are best acquainted. It is my firm belief, founded both on the general shrewdness of their observation, and my acquaintance with their particular opinions, that not a few of them knew something of the divine purity and excellence of the Christian faith, and were not indisposed that their offspring should be become acquainted with its doctrines and precepts, in connexion with their general studies. Others, I have no doubt, had little regard to any object but the advancement of their children in secular knowledge, for the promotion of which our Institution offered many advantages. We expected conversion in some instances, as the most blessed result of our benevolent labours. Some of the Pársís were indifferent about such an issue; and most of them, it may be readily admitted, had such confidence in the traditions of their own tribe, that they never made it a matter of expectation. As we practised no concealment, our duty was plain. We taught what we considered most advantageous to our pupils without restraint.

The happy effects of the system of Scriptural instruction which we pursued both in our scholastic and extra-scholastic engagements, were not long in becoming apparent. A considerable number of Pársí youths, as they grew in the knowledge of the word of God, became deeply impressed with the necessity of attending to their eternal interests, and greatly attracted by the Gospel of Christ. The simple and affecting narrative of the actual conversion of one of their number, Dhanjíbhái Naurojí, exactly as it was put into my hands, may be here introduced.

"Two days after Dr Wilson in 1835 established the General Assembly's Institution, I applied to him for admission, which was immediately granted to me. At this time I was ignorant of the Bible, and of all the doctrines of the Christian religion. But I soon began to read the Bible. At first I did not think much about it, but when I advanced in my studies, I began to understand it, and had a great love for it. I read also in Thomson's Collection, which contains many interesting subjects, and which I found to be very useful. I got more knowledge of Christianity while attending Dr Wilson's Wednesday lectures at the Mission House. Mr Payne, one of the teachers in the Institution, took me to the Sunday School, and I sometimes attended with him at the Scotch Church, to hear the preaching of the Gospel. About two years ago, I was thinking about Christianity very much, but through the fear of my relations, and of my countrymen, I did not express my ideas to any one. When any thoughts about Christianity would occupy my mind, I would try to put them out, by thinking that if the Pársí religion were false, it would not have continued to this time; but this notion only lasted a short time, for I would feel something within warning me against the path which I was pursuing. I was somewhat convinced of my folly in worshipping the elements which is quite contrary to reason, and the first and second commandments of God, which he gave to Moses. I afterwards read Dr Wilson's lecture on the Vandidád Sádé, and became convinced of the fallacy of the Pársí religion.

"My uncle ordered me to leave the Institution, and to assist his munshí in some work. Mr Payne came often to ask me to return to the Institution, and Dr Wilson having requested a Pársí gentleman to speak to my uncle about my absence, and that gentleman scold[ed] him very much, and he sent me back.* I again read Scripture with Mr Payne, and

* With reference to this matter, Dosabhái (Tálim-i-Zartusht, p. 27) says, that we pursued the youth like a "huntsman." He ought to know well that no educational institution can prosper in which there is any indifference about the regular attendance of its pupils, or the completion of their studies.

studied Mathematics and Natural History with Dr Wilson, and Mental Philosophy with Mr Nesbit. Not knowing how to acknowledge the Saviour, I proposed to enter into friendship with Mr Johannes Essai, whom I saw Dr Wilson admit into the Church, and whom I always found speaking in defence of the faith which he professed, and willing to assist any one in finding out the truth. One day he asked me to walk with him to Dr Wilson's Friday evening lecture, and I had much talk with him. I did not tell him the state of my mind, until he told me, that he intends to become a preacher of the glad tidings of salvation. At the same time, I expressed my fear of my relations, and of my countrymen, but he pointed out to me some passages in the Scriptures, by which I was quite satisfied; and in keeping his friendship I gained many advantages. Mr Smith, one of my worthy teachers, who instructed me in Geography and History, discovered what my feelings were, and he wrote on my behalf to Dr W., who received me as an inquirer after true religion. I was very much with Dr W. both by day and night, and he took me with him on his tour to the jungles, when he gave me many instructions about Christianity, and Mr Mitchell of Poona, who was with us, also read and prayed with me. When I came back to Bombay, I told to my uncle that I wish to embrace Christianity, but at first he did not believe it. A month and half after, Dr W. asked me to stop with him, and to teach a lady Gujarátí, and I told that to my uncle, and he gave me permission.

"I now beg to come forward and to receive baptism, in the presence of the public, ready to suffer for my Lord and Saviour Jesus Christ, with a full assurance of the fulfilment of his promise. My eyes are open by the divine grace, and see the true light. Oh! what a great matter it is to know the true religion. I lay hold of the Lord and Saviour, Jesus Christ, who came down from heaven, and took upon himself our infirmities, and suffered on the cross, and reigns in heaven, to save sinners. And now, my Christian brethren, I ask one thing from you, to pray for me, that I may prove to be a true disciple of Christ. And now, my fellow-countrymen, I recommend to you to do one thing, and that is, to take the Bible into your hands, and to read it earnestly, and ask God to open your eyes, and show you the true way, that you may follow it. Compare the Bible with your Vandidád, and see which is true. I am certain, certain as my life, that you will find out that the Christian religion is true, and if you do, I beg of you all to enter into it. If you will not do these things before you depart from this wicked world, you will go to that place where there is weeping, and wailing, and gnashing of teeth, and where you will find no rest; therefore do these things as soon as possible."*

A perfectly similar document, I had the pleasure of receiving from another ingenuous youth, Hormazdjí Pestanjí, which I need not here insert.† In a joint letter addressed to me by him, and another of our pupils, Frámjí Bahmanjí, there is the following passage. "After a long consideration we have been convinced that Christianity is the only true religion on the earth, and we have earnestly resolved with our hearts and souls to embrace it, being the only means of obtaining eternal life. Our design in embracing Christianity, is, not that we may have riches, (which we at present are not at a loss for,) but that we may obtain an entrance into the everlasting kingdom of God, by confessing him who came from heaven to save sinners before men, that we may not be denied by him before his Father which is in heaven."

The faith of these professing converts was destined to be tried by no common ordeal. Friends, relatives, and in fact a great part of the Pársí community, seemed suddenly to rise up against them, and not only to oppose their entrance into the Christian church, but to seek their serious injury, if not destruction. Dhanjibháí and Hormazdjí, through the grace and power of the Saviour, were enabled on the one hand, to

* Dosabháí, (Tálim-i-Zartusht, p. 12), says that this could not have been Dhanjibháí's own composition, for he laid only a 'fair copy" of it, as it was termed in Dr. Wilson's affidavit, before the Judge! Does a Munshí require to be informed, that a person may take a fair copy of any thing which he himself writes?

† It appears in the appendix to my sermon, entitled, The Doctrine of Jehovah addressed to the Pársís.

shut their hearts and ears to all the worldly temptations which the sincere, but mistaken, affection of their friends presented, and on the other, to withstand all the fierce opposition with which they were assailed. They recognized the supreme authority of conscience, directed by the word of God, in matters of religious faith and practice; and the fear of God within them seemed to annihilate the fear of man. Frámjí failed under the fury of the storm. May he, and others, yet do justice to their convictions; and show that the hope of Christ can uphold, even amidst the greatest perils, his true disciples.

There was no occasion for a moment's hesitation about the course to be pursued with regard to Dhanjibhái and Hormazdjí. I gave them a refuge in my own family; and being fully persuaded, after much observation, of the sincere and enlightened nature of their Christian profession, I baptized them, under due protection, before a numerous assembly of their countrymen and Europeans, in the name of the Father, and of the Son, and of the Holy Ghost, the only living and true God. They continued to reside under my roof; but of their personal liberty there was no restraint. Their friends had the freest access to them, except when violence was threatened and attempted. Some of their relatives expressly told me that, they had no personal objections to the course which had been pursued, and which it was proposed to pursue, respecting them, and that they were compelled to seek the possession of their persons only by the heads of the Pársí community, who would tolerate no departure from the faith of Zoroaster. I begged them to allow to others the religious liberty which they claimed for themselves, and earnestly solicited them to conduct their proceedings in a legal manner.

To the law of England, they made their appeal. On the third of May, they procured, from the Supreme Court of Bombay, a writ of Habeas Corpus requiring me to produce the body of Dhanjibhái Nauroji, and a Rule Nisi requiring me to show "good and sufficient cause" why a writ of Habeas Corpus should not be directed to me, commanding me to bring up the body of Hormazdjí Pestanjí. These writs were obtained, on the allegation that the youth were under age, that I kept them under restraint, and that I had used "undue and improper means" to "convert and seduce" them from "the faith of their "ancestors and families." They were served upon me on the 4th, and the return to them was presented in Court, on the 6th of May 1839. I produced, on that occasion, a series of affidavits, which completely upset every one of the charges which had been brought against me. The counsel for the prosecutors, however, begged for time to answer these documents, alleging in particular, that they would be able to prove that no evil consequences were to be anticipated, were the youth to be handed over to the guardianship of their friends, or other parties connected with the Pársí community. Sir John Awdry, the judge, complied with their request, and in the mean time permitted the young men to go where they pleased. They intimated their intention to return with me to my own residence. When we were leaving the Court, an assault was attempted to be made upon us by a mob of Pársís, collected at its entrance; and the most diabolical threats were uttered in our hearing. The presence and interposition of a large body of our friends, prevented all evil consequences.

On the 16th of May, the case came before the judge for his ultimate decision. Five affidavits were presented in behalf of the prosecution, one of them being the joint production of nine of the members of the Pársí Pancháyat, who were the real movers in all the proceedings which were adopted; and thirteen, disproving their assertions, were presented in the defence.* A spirited and able debate ensued, conducted by Mr Campbell, who appeared for myself and the converts, and Messrs Howard and Montriou, who appeared for those at

* In the preparation of these documents, which necessity required to be got ready in a very short space of time, I enjoyed the valuable assistance of J. P. Larkins, Esquire, Solicitor, who evinced more than official zeal in forwarding our righteous cause. They were respectively sworn to by Captain N. H. Thornbury, the Rev. Dr. Stevenson, W. H. Payne, Esquire, Bápu Mazdá, Johannes Essai, the Rev. R. Nesbit and the Rev. J. M. Mitchell, Hormazdjí Pestanjí, Mr. G. S. Collett, F. Hutchinson, Esquire, R. X. Murphy, Esquire, and Nauroji Dárábjí, as well as by the convert Dhanjibhái, and myself.

whose instigation the writ had been issued. The decision sustained the interests of civil and religious liberty, the sacred right of every subject of Britain's extended empire. It was ordered that Dhanjibháí Naurojí be "at liberty to go where he pleases." The Rule Nisi in the case of Hormazdjí Pestanjí was "discharged." * Both the young men voluntarily returned to my home, in which they continue to reside. They are diligently and successfully prosecuting their studies at the General Assembly's, Institution, with a view to the holy ministry, to which, we trust, they will, in due time, be called. Their conduct has gained for them the esteem of all who enjoy their acquaintance.

With the law which vouchsafed to the youths their liberty, many of the leading members of the Pársí community were far from being satisfied. Toward the end of 1839, they presented to the Government of Bombay a libellous document, altogether adverse to it, ever since designated as the "ANTI-CONVERSION MEMORIAL," and bearing 2115 signatures, procured, after several months canvassing and misrepresentation, out of a population of about 250,000 souls residing on the island of Bombay. I have not space to insert it in full, but its objects and spirit will be sufficiently apparent from a part of the prayer with which it concludes:— "We therefore pray of your Excellency, that you will be pleased to request the Legislative Council of India, to pass a law which shall place the Christian Missionaries, who resort to this country, on such a footing with reference to the people of India, that no such case as recently happened can occur again, without redress being afforded through a Court of Law to the injured and afflicted family, and in particular that no Missionary or other schools be esta-

* I have been purposely brief in the notice of the important proceedings in the Supreme Court, both because I do not wish unnecessarily to introduce into this work any matters which may prove a source of irritation to those whom I have long ago forgiven, and because the whole proceedings, including all the documents brought forward, and the opinions of the India Press respecting them, are recorded in the Oriental Christian Spectator for June, 1839, published in Bombay, and reprinted in Edinburgh, by Mr. Johnstone, bookseller.

blished in the interior, without the previous sanction of the Governor in Council, and that no Missionary, or other person, shall be permitted to interfere or tamper with the religion of a native child, under twenty-one years of age, except with the express and explicit sanction in writing of the parent or legal guardians of such child. And farther, that if any person after the full age of twenty-one years shall become a convert to the Christian or other faith, he shall not be capable of exercising any power or control over his wife or children, and also shall be liable to provide a reasonable sum for their maintenance; and also that he shall forfeit all right and title to inherit the family or ancestorial property of his parents, except such portion thereof as may be bequeathed to him by will, and that the provisions of the Act may be guarded by proper penalties to be enforced in any Court of Justice in India."

In the comment on this document presented by me to Government, and which is inserted in the appendix (B) to this work, there will be found a reply, by anticipation, to much of what appears in the controversial works now before me. I direct to it the attention of my native readers.

The Anti-Conversion memorial was, with a simple exception, universally reprobated by the public press in India. It was impossible that it could meet with any favour from an enlightened and impartial government. In reply to it, the Governor in Council of Bombay remarked as follows: — " The principle, by which the proceedings of this Government will be regulated, in all questions connected with the labours of the missionaries is that of the strictest neutrality . . . . . Whilst, however, the Government are thus resolved to adhere to this path of strict neutrality, it will be obvious to you, that the course of argument and fair reason cannot be impeded, since its progress is a necessary consequence of the extension of education, for which, in the abstract, you are justly so anxiously solicitous. — As regards your complaints that the missionaries are allowed to locate themselves wherever they please, even at places which you hold most sacred, the Government of India will determine, whether any, or what restriction should be imposed. — You likewise complain of the extension of missionary schools, but it does not appear how Government, adhering to the principle laid down, can interfere to prevent their extension. The remedy, however, is clearly in your own hands, for, firstly, it is within your own choice to send your children to those schools, and secondly, you may send them to the Government schools, or unite among yourselves to establish schools, where Christanity shall not be taught" . . . . . .

The deliverance of the Government of India was, if possible, still more decided and satisfactory to all who respect the sacred claims of truth and of conscience. " In reply, I am desired to state," wrote the Secretary, " that his Lordship in Council has given his deliberate attention to the statements and requests contained in this memorial. It is among the first wishes of his Lordship in Council, that the just and tolerant principles, by which the British Government in India is actuated, with regard to every question connected with religion, should be well understood by all classes of the population, and especially by persons of the high respectability and character which belong to the memorialists.— His Lordship in Council is, however, entirely persuaded that the parties to the representation now before him, will, upon reconsideration, be satisfied, that they require no further assurance on this head, than that which is to be found in the uniform tenor of the proceedings of Government, and in those declarations of strict neutrality which have with much propriety been addressed to the memorialists by the Hon'ble the Governor in Council at Bombay, and which his Lordship in Council would here desire, in the most emphatic manner, to repeat and confirm.— Consistently with the rules by which the Government alone can be guided, his Lordship in Council must feel himself precluded from entertaining the question of passing legislative enactments, which would be at variance with a just regard to the rights of civil and personal liberty, with the principles sanctioned by the British Parliament, and with the express precedents of past legislation in India. * — The attendance

* Section 9, regulation 7. Bengal Code, 1832.

at missionary schools, being entirely voluntary, the remedy against any evils, apprehended from the instruction imparted at them, is in the hand of native parents, who may refrain, as is observed by his Honor in Council, from sending their children to those schools. — His Lordship in Council cannot deem it to be necessary, or proper, to prohibit the resort of missionaries to any places to which other British subjects may, without offence, have access. The law is already powerful to prevent whatever may obviously tend to the disturbance of good order, and to punish insult, and outrage, upon the native or other religions by any parties."

The avowment of these principles and determinations, had a most happy effect in the native community. An appeal which was made to England by those who wished them, and consequently the cause of civil and religious liberty, to be restricted, fell to the ground, from the belief of the friends and agents of the Pársís in that country, that no good result would follow further agitation, and that it was likely that, in that enlightened country, reproach and obloquy would be the only harvest of its promoters. It is but justice to the Pársís, and the other natives who joined with them, to say, that many of them are heartily ashamed of their proceedings in the conversion case from first to last, and that some of them have apologized to myself, and other Europeans, for their own connection with it.

By the simple narrative which I have now given, and in the appeal which I have made to incontrovertible documents, I have overturned much of what has been advanced in the controversial works now before me. I have left my native readers, in most instances, to make the application for themselves. I am persuaded that they will not fail to draw the right conclusions.

But, what, it may be now asked, has been the result of all the agitation which some inconsiderate persons have contrived to excite in connection with the conversion of the Pársí youth? Has it served to confirm the Zoroastrians in the faith of their fathers? Has it put an end to all farther religious inquiry? The very opposite effects have been its consequence. The unreasonableness of the proceedings adopted, has generated the suspicion that there is no truth in reserve to stand on its own basis? Curiosity has been widely excited and is anxiously prosecuting research. The communications on the comparative merits of Zoroastrianism and Christianity, which have from time to time issued from the press, have been eagerly pursued. Convictions of the feebleness of the one system, and the strength of the other, are not uncommon. Hence, the alarm of those who are not prepared to allow truth to take its course, and its great author, the Father of lights, to be glorified, and immortal souls to be saved. Hence, the belief of some, inordinately attached to Pársíism, that they can contribute to support its cause. Hence, the controversial works which I now undertake to answer, the products of an advocate hired by the Pársí Pancháyat, and individuals occupying the highest place of its priesthood, and others of a more obscure standing. Dosabháí, who first appeared on the arena, concludes his work by saying that he has "toiled a whole year" at it, in consequence of an order which he received from the shets of the Pancháyat, and other great men, to render *tá'zi* the *good faith*, and to answer Dr. Wilson." Edal Dáru,* says, that he writes for the purpose of showing the Mazdayasnís the foundations of their own faith, and assisting them in their controversies with the *Jud-dín*, or Gentiles. Aspandiárjí, whose book appeared in the end of November last, seems to express his gratification with the inquiry which is proceeding in the community of which he is a member. He says, "I have peculiar satisfaction to notice that the pamphlet referred to [the lecture on the Vandidád] has within the last few months, created some sensation among the Pársís, and furnished them with many topics for discussion." †

I cannot but tender my sincere congratulations, in these circumstances, to the members of the respected Pársí community. They are in a situation different from that of many of the other tribes in this great country, who are not only involved in error, but altogether unconscious of their situation, and without any attempt being made to arouse them to con-

* Preface to the Maujazát-i-Zartusht.

† Hádí-i Gum-Rahán, p. 2.

sideration. Let them do justice to the call for thorough inquiry, and devout reflection, which has been providentially addressed to them. It is certainly their duty, as it is the duty of all men to know what God reveals as religion, and requires to be practised as religion. Ignorance of the Divine Being who created us, who confers upon us our intelligence, and all our possessions and enjoyments, and who continually supports and upholds us, and to whom we are responsible for all that we have received and are capable of doing and imparting, is in the highest degree dishonorable, detrimental, and dangerous. God has created us, expressly that we may know, love, serve, and enjoy him; and when we fail to learn who and what he is, and what he requires of us, we must be considered as neglectful of the grand end of our existence, as ungrateful for the benefits which we have received, as opposed to the government of God, and as unmindful of our own best interests. Our conduct can in no degree be excused; and in the view of it, we must consider ourselves as the enemies of God, whom he will visit for neglect and indifference. I beg permission of my friends directly to address to them a few counsels on this subject, dictated by my own earnest desires for their happiness in time and eternity.

I. *Religious inquiry should be conducted by you in a teachable spirit.* Unless you be heartily disposed to learn, it is of little use for you to propose to learn. An ardent desire to attain to the truth, is necessary; and you must never resist it, when it is presented to you, or fail to seek and use the means of discovering it. "There is a listless vacuity of mind," says Dr. Abercrombie, with whose excellent work on the Intellectual Powers some of your youth are acquainted, "which prevents it from being directed with attention, or interest, to the formation of defined opinions, even on subjects of supreme importance. There is a servility of mind, which leaves it the slave of mere authority, without forming opinions for itself by personal inquiry. And there is a rude and reckless affectation of mental independence, or liberty of thinking which leads a man to despise authority, to aim at striking out for himself a system distinguished from the received opinions of those ground him — led, it may be, by a love of singularity or the vanity of appearing wiser than his neighbours ; — or perhaps impelled, by the condition of his moral feelings, to argue himself into the disbelief of what he wishes not to be true. From all such distortions of the understanding, a regulated mental discipline tends to preserve us. It induces us to approach every subject with a sincere and humble desire for truth ; to give its due influence to authority without being blindly led by it ; to give its due weight to every kind of evidence, without partial views or imperfect examination ; and to direct the whole powers, not to favour, establish, or overturn particular opinions, but honestly and anxiously to discover what is truth. This is a subject of intense and solemn interest. A slight attention to the philosophy of it, will enable you to perceive its true bearings upon us as responsible beings ; and how, on the highest of all subjects, a man may incur moral guilt in the formation of his opinions. Both as intellectual and moral beings, the great agent by which we are acted upon, is *truth*. Truth derives its power from evidence; and there are laws of evidence, which,in their nature, are as absolute and immutable as the laws of physical relations. But for the operation of them, a state of the mind itself is required, and without this, even the best evidence may be deprived of its power to produce conviction. For the result of evidence upon the mind depends on close and continued attention ; and this is a voluntary process which every one may be able to perform. It is on this ground therefore, that we hold a man to be responsible for his belief, and contend that he may incur deep moral guilt in his disbelief of truths which he has examined in a frivolous or prejudiced manner, or which perhaps he indulges in the miserable affectation of disbelieving, without having examined them at all. The remarkable fact indeed, appears to be, that the chief source of unbelief, on the greatest of all subjects, is generally to be found in a previous moral corruption of the mind. It arises from no defect of evidence, but from a state of mind on which the highest falls without power." * Pride and con-

* Abercrombie's Inaugural Address.

ceit, indeed, are most unfavourable to the progress of any learner. They infallibly blind our minds and oppose the formation of right impressions. God, it is apparent, will not honour them. "To this man will I look," says he, "even to him that is of a poor and of a contrite spirit, and who trembleth at my word." "The meek will he guide in judgment, and the meek will he teach his way." These remarks are applicable both to those who teach and to those who are taught, and who both have much to learn in reference to Him, connected with whom it has been asked, "Canst thou by searching find out God? Canst thou find out the Almighty unto perfection? It is high as heaven, what canst thou do? deeper than hell, what canst thou know? The measure thereof is longer than the earth, and broader than the sea? For he knoweth vain man: he seeth wickedness also, will he not then consider it? for vain man would be wise, though man be born like a wild ass's colt."

Religious inquiry, then, should be conducted by you under the impression of your liability to err. Men, when viewed in reference to the subjects of religious inquiry, are exceedingly limited in their comprehension; they are undoubtedly exposed to many prejudices from education, and from prevailing sentiments and customs; and they are exposed to many evil influences within and without. It is apparent, that they are connected with sin, and that its power may both restrain them in the search for that which is good, and lead them to reject that which is true, when it is presented to them. You ought not to imagine, then, that your sentiments and conduct are correct, merely because those of many persons around you accord with them; merely because they were taught you by your parents and your priests, who still approve of them; merely because they are similar to those of your remote ancestors. You ought not to suppose, that any thing is true and right, merely because it may be agreeable to you, and you may be reaping some apparent advantages from it. You ought not, on the other hand, to conclude that any doctrine is wrong, merely because it has never formerly been presented to your view; because it is difficult for you to comprehend it; because it is rejected by your countrymen; or because it may reveal to you your own folly and wickedness. Many have erred, and you may err. On this account, you ought to proceed with the greatest caution; and you ought to pray, that God may deliver you from all the temptations which surround you, and lead you into the knowledge of all truth.

2. *Religious inquiry should be conducted by you with the determination to yield to the dictates of truth.* Many difficulties, and much opposition, are frequently experienced in following the path of rectitude; and it is well to calculate upon them, and to make preparation for meeting them. Most of these difficulties originate in our own depravity. We do not naturally like to acknowledge our errors and change our customs. We do not like to subject ourselves to the scorn and hatred of those who differ from us. We do not like to expose ourselves to hardships and sufferings. Whatever may be our feelings and apprehensions, however, there can be no doubt as to our duty. *Ignorance*, we have remarked, is very sinful; but *disobedience,* when attended with *knowledge*, is more so. To resist truth, is to resist the God of truth, and to provoke his righteous displeasure. Those who know God and who glorify him not as God, are exposed to his righteous indignation, while those who act agreeably to the will of God, according as it is revealed to them, obtain his approbation and are aided in the work of inquiry. God is able to support you under all the trials which you may be called to endure. He has supported many persons in situations similar to your own; and he has enabled them to love the truth, even more than their own lives. It is infinitely better for you to suffer for an adherence to that which is good, than to remain in error, or neglect, or resist, your right convictions.

3. *Religious inquiry should be conducted by you under a deep impression of the brevity of time, and the speedy approach of the hour of judgment.* That which concerns the glory of God, and the salvation of the souls of men, must be very important; and it must be apparent that to make *it* the subject of procrastination must be highly sinful and dangerous. Your continuance in this tabernacle of clay, will be

short, and it is altogether uncertain. Now, as you must be speedily summoned to the presence of your Maker, and subjected to his unerring scrutiny, and as you may be called from this sublunary scene without any warning, you ought, above all things, to betake yourselves to immediate preparation. By following this course, you will avoid evil, and obtain good. It is not too soon for you to be delivered from the curse and power of sin; and it is not too soon for you to obtain the knowledge of God, and the Redeemer whom he has appointed, and an interest in his favour. Thousands perish because they resolve to delay. May the Lord in mercy prevent you from being added to their unhappy number!

To the controversialists whom the interests of truth require me to oppose, I trust that I cherish no feelings inconsistent with those of the purest benevolence. On the arena which they have chosen, I most readily meet them; and in contending with them, I bear in mind that the eye of God himself, as well as that of man, is directed to our movements. In the following chapters they will find, I trust, all their representations and reasonings, which legitimately bear on the controversy in which we are engaged, both fairly stated, and fairly criticized. Throughout all their works, with the exception of that of Edal Dáru, who, to his own credit, has maintained his temper, there is much asperity of language, which it is my duty to avoid, rather, than imitate. They contain much irrelevant matter, some of which I must here dismiss with the briefest notice.

1. The efforts which are made to blast the character, and disparage the attainments, of the Pársí converts to Christianity, will only redound to the discredit of their authors. For a learned munshi, like Dosabháí to speak of Dhanjibháì by the contemptuous epithet of the "Nazarene,*" and to attempt to prove that by embracing the faith of Jesus, he has broken every one of the ten commandments given to Moses, is at once to dishonour his own venerable beard, and to bring reproach on his own understanding. Broken every one

* Tálim-i-Zartusht p. 27.

of the ten commandments by his conversion! By embracing the religion of Jehovah, the self-existent God; by forsaking the worship of idols, whether natural or articifial; by refusing vainly to use the name of God, or to give it to vanities; by hallowing the space of time appointed for the worship of God, and the enjoyment of holy rest, on that day on which, since the resurrection of Christ from the dead, it is his intimation that this should be done; by honouring his relatives, and consulting their welfare, by showing them an invaluable example of deference to the will of God, whose authority is paramount; and by connecting himself with those eternal principles of mercy, purity, honesty, truthfulness, and contentment which were written by the finger of God, on the tablets of testimony! It is only in connection with the doctrine of the Trinity, that there is any thing even specious in the munshi's reasonings in support of his charge; and even here there is nothing just or substantial. Trinity, or Tri-unity, expresses merely the fact, revealed to us in the Bible that in the *one* Godhead, there are three personal distinctions and agents, the Father, the Son, and the Holy Ghost. They are not said to be both *one* and *three* in the same sense. In one sense, they are "one," and in another, "three." The doctrine of Scripture may be *above* reason,—and, on this very account, it has been revealed,—but most certainly it is not *contrary* to reason.

Neither of the converts has put away his wife. From one of them the Pársís detain his partner and child, both of whom he would be happy to receive and treat with kindness. Neither of them has denied his parentage.*

The passage † which Dosabháí quotes from the Bible forbids all profane swearing. The Christian Scriptures, however, do not interdict a judicial oath. Such "an oath," they say, is "for confirmation," "an end of all strife." ‡

2. Dosabháí is very liberal in his quotations from the

* See comment on the Anti-Conversion Memorial inserted in the Appendix [B].

† Matthew, v. 33 — 37

‡ Hebrews vi. 16.

writings of Voltaire. It is to be regretted that he has not informed his readers, that the works of this infidel have been often refuted in the most satisfactory manner in Europe; and that they are consequently destitute of all respect and authority. It may be proper to inform him that the principles of Voltaire failed him in his last moments, that he was greatly excited in the prospect of death, and that he sent for a Christian priest, to administer to him consolation; and that he professed to die in the faith of the church in which he was born.* Dosabhái, as will be seen from another part of this work, claims the authority of Gibbon in favour of the Pársí religion. It is a pity that he did not quote the following passage from his History of the Decline and Fall of the Roman Empire, which is immediately connected with that with which he has favoured his readers: —

"Had Zoroaster in all his institutions, invariably supported this exalted character,† his name would deserve a place with those of Numa and Confucius,‡ and his system would be justly entitled to all the applause, which it has pleased some of our divines, and even some of our philosophers to bestow on it. But in that motley composition [the Zend-Avesta],

* He undoubtedly penned the following declaration: — "I the underwritten, declare, that for these four months past, having been afflicted with a vomiting of blood, at the age of eighty-four years, and not having been able to drag myself to the Church — the Rev. the Curate of St Sulpice having been pleased to add to his good works that of sending to me the Abbé Gaultier, a priest, I confessed to him, — and if it please God to dispose of me, I die in the catholic religion, in which I was born, hoping that the Divine mercy will deign to pardon all my faults. If ever I have scandalized the Church, I ask pardon of God and of the Church.

"Signed, Voltaire, March the 2d, 1778, in the house of the Marquis de Villette, presence of the Abbé Mignot, my nephew, and the Marquis de Villevielle, my friend."

See this document and some others of a similar kind, with a narrative of the last days of the "philosopher" in the "Vie Politique, Litteraire, et Morale, de Voltaire, par M. Lepan."

† That, which, as Gibbon says, he had, when he "*laid aside the prophet*" and "*assumed the legislator,*" and delivered some good agricultural and social maxims.

‡ Numa was a legislator of the Romans, and Confucius of the Chinese.

dictated by reason and passion, by enthusiasm and by selfish motives, some useful and sublime truths were disgraced by a mixture of the most abject and dangerous superstition. The Magí, or sacerdotal order, were extremely numerous, since, as we have already seen, fourscore thousand of them were convened in a general council. Their forces were multiplied by discipline. A regular hierarchy was diffused through all the provinces of Persia; and the archimagus,* who resided at Balch was respected as the visible head of the church, and the lawful successor of Zoroaster. The property of the Magi was very considerable. Besides the less invidious possession of a large tract of the most fertile lands of Media, they levied a general tax on the fortunes and the industry of the Persians. 'Though your good works' says the interested prophet, 'exceed in number the leaves of the trees, the drops of rain, the stars in the heaven, or the sands on the sea-shore, they will all be unprofitable to you, unless they are accepted by the *destour*, or priest. To obtain the acceptation of this guide to salvation, you must faithfully pay him *tithes* of all you possess, of your goods, of your lands, and your money. If the destour be satisfied, your soul will escape hell tortures; you will secure praise in this world, and happiness in the next. For the destours are the teachers of religion; they know all things, and they deliver all men.'†

"These convenient maxims of reverence and implicit faith, were doubtless imprinted with care on the tender minds of youth; since the Magi were the masters of education in Persia, and to their hands the children even of the royal family were intrusted. The Persian priests, who were of a speculative genius, preserved and investigated the secrets of Oriental philosophy, and acquired, either by superior knowledge, or superior art, the reputation of being well versed in some of the occult sciences, which have derived their appellation from the Magi.

"The Majesty of Ormusd, who was jealous of a rival, was seconded by the despotism of Artaxerxes, who could not suffer

* Chief Mobed. † Saddar, Art. 8.

a rebel; and the schismatics within his vast empire were soon reduced to the inconsiderable number of eighty thousand. This spirit of persecution reflects dishonor on the religion of Zoroaster; but as it was not productive of any civil commotion, it served to strengthen the new monarchy, by uniting all the various inhabitants of Persia in the bands of religious zeal."*

It will be long before even an infidel will feel himself warranted to write in this style of the Christian Scriptures. Where do we find the apostles of Christ begging for money, under the pretence of saving the souls of those who present it, or dooming to destruction those who withhold it, as the dasturs do in the passage which has been now quoted?

3. Dosabhái has favoured his readers with several accounts of fraud and deception attributed to the Jesuits and other Roman Catholic padres. His avowed motive for so doing, is to prejudice the minds of the natives of India against the Christian missionaries who at present seek their conversion. If these missionaries either approve of, or imitate, the conduct of the Jesuits, let them certainly be held up to reproach and ignominy. That they do neither, is evident from Dosabhái's inability to bring any specific charges against them. They hold all deception in utter abhorrence. They view it in the light in which it is exhibited in the Christian Scriptures. They desire to be the humble followers of the apostles of the Saviour, who before the whole world, could thus declare themselves:—"Therefore, seeing we have this ministry, as we have received mercy, we faint not: but have renounced the hidden things of dishonesty, not walking in craftiness, nor handling the word of God deceitfully, but by manifestation of the truth commending ourselves to every man's conscience in the sight of God."†

4. Dosabhái pretends to blame the converts for not performing miracles, agreeably to his interpretation of Mark xvi. 17, &c.—"These signs shall follow them that believe: in my

* Gibbon's Decline and Fall of the Roman Empire. vol. i. chap. 8.

† 2 Cor. iv. 1, 2.

name shall they cast out devils; they shall speak with new tongues." This promise was not given to *all* believers. It was fulfilled in the days of the apostles of Christ, in the case of those to whom it refers.

In connection with his demurrer on the passage now quoted, Dosabháí repeats the following absurd story. "A missionary thus confidently asserted to his disciples: —'When I was riding on horseback, in the country of the Konkan, I saw a tiger opposite to me. The horse cast his eyes on the ravenous brute, startled, and threw me to the ground. Upon this the tiger having smelled the illustrious *pír* walked away, and this it did three times. The missionary having come into the city told the story to his disciples; and certain *blue-light* simpletons believed it, and published it to the world." The munshi is mightily pleased with this tale; and it is almost a pity to destroy his complacency. The following, however, is the true version.

"We set out for Nágotána, a little before sunset. On the road, I experienced a remarkable deliverance, which should excite my most fervent gratitude to the Father of all mercies. I had got the start of Mr. M. in passing through the jungle, and in order to allow him an opportunity of coming to me, I was just about to pull up my horse, when I observed an enormously large tiger about six yards from me. Instead of running from me, he sprung up near my horse. I then cried out as loud as I could, with the view of frightening him. I had the happiness of seeing him retreat for a little; and I gallopped from him, as fast as my horse could carry me, to Mr. M., whom I found walking with four or five natives. We passed together the spot where I had the encounter, without seeing our enemy. He was heard, however, among the trees by our horsekeepers. He has been seen by the natives for some days past, a short time after sunset, exactly at the place, (about six miles from Nágotána), where he appeared to me. The men whom I found with Mr. M. told me, that they regularly present offerings for protection from tigers to an image on Wardhan hill. I showed the vanity of their confidence; but, in their misdirected devotion, I saw the call to remember 'the

Lord, who is my refuge, even the Most High." Is there any pretence of a miraculous interposition in this narrative?*

But I must now proceed to the consideration of more important matters. It is my intention, with as much regard to order and system as the want of arrangement in some of the works to which I reply will admit, to take a calm and impartial review of the whole of the essential principles of the Pársí religion, and to compare them, when necessary, with those of the Christian faith. My observations will be directed amongst other matters, to the following subjects :—

I. The Pársí notions of the Godhead, and the relations of Zarúána-Akarana, and Hormazd.

II. The doctrine of the Two Principles, Hormazd and Ahriman.

III. The worship of the Elements, and of the Amshás-pands and I'zads, who are said to preside over them and the other works of nature.

IV. The general Polytheism of the Pársís.

V. The Historical, Doctrinal, Ceremonial, and Moral Discoveries and Institutes of Zoroaster, as contained in the Vandidád.

VI. The Pársí notions of the Responsibility, Depravity, and Guilt of Man and the means of his Salvation.

V. The alleged Mission of Zoroaster.

As I proceed, I shall uniformly state the authorities on which my remarks are founded. Should I find at the end of the course which I have laid down for myself, that I have failed to notice any parts of the publications of my opponents deserving of the least attention, I shall refer to them in the Appendix (C).

* Oriental Christian Spectator, vol. v. p. 155.

CHAPTER II.

THE PA'RSI' NOTIONS OF THE GODHEAD, AND THE RELATIONS OF ZARU'A'NA-AKARANA AND HORMAZD.

Importance of the knowledge of God—Edal Dáru on the Godhead—Remarks on his description — Are the Pársís Deists — Edal Dáru's attempt to connect his account of the Godhead, with Hormazd — Dosabháí's claim of Supreme Divinity for Hormazd — Extract from Dr. Wilson's lecture on the Vandidád, on the derivation of Hormazd from Zarúána-Akarana — Refutation of criticisms on this extract — Testimony of Antiquity as to the derivation of Hormazd from Zarúána — Testimony of the Sacred Books of the Pársís on the same subject—Testimony of the digests of the Pársí faith, in the Bundéshné and I'lmá-i-Islám — Concurrence of European Scholars—the Pársís remonstrated with on the unreasonableness of their notions of the Godhead, and of Zarúána-Akarana and Hormazd.

The knowledge of the Supreme Being, it must be universally allowed, lies at the foundation of true religion. If the attributes of his nature, and the character of his providence, be misapprehended or inadequately realized, there can not possibly be produced that right state of contemplation, and thought, and feeling, and action, in reference to God, in which genuine practical religion consists. A review of the Pársí notions of the Godhead, is consequently incumbent upon us in the very commencement of the inquiries which it is our duty to pursue. I shall permit the Pársís to speak for themselves, in the explanation of their tenets, and carefully examine the writings which they consider the authoritative standard of their faith, and devotional service.

Edal Dáru, the chief-priest of the Rasamís, in the commencement of his work entitled Maujazát-i-Zartusht, writes as follows, in the form of question and answer: —

"Q. Thou sayest that thou art a *yazdán-parast* (a worshipper of Yazdán), then to what effect art thou acquainted with God, and what dost thou acknowledge the Lord God to be?

"A. The one holy and glorious God, the Lord of the creation of both worlds, and the Creator of both worlds, I acknowledge thus.—He has no form, and no equal; and the creation and support of all things is from that Lord. And the lofty sky, and the earth, and light, and fire, and air, and water, and the sun, and moon, and the stars, have all been created by him, and are subject to him. And that glorious Master is almighty, and that Lord was the first of all, and there was nothing before him, and he is always, and will always remain. And he is very wise and just; and worthy of service, and praise, and imperative in his demand for service. Thus, according to the above precise statement, I know the Creator to to be one God, and I acknowledge him to be all-powerful over every object.

"Q. How is God in his form, and what is his nature, and can that powerful Lord be beheld by us?

"A. God has no form or shape; and he is enveloped in holy, pure, brilliant, incomparable light. Wherefore, no one can see him; and no one can adequately praise and celebrate that glorious Lord, and chief of wonders, who is without assistance and in his thought and opinion very glorious, and ગીનોઆંન ગીનો, or among the invisibles the invisible; that is to say, as the Izads and Amsháspands are invisible to us, so that they cannot be beheld by the eyes of men of the dust, so this exalted and supreme Lord is concealed from the angels and Amsháspands; because that Lord is greatly superior to the angels, and without shadow and form. We are able to inquire into that Lord by the light of the understanding, and through means of learning. We constantly observe his influence, and behold his marvellous wonders. This is equivalent to our seeing that Lord himself.* This fact is undoubted and indisputable.

"Q. Where is that God himself?

* તે નીશ્ચે તે શાહેબને જોઈઆ બરાબર છે*

"A. That God is present in every place, in heaven, earth, and the whole creation; and whithersoever thou dost cast thine eyes, there he is nigh and by no means far from thee."*

These passages prove that the learned dastur is acquainted with *some* of the attributes of the Supreme Being. I am happy to find that this is the case, — that he admits that the Creator of the universe, is an independent, eternal, omniscient, omnipotent, holy, just, glorious, and pure, Spirit, who is superior to all other existences, and who is worthy of the praise and service of all the creatures whom he has formed. But though I admit, and ever hold and teach, that God makes himself known by his word and works, I cannot assent to the declaration, — which I believe to be the foundation of many religious errors, and especially of those in which the Pársís are involved,— that when "we observe his influence, and behold his marvellous wonders, this is equivalent to our seeing himself." When we are permitted to contemplate the glory of his works and agency, we are called upon to form just *inferences* respecting his character and providence; but we must be careful not to confound his works with his own person. The very spirituality of the divine nature, which the dastur professes to admit, forbids the imagination that it has a development in matter, either gross or refined, either dark or brilliant with glory.

Some of the Pársís think, that because they admit the *existence* of God, and acknowledge *some* of his attributes, they are entitled to the name and respect of Theists (*khudá-parastáñ*). But they must not be surprised, if we somewhat closely examine their claims to the designation which they wish to assume. All the tribes of men, throughout the world, however degraded they may be in their intellect, and sunk in barbarism in their habits, they must bear in mind, admit the existence of a Supreme God, and have more or less correct views of *some* of his qualities. All of them, however, who deprive the divine character of any of its essential attributes which are plainly revealed, and who at the same time professedly recognize any *other* object of worship, besides the Supreme

* Maujazát-i-Zartusht, pp. 2, 3.

God, and who worship God through the medium of images, the elements, and selected symbols, we consider *Polytheists* and *Idolaters*; and those who confound God with his works, who teach, that besides God, there is in reality no other object existing, we consider *Pantheists*. The class to which the Pársís belong, must be determined by a calm and candid reference to their belief and practice.

A sacred regard to the cause of truth, and an earnest desire to see its interests advanced, and most ruinous errors prevailing among my fellow-men corrected, have led me, from time to time, to protest against the notions of the Divine Being entertained by the Pársís, — against the multifarious objects of worship and reverence which they suppose to exist and constantly serve, and against the mode of worship which is predominant in their community, and which is sanctioned by the books which they esteem sacred, and to which they appeal as the foundation of their religious opinions. How far my sentiments have been correct, and how far they are entitled to the reception of the Pársís, will appear from the subsequent pages. It will be seen, from the evidence which I have now to adduce, that *Hormazd, whom they set forth as the supreme object of their worship, is supposed to be not a self-existent, but a derivative and secondary being, originating in, or by, Zarúána-Akarana, or Time-without-Bounds.*

The account of the Supreme God, which we have already introduced from the work of Edal Dárú, will be kept in mind, as containing the admission of certain truths to which we shall afterwards appeal, or which we shall take for granted. The dastur, in continuing his description of God, or rather *attempting to associate his ideas of God, with the principal object of worship recognized by the Pársís*, proceeds as follows:—

"Q. How many are the *names* of the glorious God?

"A. The names of God are numerous. Of these, the glorious names are three, the first *Dádár*,* the second *Ahur-*

* [Avestan] *dátara*, (in the vocative, in which it most commonly occurs, [Avestan] *dátare*), Giver, or Creator. Anquetil erroneously renders this word by "just Judge."

Mazd, and the third *Asó.** Besides these, there are one hundred and one, which occur in the work of reading the Izashné-Gáhs by the ઈઞોખ્વદાથરેગાર (pure) Mobeds. † All these names are descriptive, that is, they are expressive of the goodness of the righteous works which are manifested both in this and the other world." In a subsequent part of his book,‡ he writes: —"In the religious books of Dádár Hormazd, many things are commanded; but I mention only those commands which are essential and necessary, and which at all times are to be observed and obeyed. In the first place it ought to be observed, that Dádár Hormazd is the Creator of the whole world." "The meaning of the word Hormazd," he afterwards § writes, "is this: — It is applied to the great wise God. The meaning of *Ahur* is Lord (*Khudá*); and the meaning of *Mazd* is 'wise' (*dáná*), and 'greatly wise.' ‖ I give one example of the meaning of the word *Ahur*. In the *Ahurmazd-Yasht*, it was said by Ahurmazd to Dádár Zartusht, અહુર નામ અહ્મે, *Ahur nām ahmé*. The meaning of this in Pahliví, is written ખુદા શંમ હુમનંમ, *Khudá sam humnam*, 'that is, *Khudá* (Lord) is my name, or in other words, I am self-produced.' [Also we have] '*Mazdâo nām ahmé*,' that is, 'my name is wise' or greatly wise, or in other words, I know all things."

* [Zand script] *ashya, pure.* M. Burnouf justly supposes this word to be like the Greek ὅσιος "holy." Commentaire sur l' Yaçna, p. 16.

† A list of the hundred and one names of God, is given at the end of the Khurdah-Avastá, and at the commencement of the Bombay edition of the Vandidád lithographed in the Zand character. A similar list, but with the names in a somewhat different order, is given in Hyde (De Vetere Religione Persarum, Cap. xi.). Many of them occur, and are explained, in the Hormazd Yasht, some passages of which we give in the Appendix (D).

‡ Maujazát-i-Zartusht, p. 13.

§ Maujazát-i-Zartusht, p. 19, note.

‖ This etymological explanation, to which I assent, agrees with that given by the learned M. Eugène Burnouf, in his Commentaire sur l' Yaçna (pp. 70—76.) The Zand form of the word is, in the nominative case, [Zand script] *Ahurô-Mazdâo.*

Dosabháí writes in a somewhat similar strain. In his preface, he says, "Dádár Hormazd is, without doubt, the great God *(Parameshvar.)*" In the commencement of his work,* he writes as follows: — "We acknowledge one God, the Lord (Khudá), who has created the heavens, and the earth, and the angels, and the stars, and the sun, and moon, and fire, and water, and all objects in both worlds. We give him *bhakti* (worship), we give him *parastash* (worship), we serve him. Beside this God, we neither acknowledge nor worship another." He thus defines the meaning of the word Hormazd: "In the Burhán-i-Kátagh the meaning of Hormazd is *Rab-ul-arbáb*, that is *Sahebno Saheb*. In Richardson's dictionary *Rab-ul-arbáb* is translated, 'Lord of Lords.'" †

* Tálim-i-Zartusht, p. 1.

† Tálim-i-Zartusht p. 134. With regard to this question, I would, in passing, make two remarks. It is not so much with the meaning of the word Hormazd in the Persian work Burhán-i-Kátagh, or any other Musalmán dictionary, as in the sacred books of the Pársís, with which we have most to do. And it may be well to take the whole rendering into account. What we find under the name is as follows: —

هرمز روز اول است از ماه شمسي نیک است درین روز
سفر کردن و جامه نوپوشیدن و نشاید وام دادن ونام فرشته
هم هست که امور و مصالح روز هرمز با و تعلق دارد ونام ستاره
مشتري ونام پسر بهمن بن اسفندیار ونام پسر نوشیروان هم
بوده است و بمعني رب الارباب هم هست

— "Hurmúz is the first day of a solar month. It is propitious on this day to travel and put on new apparel, and not proper to lend money. And it is also the name of an angel, under whom are the deeds and counsels done on the day of Hurmúz. It is also the name of the planet Jupiter, and of the son of Bahman, the son of Asfandiár, and also of the son of Nausherwán. It has also the meaning of Lord of Lords."

Here the word is declared to be the name of an *angel*, as well as of the Lord of Lords. Do the Pársís wish to have *two* super-human Hormazds? It is only because the author of the dictionary knew that the Pársís sometimes speak of Hormazd as a *creature*, that he writes of him under *two* characters.

I would here notice an absurd digression of Dosabháí, which occurs in the part of his work to which I have now referred. He blames me for

With the passages here given, the reader will now compare the following extract from my lecture on the Vandidád, founded, as far as that work is concerned, principally on the authority of Anquetil du Perron. "The Vandidád robs God of all his glory, inasmuch as it represents the Supreme God as inactive, as unmindful of the concerns of the universe, and as having surrendered the administration of affairs to Hormazd.

"Zorwan [or rather زروان *Zarúána*], the first cause of all things, is seldom mentioned; and his excellence and perfections are not described. He is spoken of as "Time-without-Bounds;" as wholly absorbed in his own excellence, and as a "bird moving on high." Near the conclusion of the third fargard, Hormazd speaks of the world as belonging 'to that being who is absorbed in his own excellence.' He is perhaps, recognized by Zoroaster in the sixth fargard, and in some other places. He is invoked as "Time-without-Bounds," in the nineteenth fargard. But this notice which is taken of him, is inconsistent with his character as the Sovereign of all. He is not set forth, as he ought to be, as the Creator, calling all things into existence by the word of his power; and as the Governor, doing according to his will in the armies of heaven, and among the inhabitants of the earth.* To Hormazd, indeed, are ascribed most of the per-

using in my lecture the words *Mazdayasnan*, *Amsháspand*, *Asmán*, *Time without-Bounds*, *Bad* or *Govad*, *Sapandarmad*, *Farohar*, and *Hormazd*, without stating their meaning to the Pársís, which he himself professes to explain on the authority of the Burhán-i-Kátagh. If he will look at my pamphlet, he will find, that though I had no occasion to discuss them *etymologically* in my lecture, I have not left the reader to be at any loss as to the sense which I attach to them; and if he will attend to his own exposition, he will find that in some instances it goes beyond the Burhán-i-Kátagh, by which he professes to be guided, as well as contradicts his fellow controversialist, Edal Dárú. Of the opposition of the latter kind, I may give one example. Mazdayasna he explains as "free from evil." Edal Dárú, with more regard to the meaning, makes it a "worshipper of Yazdán." It ought to be a worshipper of Mazdáo, or Hormazd. The correct form of the substantive, is مزدیسن *Mazdayaçna*.

* So little is Aspandiárjí attentive to my statements and arguments which he professes to refute, that he accuses me (Hadí-i-Gum-Rahán,

fections, and works, which are peculiar to God. He is called the 'pure, the just judge.' He is the 'sovereign judge, the sovereign excellence, the sovereign knowledge.' He is, 'the best, the purest, the most intelligent, who possesses the best body, and who by reason of purity is above all." (Fargard 19). He is represented in many places as the Creator, and Ruler of the visible world.

"So powerful is the objection to be urged against the Vandidád from this view of matters, that many of the *Behdín* or Lay-Pársís, have been led to deny the existence of Zorwan altogether, and to maintain that Hormazd is God, and God alone. They do this contrary to the testimonies from Greek, Latin, and Armenian authors, which I lately brought before your notice. They do this contrary to the faith of their forefathers, as expressed in the verses presented by them to the Hindú Ráná on their first arrival in Sanján, in which Hormazd is described merely as the Divine Hormazd, the chief of the Amsháspands, or archangels. They do this contrary to the doctrines of their Dasturs, and Mobeds, who, in their conversations with me, have admitted the existence of Zorwan, and spoken of him as *lárang*, the colourless, and *nirákár*, the formless. They do this contrary to the books which they esteem sacred. In the Si-Rozé, [under the day] appointed for Hormazd, he is called an Izad. In the [heading of the] Yasht which bears his name, he is spoken of as 'the depositary of the law given by Zorwan.' * In the

p. 28) of "attempting to prove that Zorwan is represented in the Vandidád, as the Governor of all things." He will see, from this extract from my lecture which was before him, that the very *reverse* is the fact.

* "Ormusd, dépositaire de l' autorité du Temps sans Bornes." Anquetil, tom. iii, p. 144. As the statement in this instance, appears to be merely that of the learned Frenchman, I am not now disposed to lay any particular stress upon it. It is somewhat curious, however, to find Aspandiárji (Hádí-i-Gum-Rahán p. 32) characterize my reference to it as "downright falsehood." A little patience in inquiry, and a little politeness in expression, are disadvantageous to no controversialist. Aspandiárjí, in the part of his work now in my eye, quotes a passage from the Hormazd-Yasht, which, he says, makes Hormazd "the Creator of Time." In the translation of the Khurdah-avastá published at the Samáchár

nineteenth fargard of the Vandidád, Hormazd is represented as having been created by Zorwan. In the second fargard of the same work, he speaks of himself as distinct from God. When Zoroaster asked him, whence cometh the light which brightens the Viráshué, which Jamshíd had perfected, he replied, I have given to him a hundred portions of the light given by God. In the nineteenth fargard, he is represented as opposing Ahriman by the word, or Honovar, and the law of the Mazdayasnans, or, in other words, by means prescribed to him by another. There is no foundation for the opinion, that, according to the Pársí religion, Zorwan and Hormazd are the same divinity. In a catechism lately published by a Mobed, the name of Hormazd, who is all in all in the Vandidad, does not once occur. The author of that work is probably ashamed to give Hormazd the honours which are conferred on him in the Vandidád, and well he may." *

It is with reference to this passage, that Dosabhái makes the statements which we have already quoted from his work.

press, (p. 253) the very words which he thus renders, are made to intimate that જમાનો હમેશે છે "Time is always". The Zand adjective which qualifies the noun, however, is 𐬓𐬀𐬜𐬁𐬙𐬀 *Khadáta*, which means neither more nor less than "self-given."

* Lecture on the Vandidad, pp. 9 — 11. The catechism to which I refer in the concluding sentence of this quotation is that of "*Sohrábjí Mobad Dorábjí*," printed at the press of the Harkárah and Vartamán in the year of Yazdajard 1202 [A. D. 1832.] Aspandiárjí unwittingly informs the public that *another* catechism has been published without the name of Hormazd. "It is highly regretting (to be regretted,)" he adds, "that the author did not foresee that the name of Hormazd would be quite undervalued in the sight of the missionaries, merely from the circumstance of its being not made mention of .... But there are several other works by the same author, in which the name of Hormazd is not omitted." The works to which he refers, are the Gujarátí translations of a section of the Dabistán, and of the Pand-Námah of Mullá Firuz, which bear the name of my friend *Furdunjí Marazbánjí*. Of the use of the name of Hormazd in these last mentioned works, I am well aware. Still, however, the omission of it in the *catechisms*, evidently intended for general use, is worthy of notice. A liturgical work alone properly speaking," says Aspandiárjí, "should contain the name of Hormazd." What extraordinary shifts some have been driven to in these discussions!

To his special comments upon it, we shall direct particular attention.

1. He accuses me of ignorance of the character of Hormazd. "About the meaning of the word Hormazd, " he says, " I produce an important proof. After we Pársís have recited the *namáz* (worship) appointed for the five watches,* we recite a species of adoration called the *Sitáíshné*, in which we praise Hormazd. The Padre will learn from it, that Hormazd himself is the most high God."†

Of this *Sitáíshné*, Dosabhái quotes only the first sentence. As many of the Pársís, however, lay great stress upon it, I give it in full, as it is published in the original language, but in the Gujarátí character, in the *Khurdah-Avastá* :—

નાંમ સેતાઇશને ઓ હોરમજદ * ઉ હુમા બુદ * ઉ હુમા હશ
ત ઉ હુમા બેદ નાંમ ઇજદ શપના મીનો * અંદરચ મેનુઆંન
મીનો * અજશ ઓદશ * ઇઅક નાંમ હોરમજદચ * ચે ખુદાઇ મે
હેશત * ઉ તવાંનાં * ઉ દાંના * ઉ દાદાર ઉ પરવરદેગાર * ઉ પાં
ના ઉ ખાવર * ઉ કેરફેગર * ઉ અવખશીદાર * ઉ વેજ વેહે દાદ
શતાંની * હુમા જોર * શેપાશ ઓઇ બજોરગ હશતીઆંન * કે
આફરીદ * અવનીદ * ઉ પખેશ અંગાંમ બતી * જોર દાનાઇ
અંવરતર શશ અમશાશપંદાંન * અવદવેશ ઇઅજદાંન * રો
શંન બેહેશત ગરોથમાંન * ઉ ગેરદ આશમાંન * ઉ ખુર તા
વા * ઉ માહ બામી * ઉ શતર વશ તોખમો * બાદ અંદર ઓઇ *
આવ * ઉ આતશ * ઉ જમીન ઉ ઊરવર * ઉ ગોશપંદ *
ઉ અઇ ઓબશશત * ઉ મરદુમ * ઇઅજશને * ઉ નીઆઇ
શને * અજ ઓઇ ખુદાઇ કેરફેગર * કે મેહે કરદ * અજ
હરગેતીહા દેહેશનાં * મરદુમ પ ગવાઇશ * માદાંમ દાદ * ઉ

* Or Gáhs. The first gáh, *Hávan*, lasts from sun-rise to noon; the second, *Rapithawan*, from noon to three o'clock; the third, *Ozíran*, from three o'clock to sun-set; the fourth *Aivishruthrem*, from sun-set to midnight; and the fifth *Ushahan*, from midnight to sun-rise. I here give the popular names of the Gáhs. Their Zand forms occur in the fourth chapter of this work.

† Tálim-i-Zartusht, p. 114.

શેહેરીઆરેસ * અંગામ ઉરાઈની દારેસ દામાંન * પ રઅમ * અંગેજસને પરહેજ દેવાંન નમાજ ઓઈ વીસપ આગાહ * અસ ખાવર * કેસ ફરેસતીદ * પ જરથુસતર સપંતમાંન અશો ફરોહર અસતશ ઓઈદામાંન દીન દાંનસને * રોસંન આસન એરદી * ગોશો સરત એરદી * ઉ દાંનાઈસ * રાઈનીદારેસ વીસપ હસતાંન * ઉ બુદાંન * ઉ બેદાંન * ફરહંગાંન ફરહંગે માંથરે સપેંત * કુબેદ રોઆંન હુંપુલ બોખતારેસ અજ દોજખ વદારદાંર * ઓદ આંને પેહેલીમ અખાંન અશોઆંન * રોસંન હુંદ * હબોઈ હમા નેકસ * પ ફરમાંનેતો ખાવર પ ફપમાંનેતો ખાવર પ ફરમાનેતો ખાવર પદીરમ ઉ મીનમ * ઉ ગોદમ ઉ વરજેમ * દીન અવેજહ * આસતુઆં હોમ પ હર કેરફે * અવાખસ અજ વીસપ બજહ * આવેજ દારોમ * ઓદસ આશુદ કુનસને * પરેહજસને * ઉ પાક સસ * જોર બકોનમ * મનસને ઉ ગવસને * કુનસને * ઉ વીર * ઉ હોસ * ઉ એરદ * પ કાંમે તો કેરફેગાર * તવાંનેમ કરદ * આંને તો પરસતરસને * પ બેહે મનસને * બેહે ગવસને * બેહે વરજસને * વસાદમ રાહે રોસંન * ઓમ નરસાદ ગેરાંન પજદે દોજખ * વદીરમ પ ચેસઅંદરગરસમ માંન બેહેસતપોર બોઈ હરવેસપ પેશીદ * ઉ હમા ખારેસ * શેતાઈસને ઓઈ અવખશીદાર ખુદાઈ * કુકાંમ કેરફેગાર * પાદાઈસને કુનંદ ફરમાંત રાઈનીદારાંન * અવદેમ બુજીદ દરઅંદાંન * ચેઅજ દોજખ * આવેજહા * વીનાંરદે * વીસપ શેતાઈસને દાદાર હોરમજદ * હરવેસપ આગાહ * તવાંના તવંગર * હફત અમશાસપંદ * બેહેરાંમ ઈજદ પીરોજગર દુસમંન જદાર * અમહે કુતાસતહે બેરસાદ *

Instead of inserting my own version of this passage, I give place to another, which was handed to me when I was lately engaged in lecturing on the Zoroastrian faith, by a Pársí, Mánakjí Pestanjí. He entitles it:—

"Translation of a short prayer from the *Zend-Avestá.*

"[In the name of the God Almighty, the bestower of gifts

and favours,*] I praise the name of the Lord Hormazd, *who has existed from the beginning, does now, and will for ever continue to exist* ; whose name is Yezd, God the excellent, the invisible, the invisible of the invisibles, *the self-created deity*, denominated by the sublime appellation Hormazd; the Great, Omnipotent, Omniscient, the Creator of all things, the Protector, the Guardian, the Superintendent, the Source of all virtue, ever vigilant, the Holy, the Distributor of upright and impartial justice! With all might, I express my thanks and gratitude to the noble Lord of the creation, who has created the universe by his own free-will and wisdom, who has created the six Amsháspands † (Archangels), that sit beside him, and numerous other angels; who created the glorious paradise, the rotatory heavens, the resplendent sun, the glorious moon, the innumerable stars, the seeds (of every thing), the wind, the air, water, fire, the earth, the trees, the animals, the metals; who has created men. I adore and praise the Lord of virtue, who has given superiority to men above the rest of the creation, and given them the inestimable gift of speech, for the purpose of managing all the worldly concerns, for arguing with the enemies of religion, and for abstaining from Satan; and created him to rule over the earth. I worship the all-wise, omniscient God, the universal Protector, who has sent (in this world) through the virtuous, pure, and sanctified (prophet) Zartusht, the Mazdayasnan faith, for the peace and harmony of the people; who has created wisdom and pure intellect, knowledge and reason, by which (men) are enabled to conduct themselves with regard to what is passing, what has passed, and what will come to pass; who has given the Zend-Avestá as the best of all other knowledges, which enable (men)

* The Pahliví for these words, I have not given above, as I do not find the readings to agree in the copies before me. અનામે ઇઝઅવદ અખ-શાઇઝઅદદ્હે અખશાઇઝઅશાગાર, are probably what the translator has had in view.

† In the Gujarátí translation of the Khurdah-Avastá, printed at the Samáchár press in the year 1818, the explanation is here added,—" as one lamp from another lamp," જેમ એક ચેરાગથી બીજો ચેરાગ.

to pass the bridge Chínavad in safety, and preserves them from hell; which guides (us) to that glorious place of gladness and felicity, which is destined for the righteous. May I, O Lord, obey thy command and profess thy (thine) faith, and meditate, speak, and do (every thing) according to thy desire and agreeably to thy will.— May I remain firm and stedfast in the path of rectitude. — I do hereby abstain from all sin, and persevere in virtuous conduct and practise abstinence. — May I, O Lord of righteousness ! adore thee according to thy desire from the bottom of my heart, by means of expressions uttered from my mouth, by my deeds, by the practice of virtue, by my unsullied conscience, by my wisdom and sense, and to the utmost extent of my ability and strength. May I walk in the path of heaven. May I not be subject to the insufferable rigors of hell. May I pass the bridge of Chínavad in safety, and reach the everlasting paradise which is adorned, full of perfume, and easy of access. I praise the ever-glorious, and ever vigilant Almighty, who rewards those who practise righteousness. I praise thee, O Lord, who art the dispenser of justice on the day of judgment, the Redeemer and Liberator of the wicked from hell, who art the Regenerator of the human race. *I offer all my praise and adoration to Hormazd, the Omniscient, Omnipotent, the Independent and Absolute (master), the Creator of the seven Amsháspands and of Behrám the powerful, who is the successful destroyer of enemies. Do thou (O Lord) lend me thy assistance.*"*

* This last sentence is more incorrectly translated than any of the preceding. In the Khurdah-Avastá published at the Samáchár press, it is thus given in the Gujarátí language :—

સરવ તારીફ અને સેતાએસથી દાદાર હોરમજદને જે સરવ હકીકતનો જાણનાર અને સરવે વાતો સકતો અને સરવેથી બેપરવા અને સાતે અમશાસપંદ અને બેહેરાંમ ઈઅજદ જે દુસમનોને મારનાર અને જોરમંદ નેક પેદા કીધેલા * તે માહારી મદદે પોહોચો *

The literal meaning is: — "With all praise and *Sitáish* (praise) to Dádár Hormazd, who is the knower of all circumstances, and who is potent

This Sítáishné, will never induce me to allow that Hormazd is the most high God, though it contains sufficient proof that many of the Pársís are accustomed to ascribe most of the attributes and honours of God to Hormazd, a fact which I have very distinctly brought to notice in my lecture on the Vandidád, and other papers treating of the Pársí religion. The Sitáíshné is not, as the translator alleges, from the *Zand*-Avastá; for it is to be found only in the *Pahliví*, and that of a comparatively modern character, not essentially different from Persian. It is not one of the prayers which are supposed to be divinely authorized by the Pársís. As allowed by Dosabhái, and as intimated in the heading prefixed to it in the Khurdah-Avastá, or minor liturgy, it is a mere *supplement* to some of the ordinary forms of worship which they repeat. It has, I suspect, been composed at a late period, in imitation of the forms of the Christians or Musalmáns.*

in every thing, and who is without the care of any one. And let the seven Amsháspands and Behrám Izad, the destroyer of enemies and the powerful, created upright, come to my assistance." This, it will be seen, nearly agrees with the Pahliví.

* The alleged specimens of *Zand* shown to Sir William Jones by the Pársí Bahman, were, I suspect, in the *Pahliví* language. It was probably on this account that he has said, (Works vol. iii, p. 116, 8vo. edit.) that "the dialect of the *Gabrs*, which they pretend to be that of Zerátusht, and of which Bahman gave me a variety of written specimens, is a late invention of their priests, or subsequent at least to the Musalmán invasion." I cannot acquiesce in this opinion even as far as the Pahliví itself is concerned; but I would certainly form a judgment in some cases, as in the present, as to the date of certain compositions, from a consideration of their proximity to modern Persian.

As this sheet is passing through the press, I have received a letter from Mánakjí Pestánji, who pressed on my attention the translation of the Nám Sitáíshné, which I have quoted above, in answer, as he thinks, to some observations " which I made upon it in a public lecture lately delivered in Bombay. "I admit," he says, "that it is in the Pahliví [why did he before say that it is in the Zand?] .... I beg to say that on consulting some of our ancient religious works [why are their names and dates not given, and specific references not made to them, and the authorities on which they rest, not extracted?] I have found that the prayer which I had sent to you, and which you were pleased to read publicly, was composed by one of our holy prophet Zartusht's disciples, not long after the divine mis-

The translation, given by Mánakjí Pestanjí, though evidently too paraphrastic throughout, I am willing to receive as a well-meant attempt to do justice to the Nām Sitáíshné. The only parts of it which bear upon the subject before us, are the opening sentences, * and especially the words which I have marked in italics, and which I have no doubt, the translator interprets as teaching the independence and eternal existence of Hormazd. The expession "self-created deity" is an inaccurate rendering of the Pahliví *ajas Khudash*, — equivalent to the Persian *Az-ash Khudá*, — which means simply " of himself the Lord." The declaration that Hormazd " has existed from the beginning does now, and ever will, continue to exist", is that only which demands our attention. What its legitimate interpretation is, — if it is to be understood in accordance with the passages in the Pársí scriptures which will immediately be produced, — we shall now see. Anquetil du Perron, consistently with what will now be mentioned, confines the expressions, "always was, and always is, and always will be," to *definite time*, or time-with-bounds. In his table, he refers to them as showing that Hormazd " a été *dans le temps* toujours, continuellement, et sera toujours."† He has the express authori-

sion of this greatest of all the prophets; and that it was incorporated in the volume, called Khurdah-Avastá by Adarbád Máhrespand, who flourished about 1700 years ago in the time of Sháhpur, the successor of the celebrated reformer Ardeshír Bábegán, king of Persia, at the time when Muhammad was not in existence. It was Adarbád Máhrespand who enjoined the injunction you pointed out that evening, that it should be repeated by every follower of Zartusht after every *Níáish* and *Yasht*." To Adarbád Máhrespand, we may afterwards have an opportunity of directing attention.

* Dosabháí renders them in Gujarátí to the following effect: — " I praise the name of Hormazd, who always was, and always is, and who always will remain, whose name is *khudàinu wardhíno karanár*, the conductor of the Divine providence, the concealed, and amongst the things that are concealed, the concealed, the Lord who is created by himself, Hormazd, who alone is the great, and powerful, and wise Lord, that is, he who knows all mysteries, and who is the Creator, and Preserver, and Overseer, and the Protector of all, and the Lord of righteousness, and who is always observant and holy, and who is himself the Lord of justice.

† Zend-Avesta, tom iii, p. 744.

ty of the Pahliví Bundéshné, for such an interpretation. In a passage, in the commencement of that work, to which we shall again advert before the close of this chapter, and in which the *origin of Hormazd in time*, (*zamán*,) is plainly stated, it is added : — " *janunid u hét u hamá janunid* — " He [Hormazd] was, and is, and will be."* This, it must be remembered, is said merely in reference to existence in *Time-with-Bounds*, as is evident from the context.

Dosabhái admits that there is such an object mentioned in the Vandidád, and other sacred books of the Pársís, as *Zarúána-Akarana*. But he says,† that, " it is the name of a *Time*, which is the attribute of Dádár Hormazd, applied to him because no one knows the beginning or end of that Lord, the Creator, or, in other words, *when* that Lord was produced, or how long he will exist." Zarúána-Akarana, he expressly says, is equivalent to " Eternity."‡ Now, with regard to this matter, I would remark, that if the Pársís really believe Hormazd to be eternal, they have no reason to speak of his being produced either *at* a time known to man, or unknown to man. To speak as they do, of his " having come *out of* eternity," is nonsense, if he exists *during* all eternity. What they should say, if their books really warrant them to consider him eternal, as they certainly do not, is, that he exists *throughout* or *during* eternity. Their acknowledgement that Hormazd "came *out of* Zarúána", is fatal to the idea that he can be considered eternal.

Dosabhái himself has seriously felt the untenableness of the ground which he here occupies. " It is true," he writes, " that Zarúána, is represented in the Vandidád as the first cause of the creation, for every thing has come out of eternity. Moreover, it is a misrepresentation of the padre when he supposes that we do not reckon him to be Lord *(Khudá)*. In the same way as in the Zand-Avastá we give worship *(ará-*

* Bundéshné, p. 1.

† Quoting from the appendix to the Khurdah-Avastá, as translated by Edal Dáru.

‡ Tálim-i-Zartusht, p. 117.

dhaná) to, that is, recognize, the four elements, and the moon, and the sun, so we worship, or recognize, Time-without-Bounds. As for example, we find it thus in the Khúrshíd-Níáish,—*Zarúánem-akaranem yazamaidhê*,* that is to say, I worship (árádhuch) or recognize (*yád karuch*)† Time-without-Bounds." ‡ In view of these admissions, I put to him the following questions, and demand of him a precise and straight-forward answer: — How can the declaration that Hormazd came out of Zarúána, be equivalent to the declaration that he is "eternal," when it is allowed that *every* created object has come out of Zarúána? Is it meant to be asserted that every created object is eternal? How can Zarúána, if it be nothing more than eternity in the abstract, be an object of invocation, or esteemed "Lord?" Are you, and the Pársís in general, not ashamed to speak to, and praise, eternity, which you allege is only an "attribute of God?" O Dosabhái, you will never get out from the meshes of the net which you have woven for yourself. The more you roll and kick about, the tighter will it become.

With a view to bewilder the reader, Dosabhái asks me, "Do not *you* recognize eternity, and do not you reckon God eternal, as in many passages of the Bible it is said, "God came from all eternity." § I reply, I do *not* recognize eternity as an

* [illegible] In an ancient MS. copy of the Khúrshíd Níáish, said by the person who gave it to me to be the oldest in India, [illegible] *d* is used for the [illegible] *dh* of the common MSS.

† This, the reader will perceive, is a disingenuous attempt of Dosabhái to soften the meaning of the preceding word, which its ancient appropriation, in the Pársí translations, to the Zand *yazamaidhê* forced him to use. *A'rádhan* from which the Gujarátí verb *árádhuch* is derived, is the Sanskrit word for worship. For an investigation of the meaning of the verb [illegible] *yazamaidhê*, see Chapter V.

‡ Tálim-i-Zartusht, p. 117.

§ This alleged quotation he gives in English, as it here stands. He translates it into Gujarátí thus: — "*Khudá Zorwán-mánthí nikalo*, God proceeded out of eternity!!" At this place, Dosabhái, I may remark, enters into a long digression from his argument, in which he introduces two Zand extracts from the Izashné, according to which the *Ahunavar* or object of invocation. God, I devoutly acknowledge, *is* eternal. I also say, that there is not a single passage in the Bible, like that which Dosabhái professes to quote from it. The words "*God came from all eternity*," and which he more than once sets before his reader, are entirely a fabrication of his own imagination.

Dosabhái further asks me, if I do not "reckon *Jehovah*, or *Almighty God*, as holy, and a just Judge, and the Lord of Justice." I answer him in the affirmative; but I deny his inference, that there is nothing improper in giving these attributes and titles to *Hormazd*. He who originated in Zarúána, can never be compared to him who is self-existent, and who has no beginning and no end, who is the same, yesterday, to-day and forever, the Father of lights, with whom there is no variableness, neither shadow of turning. But to this matter, it will be necessary again to return.

3. Dosabhái blames me for wounding the Pársí religion by making references about Zarúána and Hormazd to Greek, Latin, and Armenian authors, quotations from whose works I have not produced. I beg of him to observe, that the quotations to which I allude, I had given at length in the second of my Pársí lectures delivered in 1833, and that my lecture on the Vandidád,—the publication of which was requested and accomplished,—was only a *part* of that series. To some of the passages, as they are found in my notes, written nine years ago, he is now welcome.

In the first of them Hormazd is represented as *produced from light*. "There are others," says Plutarch, "who reckon that there are two gods, devoted to contrary practices, so

word, consisting of the twenty-one original *Núsks* of the Avastá, was created before the heavens, the earth, the water, fire, &c., and which Ahunavar he recommends me to study at the feet of the dasturs. This digression is a proof of his conscious inability to grapple with my argument. It is quite of a kin with much of what we find in his book. We shall by and by see more of the Ahunavar; but I may here ask, why it was made long before it was needed by man? Did Hormazd himself, like the Hindú Brahm with the Vedas, require to take lessons from it before the creation?

that the one effects good works; and the other evil works. Him who is the better, they declare to be God; and the worse, the Devil. Of which sentiment was Zoroaster the Magian, who they say, lived about five hundred years before the Trojan war. This Zoroaster called the better, Oromazes; and the worse, Areimanius. And he added this announcement, that among objects falling under the cognizance of the senses, the former is most like to light, and the latter to darkness and ignorance: that Mithras is intermediate between them, which is the reason why the Persians reckon Mithras the Mediator or intermedium..... They say that *Oromazes was born of the purest light, and Areimanius of darkness*, (Ὁ μὲν Ὡρομάζης ἐκ τοῦ καθαρωτάτου φάους, ὁ δ' Ἀρειμάνιος ἐκ τοῦ ζόφου γεγονὼς), and that they continually wage war against one another."*

In the second, God is represented as *distinct* from Hormazd and Ahriman, and concealed during their conflicts. Theopompus, as quoted by Plutarch, in the work from which the preceding extract is made, thus writes: — "According to the sentiments of the Magi, one of these gods must be superior, and the other must succumb, in turn, for three thousand years; and that they must carry on war with one another for three thousand years, and fight and demolish one another's works; that at last hell shall be no more, and that then men shall be happy, not using food nor casting a shadow; that the *God also who planned all these things, keeps himself in repose for a certain time* (τὸν δὲ ταῦτα μηχανησάμενον θεὸν, ἠρεμεῖν καὶ ανοπαύεσθαι χρόνῳ), an interval not too long for a God, but rather like the right and moderate time of a mortal's sleep."†

The third quotation, from the "Persian or Zoroastrian Oracles," written in the Greek language, and quoted by Psellus, Proclus, Synesius, and others, runs thus; — "All things are the *offspring of one fire*. The father, or first Deity, perfected

*De Iside et Osiride, in Plutarch. Om. Oper. vol. vii, p. 457, Lipsiæ 1817.

† Plutarch. ibid. p. 459.

all things, and delivered them to the second mind, who is that whom the nations of men commonly take for the first."*

The fourth quotation is to this effect: — "The Magi, and the whole Arian race, call (as Eudemus likewise writes) the rational universe, and the One, sometimes *Space*, sometimes *Time, from which both the good God and evil Demon have separated*; or, as some will have it even before them; light and darkness. When undivided nature had divided itself, the two-fold system of the higher powers formed itself — Oromazd forming one system, and Areiman the other." Eudemus, here quoted by Damascius, is said to have been a pupil of Aristotle.†

The fifth quotation, from the history of Vartan by Eliseeus, an Armenian writer, is composed of a proclamation issued by the Persian Government in the fifth century. I have marked in italics the passages to which attention should be particularly directed. "Mihrnerseh, grand vizier of Iran and Daniran, to the Armenians abundant greeting (A. D. 450): know, that all men who dwell under heaven and hold not the belief of the Mastesens, (Mazdayasnís) are deaf, and blind, and betrayed by the devil-serpent; for before the heavens and the earth were, the *great God Zruan* prayed a thousand years, and said, 'If I, perhaps, should have a *son named Vormist, (Hormazd)* who will make the heavens and the earth.' And he conceived two in his body, one by reason of his prayer, and the other because he said *perhaps*. When he knew that there were two in his body, he said, 'Whichever shall come first, to him will I give over my sovereignty. He who had been conceived in doubt, passed through his body and went forth. 'To him spake Zruan: 'Who art thou?' He said, 'I am thy *son Vormist*.' To him said Zruan: 'My son is light and fragrant

* Cudworth's Intellectual System, pp. 287, 8. Cudworth (p. 292) gives a brief account of the work from which this passage purports to be a translation. According to Bayle (article *Zoroastre*), an edition of the Zoroastrian Oracles was published at Amsterdam in the year 1689, with the scholia of Pletho and Psellus.

† See the original in Hyde de Vet. Rel. Pers. p. 292, and Neumann's Vartan, p. 85.

breathing; thou art dark and of evil disposition.' As this appeared to his son exceedingly harsh, he (Zruan) gave him the empire for a thousand years. When the other son was born to him, he called him Vormist. He then took the empire from Ahriman, gave it to Vormist, and said to him, 'Till now I have prayed to thee, now thou must pray to me.' And Vormist made heaven and earth; Ahriman on the contrary brought forth evil."* This passage clearly represents Hormazd as the son of Zarúâna.

The next which I adduce, is similar to that which I have now brought forward. It is from Esnik, another Armenian writer of the fifth century. "Before yet any thing was made," he says, "either the heavens or the earth, or any creature whatsoever, which liveth in the heavens or on the earth, was one named *Zeruan*, a word signifying the same with *destiny* or *fame* (fate ?). A thousand years he offered sacrifice, that he might obtain a son, who should have the name *Ormisd*, and should create heaven and earth, and all things in them. After a thousand years of sacrifice, he began to reflect and said, 'the sacrifice which I have performed, does it conduce to the end, and shall a son, Ormisd, be born to me, or do I strive in vain ? While he thought thus, *Ormisd* and *Ahriman* were conceived in the body of their mother. Ormisd was the offspring of the sacrifice, and Ahriman of the doubt. Zeruan knew this and said, — 'Two sons are in the mother's womb, he who shall first come forth to me, will I make the king. Ormisd knew his father's thought, imparted it to Ahriman, and said, 'Our father Zeruan intends to make him king, who shall first come to him;' and Ahriman hearing this, pierced through the body of his mother, and stood before his father. Zeruan looking on him said, 'Who art thou ?' And he said, 'I am thy son.' Then Zeruan spoke to him: 'My son is of odoriferous breath, and resplendent appearance, but thou art dark and of an evil odour.' While they were thus speaking together, *Ormisd was born at his proper time*, and he was bright-shining and sweet-breathing. He went forth and

* History of Vartan, by Eliseus, translated by Newmann, pp. 11, 12.

came before Zeruan: and when Zeruan looked upon him, he knew that this was his son Ormisd, for whom he had offered sacrifice. He took the vessel which he had in his hand, and wherewith he had sacrificed, gave it to Ormisd, and said, 'Hitherto I have sacrificed for thee, now and henceforward thou must sacrifice for me: and hereupon Zeruan gave his vessel to Ormisd, and blessed him. Ahriman saw this and said to Zeruan 'Hast thou not taken an oath, whichsoever of the two sons shall first come to me, him will I make king?' Zeruan, that he might not brèak his oath, said to Ahriman, O thou false and evildoer! to thee the dominion be given for nine thousand years; but I appoint Ormisd lord over thee. After the nine thousand years Ormisd shall rule, and what he wishes, that shall he bring to pass. Now Ormisd and Ahriman began to form creatures; and all that Ormisd formed were good, and all that Ahriman formed were evil and perverse."*

* Notes to the History of Vartan, p. 9. The original of this may be seen in the work of Esnik against the Heretics, printed at Venice in 1822, p. 113. Esnik's reasoning upon it, as translated by my friend Aviet Aganoor, Esq. I give in the Appendix (D). It is remarkably terse and appropriate; and shows that the Armenian writer is an excellent logician.

Somewhat similar to these Armenian notices, is a passage in the Arabic work, entitled *Sharistani*, quoted by Dr. Hyde, but the application of which, that learned author has not every distinctly perceived. "Altera Magorum Secta originalis, sunt *Zervanitæ* qui asserunt Lucem produxisse Personas ex Luce, quæ omnes erant Spirituales, Luminosæ, Dominales; sed quod harum maxima Persona, cui nomen Zervân, dubitavit de re aliquâ; et ex ista dubitatione emersit Satanas. Sunt ex eis qui asserunt, non esse dubium quin Zervân ille Magnus stetit et musitavit 7999 annos, ut posset habere Filium, et non habuit. Tum novum quid animo molitus, cogitavit secum quòd fortè hic mundus nil valet. Ideoque emersit Ahreman ex tali solicitudine unicâ: et emersit Hormus ex tali scientiâ: et quòd dum hi duo essent simul in uno ventre, et Hórmus esset exitui propior, subtiliter agens Ahreman, seu Satanas, matris ventrem diffidit, et tum prior exiens occupavit mundum." . . . .

These matters Hyde considers metaphorical, but for what reason he has not informed us. He adds:—"Et ab his non multum obludunt quæ apud Photium habet Theodorus Mopsuestiensis Presbyter, qui scripsit de Persarum Magiâ, ubi exponit nefandum Dogma quod Zasrades introduxit, sive Zaruam quem Principem omnium facit, et fortunam appellat. Deinde tradit, Hunc libationem facisse ut Hormisdam gigneret, quem et genuit, uti et Satanam. Item, de eorum Αιμομιξια ubi etiam eorum per-

Esnik, the author of this passage, had the Pársí religion before him as a practical system; and he writes as a person thoroughly conversant with its various dogmas. Moses of Chorene, another Armenian, who was nearly one of his contemporaries, refers also to Zerovanus, and says that he is mentioned in the Chaldaic books as synonymous with Zoroaster himself, the origin of the Medes and the *father of the Gods.**

Such are the testimonies to which I referred in my lectures. When coupled with those more intimately connected with the Pársí, it will be acknowledged that they are possessed of no slight importance in a historical point of view.

4. Dosabhái's reply to my allusions to the testimony of the books esteemed sacred by the Pársís, as to the subordination of Hormazd, as has been already in some degree apparent, is exceedingly lame.

I had said that Hormazd, in the Sirozah is "called *an* Izad."‡ I should rather have said is "treated as an Izad."

obscœnum Dogma verbatim exponit et refellit. De Vetere Religione Persarum, p. 298.

Abulfeda, also says, that Zoroaster taught that there is a God more ancient than the Two Principles. See Pocock. Spec. p. 143.

* "Zerovanus, quem híc ea Zoroastrem Magum, Bactrianorum regem, fuisse dicit qui fuit Medorum principium ac Deorum pater." Whiston's Translation, p. 16.

† "I beg to express my wish to know," says Aspandiárjí, (Hádí-i-Gum-Rahán, p. 31) "in what part of the Sirozé, Hormazd is called by the appellation of an Izad." I answer, *In the very first clause*, according to Anquetil, whom I quoted in my lecture on the Vandidád, and who, from this copy of the smaller collection of Raváyats, has quoted the Zand words "Eôktô nâmenô iezetehé" as his authority for his rendering, "Appellé Ized" (Zendavesta tom. iii p. 116). In the Zand MSS. now in my possession, I do not find this reading. My argument, however, remains untouched while Hormazd is there associated with the Izads in the manner above adverted to. In connection with this matter, Aspandiárjí says, "that a Pársí came to me to request me to "point out to him that part of the Sirozé, which treats of good and evil omens, and that he returned home without any satisfaction." Of this visit, I remember nothing. This I know, however, that the translation of the *Sífat Sirozah*, — not the smaller liturgical Sirozah which Aspandiárjí confounds with it, — was published in London by the Royal Asiatic Society (Journal, vol. iv.) in 1837. I now give Aspandiárjí the "satisfaction" to be derived from a perusal of it, by inserting it in the Appendix (E.)

Izad, the Mobed says, is a "name of *God*," as given in the Burhání-Kátagh. This I allow ; and if Hormazd alone had been esteemed "*the* Izad," I should not perhaps have adverted to the expression as marking the fact that Hormazd is considered only a secondary divinity in the Pársí sacred writings. Hormazd, I beg my opponent to observe, however, is viewed as an Izad, in the [Lesser] Sirozah, in the same way that Bahman, Ardebehisht, Shahríwar, Spandármad, Khurdád, Amardád, Adar, A'bán, Khúrshíd, Máh, Tír, Gosh, Meher, Sarosh, Rashne-Rást, Farvardín, Behrám, Rám, Guvád, Dín, Ashasang, Ashtád, Asmán, Zamiad, Máhraspand, and Anírán are viewed as Izads.* Each of the imaginary beings now mentioned, has a day of the month sacred to him, in the same way as Hormazd has the first, eighth, sixteenth, and twenty-third days of the month sacred to him. Is this an association and connection, I would ask, worthy of the reputed Creator of the heavens and the earth, who has "no equal," and whose glory it is impiety to give to another? It is not enough to say that he is the "chief of the Amsháspands and Izads," when they are thus suffered to be numerically arranged with him, to be reckoned his brethren, and to usurp his honour.† It is not enough

* The Zand work for *Izad* is 𐬫𐬀𐬰𐬀𐬙𐬀 *yazata,* which means an "object of worship." It corresponds exactly with the Sanskrit यजत, *yajata,* which occurs in the Rig-Veda (Sánhitá B. I. ch. iii, h. 34, st. 7), and which is explained by Sáyan, the commentator, by यष्टव्य, *yashtavya,* and rendered by Rosen *sacris celebrandus.* M. Burnouf translates it by "digne qu'on lui offre le sacrifice." See Journal Asiatique, Octobre 1840.

The Zand for Amsháspand is 𐬀𐬨𐬆𐬱𐬀 𐬯𐬞𐬆𐬧𐬙𐬀 *amesha-speñta.* The words of which this name is composed, are correctly represented, by Edal Dáru (Maujazát-i-Zartusht, p. 20), by "exalted immortal." The appellation is conferred in the Zand writings on the first six imaginary persons mentioned, as well as on Hormazd.

† Aspandiárjí thinks that the shlokas presented to Jáde Ráná of Sanján, represent the "divine Hormazd" as the "chief, or Lord, of the Amsháspands, or archangels, as he is of the mortals below." This is educing a meaning from them, which, though it is consistent with many passages in the Pársí writings, I do not perceive to be conveyed by them. Why is Hormazd uniformly represented as *one* of the *seven* Amsháspands? Why is he enumerated and classed along with his reputed *creatures* ?

to say that at the time they are worshipped, he is worshipped, either first or last; for if he were truly God, and to give a directory for his worship, it would show that there is an infinite distance between himself and all and each of the creatures which he has made, and that he presides over every day of the month, as well as over the first. On this subject, however, I shall not now enlarge, as it will afterwards devolve on me to point out the absurdity and the sinfulness of the worship, in any form, of Izads and Amsháspands, as sanctioned by the Pársí writings.

Of most of my references to the so-called sacred books of the Pársís, and other authorities which mark the derivative rank of Hormazd, Dosabháí has found it convenient to take no notice whatever.* But while I call the attention of the Pársís to the fact that they are not disallowed, or shown to be irrelevant, or proved to be the foundation of erroneous conclusions, I may also give a few more proofs of the fact that the authorities on which the Pársí religion rests, represent Hormazd as a secondary and derivative God.

(1). In the "sacred books" of the Pársís, there is a class of beings denominated *Farohars*† frequently spoken of, and set forth as objects of worship. Anquetil du Perron, the French translator of these books, thus describes them: 'Les Ferouers sont comme l'expression la plus parfaite de la pensée du Créateur appliquée à tel object particulier. Ils ont d' abord existé seuls. Réunis ensuite aux êtres quils représentoient, ils ont fait partie, si je puis m'exprimer ainsi, de

* Aspandiárjí (Hádí-i-Gum Rahán pp. 28, 29) gives what he considers five positive "proofs" of the identity of Hormazd with God." Not a single one of them refers to the question about the origin of Hormazd, either negatively or positively. The first of them is the first verse of the first Há of the Izashné, to which we shall refer under another head. The others are all Pahliví, though Aspandiárjí has cunningly marked them as from the "Avastá," which (p. 5) he calls the *language* of the sacred books of the Pársís! My observations on the Nãm Sitáíshné supersede further notice of the passages quoted.

† The nominative singular is in Zand 𐬟𐬭𐬀𐬎𐬀𐬱𐬌𐬱 *fravashis*. The noun is feminine.

l'ame des Creatures."* M. Eugène Burnouf, the author of the learned and elaborate commentary on the Yaçna, says of them: — "Par ferouer les Parses entendent le type divin de chacun des êtres douées d' intelligence."† In Guigniat's translation of Creuzer on the Religions of Antiquity, they are called "les idées, les prototypes, les modèles de tous les êtres."‡ English writers give a similar account of them. "The Faruhers," says Mr. Erskine, the author of a very able essay on the Sacred Books and Religion of the Pársís, "are the angels and unembodied souls of all intelligent beings."§ Mr. Shea, in the translation of Mirkhond's History of the ancient Kings of Persia, calls them "models of existence."|| In a former publication, I have referred to them in similar words, and also called them the "prototypes of spirits."¶ Dosabhâí has favoured us, with the following explanation. "*Faruhar* means *johar*. They call that *johar*, which is in English called *Essence*. It is a *mantak*, or logical word. In Arabic, they apply *johar* to an article which is composed of its own substance; and they apply the word *araz* to an object which is composed of another object. Take for example the sun and sunshine: — The *johar* is the sun and the sunshine is *araz*. Take another example, of wood, and a chair: — the wood is *johar* and the chair is *araz*, for the chair is made from wood, and if there were no wood, there would be no chair."** This statement I do not particularly oppose, except so far as to say that *johar* means more commonly the primitive state of an object, and that *araz* is applied to its accidents or proper-

* Zend-Avasta, tom. ii, p. 83, n. 6.

† Commentaire sur le Yaçna, vol. i, p. 270.

‡ Tom. i, p. 326.

§ Transactions of the Bombay Literary Society, vol. ii. p. 318.

|| p. 41.

¶ Doctrine of Jehovah addressed to the Pársís, p 27.

** Tâlim-i-Zartusht, p. 134.

ties.* Dosabhái, by his stroke of logic, neither confirms nor illustrates his opinion.

In none of the books of the Pársís, have I observed *Zarúána-Akarana* spoken of as having a *Faruhar*. The reason is obvious. "Time-without-Bounds," says Anquetil du Perron, "has no Faruhar, because it is self-existent, and is consequently without a prototype."† That *Hormazd*, however, is represented as having a Faruhar, or prototype, and is therefore not self-existent, can easily be proved. In the nineteenth fargard, or section, of the Vandidád, addressing Zoroaster, he gives this commandment:—

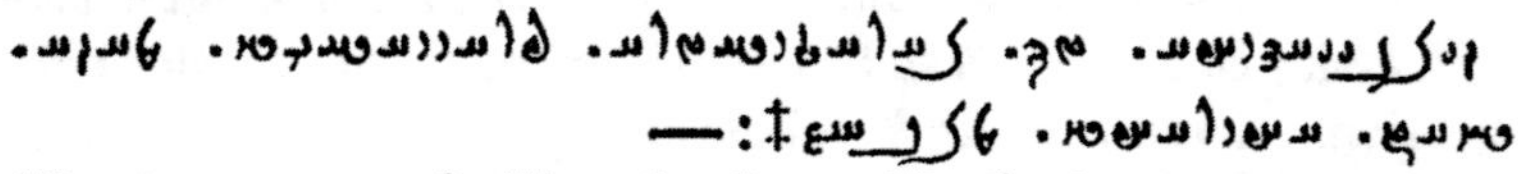

Ni-zbyanguha tú Zarathushtra Fraúashîê mana yat Ahurahê Mazdâo:—"Invoke thou, O Zoroaster, the Faruhar of me, that is, of Hormazd:"—An example of this worship, we find in the twenty-second Kardé of the Yasht-Farvardín, in which it is said, "I make Izashné to all the Faruhars which have been from the commencement, with that of Hormazd; the most perfect," &c.§ In the twenty-third Há of the Yaçna, or Izashné, we have another:—

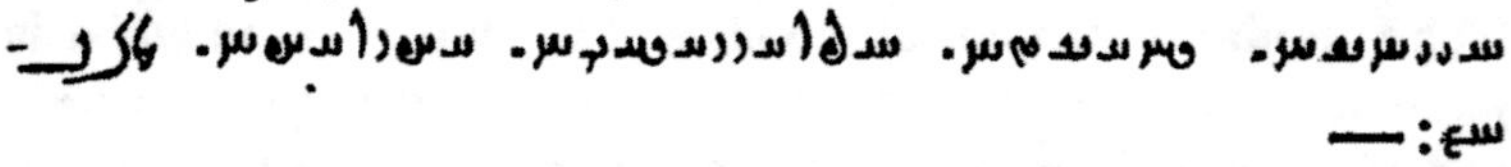

—*A'yêçê yaztê áfraúsahîê Ahurhê-Mazdâo:*—"I express-my-love-to, I sacrifice-to the Faruhar of Hormazd." Many other passages of a like nature can easily be produced.

Now the question comes to be, How has the recognition of the Faruhar of Hormazd come to be made? If he is to be viewed as an uncreated being, there can neither have been, nor can there be, an "original idea," or a "type," or a "pro-

* Of this fact, Dosabhái himself is well aware. In another part of his work, when treating of another subject, he says, that the logical word accident is properly rendered by the Arabic word *araz*. Tálim-i-Zartusht, p. 130.

† Anquetil, tom. iii, p. 262. ‡ Lithographed Vandidad, p. 510.

§ Anquetil. iii, 262.

totype" of himself, to be distinctly recognized or addressed by man. It is only when he is supposed to be the production of another being, —of Zarúána-Akarana,—that there is any meaning whatever in the language which the Pársís have used in their sacred books. The authors of these works have undoubtedly viewed him as a derivative being.

(2). Near the commencement of the nineteenth fargard of the Vandidád, the Word, or Ahunavąr, is particularly praised, and it is there expressly said to have been given by Zarúána-Akaran.

The words of the original Zand are :—

[illegible]

—*Datḫaṯ speñtó-mainyus datḫaṯ Zaruáné-Akaranahé.*— These words are used in reference to the Word given to Zoroaster. They have been tolerably correctly rendered into Gujarátí by the dasturs, આપીઓં સપેના મીનો આપીઓં જમાનો અકનારે*—"It has been" given to me by the high invisible, (or intelligence, Hormazd ;) *it has been given to me by* Time-without-Bounds." This is an unequivocal instance of Zarúána being set forth as a *personal agent*, having dealings with men, a fact utterly inconsistent with the notion of Dosabháí, that Zarúána means simply "eternity," or an "attribute of Dádar Hormazd," and it is consequently subversive of his whole theory. He himself must clearly see that this is the case, for in no sense can it be said that eternity has given the word to Zoroaster. A similar proof may be found in the representation which is given of Zarúána, in the nineteenth fargard of the Vandidád, in which it is said that he has formed the way which leads to the bridge of Chinavad, on which the souls of men are said to be compelled to enter at death. That way is spoken of in Zand as † [illegible] *pathãm Zarúódátanãm* " the path given by Time."

* Lithographed Vandidád, p. 508.

† Author's MS. Vandidád, vol. ii, p. 226.

‡ Vandidád, lithographed, p. 516.

(3). Dosabháí has himself quoted a passage from the Khúrshíd Níáísh, in which Zarúána-Akarana is represented as an object of worship, or, as he would have it, an object of recognition.* In the nineteenth fargard of the Vandidád a little in advance of the passage which we have quoted above, the command is expressly given to Zoroaster that he may be invoked: —

[illegible]

[illegible] —:

—*Ni-zbyaênguha tú Zarathushtra thwásahê Khadhátahê Zarúánahê Akaranahê*:— " Invoke thou, O Zoroaster, the self-given Time-without-Bounds." A little onward Zoroaster thus expresses his consent: *Nizbyêmí Thwásahê Kadhátahê Zaruánahê Akaranhê*, " I invoke the self-given heaven Zarúána-Akarana.*

In the small Sirozé, under the day of the Izad Rám, Zaruána-Akarana receives the [illegible] *khsnaothra*, " the prayer which-renders-favorable;" and in the great Sirozé, under the same day, the supplicant says to him, or it, *Yazamaidhê Zarúánem-Akaranem*, " I worship Zaruána-Akarana." It is addressed in the same terms in the *Nirang-Dast-Sho*, or the formula for recitation on the occasion of washing hands.

So much for the testimony of the sacred books of the Pársís as to the secondary, and derivative, character of Hormazd. If it is not so extensive as some may expect, it must be borne in mind that these books are reckoned incomplete of themselves, and considered mere fragments of works which have perished. It is quite consistent, I would now remark, with the *digests of their cosmogonies and doctrines* which the Zoroastians have from time to time given to the world.

The most ancient of these digests is the *Bundéshné*, which till lately was so highly esteemed among them that it was

* *Yazamaidhê*, the word used, literally signifies "sacrifice with prayers."

† Vandidád lithographed, p. 411.

generally considered a work written by divine inspiration. It exists in Pahliví, and is supposed by Anquetil du Perron to have been written about the seventh century of the Christian era. Though it is in the highest degree absurd in many of its statements, it is scarcely less so than the Vandidád itself, and may well be referred to, not for the proof of the correctness of the opinions of the Pársís, but for a statement of what they were when it was composed. In the very commencement of this work, we find the following passage :—

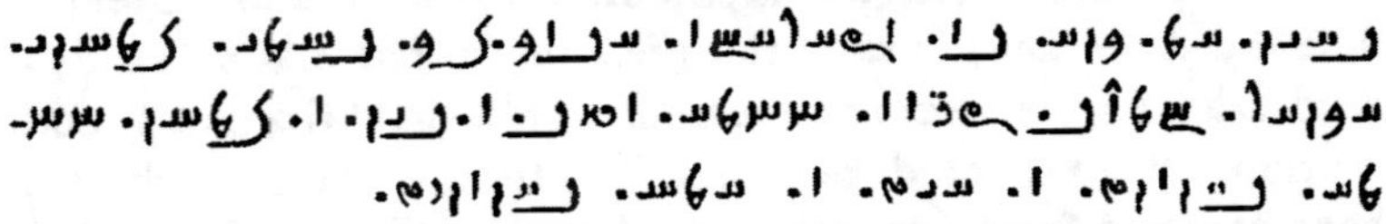

—*Dain ham kana du vajarashna advak zak dámé zamáné akanar humnad jagun Anhuma ved u dén, u zamán Anhuma janunid u hét u hamá janunid*, "With regard to the existence of both [Hormazd and Ahriman] in time, each is the production of Time-without-Bounds [Zamán Akaran], namely Hormazd the most excellent, and the law, and [in] time Hormazd was, and is, and always will be."

Another work entitled the I'lmá-í-Islám, containing the replies of a Pársí Dastur to the questions of a Musalmán inquirer, and of great repute among the Pársís, and supposed to have been composed about the year 1126 of the Christian era,* contains the following passage :—

در دین زرتشت چنین پیدا است که خدا از زمان دیگر هم آفریده
است و آفریدگار زمان است و زمان را کناره پدید نیست و بالا پدید
نیست و بن پدید نیست و همیشه بوده است و همیشه به شد و هر که
خرد دارد نگوید که از کجا پیدا آید و این بزرگواري که بود کسي نه
بود که در آفریدگار خواند چرا زیرا که آفرینش نه کرده بود پس آتش و
آبرا بیافرید چون بهم رسانید هرمزد وجود آمد زمان هم آفریدگار بود
و هم خداوند بسوي آفرینش که کرده بود و مادر و اول گفته این که
هرمزد و آهرمن هردو از زمان موجود شده اند

* Anquetil, Zend-Avasta, tom iii. p. 339. Of the *I'lmá-i-Islam*, Sir William Ouseley says "A copy of it I procured, but not without difficulty

"In the religion of Zoroaster, it is to this effect declared, that God (*Khudá*) created every thing from Time; and that the Creator is *Time*. And for *Time* no limit has been made, and no height has been made, and no root has been made. And it always has been, and it will always be. He who has intelligence even, will not be able to tell whence it has been made. So great is its glory that there is no other being who can be called Creator, because the creation was not then made. Afterwards, fire and earth were created; and from their union *Hormazd* was created. *Time* was the Creator and this Lord has guarded the creation he has made . . . . . . And I have in the commencement said, that Hormazd and Ahriman were created by Time." In the same work, we have also the following passage respecting Hormazd :—

و هرمزد هرچه کرد بیاری زمان کرد و هرنیکی که در هرمزد با عث
بداده بود و زمان درین خدای هرمزد پیدا کرد وبر اندازه دوازده
هزار سال باشد

—"And whatever Hormazd created, he created by the aid of *Time*; and all the righteousness that was in Hormazd was given to him. And *Time* had created it in the divine Hormazd, and had established him king for the space of twelve thousand years."

Plainer language than this it is impossible to conceive. It is quite consistent with my account of the Pársí religion to which Dosabhaí has objected; with the quotations which I have adduced from Greek and Armenian authors; with the testimonies which I have extracted from the reputed sacred writings of the Pársís; and with all the considerations which I have brought before the notice of the reader.

among the fire-worshippers, by whom as Anquetil justly observed, it is considered extremely valuable and ancient; some of them tracing it up to the time of ALI, who died in the seventh century. But from this supposed antiquity, I am inclined to deduct at least six hundred years, and to believe it a work of the thirteenth century, for reasons which shall hereafter be assigned in a descriptive catalogue of my oriental MSS." Ouseley's Travels, vol. ii, p. 270.

I must now be allowed to hold, that I have established the proposition which I have placed near the commencement of this chapter, — that I have proved that the Pársís, who are guided by the authorities on which their religion is founded, acknowledge Hormazd, the supreme object of their worship, to be not a self-existent, and independent, but a derivative and secondary being. I am by no means singular in the opinion which I entertain on this subject. It is that, almost without exception, of every European scholar who has devoted his attention to the Pársí religion. To a few of the testimonies on this subject, I now request the attention of the Pársís.

I need scarcely make any reference to Anquetil du Perron, as it was principally on his authority that I made the statements to be found in my lecture on the Vandidád. A reference to the table of contents appended to his translation of the Zand-Avastá, under the head of "Temps sans Bornes," will show both the conclusions at which he has arrived, and the grounds on which he has rested his opinion.

"The first and original Being, in whom, or by whom, the universe exists," says Gibbon, "is denominated in the writings of Zoroaster, *Time-without-Bounds*;* but it must be confessed, that this infinite substance seems rather a metaphysical abstraction of the mind, than a real object endowed with self-consciousness, or possessed of moral perfections. From either the blind, or the intelligent operation of this infinite Time, which bears but too near an affinity with the chaos of the Greeks, the two secondary but active principles of the universe, were from all eternity produced, Ormusd and Ahriman, each of them possessed of the powers of creation, but each disposed, by his invariable nature, to exercise them with different designs. The principle of good is eternally absorbed in light; the principle of evil eternally buried in darkness."

* Gibbon's Decline and Fall of the Rom. Empire vol. i, chap. viii. "Zeruáné Akerene, so translated by Anquetil and Kleuker. There is a dissertation of Foucher on this subject, Mem. de l' Acad. des Inscr. t. xxix. According to Bohlen (das al Indien) it is the Sanscrit *Sarvam Akaranam*, the uncreated whole; or according to Fred. Schlegel, *Sarvam Akharyam*, the uncreated indivisible. Note by the Rev. H. H. Milman.

* "The cosmogony of the Zendavesta," says Lord Woodhouselee, "according to the account of these expositors, supposes the first principle of all things to be time-without-bounds, or *eternity*. From this first principle proceed (but in what manner is not explained) the first light, the first water, and the original fire. From this first principle likewise sprung Ormusd and Ahriman, secondary principles, but active and creative of all things; Ormusd, a being infinitely good, and Ahriman, a being infinitely wicked." † "God, he [Zoroaster] taught," says Sir John Malcolm, "existed from all eternity, and was like infinity of time and space."‡ "It may not be uninteresting to observe," says Sir Graves Haughton, "that the word *sarva* employed here [in Manu] to signify the universe, in its original and primary sense implies *all*, or the *whole*..... In the account given in Enfield's History of Philosophy, it will be seem that Zarva was the chief of all the gods among the Persians, and produced the good and evil principles, Hormisda and Satana. I think, from the evident connection between the religious systems of the Persians and the Hindus, the identity of the good Zarva and the Sarva of India must be incontestible; and we are thus enabled to take a new and most accurate view of the real nature of the Magian religion. In it we find the same prevailing idea common in all the theogonies of the ancients, namely, the finite nature of their gods, and their subordinate rank, as the personifications or power of the *boundless whole*, that is, of *nature*."§ Dr. F. Creuzer, the author of a most important work on the religions of antiquity, writes as follows: § "On voit donc que le doctrine des Perses ne s'arrêta point au dualisme, comme nombre de savans l'ont pensé : elle aussi,elle reconnut un principe suprême de la dualité, la durée sans bornes, l' E´ternite

* Universal History, vol. i, p. 227, 228.

† History of Persia, Vol. 1, p. 495, 8vo edition.

‡ Institutes of Menu, vol. ii, pp. 434—5.

§ I copy the French translation of Guigniaut, not having the original work beside me.

ou l' E'ternel, *Zervane-Akerene*, créateur d'Ormuzd et d'Ahriman. C'est Zervane-Akerene qui a donné la naissance à tous les êtres; c'est lui qui au commencement fit *Zervane*, le Temps ou le long temps, la grande période ou année du monde, qui durera douze mille ans jusqu'â la résurrection. Dans Zervane repose l'univers, et comme lui de Temps fut créé, tandis que Zervane-Akerene et la durée incréée, qui n'a point eu de commencement et qui n'aura pas de fin." * Professor Stuhr, in his highly philosophical work on the Religions of the East, says; — "As an idea of the Supreme Being, that of Zerouane-Akerene, or uncreated time, † occupies the first place [in the Zand-Avastá.] This original being, from which Ahriman as well as Ormazd are said to derive their existence, the first beginning of every thing, was sometimes called *fate*."‡

Many similar passages are now before me; but it is of little use to multiply extracts of this nature. The Abbé Foucher, and Mr. Erskine, as far as I know, are the only writers of any consequence on the Pársí religion who have entertained opinions somewhat different from those now introduced. The worthy Abbé, it must be borne in mind, however, wrote under a feeling of great disappointment with the Zand-Avastá as a human composition; and he was surprised to find that Zarúána-Akarana is so seldom alluded to in its pages, while Hormazd appears supreme both in honour and service.§ If he had kept the distinction which he himself at first recognized in view, he would not perhaps have felt the force of

* Tom. i, p. 323. "D'après le Zendavesta. *Conf.* Gærres *Mythengesch*, 1. p. 219 seq.; et la note 4 sur ce livre, § 2, que donnera de nouveaux développemens." Guigniaut, in the note here alluded to, refers for illustrations of his opinion to Frederick Von Schlegel, M. de Hammer, and Gærres, &c.

† Or *uncreated universe*. (सर्वम् अकरणम्)

‡ Translation by the Rev. Mr. Weigle, in the Oriental Christian Spectator, Sept. 1840.

§ Mem. de la Acad. des Inscript. tom. xxxix, p. 727 &c.

the difficulties by which he was overcome.* As soon as the Pársís conceived of the origin of all thanks as existing in a state of insensibility or repose, it was easy for them to give the preference over it to the active principles, Hormazd and Ahriman, in both their regard and aversion. Mr. Erskine does not appear to have come to a very decided opinion on the point to which our attention is now directed. "Different opinions are held among them [the Pársís] concerning the nature of things, and the writings ascribed to Zertusht are very imperfect on that subject. All the laity, or Behdıns, consider Ormazd, and Ahriman the author of evil, as having existed from the beginning; and Zerwan, or Time, as a production of Hormazd; an opinion which seems to be favoured by the *Avesta* [where ?]. But many of the dasturs, following the expositions of later authors, hold that every thing has originated from Zerwan, or Time, and that Hormazd was the first active and creative being produced by that original principle."†

There is certainly *imperfect* information on the principal subject of this chapter in the sacred books of the Pársís; but I cannot see that these books bear an interpretation different from that which I have put upon them, and which is so consistent with what is furnished from independent sources, and from the Bundséhné and I'lmá-i-Islám, acknowledged by the Pársís themselves. To the existence of the errors which these books have begotten, and which Mr Erskine in the case of the priests so distinctly notices, I myself can bear my personal testimony. Though, when ashamed of the peculiar regard which they show to Hormazd, the Pársís keep Zarúána as much as

* Les Ghèbres croient encore aujourd'hui que l' Univers est composé d'une *matière insensible*, et de deux principes actifs qui lui donnent le mouvement et la vie. De ces deux principes, l'un est essentiellement bon: c'est la lumière ou le feu, c'est Ormouz ou Oromaze; c'est l'ame primitive du monde, dont le Soleil, la Lune, les Astres, et le feu terrestre sont des détachemens. L'autre principe qui s'est insinue dans l'Univers, est essentiellement mauvais; c'est la mauvais ame, source de tous les mauvais esprits, c'est *Ahriman*, *satan*, le diable.—Mem. de la Acad. des Inscr. tom. xxxi. pp. 496—7.

† Bombay Transactions, vol. ii, p. 317.

possible out of sight, they are no sooner charged with the doctrine of unmitigated *Dualism*, involved in their notions of the two principles Hormazd and Ahriman, than they immediately hint at Zarúána, the reputed parent of these implacable foes. Even Dosabhái, as has been already seen, shrinks from the absolute dismissal of Zarúána, and declares that he is *Khudá*, Lord in a personal sense, and sometimes viewed as an object of worship. When the *evasions* which they have practised in this controversy are overlooked, the Pársís, I fear, will again yield themselves to the dogmas of their own books. To such of them, then, as hold Hormazd to be a derivative being, I say, that the ascription to him of divine names, and attributes, and titles, and works, and honours, as is done throughout the whole of the Vandidád, the Izashné, the Yashts, Níáíshes, &c. will appear to them, if they will grant the matter a rightful consideration, to be nothing short of absolute blasphemy. With a reference to their case, I repeat the expostulation which I have elsewhere addressed to them. "The fundamental truth of religion they have yet to learn, admit, and apply in their devotional and practical services. They must be considered, in the view of the claims of the Creator, as robbing him of that honour and glory which necessarily belong to him, as practising the sin than which none greater can be imagined, and as provoking the righteous indignation of Heaven. I call upon them to consider the position in which they stand, and to mark their guilt and danger; and cherishing the deepest compassion for their immortal souls, and entertaining the most fervent desires for their welfare in time and eternity, I earnestly beseech them to beware of prejudice and sophistry when they attempt to form a sober judgment of their circumstances. Let them take no encouragement in their errors from the similarity of their creed to that of the Hindús, who view the divine nature, as essentially *nirguna*, or devoid of qualities, and to be recognized in worship only in its circumstantial manifestations, and effluences; for it can be shown that their theories and speculations are both inconsistent with themselves, and altogether destructive of the divine honour. I warn them against the delusion which is so prevalent in this country, that if confidence be fairly placed in any one God, it is of no great consequence that erroneous notions are entertained of his character. He who has not "life in himself" is no God at all; and the sin of failing to recognize that God who has life in himself, however much it may be concealed through the influence of the temptation through which it is produced, is almost equivalent to absolute Atheism." *

To this I add, that the ideas which the Pársís have of the first principle, or Zarúána, are such as to show that in their notions of it, or him,—for I really know not what pronoun it is best to apply in the case,—there is nothing corresponding with right conceptions of the one only living and true God. If Zarúána be indeed the Supreme Divinity, then to talk of him as merely Time, or Fate, or Destiny, or Eternity, to ascribe the principal works of creation and providence to one of his creatures; to rob him of the actual government of the Universe; and to exclude him from all but occasional worship, is the quintessence of impiety. A God who has not divine attributes; who has not performed, and who does not perform, the divine works of creation and providence; who is not entitled to be considered paramount in the inquiry and contemplation, and love, and worship, and service of man, is a monstrous birth of the depraved imagination of man, from which every pious mind must revolt with horror.

I do not wonder that the Pársís who are ignorant of the contents of their sacred books, are ashamed to admit that it is there to be found, and that there can be any being prior or superior to that Hormazd, whom they principally recognize and adore. Let them examine, however, the matter in all its relations; and let them come to that conclusion which the interests of truth imperatively demand. Before repelling my reasonings on the subject, let them carefully examine the statements which I have submitted to their notice. Let them particularly remember that Dosabhái, the champion of the pancháyat, in his eagerness to excuse what cannot be defended,

* Doctrine of Jehovah addressed to the Pársís, pp. 22, 23.

has even admitted, in the passage to which I have more than once referred, that Zarúána-Akarana is to be *sometimes* worshipped,—a fact which is perfectly irreconcilable, with the interpretation which he has given, in other parts of his work, that it means simply "*Eternity.*" If they should overlook the whole of what I have now written, let them not withdraw their eyes from these plain truths: — *To conceive of the origin of all things as merely "infinity-of-time," is to dislodge God from his throne. To address "infinity-of-time," as intelligent, and observant, and able to hear and answer prayer, is to trample in the dust the reason of man.* Of this sin and folly, in both, or either, of its instances, *every* Pársí who uses the Zand-Avastá is undoubtedly guilty. Let that book, consequently, be henceforth viewed and treated, merely as a monument of the errors of the human mind.

CHAPTER III.

THE DOCTRINE OF THE TWO PRINCIPLES, HORMAZD AND AHRIMAN.

Testimony of Greek and Armenian Writers — Remarks upon this Testimony — Extract from lecture on Vandidád — Dosabhái's interpretation of Ahriman — Extract from the Dabistán — Concurrence of Aspandiárjí with Dosabhái — Refutation of the reasonings of Dosabhái and Aspandiárjí — Appeal in nineteen instances to the Vandidád, with an exhibition of its demonology — Edal Dáru's views of the Devil. Criticism on the interpretations of the Dabistán, Sháristán, and of the Sipásí Sufis in general — Demonology of the Bundéshné — The Accounts of Hormazd and Ahriman contained in the Sacred Books of the Pársís shown to be impious and absurd in whatever way they may be interpreted — Notice of the information contained in the Bible respecting the origin and operations of physical and moral evil.

One of the most difficult questions which the mind of man has ever proposed to itself, and which it is most anxiously inclined to urge, is, How has physical, and especially moral, evil been introduced into the world in which we dwell. The religion of the Pársís, according to the views which have been generally, nay almost universally, taken of it, both in ancient and modern times, has professed to give as the reply, that evil has had its own peculiar author, who is quite distinct from that being who is essentially good in his own nature, and the origin of all the good which is diffused throughout the universe. This doctrine has not inappropriately been said to be the "foundation-stone of the whole structure, both of Zoroaster's religious and political philosophy."* Before making any remarks on its reasonableness, or unreasonableness,

* Hetherington's Fulness of Time, p. 210. This work is characterized by great vigour both of thought and expression. It ought to be read by every person as a supplement to the Researches of Heeren.

it may be proper for us to refer to some of the accounts which we have of the form in which it has been propounded, and to the attempts which have been made, by more than one of the controversialists to whom it is my duty to reply, to disguise and conceal it.

The prophet Isaiah, when addressing Cyrus, or Kai-Khosru, says to him, in the name of God,—who was afterwards to raise up that king for the deliverance of the Jews from the bondage of Babylon,—"I form the light and create darkness: I make peace and create evil: I Jehovah do all these things."* It is generally supposed by commentators on the Sacred Scriptures,—and the conjecture is not unreasonable,—that he thus takes for granted the existence, in that monarch, of the notion, which he condemns, that evil has a separate and distinct principle.

Xenophon, the Greek,† who wrote a work, partly historical and partly imaginative, on the life of Cyrus, represents that king as challenging Araspes, a noble Persian youth, for his attachment to Panthea, a beautiful captive, and as receiving from him the following answer: —"I have plainly, he said, O Cyrus, two souls (Δύο ψυχάς). I have now philosophized this point, by means of that wicked sophoster Love. For, a single soul cannot be good and bad at the same time, nor can it at the same time affect both noble actions and base; yet these at the same time it wishes to do and not to do; but it is plain there are two souls; and when the good one prevails, it does noble things; when the evil one prevails, it attempts base things."‡ This doctrine seems to harmonize, to a certain extent, with that which is commonly laid to the charge of the ancient Persians, inasmuch as it takes it for granted that good and evil, even in the constitution of man, have each a distinct origin.

* Isaiah xlv. 7. The prophecy of which this forms a part, was delivered about 712 years before Christ.

† Born about 450 years before Christ.

‡ Cyropœdia, lib. vi.

We have already introduced into our pages several passages in which the alleged principles of both good and evil are brought to our notice.* Plutarch † denominates them, as we have seen, respectively Oromazes and Areimanius, and represents them as devoted to contrary practices, and effecting works corresponding with their nature. "Of plants," he says, "they [the Persians] reckon some to belong to the good God (ἀγαθοῦ θεοῦ), and some to the evil Demon (κακου δαίμονος) and of animals some, as dogs, birds, and land urchins, they attribute to the good being, and certain aquatic [urchins], to the evil one, and bless him who slays the most of them." Proceeding in his account of them, he attributes to each of these principles the power of creation. "Oromazes" he says, "made six gods; the first that of Benevolence, the second of Truth, the third of Equity, and the others of Wisdom, Wealth, and the Joy which follows the doer of the things which are honest. Areimanius made an equal number opposed to them. Oromazes then magnified himself three-fold, and removed himself from the sun, as far as the sun is removed from the earth, and decorated the heaven with stars, and appointed one Sirius, the guardian and observer of the others. Then he created twenty-four other gods, and placed them in an egg; while Areimanius created the same number which perforated the egg, and hence evil became commingled with good."‡ The final triumph of Hormazd, he anticipates. His testimony wonderfully accords with the notions of the Pársís as contained in their sacred books. The good and evil intelligences which he mentions, are evidently the Amshåspands and Izads of Hormazd, and the evil genii of Ahriman which correspond with them.§ To the opinion of Theopompus, who lived about

* See the preceding chapter.

† Born A. D. 50.

‡ Plutarch. de Iside et Osiride, in Plut. Om. Op. Reiskii, vol. vii, p. 457.

§ For a full comparison of the passage from Plutarch with the doctrine of the Pársís, see an article by Anquetil du Perron in the Mémoires de Littérature, tom. xxxiv, p. 393, &c, and also Burnouf's Commentaire sur l' Yaçna, vol i, p. 148, &c.

350 years before Christ, as quoted by Plutarch, we have already referred. *

Diogenes Laertius, who wrote about 147 years after Christ, in his preface to the Lives of the Philosophers, writes as follows: — "Aristotle, in his first book on philosophy, teaches that they [the Magi of Zoroaster] are more ancient than the Egyptians; and that according to them there are two principles, a good demon and an evil demon (*κὰι δύο κατ' αὐτοις ἔιναι ἀρχὰς αγαθὸν δαίμονα και κακον δαίμονα*), and that one of these is named Jupiter and Oromasdes, and the other, Pluto and Areimanius. Which thing Hermippus also declares in his first [book] on the Magi, and Eudoxus in the Period, and Theopompus in the eighth [book] of the Philippians."† Here is a series of authorities of a very express character, and extending through nearly five centuries before the days of Diogenes.

Eubulus, as quoted by Damascius, we have referred to, as declaring that the Iranians declare that there is both a "good God and an evil Demon," of whom "Time," or "Space", is the author.‡

The testimony of several Armenian writers, we have given at length. It conclusively proves that they believed that the Pársís reckon Hormazd and Ahriman to be beings of opposite character and principles, who were coetaneously produced by Time. This testimony quite accords with the less extended one of Theodorus of the fifth century, that Zaruam offering a libation to engender Ormisdas, produced both him, and Satanas.§

The influence of the tenets of the ancient Persians is conspicuous in the doctrines broached and propagated by Manes, and other heretics, who were extensively instrumental in cor-

† See page 124 of this work.

* Diogenis Laertii Procemio, seg. 8.

‡ See page 125 of this work.

§ See page 127 of this work,

rupting several portions of the early Christian Church.* The resemblance of the Doctrines of the Persians and Manicheans is noticed by Agathias, the historian of the affairs of the emperor Justinian. He says, "They [the Persians] agree in most respects with those called Manicheans, since they hold that there are two first principles, one of whom is good, producing whatever is best from himself; and that the other, the second, in a directly contrary method produces what is opposite; and that they give barbarous names to them taken out of their own language. The God, or the Creator, they call Hormisdates; but Arimanes is the name of him who is evil and pernicious." He goes on to mention their slaughter of noxious animals as injurious to Ahriman and agreeable to Hormazd.†

* Of Manes the following notice is perhaps sufficient. "As the Christianity of the Gnostics had so much in common with the system of Zoroaster, it is not wonderful that the Persian Christians, amongst whom Gnosticism had long prevailed, should have been led to combine them. The religion of the Zend having degenerated into a gross Dualism and mere ceremonial worship under the Arsacides, their successors, the Sassanides, were now making every effort to restore its ancient purity (A. D. 227 seq.); and in the assemblies of the Magi the supremacy of the one great first principle (*Zeruane akerene*) had been acknowledged, and Dualism with its adherents (Magusæans) condemned. It is probable, that this division amongst the believers in Parsiism first suggested to Manes the idea of uniting Chrstiainity with the system of the rejected Magusæans. In the name of this man (*Mani — Cubricus, Manes, Manichæus*) as well as in their accounts of him, the writers in the East differ from those in the West; agreeing only in the following particulars:— that he was hated by the Magi, persecuted by the Persian kings, compelled to flee, and at length, according to the Orientals, by order of king Baharam, or Vararanes, (A. D. 272–275,) most barbarously put to death as a corrupter of the national religion, in a castle which the Eastern writers call Dascarah, and the Western, Arabion.

"The system of Manes begins with supposing two eternal and coexistent kingdoms, the kingdom of light, and the kingdom of darkness. These border on each other, and are under the dominion, the one of God and the other of the Demon, or Hyle." Gieseler's Ecclesiastical History, vol. i, p. 131.

† Vid Agathiæ Scholastici de Imperio et Rebus gestis Justiniani lib. ii. Agathias flourished about the middle of the sixth century after Christ. His account of the Persian religion, to which we shall afterwards have occasion to refer, is particularly interesting.

I am not aware that any passages can be quoted from ancient authors which essentially differ from those which have now been given respecting the belief of the ancient Persians both in a good and evil principle, though others, perhaps, may be brought forward to show that a variety of opinion may have existed as to the exact *origin* of these principles. Some writers may have considered them eternal; some as respectively originating from primitive light and darkness; and some, as the productions of Zarúána-Akarana, or Time-without-Bounds. All have given the same general accounts as to their supposed relation to one another; and of the production by them of the good and evil which exist in the world. According to the universal testimony of antiquity, the ancient Persians must be considered as *Dualists*, holding the existence of two independent principles, either secondary to another being from whom they are said to have originated, or themselves eternal in their own nature. The stress of the evidence, as will have been seen from the last chapter, is in favour of their being viewed as secondary existences. Those who reject it will be obliged to admit the dualism of the Pársís in its most unmitigated form. Those who receive it, while they consider Hormazd and Ahriman the active lords of creation and providence, will still be held to be *practical Dualists* in the proper sense of the term. Whatever choice the Pársís may make in the case, most serious error must be laid to their charge, and secure their conviction before the bar of both reason and conscience.

The doctrines of the Vandidád remarkably harmonize with the testimony of antiquity as to the opinion of the Pársís on this subject. "The Vandidád Sade," I remark in the lecture which Dosabhái and Aspandiárjí have made the subject of their criticism, "gives a highly irrational account of the origin and operations of natural good and evil. Hormazd was opposed by Ahriman in all his works. When Hormazd created Eriáné Véjo, similar to Behisht, Ahriman, according to the first fargard, produced in the river the great adder or winter; when he created Soghdo, abundant in flocks and men, Ahriman created flies which spread mortality among the flocks;

when he created Bakhdí, pure and brilliant in its colours, Ahriman created a multitude of ants which destroyed its pavilions; when he created any thing good, Ahriman was sure to create something evil. 'Ahriman, this chief of death,' it is said in the beginning of the nineteenth fargard, 'this chief of the Dews,* comes from the north, he proceeds from the places which are north. Ahriman full of death, the master of the evil law, runs continually everywhere producing devastation. He is the author of evil."...... "They see," it is said in the same chapter, " running in crowds, and running separately and apart, Ahriman full of death, chief of the Dews, the Dew Andar, the Dew Sával, the Dew Naongs, &c. The author of evil has produced and engendered in time these Dews." †

This is but a brief reference to the doctrines of the Vandidád on the subject to which it refers; but it has attracted the particular attention of Dosabháí. That no injustice may be done to his comments upon it, I shall lay them at length before the reader in a faithful translation.

" What is written in the Vandidád about Hormazd and Ahriman, and light and darkness, is a *parable* of our prophet Zartusht. He has declared a matter in secret science, which, if its explanation were known to the padre, would not be declared by him to be nonsense. But being wretched and ignorant, he looks at the outward narrative, and does not understand its meaning. The explanation of the matter is this. The description is of the [good] qualities and evil qualities which are in a man, and which in Arabic are called *fazílat* and *razílat*, and in English *virtue* and *vice*. Hormazd and Light are good works; and Ahriman and Darkness are evil works; as what is good is Hormazd, and what is bad is Ahriman. Liberality is light, and Stinginess darkness; the restraining of Anger is Hormazd, and indulging it is Ahriman; Humility is Hormazd, and Pride is Ahriman. So, in like manner, may the other good and evil qualities be spoken of. The explanation of

* دیو *dew* in Persian, and 𐬛𐬀𐬉𐬎𐬀 *daēva* in Zand.

† Lecture on the Vandidád, p. 12.

what is written in the Vandidád about Ahriman running forth with the other Dews is, that to each side of a good quality there is an evil quality attached. For example, to Humility there are two evil qualities attached; for if it exceeds its proper bounds, it becomes Lowness and Meanness; and if it fall short of its bounds, it is not Liberality but Extravagance and Immorality, as it is called in English; and if Liberality falls short of its bounds, it becomes Pride. In like manner, if Liberality is, in excess it is Stinginess. In this way, every good quality which is in man has its opposing bad quality. Connected with this the Vandidád has given a parable; and learned Pársís and Musalmáns have consequently written in their books that the prophet Zartusht is a speaker of parables. Why does the padre not acknowledge all this, and why does he speak of it as nonsense? It is a pity that the accomplished Parsí, whose assistance the padre has acknowledged in his pamphlet on the Vandidád, did not point out to him this explanation; but if that wretch also did not know it, what could be done? Now if the padre wont approve of what we have above written, let him read what is to be found in the fourteenth chapter of the celebrated book called the Dabistán about the secrets of Zoroaster, and be convinced. I shall here show one article on the subject. In the 642d page of the Gujarátí translation of the Dabistán by the accomplished Pársí Mullá Firuz,* there is the undergiven account. "The author of the Dabistán says, 'I will now reveal whatever secrets, and signs, and nice distinctions, are among the Pársís, because the exalted prophet Zartusht Sáheb, has set forth many secret matters through means of signs and nice distinctions, that by declaring wisdom in a secret way, it might be in safe-keeping and trust-worthy, and not fall in to the hands of the ignorant, while the wise only should understand its full meaning and import.

"'*Ramáz*, or *Mysterious Science*. It is said that the Běh-

* The translation bears the name of Fardunjí Marazbánjí. Mullá Firuz is only introduced into the preliminary notices, as certifying as to the accuracy of the version.

dins (the followers of the good faith) have written that there are two Creators, the one Hormazd and the other Ahriman. And it is said that God (*Khudá*) entertained this imagination: — Perhaps some other [being] may be created to oppose me, and maintain enmity against me. At that time, Ahriman was produced from this imagination of God. And in another place, it is written, that God was alone, and got afraid, and that God formed an imagination, from which Ahriman was produced. And it is written that Ahriman was in this world, and beholding from a hole, that the most high God is possessed of great nobility, and glory, and dignity, he became jealous, and began to practise wickedness and deceit. Then God created an army of angels, with which he carried on war with Ahriman; but Ahriman was not broken down by Hormazd, and Hormazd made with him a covenant of peace, that he should remain in the world for a certain number of years, and that afterwards, when this space might be expired, Ahriman should be destroyed from out of this world, and that the whole world should be filled with righteousness and goodness, and evil deeds should leave the world.'

"' *The explanation of this Mysterious Science. World,* the body of man. *Hormazd,* the spirit which performs good works in man. *Ahriman,* the evil disposition of man. *Imagination,* the evil habits of that spirit. *The evil and deception of Ahriman,* the power of the evil disposition of man upon the soul, and the desire of the evil disposition to keep the soul under its own authority. *The army of angels created by God,* the soul's imprisoning, by the strength of its righteous habits and abstinence, the army of the evil disposition. *God made peace with Ahriman,* the fact that bad and evil habits do not leave man in an instant, but have their remedy effected by degrees. *Ahriman will remain a certain space in this world,* the fact that the evil disposition of man's nature will not always remain, but it continues only in his body while ignorance exists. Afterwards, if the soul of man become strong, through the strength of the soul's righteousness, the evil disposition will be removed. And the evil disposition remains in some bodies as long as they are not dead. *After the time of Ahri-*

man has expired, he will be removed, the world will become righteous, and iniquity will depart from the world,—is thus to be explained :— It occurs, in the first place, when persons by the power of abstinence and austerity (*tap*) strike their breath, so that though alive they are as dead, and restrain their souls as when they are under the power of death ; and, in the second place, when, according to the death to which every man is subjected, a person dies, and with a perfect and righteous soul, he becomes freed from the world, and proceeds to, and remains in safety in, the heavenly world filled with righteousness and goodness.' See the statements which are in the Vandidád about this matter." *

So much for Dosabhái's attempted explanation of the Good and Evil Principles of the Pársí religion. He denies the personal existence of Ahriman and his hosts altogether ; and says that the accounts which are given of his actings are merely parabolical descriptions of the power and operations of the evil nature and disposition and habits of man. Aspandiárjí's sentiments are not dissimilar. "Ahriman," he says, "has no real being, but is (merely) an emblem of vice or evil." † Now, while I allow to these writers, that most important instructions may be conveyed by appropriate parables, as has been frequently done in the case of the most distinguished teachers who have appeared in the world, I deny that they have been successful in defending the Pársí religion by pleading for a parabolical interpretation of the passages in the Vandidád, and other Pársí books which refer to Ahriman. It requires no great effort to shew, that their explanation is altogether unsuited to the representations made in these books ; and that by resorting to it they force us to come to the conclusion, that the Pársí doctrine of the Two Principles, as commonly understood and declared, is *wholly indefensible.* I am hopeful that the criticism to which I am about to submit it, and the references which in connexion with it I shall make to the Vandidád, will lead all the Pársís, who will give the subject

* Tálim-i-Zartusht, pp. 62—65.

† Hádi-i-Gum-Rahán. p. 36.

the serious and attentive consideration of which it is deserving, for ever to abandon the faith of Zoroaster.

I beg my readers to ask themselves, as we proceed, Is Dosabhái's and Aspandiárjí's explanation consistent with the doctrines and narratives of the Vandidád, and does it enable us to see that they are agreeable to reason, and common sense? Or, is it not altogether opposed to reason and common sense, and exhibits the absurdity of the statements of the Vandidád in a more conspicuous manner than when they are literally interpreted?

1. If Ahriman be only the evil dispositions and habits of man, and have no personal existence, then who is Hormazd, who is set in direct opposition to Ahriman? Does Dosabhái wish it to be understood that *he* is only the *good* disposition of man, and has also no personal existence? If he does not abandon his parabolical interpretation, he will answer the latter of these questions in the affirmative. If he answers it in the affirmative, he will bring down upon himself the wrath of the whole Pársí community, and render even to them the language of the Vandidád an unmeaning jargon. He is plainly between the horns of a dilemma, and I leave him to choose the one by which he may wish to be transfixed. Let him boldly move to the one side or the other. Aspandiárjí has not shrunk from destruction in this case. He distinctly says, with reference to the creations of Hormazd in the first fargard of the Vandidád, that "Hormazd is here represented as an emblem of the principle of good or virtue, which being inherent in the nature of man, inclines him to do what is good or virtuous." He deprives the world of even a nominal Creator altogether!*

2. In the first fargard of the Vandidád, we are informed that when Hormazd created 𐬀𐬌𐬭𐬌𐬌𐬀𐬥𐬆𐬨. 𐬬𐬀𐬉𐬘𐬋 *Airyana-Vaêjô*, or Irán-Vejo, a holy and beautiful place, fit for the abode of man, Ahriman created what was entirely of an opposite character, a mere jungle.† Does Dosabhaí consider

* Hádí-i-Gum-Rahán, p. 35.

† This passage of the Vandidad, I refer to as it is interpreted by the

Irán-Vejo, a country, and the jungle of Ahriman, only man's evil nature and its effects? If his parabolical interpretation is not to be thrown aside, this he must do, and still leave it to be explained, how it is declared in the Vandidád that the first work of the Paityárem (Ahriman) was the counter part of the work of Hormazd. Is an "evil disposition" the counterpart of a country? "Irán-Vejo, "says Aspandiárjí, "is typical of faith or belief.*" He afterwards, however, speaks of "every *town*" mentioned in the Vandidád as filled with serpents and noxious animals, the emblems of evil passions; and thus forgets that he had made the first of them a mere type also.*

3. In the same fargard of the Vandidád, we are told that Hormazd created in Irán-Vejo, a delightful river (called by the Pársis the Veherod); and that Ahriman created in this river a great serpent. Do Dosabhái and Aspandiárjí interpret this serpent as merely the evil disposition of man? If they do so, according to their boasted explanation, they directly contradict the Vandidád, which expressly declares the monster to be† *Zyāmcha daēúo dátem,* "even winter given by the devils."

4. In the same fargard, we are informed that the second place created by Ahriman was *Çughdhó,* or Shurik, and that Ahriman created in it a multitude of *çkaitím,* or flies, which destroyed its flocks and herds. Are these flies the evil dispositions of man? What have *they* to to do with sheep, and goats, and cows, which the Pársís allow to have been given by God as food to man?

5. The fourth place created by Hormazd is said to be *Bákhdí,* or Bokhara. Ahriman, according to the Vandidád, there created ants to carry off its corn and grain. Are these industrious, but frequently troublesome, little creatures, also the evil dispositions of men?

Gujarátí translators of that work. *Irán-Vejo,* they denominate a શેહેર or abode, and its opposite a ઉજાડ or desert. Author's MS. vol. i. p. 2.

* Hádí-i-Gum-Rabán, p. 35. † Ibid.

6. In *Haróyúm,** or Háláb, the fifth reputed creation of Hormazd, Ahriman created "diverse wasps."† "Between these [the evil passions]", says Aspandiárjí, "and the noxious insects which commit such dreadful ravages, there is an apparent analogy, inasmuch as the first are calculated to molest or destroy the principle of virtue inherent in the constitution of man." But if these noxious insects are indeed the evil dispositions of man, they are certainly not confined to Aleppo.

7. In *Ranghayáo,* or Khorásán, the sixteenth place said to be the work of Hormazd, the murderous Ahriman created the Devil of winter. Is this supposed plague also the evil disposition of man? Is even the winter, over which the fiend is said to preside, in its own season, ever a positive evil? O Dosabhái, you will have some difficulty in retreating from the arena of controversy in your parabolical chariot. Avoid being upset in it, like your friend Aspandiárjí, who, after declaring that "the sayings of our Lord Zoroaster, are full of divine or philosophic truths, *buried in some mystic terms*, each of which is susceptible of *various interpretations*;" that "it is asserted that the whole Avastá can thus be resolved into *two opposite meanings;*" and that "Ahriman has *no real being;*" to complete his self-sacrifice as a reasoner, says, of the nineteenth fargard of the Vandidád that "it is distinctly stated therein that *Ahriman is a creature of the Almighty God ! !*"‡

8. In the third fargard, we are informed that there are certain Kharfastars, or noxious animals, which offend the earth, by making holes in it. Are the evil dispositions of man, the vermin and reptiles which breed and take refuge in the ground?

* This is the accusative case.

† *çaraçkemcha dariwikácha.* Anquetil translates these words by "une pauvreté absolue." The place referred to, he considers to be Herát. The Dasturs consider it to be Aleppo.

‡ Hádí-i-Gum-Rahán, p. 36.

9. Is the Devil Nasush, who according to the same fargard, takes possession of the nose, eyes, tongue, mouth, and other members, of a man who carries a dead body, only an evil disposition in the mind of man ?

10. Is the same Devil, who according to the fifth fargard renders criminal the soul of a man, a part of whose body a dog, bird, tiger, wolf, or fly, may have carried away, only an evil disposition in the mind of man. ?

11. In the fifth fargard, we have the following extraordinary statements :—

[illegible] *

— Dátare áfs narem jaiñti vá ? A'aṭ mraoṭ Ahuro-Mazdâo, áfs narem nôiṭ jaiñti. Açtó-vídhaotus dim bañdayêti vayó dim baçtem nayêiti. A'fs uzúazaiti, áfs niúazaiti, áfs paiti raêchayêiti. Vayó dim paçchaêta frañguhareñti. Athra adháṭ frajasati bakhta adháṭ nijaçaiti.— Dátare átars narem jaiñti vá ? Aaṭ mraoṭ Ahuró-Mazdáo átars narem noiṭ jaiñti. Açto-vidhaotus dim bañdayêti. Vayó dim bastem nayêiti. A'tars hañdajaiti açta ustánemcha athra adhāṭ frajaçaiti bakhta adháṭ nijaçaiti.

* Lithographed Vandidád pp. 176, 177.

"O *Dádár* [Hormazd], does water kill a man? To this effect Hormazd replied, 'Water does not kill a man; the devil Asto-Guvád binds up his breath, [and the devil] Naevatar having bound him carries him off. The water raises him; the water takes him down; the water takes him forward [in the attempt to save him]. The Naevatar [devil possessing the fishes] voraciously consumes him from behind that place, and when his fate is completed, arrives.' — 'O Dádár, does fire kill a man?' To this effect Hormazd replied, 'Fire does not kill a man. The [devil] Asto-Guvád binds his breath, and the Náevatar having bound his breath carries him off. After this the fire burns his body and life and then takes him aloft. When his fate is completed he arrives."*

This passage has proved rather troublesome to our parabolical friend, for he has condescended to give it special notice. "That fire kills not a man; the devil Asto-Vád binds him," he observes, "is written in the Vandidád. The explanation is this: — the great wrath and quarrelsomeness that are in a man, are represented by the figure of a devil which misleads a man. For a man, on account of his wrath and quarrelsomeness, falls into fire and water. His wrath is denominated Asto-Vád in the Vandidád; for the evil dispositions and evil deeds that are in a man, as lust, wrath, covetousness, affection, &c. are all spoken of as devils by our master the prophet [Zoroaster], though they are not like those whom you ostentatious worshippers imagine to exist, and whose pictures and frightful images you draw with horns and tails."† No such interpretation as this is once hinted at by the Gujarátí translators of the Vandidád. The difficulty, Dosabhái should have borne in mind, is not in showing how people may occasionally get *into* fire and water, but in explaining the strange treatment which they receive *after* they are involved *in* these

* This rendering I give according to the Gujarátí translation and paraphrase of the dasturs. MS. vol. 1. pp. 119—121. For some critical remarks on the passage, see Burnouf's Commentaire sur l' Yaçna, pp. 464—467. There is little difficulty in making a literal translation.

† Tálim-i-Zartusht, pp. 83, 84.

elements. Asto-Guvád begins his mischievous work *after* the unfortunate folks are enveloped in the flames, or covered with the waves. Is he then merely an evil disposition in the mind of man? Is it anger and wrath, which according to Dosabhái, choke a drowning and a burning man? Aspandiárjí, who writes a great deal of absolute nonsense on this subject,* makes Asto-Guvád the "angel of death," and remarks, "that until fate comes no one dies." But why, according to his theory, does Zoroaster confine his interrogation to *water* and *fire*? His question, according to Aspandiárjí's interpretation, ought to have been, Can *any thing* kill a man; for it is to this question, that "No one can die before the time appointed," is the reply.† It is the *deification* of the elements by the Pársís, to which we shall afterwards direct attention, which has led them to mantain that water and fire kill not a man, and to ascribe to a devil the work of destruction, which the common sense of man attributes to their instrumentality.

12. Dosabhái seems to have some joke lurking in his mind about devils with *horns* and *tails*, a notion of which he has probably acquired from the pictures usually contained in the Ardái-Viráf-Námah, and Sháhnámah, or in prints made for the amusement of children. What does he make of the [illegible] *drúâo bizañgró aúatha ashemaógħó* "the accursed [devil] the *two-foot-*

* Hádí-i-Gum-Rahán, pp. 40, 41.

† That Aspandiárjí is not satisfied with his theory, is evident from the following appendage which he has attached to it.—"But here I may take the liberty of asking one question to (of) my learned friend; that whether he is perfectly aware that the injury thus sustained is solely attributable to the agency of Fire and Water? For it is a well known fact, that no good or bad is effected without the combination of three causes; as for instance, to continue with the same element, fire, it cannot be supposed to be capable of burning except through the agency or help of some inflammable substance, and also through that of the wind or air...... The same remark might as well be applied to water." So say I; and I now ask Aspandiárjí, if he is willing to represent his "prophet" Zoroaster as asking Hormazd, Does fire burn without some inflammable substance? If Zoroaster put such a question, he was certainly not so wise as some of his infantile disciples in Bombay?

ed Ashmogh" mentioned in the fifth fargard of the Vandidád? "*Hesam* Dew," he tells us,* "is anger; *Niáz* Dew, covetousness; *Rasak* Dew, envy; *Dir* Dew, sickness and laziness; *Khasam* Dew, wrath and enmity; *Warun* Dew, lust, or mockery, or pride; *Busiásp* Dew, somnulency; *Padmuj* Dew, lamentation or sorrow; *Pas* Dew, procrastination about the accomplishment of good works."† What evil passion has he left for Ashmogh? How can an evil disposition in the mind of man do what Ashmogh is said to do in the Vandidád,—‡take possession of *food*, and *clothes*, and *trees*, and *herbage*, and *metals* and so forth, as well as of a pure man?

13. Dosabháí speaks of evil dispositions remaining in a man *till* his death. Is the devil Nasush who enters a body in the form of a fly, *after* the life is departed from it, § also an evil disposition?

14. Are the Devils, male and female, who in crowds of fifties, hundreds, thousands, and tens of thousands, run about the dukhmas, or depositaries of the dead, ‖ only the evil habits and dispositions of men? The bázárs and tippling-houses, one would think, would be the favorite haunts of the vile passions.

15. Is the cursed devil Nasush who comes from the North, "and who according to the eighth fargard of the Vandidád, is frightened away by the white dog, with four white eyes ¶ and yellow ears," also an evil disposition of man? Can the barking of dogs destroy the evil habits of men?

16. Dosabháí is acquainted with Richardson's Persian Dictionary. The author of this work, in a note to his preface, writes in the following strain respecting a passage contained in the eighth fargard of the Vendidád:—"Ormuzd (Omni-

* Tálim-i-Zartusht, pp. 68, 69.

† Quoting the *Farziát-i-Zartusht* of Aspandiárjí Framjí, p. 208.

‡ Vandidád, fargard v.

§ See Vandidád, fargard vii.

‖ Vandidád, Fargard vii.

¶ The Dasturs explain this by saying that two of the eyes are real, and the other merely "spots" resembling eyes.

potence) and Zoroaster are introduced in dialogue. The law-giver wishes to know how a man should get rid of a demon called *Daroudj Nesosch*, supposing him in the shape of a fly, to have taken possession of the crown of his head. *Ormuzd* directs him to wash the parts, which would drive the fiend between the eye-brows ; from thence he is to be forced, by another ablution, to the back of the head, from that to the ear, then to the nose, the mouth, the chin ; till at length, fighting every inch of ground, the poor devil is successively driven over every part of the body, till we find him stationed on the left foot ; when Zoroaster thus proceeds in his catechism ; (what is between hooks being M. Anquetil's explanatory interpretations, and not in the original).

" ' When the water has reached the top of the left foot, where does the *Daroudj Nesosch* retire ?' Ormuzd replied : '(The *Daroudj Nesosch*) under the form of a fly, places himself under the foot ; it must be raised, letting the toes rest on the ground, and thus wash the under part of the right foot. When the under part of the right is washed, the Daroudj Nesosch retires under the left foot. When the under part of the left foot is washed, the Daroudj Nesosch, in the form of a fly, places himself under the toes. Allowing the sole of the foot (to rest upon the ground) the toes must be raised, and those of the right (foot) washed. When the toes of the right foot are washed, the Daroudj Nesosch is overthrown (conquered, and returns) towards the North, he who under the shape of a fly places himself upon (the impure man) and strikes him like the Djodje (dog) of the desert, destroys the productions of the Dews and their dwellings,' &c. (Zend-Avesta par M. Anquetil Du Perron, Vol I, part. II. p. 341). Can human credulity suppose this to be the composition of Zoroaster, or of any man who had pretensions to common sense ? "

I have carefully compared this passage with the original Zand, and I find that it conveys the sense with sufficient accuracy, and that a more literal and complete version will only enhance the absurdity. * Dosabhâí has ventured to apply to

* Another passage of almost the same import, is given in the ninth fargard.

it his far-fetched theory! "The explanation of it," he says, "is this: — In the nature of man whatever bad works, bad habits, bad manners, and bad ways there are, they are this devil Nasush. They don't leave the mind of man in an instant; they must be extracted gradually by purity of heart, and holiness of mind, until they come to a man's toes and take their flight in the form of a fly." I am certain that in making this statement Dosabhái was conscious of its inapplicability. The defilement spoken of in the Vandidád, which is said to give occasion to the possession of the devil, is not spiritual but corporeal. It follows defilement by a *dead body*.*

17. We read in the eighth fargard of the smell of a certain fire carried to the dadgáh, frightening away and destroy-

* The passage on which we have now commented, is probably that to which reference is thus made by Mr. J. A. Pope, the translator of the Ardái-Viráf-Námah: — "That they [the alleged writings of Zoroaster] abound in absurdities cannot be doubted, but that many of them seem to inculcate and impress on the minds of the vulgar, some moral duty, is evident from the following fact. Conversing with one of their priests about the Zend-Avesta, I pointed out to him the dialogue between Ormazd and Zoroaster as a specimen of great absurdity; to which he agreed. 'But this,' he said, 'must not be taken in a literal sense; this is only meant to impress the necessity of ablution and bodily cleanliness, and in this sense it is understood by us and so explained to the people. There are no doubt,' he continued, 'great incongruities in it, but we suppose it to be the work of our prophet Zeratush.'" *Preface to Ardái-Viráf Námah, pp.* xii. xiii. It is a curious fact that Dosabhái seems at one time to have been inclined to adopt the theory contained in this passage. He quotes a part of it (Tálim-i-Zartusht, p. 84); but he refrains from drawing the inference which it suggests, no doubt because of its opposition to his own theory about Ahriman and his hosts being the evil passions of the mind, which it entirely upsets. According to the explanation given by the priest to Mr. Pope, the story of the diabolical possession, and the minute directions given about the expulsion of the fiend, are pure inventions for the deception of the vulgar, made for the express purpose of frightening the people into the observance of cleanliness. The *absurdity* is not lessened by this view of the case. They receive only the additional character of "*pious frauds*," which however congenial they may be to systems of false religion, must lead to the execration of their authors.

Aspandiárjí's absurd comment on the passage, we shall notice in our sixth chapter.

ing various "devils with two feet," such as the Darvands Paris, and so forth. What kind of evil passions are those which are to be ranked among the *bipeds*, and which odoriferous fumes expel from their hiding-places?

18. According to the tenth fargard, the devils Andar, Sával, Náoang, and others (who according to the Gujarátí translation of the Vandidád are the counterpart of the Amsháspands Ardebehisht, Sháhravar, &c.); and the devils of houses, streets, villages, and provinces ; and the devils of a person's own body, and of a dead man, and of a dead woman ; and the devils of lords of houses, streets, villages, and provinces, are all to be expelled by the recitation of a certain part of the Avastá. O Dosabhai, see for a moment how the matter will stand, according to your theory : —

Ander Dew, an evil desposition. *Siväl Dew*, an evil disposition. *Náoang Dew*, an evil disposition. *House devil*, an evil disposition. *Provincial devil*, an evil disposition. *Dead man's devil*, an evil disposition. *Dead woman's devil*, an evil disposition. *Devil of a lord of a house*, an evil disposition. *Devil of a lord of a street*, an evil disposition. *Devil of a lord of a village*, an evil disposition. *Devil of a lord of a province*, an evil disposition. *Other kinds of devils*, evil dispositions.

Here you have specific devils, and generic devils, the devils of persons and places, of males and females, of the living and the dead, of bodies and souls, and what not, all evil dispositions, and all ready to take their flight at hearing certain sounds, as they have been already represented as disposed to fly when regaled with certain sweet odours. You will find the parable somewhat troublesome in the explanation. I suspect that like the priest who conversed with Mr. Pope, you will be forced to admit after all your efforts that it contains "great incongruities."

19. Were I to proceed to bring forward all the passages in the Vandidád which are inconsistent with Dosabháí's theory, and at the same time supremely absurd in whatever way they may be interpreted, and briefly comment on them, I should be required greatly to extend this volume. Leaving several notices till we come to give an analysis of the Vandi-

dád,* I can here make only a general allusion to a few more of those which I have observed. The devils of Mázandrán can be opposed by the cock of the morning, by lances, poignards, bows, arrows, pikes, and slings. † The devils produce evil passions and dispositions, ‡ and consequently must be as distinct from them, as the workman from his work. The devils carry on a long and filthy conversation, with the Izad Sarosh, about their own progeny. § Ahriman comes from the North, the peculiar place of his residence. He invents an evil law, in the same way that Hormazd is said to make one of an opposite character. He begs Zoroaster not to destroy his people. He infests a dead body, behind and before, for three nights after the decease. He creates a great many other devils,— through one of whom he forms winter,—and who exercise a variety of functions, and who after doing much mischief betake themselves to hell. These descriptions, and others of a like kind, leave not a shadow of doubt, that the framers of the Vandidád conceived the devils of whom they wrote to be malevolent spirits, the authors of all the moral and natural evil which exists.

Dosabhái's interpretation, I have now more than sufficiently shown, is altogether opposed to the doctrines of the books esteemed sacred by the Parsís. It is directly opposed also to the work of his fellow controversialist Edal Dáru, the chief-priest of the Rasamís, their larger sect. This Dastur tells us that by the "influence of the *kustí*, the Dews, Darujes, and magicians are destroyed;"‖ that "the *sadra* (sacred vest) and *kustí* (sacred cincture) preserve the [departed] soul from the calamities accruing from Ahriman;"¶ that the "souls of dead children" are prevented by them from becoming devils, *khavís* and *jíns*," "while many of the souls of the Jud-dín, become devils, *khavis* and *jíns*;"** that Dúrásarún the magi-

* See Chapter vi.

† Fargard xii.

‡ Fargard xviii.

§ Fargard xviii.

‖ Maujazát-i-Zartusht, p. 4.

¶ Ibid. p. 8.

** Maujazát-i-Zartusht, p. 8. I beg the reader here to notice the absurd importance which the dastur of the Rasamís attaches to the wearing of the *sadra* and *kusti*. One of his disciples, when in England, gives a very different account indeed of the matter. "The girdle and gar-

cian found out through the wiles of Ahriman, that Zoroaster was to be born in the town of Reí;"* and that Búrántrús,

ment may appear superstitious," he says, "but it is no more than the baptism of the Christian, or the circumcision of the Mahometan..... Why does a Christian priest wear a white neckcloth, slit into two parts under his chin? Why does he wear a white surplice in the reading desk, and a black gown in his pulpit?" Colonial Magazine, June 1841. We content ourselves by giving a negative answer in this case. Nothing of the kind is done to prevent us from "becoming devils, *khavís* and *jins*" after death. "The kustí, according to the institutes of the Pársís, should consist of seventy-two interwoven filaments, and should three times circumvent the waist. The appointed time for investiture, is when a child has arrived at the age of seven years, seven months, and ten days. It sometimes takes place at an earlier period, in order to facilitate infantile marriages, of which the Pársís are as fond as any other class of the natives of India; and also at a later period, when the families are unable to pay for the necessary ceremonies. In the third *shloka* addressed by the mobeds to the Rájá of Sanján, on the arrival of the Zoroastrians in Gujurát, the kustí, and other 'sacred' parts of Pársí dress are thus alluded to. "They who wear a shirt, that is to say, the sadar, and who have round their loins, like the head of a serpent, of good woollen thread, the sacred kustí; and who cover the crown of the head with the cap of two-folds, are we, the fair, the fearless, the valiant, and athletic Pársís." These articles are assential to the preservation of the purity and safety of the Zoroastrians, and are the panoply in which they can successfully encounter the assaults of Ahriman. The kustí bears some analogy to the Brahmanical *munjh*. It is evident frum the figures at Persepolis, that it, or something corresponding with it, must have been in use among the ancient Persians." The Doctrine of Jehovah addressed to the Pársís, p. 43.

Edal Dáru says that each of the threads of the kustí is equal in value to one of the seventy-two Háhs of the Izashné; that each of the twelve threads in the six lesser cords is equal in value to the *dawúzdih hamáist* [supposed to be the fifth núsk of the Avastá, and the service used for the purification of women]; that each of the six lesser cords is equal in value to one of the six *Gahambárs*, or periods of creation; that each of the three circumventions of the loins is equal in value to *humat* good thought, *hukhat* good speech, *huaresta* good work; that the binding of each of the four knots upon it confers pleasure on each of the four elements, fire, air, water, and earth!! He also mentions, according to the *Saddar*, that a person when tying the knots, should think that Hormazd has no companion, that the Mazdayasní religion is true, that Zoroaster is a prophet, and that virtue should be practised. See Maujazát-i-Zartusht, p. 4—6. He says that the proper time for the investiture, is when a child is seven years old from its conception, p. 11.

* Maujazát-i-Zartusht, p. 32.

another magician, through the same aid, made a similar discovery.* He gives us this information about an interview which Zoroaster had with the devil:—"When he came into this earthly world from the other [which he is said to have visited] the unholy Ahriman laid wait for him and began to repeat the words of fraud, pretence, and deceit. Then the prophet Sáheb replied, 'Dádár Hormazd is the Creator of the whole world. I am strong and established in the faith of the pure and excellent Mazdayasní religion, and through this religion I shall trample thee under foot, and the words of thy proud pretence, and deceit, I am able to reject.' Having said this, he read aloud a *karda* (small section) of the Zand-Avastá, upon hearing of which the impure murderer, and his devils were reduced to nought. † He tells that the *nirang*, or consecrated urine of an ox, is a specific for all the disturbance, filth, and nastiness of Ahriman,"‡ &c. He declares that Ahriman after death reproaches all that come into his power.§ It is manifest from all this information, that the dastur, like the Vandidád, considers Ahriman and his associates to be malevolent and injurious spirits, and not the evil dispositions of man, which they seek to inflame.||

Dosabhái, as we have seen, endeavours to support his theory, by referring to the *Dabistán*. He might have saved himself this trouble, for the author of that work, though he enters into descriptions of, and discussions about, what he conceived to be the religion of the Pársís, as it was represented to him by the conversation of priests, and certain books which he saw, had I suspect, never seen the Vandidád, or any of the other works comprised in the Zand-Avestá, and of course was quite incapable of interpreting them, or commenting upon them. The Zand-Avesta, in fact, was a word of which the Sipásí Sufis,

* Maujazát-i-Zartusht, p. 44.

† Maujazát-i-Zartusht, pp. 68, 69.

‡ Maujazát-i-Zartusht, p. 84.

§ Maujazát-i-Zartusht, p. 103.

|| Edal Dáru is much guided in his notices of the Ahriman and his hosts by the Zartusht-Námah, a translation of which appears in the Appendix (A). This work throughout, is a testimony against Dosabhái's interpretation of the Devil.

or followers of Azar Kaíwán, to whom the author of the Dabistán belonged, knew not the meaning. Both in the Dabistán and Sháristán, as I have noticed in many instances, the Avastá and Zand, or the Zand and Avastá, are spoken of as *distinct books*, while the Pársís generally consider the Zand to be the name of a language in which the *Avastá* or *word*, is written !* The absurdity of an appeal to the Dabistán, Sháristán, and other works of the Sipásí philosophers, must now be apparent. Their authors had neither seen nor studied, and consequently could not expound, the Zand-Avastá.

There are two other most important facts connected with this subject, which remain to be taken into consideration. The Sipásí Sufis interpreted the *Shaitán* of the Muhammadans and Christians in the same way that they interpreted the *Ahriman* of the Pársís, thus doing the utmost violence to the meaning attached to the word by these communities.† The general system of parabolical exposition to which the Sipásís resorted, outrages common sense. To this fact the attention of oriental students has been particularly directed by Mr. Erskine. When referring to the writers of the Dabistán, Dasátír, &c, he says of them :—"They allegorize the whole of their

* *Avastá* is a Pahliví noun corresponding with the Zand *māthra*, or Sanskrit *mantra*.

† In support of this statement, I quote the following passage from the Shàristán.

گویند مذهب مجوس آنست که عالم را دو صانع است یزدان واهر
من یزدان خدارا گویند واهرمن شیطان را انچه در مصحف آمد—هوالاه
في السماء اله وفي الارض اله — مارا غرض از آوردن آیته نه آنست که
دو اله اعتقاد میکنم بلکه مراد آنست تا معلوم شود عقلا را که قران نیز
محتاج بتاویل است

"They say that in the Majus religion there are two Creators of the universe, Yezdán and Ahriman. They call God Yesdán, and Satan, Ahriman What is found in the Mushif [the book, i. e. ; the Korán]— '*Gods* are in heaven, and on the earth' — does not mean that there are two Gods ; but the meaning is this, that it should be known to him who has sense that the Korán, too, is in want of explanation." Author's M S. p 129

ancient history; whenever a *div* is mentioned, understanding by it a wicked man; and the conquest and destruction of the demons, they hold to mean only the conquest of man over his passions. In like manner the whole history of Khy-Khusro, and of Alexander the Great, is reduced to a moral and allegorical romance."* To some of their other achievements and qualities, we shall afterwards have occasion to advert.† Fit helps are they indeed for the sinking cause of the religion of Zoroaster in Bombay! Drowning men snatch at the foam.‡ This is the real explanation of Dosabhái's grasping at them. If Mullá Firuz, and others, did the same before he took up the pen to do battle for the pancháyat, it is only because like him they had discovered that no defence can be offered of the doctrines of the Vandidád respecting Ahriman, when they are properly interpreted. They resorted to an allegorical meaning from sheer necessity, but even in it, they have found no refuge. The theory about the evil dispositions of men, as I have fully shown, and as Edal Dáru seems to admit, from his using the terms for Ahriman and his associates in a personal sense, cannot in the slightest degree explain the demonology of the Vandidád, — give any interpretation of it at all agreeable to common sense.

That theory is equally impotent with regard to the Bundéshné, which in a cosmological and doctrinal point of view, is by the Pársís considered next in authority to the Vandidád itself, and according to some persons the only key to the right understanding of that volume. The Bundéshné represents Ahriman in his essential character of the author and prince of evil, as the production of Time-without-Bounds, co-etaneous with Hormazd; as existing with his evil law in primeval darkness, while Hormazd existed with his good law

* Bombay Transactions, vol. ii, p. 367. The Pársís may see the foundation of Mr. Erskine's remark, by examining the Gujarátí translation of the Dabistán, pp. 112—116, &c.

† See Chapter viii. of this work.

‡ This is a Gujarátí improvement of the English proverb, "Drowning men catch at straws."

in primeval light; and as peopling the abode of evil with evil beings, Dews, and Darvands, as soon as he had discovered that Hormazd, during the first three thousand years of his existence, had peopled heaven with beings of an opposite character. It represents Hormazd as first proposing terms of peace and forbearance to Ahriman, entreating him to render his aid to his productions, and informing him that after nine thousand years,— during a third of which he should be alone, a third with his works confounded, and a third in subjection to Ahriman,—Ahriman should come to nought. It represents Hormazd and Ahriman as each repeating their own law for their own protection. It represents them as respectively engaging in the work of creation, —Hormazd, for instance, as creating the Amsháspands, Bahman, Ardebehísht, Shahravar, Sapandormad, Khurdád and Amardád; and Ahriman as creating the arch-devils, Akuman, Andar, Sával, Nikáid, Tárik, and Járik; and as encouraging their respective productions to mutual war. It represents Ahriman and his hosts as breaking in upon the work of Hormazd in this world, and attempting to commit in it all kinds of devastations, as assaulting the primitive Bull, and Kaiomars, the first famous king, and polluting fire, and creating the smoke which obscures it; as spreading abroad the darkness of the night; as forming and scattering about serpents, scorpions, toads, and other noxious animals; as scorching the trees; and, in short, as doing unspeakable mischief, which required the utmost exertions of Hormazd to defeat and repair.* It represents Hormazd and and Ahriman, and their respective followers, as, after innumerable combats and a brief experience of the torments of hell, reconciled at the end of the world.† It does all this with a particularity, and sincerity, and absurdity of description, which must baffle the most ingenious parabolical interpreter who has ever appeared.

Nothing is now left for me but to charge the Pársí "sacred writings" with the errors respecting the origin and operation

* See Bundéshné, near the beginning.

† Bundéshné, near the end.

13

of natural and moral evil which they so abundantly contain. These errors are so ruinous in practice, that a late most able Governor of Bombay, well acquainted with the Zoroastrians of this place, has correctly characterized their religious observances as principally guided by their demonology. "Their religion itself," says the Hon. Mountstuart Elphinstone,* "has nothing inspiring or encouraging. The powers of good and evil are so equally matched, that the constant attention of every man is necessary to defend himself by puerile ceremonies against the malignant spirits from whom his deity is too weak to protect him." That no misunderstanding of the matters of this chapter may be thought excusable, and that no further evasion may be practicable, I shall submit my observasions in the plainest terms, and with reference to the different views which have been, or can be taken, of the case.

1. If it be held that the sacred books of the Pársís represent Hormazd and Ahriman as both eternal and self-existent beings of opposite characters, and to be both supreme in their own connections, then these books must be considered as setting forth the doctrine of *Two Principles,* — which is both monstrous and supremely unreasonable. This is a dogma altogether inconsistent with the order, regularity, and beneficence, and the unity and harmony of the laws, which pervade and guide the world, nay the whole extent of the universe with which we are in any degree acquainted. It is a dogma which the sun in its glory, the moon in its brightness, all the heavenly bodies in their courses, the earth full of the divine goodness, and every creature, primarily connected with physical good, and only incidentally with evil, extinguish in the rational mind. It is a dogma, according to which God is robbed of his essential and peculiar glory. If it be true, God is not alone without a Creator; for the author of evil also exists without an origin. God is not alone without beginning of days and end of years; for the devil also knows not the measurement of time. God is not alone infinite in knowledge; for the counsels of iniquity are independent of him, and

* Elphinstone's History of India.

uncontrolled by him. God is not alone possessed of underived and boundless power, doing according to his will in the armies of heaven and among the inhabitants of the earth, and making the permitted and restrained wrath of man and devils to praise him ; for the devil too has power which was not bestowed, and which cannot be restrained. God is not the universal Creator, for the devil has formed many of the beings which exist, and many of the objects which are to be found in the frame of the world. God is not the universal Sovereign ; for the devil has millions of agents who are subject to his undivided control, and who in their every action acknowledge him as the only king. It is a dogma, according to which there is actually no being of infinite perfection, whom the mind of man can contemplate with holy reverence and fear, in whom it can supremely delight, and whom it can love, worship, and obey, under the influence of the conviction that he is possessed of every possible excellence.

2. If it be held that the Pársí "sacred books" teach that Hormazd and Ahriman, with the names which they now possess, are both the productions in time of a being existing from all eternity, then, while their mutual acts and relations refer both to creation and providence, the Pársís are to be still considered as *practical Dualists,* * and the charge is also originated and substantiated, that the being possessed of supremacy of nature, and therefore to be recognized as God, has directly created an evil being, a being evil from the beginning, and the source of all the evil which exists, or ever will exist. The framers of this doctrine have "darkened counsel by words without knowledge." While endeavouring to show that the God of active providence, whom they denominate Hormazd, is *not* the author of evil, they have made the God in whom *he originated,* the parent of Ahriman with his essential wickedness, and of all that he is supposed to gene-

* The Abbe Foucher (Memoires de Litterature, tom. xxxi, p. 499,) calls this "le dualisme mitigé ;" but he properly adds, "c'est néanmoins un véritable dualisme, puisqu'on y reconnoît une nature essentiellement mauvaise, que Dieu peut seulement réprimer, et non pas anéantir."

rate. If this is not the highest blasphemy, let the Pársís declare in what the most heinous sin consists.

3. If it be said that the Pársí sacred books teach that Hormazd is the supreme God ; and that Ahriman is only one of his *creatures*, who has always possessed the character ascribed to him in the Vandidád, then the charge of blasphemy to which I have above alluded, is equally just and surely established. The matter is simply this : — the God Hormazd made the devil Ahriman as a devil ; and God is thus the direct author of evil ! Are the Parsís prepared to make this impious affirmation ?

4. If it be maintained that the Pársí sacred writings represent Ahriman as a *creature*, then they cannot with any consistency ascribe to him, as they actually do in the passages which we have quoted, works of creation, and represent him as in some respects equipotent with God himself. Can any being however exalted in station and dignity, but God himself, call into existence from absolute nothingness, and confer life ? Can any created being call the meanest insect, or worm, or serpent, or toad, into existence, as Ahriman is said to have done ? Can any created being create other beings possessed of the intelligence and power of the angels and archangels of God, like those who are declared to be the progeny of Ahriman ? Can any created being, as Ahriman is supposed to have done, so contend with God as positively to divide with him the sovereignty, and that against his own will and determinate effort ?

5. If it be said that the Pársí sacred writings seek, as undoubtedly they do, to set forth the works of Ahriman, as evil and that continually, then it must be admitted that their authors have been most wretched philosophers ; — and have in many instances altogether mistaken the nature of physical evil. Darkness, the original abode of Ahriman, and the substance which he is said to distribute over the earth, as I have formerly observed to the Pársís, is merely the absence of light, and is the consequence of God's creative and providential energy and arrangements. Its recurrence and continuance is fraught with distinguished blessings to the human race, in-

asmuch as it furnishes and secures that repose, rest, and refreshment, which independently of it, cannot be obtained. The winter which is said to have been created in Irán-Vejo, occurs according to the established laws of nature, connected with the declination of the poles of the earth, and the sun's place in the ecliptic ; and, notwithstanding certain inconveniences which attend it, when the prudence of man neglects to make proper provision for it, it is in the highest degree beneficial, as it forms a diversity in the seasons, and purifies, and restores, the earth and atmosphere. * The flies, and ants, which make devastations in Sughdḫó and Bakḫdí, bear in their own constitution the marks of benevolent workmanship ; are happy in their own existence, the enjoyment of what providence has furnished for them, and the humble functions which they exercise ; and have even their use to man, as they consume minute, but abundant, impurities, which could not perhaps be removed conveniently without their aid; and are only in particular circumstances actually injurious.† Smoke is the natural result

* Let the Pársís note the simple, but sublime, praise of the Psalmist addressed to Jehovah :—" The day is thine, the night also is thine: thou hast prepared the light and the sun. Thou hast set all the borders of the earth : thou hast made summer and winter. " Psalm lxxiv : 16, 17.

† Respecting the ant there is a very beautiful couplet in the Sháh-Námah of Firdausi, under Faridun, worthy of the attention of the Pársís.

میازار موری که دانه کش است

که جان دارد و جان شیرین خوش است

These lines have been thus paraphrased :—

" Kill not the little ant that toils with pain
To drag along and hoard the golden grain ;
It too has life, and ah ! despite of care,
How sweet is e'en to it the vital air. "

More worthy than this of the attention of the Pàrsís, is the following extract from the Confessions of Augustine, bishop of Hippo, who flourished at the commencement of the fifth century after Christ, and who before his conversion was a follower of the heretic Manes, to whom we have already alluded. "I now began to understand that every creature of thine hand is in its nature good, because every thing individually, as well as all things collectively, is good. Evil appeared to be a want of

of the decomposition of bodies, subjected to the process of combustion, and is merely the conspicuousness of the ascending particles, borne up by, or composed of, the emitted gases. The bark of trees is *not* from the scorch, or creation, of Ahriman ; but it is an essential part of their organization, answering most important ends, and facilitating their vital functions. "It acts", says a celebrated botanist, " as a protection to the young and tender wood, guarding it from cold and external accidents. It is also the medium in which the proper juices of the plant, in their descent from the leaves, [which are a mere dilitation of itself], are finally elaborated, and brought to the state which is peculiar to the species. It is from the bark that they are horizontally communicated to the medullary rays, which deposit them in the tissue of the wood," * even in the centre of the trunk. Some of the most useful substances, as gums and resins and the astringent principle used in tanning, are to be found in it in their greatest abundance. Its powders and extracts, as in the case of the Peruvian bark, quinine, etc. — which the Pársí mobeds, merchants, and mechanics, both know and appreciate,—are most useful in medicine.

6. If it be said, as Dosabhái and Aspandiárjí maintain, that the Pársí scriptures set forth Ahriman and his hosts, as merely the evil passions and dispositions of man, then it is absolutely necessary that they be interpreted throughout in consistency with this explanation. I have in this chapter shown some of the difficulties which exist ; and I call upon Dosabhái and his friends to solve them and the many others of a like

agreement in some parts to others. My opinion of the two independent principles, in order to account for the origin of evil, was without foundation. Evil is not a thing to be created ; let good things only forsake their just place, office, and order, and then, though all be good in their nature, evil, which is only a privative, abounds and produces positive misery. I asked what was iniquity, and I found to be no substance but a perversity of the will, which declines from thee the Supreme Substance to lower things, and casts away its internal excellency, and swells with pride externally." Augustine's Confessions, book vii, in Milner's Church History, vol. ii. pp. 342, 343.

* Lindley's Introduction to Botany, p. 310.

kind which will attract their attention in subsequent parts of this work. Were I to grant, which I do not, the correctness of their explanation, the essential absurdity of the passages in which Ahriman and his associates and his works are spoken of, would still remain. There can be such a thing as incoherent, incongruous, and ridiculous parable, as well as incoherent, incongruous, and ridiculous narrative. There is not an intelligent Pársí in Bombay, who can read with gravity the descriptions of Ahriman, Nasush, and their company, which are contained in the Vandidád. Instead of claiming God for the author of the book, the candid reader, will be disposed like Richardson, to ask, " Can human credulity suppose this to be the composition of Zoroaster, or of any man who had pretensions to common sense ?"

I commenced this chapter by saying, that "One of the most difficult questions which the mind of man has ever proposed to itself, and which it is most anxiously inclined to urge, is, 'How has physical, and especially moral, evil been introduced into the world in which we dwell.'" I have shown at length, that, notwithstanding the professions of its votaries, the Pársí religion has signally failed to give the reply, and that it has left the inquiry involved in far greater difficulties that it was found. I hope that the Pársís will bear with me while I make a few further observations on the subject, guided by the revelation of God's character, and will, and works, contained in the Scriptures of the Oldand New Testaments. They are substantially those which, I have already in another publication, submitted to their consideration *

Though we charge the Pársís, as in the case to which we have now referred, with frequently considering what is essentially good to be actually evil, we can of course have no dispute with them as to the fact that much evil exists in the world. Our controversy with them refers to the nature of evil, and the arrangements under which it is produced.

The ancient Persians, as we have shown by the quotations which we have made from the classical writers, attributed

* See Doctrine of Jehovah addressed to the Pársís, pp. 39 — 41.

good and evil to different authors; and the modern Pársís, who interpret their own reputed sacred books in their proper sense, assent to the general tenets which of old were promulgated on this subject. The Bible teaches us, that in a most important sense, good and evil have one origin. But in doing this, it does not represent God, in any degree, as the culpable author of sin.

The moment that we admit, that man is the lord of the creation of this lower world, and that he has been involved and continues in sin, or the transgression of the law of God, the existence of *physical evil* under the government of a holy and righteous God, is most satisfactorily accounted for. It is neither more nor less than God's emphatic testimony against iniquity, the proclamation to the universe of his unsullied purity. It was sin, we must admit in this view of the case, which inflamed the wrath of God, whose blast has consumed much of the beauty of this fair creation. It is sin which commissions the storm, and the tempest, and the hurricane, and the earthquake, to spread devastation and woe among our race. It is sin which generates the fear, and shame, and trouble, and horror, and distress, and disease, which are everywhere committing their dreadful ravages. It is sin which sharpens the arrows of death, and sends them with unerring aim into the vitals of its victims. It is sin which hath kindled that fire which shall not be quenched, but which shall consume the wicked throughout the endless ages of eternity.

Some have attempted to modify this view of physical evil, by maintaining that its ravages are not discriminative, that they do not realize the distinctions which actually exist in the moral goodness of individual men. In point of fact, however, they are, in a great degree, discriminative. Suffering is so closely connected with many vicious courses, as those of intemperance and profligacy, that it is universally admitted to be their direct and legitimate fruit. There is unspeakable happiness, and, as its consequence, freedom from many bodily ailments, and frequently a protraction of life, from the exercise and cultivation of holy affections. The afflictions of the righteous, even when they appear to equal or exceed in severity those of the wicked who are living in absolute rebellion against God, are associated with special heavenly support and consolation, and are more corrective than punitive, more fitted to purify than destroy. Even though malignant spirits, according to the notions of the Pársís, may, in a way unknown to us, be in some degree instrumental in their application or distribution, they are all administered under the direct control and guidance of God himself.

It is in reference to our accounting for the existence of *moral evil*, that any real, that in fact an insuperable, difficulty is experienced. When we consider that God hates sin, and that he has the power to prevent it, we cannot, in our present state, see *how* it could at first have been introduced into the universe. That it *has* been introduced into the universe, however, and even into the world which we inhabit, we have too sure evidence in our own consciousness, in our unvarying observation, and in every page of history. That it has not been caused, according to the allegation of the Pársís, by a principle of evil existing from eternity, or coetaneous with the providence of God, is manifest from the facts, that it has no independent support, which a God of goodness cannot destroy, and which in all who are sanctified, he actually destroys ; and that it is not incompatible with the creative energy, which it is admitted the God of goodness has displayed, to destroy the whole system of things in which it is found. That its guilty origin must have been in the creature and not in the Creator, is evident from the fact, that it is not viewed with complacency, but with wrath and indignation, by God, as is certified to us by the suffering which he fails not to inflict as part of its punishment. The divine revelation of the Bible, while in innumerable passages it exhibits and vindicates the holiness of God, directly informs us that sin was first voluntarily committed by angels, who kept not their first estate, and afterwards by man, who offended God by also voluntarily breaking his commands, which had been expressly made known, and supported by sanctions suitable to the authority of the Most High, on which they were founded. The same infallible standard of faith, however, assures us that all events occur according to the appointment of God, and that even the greatest sin which was ever committed, the crucifixion of the Lord of glory, took place according to "his foreknowledge and determinate counsel." Though it attempts not to relieve our metaphysical perplexities, it supports the unlimited sovereignty of Jehovah, both in the permission and control of that which is evil. It exhibits God as frustrating the tokens of the liars, and making diviners mad ; as turning wise men backward, and making their knowledge foolish. It shows us "that the Lord hath made all things for himself, yea even the wicked for the day of evil ;" that he brings light out of darkness, strength out of weakness, and order out of confusion ; and that he makes the wrath of man to praise him, as well as restrains the remainder of his wrath. It saith in the name of God, unto Pharaoh, a most wicked and abandoned prince :—"Even for this same purpose have I raised thee up, that I might show my power in thee, and that my name might be declared throughout all the earth." It shows that the existence and continuance of evil will be overruled by God for the manifestation of his praise, both through the developement and execution of the glorious scheme of redemption, and the awful visitation of the divine justice on the children of destruction, who go to their own place, the world of interminable woe.

These observations, I respectfully commend to the consideration of the Pársís. If the statements of the Bible do not afford all the information which they ask, they certainly furnish all that can be reasonably demanded in this sublunary world, where the wisest "know only in part." For the portion of light communicated by God, we ought to be grateful, while we patiently wait for such accessions to it, as our happiness in the other world may require. To this subject, we shall have occasion again to advert. *

* See Chapter vii.

CHAPTER IV.

THE WORSHIP OF THE ELEMENTS AND HEAVENLY BODIES, AND OF THE AMSHA'SPANDS AND IZADS, WHO ARE SAID TO PRESIDE OVER THEM AND THE OTHER WORKS OF NATURE.

Statement respecting the Polytheism of the Pársís — Their Worship of the Elements and Heavenly Host — Alleged explanation of Gibbon — Testimony of the Greeks and Romans — Testimony of the Fathers and Historians of the Christian Church — Difficulties of Gibbon and confession of Hyde — Testimony of the Musalmáns — Perversion of that of Fardausí by the Pársí controversialists — Notions of the present Pársís on the Worship of the Elements, Angels, and Celestial Bodies — Explanations and attempted vindications of Edal Dárú — Perversions and explanations of Dosabhái, Aspandiárjí, etc. — Comparison of the views of the controversialists with the admissions of the Kadím Táríkh, Sanján Shlokas, Kissah-i-Sanján, the dastur who instructed Mr. Lord, and the Zartusht-Námah—Refutation of the defences and apologies of the controversialists — Fire not the Glory or Substance of God — Impiety and unreasonableness of the worship of Angels said to preside over Fire or any of the other works of God — Errors respecting the number and combination of the Elements — Fire not a superintendent and preserver of man—Dosabhái ashamed of the honours conferred on fire in the Vandidád—Specimen of these honours — Blasphemous Worship of Fire illustrated by a translation of the A'tish-Behrám Niáish, etc.—Comment on this form of prayer — Unreasonableness of legend in the Sháhnámah respecting the discovery of Fire by Hoshang — Explanation of the unquenchable fires of A'zar-Baiján — Worthlessness of the legend of the Sháhnámah respecting the Atish-burjín-Meher — Theories respecting the origin of the Worship of the Heavenly Host and the Elements—General remarks on the unreasonableness and sinfulness of worshipping any of the inanimate or intelligent Powers of Nature.

THE charges which in the two preceding chapters I have brought against the Pársí religion, as unfolded in the books on which it professes to be founded, and which, I trust, I have clearly established, are of a very serious nature. I hope that not a few of those for whose benefit this work is particularly intended, will consider them in this light, and perceive that the system of faith to which they have been hitherto particularly attached, is fundamentally wrong, both as it sets forth as the object of supreme worship, an imaginary God, Hormazd, who is represented not as self-existent and independent, but secondary and derivative in his being, and as it degrades even him by recognizing an evil principle, or Ahriman, who is coetaneous, and, in some respects, equipotent, or, in other words, his equal both in duration and power. I hope, also, that they will see, that the accounts which are given in the Vandidád and other reputed sacred books of the Pársís, both of Hormazd and Ahriman, are so unreasonable and absurd, as to show, not only that these books have no claim to be considered as given by inspiration of God, but that they have even no claim to be considered as the productions of philosophical and enlightened men.

Another heavy charge against the fundamental principles of the Pársí religion remains to be made; and I bring it forward with the fullest confidence that it can be substantiated. That religion is decidedly *polytheistic.* Not only does it set forth an erroneous object of supreme worship, and circumscribe the glory and the power of that object by an imaginary being of an opposite character; but it recognizes a vast, an almost uncountable, number of objects of religious worship and reverence. The full extent of its polytheism, I shall notice in our next chapter. I shall advert at present principally to the *Elements of nature, and the Amsháspands, and Izads, and other beings*, who are supposed to preside over them, and the works of God into the composition of which they enter. As in former instances, I shall, as introductory to the remarks which it is my duty to submit on the subject, as it is set forth in the Pársí sacred writings, refer to the testimony of antiquity on this subject. This is the more necessary as Dosabháí himself has, in one instance at least, made an erroneous appeal to that testimony. Quoting Gibbon, he says;—"The theology of Zoroaster was darkly comprehended by foreigners, and even by far the greater number of his disciples; but even the most careless observers were struck with the philosophic simplicity of the Persian worship. 'That people,' says Herodotus, 'rejects the use of temples, of altars, and of statues, and smiles at the folly of those nations, who imagine that the gods are sprung from, or bare any affinity with, the human nature. The tops of the highest mountains are the places chosen for sacrifices. Hymns and prayers are the principal worship; the supreme God who fills the wide circle of heaven, is the object to whom they are addressed. Yet at the same time, in the true spirit of a polytheist, he accuses them of adoring Earth, Water, Fire, the Winds, and the Sun and Moon. But the Persians of every age have denied the charge, and explained the equivocal conduct, which might appear to give a colour to it. The elements, and more particularly Fire, Light, and the Sun, whom they called Mithra, were the objects of their religious reverence, because they considered them as the purest symbols, the noblest productions, and the most powerful agents of Divine Power and Nature.''*

Herodotus, to whom reference has now been made, is known, I doubt not, to some of my native readers, as the "Father of Grecian History." "With an ardour in the pursuit of knowledge very rarely equalled," says his latest and best translator, Mr. Isaac Taylor, "when in early life he devoted himself to the task of collecting the scattered materials of universal history, did not think himself qualified for the work until he had visited every country to which the Greeks of his time had access:—everywhere examining documents, conversing with the learned, and collecting connected evidence. The fruits of his industry we have before us; and it may confidently be affirmed that, after every exception has been admitted which the most sceptical criticism can substantiate, there will remain, in the nine books of Herodotus, a mass of information more extensive, important, and instructive, than is to be found in any other author of antiquity. Unaffected,

* Gibbon's Decline and Fall of the Roman Empire, vol. i, p. 322, quoted in the preface of the Tálím-i-Zartusht, p. 16.

unambitious, mellifluous, perspicuous, in his style; bland, candid, and gay, in his temper; laborious in his researches; judicious, for the most part, in his decisions; and apparently free from sinister intentions and national prejudices — he holds up a mirror in which is seen, without obscurity, or distortion, the face of nature — the revolutions of empires, and the characters of statesmen. This great writer brings down the history of Greece to the end of the year 479, before the Christian era, when the Persians were compelled for ever to abandon their long-cherished hope of crushing liberty in its birth-place."*

In the course of his great work, Herodotus gives a very curious account of the laws and manners of the Persians; and though it may not in *every* respect be correct, it must be considered as generally so, and extremely valuable. The part of it which refers to the Pársí *religion* is as follows. I use the translation of Mr. Taylor, referring to the original only in a few instances connected with the terms expressive of worship and reverence.

"I have informed myself," says Herodotus, "of the Persian Institutions, which are such as follow. — They think it unlawful to form images or to construct temples or altars — imputing extreme folly to those who do so: — I suppose not believing the gods to be allied to humanity, as the Greeks imagine. Their custom is to ascend the highest mountains, where they perform sacrifices to Jove, and they call by this name the whole circle of the Heavens. They sacrifice (θύουσι) also to the *sun*, to the *moon*, to the *earth*, to *fire*, and *water*, and to the *wind*,— to those only they anciently sacrificed; but in latter times they have learned from the Assyrians and Arabians, to worship also Urania; — the Assyrians called Venus, Mylitta —the Arabians, Alytta, but the Persians, Mithra. The mode of performing sacrifice to the above-mentioned divinities (θεοὺς) is as follows: — when about to sacrifice, the Persians neither erect altars, nor kindle fire: they neither make libations, nor use the flute, nor have garlands, nor cakes.

* Preface to the Translation of Herodotus, p. v.

If any intends to offer to a god, he leads the animal to a consecrated spot:—there he invokes the god, having his tiara girt with a wreath—generally of myrtle. Nor does the worshipper implore blessings for himself alone, but prays that it may be well with all the Persians, and with the king:—thus he prays for himself only as included in the petition for all the Persians. Then dividing the victim into parts, he boils the flesh, and lays it upon the most tender herbs, especially trefoil. This done, a magus—without a magus no sacrifice may be performed,—sings a sacred hymn (ἐπαίεδει θεογονίον), called by them an incantation, (ἐπαιοιδήν). After a little time, the worshipper carries away the flesh, of which he makes what use he thinks fit..... Whoever of the citizens is afflicted with the leprosy, is forbid to enter the city, or to hold intercourse with other Persians; for they affirm that this disease is inflicted in punishment of some sin against the *sun.* Any foreigner so diseased is expelled by the mob from the country; and on the same account they drive away white pigeons. They are careful to preserve a *river* from every pollution, even that of washing the hands in it; nor do they permit others to do so; as in fact they have a great veneration (σέβονται) for all *streams*.... Thus far I have been able to speak accurately of what has fallen under my own observation; but of another custom I cannot speak so positively; I mean the rite of burial, in which more secrecy is observed. It is said that the corpse of every Persian, before interment, is torn of birds or dogs. This practice is, I certainly know, observed by the Magi, for it is done openly. The Persians having inclosed the body in wax, bury it in the earth. The Magi, as they differ much from other men, so also from the Egyptian priests; for these scrupulously abstain from killing any animal, except such as they sacrifice; but those, with their own hands, slay all animals, except *dogs* and *men*; indeed they use great diligence in destroying ants, serpents, and various reptiles and birds; there might be some peculiar reason originally for this custom which we leave as it is, and return to the course of the history."*

* Taylor's Translation of Herodotus, pp. 65, 67, 68.

To these brief notices, I am disposed to attach considerable importance. It will be observed that the father of Grecian history, whose veracity and general accuracy of personal observation and description are universally admitted,* declares that his own observation and particular inquiries were the sources of his information. His formal testimony is in all essential points corroborated by various incidental allusions and intimations given in the course of his work, to some of which we shall now advert.

1. *Temples* and *altars*, as we shall immediately see, came into use among the Persians shortly after the days of Herodotus; but that they anciently adored the "whole circle of the heavens," in the manner which he describes, there can be little doubt. Herodotus says that this object of worship was denominated *Jove.*† To the same god, according to the information which be gives in his historical narrative, were dedicated the sacred white horses, and chariots of which, when describing the march and muster of the Persian host under Xerxes, he gives the following account: — "After these (the spearmen) came ten sacred Nisoean horses, gorgeously caparisoned. . . . . Close behind the ten horses, followed the sacred chariot of Jupiter drawn by eight white horses, and behind them walked the charioteer holding the reins, for no mortal ascends this seat."‡ This chariot was left in Pœonia when Xerxes advanced against Greece.

The deification of what were conceived to be the *elements* of nature, is expressly intimated by Herodotus. The historian himself frequently refers, in the course of his history, to a treatment of these elements which could originate in nothing else but in the belief that they are sentient or divine. "When Cyrus attempted to pass the river Gyndes, which could only be done by boats, one of the white horses called sacred,

* In reference to accounts received from others, he was sometimes singularly credulous.

† Jove, according to the Greeks, the god of the firmament, corresponded in some respects with the *A'smán* of the Pársís.

‡ Taylor's Translation, p. 495.

full of mettle, plunged into the stream, and endeavoured to reach the opposite bank; but being submerged in the current, it was borne away. Cyrus, enraged at the river for this injury, threatened to reduce it so low that in future women should ford it with ease,— not wetting their knees. Having uttered this threat he delayed the progress of his army towards Babylon, and dividing his forces into two bodies, measured out one hundred and eighty channels to be cut from both banks of the river, thus diverting the Gyndes on all sides. He enjoined upon his army the work of digging these trenches, and by their numbers they completed it; but the whole summer was spent there in the labour. Cyrus, having in this manner *punished the river* Gyndes, by distributing its waters into three hundred and sixty trenches, advanced towards Babylon."* Foolish as was this conduct of the great monarch, it proceeded from the belief that there was something *sentient* in the waters. It was more than surpassed by that of Xerxes. When he had constructed his bridges at Abydos, "there arose a hurricane, which rent and dissipated both of them. Xerxes, on hearing of this accident was filled with rage, and commanded three hundred strokes of the whip to be inflicted on the Hellespont; and also that a pair of fetters should be thrown into the deep." "I have indeed heard," continues the historian, "that he sent persons to brand the Hellespont with a hot iron; at least he directed that when the flogging was inflicted, the following barbarous and outrageous words should be pronounced—'O thou bitter water, thy lord inflicts on thee this punishment for having injured him, though uninjured by him. Yet the king — even Xerxes will pass over thee, whether thou wilt or not. Justly no man offers sacrifice to thee, for thou art a perfidious and brackish stream.' He also directed his officers to *punish the sea* in like manner, and he caused the overseers of the bridges to be decapitated."† This was what the Hindús call the *viroddhi-*

* Clio, Taylor's Translation, p. 90, 91.

† Polymnia, Taylor's Translation, p, 491,

bhakti, or worship of opposition, with a vengeance ! * Threatenings and punishments, however, did not always continue the order of the day. Recourse was afterwards had to *praise*, and *offerings*. When preparations were again made for the passage of the army, " the rising of the sun was eagerly desired ; meanwhile incense of all kinds was offered to the gods upon the bridges, and the road was strewed with branches of myrtle. At the instant of sun-rising, Xerxes poured a libation from a golden cup into the *sea*, at the same time addressing a *prayer to the sun*, intreating that no accident might prevent his continuing to vanquish the nations of Europe, until he had reached its utmost limits. As he finished this prayer, he threw the cup into the Hellespont, together with a golden vase and a Persian sword of the kind called a scimitar." "Whether this was done," says Herodotus, "as an offering to the sun, or whether, repenting of the stripes he had inflicted on the Hellespont, he wished to make amends to that water by these gifts which were thrown into it, is a question I cannot certainly determine."† Under the auspices of Xerxes, the Magi, (Mobeds) on the banks of the Strymon, " sacrificed some white horses, and obtained lucky omens. After the performance of various rites of divination, addressed to the *river*, the host marched through what are called the Nine ways of the Edonians. "‡ These instances of the worship of *water* are decided. It was probably owing to the regard which was paid to this element, that few or none of the Persians were able to swim. Herodotus simply alludes to the fact. § The deification of *fire* he plainly intimates. He notices, as an act of impiety, the burning of the body of Amasis by Cambyses, because " the Persians think fire to be a god," and they " think it wrong to offer the dead body of a man to a god." || We have already referred to Xerxes as

* A reference to the practice of the Hindús, who cajole or defy their gods in turn, throws considerable light on the conduct of the Persian monarch.

† Polymnia, Taylor's Translation, p. 501.

‡ Polymnia, Taylor, p 521.

§ Polymnia, Taylor, p 260.

|| Thalia, Taylor p. 194.

pouring out a libation to the *sun*. Another instance of his acting in a similar manner, was before the commencement of the engagement in which Leonidas fell.* The following narrative connected with him represents the *moon* as an object of devotion among the Persians. "Xerxes, after passing the winter at Sardis, mustered the host after the commencement of spring, and advanced towards Abydos. While on his march, the sun, leaving its place in the heaven, disappeared; and, though the sky was cloudless, and perfectly serene, day was exchanged for night. Xerxes in beholding and considering this event was filled with inquietude, and sought from the Magi the meaning of the portent. They declared that 'God predicted to the Greeks the extinction of their state'; for said they, 'the sun is the tutelar of the Greeks, as the *moon* of the Persians.'" † Of the deification of the *winds* also, there is an illustration given. "The gale [which destroyed a great part of the fleet of Xerxes] raged during three days; at length the Magi, by making incisions, and by performing incantations to the wind, and moreover by sacrificing to Thetis and the Nereids assuaged the storm on the fourth day;—or it might be that it abated of its own accord."‡

2. Herodotus states that the Persians had learned to worship some of the *gods of other nations*. Darius was so far affected by the "glory of images," that he wished his own image to be placed in an Egyptian temple. "The king Sesostris, alone of the Egyptian monarchs," says the historian, "ruled over Ethiopia. He left monuments of himself in figures of stone, placed in front of the temple of Vulcan. Two of them, representing himself and his wife, are thirty cubits high; the others are of his four sons, twenty cubits high. A long time afterwards a priest of Vulcan refused to permit a statue of Darius the Persian to be placed in front of these colossal images." § Xerxes appears to have been smitten with a similar devotion. "He sacrificed a thousand oxen to the Trojan Minerva; at the same time the Magi performed libations to the heroes of

* Polymnia, Taylor, p. 572.

† Polymnia, Taylor, p. 493.

‡ Polymnia, Taylor, p. 560.

§ Euterpe, Taylor p. 148.

the place."* Datis would not allow the Persian fleet to approach Delos, because it was the birth-place of Apollo and Diana. †

3. The mode of disposing of the dead, observed by the ancient Persians, corresponded with the accounts which were given to Herodotus, and did not essentially differ from that in use at the present day. The treatment of the dead had its origin in respect to "the god of the *earth*." Herodotus says, that this deity was honoured by the burial of the living. The Persians under Xerxes at the Nine ways of the Edonians, "buried alive in it nine boys and nine girls, the children of the inhabitants; for it is a Persian custom to bury the living; and thus, as I have been informed, Amestris, the wife of Xerxes, when advanced in years, buried alive fourteen youths taken from the most illustrious Persian families, in order to gratify the god who is said to be under ground." ‡

4. The Magi, to whom we have seen Herodotus referring, were the Mobeds or ministers of religion. They are men-

* Polymnia, Taylor, p. 496.

† Errato, Taylor, p. 450.

The Persians, however, were not on all occasions thus the slaves of superstition. Darius Hystaspes wished to take the "statue of solid gold, twelve cubits in height," but "dared not execute his wishes; but his son Xerxes not only took it, but put to death the priest, who endeavoured to prevent its removal." (Clio, Taylor, p. 87.) When the priests of Egypt introduced Apis to Cambyses, "as in a fit of fury he drew his dagger, intending to strike the belly of Apis; but instead he struck the thigh, and then laughing said to the priests—'O you blockheads! do the gods become such — consisting of blood and flesh, and that may feel iron? Yet such a god is worthy of the Egyptians. But now you shall have no reason to rejoice at having mocked me." So saying, he commanded those whose business it was, to scourge the priests, and gave orders that all the Egyptians who might be found feasting, should be put to death. Thus ended this festival, and the priests were punished. As for Apis who was wounded in the thigh, he wasted as he lay in the temple, and at length dying of his hurt, the priests buried him, without the knowledge of Cambyses." (Thalia, Taylor, p, 201.) During the devastation of Phocis, the Persians destroyed several temples, to one of which there was an oracle of Apollo. (Urania, Taylor, p. 595.) The Athenians accused Xerxes of having burned the "dwelling-places and statues" "of their heroes, without dread."

‡ Polymnia, Taylor, p. 521.

tioned by Herodotus as a people of Media united under the sway of Dejoces with the Budi and other tribes. * He ascribes to them the interpretation of dreams, † and omens, and the incantation of winds, &c. On them probably devolved the exposition of the ancient constitutions to which he alludes, when speaking of Cambyses's marriage of his sisters. ‡ One of them was guardian of the royal palace during the absence of Cambyses in Egypt, and united with his brother in the usurpation of the government.§

5. The respect which the Pársís of old paid to *dogs*, and their anxiety to destroy *noxious animals*, have continued among their successors to the present day. The injunctions of the Vandidád respecting them, we shall have frequently occasion to notice in our sixth chapter.

The Pársís of Bombay, I am sure, will now be prepared to perceive the want of candour evinced by Gibbon, when he represents Herodotus as bringing a charge against the ancient Persians, on the score of the worship of the Elements and of the Heavenly Host, which cannot be substantiated. The venerable historian writes with all the simplicity of truth. As he was himself a polytheist, it is absurd to speak of him as "*accusing*" the Persians, when he refers to their polytheism. He evidently relates facts with which he was acquainted; and he praises the Persians, when he esteems them praiseworthy. He mentions numerous circumstances which illustrate his general statements; and they are so minute and circumstantial, as to establish his accuracy. In the very "*religious reverence*" of the elements which Gibbon admits, there is essentially that deification which he denies. Of this fact Dosabháí, the hero of the Pársí pancháyat, seems to have been well aware, for he renders "*religious reverence*" by *kibláh*, which is merely a "centre-of-worship." Why did he hesitate to give a faithful translation of Gibbon, when he claimed his patronage? Only, I fear, because he knew that it would not suit his purpose.||

* Clio, Taylor, p. 48, 49. † Clio, Taylor, p 51.

‡ Thalia, Taylor, p. 202. § Polymnia, Taylor, p. 52.

|| Gibbon is not the only apologist of the Pársís who has unreasonably

Ctesias, another Greek historian, who died about the year 384 before Christ, represents Darius Hystaspes (or Gushtásp) as erecting an altar to Jupiter, the god of the firmament, and sacrificing upon it.

Xenophon also a Greek historian, who wrote a few years later than Ctesias, takes occasional notice of Cyrus (or Kai-khosru), and his followers, as sacrificing to Jupiter (the god of the firmament), and to the sun, and to the earth, and addressing them in prayer, and pouring out to them libations. Thus for example, we find him saying, "Cyrus sacrificed first to the regal Jupiter, then to the other deities..... As soon as he had passed the borders, he propitiated the earth by libations, and the gods by sacrifice."* "When they came to the sacred enclosures, they sacrificed to Jupiter and burnt the bulls entirely. Then they sacrificed to the sun, and burnt the horses entirely; then killing some victims for the earth, they did as the Magi directed."†

Strabo the geographer, who flourished in the middle of the first century after Christ, gives a particular account of the Persian religion and customs. He says, "The Persians erect neither statues nor altars; they sacrifice in a lofty place, reck-

detracted from the testimony of Herodotus. Dr. Hyde, who was nearly as much a Zoroastrian as a Christian,—who could venture to say in reference to certain reported predictions of Zoroaster, "*quæ omnia suadent et persuadent Zoroastrem, hac in parte, vere divinam revelationem habuisse*,—waxes quite wroth respecting it, and modestly exclaims, "*Dolendum quod antiquissimus scriptor addictus fuit mendaciis.*" This learned divine, however, was accustomed in this way to characterize whatever was adverse to his own unfounded theories. After alluding to the testimony of the fathers of the Christian church, and others, he completely loses self-control, and breaks out into profane swearing, "*Bone Deus, quanta sunt hæc mendacia!*" (De Vet. Rel. Pers. Cap. vi. p. 136.) The unfaithfulness of Hyde in dealing with his authorities, has been noticed by many writers since his day, and particularly by Anquetil du Perron, Foucher, and Mosheim. The admitted learning of his work, probably on this very account, did not secure for it the favour which was expected. It "was so ill received by the public, that the Doctor boiled his tea-kettle with the greatest part of the impression." See Pinkerton's Voyages and Travels, vol. ix, p. 196.

* Cyropæd. lib. iii. † Ibid. lib. viii.

oning the sky to be Jupiter. They worship (τιμῶσι) the sun whom they call Mithra, and the moon, and Venus, and fire, and the earth, and the winds, and water. They sacrifice in a clean place * . . . . . They sacrifice particularly to fire and to water, placing dry wood upon the fire with the bark taken off and with fat thrown upon it; then, oil having been infused, they cause it to blaze, not breathing upon it but ventilating it. If any one breathes, or throws any thing dead or filthy, upon the fire, he is punished with death. With regard to water, they thus act; coming to a lake or river or fountain they make a trench, and they cut the throat of their victim, taking care lest any of the adjoining water should be touched with the blood, lest the whole should be polluted; afterwards having placed the burnt-offerings upon myrtle and laurel, the Magi burn them with slender twigs." Having noticed the fire-temples in Cappadocia and the altar which is in the midst of them, he says, "The Magi keep upon it a quantity of ashes and an immortal fire, and going there daily for an hour they repeat their prayers, holding a bundle of twigs before the fire." He says that their tiaras were pendent on each side, that impurities might be avoided. "The Persians," he continues, "do not go into a river, nor do they wash in it nor bathe in it, nor cast a dead body into it, nor any other thing which appears to be impure. To whatever god they sacrificed, they first address fire."†

Quintus Curtius, who flourished about the year of Christ 64, and who writes the life of Alexander the Great, when speaking of the army of Darius, says, "The fire which they called eternal was carried before them on silver altars: the Magi came after it singing hymns after the Persian manner; three-hundred and sixty-five youths clothed in scarlet followed them, according to the number of the days of the year as the Persians compute it." He also represents Darius as conjuring his soldiers by this "eternal fire," and the shining of the sun.‡

* He here quotes Herodotus. † Strabonis Geograph. lib. xv.

‡ Curt. lib. iii, cap. 3. Lib. ii, cap. 14.

Pliny, the natural historian, who flourished about 100 years after Christ, represents the Persians as averse to sailing on the sea, from the fear of polluting it, and as refraining to spit into water.*

Diogenes Laërtius, about A. D. 147, in his Lives of the Philosophers, says, "The Magi descant on the origin and nature of the gods, whom they [reckon to be] fire, and earth, and water. They reject symbols and statues.... They think it wrong to dispose of the dead by fire."†

Sextus Empiricus, the Pyrrhonic philosopher, who is supposed to have lived in the early part of the second century, says that the "Persians reckon fire to be a god (θεοφοροῦσιν)."‡

Agathias, to whom we have already referred, says of the Persians, that "they particularly venerate water;" and that "fire is most honoured by them, and seems the most sacred."§

Procopius, an imperial counsellor in the Roman service, and who is supposed to have died A. D. 560, represents Perozes (Firuz) the Persian king as worshipping the rising sun;‖ and Chosroes (Khosru) repairing to the province of Ardabigana, "where there is a large pyreum, which the Persians worship as the chief of the gods, and where the Magi nourish the unextinguished fire."¶ He notices it as a custom of the Persians, that they abstained from burying the dead.**

Justin, a Latin author who wrote a Compendium of the History of Trogus Pompeius, says that "the Persians esteem the sun to be the only one God (solem unum Deum), and suppose that horses should be sacrificed to the same God."†† Long before his day, Ovid gives a similar intimation.‡‡

* Hist. Nat. lib. xxx, cap. 2.

† Procem ii, segm. 6, 7.

‡ Sexti Empirici lib. ix, adversus Physicos.

§ Agath. Schol. lib. ii.

‖ Procop. de Bello Pers. lib. i. cap. 3.

¶ Ibid. lib. ii, cap. 23.

** Ibid. lib. i, cap. 11.

†† Justin. Hist. lib. i, cap. 10.

‡‡ Fast. lib. i. v. 355.

Placat equo Persis radiis Hyperiona cinctum,
Ne detur celeri victima tarda Deo.

These authorities most decidedly prove that divine honours were conferred by the ancient Persians on the Elements of nature, and on the Heavenly hosts. Many others testifying to the same fact, could easily be produced. To some of those found in the writings of the fathers and historians of the Christian church, we may now advert. It will be seen, that like those already quoted, they are altogether unequivocal. Clemens Alexandrinus, at the beginning of the third century, refers to Diogenes, as saying, that the Magi of Persia "confer divine honours on fire (τὸ πῦρ τετιμήκασι), and asserts, on the authority of Dio, that they reckon fire and water to be the only resplendencies of the gods, "(θεῶν ἀγάλματα)."* Chrysostom, of the fourth century, says, "Fire is reckoned among the Persians to be God; and the barbarians inhabiting those regions, honour it with great veneration."† Socrates, the church historian, says, that "the Persians worship fire; and the king is accustomed to adore fire burning upon a perpetual altar."‡ Sozomenus gives a similar testimony, and represents the second Sháhpur as grievously persecuting the Christians, because they would not unite in this idolatry.§ Theodoritus in the fifth book of his Ecclesiastical History,‖ says of the Persians in the reign of Yazdajard, that "they reckon fire to be a god;" and that the Persians are accustomed to call those Magi, who deify the Elements, (μάγους δὲ καλοῦσιν οἱ πέρσαι τοὺς τὰ στοχεῖα θεοποιοῦντας). Elisæus, the Armenian author of the history of Vartan, represents the Persian king as sacrificing to the

* Clementis Cohortatio ad gentes, 19. Bishop Potter in his edition of Clemens adds to this testimony the following: — "Auctor Recognitionum Clementis lib. 4. cap. 29. de Zoroastre agens, *Busti cineres*, inquit, *tanquam fulminei ignis reliquias, qui primitus erant decepti, deferunt ad Persas, ut ab eis, tanquam divinas è cœlo, lapsus ignis conservaretur excubiis, atque ut cœlestis Deus coleretur.*

† Chrysost. ad populum Antioch. Hom. iv.

‡ Socratis Hist. Eccles. lib. vii. cap. 8.

§ Sozomen. Hist. Eccles. lib. ii, cap. 9. A notice of the persecution here referred to, the Pársí reader may see in The Doctrine of Jehovah addressed to the Pársís. pp. 14, 15.

‖ Cap. 39.

holy fire in the year A. D. 450, and as issuing the command, "All people and tongues throughout my dominions must abandon their heresies, worship the sun, bring to him their offerings, and call him god; they shall feed the holy fire, and fulfil all the other ordinances of the Magi."* The translator of this work informs us, that the Armenian writers of the eleventh and twelfth centuries, call the followers of Zoroaster, the "sons or servants of the Sun."† Esnik, from whose work, written in the fifth century, a quotation is given in the appendix (D), uses a similar epithet, as do many of the Syrian writers referred to by Assemanni in his Bibliotheca Orientalis.

Gibbon, in the passage quoted by the author of the Tálim-i-Zartusht, says that the "Persians of every age have denied the charge of [fire-worship], and explained the equivocal conduct." Such an assertion is more easily made than established. I confidently challenge any of the supporters of his opinion to produce a single proof of its accuracy applicable to the age of the authors to whom I have now referred. Their testimony is absolutely uncontradicted by any of their contemporaries. This we are inclined to believe Gibbon knew right well, for he is forced to admit, as we have seen, that they viewed fire, light, and the sun, as "*objects of religious reverence.*" Dr. Hyde, who was also a willing, but unsuccessful, apologist of the Pársís, was likewise compelled to admit that they believe in its intrinsic sacredness. He thus writes: — "Omnis Ignis, sive sit cœlestis et superior Planetarum et Meteorum; sive terrestris, aliquid Sanctitatis et Beatudinis in se habere creditur;"‡ that is, "All fire, whether it be celestial and superior, of the planets and meteors; or terrestrial, is believed to have some sanctity and blessedness in itself."

That the Musalmáns have esteemed the Pársís fire-worshippers, is evident from thousands of passages in their writings, and from the designations which they have usually conferred

* Neumann's Translation of the History of Vartan, pp. 6, 8.

† Preface, pp. xx.

‡ De Vetere Religione Persarum, p. 21.

upon them, such as *Atash-parast* and *Gabar*. The former of these means literally a *fire-worshipper*; and the latter is always used as synonimous with *fire-worshipper*; as may be seen by a reference to any of the Persian dictionaries, to any book of travels in Persia, or to any of the Persian poets. Shaikh Sádí says in the Gulistan: —

اگر صد سال گبر آتش فروزد   چو یکدم اندر ان افتد بسوزد

"Though the Gabar may serve fire a hundred years, yet the moment he falls into it, he will be burned." That the Gabars were Pársís is evident from the fact, that the Musalmáns in Persia so denominate the followers of Zoroaster in that country at the present time, and speak of the remains of their forefathers as the works of the Gabars. * In the course of time,

* Will it be credited that *Kalam Kas* in the *Nirang-Há*, has occupied nearly ten pages of his book, in denying that the Pársís are Gabars, and in railing against me for asserting the fact! Another Pársí writer in the Bombay Samáchar has acted a similarly absurd part. Though the matter has no great importance, I beg to request the attention of any Pársí who may have been influenced by them to the following note, which I extract from Ouseley's Travels: —

" *Gabr*, according to the manuscript dictionary, *Berhán Kattea*, ' is used in the sense of *Magh*, which signifies a fire-worshipper ': —

گبر بمعني مغ باشد که آتش پرست است

This is sometimes written, and very often pronounced *Gavr*, by a change of letters frequent in Persian, as in other languages. ' *Gavr*, ' we learn from the dictionary *Jehángíri*, means ' those fire-worshippers, who observe the religion of *Zardusht*, (or Zoroaster), and they are also called *Magh*:'—

کور — آتش پرستانرا گویند که در دین زردشت باشند و انهارا مغ نیز نام نهند

But Origen, in the third century, defending Christianity against Celsus, an Epicurean, who had alluded to the mysteries of Mithra, uses *Kaber*, as equivalent to *Persians*. , Let Celsus know, ' says he, ' that our prophets have not borrowed any thing from the Persians or Kabirs, " — Ιστω δε Κελσος — ουτ' απὸ Περσῶν ἢ Καβείρων λαβόντες ἡμῶν όι προφῆται λέγουσι τινα. — (Orig. contr. Cels. Lib. vi. p. 291. Cantab. 1658). A Jewish writer, quoted by Hyde, (Hist. Relig. Vet. Per. Cap. xxix.) declares that the Persians call their Priests (in the plural) *Chaberin*, (or *Khaberin*) פרסיים קורין לכומרין חברין, whilst the singular חבר

when some of them began to be affected by the principles of Sufiism, and when they erroneously viewed all the different forms of religion as nearly upon a point of equality, and inward contemplation as independent of outward profession, they may have occasionally taken a more indulgent, though not a more correct, view of the ancient Persians. Firdausí, * the author of the Sháhnámah, is represented by Edal Dáru as writing of them thus: —

مپندار کاتش پرستان بد ند   پرستندهٔ پاک یزدان بد ند

That is to say, "Think not that they were fire-worshippers; they were the worshippers of the holy God." This passage, as it is here given, I have not found in the Sháhnámah, But much dependence cannot be placed on the manuscripts of that work. "They differ from one another," as observed by Sir William Ouseley, "in every part of the Sháhnámah, and exhibit such a variety of readings, as would weary the most patient and persevering drudge who should undertake to collate several copies of a work, comprising more than one hundred and twenty thousand lines." Speaking of Kai-Khosru, and his maternal uncle, Firdausí, however, says: —

ایک هفته در پیش یزدان بد ند   مپندار کاتش پرستان بد ند
که اتش بدانگه مهراب بود   پرستنده را دیده پر اب بود
اگرچند ت اندیشه با شد دراز   هم از پاک یزدان نه بي نیاز

"They were a whole week before God; think not that they were the worshippers of fire, because fire was a conspicuous object at that time. The eyes of the worshippers were full of tears. If thou hast got so much thought, then [thou wilt

Chaber or *Khaber*, (occurring in the Talmud), is explained by Hebrew commentators, as signifying פרסאי *Parsái*, or Persians. On this subject Hadrian Reland has offered some remarks, in Dissert. ix. de Persicis Talmudicis. (See his 'Dissert. Miscell. Part. ii. p. 297. Traj. ad Rhen. 1706). Dr. Hyde, however, as above cited, thinks that *Chaber* or *Chaver*, denoted both a priest and a layman; any person 'modo sit hujus religionis; namque non notat Persam gente sed Persam religione; nec statum civilem spectat.'" Ouseley's Travels, vol. i, pp. 105, 106.

* Firdausi was born in the year of Christ, 946.

see that] thou art not independent of the glorious God." The poet does not apply this description, it is to be observed, to *all* the ancient Persian kings and heroes ; and even if he did, there would still be left room for his idea, that Zoroaster was actually the patron of the fire-worshippers.* The assertion which it makes, is altogether inconsistent with the particular statements of Firdausi. Some of the oldest Persian kings, he expressly declares to have been fire-worshippers. When speaking of Hoshang, the grandson of Kaiomars, the first king of the Peshdadian dynasty, who, as mentioned in a passage which we shall afterwards quote, is said to have first discovered the method of producing fire by friction, he represents him as commanding his subjects to reckon it the " divine glory, " and to give it the highest worship, or "*parastish.* " The passage is given in full by Edal Dáru, when he sets forth the glory of fire in the *Maujazát-i-Zartusht*. Firdausí also, after having mentioned the erection of the city Dáráb-gird, by Dáráb, proceeds as follows: —

یا کہ اتش افروخت از تیغ کوہ　　پرستندہ آزر آمد گروہ
زهر پیشہ کارگر هاستدند　　همہ شهر از ایشان بیارستدند

" He then kindled a fire on the summit of a mountain. The *worshippers-of-fire* came in crowds ; and they procured the most skilful artists of every kind, by whom the whole city was adorned."

The testimonies which we have now brought forward, prove that the Persians have from time immemorial been addicted to the worship of the elements, and particularly of fire. Had the practice, however, been a mere matter of history, we should not have adverted to it with this particularity. But it is a melancholy fact, that to this day, fire and the other elements are regularly regarded as objects of worship and reverence, by the followers of Zoroaster. The following extracts from the work of Edul Dáru, the chief priest of the Rasamís, their larger sect, while they reveal the existence of the feeling of a certain degree of shame on account of what is done, clearly unfold the sacred importance which they attach to fire,

* See extract from Firdausi in Chapter viii.

and the service which they render, to it. I give a literal translation of what he has written on the subject.

[1]. — " We Zoroastrians reckon fire, and the moon, and other glorious objects filled with splendour and light, centres-of-worship (*kibláh*) ; and in their presence we stand upright and practise worship (*bandagí*), for the most High God has declared that they are *his* glory. On this account, the sun and fire are the divine glory (*khudái-nur*); and it is fit that at the time of worship (*bandagí* and *àbádat*) such glorious objects should be considered a kibláh.

[2]. — "And it ought to be known, that over every object in earth or in the heavenly worlds created by God, there is a glorious angel appointed to preside, and exercise superintendence. For example, Khurshíd Izad is over the sun ; Mohor Izad, the moon ; over the soil, is Aspandarmad Amsháspand ; over fire, Ardebehisht Amsháspand ; over water, A′wā Izad ; over air, Gowad Izad ; over rain, Teshtar Tír Izad ; over trees, Amardád; over cattle, Bahman Amsháspand. In this way they preside and superintend, and in this way God has committed all these objects wholly to the charge of angels. Wherefore, when reciting the Zand-Avastá, they praise these objects of the universe, it ought to be certainly known that they praise the angels who preside over them.

" I give a proof of this from the Zand-Avastá, by writing below the báj [the muttering] which we use when we sit down to eat, along with its meaning :— *

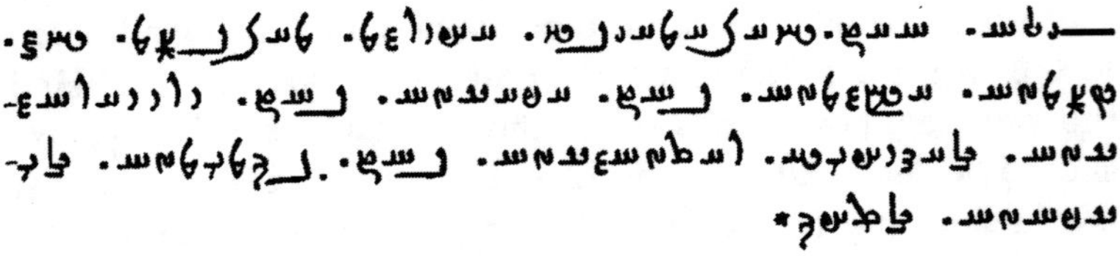

— ***Ithá áaţ yazamaidê Ahurĕm-Mazdãm, yé gãmchá ashĕmchá dáţ, apaçchá dáţ, urúaráoçchá vanguhís raochâoçchá dáţ, búmímchá viçpáchá vóhú.*** [***ashem vóhú***]. :—

* The dastur gives this in the Gujarátí character. I have substituted the original Zand, for the sake of precision. The passage occurs at the commencement of the fifth Há of the Yaçna. It is also given in the commencement of the Khurdah-Avastá.

"—' Here, in this manner, I worship (*árádhunch*) (that is glorify and remember) Hormazd, by whom the cattle and the *asoí* [purity], (that is Bahman Amsháspand, and Ardebehísht, who is even over the *asoí*,) have been created, and by whom the water has been created, and the good vegetation and the light have been created, and the earth and all that gives delight (*ná'mat*) from first to last have been created.— This Lord, in this place, I remember, and glorify; and I praise him for this pleasant food which he has given to me.' *

"Now, according to the above-mentioned proof, it is evident that there is an angel presiding over every object in the world. Consequently, when in the course of reciting the Avastá, there is the praise of any object, there is the praise of the angel, who presides over that object. This ought to be rightly understood; and also it ought to be known, that when the angel is praised, Dádár Hormazd, the creator of that angel, is praised. This ought certainly to be recognized, for there is no doubt of it.

[3.] — " Concerning this matter, I give another proof:— 'The reason of making light and fire a centre-of-worship (*kibláh*) is, that whatever under the first heaven is created in this world, is made from the four elements — fire, and air, and water, and earth. Therefore, there are four substances particularly glorious, from which even all men are created. Of these, fire is particularly brilliant, and pure, and pregnant-with-light, and consequently, fire is several times superior to air, water, and earth, and on account of this superiority, it is quite right that fire-temples should be made, and the fire esteemed a centre-of-worship; and in like manner it is even

* The passages within parentheses are so given by Edal Dáru. An exact verbal translation of the Zand is the following:—" Here, in-this-manner, I worship Hormazd who has created [or given] both cattle, and the purity [on which they feed], and created water, and created vegetation, and the good light, and the earth, and all delight." *Ashem Vohu* are the catch words of another short *báj*, which follows. The references by the dastur to the Amsháspand, it will be observed, are in this instance *mere interpolations*!

more proper that the heavenly bodies, as the sun and moon, should be esteemed centres-of-worship.' So much is taken out of the Shâristán.

[4].—"Moreover, I give another proof. There is an honnorable fire, which either *manifestly*, or *secretly*, exercises superintendence and preservation over the body of man. That fire, in the language of the Avastá, is called *atarem vohu farianem*; * and in the Pahlivi and Pázand † languages, *átish vohu farián*; and in the Arabic language *gharezí* and *harárati gharezí*. ‡ From the blessing of that fire, every man lives, for to all the food which he eats, and the drink which he takes, that fire imparts heat. It also is the power which imparts the hunger, which succeeds eating. As long as that fire, possessed of light and heat, remains in the body of men, he preserves the ability of living, and remains comfortable; and when the heat of this invisible fire goes out of a man, then the appetite for eating and drinking is stopt and the hope of living is lost. Now a sensible view ought to be taken of the fact, that the venerable fire which is found within a man, imparting this power, confers happiness, and day and night is the cause of man's life, as long as it is not separated from him; and it keeps man in happiness as long as he lives. And the fire which *manifestly* exercises superintendence, is that which forwards the works of the whole human race during the night. From its assistance, for example, meetings are held at night, and there is eating and drinking and enjoyment. All this is from the blessing of light. And even during the day, for all eating and cooking, and for putting away the cold and damp of snow from the body of man, it unfailingly communicates heat, and activity. And

* Here the dastur uses the accusative for the nominative. His language approaches that of the Bundéshné, which professes to describe all the different kinds of fire. See Gujarátí translation of Bundéshné, pp. 310—344.

† There is no such distinctive language as the Pázand. It is the explanatory language written along with, or underneath, the Zand,—Pahlivi, Persian, or whatever else it may be.

‡ Literally, latent heat.

besides, the arts and handicrafts, the making new inventions, and projections and trades followed by men, are practised through the blessing of this venerable fire, and every thing requiring heat is performed through the help of this fire. Moreover, the excellence of this fire in behalf of man is very great. Wherefore it is proper that this venerable fire should be made a *kibláh.* There are many proofs of the matter, which if I were to give, there would be prolixity. I only briefly give a few proofs from the Avastá.

[5] — "Now, I give a testimony about making the holy fire a kibláh from the Avastá. In the *Ardebehisht Yast* of the Avastá, Dádár Hormazd represented to the honorable Zoroaster to this effect ; — 'It is proper to make my Ardebehisht a kibláh.' I write the passage below, along with its meaning : — *

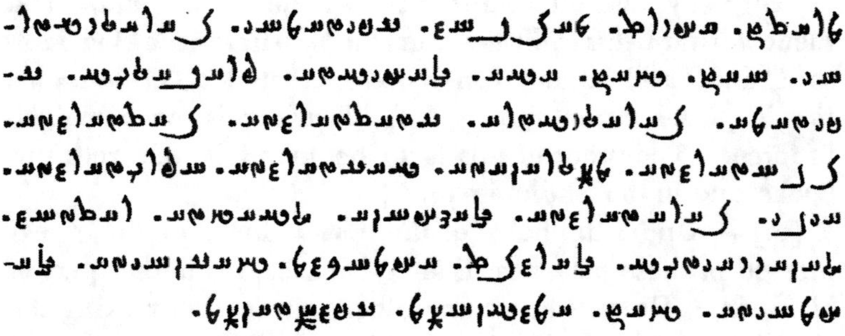

— *Mraot̰ Ahuró-Mazdáo çpitamái Zaraṯhustrái, A'at̰ yat̰ asa vahista fradathís çpitama Zaraṯhustra çṯaotarěcha zaotarěcha zbátarěcha mãthranacha yaçtarěcha áfrítarěcha aibi zaratarěcha vanghána kẖsaêta raochâo kẖanavaitís varězó ahmákěm yaçnáicha vahmáicha yat̰ aměsnãm-spěñtanãm :* —

— " 'Hormazd said to Spitaman [the exalted] Zoroaster (that is to me who am Spitaman Zoroaster), I have created the exalted and the just (that is, Ardebehisht) worthy of praise, and worthy of being made a *kibláh,* (that is, worthy of being

* As in a former instance, I substitute the Zand letters for the Gujaráti of the dastur.

served by a person standing upright in its presence,) and worthy of being remembered, and worthy of having the Avastá language read and obeyed, and worthy of adoration, and worthy of the *áfrins*, and worthy of being raised aloft, (that is, exalted), and worthy of having a glorious, excellent, and brilliant place made ; likewise worthy of the Izashné, and worthy of the *Niáísh.* — Such are the Amsháspands, and my Ardebehisht Amsháspand is of them.' *

" According to the preceding testimony from the Avastá, the Ardebehisht is a kibláh ; and in this manner respecting the other Izads and Amsháspands, the order was given by Dádar Hormazd to the exalted Zoroaster, that they should be adored and praised. This doubtless ought to be known. And it ought to be known, that from the time of the Peshdádian king Hoshang, and according to the order of the most High God to Hoshang, he formed *atish-khánahs* [fire-temples] in every city, and ordered that fire should be a *kibláh*, and thenceforward this right law remained. Afterwards king Jamshíd and Faridún and Kai-Khosru erected *atish-khánahs*, that is, places for enthroning fire. Their regulations remained in force. The proof of this is to be found in our religious books, and in the Sháhnámah. "†

[6.] — Under the belief of the " sacredness of fire," expressed in these passages, Edal Dáru asks, in another part of his work, " Do you know any other warrants for making the sacred fire a kibláh ?" And he gives the following reply : —

" Yes, I know that in the Sháhnámah of the poet Firdausí of Tus, Hoshang, the son of Saiámuk, went out with the sages of his court to walk in the direction of a mountain. Suddenly he saw a serpent at a great distance. It immediately made an attack upon Hoshang, who instantly lifted up a large stone with which to kill it, when the serpent having

* It will be observed, from the remarks on part of this passage, afterwards given in this chapter, that I have some objections to this translation. The quotation is a very important one, and a critical investigation of some of the words here used as expressive of religious honour, will be found in our fifth chapter.

† Tálim-i-Zartusht, pp. 14—21.

leapt and ran away, hid itself in the grass. The stone having been smashed upon another stone, both flew into pieces; and from the midst of them the light of fire became manifest, and from it all the dried grass and sticks were burned, and the fire blazed with light. Upon this the holy Sarosh Izad, having come from concealment, gave orders to king Hoshang to this effect: — O exalted king, make this glorious fire a *kibláh*, for the fire is divine in its glory (*nur-i-khudáí.*) Hoshang having heard this, gave thanks and praise to the most High God in his temple, because his glorious fire was given to him as a kibláh. Then at this time, he enthroned fire at the place of a kibláh, and commanded every person, as follows: — *This fire is the glory of God, wherefore it is necessary to worship it*, (*parastish kidhí joie.*)'* At that time king Hoshang instituted a great festival, and having made a great rejoicing, he established the festival under the name of the *Jasan-i-Saddah.* In this manner having made fire a kibláh, the directions which he gave about attending to it have been observed till the present time." †

In this passage Edal Dáru, as will be afterwards shown, has used considerable liberty with the Sháhnámah. A similar extract is given by Dosabháí from the *Shárístán*, to which we shall also subsequently advert.

There are a few other passages in the chief-priest's work, which throw additional light on the Pársí fire-worship, and which I insert, before making any comment on his opinions.

[7.]— "The fourth glorious and grand object given to the exalted Zoroaster [when he was said to be in heaven], was the fire named *A'dar-burjín-Meher.* So wonderful was this fire, that it blazed of itself without fuel; and it had no need of a human servant to make it burn with brilliancy. Nothing could do it harm, that is to say, neither fire nor earth could injure it; and from throwing earth and water upon it, it blazed with great brilliancy." ‡

[8.]—" Afterwards, Ardebehisht Amsháspand, having ap-

* These are the Gujarátí words used by the dastur.

† Maujazát-i-Zartusht, pp. 24, 25. ‡ Maujazát-i-Zartusht, p. 63.

proached the holy Zoroaster said to him, Convey my message to king Gushtásp to this effect : —'I have committed to you the charge of the fire of every place. Wherefore, in every city and place-of-abode, erect *átish-khánahs,* that is places for its residence, and grant a settled provision for its support, and appoint Mobeds for perpetually guarding it, and also for nourishing it, for *fire is produced from the glory of God.* And thou knowest well that at every instant it is useful to the whole population of the world, and no person can do without it, and he who always places fuel and odoriferous articles upon it, will always remain young, and never become old. It reveals to man the property of every thing. If thou wilt place sweet-smelling articles upon it, it will emit sweet odours ; but if thou wilt place bad smelling odours upon it, it will emit bad odours. From this my fire, the pain and suffering from cold, damp, and shivering, is removed. Besides, in it there are many benefits. In the same manner that the holy Providence hath placed fire under my charge, I place it under thy charge, O Zartusht. Wherefore, advise all the inhabitants of the world in my name, to this effect : — Serve, and preserve fire. If you do not act according to my counsel, then the most High God will be displeased with you. "*

[9.] " The wonders of the *A'dar-burjín-Meher* are these. When any person took that fire into his hand, it was not burned. The exalted Zartusht having taken it into his hand, put it on the hand of Gushtásp, † and the hand of Gushtásp was not burned. Gushtásp put it into the hands of his wazír Jamásp [the minister of Gushtásp], and the hand of Jamásp was not burned. In this way, Jamásp put it into the hands of all the nobles who were present in the royal company ; but its heat affected none of them. [Here follows a passage in almost the same words as those given above.] Another wonder of this fire was, that when the religion of Zoroaster was spreading in the

* Maujazát-i-Zartusht, pp. 64, 56. The dastur is here, with some alterations, following the Zartusht-Námah.

† It was in the reign of Gushtásp, supposed to be Darius Hystaspes, that Zoroaster lived.

world, and king Gushtásp went to the country of Jabulistán where the hero Rustam was residing, for the purpose of embracing it, and when he had resided there for a long period, Arjásp the grandson of Afrásiáb the king of Turkistán, having obtained leisure and opportunity, came into the country of Irán to make war, and wished from hatred and enmity to destroy the good faith. A considerable time before this, on a certain day, king Lohrásp was engaged in adoring the fire A′dar-búrjín-Meher, when this concealed voice came forth from the light, 'O Lohorásp, hear, consider this my word, you have served me in a very excellent manner. Upon your body great trouble and labour have come; you have to fight with your enemies; the war is such that you will be forced to hold the sword, and through fear you will fail to remember God.' In this manner, an invisible voice came out from the glory of the fire; and in this manner the holy fire foretold to Lohrásp the war of Arjásp the Turkí.

"But some persons will say that the exalted Zartusht had applied some medicament to his hand, and that on this account the heat of the fire did not affect him. The reply is this:— Consider, according to your excellent wisdom, the exalted Zartusht first took the fire into his hand, and gave it into the hand of the king Gushtásp; and Gushtásp gave it to his wazír Jamásp; and Jamásp gave it into the hand of the other nobles who were present in the royal company; and nevertheless the hand of no one was burned! It is certain that king Gushtásp and his nobles, applied no medicament to their hands or bodies, and had no necessity to apply medicaments, because they did not wish to oppose the plea of the prophet. Since their hands were not burned, it undoubtedly appears that God gave fire to the exalted Zoroaster with such properties, that a distinguished prophetical mission might be manifest to the world.

[10.] — "Moreover, I give a testimony about this fire from the Sháhnámah. In the Sháhnámah it is written, that the exalted Zartusht was a prophet from God. In the days of king Gushtásp, an altar with a splendent fire was brought from the presence of God, and the name of that fire was *A'dar-burjín-Meher.*"*

Such are the explanations, and confessions, and attempted vindication of the honours rendered to fire by the Pársís, which have been lately set forth by the gentleman occupying the highest position in its priesthood, and at the pecuniary charge of the most wealthy individual of their community. Dosabháí, the advocate of the pancháyat, writes on the subject with a great deal more caution, but with a great deal more disingenuousness and inconsistency.

We find him, indeed, giving the most contradictory accounts of the matter, and at the same time actually establishing the very charge which he professes to be anxious to repel. When scolding Dhanjibháí Nauroji, for accusing the Pársís of fire-worship, he mentions * that they view them merely as a *kibláh*, or centre-of-worship, and "visible symbols of the invisible God." He then brings in Gibbon to support his theory; and while he quotes the passage from that author which we have already given, in which it is said that the Persians consider, "the elements, and more particularly Fire, Light, and the Sun, whom they called Mithra, as *objects of religious reverence*," he gets afraid, as we have seen, to translate the passage aright, and actually renders the words which we have marked in italics by *dín dharmno keblo*, [religious *kibláh*.] He forgets all this scrupulosity and evasion, however, in subsequent parts of his work. In order, as he thinks, to evince that Dhanjibhái perverts the second commandment written on the tablets given to Moses, when he applies it to the Pársí treatment of fire, he says that the commandment refers only to images "made by the *hand of man*," ‡ and thus shows that the Pársís view fire, and the other supposed elements, in a light which would be condemned by the second commandment, if it had, as it assuredly has, a more extensive meaning, and is applicable to the worship of the works of

* Maujazát-i-Zartusht, pp. 71—73.

† Tálim-i-Zartusht, p. 18.

* Tálím-i-Zartusht, p. 15.

‡ Tálim-i-Zartusht, p. 20.

God as well as to the works of man.* Afterwards, when replying to his own question, "Why do you, professing to acknowledge only one God, honour fire, and water, and the moon and the sun, and call fire the *Son of God*, and water and the earth, the *Daughters of God*," he presents us with some statements similar to those which we have already quoted from Edal Dáru. "As fire," he says, "and water, and the moon, and sun, &c., have been created, so over each of them an angel has been appointed to preside. As for instance, Ardebehisht is over fire; Khurdád, over water; Khúr, over the sun; Mahbokhtar, over the moon; and other angels, over other objects of the world, presiding and superintending, and to be adored. So we do adore (árădhunch) the glorious angels, and according to the commandment of God, repeat the A'tish [Fire] Níáísh, and the A'wă [Water] Níáísh, and the Khurshíd [Sun] Níáísh, and the Mah [Moon) Níáísh; we honour not fire, nor water, nor the sun, nor the moon. We reckon them our kibláh. In the same any that the Musalmáns, when they worship, turn their faces to the Ká'bá, so we reckon the brilliant angels a kibláh. And the explanation of the fact that in our Zand-Avastá fire is called the Son of Hormazd, and the earth and water, the Daughters of Hormazd, is this, that an object created by God is his offspring. Wherefore, we worship the angel that is over that object. What, do you not acknowledge the angels, of whom it is said in the Bible, in various places, that they appeared to Christ and to Mary, &c"? In a subsequent part of his work, p. 11, he endeavours, on the authority of some author, whose name he does not give, to prove that there is a connection between the Pársí religion and Free-Masonary, and quotes, amongst others, this passage: "To come then at once to the point, Masonry (as it appears from the customs, ceremonies, hieroglyphics, and chronology of Masonry) is derived from, and is

* In the fifth book of Moses, it is thus written: — "Take ye therefore good heed. . . . lest thou lift up thine eyes unto heaven, and when thou seest the sun, the moon, and the stars, even all the host of heaven, shouldest be driven to worship them and serve them, which the Lord thy God hath divided unto all nations under the whole heaven." Deut. iv: 15, 19.

the remains of, the religion of the ancient Druids, who like the ☞ Magi of Persia and the priests of Heliopolis in Egypt were priests of the Sun.* ☞ They paid worship to this great luminary, as the great visible agent of a great invisible first cause, whom they styled time-without-limits." This statement he reckons a sufficient answer to the remark in the 18th page † of my Lecture on the Vandidád:—"The Pársí looks up to the heavens, and having perceived the great light which God has given to enlighten the path of man, he presents it with his adorations. He forgets that it has no life. He acts just as absurdly as any man would do, who instead of going to the Governor with a petition, should go and pray to the lamp which is burning on his table." He afterwards, however, returns, ‡ to the passage now quoted from my lecture, and its context; and in reply to the charge which it brings against the Pársís, he says, "We reckon the sun a glorious object created by God, and a visible sign of the invisible Lord. The name of the angel who is over it is *Khúr*; in the Burhán-i-Kátagh dictionary *khúr* means a symbol; §" and he adds, ‖ "We say that an angel is the glory of the most high God, and we honour and worship God's glory and his [the angel's] glory, which is right and proper." In the 158th page of his work, he says "Fire is the glory of God, wherefore in the Zand-Avastá it is figuratively called the Son of God." In the 160th page, he quotes a passage from the *Sháristán* respecting Hoshang, similar to that which Edul Dáru professes to quote from the *Sháhnamáh*. In page 163, he says, "In the Vandidád, it is truly written that the master of a house should reverence the fire given by Hormazd; but this fire is the presiding angel *Ardebehisht* or *A'dar*, whom we reverence; for fire is the meaning of the word *ádar*, or *ázar*; and the angel who is over fire is called *A'dar* or *A'zar*. . . . Look to the Burhán-i-Kátagh and you will be convinced that

* These hands directing attention to this passage, are those of Dosabhái.

† Dosabhái quotes it as the fourteenth.

‡ p. 126.

§ I do not find this to be the case.

‖ p. 128

this is the meaning." All these passages, — some of which are not very consistent with one another, — show anxiety on the part of Dosabhái to vindicate the Pársís from the charge of fire-worship, while they evince also, that he wishes fire, and the angels who are said to preside over it, to be received with holy reverence. It will be seen from the quotations which we have already introduced from Edal Dáru, how far he differs from that dastur. Both of them are more disinclined to admit the absolute fire-worship of the Pársís than many of their countrymen.

Aspandiárjí is, if possible, still more ashamed of the manner in which the elements are treated by his friends and by himself, when he officiates in the *átishgáh.* He says that "the sun, moon, and fire, are viewed in the Pársí religion in no other light than that of a Kibláh."[*] He quotes some passages from the Avastá in which he thinks that the elements are said to be *created* ; but these passages have nothing to do with the *worship* of the elements, except as suggesting a reason for its condemnation to all but genuine Zoroastrians, who hold that the elements are made of the essential glory of God, and who give to God himself the name of [illegible] *A'tars* or FIRE,[†] and to a priest the name of [illegible] *A'thrava* or FIREMAN.[‡]

I have just said that the Pársí controversialists are more disinclined to admit the elemental worship of their tribe, than many of their countrymen. In connexion with this assertion, I cannot withhold the following important testimonies, belonging both to ancient and modern times, which must satisfy every considerate mind.

Dastur Aspandiárjí Kámdínjí of Baroch, in his controversial work entitled the *Kadím Tárikh Párshioní Kasar,* published at Surat so late as 1826, in his translation of the Sanskrit *shlokas* said to have been presented to the Hindú Ráná at Sanján, where they first landed in Gujarát, broadly represents

* Hádí-i-Gum-Rahán, p. 44.

† The Hundred and One Names of God, No. 54.

‡ Vandidád, passim.

them as અગનીની પુજાના કરનારા "*agniní pujáná karanárá*," or *Fire-worshippers* * He could not have done otherwise, as the first *shloka* clearly mentions their elemental worship, and that even before their worship of Hormazd : —

—सूर्यं ध्यायंति ये वै हुतवहमनिलं भूमिमाकाशमाद्यं तोयेशं पंचतत्वं त्रिभुवनसदनं न्याशष्मंत्रैस्त्रिसंध्यां श्री होर्मज्दं सुरेशं बहुगुणगरिमाणं तमेकं कृपालुं गौरा धीराः सुवीरा बहुबलनिलयास्ते वयं पारसीकाः १

— "They who worship the sun, fire, wind, earth, ether, water, — the five principal elements, the three worlds, three times a day, through the *Niáish mantras*, and [who worship] the divine Hormazd the chief of the *Suras* (angels), the greatly endowed, the exalted, the compassionate one, are we, the fair, the bold, the heroic, the powerful, the Pársís." The eleventh shloka also alludes to their "Worship of the Sun," or as Kámdín has it *surajní pújá*. The twelfth refers also to their worship of all the elements, even placing it, as in other instances, before that of Hormazd.

In the *Kissah-i-Sanján*,† the principal document in the hands of the Pársís detailing the particulars of the arrival of their ancestors in India, and composed by a priest of Nausárí in the year A. D. 1590, it is said that the Pársí exiles when off Sanján, the place where they first settled in Gujarát, escaped from a dreadful storm.

ز ایمن اتش بهرام فیروز

— "By the blessing of the *fire of Běhrám* the victorious." In the same work, they are set forth as expressly declaring themselves to be fire-worshippers to Jádé [Jayadeva ?], the Hindú Ráná of the place, when they solicited from him the liberty of settling in his country. The whole of what passed between the chief Mobed who represented them, and the prince to whose protection they looked, is worthy of attention. I here give it a place in the original Persian, with a plain trans-

* See the Kadím Táríkh, pp. 129, 130.

† Of this little work a translation, I believe, will soon be published by Lieut. E. B. Eastwick.

lation, marking the passages which more immediately refer to the subject at present under discussion.

من اول بیذم ارین دین شمایان   ازان پس جای تان سازیم مایان
دیگر آنکه زبان ملک خود را   گزارندش که بد هیم ماوا
گبان شهر ایران دور دارند   زبان ملک هندی را بر آرند
سدیگر انکه از پوشش زناهان   بپوشد چو زنان ما زا نهان
چهارم آنکه این آلات و شمشیر   کشایند و نه بندند هیچ جا گیر
به پنجم چونکه کار خیر فرزند   کنند آن شامگه کابین به بندند
زر این قول شما اول بود راست   بشهر من شما را جای و ماواست

چو دستور این همه راز از رای بشنید
بناچار این همه گفتار بگزید

ازان پس گفت باوی موبد سر   زدین گویم شنوی رای پرویر
در اینجا مشو خود دلگیر از ما   زما خود نیاید بدی هرگز در اینجا
همه هندوستانرا یار باشیم   سر خصمانت را هر جا بپاشیم
یقین دانی که ما یزدان پرستیم   برای دین از در دندان پرستیم
همه بگذاشتیم از هرچه بوده   بره بسیار دشواری نموده

همیدون خان مان ملکت و رخت
همه بگذاشتیم ای شه نکوبخت

غریبانیم ما از تخم جمشید   ادب داریم از مهتاب و خورشید
سدیگر کاو را با آب و آتش   نکو میدارمش از کای ناتش
پرستش میکنیم از آتش و آب   همان از کاو خورشید و مهتاب

خدا در دهر هرچه آفرید ست
نمازش می بریم او خود گزید ست

همان کستی ما هفتاد و دو تار   ببندیم و بخوانیم با دل ابرار
زنانهای که او دستان نشیند   بخورشید و سما و مه نه بیند
هم از اب و هم از اتش بود دور   زیرا کان بود از خاصه نور
ز هر چیزی کند پرهیز بسیار   بروز روشن و اندر شب تار
نشیند تاکه زود ستان شود دور   چو شوید سر به بیند آتش و هور
دیگر آن زن که او فرزند زاید   چهل روزش همی پرهیز باید
چنان پرهیز شاید چونکه دستان   بپرهیزد نشاید خوار و گردان
ز زن فرزند اندک مه که آید   ازان فرزند کو مرده بزاید
ندهد هر جای رود یا او بتازد   ا باکس گفتگو میهم نسازد

همان زن نیز با پرهیز بسیار   چهل و یکروز بنشیند در ینکار
دگر هر چه کە رسم و راه بودە   هە در پیش او یکیک نمودە

—"First, let us know the faith that is yours; after that we shall make a place ready for you. The next condition is, that in order to remain here, you leave off the language of your country, that you give up the language of Irán, and acquire the language of Hind. The third condition regards the dress of women, which must be like that of our women. Fourthly these weapons and these swords must be unopened and unworn in any place. Fifthly, when a child is married, the marriage procession must be at night. If these conditions are accepted by you, my city is open for your reception. When the dastur heard all these things from the Ráí (prince,) being without resource he accepted the proposals. Then the chief Mobed thus addressed him, "Listen, O wise prince, to what I relate of our faith. Be not thou afraid of us; no evil will accrue from us in this place. We shall be friends to all Hindustán. We will scatter the heads of your enemies in every place. Be assured that we are the worshippers of Yazdān. On account of our faith have we fled from the unbelievers [the Musalmáns]; we have abandoned all our possessions; we have encountered many difficulties by the way; house, and land, and possessions, all we have abandoned. O prince of excellent fortune, we are the poor descendants of Jamshíd. *We give reverence* (adab dárem) *to the moon and sun. Three other things we hold in estimation* (nekú medáram,) *the cow, water, and fire. We worship* (parastish mekunam) *fire and water; also the cow, the sun, and moon.* Whatever God has created in the world, we bear worship to it (*namázash mebarem.*) This *kusti* (cincture) composed of seventy-two threads, we bind on with a heart full of gladness. Our wives when they are in their courses *look not on the sun, nor on the skies, nor on the moon. From fire and water, they remain at a distance, since those things are of the essence of glory.* From all things they carefully ab-

* Kissah-i-Sanján, Author's M.S, pp. 12, 13.

stain in the light of day and the darkness of night; they abstain till their courses are completed. *When they have purified themselves, they look on fire and on the sun.* Moreover, the woman who bears a child must observe restriction forty days, the same restriction as a woman in her courses; and she must remain retired and in seclusion. When a woman bears a child before her time is fulfilled, she is not permitted to go abroad or move out; nor is she allowed to converse with any one. That woman must observe a strict abstinence; forty-one days must she therein abide. And whatever besides were their observances and rites, the same did the dastur recite to the Rájá."

The Pársís gave a similar account of themselves to the English who particularly examined into their creed, when they first came into contact with them in India. Mr Lord represents a Dastur as saying, that "Forasmuch as fire was delivered to Zartusht their lawgiver, from God Almighty, who pronounced it to be His virtue and His excellency, and that there was a law delivered for the worship of this fire, confirmed by so many miracles, that therefore they should hold it in holy reverence, and worship it as a part of God, who is of the same substance; and that they should love all things that resemble it, or were like unto it, as the sun and moon which proceeded from it." *

In the *Zartusht-Námah,* which I criticize at length in the eighth chapter of this work, and a translation of which is given in full in the appendix (A), there are many direct intimations of, and unequivocal references to, the elemental worship of the Pársís. The writer of the Persian copy in my possession, made two hundred years ago, declares himself to be *parastár átish wa Behrám,* a "worshipper of fire and Behrám."†

If in times later than those to which these notices refer, the Pársís have given contrary representations of their religious

* Lord's Discovery of the Banians and Pársís, in Pinkerton's Voyages and Travels, vol. vii, p. 506.

† Zartusht-Námah, author's MS., last page.

opinions, it is only because of the consciousness of shame, produced by the light reflected from a Christian community. Though they may have misled some travellers, who have made little inquiry into their religious doctrines and practices, they have to this day most diligently continued the adoration of the elements and heavenly bodies in the manner which will immediately be noticed, and endeavoured, when pressed on the subject, to vindicate, like the controversialists now before us, the religious reverence which they have extended to these the sacred objects of their regard.

But I must now proceed to comment on the extracts which I have made from the works of Edal Dáru and Dosabháí. I shall offer my remarks on the different considerations which they have brought before our notice with reference as far as possible to the order of arrangement which they themselves have adopted. I indulge the sincere hope, and offer up the earnest prayer to God, that the Pársís who may attentively and candidly peruse what I have to present to their reason and conscience, will clearly see that their sacred books and religious teachers, have fallen into the most foolish, but at the same time grievous and dangerous mistakes, respecting the nature of fire and the other elements, and are guilty of the greatest sin against that God who has declared that he will not give His glory to another, whenever they act according to the directions of these books.

1.* Both Edal Dáru and Dosabháí "reckon fire and the sun, and moon, and other glorious objects filled with splendour and light" "to be produced from the glory of God," and to be literally the "*glory of God*;" and in doing this, as has been already seen and will yet appear, they do not go beyond their sacred books. This, however, is not their character. *Light* is only the *work* of God; and however wonderful it may be, — whether it be matter, or a state of matter,—it has *nothing of a divine nature*, and forms *no part of the divine substance*. It has neither intelligence, nor sensation, nor life.

* The divisions which follow correspond with those which I have used in bringing forward the opinions of the dasturs.

Combustion, in which the Pársís so much rejoice, when they try to promote it by odoriferous fuel, every one of them who has studied chemistry knows, is caused merely by a union of substances having strong attraction for each other, and which during their combination evolve heat and light ; and most frequently it arises from the combination of any body with oxygen. *Flame,* which the Pársís view as the most intense glory of God, is merely gas or vapour heated to a temperature sufficiently high to become luminous. God is present where light is absent. It is subject to motion and change and even extinction ; but God is the same yesterday, to-day, and forever. Though in the language of man, light may be figuratively referred to as illustrating the glory of God, it does not constitute that glory. When the objects in which it is most apparent are contemplated in their greatest splendour, let their *Maker* be addressed in the language of the Psalmist : — " Of old hast *thou* laid the foundation of the earth, and the heavens are the work of thy hands : they shall perish, but *thou* shalt endure ; yea all of them shall wax old like a garment : as a vesture shalt *thou* change them, and they shall be changed, but *thou* art the same, and thy years shall have no end."*

2. The existence and ministry of *angels,* Christians of course allow ; but they *neither attribute to them divine works, nor confer upon them divine honours.* They represent them as the humble, and cheerful, and obedient *servants* of God, and *not his associates* who participate in his praise and honour. They hold, that though he employs them in the fulfilment of his counsels and the execution of his commands, he himself, from the necessity of his own nature, and the absolute dependence of every object which exists on his power and goodness, sees all, upholds all, and directs all, for the accomplishment of his own purposes, and the manifestation of his own glory. They view God himself as the universal Sovereign, who doeth " according to his will in the armies of heaven and amongst the inhabitants of the earth."

* Psalm cii : 25 — 27.

His providence they consider as universal and ever active, extending to every province of nature, to every individual creature, and to every action and event. It comprehends, according to the Scriptures which they receive as true and faithful, all the arrangements and distributions which are made connected with the family of man. God "hath made of one blood all nations of men to dwell on all the face of the earth, and hath determined the times before appointed and the bounds of their habitation; that they should seek the Lord, if haply they might feel after him, and find him, though he be not far from every one of us; for in him we live, and move, and have our being."* His knowledge of our circumstances, is so great, that "he understandeth our thought afar off;"† and "the very hairs of our heads," our most insignificant members, are by him "all numbered."‡ His care extends beyond the human race, and all its diversities; for all the cattle of the fold, all the beasts of the forest, all the fowls of the air, and all the innumerable tenants of the deep, wait upon him that he may give them their meat in due season: that he giveth them, they gather: he openeth his hand, they are filled with good.§ "The earth is satisfied with the fruit of his works."¶ "The heavens," also, "declare the glory of God; and the firmament showeth his handy-work." ‖ These heavens he "stretched forth alone."** His sublime invitation to the children of men is, "Lift up your eyes on high, and behold who hath created these things, that bringeth out their host by number: ‡ he calleth them all by names, by the greatness of his might, for that he is strong in power; not one faileth."†† "No magnitude, however vast, is beyond the grasp of the divinity:" "no minuteness, however shrunk from the notice of the human eye, is beneath the condescension of his regard.‡‡ Men, in their boasted wisdom, have thought that they have exalted God, when they have repre-

* Acts, xvii: 26, 27. † Psalm, cxxxix: 2. ‡ Luke, xii: 7.
§ Psalm, civ: 27, 28. ‖ Psalm, xix: 1. ¶ Psalm, civ: 13.
** Isaiah, xliv: 24. †† Isaiah xl: 26.
‡‡ Chalmers's Astronomical Discourses.

sented him as not himself deigning to uphold the constitution of the universe, and to direct the works of his hands, and when they have attributed the government of the world, and the guardianship of the various departments of nature, to subordinate deities and powers. While they have professed themselves in this way to be wise, however, they have proved themselves, by the imaginations of their heart, to be fools. They have greatly degraded Him whose kingdom is over all; and they have attributed His works and providence to those, who, without his inspection and recognition and continued support, could not be connected even with their humblest movements. They have committed great sin, and they have exposed themselves to great danger, by their unhallowed and presumptuous speculations. I desire to see all who coincide with them in their errors, and especially the Pársís, who have committed every province of nature to the care of the Izads and Amsháspands, to whom we have already referred, awakened to a sense of the perilous situation in which they stand, and led, in the fulness of penitent and devotional hearts, to exclaim, "*Thine*, O Jehovah, is the greatness, and the power, and the glory, and the victory, and the majesty; for all that is in the heaven and the earth is *thine*; *thine* is the kingdom, O Lord, and *thou* art exalted as head above all. Both riches and honour come of *thee*, and *thou* reignest over all; and in *thine hand* is power and might, and in *thine hand* it is to make great and to give strength unto all."*

The Pársí notion of the appointment of Izads and Amsháspands to "preside over and superintend, every object in earth, or in the heavenly world created by God," I beg them to notice, is *irrational and absurd*, as well as impious. It is impossible that created beings can do the work which the Pársís have assigned to them. Take, for example, the case of Khurshíd, and Ardebehisht, and Mohor, and Máhbokhtar, and A'wā who are said to preside over light, and fire, and the firmament, and the moon, and water. What must be their dimensions, what their intelligence, and what their

* I Chronicles xxix: 11, 12.

power, and what their co-operation by consent, before they can fulfil their duties? Do not light and heat come from the sun which is 95,000,000 of miles distant from the earth? and do not light and heat proceed from the sun to Herschel, the most remote planet of the solar system, which is 1800,000,000 miles distant from the sun's disc? Does not light come from the stars, which are countless in number, and the suns of other systems immeasurably distant from our world?* Does Khurshíd cover the whole surface of the sun, from which light proceeds? Is that orb the centre of his being? And does he fill the space which intervenes between the sun and the earth, and the planets, which are still more remote? If his presence is confined to the sun, and if sound travel at the rate of about 1,107 feet in a second, how many years will be required for a Mobed's prayers to reach that luminary? † How many followers of Zoroaster can Khurshíd listen to at the same moment, and regard, without confusion and distraction? Does he know the thoughts, and desires, and purposes of man's heart, in which prayer originates? Does Máhbokhtar borrow from him the light which is reflected from the moon? How does Ardebehisht, who is said to preside over *fire*, divide the sovereignty between Khurshíd, who is declared to be set over *light*? Is there a consultation held between Ardebehisht the Amsháspand of *fire*, A'wā the Izad of *water*, and Mohor the Izad of the *firmament*, when water is to be heated, or boiled, or evaporated, or cooled, or showered down on the earth, or frozen? Or, do Ardebehisht and Mohor combine together to effect all these changes in its state without A'wā's consent? or, do they absolutely make war against him when they are accomplishing them? When *air* enters the lungs, or has its oxygen extracted and consumed by *fire*, or putrefaction, is Mohor the Izad of the *firmament*, perfect-

* Professor Bessel, who thinks that he has discovered the parallax of the star 61 Cygni, estimates its distance, from the earth at 657,700 times that of the sun, which gives the inconceivable distance of 62,481,500,000,000 miles!

† Our hasty calculation gives us somewhat more than fourteen years.

ly satisfied to have it treated in this manner, and so rendered impure? What saith Mohor Izad when a mixture of the two airs, or gases, oxygen and hydrogen, are through an explosion of *fire*, the charge of Ardebehist, entirely stolen from him, and converted into *water*, the charge of A'wā Izad? Is Khurshíd quite pleased when the *light* which he sends forth in straight lines, is refracted and reflected and absorbed by the *atmosphere*, and *water*, and the *earth*? Would the *water* which is taken up to the firmament by *heat*, ever return to the earth in copious and refreshing showers without the *cold*, by which its vapours are condensed, and which the followers of Zoroaster attribute to the devil? Don't *fire*, and *heat*, and *light*, and *water*, and *earth*, mutually act upon one another, according to established laws, which show that they are under the guidance of *one Supreme Ruler*, and not under that of separate superintendents?* These questions, I submit to the intelligent Pársís of Bombay. If they will calmly consider them, and others of a like nature which will readily suggest themselves, we shall hear less than we have been accustomed to do of the doctrine of

* This consideration was pressed on the attention of the Pársís so early as the year of Christ 450. The Christian Armenians at that time, thus addressed the prime minister of Persia. "The four distinct elements exercise alternately the elemental service, and the four are seen, although irrational, still not omitting the duties allotted to them by the will of their Creator, but on the contrary obeying it in reverence according to the order. Behold, easy and manifest to all eyes is the explanation of this simple proposition; for that which is fire is, according to its being and power, mingled with the three other elements : so, for example in stone and in steel we find heat in abundance, less in the air and water, and of itself it never appears. Water is existent of itself, and exists in conjunction with the three other elements: we find it in abundance in the earth, and in smaller quantities in the air and in the fire. The air penetrates fire and water, and by means of water all edible substances. And thus the elements are mixed and combined as a body; their natures are mutually unopposed: they have never taken an hostile position. Whence it is manifest that there is one only Lord who mingleth them, who arranges the objects mingled according to one rule suited to the nature of all things living, and to the enduring existence of the world". — Elisæus's Hist. of Vartan by Neumann, p. 17.

the Avastá, that God has "committed all objects wholly to the charge of angels;" and there will be some hesitation about declaring, that "when reciting the Zand-Avastá, they praise the objects of the universe, they praise the angels who preside over them."

On this latter point, I would again observe, that if an inanimate object is praised as if it had life and intelligence, he to whom it belongs will not thank him who extols it; and I would add, that if an *angel* receive any of the honours which belong to *God*, — if it be said, for instance, that he is present where he is not present, that he can know the thoughts and desires of men's hearts, and that he can hear and answer in heaven the prayers which are offered on earth, and that he can give that help which God alone can bestow, — God who alone is omnipresent, omniscient, and omnipotent, must be greatly displeased.

3. Edal Dáru tells us that "whatever under the first heaven is created in this world, is made from the four elements — fire, and air, water, and earth." He states that fire, the most glorious of these elements, is consequently rightly made a *kibláh*. He is altogether wrong in his philosophy, I tell him; and I call in a Pársí youth to correct his error. The intelligent editor of the useful Gujarátí magazine, the Vidyá-Ságar, in his first number, writes as follows: —

"The ancients have said that in this world there are four elements, — first, fire; second, air; third, earth; and fourth, water; and all things are made from the union of these four substances. They have also said that in these four substances, no other thing is compounded. But the moderns, — the English and other learned men, — say, that air, and water, and earth, are *not* elements, not originally simple substances. Water, for example, is made of two airs (hydrogen and oxygen); atmospheric air is composed of two substances (oxygen and nitrogen); and earth is composed of a great variety of substances. Chemistry informs us that there are 54 elements; and that all the substances which exist in the world are formed from them."

Water and air, many of the Pársí youths in Bombay

have seen decomposed by chemistry. No person, instructed in this science, will speak of fire as an element, or forget that the very soil of the earth is composed of the gases, or airs, as well as other simple substances. The science of Zoroaster and that of the educational institutions in Bombay, do not correspond. Even the plea of "popular language," sometimes available, cannot be urged in favour of Zoroaster; for, as has been seen, he has given to each of the supposed elements, a distinctive angel to preside over it. The doctrine which is here confuted, the dastur tells us, is contained in the *Shâristân*. This does not in the slightest degree support its credit; for the author of that work, though perhaps an accomplished juggler, was but an indifferent chemist. Both Edal Dáru and Dosabhái may depend upon it, that they do not support their cause by referring to it, for neither in a philosophical nor a historical point of view, is it entitled to the slightest attention. Dosabhái, I would remark in passing, has been at the trouble of lithographing a passage from it in the original Persian, giving the reader to wit, from the use which he makes of it as testifying to matters which happened many thousand years ago, that it is a very ancient book. This, however, is not its character. It is quite a modern work, as is known to every orientalist. The late Mulláh Firuz, the most learned Pársí of his day, says "Behram Ferhad, the author of the Sháristání Chár Chamen, flourished in the reign of Akbár, and died about A. D. 1624, in the reign of the emperor Jahángír. This author, who appears to have been a native of Shiráz, though outwardly a Musalmán, was really a Pársí, or rather a disciple of Azer-Keiwán, a philosophical ascetic, who founded a new sect on the foundation of ancient Pársí tenets." *

4. Edal Dáru is not content by saying, that there is an angel who presides over and superintends fire; but he will have it that *fire itself is a superintendent.* He says that "there is an honorable fire, which either *manifestly*, or *secretly*, exercises

* Preface to the Dasátir, p. vii.

superintendence and preservation over the body of man." To this fire, he says, the Avastá has given the name of *atarem vohu farianem*. As to what is acknowledged to be *secret*, we can say but little ; but this we would observe, that what enters the stomach gives heat as well as receives it, and that we have never yet seen a Pársí make a kibláh of his stomach, except by eating and drinking. As to the light and heat which are *manifest*, we think them very important blessings given by God to man, not however that he may serve *them*, and worship *them*, but that they may serve *him*. Let lamps, and torches, and candles, by all means dispel the darkness of night. Let the man shivering from cold approach the fire that he may be warmed, in the same way that a person oppressed with heat should fly to the shade. Let hammers, and chisels, and hatchets, and other tools for labour, be fashioned in the fire. Let the *tapelo*, and *degadi*, and *kadai*, and *lori*, and *kitali*, and other cooking pots, and pans, and kettles, ever rest upon the fire. But, oh! let no rational being speak to it, no prayer be addressed to it, no reverence be tendered to it.

5. Dosabháí, in a passage which we have already quoted, says, the Pársís "honour not fire, nor water, nor the sun, nor the moon ;" and that the fire which the Vandidád commands a master of a house to serve "is the presiding angel, Ardebehisht."

The extracts which we have already given from his own pages, and those of his fellow-controversialist Edal Dáru, will show with what exceptions and limitations his language is to be understood. I most positively deny his assertion ; and refer him in support of my denial to the passages in the eighteenth fargard of the Vandidád, from which I have made extracts in my lecture, but which I shall now present in the original, with a literal translation : —

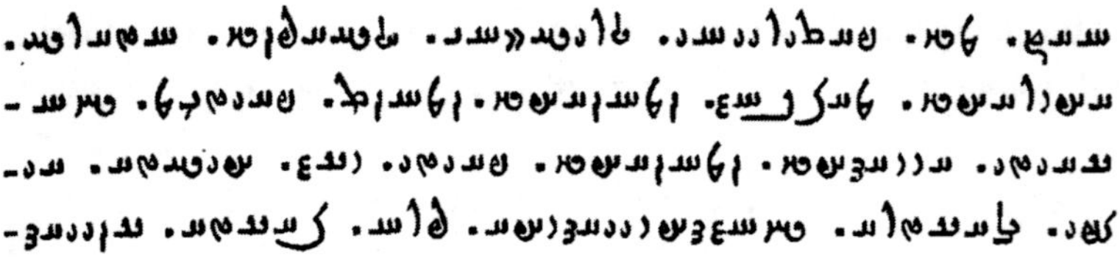

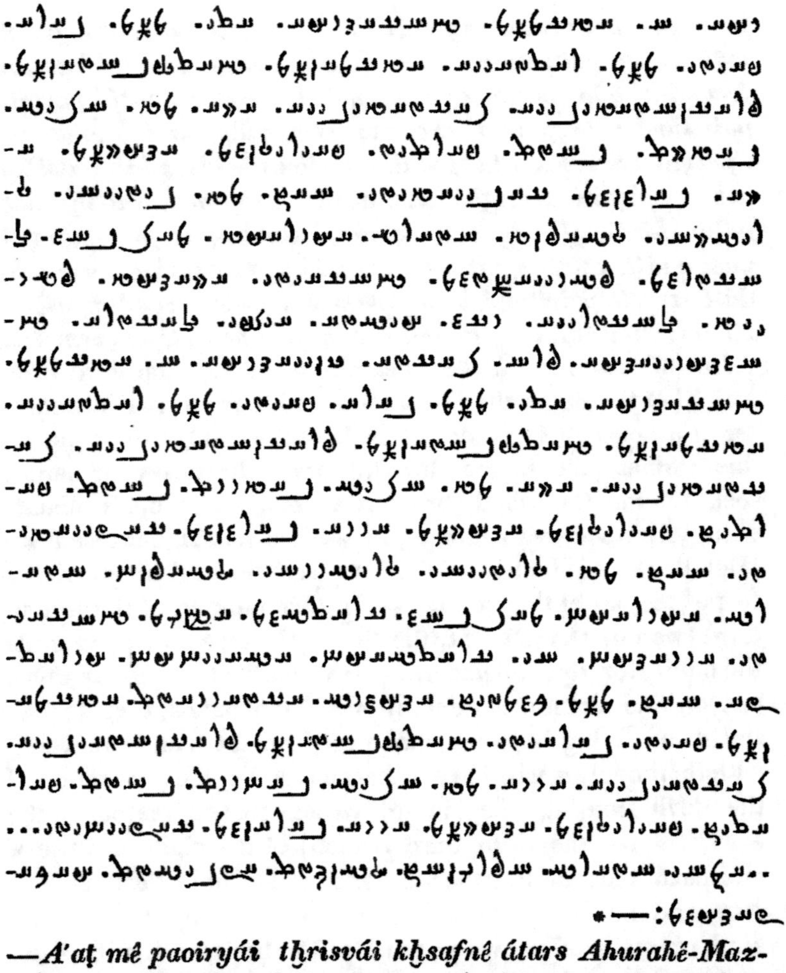

—A'aṭ mê paoiryái thrisvái kẖsafnê átars Ahurahê-Mazdâo nmánahê nmánó pailím yáçaiti avanghê nmánah paiti, uçĕ hista aiwi vaçtra yâonghuyanguha frazaçta çnyanguha á áêçmãm yáçanguha aoi mãm bara paiti mãm raochaya aêçmanãm yaozhdátanãm fraçnátaêibya zaçtaêibya ava mê A'zis daêvó-dátó paróiṭ pairithnĕm anghvãm ava darĕnĕm çadyaêiti. A'aṭ mê bityái thrisvái kẖsafnê átars Ahurahê Mazdâo váçtrĕm fsúiyañtĕm yáçaiti avanghê fsuyê váçtrya uçĕ-hista aiwi vaçtra yãonghu-

* Vandidád lithographed, pp. 480, 481, 483.

yanguha fra zaçta çnyanguha á aêçmãm yáçanguha aoi mãm bara paiti mãm raochaya aêçmanãm yaozḫdátanãm fraçnátaêibya zaçtaêibya ava mê A'zis daêvôdátô parôiṭ. pairithnĕm anghvãm ava darĕnĕm çadhyaêiti. A'aṭ mê tḫrityái tḫrisvái kḫsafnê átars Ahurahe-Mazdâo çraosĕm ashím yáçaiti avanghê ái çraosahê asayêhê huraodḫa áaṭ mãm kĕm-chit anghéus açtavató aêçmanãm paiti baraiti yaozḫdátanãm fraçnátaêibya zaçtaêibya ava mê A'zis daêvódátóparaoiṭ pairithnĕm anghvãm ava darĕnĕm çadḫyĕiti. . . Ahmái átars afrínáṭ kḫsnútó adḫbistó hakadḫanghem &c.

"In this manner, at the beginning of my first third [i. e. watch] of the night, the fire of Hormazd thus requests the master of a house: 'O master of the house, quickly arise; put on fine clothes [the sacred dress], thoroughly wash your hands, seek for me the wood, bring it to me, make me brilliant, with pure wood, with thoroughly washed hands, because A'zis [Dew], the production of the devil from the beginning, wishes to put me out of the world.'* — In this manner, at the second third [watch] of the night, the fire of Hormazd thus requests the cultivator, the benefactor: — 'O cultivator, quickly arise, put on fine clothes, thoroughly wash your hands, seek for me the wood, bring it to me, make me brilliant with pure wood, with thoroughly washed hands, because A'zis, the production of the devil from the beginning, wishes to put me out of the world'. — At the third third [watch] of the night, the fire of Hormazd thus desires the assistance of the pure Sarosh: 'O pure and beautiful Sarosh, let some one bring to me some kind or other of my wood produced in the world, with clean washed hands, because A'zis, the production of the devil, wishes to put me out of the world.'. . . . . . The fire thus blesses him [who carries wood to it with pure hands.] 'Be thou happy, free from disease, and filled with good, &c.'" †

* Or, as the dasturs explain it, "to extinguish me by damp."

† This passage, I have translated as literally from the Zand as intelligible idiom will allow. The Gujarátí translation of Frámjí Aspandiárjí is quite consistent in meaning with the closest rendering. Author's MS. vol. ii, pp. 286 — 289.

Here there is certainly no mention, direct or indirect, of the *amsháspand* Ardebehisht. *Fire,* and fire alone, is the speaker. It is *fire* which is afraid of extinction from damp, and the want of fuel. It is *fire* which calls for renewed aid at the different watches of the night. It is *fire* which asks that it may be made brilliant. It is *fire* which promises rewards. It is *fire* which dispenses blessings. Nothing but *fire* is brought before our notice in the passage. Whether the language expressive of its desires for assistance is literal or figurative, I do not here inquire. I say, however, that it conveys the meaning that *fire* is to be religiously served by the Pársís.*

* In these remarks which were penned before the publication of Aspandiárjí's *Hádi-i-Gum-Rahán,* Aspandiárjí will find an answer by anticipation to whatever worth notice he has alleged in the 45th and 46th pages of his work.

Aspandiárjí accuses me of omitting the translation of a sentence in the Vandidád occurring immediately before the blessing dispensed by fire. "It is the third sentence," he says, "which runs thus: he who about the last watch of the night gets up, after having put on clean clothes, and the kusti, and having washed his hands, stirs the fire and puts fragrant combustible on it, and then offers his prayers, receives the good blessings from Ardebehisht, one of the Amsháspands, who presides over fire." No such sentence, is to be found in this part of the Vandidád. Why, if it exists, did not Aspandiárjí bring it forward, when professing to correct me?

Aspandiárjí thinks that he has discovered something similar to the Pársí treatment of fire in the use of incense in the Jewish worship. He is entirely mistaken. The Jews used incense in their worship as symbolical of the acceptableness of the sacrifice to be presented by Christ, and of the prayers presented in faith in his name, but they never rendered to it either prayer or service.

Why Aspandiárjí has referred to the fact that the angel of the Lord [i. e. Christ] appeared to Moses in a flame of fire, he has not informed us, and I cannot guess, unless I suppose that it be to suggest to the mind of the reader, that it is the Lord who appears to the Pársís in the flame of their A'tishgáhs. But such an idea is not only inconsistent with the utter want of any manifestation of the divine glory in these places,—as for example, was the case when the bush burned and was not consumed, and an audible voice proceeded from it,—but with Aspandiárjí's notion that fire is merely a *kibláh.*

With regard to John's vision of seven lamps of fire before the throne, to which Aspandiárji (p. 48) also refers, I would observe, that they

A similar remark is applicable to the passage which I have given from Edal Dáru in the paragraph which I have marked [5]. In the Zand there is not the slightest mention made of an *amsháspand*, as an object of worship. The translation of Edal Dáru himself is inconsistent with his own interpretation; for it is not an Amsháspand or archangel, that can, as he alleges, be "raised aloft, and is worthy of having a glorious, excellent, and brilliant place made."* His translation, moreover, however much in accordance with the traditional renderings of the Pársís, is decidedly erroneous. It should have run in the following form: —"Hormazd said to the exalted Zoroaster, in this manner, this best creation, (or this creation belonging to, or under the charge of, Ardebehisht†) O exalted Zoroaster, the praiser, the chaunter, the invoker, the reciter, the sacrificer, the delectifier, the great-extoller, [this] good, royal, splendid article, [or existence applied to fire] is the work of us the Amsháspands for the Izashné and the Níáísh?" The Zand words *çtaotarĕcha zaotarĕcha zbátarĕcha mãnthranacha yaçtarĕcha áfrítarĕcha* and *aibizaratarĕcha*, omitting the *cha*, — corresponding with the Sanskrit च *cha*, — have all their Sanskrit equivalents of an almost literal accordance. Thus, we have in Sanskrit स्तोतृ *stotri*, a praiser; होतृ *hotri* ‡ "a priest, who at the sacrifice recites the prayers of the Rig-Veda;" § ह्वातृ *hvátri* || an

were symbolical of the perfect Spirit of the Lord, who is an object of worship. Aspandiárjí will find no countenance of the *worship of lamps* in the new Testament.

* See his translation, quoted in p. 201 of this work.

† In referring again to Edal Dárú's work I find that he reads *asahĕ vahistahĕ fradathĕis* for the *asa vahista fradathĕis* of my Zand MS., from which I have quoted. If he be correct in this reading, as I think he is, then the translation within parentheses above is the correct one.

‡ The ह *h* of the Sanskrit, it is to be observed, is almost uniformly the correspondent of the Zand ζ *z*. Thus we have *hasta* "a hand" in Sanskrit, for *zasta* in Zand; and *him a* "cold" in Sanskrit, for *zima* in Zand.

§ Wilson's Sanskrit Dictionary.

|| Here the Sanskrit *v*, as is commonly the case, is used for the Zand *b*.

invoker; मंत्रिन् *mantrin* an adviser, or reciter of the *mantras* or initiatory texts; यष्टृ *yashṭri* a sacrificer; प्रीतृ *pritri* a delectifier or satisfier; and अभि-जरतृ *abhi-jaratri** an extoller. I suppose that Edal Daru himself will admit that the words *varĕzó ahmákĕm amĕsnãm-spĕntanãm* mean "the work of us the Amsháspands." It is to be regretted that he did not perceive that the whole passage establishes the very reverse of what he adduces it to prove. I hereby publicly challenge him to point out a single Zand word in his quotation equivalent to the Arabic Kibláh.

No doubt can now remain of the practice of absolute fire-worship by the Pársís. It may be well, however, before we proceed farther, to refer to the exact form in which their pyrolatrous prayers are presented. I beg to call their attention, with this view, to one of the most frequent supplications which they address to fire, the *A'tish-Niáísh*; and that I may not be accused of dealing unjustly with them, I shall content myself with giving a literal translation of the Gujarátí version and paraphrase of that prayer as set forth by the chief-dastur Edal Dáru himself in the ખોરદેહ અવસતાનો તરજુમો, or *Translation of the Khurdah-Avastá*, printed in Bombay in the year A. D. 1817, subjoining, when necessary, a few explanatory notices, and making a couple of references to the original Zand. The passages within parentheses, it will be observed, contain the paraphrastical explanations of the dastur. One or two words I have myself introduced, marking them by "supplied parentheses." How derogatory the prayer is to the majesty and glory of God, the reader will perceive as he advances.

* This word, omitting the inseparable prefix, is evidently from the root जृ *jri*, which, though not of frequent occurrence, is still to be met with in the Vedas, and in the sense given above. "Tanquam a radice जृ deductæ, inveniuntur, canere, laudare, जरते (*jaraté*) Nigh. iii, 14, iv, 1. &c." See Westergaard's Radices Linguæ Sanscritæ, p. 74. When criticizing the passage of the Ardebehisht Yaçt now before us, I may here mention, I have had an opportunity of personally consulting Mr. Westergaard.

"(I commence) in the name of Yazdān, the wise Lord, created of himself,* the author of encrease. Let the glorious and resplendent *A'tish Bĕhrám* encrease. (If the Níáísh be made near the A'darán the meaning of its *pad* is,) Let the glorious and resplendent *A'tish A'darān* encrease! *Iz hamá gunáh; pa patiti hóm.* †

"O Hormazd, give to me a thoroughly perfect mind, (that is wholly a righteous desire), and health-of-body. And from the inflicter of wounds (Ahriman) me (keep free). O glorious, invisible Hormazd, I lay hold of Bahman (that is, a good disposition‡); that good disposition impart to me. The merit which is very strong over the oppressive (Ahriman), is through the mastership of a good disposition;(and) the pleasurable desire I experience and dispense, is from a good disposition. And, O Hormazd, give me thy strength; and over him who through a good disposition is an obedient pupil, give me the kingship and mastership. And make (my) habits, in merit and works of religion, glorious and perfect. (That is, make my habits righteous). O Hormazd, I Zoroaster, henceforth devote the liberality of my body and soul to Bahman Amshấspand. (That is, I devote my body and soul). And I do the work of purity (so that Ardebehisht may become pleased. §) And whatever word I shall speak (let me speak it in such a manner that it shall be worthy of being heard by Shahravar (that is acceptable to the king). And I delectify Hormazd.

"And I give worship, [namáz in Gujarátí,] (to thee), O fire of Hormazd, who art the giver of righteousness, the glorious

* This should be the "Lord Hormazd," the words of the original *Pahlivi*, preceding the proper commencement of the Níáísh, being [illegible] *Ahoramazda-khudái.*

† A reference to other prayers here introduced.

‡ An interpolation.

§ This clause, it will be observed, is a pure interpolation. It is not even *explanatory* of what precedes.

Izad. (*Fravárâné.**) Fire the Son of Hormazd, thee, O Fire the Son of Hormazd, and Fire the Son of Hormazd, very resplendent, and profitable, created of Hormazd,† the fire that is the (*A'tish Farobá*)‡, thee; and the Iranian splendour§

* This is a reference to a clause of the prayers of the *gĕhs* or watches, to be here introduced.

† The original of the passage beginning with this paragraph, properly speaking the commencement of the Níáísh, is the following: —

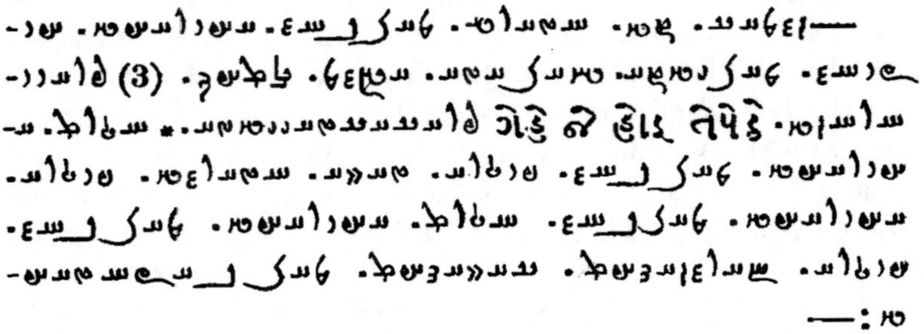

Namas tê átars Mazdâo-Ahurahê hudhuâo, mazista yazata. Ashem Vóhû (3). fravárâné fraçaçtayêcha. (Here in Gujarátí is the direction to recite these pieces). *A'thró Ahurahê-Mazdâo puthra, tava átares puthra Ahurahê-Mazdâo. A'thro Ahurahê-Mazdâo puthra. Kharenanghó savanghó Mazdadhátahê.*

The literal translation is this: — "Salutation to thee, O fire of the multiscient Lord, the knower of good, the greatest Izad. (*Ashĕm Vóhú* thrice. Let the *Fravárânĕ* of the *Gĕh* be recited and also the *fraçaçtayêcha.*) O Fire the Son of Hormazd, thee O Fire the Son of Hormazd, the fire the Son of Hormazd, the glorious *Çavanghó* made of Mazd (Hormazd), [I worship"]. Fire, it will be observed, is here called the greatest Izad (or "object of worship," as shown in page 129 of this work), the "Son of Hormazd;" and "the glorious *Çavanghó* made of Hormazd." The words 'I worship,' I have marked as supplied; but the verb *yazamaidê*, exactly corresponding, is given as the governing verb of the nouns in the objective case in a subsequent part of the *Niáish*. In the Bundéshné (Gujarátí version page 331), it is said that the *Çavangh* is one of the five kinds of fire; and that it is "always increasing in the presence of Hormazd." The other great kinds of fire are there said to be *Vóhú Farian*, the *Orvá-zest*, the *Vazest* and the *Spenest*, or the *At'ish Bĕhrám*.

‡ Or *A'dar frá.* Edal Darû, in the appendix to his Translation of the Khurdah-Avastá, says, that it is a kind of fire "which presides over Dasturs, Mobeds, and watchmen, whose wisdom and glory i sderived from it."

§ Edal Dáru says in his appendix to the Khurdah-Avastá, that is the glory of the Mázdayaçní religion.

created of Hormazd; and the Kaianian splendour* created of Hormazd; and Fire the Son of Hormazd [the fire A'dar Gosasp;]† and [the king] Kai-Khosru; and the cave of Kai-Khosru, which is in the city of Adarbádagán; and the mountain Asnuand‡ created of Hormazd, and the cave called the Chechast§; and the Kaianian splendour created of Hormazd; and the Son of Hormazd, the fire A'dar Burjín, and the mountain Rewand ‖ created by Hormazd, and the Kaianian splendour created by Hormazd; and Fire the Son of Hormazd, the Fire the glorious increaser, the mighty and resplendent Izad, and the Izad who is the giver of perfect health-of-body; and Fire the Son of Hormazd, of all the fires and kings the chief, who is the Izad Nariosangh;— for delectifying all these fires, I perform the Izashné and the Níáísh, and please (them), and make them conspicuous.¶ *Yathá ahú vairyó athá ratus ashát aoít hachá* &c.**Through the Izashné and through the Níáísh,

* *Kaiání nur.* This, says Edal Daru, in the appendix above referred to, "is one of the glories of God," which imparts wisdom, and art, and power in the Izashné, and gives judgment to judges and kings.

† This Edal Dáru says, is the fire which presides over heroes, which makes a noise in the presence of Hormazd, and which is the fire of thunder. For his notions of fire, the dastur seems principally indebted to the Bundéshné.

‡ The mountain on which it is supposed that the fire Gosasp resides.

§ The cave, according to Edal Dáru, in which Kai-Khosru was concealed, and which both in length and breadth was four parasangs. It would be well if the Pársís would send forth some of their own youngsters on a voyage of dicovery, as this large cave has entirely escaped the purblind eyes of the Firangís. Who knows but a deputation of zealous Zoroastrians might yet successfully survey the cave *Orvast*, said in the Bundéshné (Gujarátí translation p. 260) to be 700 parasangs long!

‖ The mountain on which the Atish-Burjin was said to be found.

¶ The nouns which the dastur through the whole of this paragraph has rendered as in the objective, are actually in the genitive, case; and this last clause should be thus rendered, "Let there be the delectification, of &c. through the Yaçna, the Vahma (Níáísh)." The dastur's version, I allow, substantially conveys the sense.

** This mantra is here to be introduced in the recitement.

and through the well-brought-thing (that is the sweet odour imposed), and right-brought-thing (that is through watchful attendance), and the help-brought (that is the service) rendered, I perform to thee the *áfrín* (that is praise.)* Thou art worthy of having the Izashné and the Níáísh performed ; and be thou worthy of having the Izashné and the Níáísh performed in the houses of men. And let the man who has always the *isam*† in his hand, and the *bars.m*‡ in his hand, and the *jivám*§ in his hand, and the *hávnim*|| gloriously worship thee ; and let that man be blessed. And let him place wood (upon thee,) and give (that is place upon thee) what yields sweet odours. And let him give (thee fat), and let him place bundles [of wood ?], (upon thee), and let him remain a youthful master, and a blessed master. Do thou (who) during the *Der-mudat*¶ [the long time] the high, immortal, magnificent, weapon (who) with a good weapon makest (all) immortal (that is till thou makest the resurrection), remain burning in that house, and always remain burning in that house, and remain splendent

* The Zand word here used is [illegible] *áfrinámi*, equivalent to the Sanskrit प्रीणामि *prinámi*, I satisfy, delectify, or fulfil the desires of.

† A stick, or wood, and particularly the three pieces of sandal wood and three pieces of frankincense, which are put aside, to place on the fire-stand, at the time of the recitation of the Izashné.

‡ The rods, 22 or 35 in number, of the pomegranate, or *Hom*, or *Gaz* (tamerisk) tree, or of silver or brass, and which, tied together, the Mobed holds in his hands when reciting the Izashné and Vandidád, or muttering the *bázhes*.

§ A mixture placed in a cup used in the Izashné, composed of one-fourth of goat's milk, and three-fourths of water.

|| A cup used in the Izashné for containing the juice of the Hom. In the Burhán-i-Katagh the Hom, which is found in Persia, is said to resemble the tamarisk. For an illustration of the instruments and vessels of the Izashné, see the accompanying lithograph.

¶ The *Der-mudat*, or the *Der-khudá-zamán*, Edal Dáru, in his appendix to the Khurdah-Avastá, makes the period of 12,000 years, which is now advancing, and at the termination of which the resurrection is to take place.

in that house, and remain the increaser in that house. And give to me, O Fire the Son of Hormazd, speedy (that is quick) ease, and a speedy nourishment, and a speedy livelihood, and great ease, and a great nourishment, and a great livelihood. (That is, let not these things be lessened to us.) And (give to me) the wisdom of foresight, and (of wisdom) the increase, (which from one thing understands many things) ; and eloquent speech ; and for my soul (heaven) ; and understanding (that may remain fixed), and the greatest intelligence (which is the intelligence acquired from listening) ; and lofty valour in the destruction of enemies, and besides (in the words of religion and justice) bravery and strength, and power of foot; and wakefulness, (so that I may sleep) in the third part of the day and night, and rise quickly at the [appointed] time ; and strength of arm ; and children renowned for their natural understanding, who shall be ornaments of the city, and sit in the assemblies, and be beautiful, and righteous, and respectable, and givers of relief from difficulties, and rightly wise, who (that is my children) in the house, street, town, and country, may make me conspicuous. And, O Fire the Son of Hormazd, give to me what is necessary,— the everlasting high abode of the pure, filled with all splendour and ease [happiness ?], (that is the heaven on high), in which now (there is only life). And make me fit for the lordship, and an excellent devotee, (of the other world), and of (this world) an excellent righteous [person], with a right soul. O Çpitama Zoroaster, whosoever morning or evening cooks a pleasurable and delightful meal, to him the Fire of Hormazd makes his address, and entertains the wish with every person of having sweet odours placed [upon it], and care being executed, and the *zandgoí* [ceremonies] being done. And as a friend goes near a friend, (and for that friend) takes something, (and a friend looks upon the hand of a friend), so upon all persons who go near any of (the fires), the fire casts a look. The fire is lame [i.e. without the power of motion], (but a hero it is called) ; I worship it the glorious fire, the powerful hero. * If any person, with purity, having placed wood (upon the fire), and having, with purity, bound the *barsam*, and having put fragrant wood, worship the fire,—then the fire of Hormazd thus blesses him, 'Remain thou happy, (and) without disease, (and) satisfied. And let thy great herds of small cattle, and the great posterity of thy children, increase.' And whatever wish may be manifest in thy mind, if it be like the wish of Hormazd, and if it should be that thou shouldst live to the last night, then thou wilt remain alive with life, according to the wish of Hormazd. And whosoever, in the expectation of his own righteousness, places wood upon the fire, the fire thus blesses him [in the manner aforesaid ?]. — *Horamazda-khudái*, &c. as in the *Khurshid Níáísh*, silently. *Yathá ahú vairyó.* (2).† — By means of the Izashné and Níáísh, and of superior and strong power, I bless Fire the Son of Hormazd. Fire the Son of Hormazd, thee; O Fire the Son of Hormazd, thee; O Fire the Son of Hormazd, and Fire the Son of Hormazd, very resplendent and profitable, created of Hormazd (the fire that is the A'tish Farobá,) thee; and the Iránian splendour created of Hormazd; and the Kaiánian splendour created of Hormazd; and Fire the Son of Hormazd (the fire A'dar Gosasp); and (the king) Kai-Khosru; and the cave of Kai-Khosru (which is dug in the city of A'darbádagán); and the mountain Asnuand created of Hormazd; and the cave called Chechast; and the Kaiánian splendour created of Hormazd; and the Son of Hormazd, the fire (A'dar-Burjín); and the mountain Rewand created by Hor-

* I here give the dastur's Gujaráti for this sentence: —

બુજોરગ આતશ જોરાવર પેહેલવાંન છે તેહેને આરાધું *

The original Zand is: —

𐬁𐬙𐬀𐬭𐬆𐬨 · 𐬯𐬞𐬆𐬧𐬙𐬆𐬨 · 𐬫𐬀𐬰𐬀𐬨𐬀𐬌𐬛𐬉 · 𐬙𐬀𐬑𐬨𐬆𐬨 · 𐬵𐬆𐬧𐬙𐬆𐬨 · 𐬭𐬀𐬚𐬀𐬉𐬱𐬙𐬁𐬭𐬆𐬨 : —

— *A'tarĕm spĕñtĕm yazamaidé takhmĕm hĕntĕm arathistárĕm.* This literally means, "I worship-with-sacrifice the glorious fire, which is the powerful hero."

† In the recitation, the prayers here referred to are to be introduced.

mazd ; and the Kaianian splendour created by Hormazd ; and Fire the Son of Hormazd, the fire the glorious encreaser, the mighty and resplendent Izad, and the Izad who is the giver of perfect health of body, and Fire the Son of Hormazd, of all the fires and kings, the chief, who is the Izad Nariosangh ;— (I bless all the fires).* *Ashĕm Vóhú* (thrice). O Hormazd, as thy fire, the exalted Lord, is (well) pleased with the pure people, and is the Lord of bravery, and publicly advances the happiness of him who assists it (that is gives),— so the person who gives affliction to fire, it afflicts ; Hormazd, according to his will, visits him with resentment (that is punishes him). *Ahmái-riçcha* (as in the *Khurshíd Niáísh*). *Kĕrĕbá-mazda. Ashĕm Vóhú* (once). (On such a month, such a *gĕh, &c.*) Let there be increase of the high and resplendent fire *Bĕhrám*, the glorious fire ; or, of the *A'tish A'darān*,† the glorious fire, and the A'darān ; which is the victorious master ; and of the fire *Gosasp ;* and of the fire *Khurdád* ; and of the fire *Burjín-Meher ;* and of the exalted fires, and the fires which are settled in the Dádgáh (that is in the place formed according to religion). And let there be the increase of the glory and splendour of *Mino-karko.*‡ *Ashĕm Vóhú* (once)."

Such is a literal rendering of the chief dastur's translation of the A'tish Níáísh,—a translation, which though evidently more founded on the traditional Pahliví and Persian renderings of the Pársís, than on a grammatical construction and philological investigation of the Zand, it must be admitted, substantially conveys the meaning of the original, with which throughout, for my own satisfaction, I have carefully compared it. I have another Gujarátí translation before me, which I have also done into English ; but it it is not necessary for me to insert it in this place. It is that of the late learned Dastur Dasturán Frámjí Sohrábjí of Nausárí, contained in his

* It will have been observed that the preceding adoration is a mere repetitition of what occurs in the commencement of the Níáísh.

† Literally, the fire of fires.

‡ "This," according Edal Dáru (Appendix to his Translation of the Khurdah-Avastá, p. 769), "is a splendour near Dádár Hormazd."

edition of the Khurdah-Avastá, published in 1818, and which is principally in use among the Kadímís of Bombay. As far as it exhibits fire as an object of worship among the Pársís, it agrees with that of Edal Dáru.

Many of my readers, I have no doubt, will be *astounded* at the blasphemous worship of fire, as set forth in the A'tish Níáísh, which has now been brought to their notice. No translation which can legitimately be made of the Zand, can render this worship in the smallest degree less revolting to the understanding and reason of man. Throughout the whole of the Níáísh, fire is praised and adored as the Son of Hormazd; not simply because it is said to have been created by him, as some of the controversialists allege, — for *every thing in the universe* may in this sense, according to the views of the Pársís, be said to be the Son of Hormazd, — but because it is considered to be the manifestation of his greatest glory, — the essence or emanation of that glory itself. Here it is celebrated, not as under the control of an Amsháspand or Izad, but as itself the 𐬨𐬀𐬰𐬌𐬱𐬙𐬀 𐬫𐬀𐬰𐬀𐬙𐬀. *mazista* * *yazata*, the "greatest Izad," or object of worship. Here, it is addressed, as sentient, intelligent, and divine. Here, it is addressed as differing in its kinds, and qualities, according to the mountains and combustibles in connexion with which it may be developed. Here, it is addressed as the "glorious author of increase," and the "giver-of-perfect-health-of-body." Here it is represented as ambitious of "delectification," and craving in its desires for "wood," and "sweet-odours," and "fat." Here, it is set forth, as worthy of the most solemn services, laudations and supplications, of the Pársís, — the Izashné, the Níáísh, and the A'frín, and so forth; and here it is set forth as reverenced, and worshipped, and adored. Here, it is viewed as dispensing "foresight," "wisdom," "strength," and "victory;" as bestowing distinguished "posterity," and abundance of flocks and herds; and imparting happiness in this world, extending preserva-

* The resemblance of this superlative to the Greek μέγιστος will be noticed by the European scholar.

tion till the resurrection, and conferring eternal bliss. Those who serve it, according to its demands, are assuredly, in the grossest and strictest sense of the term, FIRE-WORSHIPPERS. I do not wonder that the intelligent descendants of the Medes and Persians in India, are beginning to revolt from this designation ; and I look forward with joy to that day, when the "sacred fire" shall no longer blaze on their hearths, but to cook their victuals or aid them in their manufactures ; and when the fire-temples throughout Bombay and Surat, shall, by their own hands, nerved by the truth and Spirit of God, be levelled with the dust or converted into cotton godowns. Let them not, I even now beseech them, blind their eyes to the enormities of the Zand-Avastá. Let them not palliate their idolatry of nature,by alleging that they commence and end their services in the name of Hormazd ; for were he the true God, — as he is not, — it would only be a degradation of his honour and glory, to conduct idolatrous worship under the pretence of his countenance and authority. Let them never for a moment think of worshipping even the most glorious *works* of God, under the imagination, that their prayers and praises addressed to them, will recoil upon God himself. Let them remember that, as there is an *infinite distance* between the Creator and creature, there should not be the attributing to the creature of the smallest respect or reverence which belongs to GOD.

Not content with dealing out abundance of erroneous *theology* and *philosophy* on the subject of fire, some of the controversialists have tried to bolster up their cause by a mass of absurd *legendry*. Edal Dáru, makes a calm appeal to the Sháhnámah, with reference to the alleged discovery of fire by Hoshang; but he has considerably smoothed and rationalized the narrative contained in his authority. The following is what we actually find on the subject in the poet of Tus : —

یکي روز شاه جهان سوي کوه　　گذر کرد با چند کس هم گروه
پدید آمد از دور چیزي دراز　　سیه رنگ و تیره تن و تیز تاز

دو چشم آز بر سر چو دو چشمه خون   زدود دهانش جهان تیره گون
نگه کرد هوشنگ با هوش و هنگ
گرفتش یکی سنگ و شد پیش جنگ
بزور کیانی بیازید دست
جهان سوز مار از جهان جو بجست
برآمد بسنگ گران سنگ خورد   همان و همین سنگ بشکست خورد
فروغی پدید آمد از هر دو سنگ
دل سنگ گشت از فروغ آذرنگ
نشد مار کشته ولیکن زراز   پدید آمد آتش ازان سنگ باز
هر آنکس که بر سنگ آهن زدی   ازو روشنائی پدید آمدی
جهاندار پیش جهان آفرین   نیایش همی کرد و خواند آفرین
که اورا فروغی چنین هدیه داد   همین آتش آنگاه قبله نهاد
بگفتا فروغی است این ایزدی   پرستید باید اگر بخردی
شب آمد برافروخت آتش چو کوه
همان شاه درگرد او با گروه
یکی جشن کرد آن شب و باده خورد
سده نام آن جشن فرخنده کرد
زهوشنگ ماند این سده یادگار *

"One day the king of the world (Hoshang), passing by the side of a mountain attended by his followers, perceived at a distance a long creature, black-coloured and black-bodied, and very quick in its march. Its two eyes resembled two fountains of blood. From the smoke of its mouth, the world was covered with black vapour. He observed it by his wisdom and prudence. Having taken a stone in his hand, he went forward to combat it. With royal force, he hurled the stone at it. But the world-consuming serpent crept away from the king. The small stone struck against another stone,

* Lumsden's edition of the Sháhnámah, vol. 22, 23.

and broke into pieces. Light issued from the two stones. The heart of the stone turned bright with light. The serpent was not killed, but from the blow of the stone the fire was produced. Since that time, whoever has struck iron against a stone has got light by it. Then the king before the Creator, uttered praises, and acknowledged him as the Creator, because he granted him the gift of this light; and then at that place he made it his kibláh. And he said, *this is a divine splendour, let it be worshipped*, if ye would be wise. At night he kindled a fire like a mountain; the Sháh was with all his people round about it. That night he made a great feast and drank wine, and named it (the feast) *Saddah*. From Hoshang is the observance of the Saddah." A comparison of this rendering with the Dastur's version, will show, that if he had the Sháhnámah really before him, he was actually ashamed of the legend which is there to be found.* I do not wonder at his feelings. However much that legend may minister to the amusement of the reader, it cannot be received as in any degree veritable. It is absurd to suppose that the method of obtaining fire by friction, was unknown till the days of Hoshang; for the common business of life could not have been carried on without its discovery. The monstrous serpent darkening the world with the smoke of its vapour, and its concomitant circumstances, are evidently fabulous. Poets such as Firdausí, who indulged their fancy to an extreme degree, and who lived thousands of years after the time of the kings whom they celebrate, are not to be viewed as historical authorities. They are no more than writers of romance, and are spoken of as such by all European scholars, who, however much they may be interested in their writings as works of taste and curiosity, lay little or no stress on their testimony as to the ages of antiquity. Sir William Ouseley rightly says, that "Firdausí relates the ad-

* It is still more perverted by the author of the Nirang-Há, (pp. 239—241. He professes to quote the Sháhnámah; but it is plain, either that he has had not that work before him, or that he has deliberately perverted its narrative.

ventures of personages who never existed but in the poets imagination: and of others whose existence is dubious though not improbable."* General Vans Kennedy, of whose learning the Pársís are well aware, and who is not disposed to undervalue the Persian accounts, says of them: — "The native accounts of Persia (by Firdausí and others), can neither convey any satisfactory knowledge of its own history, nor in the slightest tend to illustrate that of any other nation. For they contain nothing but the names of the kings; the notice of a very few events; and a general character of each king, of which it is difficult to decide whether it has been collected from original materials, or is merely the composition of the Muhammadan historian. To erect systems on such a foundation, or to deduce any conclusion from such premises, must be considered inconsistent with every principle of sound reasoning."† Having said this much, and already alluded to the age of the Sháristán, which is even later than the Sháhnámah, we need not comment on the passage about the discovery of fire by Hoshang, which Dosabhái quotes from that work. It is probably founded on what is in the Sháhnámah, though in some respects it contradicts both it, and Edal Dárú's account of the reputed miracle, and that in several particulars. I give a single example of this inconsistency. The Sháhnámah says that Hoshang was "attended by his followers," and Edal Dárú, that he was "with the sages of his court," when he discovered the monster; while the Sháristan and Dosabhái say that he was "alone."‡

Edal Dárú's reference to the legends respecting the *A'tish-Burjín Meher*, are similar in character to that which I have now noticed. In a subsequent part of this work, I shall show, that the account given by Edal Dárú of Zoroaster's journey to heaven, of his doings there, of the articles which he is said to have brought from it, and in fact of all his reputed miracles, is totally unworthy of credit. In the meantime, I must ex-

* Persian Miscellanies, p. 95.

† Bombay Transactions, vol ii, p. 143.

‡ Tálim-i- Zartusht, p. 161.

press my conviction, that even to many of the Pársís the legend respecting the *A'tish-Burjín-Meher* must appear to be altogether unworthy of the slightest credit. A few words, explanatory of what may have been its origin, may not be unacceptable.

In *A'zarbaizán*, or Media, "the country of fire," and in other districts of Irán,. there were several gaseous currents proceeding from crevices in the rocks, and openings in the ground, which were capable of ignition, and which superstition, directed by priestly wiles, could easily represent as supernatural and miraculous. When it had done this, the people under its influence, would not scruple to receive any stories respecting the origin and effects of the actual phenomena which might be proposed for their credence.

Of some of the fires, produced in the manner now referred to, I would solicit attention to the following curious account by Mr Jonas Hanway, an English traveller : — "This object of devotion to the Gabars" [their reputed 'everlasting fire'] "lies about ten English miles north-east from the city of Baku, on dry rocky land. There are several ancient temples built with stone, supposed to have been all dedicated to fire; most of them are arched vaults, not above ten to fifteen feet high. Amongst others there is a little temple in which the Indians [or Pársís] now worship: near the altar, about three feet high, is a large hollow cane, from the end of which issues a blue flame in colour and gentleness not unlike a lamp that burns with spirits, but seemingly more pure. These Indians affirm, that this flame has continued ever since the flood; and they believe it will last to the end of the world; that if it was resisted, or suppressed in that place, it would rise in some other. There are generally forty or fifty of these poor devotees, who come on a pilgrimage from their own country, and subsist upon wild sallary, and a kind of Jerusalem artichokes, which are very good food, with other herbs and roots found a little to the northward. . . . . . A little way from the temple is a low clift of a rock, in which there is a horizontal gap, two feet from the ground, near six long, and about three feet broad, out of which issues a constant flame, of the colour and nature I have already described: when the wind blows, it rises sometimes eight feet high, but is much lower in still weather: they do not perceive that the flame makes any impression on the rock. This also the Indians worship, and say it cannot be resisted, but it will rise in some other place about twenty yards. On the back of this clift is a well cut in a rock about twelve or fourteen fathoms deep, with exceeding good water. The earth round the place, for about two miles, has this surprising property, that by taking up two or three inches of the surface, and applying a live coal, the part which is so uncovered immediately takes fire, almost before the coal touches the earth: the flame makes the soil hot, but does not consume it, nor effect what is near it with any degree of heat. Any quantity of this earth carried to another place does not produce this effect. Not long since eight horses were consumed by this fire being under a roof, where the surface of the ground was turned up, and by some accident took flame. If a cane or tube, even of paper, be set about two inches in the ground, confined and closed with earth below, and the top of it touched with a live coal, and blown upon, immediately a flame issues, without hurting either the cane or paper, provided the edges be covered with clay, and this method they use for light in their houses, which have only the earth for the floor: three or four of these lighted canes will boil water in a pot; and thus they dress their victuals. The flame may be extinguished in the same manner as that of spirits of wine. The ground is dry and stony, and the more stony any particular part is, the stronger, and clearer is the flame; it smells sulphurous like naptha, but not very offensive. Lime is burnt to great perfection by means of this phenomenon; the flame communicating itself to any distance where the earth is uncovered to receive it. The stones must be laid one upon another and in three days the lime is completed. Near this place brimstone [bitumen ?] is dug, and naptha springs are found."* These curious phenomena,—if we make due allow-

* Hanway's Historical account of the British Trade over the Caspian Sea, vol. 1, p. 263, 264.

ance for exaggeration consequent on the accounts which Mr Hanway received from the natives of the country, — are explicable by referring to the ignition of the gas proceeding from the carbon and hydrogen, of which the mineral oil and mineral pitch, or bitumen, abounding in the locality, are principally composed.* Any Pársí who has studied chemistry will admit this fact; and he will also see how readily in an age of ignorance, these phenomena, and others of a like kind, could be misunderstood and misrepresented, and how, though they are merely natural, they would be supposed to be the result of a miraculous interposition of divine providence.† If at any time he will put a little naphtha into a bason and ignite it, and then pour water into the bason, he will immediately see the flame rise, and increase with great brilliancy, exactly as the A'tish-Burjín-Meher is said to have done. This is because the naphtha being lighter than water, remains uppermost, and has its surface disturbed and increased by the addition of the water, which also, from the sudden application of the heat, parts with some of its hydrogen for consumption by the flame. If he will conduct a stream of gas from the naphtha through a small tube, and ignite it, it will burn like the "everlasting fire" fed by the streams of gas proceeding from the crevices near Báku. If he will pour a little naphtha upon a small quantity of clay and ignite it, he may hand the clay from man to man, without injuring them by the heat. If he will throw bituminous earth into a fire, he will only increase the flame. With experiments of this kind, I have at a public lecture satisfied many of the natives of India, including Pársís, that the legends about the A'tish-Burjín-Meher, are merely perversions of *natural phenomena*. If it be denied that this is

* The constituent parts of naphtha are carbon 82.2 and hydrogen 14.8. The elastic mineral pitch, according to Henry, consists of carbon 52.25, hydrogen of 7.49, oxygen 40.10, nitrogen 0.15. — Jameson's Mineralogy (Encyclopædia) p. 269.

† In the Burhán-í.kátiagh, the *Azar-Burjín-Meher* temple is said to have been founded in Fárs by Kaí-Khosru.

their character, I should like to see the attempt made to prove that they are not absurdities. As to alleged voices proceeding from fire, I shall by and by have some questions to put about the *authority* on which the statement respecting them is made to rest. In the mean time I beg to refer the Pársís to the Church History of Socrates, in which they will see a particular account of the manner in which their forefathers could manage such miracles. They will there find Maruthas, a Christian Bishop of Mesopotamia declaring to Yazdejard, that a voice which addressed him proceeded from a mobed concealed behind the altar, and the king actually ascertaining the fact, and signally punishing the culprit and his fellow conspirators.*

Edal Dáru declares that the Sháhnámah states that "Zoroaster was a prophet from God," and that he brought from heaven the A'zar-Burjín-Meher, of which we have now been treating. The testimony of the Sháhnámah, written about fifteen hundred years after Zoroaster is said to have lived, is of little use in a case of this kind. It so happens, however, that it sets forth Zoroaster as an impostor, or the dupe of the devil. In proof of this assertion, I refer the reader to Firdausí's account of Zartusht as contained in the eighth chapter of this work.

The legendary explanations of the worship and reverence of fire by the Pársís to which I have now adverted, it must appear evident, are altogether unsatisfactory, and unworthy of credit.

The preceding observations have, of necessity, particularly, though not exclusively, referred to fire, and light, and the heavenly bodies, and the genii who are supposed to preside over these works of God, the objects of worship and reverence to which the controversialists with whom I have called to contend, have especially directed their attention. They are applicable, however, *mutatis mutandis*, to all the elements, and Izads and Amsháspands, which the Pársís suppose to exist. Throughout every part of the Zand-Avastá, — whether doc-

* Socratis Eccles. Hist. lib. vii. cap. 8.

trinal or liturgical, — water, earth, and air, and their most remarkable embodiments, are made the objects, not only of admiration and recognition, but of adoration and worship, in the very highest sense of the terms. Many proofs and illustrations of this assertion will be found in our next and subsequent chapters.

Some ingenuous Pársís, especially those of them who have received a liberal education, I have no doubt, will now be inclined to ask, How, if the worship of the heavenly host, and the elements of nature, cannot be defended, it ever came to be so generally practised in the ancient world. The reply is to be found in the indisposition of the depraved mind of man to engage in the contemplation and recognition of a spiritual God, to preserve the direct revelations which God must have originally given of himself to the human race, and to attend to the discoveries of his own character, and providence, and grace, which from time to time he has given to the world; and to a proneness to confound the works of God with the Creator himself, and proximate and instrumental agencies with the first Great Cause, and to rest satisfied with objects of reverence and adoration in some degree within the grasp of the human intellect, and suited, as was supposed, to its weakness, and corrupted tendencies. How the temptations to error may have operated jointly and severally, it is not very difficult to perceive. "The perplexity in which most writers" [on the origin of idolatry,] I have elsewhere observed, have involved themselves, is in a great measure to be attributed to their desire to give undue prominence to one particular theory. There surely can be nothing unbecoming, however, in the absence of direct historical testimony, in the admission that its rise in the various countries of the world, may be sufficiently accounted for on various suppositions. Those which I consider the most entitled to attention in regard to the heavenly host, and the elements of nature, are the following: —

1. '"In the days of Enos the son of Seth,' says Maimonides, 'men fell into grievous errors, and even Enos himself partook of their infatuation. Their language was, that, *since God had placed on high the heavenly bodies, and used*

them as his ministers, it was evidently his will, that they should receive from man the same veneration as the servants of a great prince, justly claim from the subject multitudes. Impressed with this notion, they began to build temples to to the stars, to sacrifice to them, and to worship them, in the vain expectation, that they should thus please the Creator of all things. At first indeed, they did not suppose the stars to be the only deities, but adored in conjunction with them the Lord God Omnipotent. In process of time, however, that great and venerable name was totally forgotten; and the whole human race retained no other religion, than the 'idolatrous worship of the host of heaven.'* 'With this superstition,' says Mr. Faber, 'the patriarch Ham seems to have been tainted, and to have conveyed the knowledge of it to his own particular descendants.' "

2. " The *typical* reference to the heavenly bodies, and elements, and the confusion which would afterwards follow it, has been adverted to by numerous writers. Lieut. Colonel Vans Kennedy supports the theory which is founded upon it with very considerable ingenuity. After stating that the fundamental truths of religion must have been *revealed* to the progenitors of the human race, he remarks that, 'If these postulata be once admitted, the origin of idolatry becomes immediately obvious. For the impressions made on the minds of the first men by their immediate communication with God would become fainter in each succeeding generation; and as the human mind is scarcely capable of devotion to an invisible and incomprehensible Being, their descendants would be naturally led to adopt some sensible object, as the type of that one self-existent and eternal God whom their fathers had adored. But in this case, what other object could Nature present so typical of divine excellence and supremacy, as —

> 'The orb that with surpassing glory crown'd,
> Look'd from his sole dominion, like the God
> Of that new world, at whose sight all the stars
> Veil'd their diminish'd heads.'

* I do not quote this passage as affording historical evidence, but as explanatory of a theory.

The sun, however, was not always visible, and the sacred fire obviously suggested itself as its adequate representative; nor if idolatry originated in Asia or Egypt, could the inhabitants of these countries have long contemplated the serene and brilliant expanse of the heavens, without imagining that it also might be a God, and hence,

'Aspice hoc sublime candens, quem invocant omnes Jovem.'

"'The earth was the next object that impressed on the minds of men the idea of divine nature; and the cause seems evident from all nations having, on account of its fruitfulness, represented it under the female character. The deification of sensible objects having thus commenced, its extension to the other elements is easily conceivable; and to evince that this was actually the first form of idolatry, there seems to be sufficient evidence.'"

3. "Perhaps, the opinion of some of the Christian Fathers, that when the knowledge of the divine glory and spirituality, which had been communicated by revelation, became obscure, men imagined the sun from his station in the heavens, and from his enlightening and vivifying powers, to be *actually* the Supreme God, and the other heavenly bodies inferior deities, is entitled to the highest respect. When the depravity of man is considered, the tendency to this corruption is at once perceived. It is probably that which is recognized by Job, when he says, 'If I beheld the sun when it shined, or the moon walking in brightness; and my heart hath been secretly enticed, or my mouth hath kissed my hand: this also were an iniquity for-the-judge; for I should have denied the God that is above.' It is an indubitable fact that in many countries of the world the heavenly bodies are believed to be actually gods."*

4. The preservation of the "sacred flame" of the altar, as it has been called, may have originated in the use of fire to consume the sacrifices which God commanded to be offered up by man and to be burnt before their view, to symbolize his

* First Exposure of Hinduism, pp. 147—149.

displeasure against the commission of sin and to impress the worshippers with a deep sense of its demerit, and to prefigure the great sacrifice, which was in due time to be made by Christ for the sins of the world. It may at first have been preserved simply for the sake of convenience, without any reference to its own supposed sacredness ; and the vain idea may have afterwards been entertained, that being employed in sacred services, it must itself be intrinsically sacred, and worthy of special regard and service. I here refer to a possible corruption, not so much of Jewish, as of Patriarchal, worship.

5. " Fire was *originally* worshipped by the natives of Irán," says Professor Stuhr, " neither as the elemental power, which had given origin to the world, nor as the fire of the hearth, conveying the blessings of family life, nor even as the flame of the forge, including the idea of mechanical skill and fabrication. The fundamental idea appears to have been that of the luminous nature of fire, by which it overcomes the power of darkness and its bad spirits. The light, as it dissipates the terrors of night, and relieves the mind from the fear of the ghosts which it fancies reside in darkness, gives rest and comfort to the disquieted soul. This seems to be the original meaning in which fire was worshipped by the Iranians. So it was raised in their imagination to a type of what was good in itself . . . . In opposition to it, darkness became the representative of evil. "* There are certainly allusions in the Pársí scriptures as to the effects of light such as are here noticed.

Observations of this kind, it would be by no means difficult to extend. What were the *temptations* to the sin of the worship of the elements and the heavenly hosts, intelligent Pársís themselves may understand, by referring to what the writers against whom we contend, vainly set forth as *apologies and defences*. Temptations, however, they must see and remember, form no vindication of error and transgression. They are not to be yielded to, but opposed. However apparent may be

* The Iranian fire-worship, translated by the Rev. Mr. Weigle from the Religions-Systeme des Orients, in Oriental Christian Spectator for 1840, p. 417.

the influences and effects of the elements; whatever may be the usefulness of fire and light; and however glorious and wonderful may be the sun, and the moon, and the stars, both in their appearance and movements; however exalted may be the angels and archangels of God, both in their endowments and service, — they are merely the *creatures* of the Almighty, possessed of a derivative excellence, and not worthy of receiving the smallest portion of our worship, but fitted to call it directly forth in behalf of Jehovah, the Lord of all. All that I have said to the Pársís on this subject, I most affectionately and solemnly beseech them to consider. When in expectation of being heard, they address one of the elements, they speak to what may be present, but to what cannot listen, what has no intelligence, what has no life, and what can give them no reply. When they address an angel, they speak to one of whose presence they can have no assurance, who may be millions of miles distant from them when they call upon him; with whom no communication can be maintained; who may be engaged, and wholly occupied, with other concerns than those to which they may be directing his attention; who according to their own notions may have several thousand persons all begging for his favour and assistance at the same moment; who may be waiting to minister in some far distant world, according to the express commands of God; and who may be thus altogether unable to render the least assistance. The calling on the name of the creature in supplication, it must consequently appear, is unreasonable, and in the highest degree derogatory to God, who alone has the knowledge, presence, goodness and power, required by the hearer and answerer of prayer. If figurative language is at any time to be used in worship, it must declaratively enhance, and not detract from, the glory of God. A truly pious spirit, when led in the highest ecstacy of devotion, to employ such language, instead of *praying to* the works of God, and *looking to them for help, will call upon them to praise the Lord.* "Praise ye the Lord. Praise ye the LORD. Praise ye the LORD from the heavens: praise him in the heights. Praise ye him, all his angels:

praise ye him, all his hosts. Praise ye him, sun and moon: praise him, all ye stars of light. Praise him, ye heavens of heavens, and ye waters that *be* above the heavens. Let them praise the name of the LORD: for he commanded, and they were created. He hath also stablished them for ever and ever: he hath made a decree which shall not pass. Praise the LORD from the earth, ye dragons, and all deeps: Fire, and hail; snow, and vapours; stormy wind fulfilling his word: Mountains, and all hills; fruitful trees, and all cedars: Beasts, and all cattle; creeping things, and flying fowl: Kings of the earth, and people; princes, and all judges of the earth: Both young men, and maidens; old men, and children: Let them praise the name of the LORD: for his name alone is excellent; his glory *is* above the earth and heaven."*

* Psalm cxlviii: 1—13.

CHAPTER V.

THE GENERAL POLYTHEISM OF THE PA'RSI'S.

Origin of the Polytheism of the Pársís — Attempt at classifying and enumerating the principal objects of their worship — Quotations in proof and illustration from the Zand-Avastá — Extract from the Vandidád — Translation of the first Há of the Yaçna, according to Burnouf — New translation of the seventy-first Há of the Yaçna — Comment on the Polytheism of the Pársís — Jumbling together and confusion of the objects of worship — Illustration from a supposed congratulatory address to a Governor of Bombay — The same terms of respect, prayer, praise, supplication, etc. applied to all the different objects of worship — Criticism on the meaning of these terms, as employed in the Zand writings, and used by the Pársís — The service of the inferior objects of worship occupies more space in the Zand-Avastá than that of the highest — Unsuccessful vindication af the Polytheism of the Pársís by the controversialists— Expostulation with the Pársís on the subject of their Polytheism — The instructions of Christ relative to prayer recommended to their attention.

One error respecting the nature of God, and the honour which is exclusively his due, is frequently the prolific parent of a multitude of errors of a similar character. As soon as men imagine that the Creator has little or no concern in the direct support and government of the works of his almighty power, and as soon as they permit any of these works, of whatever character they may be, to share in the reverence, love, praise, adoration, and service, which belong to himself as the universal Lord, there is no end to the *number*, and there is scarcely any restriction as to the *kind* of the objects of their worship. This observation is strikingly applicable to the religious degeneracy which appears among the Pársís. When they conceive of God as absorbed in his own being and unmindful of the concerns of the universe, and introduce imaginary beings to act as the guardians and superintendents of the different departments of nature, they do not hesitate to multiply these beings, according to their views of the extent of the number of the departments over which they are required to preside. When, forgetting the spirituality of God, they conceive the elements around them to be substantially his soul, his glory, and his power, they do not hesitate to recognize, as an object of worship, every object in which they appear to be particularly developed, or even embodied. In this way, they deify the whole of the material world, and the different agencies by which it is acted upon, giving their special regard to what appears in their own eyes the most brilliant and useful. And, in the same manner, they deify the imaginary prototype and the intellect and soul of man, and the soul or life of the various sentient and intelligent creatures which they suppose to exist throughout the earth and the heavens, and, some of which, like the Bráhmans, they conceive to have existed long before they appeared in their present forms. The objects of their religious worship and reverence may consequently be said to be ***innumerable.*** It is no easy task even to ***classify*** them. When hastily making the attempt on a former occasion, I wrote as follows: —

"Among the objects of their worship, they recognize the seven Amsháspands (including Hormazd), to whom the seven first days of the month are sacred; a multitude of Izads, to the chief of whom, Depádar, A'dar, A'wā, Khúrshíd, Mohur, Tír, Gosh, Dépméher, Méher (Mithra), Sarosh, Rashné, Farvardín, Běhrám, Rám, Govád, (Vád), Depdín, Dín, Ashasang, A'stád, A'smán, Zamiád, Máhraspand, and Andirán, the remaining days of the months are sacred, and to whom they ascribe the presidence over various localities and pursuits; the five Gěhs and other divisions of Time with-Bounds; Zarvána-Akarana, or Time-without-Bounds; the five Elements of nature —fire, earth, water, air, and ether*; the mighty Wind of Sapandár; Anagar Rochâo, or Primitive Light; the Sun, especially at its rising and setting; the Moon, particularly when

* The idea of worshipping ether, they seem to have got from the Hindús. It is specified in the Sanján Shlokas; but it does not occur in the ancient writings of the Pársís.

first visible, and when at its full; the Stars, and particularly the Tashtar, and all the other heavenly bodies; the sacred fires of Bĕhrám, and A'darán; the Ocean, and the Rivers of the earth; the exalted Mountains and wide-spreading Valleys; the whole World on which we dwell; the trees, plants, and other Vegetables by which it is adorned, and especially the favorite Hom and its juice Perahom; the Flocks and Herds, which are the children of Bahman, and particularly the sacred white bull, and all the irrational animals, terrestrial and aquatic; the intelligent and brave companion of man, the Dog, the great protector from the assaults of devils, and which if it does not receive the first portion of food taken into the hand at every meal, will oppose the passage of departed souls over the bridge of Chinavad; the bridge of Chinavad itself; the Resurrection; the mystical word Hunavar,* by which Hormazd fought against Ahriman; Zartusht, and the whole law of the Mazdayasnians imparted to Zartusht, and the holy Dasturs by whom it is recited; departed Spirits, of whom forgiveness is entreated for injuries inflicted on them; the Faruhars, or prototypes, of these spirits, the Faruhar and body and throne of Hormazd himself, and all the Faruhars of all the imaginary celestial and terrestrial beings; and, in short, the whole visible and invisible Creation attributed to Hormazd. Though they do not worship idols, the 'works of men's hands,' more determined and devoted polytheists than they are, the page of history does not reveal to us; and were it not that they abhor what they conceive to be the evil Principle and his works, and seem, in this country at least, to have generally avoided the metaphysical subtleties by which many around us are bewildered, they might be set down as pantheists, both spiritual and material, mystical and practical."†

I formerly remarked that I did not lightly bring these charges against the Pársís; and I am now prepared to establish every one of them, by an appeal to their own reputed sacred books.

* The *Bázh* commencing with the words *Yathá áhú vairyó.*

† Doctrine of Jehovah addressed to the Pársís, pp. 24—26.

In doing this, I shall show both what are some of the *injunctions* respecting their polytheism, and what are some of the *actual forms* in which is *practised*.

The following is from the nineteenth fargard of the Vandidád, where a great deal more matter of a similar kind is to be found:—

[illegible]

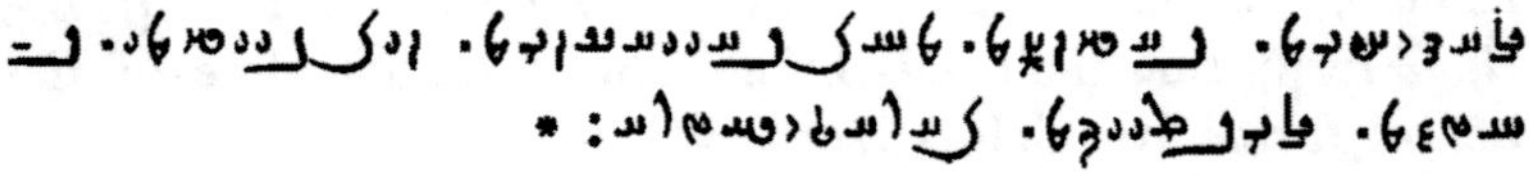

A'aṯ mraoṯ Ahuró-Mazdáo: Nizbyanguha tú Zaratẖustra vanguhím daênãm mázdayaçním; nizbyanguha tú Zaratẖústra aváon amesaçpeñti aoui haptó-karasvairím zãm; nizbyanguha tú Zaratẖustra tẖwásahê kẖadẖátahê Zaravánahe-Akaranahe vayóis uparó kairyêhê; nizbyanguha tú Zaratẖustra vátó takẖmó Mazdadẖátó çpeñta çríra dughẖdẖa Ahuró-Mazdáo; nizbyanguha tú Zaratẖustra fravasís mana yaṯ Ahurahê-Mazdáo avãm yãm mazistãmcha vahistãmcha çraêstãncha kẖraozẖdistãmcha kẖaratẖwistãmcha hukereftamãmcha asáṯ apanótemãmcha yênghé urvaê mãthró çpeñto kẖató; nizbyanguha Zarathustra imaṯ dãmi, yaṯ Ahuró-Mazdáo vákẖsem mê açãçaṯ Zarathustró nizbyêmi Ahuró-Mazdáo asava dámi dátem, nizbyêmi mitẖrem vaouru-gaoyóitím huzaênem kẖarenanguhçtem zayanãm verethrvaçtem zayanãm; nizbyêmi çraosem asím Ahuraodẖem çnatẖis zaçtya drizẖimnó kameredẖa paiti daêvanãm, nizbyêmi mãtẖró çpeñtó yó as kẖarenáo, nizbyêmi tẖwasahê khadhátahê, Zaravánahê-Akaranahê vayóis uparokairyêhê, nizbyêmi vátó takẖmó Mazdadátó çpeñta çríra dughẖdẖa Ahúró-Mazdáo, nizbyêmi vanguhím daênãm Mázdayaçním dátem vídóyúm Zaratẖustra.

—"Invoke, thou Zoroaster, the good law, the Mázdayaçnian. Invoke, thou Zoroaster, the mino [unseen] Amsháspands, who are over the seven keshvars [divisions] of the earth. Invoke, thou Zoroaster, the Thwása Khadáta [the heaven self-created], Zarvána-Akarana [Time-without-Bounds], Váyi [Izad] who is over the works above. Invoke, thou Zoroaster, the strong wind created by Mazda, Sapandár, the pure daughter of Hormazd. Invoke, thou Zoroaster, the Faruhar of me who am Hormazd, which [Faruhar] is the greatest, the highest, the best, the most powerful, the most splendid, and the best bodied, and the purest of all, whose [Hormazd's] soul is the word exalted by itself. Invoke, thou Zoroaster, the crea-

* Lithographed Vandidád, pp. 509-511.

tion of me who am Hormazd. Let Zoroaster love what has now been uttered by me. I invoke [rejoined Zoroaster] Hormazd, who has created the pure world. I invoke Mithra*, the protector of the earth, the good mover [charioteer?], the most splendid of movers, the strongest of movers. I invoke Çraos, the pure, who in his hand holds a weapon over the heads of the devils. I invoke the exalted word, the very splendid word.† I invoke the Twása Khadáta, Zarvána-Akarana, Váyi who is over the works on high. I invoke the strong wind created by Mazda, Sapandár the pure daughter of Hormazd. I invoke the good law, the Mazdayaçnian,‡ I invoke what is given against the devils, O Zoroaster."

The following is an English rendering of the French translation from the Zand, of the first Há of the Yaçna, the greatest liturgical work of the Pársís, by Monsieur E. Burnouf, whose elaborate researches connected with the Zand language, are well known to the Pársís themselves. The commentary of the learned Frenchman, on this prayer, in which his version is almost uniformly successfully vindicated, occupies a large volume, printed at the Royal Press of Paris in 1833 and 1835. I request the reader to cast his eye on the notes which I have subjoined as he passes along.

1. "I invoke,§ and I celebrate ‖ the Creator *Ahura-*

* This is evidently one of the passages which prove that among the ancient Persians Mithra was sometimes represented as the sun. The Modern Pársís understand by it Meher Izad, in contradistinction to Khurbeshíd, the Sun.

† In the Pársí traditional translations, this passage is always applied to Máhraspand Izad. Have they not been led into this error from their ing ashamed of the worship of inanimate objects?

‡ This is one of the many instances from which it appears that the law which Hormazd is represented in the Vandidád as in the process of giving to Zoroaster, had been already established, when the Vandidád was written. The framers of that work, though personating Hormazd and Zoroaster, were not able to preserve consistency.

§ [illegible] *nivaêdhayêmi* in Zand.

‖ [illegible] *hankárayêmi* in Zand.

Mazda, luminous, resplendent, very great and very good, very perfect, and very powerful, very intelligent and very beautiful, eminent in purity, who possesses the good science, the source of pleasure, him who has created us, who has formed us, who has nourished us, who is the most accomplished among intelligent beings.

2. I invoke and I celebrate *Bahman* (benevolence); *Ardebehisht*, (the excellent purity); *Shâhrivar*, (the desirable king); *Sapandomad*, (her who is holy and meek), *Khordad* and *Amerdad* * (her who produces every thing, and her who gives life) ; the *body of the Bull*, and the *soul of the Bull* ;† the *fire of Hormazd*, the most swift of the holy immortals.

3. I invoke, I celebrate him, who is given in this world, given against the Daevas, the pure *Zoroaster*, the master of purity.

4. I invoke, I celebrate the parts of the day (genii.), the masters of purity, the pure Oshen (*ushahina*),‡ master of purity.

5. I invoke, I celebrate him, who is exalted and who protects houses, the pure, master of purity.

6. I invoke, I celebrate Sarosh § (*Çraosha*), the holy, endowed with holiness, the victorious, who gives abundance to the world, Rashné (*Raçnu*), the most just, and Ashtad (*Arstât*), her who gives abundance to the world who gives good things to the world.

7. I invoke, I celebrate Hâvan (*havant*),‖ the pure, master of purity.

8. I invoke, I celebrate him, who gives fecundity, and who protects the villages, the pure, master of purity.

9. I invoke, I celebrate *Mithra*, who multiplies the pairs

* The beings mentioned above are with Hormazd himself, those which form the seven Amshâspands.

† According to the mythology of the Bundéshné, the elements of the different existing terrestrial objects were embodied in a Bull before their present developement. See Gujarâtî translation of the Bundéshne p. 176.

‡ The first Gěh or watch.

§ The *hamkâr*, or companion of the first Gěh. ‖ The second Gěh.

of oxen,* who has a thousand ears, ten thousand eyes, denominated an Izad; [I invoke, I celebrate] *Rámashné Kharom* (the pleasure of the palate).†

10. I invoke, I celebrate Rapitan (*rapithwina*,‡ the middle of the day), the pure master of purity.

11. I invoke, I celebrate *him who extends propagation*,§ and who *protects the villages*, the pure, master of purity.

12. I invoke, I celebrate *Ardébehisht* (the excellent purity), and the *fire of Ahuramazda*.

13. I invoke, I celebrate Osiren (*uzayeiren*),‖ the latter part of the day, the pure, master of purity.

14. I invoke, I celebrate him, *who multiplies mankind*,¶ and who *protects the provinces*, the pure, master of purity.

15. I invoke, I celebrate the *height*, the divine summit, source of water, and the *water* given by Mazda.

16. I invoke, I celebrate Evesrutem (*Aiwiçrúthram*),** him who watches over life, the pure, master of purity.

17. I invoke, I celebrate him *who multiplies the means of good living*††, and him who comes nearest to Zoroaster, the pure, master of purity.

18. I invoke, I celebrate the *Faruhars* of the saints and the *females* who have men for their protectors; and the *Gahanbár* favorable to houses; and the energy with a good constitution, and of an exalted size, and victory (*Behrám*), given by Ahura; and superiority the protectress.‡‡

* Lord of the jungles, according to the dasturs.

† The worshipper seems here to have an eye to his breakfast.

‡ The third Gĕh.

§ Or, according to the dasturs, Frádádár-Fasé the *hamkár* of the preceding Gĕh.

‖ The fourth Gĕh.

¶ Or according to the dasturs, Frádádár Vír, the hamkár of the fourth Gĕh.

** The fifth Gĕh.

†† The Dasturs apply this to Frádádár Visp, the hamkár of the last Gĕh, which is considered particularly favourable for religious recitations.

‡‡ This paragraph in most MSS. is followed by the repetition of the paragraphs 4, 5, and 6.

19. I invoke, I celebrate the *parts of the month*, masters of purity; the *new moon* (the genius) pure, master of purity.

20. I invoke, I celebrate the *full moon* which makes every thing to grow, (the genius) pure, master of purity.

21. I invoke, I celebrate the *Gahanbárs*,* masters of purity, Mediozerem *(mardhyoi zaramaya)* the pure, master of purity.

22. I invoke, I celebrate, Mediosham *(maidhyo shama)*, the pure, master of purity.

23. I invoke, I celebrate Patasham *(paetishahya)*, the pure, master of purity.

24. I invoke, I celebrate Eiathrem *(ayáthrama)*, the time of fertilizing, and the unfolding of birds,† the pure, master of purity.

25. I invoke, I celebrate Mediareh *(maídhyâirya)*, the pure, master of purity.

26. I invoke, I celebrate the Hamaspethmedem *(hamaspathmaédhya)*, the pure, master of purity.

27. I invoke, I celebrate the *years*, (the genii) masters of purity.

28. I invoke, I celebrate *all the masters who are masters of purity*, and the *thirty-three genii* nearest to Hávan, who are of an excellent purity, which Mazda has revealed and whom Zoroaster has proclaimed.

29. I invoke, I celebrate *Ahura* and *Mithra*, exalted, immortal, pure; and the *stars*, the holy and heavenly creations; and the star Teshtar *(Tistriya)*, luminous, resplendent; and the *moon* which watches over the germ of the Bull; and the *Sun*, the sovereign, the rapid courser, the eye of Ahura-mazdá; *Mithra*,‡ the chief of the provinces.

30. I invoke, I celebrate the genii, (Izads) of the day and of the month in which the Izashné may be recited.§

* The six periods of creation, comprising together the lunar year, which are immediately afterwards enumerated.

† This clause, I have slightly altered from Burnouf.

‡ This word is applied by the dasturs to Meher Izad and not to the Sun.

§ This supplement is given in the MSS. in Gujarátí.

31. I thee celebrate, I thee invoke, O thou *Fire*, Son of Hormazd, with *all the fires.*

32. I invoke, I celebrate the pure [good] *waters*, and *all the waters* given by Mazda, and all the *trees* given by Mazda.

33. I invoke, I celebrate the excellent *word*, the pure, efficacious, given against the Devas, given through the interposition of Zoroaster, the good law of the worshippers of Mazda.

34. I invoke, I celebrate the *mountain*, the depository of intelligence,* given by Mazda, brilliant with purity and *all the mountains* brilliant with purity, completely brilliant, given by Mazda; and the royal splendour given by Mazda, and the unborrowed splendour given by Mazda.

35. I invoke, I celebrate the excellent *purity*, the excellent *knowledge*, the excellent *understanding*, the excellent *thought*, the *splendour*, the *good* given by Mazda.

36. I invoke, I celebrate, the excellent, the perfect *blessing*, and the excellent *man* who is pure, and the *thought* of the wise man, the formidable, powerful, Izad.

37. I invoke, I celebrate both these *places* and these *countries* and the *fields* for cattle, and the *houses* and *places* where they watch the corn, and the *waters*, and the *lands* and the *trees*, and this *earth* and this *heaven*, and the pure *wind*, the *stars*, the *moon*, and the *sun*, lights which are without a beginning, uncreated,† and *all the creations of* the pure and heavenly beings, and whomsoever are the pure genii, the masters of purity.

38. I invoke, I celebrate the exalted *master*, who is master of purity, the masters (who are) the *days*, the *watches*, the *months*, the *epochs of the year* (the Gahanbárs), the

* The dasturs make this to be the hill Hostdástár, said in the Bundéshné to be in Seistán.

† The Zand here is worthy of particular notice by the reader. The lights mentioned are said to [illegible] *anaghrinãm raochanghãm khadhátanãm* without-a-begining, and self-given, or uncreated. The explanation of this language is to be found in the belief of the Pársís that they are of the substance or essence of Hormazd. Their complete deification is thus set forth.

years (genii) who are the masters of purity, that which is here given, given against the Devas, the *word of Zoroaster*, the lord.

39. I invoke, I celebrate the awful, the powerful *Faruhars* of pure men, the Faruhars of men of the ancient law, the Faruhars of modern men, my parents, the Faruhars of my soul.*

40, 41. I invoke, I celebrate all the *masters of purity*. I invoke, I celebrate all the *Izads*, both celestial and terrestrial, who distribute riches, who ought to be both adored and invoked by the purity which is excellent.

42. O thou who hast been given in this world, given against the Dévas, *Zoroaster*, pure, master of purity, if I have offended thee, either in thought, or in word, or in action, whether it be voluntarily or involuntarily, I address anew this praise in thy honour; yes, I invoke thee, if I have come short before thee in this sacrifice and this invocation.†

43. O all you vastly great masters, pure masters of purity! If I have offended you either in thought, or in word, or in action, whether it be voluntarily or involuntarily, I address anew this praise in your honour; yes, I invoke you, if I have come short before you in this sacrifice and in this invocation.

44. Worshipper of Mazda, follower of Zoroaster, enemy of the Dévas, observer of the precepts of Ahura, let me address my homage to that which is here given, given against the Dévas, to Zoroaster, pure, master of purity, for the sacrifice, for the invocation, for the prayer which renders favorable, for the benediction. Let me address my homage to the masters (who are) the days, the watches &c, for the benediction. That is to say, Let me address my homage to the masters who are the days, the watches, the months, the epochs of the year (Gahanbárs), the years, for the sacrifice, for the invocation, for the prayer which renders favourable, for the benediction."

* Let Dosabháí and others observe that the soul, instead of being a Faruhar, is represented as *having a Faruhar*.

† This passage and what follows, the Pársís, I should think, will allow, has not been composed by Zoroaster.

The following is an original translation from the Zand of the seventy-first Há of the Izashné [numbered seventy-second by Anquetil], made with the help of the Gujarátí version of Frámjí Aspandiárji, and an examination of the Sanskrit corresponding vocables, and other authorities.

"The pure Farshostar asked the pure Zoroaster: Reply, O venerable Zoroaster. What is the [religious] duty toward the masters, and what is to be done at the Gáthas?"*

Thus spoke Zoroaster: —

"I worship [*yazamaidĕ* in Zand, *árâdhun*, in Gujarátí], *Hormazd,* the pure, master of purity.

"I worship *Zoroaster,* the pure, master of purity.

"I worship the pure *Amsháspands.*

"I worship the *Faruhar of the pure Zoroaster.*

"I worship the excellent, wonderful, exalted *Faruhars of the saints.*

"I worship publicly and privately the *most exalted of the masters.*

"I worship the *most active of the Izads,* the most worthy of the masters of purity, the most praise-worthy, the most pervading, the delight of the master, the pure master of purity.

"I worship *Hormazd,* the pure, master of purity.

"I worship the whole *body of Hormazd.*†

"And I worship all the *Amsháspands.*

"And I worship all the *masters of purity.*

"And I worship the whole Mázdayaçní *religion.*

"And I worship all the *áfsmanĕm* (or andájah paimân).‡

* The Gáthas here alluded to, are probably the five days, after the expiration of the lunar year, which supplement the solar year, and are observed as a festival.

† 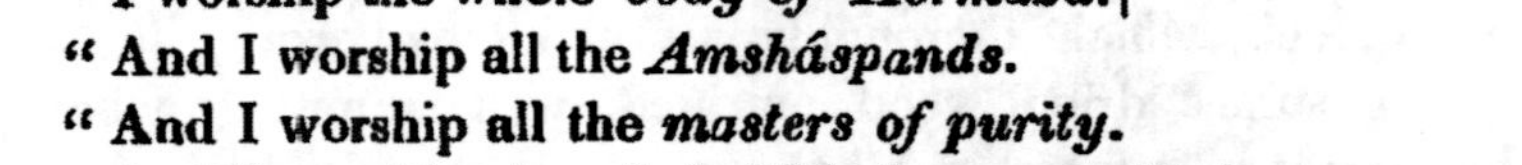

Viçpĕm kĕrĕfs Ahurahĕ-Mazdâo yazamaidĕ. The word *kĕrĕfs* here is evidently equivalent to the Latin *corpus*, and its use seems favourable to the theory of the antiquity of the Zand language. Its application to Hormazd, being adverse to his omnipresence, is one of the tokens of his being only a secondary divinity among the Pârsís.

‡ Anquetil du Perron supposes this to be the expression of the Law.

"And I worship all the exalted *mañthra* [the language of the Avastá].

"And I worship all that is given against the devils [the Vandidád].

"And I worship all the *long existences* [the beings which are to exist during the present *aión* of 12,000 years ?]

"And I worship all the pure celestial and terrestrial *Izads*.

"And I worship all the excellent, wonderful, exalted *Faruhars* of the saints.

"I worship the *whole pure creation* given by Hormazd, that is pure given, pure created, pure by the law, that is to be extolled as pure.

"I worship the whole five pure *Gáthas*, with the pure one among the pure.

"I worship all the *Izashné* and *Fráiti*, and *Paititi*, and *Aibicharěti*.*

"I worship all the *hymns af the Izashné* [or the Satut Yaçt, according to the dasturs].

"I worship all the *words* uttered by Hormazd, which destroy evil thought, which destroy evil speech, which destroy evil work; which are of him [Hormazd] who prevents evil thought, who prevents evil speech, who prevents evil work; which thoroughly cut of all evil thought, which thoroughly cut off all evil speech, which thoroughly cut off all evil work, like as fire consumes dried wood, purified, well-examined, wholly burning it. I worship *all the words* endowed with power, victory, glory, and strength.

"I worship all the *fountains of water*, flowing and stationary. [?]

"I worship all the *trees*, and the trunks, and lofty branches, and fruit.

* 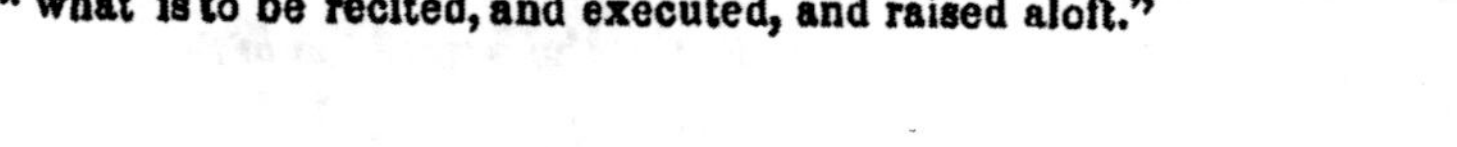

Mr. Westergaard has suggested to me that these words, being coupled with the Yaçna, probably refer to different liturgical formulæ now lost. In the Gujarátí translation of Frámji Aspandiárjí, they are rendered by "what is to be recited, and executed, and raised aloft."

"I worship the whole *earth.*

"I worship the whole *heaven.*

"I worship all the *stars,* the *moon,* and the *sun.*

"I worship the *primeval* [or boundless] *lights.*

"I worship all *the animals,* both aquatic and terrene, and that dwell in the wilderness, and changhranghachasach [?]

"I worship all the *girambár* of Hormazd, the good creation, the pure, which he [Hormazd] has created abundant and excellent, and which is worthy of the Izashné, and of the Níáísh, on account of the purity which is the best.

"I worship all the *mountains,* the purely pleasurable.

"I worship all the *caves* given by Hormazd.

"I worship all the *fires.*

"I worship all the *words of righteousness.*

"I worship all that in introducing, introduces [in worship]; let them be to me for superintendence, support, and perfect preservation.

"I invoke [𐬰𐬠𐬀𐬌𐬌𐬈𐬨𐬌 *zbayêmi* in Zand, પઢું *padhún* in Gujarátí] and worship the *Gáthas,* the exalted, the mighty lords, the pure; let them be to me for protection, superintendence, support, and perfect preservation.

"I invoke and worship *my own soul;* [let it be to me] for protection, superintendence, support, and perfect preservation.

"I worship *Khurdád,* the pure, the master of purity.

"I invoke the divine *revelation* [Zand-Avastá], the pure, master of purity.

"I worship *Amardád,* the pure, master of purity.

"I worship the *law of Hormazd,* the pure, master of purity.

"I worship the wonderful *Haftanghát,** the pure, master of purity.† . . . . .

* This is a portion of the Izashné, (35th — 40th Há) which is commanded to be repeated by dying men, and by their friends on their behalf. The objects of reverence and worship which it sets forth, are mostly the same as those exhibited in the Há which we now translate.

† Here follows a paragraph, about the recital of the word at the moment of death, and the passage of the bridge Chinavad. The meaning is very obscure in the original; and I do not find that the commentaries of the Dasturs cast any light upon it.

"I worship the *active* and *good-minded.* The good-minded and active, I worship, for the opposing of darkness, for the opposing of grief and vexation.

"I worship *health and soundness of body.* I worship *creation*, and *encrease.*

"I worship all the *words* for removing diseases, and laziness.

"I worship the recurring *Gáthas.* I worship the *Gáthas*, the exalted, the glorious masters, the pure.

"I worship the *hymns of the Yaçna*, [or *Satut Yaçt*]. I worship the whole collection of the hymns of the Yaçna, which was given to the ancient world.

"I worship *my own soul.*

"I worship my own *Faruhar.*

"I worship the *righteous good delectifier.*

"I worship the righteous man [*Dahman*], the pure.

"I worship the strong power of *Dámi* [?], the Izad of exalted mind.

"I worship these *waters*, and *grounds*, and *trees.*

"I worship these *places*, and *fields*, and the *folds* of cattle in the wilderness, and the *abodes*, and the *water-courses* [?].

"I worship the *lord of the fields*, who is Hormazd.

"I worship *Hormazd*, of all masters the greatest.

"I worship the *days*, the *watches*, the *parts of the months*, the *Gahanbárs*, and the *years.*

"I praise (*çtaomi*), invoke (*zbayêmi*), extol (*ufyêmi*) and worship (*yazamaidê*), the good, wonderful, exalted *Faruhars* of the pure, of the houses, streets, cities, provinces, devoted to Zoroaster.*

"I worship thee *fire*, the Son of Hormazd, the pure, master of purity.

"I worship the *reservoirs of waters.*

"I worship *Nariosangh.*

"I worship the powerful *Dámí*, [?] the lofty-minded Izad.

"I worship *departed souls.*

* The condition of the fire before which the Izashné is recited, is here to be looked at.

"I worship the *Faruhars* of the saints, and the *strong master*, who is Hormazd, who is highest in purity, who is the most advanced in purity.

"I worship the *whole word of Zoroaster*.

"I worship all the *good deeds* which I have now done, or will ever do."*

Hundreds of passages, similar to the three which I have now quoted, are to be found both in the liturgical and doctrinal works contained in the Zand-Avastá; but it is not necessary for me to produce others of a like character. Let the attention of the reader be directed to those which are now before him; and I am certain that be he a Native, or a European, he will cordially assent to the statements which I have made respecting both the *number* and the *nature* of the objects of worship recognized by the Pársís. There is no person, indeed, in the slightest degree acquainted with their religious tenets and practices, as they are thus set forth in the works which they esteem sacred, but will readily admit that the Pársís are truly polytheists in the most rigid sense of the term.

If any person should ask, What is the *kind* of worship rendered by the Pársís to all these deities, and deified objects, I would beg him again to look to these and similar passages for the reply. The more fully they are examined in the original Zand, or in any of the Pahlaví, Sanskrit, Persian, Gujarátí, French, or English translations, which have been, or can be made of them, the more clearly will they be seen to illustrate and establish the following observations, to which I request particular attention.

1. The objects of worship are *jumbled and confounded together* in such a manner as must lead to the degradation, — supposing them to be capable of it, — of those of them who possess the highest station and character, and the consequent exaltation of those who are of the lowest rank and influence.

The worshipper at one moment calls upon Hormazd, at the next, upon his own ghost; at one moment on an archan-

* This recitation is followed by the muttering of various minor pieces.

gel, at the next on a sturdy bull; at one time on the brilliant sun, at the next on a blazing fire; at one moment on a lofty and stupendous mountain, at the next on a darksome cave; at one moment on the ocean, at the next on a well or spring; at one moment on Time-without-Bounds, at the next on the passing hour; at one moment on the greatest master of purity, at the next on every master of purity; at one moment on the whole creation given by Hormazd, at the next on the five pure Gáthas; at one moment on the whole Vandidád, at the next on the Satut-Yaçt. If the great thus mentioned have any understanding, they must view themselves reproached, and if the mean have any modesty and shame, they must view themselves as wantonly and cruelly exposed, by the company in which they are placed.

To give my Pársí friends a more distinct comprehension of what I now wish to be impressed upon their minds, we shall suppose them to betake themselves to some respected Governor of Bombay, in order to express the regard which they cherish for his character and their gratitude for the favours which they have received from his administration, and thus to proceed with their loyal address: —

Right Honorable Sir, — We invoke and celebrate thee, because of thy justice, liberality, and bravery. We recognize thee as our good and gracious Governor. Thou are the bravest, and most intelligent of the intelligent of the Sáhebs, who have reigned over us in this great country.

We invoke and celebrate our own souls, and our own wealth, and our grandfathers' souls, and their wealth.

We invoke the Commander-in-chief, the brave, master of bravery; and the Superintendent of the Indian Navy, the exalted genius who presides over the fires of furnaces and steamships; and his *hamkár*, Ardeshir Khurshídjí, the clever and powerful.

We invoke and celebrate lance-corporal Tom, the brave, the master of bravery.

We invoke and celebrate the chandeliers of Parell-House, and the lamp of Arjun, the náyak of peons, the Kulábá lighthouse, and all the fires and lamps of Bombay.

We invoke, celebrate, and reverence the Chief-Secretary to Government, and all the Secretaries, private and public, military and civil, the pure, the great, the benevolent, and the generous. We invoke and celebrate them.

We invoke and celebrate Malabar Hill.

We invoke, celebrate, and praise the Fort ditch.

We celebrate and invoke thee, Right Honorable Sir.

We invoke, celebrate and praise the Governors of Daman and Díva, the greatest masters of bravery.

We celebrate, and invoke, and praise every European in India.

We invoke, celebrate, and adore the Indian Ocean, and the China Seas.

We reverence, and supplicate all the tanks and wells of Bombay.

We invoke the whole Regulations of Government, and we invoke the Commander-in-chief's General Orders, and every other order.

We invoke praise, supplicate and extol thy riding horses and thy carriage horses, thy dogs, and cows, and goats.

We invoke thy fields and gardens, and we invoke all thy residencies.

We invoke, praise, adore, and celebrate every person and thing that exists.

O Governor of the governed, we praise, laud, and extol thee.

Were the Mobeds to prepare an address of this kind, they could not get a single individual among their intelligent countrymen to adhibit to it his signature; were it ready for delivery they would not and could not present it, from their consciousness that instead of its being the expression of peculiar regard, it is nothing else, from its order and association, but ridiculous mockery; were they to put into the hands, or to read it in the presence, of the governor, they would infallibly be shown to the door. In reference to their dealings with their fellow-men, their proceedings are characterized by propriety and prudence. Let them reflect and repent, and let the same attributes, in their highest degree, appear in their professed communion with God.

2. Not only are all distinctions among the different objects of worship referred to in the liturgical and doctrinal works of the Pársís nearly, or altogether, levelled by their being jumbled and confounded together by the strangest and most unsuitable associations; but the same result is brought about by the fact, that *the different objects of worship, of whatever nature they may be, have actually applied to them, without the least distinction, the same terms expressive of respect, of worship, prayer, supplication, praise, invocation, glory, reverence, adoration, celebration, exaltation, recognition, commemoration, and benediction.*

This proposition is easily established. To *every one* object mentioned in the preceding extracts from the Vandidád, and Izashné, and in hundreds of other passages of a like nature are applied the following Zand words and expressions, which, with a reference to proper authorities, I shall endeavour briefly, but faithfully, to explain.

𐬫𐬀𐬰𐬀𐬨𐬀𐬌𐬛𐬉 *yazamaidé*. This verb, I have rendered, *I worship*. In the Gujarátí translation of the Vandidád and Izashné, etc. it is, as far as I have seen, uniformly rendered by આરાધુંછુ or આરાધના કરૂંછુ words exactly of the same meaning.* By Nariasangh the Sanskrit translator of the Yaçna, it is rendered आराधये, I worship. Edal Dáru renders it by *árádhunch*, which he softens by giving as its synonym *bazurg kari jánunch*, "I esteem glorious." Dosabhái also condescends to use for it *arádhunch*, the sense of which however, he endeavours to lower, by making it equivalent to *yád karunch*, I remember!"† The root of the verb, is evidently found in the Sanskrit यज *yaj* to sacrifice. M. Burnouf considers the noun 𐬫𐬀𐬯𐬥𐬀 *yaçna*, applied to the Izashné, equivalent to the Sanskrit यज्ञ *yajna*, sacrifice, and

* आराधनी, in Wilson's Sanskrit dictionary, is rendered, "worship, adoration, propitiation of the deities. E आङ्., राध to finish, ल्युट् aff." आराधना, it may here be stated, is translated "worship" by Aspandiárjí Frámjí. *Hádí-i-Gum-Ráhán*, p. 151.

† Tálim-i-Zartusht p. 117. In this place, *yazamaidé* is applied to Zaraváua-akarana, or Time-without-bounds.

he renders it "sacrifice with prayers,"* which, it must be admitted, is the highest kind of worship. There can be no doubt, that as far as etymology goes, the learned professor is correct. The reader will remember that Edal Dáru quotes a passage from the Avastá according to which the Ardebehisht fire is represented as worthy of the *yaçna* or Izashné.† Hundreds of other objects are thus honoured, in the use of the highest liturgical forms which the Pársís possess.

nivaēdhayēmi. This word, according to Bournouf,‡ I have rendered "*I invoke.*" Nariasangh, the Sanskrit translator of the Izashné, makes it equivalent to निमंत्रयामि *nimantrayámi,* "I summon or invite;" but he might have got a word nearer to it in etymology and meaning in निवेदयामि *nivedayámi*; "I inform entrust, address," or "I present offerings to." Frámjí in his translation of the Izashné uniformly renders it by ઈઝન કરૂંછ *izan karunch,* to which I do not object. With this verb almost all the addressess in the first Há, which we have quoted from the Izashné, and thousands of others of a like nature, commence.

hañkáiryēmi. This verb has been properly rendered, *I celebrate.* Nariasangh makes it संपूर्णयामि *sampúrnayámi,* which in meaning is close to what is given to it by Aspandiárjí, "I pray thee with all supplication,"§ or આરાધુંછ તમામ ઈઝશનેમાં,‖ *árádhunch tamám izashnemã.* It generally follows nivaēdhayémi, and is applied with equal frequency, both to the highest and lowest objects of worship.

çtaomi, and *çtáem* in Pahliví. Like the corresponding verb स्तौमि *staumi* in Sanskrit, this word is ren-

* *Sacrifice avec prières.* Commentaire sur le Yaçna, vol. i, p. 24.

† See page 200 of this work. ‡ Comment. sur le Yaçna, p. 121.

§ Hádí-i-Gum-Rahán, p. 28, English version.

‖ This is very near the rendering of Burnouf, "Idjuni absolutam faciam." Commentaire sur le Yaçna p. 121.

dered I *praise.* It is properly rendered વખાણું *vakhánun* in the Gujarátí translation of the Izashné. It is applied to all the dependencies of Hormazd as well as himself.

zbayêmi. This word, corrupted into *zabáem* in Pahliví, I have rendered "I invoke." It is translated પઢું *paḍhun* in the Gujarátí version of the Izashné, in the seventy-second Há of which, as will have been seen, it is applied, like that which here follows it, to the Faruhars. With the inseparable particle *ni* prefixed, it occurs frequently in the nineteenth fargard of the Vandidád.* M. Burnouf shows that, according to the usual transmutation of letters, it is the Sanskrit ह्वयामि, *hvayámi.*†

ufyêmi. I have rendered this word "*I contemplate.*" પોતાનું કરૂં *potánun karun*, the Gujarátí translation of the dasturs, is not erroneous. In the Persian it is rendered by *khwáham.*

áfrínámi, we have already observed, is equivalent to the Sanskrit प्रीणामि, *prínámi* "I delectify, or fulfil the desires of." It is particularly used in the worship of fire.

áyêçê This is evidently a verb in the perfect middle, equivalent to the Sanskrit आयेजे *áyéjé*, rendered by Westergaard "deos colo."‡ Burnouf renders it by "I glorify;"§ and Bopp by "celebro."|| In the Persian translation, of the Zand-Avastá, it is rendered by *khwáham*, and in the Gujarátí by *cháhun*, "I love, or desire." It is applied indiscriminately to Creator and creature, throughout the prayers of the Pársis.

vahma. This noun is uniformly rendered by نیایش *niáish* by the Pársís. The word, which literally signifies "praise," is applied by them by way of distinction to

* See extract, p.ix, 253 of this work.

† Alphabet Zend, p. 69.

‡ Radices Linguæ Sanskritæ, p. 116.

§ Commentaire sur le Yaçna, p. 40.

|| Vergleichende Grammatik, p. 155.

five of their liturgical pieces, addressed particularly to the sun, Meher, moon, fire, and water. In all of these prayers and addresses, as will be seen from that of fire, a translation of which we have inserted in full, the alleged works of Hormazd, animate and inanimate, have a place as well as himself.

nemó. This is the Sanskrit नमः *namah.* It is rendered by the equivalent word नमस्कार *namaskára,* "salutation or reverence," by the Pársís; and is indiscriminately applied to all their divinities.

kh͟snaoth͟ra. For this word the Pársís use the Persian خوشنومن *khushnuman,* "fulfilling the desires of," which has been introduced into Gujarátí by the Pársís. It is generally used in connexion with *vahma* above-mentioned.

fraçaçti. This noun is also principally used in connexion with *vahma.* It means celebration. It is from the Sanskrit root शंस् *shans,* "to celebrate," with the prefix प्र *pra* added.

This list might be easily extended. It may now be sufficient to remark, however, that the terms of which we have given specimens, and which we have said are indiscriminately applied to *all* the Pársí divinities, are used to express not civil, but religious, respect and honour. They are employed in the most solemn forms of devotion which the Zoroastrians possess; and the use of them in their actual connexions, leaves nothing peculiar to be addressed to the only living and true God, the Creator of heaven and earth, the supreme Sovereign and Governor, the supplier of all the wants of his creatures, and the only Saviour.

3. Not only are the different objects of worship recognized by the "sacred" books of the Pársís, unsuitably confounded together in these books, and the same terms of worship indiscriminately applied to them; but the *service of the inferior objects occupies more space in them than that of the highest.*

I have already proved, that the authorities on which the Pársí religion is founded, represent Hormazd as a secondary divinity. But allowing, for the sake of argument, that he is the primary deity of the Zoroastrians, I would ask, how it appears, that compared with that of his alleged animate and inanimate *creatures*, his service, in point of extent, occupies so often only an inferior place in the liturgical forms of the Pársís. In most of these professedly devotional pieces, his worship has only the twentieth, or thirtieth part of the space devoted to it that is assigned to that of the amsháspands, izads, elements, and other objects which are addressed. In some of the articles in fact, he his set aside, by a mere apocryphal address, or *satáishné*, at the beginning, and is not again once mentioned throughout. Let the Pársís consider the words which they utter when they pray, and they will be convinced that this is the case. Let them, respecting each sentence, ask themselves, To whom does it appertain? and they will find that the general answer must be the "creature," and that too without any reference to the Creator! The mention of God's works, real or imaginary, which they will find in their books, is not that in which these works are indirectly referred to as proofs and illustrations of the wisdom, power, goodness, and faithfulness of God, but that in which the works, are directly and expressly addressed, and praised, and supplicated.

The charge of an extensive polytheism, which I have deliberately brought against the books of the Pársís, I now hold to be completely and irrefragably established. But before making this subject the matter of further remonstrance with the Pársís of Bombay, I shall introduce to the notice of the reader all the explanations and attempted defences which I find in the controversial works to which I am replying, and which are but few, short, and insignificant.

Respecting the *Mázdayaçní religion* Dosabhái thus emphatically delivers himself:—"We ask the padre, is it improper to continue to remember (or recognize) the pure and holy Mázdayaçní religion, according to the declaration of God Almighty to the exalted Zoroaster. What! do you reckon it improper to remember your Christianity, and honour it? And do you not reckon any person an infidel, who says, I do not recognize Christianity? Now, O gentle reader, inquire, and see what is the weight of the padre's story."* If this advice be followed, I reply, the result will thus be stated:—"We do not find that the padre, or any other Christian is ever so demented as to speak to Christianity, to address it in worship as having a personal embodiment, or even to suppose that it has any life or intelligence. The followers of Christianity think it enough to admit its authority on the sure evidence presented, to believe its doctrines, to follow its injunctions, and to praise God for it as a gift to man. They are not like the Pársís who invoke the Vandidád, and who give it personal reverence, and praise, and who address to it their supplications, as if it could directly confer the blessings of which they stand in need." Aspandiarjí says, "The object of the Vandidád in enjoining to invoke the Mázdayaçní religion, by which is implied the pure worship of Ijdan, or the supreme being, is to wake (awaken ?) those who are the followers of it to the constant exercise of that piety which is inculcated in it." We have to learn how the calling on the name of a religion will accomplish this object. It is by studying the contents of the books of religion, and making them the subjects of prayer, and the rule of faith and obedience, which if the books have been given by God, will enable a person to make progress in piety. It is not by speaking even to Christianity, that a man can become a Christian. It is curious to find Aspandiárjí, who here admits the invocation of the Mázdayaçní religion, afterwards thus delivering himself:—"'I (replies Zoroaster) invoke the pure law of the Mazdayaçnans given to Zoroaster, and which removes the Devas.' But this is absolutely groundless." Will the words of the original, as given by his own father, satisfy him or will a more literal translation than the above suit him ? "I invoke the good Mázdayaçnian religion, given against the devils, the Zoroastrian."†

* Tálim-i-Zartusht. p. 135.

† Vandidad, nineteenth fargard, authors MS. vol, ii, p. 232. In the lithographed Vandidád, p. 511.

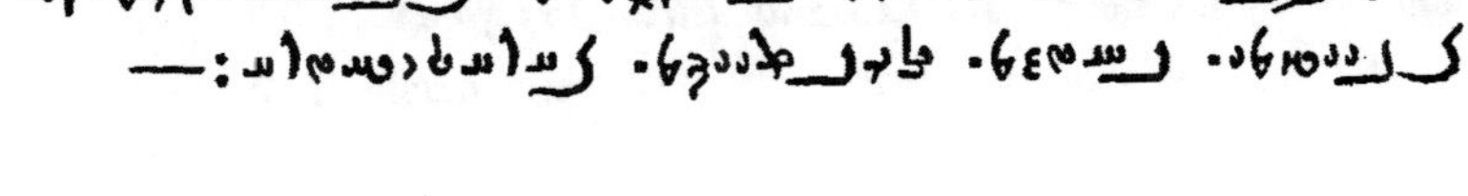

Of the *angels*, the same author thus writes : — "What is there improper in the injunction of the Vandidád about the remembrance of the angels ? Do not *you* remember the angels, and honour the Holy Spirit, without thinking it improper ?"* The reader ought to keep in mind what we have already said on the worship of angels and archangels in the preceding chapter ; and if he does this, he will readily admit the impropriety and sin of making them objects of worship, like the Pársís, who are not content simply to remember their existence, and the service they may render, when commissioned by God to execute his will, but who worship and serve them, as if every where they could hear their prayers and render them assistance, and as if God, on whom they are absolutely dependent for their existence, endowments, and support, could permit them to share in his own glory and honour. Christians may love the angels, as they love all holy beings ; and were they to receive a visit from these heavenly messengers in a visible form, they might show them becoming civil respect, as they do in the case of their fellow-men ; but most assuredly they would be violating the spirit, the precepts, and the examples of the Bible, as well as the dictates of reason, were they, for one moment, to recognize them as objects of divine homage. In the book of Psalms, which contains the great body of the inspired devotions of Christians, the angels themselves are called upon to worship God, instead of being worshipped by man. "Praise ye the Lord," says David, in his sublime poetical strain. "Praise ye the Lord from the heavens : praise him in the heights. Praise ye him, all his angels : praise ye him, all his hosts."† When a departed spirit appeared as an angel to John, and when that apostle, mistaking him for a divine person, was about to worship him, he received a decided rebuke. "When I had heard and seen,"

nizbyêmi vanguhím daênám mázdayaçním ; nizbyêmi dátem vídoyúm, Zarathustra : — "I worship the good religion the Mázdayaçní, I worship what-is-given-against the devils, O Zoroaster." There is probably some error here committed by the transcriber. *Dátem* would seem to require some masculine noun, such as *Zarathustrem*, to agree with it."

* Tálim-i-Zartusht, p. 137. † Psalm, cxlviii : 1, 2.

says the recorder of the revelation, "I fell down to worship before the feet of the angel which showed me these things. Then saith he unto me, See thou do it not: for I am thy fellow-servant, and of thy brethren the prophets, and of them which keep the sayings of this book: worship God."* The highest created intelligences and powers in heavenly places, are as dependent upon God as the meanest worm which crawls in the dust; and instead of claiming or receiving divine honours, they would, if permitted to address man, enforce the divine precept, proclaimed by Moses, and repeated by Christ, "Thou shalt worship the Lord thy God, and him only shalt thou serve."† The holy Spirit is worshipped by Christians, because, like Christ, — who is sometimes denominated the "angel of the covenant," — and the Father, he is one of the divine persons of the glorious Trinity — of the three personal united agents forming the one Godhead.‡

* Revelation, xxii. 8, 9. † Deut. vi. 13. Matth. iv. 10.

‡ In my lecture on the Vandidád, I quoted the following passage from the nineteenth fargard, "Invoke, O Zoroaster, the amsháspand who gives abundance to the seven *keshwars* of the earth." The clause, as given by me, Aspandiárjí says "has undergone some alteration; for in the Vandidád, it is stated, that the amsháspands who are the presiding genii over the seven planets, have ordained the establishment of the seven keshwars of the earth." (Hádí-i-Gum-Rahán, p. 61) It would have been only fair for him, when professing to correct my translation, had he produced the Zand words on which his criticism is founded. I here supply his lack of service. *Nízbyanguha tú Zarathustra avaon amĕsáçpeñti aoui haptó karasvairim zám.* The literal rendering of these words is simply, "Invoke, O Zoroaster, the minor amsháspands who are over the seven keshwars of the earth." From this, it must appear, that my former translation, which I made, as I intimated, principally on the authority of Anquetil du Perron, is much nearer the original than that of the mobed. Why has he said so little about the *worship* of the amsháspands, which was the principal topic to which I referred, when I quoted the passage? "To invoke these amsháspands means to bring to recollection," he says, "the innumerable advantages imparted by them to the earth, and thus be insensibly led to the worship of that Being who has created these amsháspands." (Hadí-i-Gum-Rahan, p. 61). According to this mode of reasoning, it would be proper to invoke Sir Jamshídjí Jíjíbhái's peons, that you might bring to remembrance the innumerable advantages imparted by them to one of his country mansions, that you might "insensibly" be led to respect that

Of *heaven* Dosabhái, asks "What is there wrong in remembering heaven, which God has created." * As the reader will have observed, from the authorities which we have already produced in this chapter, there is more than the simple "remembrance" of heaven practised by those, who use the sacred books of the Pársís ; and it is just because heaven, with all its glory, is merely the creation of God, that it is not to be worshipped as God. The munshi quotes a passage from Luke (Chapter xv. 21), in which he thinks the word "heaven" is used as a name of God. He is perhaps right in the opinion which he has formed. I say "perhaps," because the words rendered, "I have sinned against heaven," ἥμαρτον ἐις τὸν ὀυρανόν, may be translated literally, "I have sinned to hea-

opulent knight, from whom they have received their appointment and employment!

Aspandiárjí thus comments on another passage of the lecture on the Vandidád. "'I invoke the pure Sarosh, who strikes with extended arm the congregated Devas' is not fully comprehended, though in the Vendidád it is only, that Sarosh raises his weapon to strike Daroj. Sarosh is here substituted for Reason, which, when duly exercised curbs the evil propensities of the mind of man. Sarosh is also the name of an angel. And if our friend be still inclined to his own understanding, I would only observe that the actions which are ascribed in the Bible to the angels, are in many respects more absurd and unreasonable, than those attributed to Sarosh." What we find in the Vandidád are these words, "*Nizbyémi Çraosĕm asím ahuraodhĕm çnathis zaçtya drizhimno kameredha paiti daĕvanám*" The sense of this, I maintain, I have substantially given. The Mobed puts daruj, a word of like meaning for daĕva, which he will see, is the last word in the sentence. It is "over the head of the Daĕvas," that the weapon of Sarosh is to be held. The Gujarátí translator of the Vandidád applies the word "Sarosh" to the alleged angel of that name ; but it is not with the conduct attributed to Sarosh, but with the *conduct of the Zoroastrians to Sarosh,* when they worship him, that I here find fault. I know of nothing "absurd and unreasonable" ascribed to angels in the Bible.

Respecting another of the Pársí Izads, Aspandiárjí says, "There is no crime in invoking Márespand, who is represented as a shining angel, when by invocation it is meant to praise and admire that great being who is the source of all light." It is a great crime, however, to praise any angel instead of God, or as God, as the Pársís do when they call upon their Izads.

* Tálim-i-Zartusht, p. 135.

ven," that is to the highest extent, or may be interpreted as intimating that the sin of the prodigal was offensive to God and to all holy beings in heaven. If the word "heaven" be considered a name given to God, because he is the supreme and only authority in that blessed region, where the effulgency of his glory is displayed, it must be clearly seen that it is used not in an absolute, but in a figurative sense, which cannot be mistaken any more than the use of the word "throne" of England or any other country, for the king or queen who may be entitled to sit upon it, and dispense judgment. When Dosabhái translates the words, "In them [the heavens] hath he set a tabernacle for the sun," by શુરજને પરમેશ્વરે આ કાચનો દેવલ બાંધિછે, or "God has built a divine temple for the sun,"* he is guilty of a gross perversion, from which after all, he is unable to draw any inference in support of the worship of heaven. Aspandiárjí is, if possible, more inconsiderate and feeble in his attempt to vindicate his cause than his friend the munshi. In reference to a quotation of mine,—"Invoke, O Zoroaster, the heaven given-by-god," he says, "I have simply to state that such reading is not to be found in the Vandidád. The only direction given therein by Hormazd to Zoroaster is, 'Contemplate, O Zoroaster, the heaven, and thus bring to thy recollection the power and energy of me, who have sustained it without any support.'"† My quotation, I maintain, is correct, though for "given-by-God," I now prefer "self-given" as a translation of khadáta. I have referred to the original Zand, of which it is the translation in my sermon entitled "the Doctrine of Jehovah;" and I here repeat it as found in the nineteenth fargard of the Vandidád,—

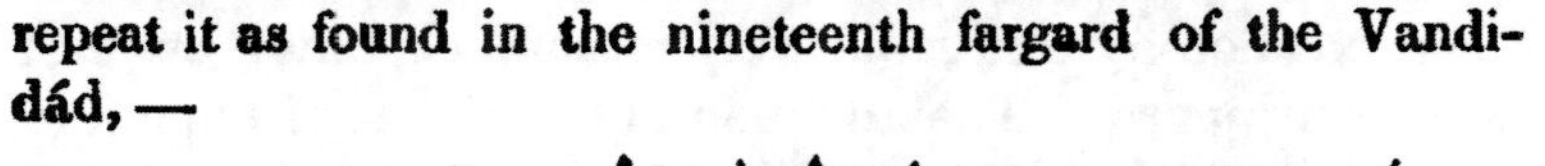

nizbyanguha tú Zarathustra thwásahê khadhátahê.‡ These

* Tálim-i-Zartusht, p. 737.

† Hadí-i-Gum-Rahán, p 60. English version.

‡ Author's MS. vol ii, p. 229.

words are thus rendered into Gujarátí by Aspandiárjí's father, *Padh tu Zartusht asmán khadád*,* which means, Invoke (or worship) thou O Zoroaster, the heaven *khadád* or self-existent heaven. I publicly challenge Aspandiárjí to produce from the Vandidád any passage in Zand corresponding with *his* alleged quotation. If I am not mistaken, he anticipated something like the reply which I now give, for he adds to his critique the assertion, that "there is also an angel by name *ásmán*, who presides over the heaven, or sky," evidently wishing to insinuate that the worship recommended, and which at first he wished to conceal, is only angelic worship. I am the more confirmed in this opinion by the conclusion of the notice which he takes of the matter. "If there is any impropriety," he asks, "in invoking heaven, why should the Christians themselves resort to it in their prayers." † The allegation which he here makes, I need scarcely observe, he leaves without proof. "Heaven is a term," he goes on to say, "which is not unfrequently employed in the Bible as an emblematic (emblem) of God." Were "heaven" invoked, then, in the instances in which this is the case, it ought to be clearly seen that it is not the region of heaven, but its glorious occupant, even God himself, who is invoked. The two texts which he quotes from the New Testament are altogether inapplicable to his argument. "Swear not at all; neither by heaven, for it is God's throne; nor by the earth, for it is his footstool." ‡ If we are not to swear by heaven or earth, far less are we to pray to them or to worship them. "Thou, Lord, in the beginning hast laid the foundation of the earth; and the heavens are the works of thy hands." § Their creation by God is the very reason why they are not to be worshipped. The attention of the Mobed, I request to the verses which follow. "They [the earth and heavens] shall perish, but thou [the Son of God] remainest: and they shall wax old as doth a garment; and as a vesture shall thou fold them up, and they shall be changed: but thou art the

* Ibid. p. 229. † Hádí-i-Gum Rahán, p. 60. E. V.

‡ Matth. v. 34, 35. § Heb. i. 10.

same, and thy years shall not fail." There is an essential, an infinite, distinction between God and his most glorious works here recognized, which ought never to be overlooked, and which ought to be viewed as discouraging and interdicting all idolatry.*

Zarvána-Akarana or *Time-without-Bounds*, we have seen from a former part of this work, Dosabhái generally interprets in an impersonal sense, — as equivalent to *eternity*, for which he pleads for nothing more than a "remembrance."† Unfortunately for his argument, however, he himself, in another page, has quoted from the Zand-Avastá this sentence, — *Zarvánem akaranem yazamaidê*.‡ The last word here used, as we have already shown, is expressive of the highest act of worship, which, as addressed to eternity, must be considered in the highest degree unreasonable and absurd.

The defence which Dosabhái offers of the worship of *Bád*, the angel who is supposed to preside over the wind, and of *Sapandarmad*, or *Sapandar*, a female angel who is supposed

* Aspandiárjí, in the context of the extracts which we have now produced from his publication, charges Christianity with the encouragement of idolatry. "The God of the Christians," he says (p. 61), "is invested with the perfect shape of a human being, since he has a throne to sit upon, and the earth is his footstool to lay his foot upon; and his Son Jesus sits beside him at his right hand." The inference which he here makes, is both incorrect and indecorous. The language employed by the sacred writers, is evidently figurative, and used in condescension to the imperfect conceptions of man. Heaven is described as God's throne, for his glory, and majesty, and grace are there most conspicuously displayed. The earth is his footstool, as comparatively mean and remote, when viewed with reference to heaven. Christ is said to sit at God's right hand, because in his human nature, and in his exalted state, as ascended on high, he occupies the place of greatest honour and power. The references which the Mobed makes to a "couch," and "plate," and "cup," are quite degrading, when compared with the scriptural image of a "throne," the seat of sovereignty. I am not surprised that he here speaks of the "innocent religion of the Hindús," for his own is so much allied to it in erroneous doctrine and practice, that the one cannot be blamed without the other being condemned.

† Tálim-i-Zartusht, p. 137.

‡ Tálim-i-Zartusht, p. 117.

to preside over the *earth,* * is exactly similar to that which we have noticed in the preceding and other paragraphs, and is in a similar manner to be repelled. Aspandiárjí thus delivers himself: — "The term *Zamín*, or earth, which in the Avastá language is in the feminine gender, in the same manner as the word moon in English, is here [in the Vandidád] supposed to be the daughter of Hormazd, whose production surely it is. To invoke her and the wind, no doubt, implies the contemplation of the various benefits flowing from the earth to man, as also of those which belong to the wind or air." † We have no wish to frown upon geographical, geological, or meteorogical inquiries, far less upon making the works of God, and their various phenomena, the objects of devout contemplation ; but we do object to praying either to the earth and winds, or to the angels who are said to preside over them. It is personal invocation and praise, in professedly solemn worship, which the Mobed has to explain ; but which he never can explain, without departing from the right interpretation of his sacred books. In the sense in which, he says, the earth is called the "daughter of Hormazd," every existing thing may be parabolically said to be the daughter, or son, of Hormazd, by those who conceive that every thing is his "production." He ought to know, however, that according to the Vandidád the earth is the "daughter," and fire the "son," of Hormazd, in a *peculiar* sense, being not simply alleged products of his will and power, but portions of his spirit and substance, as has been already set forth.

Faruhar, as applied to God, Dosabhái wishes to be considered equivalent to *johar*, or "*essence.*" ‡ We have already shown that it means a prototype, and is applicable to Hormazd, only when he is considered as the creature of *Zarvána-Akarana.* The worship of Hormazd's *faruhar*, which is proved by the terms employed, the munshi vainly wishes to set forth merely as the "remembrance" of the divine essence. The essence of God, better metaphysicians than Dosabhái,

* See Tálim-i-Zartusht, pp. 137, 138.

† Hádí-i-Gum-Rahán, p, 61.

‡ Tálim-i-Zartusht, p. 138.

hold to be entirely beyond the knowledge of man. On all the Faruhars, but that of Hormazd, the munshí is silent. He truly felt the unsatisfactory nature of his limited reference, for though the doctrine of the Trinity has no connexion with it, he cannot refrain from scoffing at it as equivalent to the doctrine of Tritheism, an imputation, which the very meaning of the word Trinity, which he knows right well, altogether forbids.

In connexion with the matters on which I have now commented, Dosabhái repeats what he conceives to be the claims of Hormazd to divine worship. I have already at length shown the place which he really occupies in the sacred books of the Pársís* ; and I need not trouble the reader with unnecessary repetition. Were I to admit, which I do not, that Hormazd is represented in the Zand-Avastá as the supreme God, all that I have said about the impropriety and sin of the recognition of the other objects of worship, which have been brought before the notice of the reader, would still have its unqualified and undiminished force and application. Aspandiárjí thinks that he has found a final and satisfactory vindication of his sacred books in the following declaration.— "That the religion of the Pársís includes the worship of the only one God, may appear quite evident from the following quotation in the Avastá.

"(Avastá). *Ianghe hàtáma äada iasne pete vangho majdá ahuro vethä ashád hachă*.†

"(Meaning). In the same manner it may be commanded, that in preference to the other Izads the great Dádar Hormazd alone should be worshipped and prayed (to), for he alone distributes the proper rewards."‡

The Mobed has not told us whence he has taken the passage. I beg to inform the reader, however, that it is among the Pársís as a *mantra* among the Hindús, and that it occurs at the conclusion of the fourth and other *Hás* of the Izashné, and is used frequently in their liturgical services. The

* See Chapter ii. † Sic scribit Magus.

‡ Hádí-i-Gum Rahán, p. 62.

20

translation of the Zand given by Aspandiárjí, is altogether incorrect. I defy him, and all the dasturs of India, to produce a single word or clause here warranting the comparison of Hormazd with the other Izads. I do more than this. I maintain that the passage, as is proved by the subjoined note,*

* The passage, when exactly represented according to the Zand letters, and given in full (for Aspandiárjí has omitted some words), is as follows:—

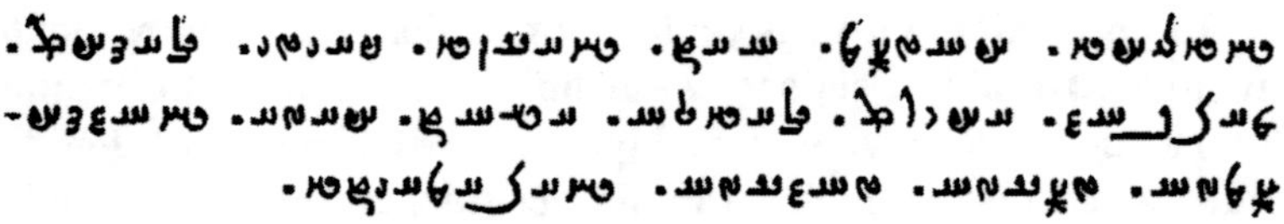

Yênghê hátãm áat yaçnê paiti vanghó mazdâo ahuró vaêthá asát hacha yâonghãmchá tãçchá tâoçchâ yazamaidhê.

The translation of these words, if we may judge from the unsuccessful attempts which have been made, has long been felt to be a difficulty both by learned Asiatics and Europeans. The difficulty does not arise so much from inability to attach a specific meaning to each of the vocables employed, for such a meaning is apparent, but from the awkwardness of the grammar and construction.

'The following is Nariosangh's Sanskrit rendering, or rather paraphrase :

ये वर्तमानेभ्यः एवं इजिस्न्या उपरि उत्तमे महाज्ञानिनः स्वामिनः किल इजिस्नीः होर्म्मिज्दस्यार्थे प्रचुराः कुर्वन्ति चेतरि पुण्यात् यत् किंचित् पुण्यं प्रसाददानं होर्म्मिज्दो वेत्ति समवायकान् तान् तांश्च आराधये नरस्त्रीआकृतीन् आमिश्रास्थितान्

Respecting this gloss, professor Burnouf justly says, "Est en particulier d'une barbarie extrême."

In the Gujarátí version of the Izashné we have this rendering of the passage:—

કે છે એરવશે ઈજશને બોલાનાર ભલી મજદ અહોર ખબરદાર શવાબનાં કામથી કેઅંનજુમનંને નર નારીનાં આરાધું*—Author's Ms. vol. 1st. pp. 74, 75.

The translator, who is partly correct in the words he here uses, paraphrases the passage much in the same way that the controversialist Aspandiárjí does; but this he does without a warrant.

Anquetil du Perron, following Nariosangh to some extent, gives this translation:—

is one in which the Pársís worship *all* the objects collectively which we have already enumerated. I do more still: I suppose for the sake of argument, that Aspandiárjí's rendering is correct; and I claim it as an unwilling, but direct, *admission* of the truth of the principal fact which I have endeavoured to establish in this chapter,—that Hormazd is not the only god of the Pársís. If he be the Supreme Being, why is he ranked among the Izads at all, and why is his worship not recommended and practised, not merely in *preference to* that of the other Izads, but to its entire *exclusion?*

We have now seen that the Pársís, who follow their sacred books, "have lords many and gods many," whom they indiscriminately worship and serve, and also that when engaged in their devotions, their time is principally spent in addressing the creature to the neglect of the Creator. We are consequently authorized, nay we are imperatively called upon by the interests of truth, to class them among Polytheists, against whose errors, with zeal for the glory of Jehovah and the benevolent desire to promote the best inte-

"Ceux qui récitent ainsi les Hás de Izashné, Ormuzd veille sur eux, il les récompensera, soit que ce soient des hommes ou des femmes, je leur fais Izashné."—Zand-Avastá, vol. ii, p. 101.

M. Burnouf, after an able grammatical and etymological analysis of the passage, thus literally renders it into barbarous Latin:—

"Quicunque existentium tunc in sacrificio bonum multiscius Ahura declaravit per puritatem, et quarumcunque (feminarum existentium tunc etc.) illosque hasque adoramus."

His French translation is as follows:—

"Tous les êtres mâles et femelles à qui le tout savant Ahura a enseigné alors que le bien s'obtenait dans le sacrifice par la pureté, nous leur adressons le sacrifice," that is, "All the beings male and female to whom the omniscient Ahura has pointed out that good is obtained in sacrifice by purity, we address our sacrifice."—Commentaire sur le Yaçna, pp. 108—116.

I think that the learned professor has given the meaning of the passage. And I shall adhere to it till such time at least as the Pársís are able by a grammatical analysis to point out its inaccuracy. All will see that Aspandiárjí is guilty of a gross,—I shall not say a willing,—perversion of the passage.

rests of our fellow-men, we must ever protest. I beg my native readers attentively to consider the line of argument which we have pursued, impartially to weigh the evidence which we have adduced, and solemnly and prayerfully to view the conclusion at which we have arrived. I especially beg those of them whose understandings have been in some degree enlightened, who are beginning to be so ashamed of the religious services of their tribe as if possible to consider them entirely symbolical, or commemorative, and who have any anxiety about the infinitely precious interests of their never-dying souls, to avoid contributing in the smallest degree to the evasion of the truth. The fundamental principle of religion, as handed down by tradition, as proved by the unity and harmony and regularity which prevail throughout the whole extent of the vast universe falling under our notice, or set forth in the book of real inspiration, is, THERE IS ONLY ONE GOD. This God alone is able to hear and answer prayer. He is to be supremely honoured, and he is to be exclusively honoured, in divine worship. His inalienable glory is thus to be recognized, and devoutly acknowledged. It is essential to his right service, that he should ever meet with this regard. Nothing but an indisposition to hold communion with him, an aversion to view the glory of his infinite majesty and unspotted holiness, a disregard of his omnipresence and omniscience, and a distrust of his compassion and grace, have led mankind to worship other gods, to call upon the names of angels, archangels, or men, — upon the elements or energies of that nature which He appoints and controls, and which is merely the index of his will, — or upon any of the multifarious works of his boundless wisdom and power. May men everywhere recognize his character, providence, and law, and see their responsibility for all their gifts, endowments, capacities and possessions! May they believe the revelation of his will! May they repent of their sins, receive the Saviour into their hearts, and obtain the pardon of their transgressions, and the sanctification of their whole man, through his infinite merits, and love and serve God, and God alone, with their whole souls!

In connexion with the observations which I have now

made on the objects and mode of worship of the Pársís, I may here briefly advert to Dosabháí's attempt to disparage the model of prayer which Christ taught his disciples. Quoting the second volume of Voltaire's so-called Philosophical Dictionary, he writes thus: —

"Perhaps it will hardly be believed, that Dr. Tamponet one day said to several other doctors, I would engage to find a multitude of heresies in the Lord's Prayer, which we know to have come from the Divine mouth, were it now for the first time publishing [published ?] by a Jesuit.

"I would proceed thus: 'Our Father which art in heaven' — A proposition inclining to heresy; since God is every where. Nay, we find in this expression the leaven of Socinianism; for here is nothing at all said of the Trinity.

"'Thy kingdom come: thy will be done on earth as it is in heaven'— Another proposition tainted with heresy; for it is said again and again in the Scriptures that God reigns eternally. Moreover, it is very rash to ask that his will may be done; since nothing is, or can be done, but by the will of God.

"'Give us this day our daily bread'— A proposition directly contrary to what Jesus Christ uttered on another occasion: —'Take no thought, saying what ye shall eat? or what ye shall drink . . . . for after all these things do the Gentiles seek . . . . But seek ye first the kingdom of God and his righteousness, and all these things shall be added unto you.'

"'And forgive us our debts, as we forgive our debtors' — A rash proposition, which compares man to God, destroys gratuitous predestination, and teaches that God is bound to do to us as we do to others. Besides, how can the author say that we forgive our debtors? We have never forgiven them a single crown. No convent in Europe ever remitted to its farmers the payment of a single sous. To dare to say the contrary is a formal heresy.

"'Lead us not into temptation'— A proposition scandalous and manifestly heretical; for there is no tempter but the devil; and it is expressly said, in St. James's Epistle — 'God is no tempter of the wicked; he tempts no man.'

"You see, then, said Doctor Tamponet, that there is nothing, though ever so venerable, to which a bad sense may not be given. What book, then, shall be liable to human censure, when even the Lord's prayer may be attacked by giving a diabolical interpretation to all the Divine words that compose it."

Both Dr Tamponet and the author of the Dictionary, were well aware that this is an *unfair* criticism on the prayer which Christ taught his disciples. It is rightly stated by them, though Dosabhái cunningly omits the translation into Gujarátí of the words expressive of their opinion, that it is only a suppositive "*diabolical interpretation of the divine words.*" Little need be said, in consequence, in refuting what they insincerely advanced. Though it is intimated in the prayer, that God is in heaven, it is not asserted that his presence is confined to that locality. We have many scriptural warrants for addressing either the Godhead in its unity, or as composed of the three persons who form the Trinity, or each of these persons individually. The reign of God is, like himself, from everlasting to everlasting; but it cannot be denied that man has rebelled against his authority, and that the moral kingdom of God advances in this world, with the progress of heavenly truth. While the will of God's determination cannot be opposed, the will of his complacency, as adverse to sin, is disregarded by every transgression. When we limit our requests to "daily bread," we are certainly far from anxiously asking, "What shall we eat? or what shall we drink? or wherewithal shall we be clothed?" When we pray for the remission of our "debts," it is the pardon of our sins which is the burden of our supplication; and the forgiveness of our debtors to which we refer, is the forgiveness of those who injure us. All this is clear from the words of Christ himself, "For if ye forgive men their trespasses, your heavenly Father will also forgive you: but if ye forgive not men their trespasses, neither will your Father forgive your trespasses,"— which have a very different meaning from that attached to them by Dr. Tamponet. As to the convents in Europe, we know not what may, or may not, be their duty, in particular circumstances, in reference to their farmers; but the divine injunction, and not the practice of any particular class of men, is the rule of Christian conduct. When we pray, "Lead us not into temptation," we emphatically ask that God may prevent us from being led into temptation, or deliver us when we are tempted. God tempteth no man, in the sense of enticing them to sin, though he trieth the faith, and love, and obedience of his people. The devil is not the only tempter. "Every man is tempted, when he is drawn away of his own lust, and enticed."*

So much for Dr Tamponet, and his patron, Voltaire. I am unwilling to dismiss the subject on which they comment, without inviting the attention of Dosabhâí to our Lord's general instructions on the subject of prayer, as they are recorded in Matthew vi. 5 — 15. They are of the highest importance; and all classes of the heathen in this country will find them peculiarly suited to the circumstances in which they are placed.

When surrounded on the mountain by multitudes from all the provinces of the country in which he ministered,— from Galilee, and Decapolis, and Jerusalem, and Judea, and beyond Jordan,— Christ plainly and solemnly taught them how they were to hold acceptable and profitable communion with God, the only object of divine worship. Addressing each of them in his individual capacity,— he gave the emphatic charge, *When thou prayest thou shalt not be as the hypocrites are, for they love to pray standing in the synagogues, and in the streets that they may be seen of men.* Sincerity, heartfelt sincerity, and the deepest humility, and reverence, are demanded of thee; and all pride and ostentation must be put far away. When engaged in holding converse with the Most High, it is to Him that thy meditation and praise must be directed, and to Him that thy desires must go forth. The hypocrites *have their reward.* They are noticed, and perhaps applauded, by the children of mortality; but they are condemned, and rejected, by the Hearer and Answerer of prayer. His

* James i. 14.

glory passes not before their view; his grace is not diffused on their souls, and his blessing is not vouchsafed to their cry. Profit, then, by their disappointment, and avoid their example. Withdraw thyself from the observation of thy fellow-men, which entices thy heart from God. *When thou prayest enter into thy closet*, a place of secret retirement, *and when thou hast shut the door*, excluding the world, and the things of the world from thy view, *pray to thy Father which seeth in secret*, to whom the darkness, and the light are both alike, and who searcheth the hearts, and trieth the reins of the children of men. Though he is invisible to thy sight, the eye of his regard is upon thee, and his ear is open to thy supplication; *and thy Father who seeth in secret shall reward thee openly*, manifestly grant thy requests and lead thee to rejoice in his goodness.

And, whilst in thy solemn worship, thou excludest the consideration and praise of men, imagine not that thy adoration, and thanksgiving, and confession, and supplication, possess the least intrinsic merit in the sight of God. "Let thy words be few and well chosen." *When ye pray, use not vain repetitions as the Heathens do: for they* foolishly *think that they shall be heard for their much speaking;* that by the amount of their service they can purchase the divine favour, and compel God in equity to grant their desires. *Be not ye, therefore, like unto them*, imagining that God requires to be informed of your wants, and that you, by your repeated requests, can extort his blessing. *Your Father knoweth what things ye have need of, before ye ask him.* It is to mark your absolute dependence, and to encrease your own devotion, that he graciously says unto you, "Ask and ye shall receive, seek and ye shall find, knock and it shall be opened unto you." An example of prayer, I now impart to you. *After this manner*, therefore, not confining yourselves to a mere form, but expressing the desires of your hearts, *pray ye:*—

Our Father which art in heaven, hallowed be thy name: thy kingdom come: thy will be done in earth as it is in heaven: give us this day our daily bread: and forgive us our debts as we forgive our debtors: and lead us not into temptation, but deliver us from evil: for thine is the kingdom, and the power, and the glory for ever. Amen.

Appropriate, indeed, is this form of devotion. The supplicant, with filial confidence and boldness, addresses God, as the author and supporter of his being and that of his fellow creatures, and as his reconciled Father. Standing on the orb of this earth, and lifting up his heart and his voice to God, he fully recognizes the omnipresence and omniscience of Him with whom he has to do, and remembers that He is in heaven displaying the effulgency of his majesty, his glory, his bounty, and his grace. Seeing that, in the character of God, there is every perfection and excellency, and that He is glorious in holiness, fearful in praises, ever doing wonders, he prays that His name may be hallowed, or esteemed holy, and admired in all its excellence, by the children of men. Jealous for the honour of God, and mourning over the disobedience, and rebellion, and misery of the world, he prays that that kingdom which is righteousness, and peace, and joy in the Holy Ghost, may speedily come; that men, delivered from the bondage of Satan, may acknowledge God as the Supreme Sovereign, and, subject to his authority, devote to him the affection of their hearts and the service of their lives. Knowing how joyfully, and promptly, and constantly, the principalities and powers in heavenly places act agreeably to the divine will, he supplicates that it may be done on earth as it is done in heaven. Feeling his absolute and entire dependence upon God, but not anxiously caring for the future, or distrusting the Divine providence, he asks merely an humble and present supply of his bodily wants. Groaning under the burden of sin, and trembling under the amount and aggravation of his transgressions, and fearing the wrath and judgment of God on their account, he implores for pardon, and prays that the record of his debt may be erased from the book of God's remembrance; and, while he asks forgiveness for himself, he acknowledges his own obligation to impart it to his fellow-men. Grieving over the power of sin, as well as fearing its curse, he prays that he may not be tried above his strength, nor led into temptation, but delivered from all evil and the evil one, from indwelling and surrounding sin, and from the assaults of the devil. And he concludes with the ascription of the kingdom, and the power, and the glory, to God, for ever and ever: Amen.

How comprehensive and important are the petitions thus addressed to the seat of heavenly grace! Three of them, it will be observed, respect the glory of God, as it refers to his character, his government, and his will. Three of them respect the wants of the unworthy supplicant. One of these is connected with the interests of time, and two of them with the interests of eternity. The subordination of temporal to spiritual blessings is thus exhibited, and all is consistent with the actual necessities of man, and his relation to God. Will any Pársí venture to say that this is the case with a single prayer contained in the Zand-Avastá?

CHAPTER VI.

REVIEW OF THE HISTORICAL, DOCTRINAL, AND CEREMONIAL DISCOVERIES AND INSTITUTES OF THE VANDIDAD, EMBRACING AN ANALYSIS OF THAT WORK, ACCORDING TO THE ORDER OF ITS FARGARDS.

1— *The creation by Hormazd of sixteen blessed localities — The devastations produced in them by Ahriman, the reputed author of evil, and the creator of winter and noxious animals* —2— *Wonderful proceedings of Yimó, or Jamshid, in Irán, in promoting agriculture, controlling the atmosphere, and banishing disease, death, and other evils* —3— *Various matters please the earth, as the performance of the ceremonies of the Mázdayaçní faith, building lofty houses, and having thriving families — Various matters displease the earth, as having holes in it, which allow the devils to come to it from hell, the burial in it of dogs and men, the construction of dakhmas, the existence of vermin, and particular lamentations for the dead — How the dead should be disposed of — Calamities which accrue to a person defiled by the dead — Agriculture, the primary duty of a Mázdayaçna — Land to be presented to priests — Prescription of stripes for defiling it by the carcases of men and dogs —* 4— *Untruthfulness and violence, how to be punished — Want of equity in the prescriptions respecting them —Atonements to be made by offenders* —5— *Consideration of various impurities — Defiled wood not to be presented to the sacred fire — Fire and water kill not — Dead bodies, how to be disposed of when they cannot be taken to the dakhmas — Moral purity of man at his birth — Extravagant praise of the Vandidád —Possession of the companions of the corpse of a man or dog by the devil Naçus — Untimely births* —6— *Defiled land, how long to be kept from cultivation — Funeral of bones, hair, nails, etc. how to be conducted — Prescription of stripes for allowing marrow to escape from the bone of a dead dog or man — Defilement of water, snow, and trees by corpses — How corpses should be carried to the dakhma* —7— *Invasion of corpses by the devil Naçus — Wonderful effects of water — Purification of defiled mats, wood, grass, etc. — Physicians must try their skill on the worshippers of demons, before they practise among the Mâzdayaçsnas — Physicians' fees — Cures performed by the lancet, and by the word, etc. — How ground defiled by the dead is to be dealt with, and the great merit of erasing old dakhmas — Premature births — How the cattle who eat dogs or men should be dealt with* — 8 — *How impurities are to be removed from houses, and funerals to be conducted, with the help of dogs and priests — How adultery should be punished — Expulsion of the devil Naçus by ablutions with water — Cooking and burning the dead condemned — How fire which has been defiled may be purified and taken to the dâdgâh — A man defiled by a corpse in the jungle may be purified by cow's urine, or repair to the priest — Sin of entering water with an impure body* —9— *Ceremony of the Barashnom — More about the expulsion of the devil Naçus by ablutions, and the frightening of devils by the word — Presents to be given to the person who performs the Barashnom* — 10 — *Frightening of devils by the word — Place for the Barashnom* —11— *Purification of natural objects terrestrial and celestial — Extermination of devils by the word* —12— *Ceremonies for the dead, and purification of articles and places defiled by corpses — Special prayers prescribed for dead relatives — Purification of places defiled by corpses* — 13 —*Character and treatment of living dogs — Character and treatment of cocks* —14— 10,000 *stripes to be inflicted on the murderer of a water-dog — Extraordinary atonements to be made by the criminal* — 15 — *Crimes of praising a foreign faith, feeding dogs with hard bones and too hot food, etc.— Obscenities alluded to* —16— *Treatment of women* —17— *How to cut off hair, pair the nails, and conduct the funeral of the refuse* — 18 — *Equipment of a priest — Destruction and mortality by the devil — The morning occupation of the bird Parodars — Cravings of Fire — Feeding the bird Parodars — Conversation between Sarosh and the devil Hashem — Extraordinary atonements* — 19 — *How Zoroaster encountered the devil — Zoroaster informed as to a method of destroying the works of the devil — How the Izashné is to be performed — Purification of a person defiled — The doom of man and devils discoursed of — The Resurrection — Polytheistic worship enjoined* — 20 —*Additional legends respecting Jamshíd — Worship of the exalted Bull recommended — Its wonderful influence, particularly with regard to rain — Rain discoursed of* — 22 — *Hormazd contrasts himself with Ahriman — Creation of Ahriman — Mission of Zoroaster — General remarks on the character of the Vandidád.*

A VERY appropriate and convenient division of Pagan theology was made by the ancients. They distributed it into the *mythical* or fabulous, used by the poets; the *physical*, or natural, used by the philosophers; and the *political*, or civil, used by the people.* We have hitherto had principally to do with the two first kinds, in our notices of the Pársí religion; but the third must now be introduced to our attention, though not in a separate form. We have seen what the Zoroastrian faith is in reference to the multifarious and diversified *objects of worship* which it recognizes. It is now incumbent upon us to direct our attention to its *historical, doctrinal, moral, and ceremonial discoveries and institutes, as they are unfolded in the books which it considers sacred.* Our object will be best accomplished, by taking a calm review of the Vandidád, which, with the liturgical works with which it is connected, and to which it may be proper for us occasionally to refer, forms the only authoritative standard of faith to which the Pársís make their appeal.

The Vandidád, as I stated in my lecture, "professes to report the result of an interview of Zoroaster with Hormazd."† It contains twenty-two *fargards*, or sections, which, for the sake of convenience, we shall consider in their order, before we offer any general remarks on its contents. Should any repetition be the consequence of our following this method, it will be owing to the Vandidád itself; and though it may be attended with some inconvenience, it will not be without its advantages, as it will confirm and illustrate many of our preceding representations and reasonings.

1. The first fargard of the Vandidád gives us an account of the reputed creation, by Hormazd, of sixteen holy and

* See Gale's Court of the Gentiles, vol. i, p. 213.

† Aspandiárjí (Hádí-i-Gum-Rahán, p. 8.), when referring to this statement, drops the words "*professes to report*," and says, "He (Dr. Wilson) further states that the Vandidád is the result of an interview of Zoroaster with Hormazd." Having been guilty of this deception, or oversight, the Mobed adds, "This will clearly show that the Vandidád which is extant among the Pársís to this day, is the *the real production of Zoroaster* and of no other person!!"

blessed localities, which are supposed by the Pársís to be Irán (the Ariana of the Greeks), Shurik, Marva, Bokhárá, Nesápur, Hálab (Aleppo), Kábul, Orwe, Gurgán (or Jurján), Hermand, Sistán, Rei, Chin (China), Kirmán (or Padashkhargar), Hindustán, and Khorásan. The Zand names of these places, as given in the accusative case, in which they occur in the Vandidád, are the following:—

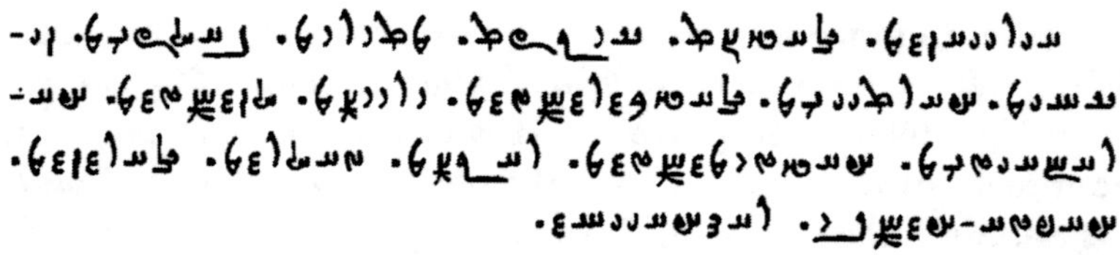

Airyanem-Vaêjo, Çughdhô, Môurum, Bakhdhím, Nisáim, Haroyím, Vaêkereñtem, Urvãm, Khneñtem, Haraqaitím, Haêtumeñtem, Raghãm, Chakhrem, Varenem, Hapta-Hendu, Ranghayâo. It must be evident that there must be some difficulty in identifying the Zand names with those of places known to the moderns. The Pársís, however, as we have seen, have made the attempt; and for this they are not to be blamed.

As the above-mentioned places came from the hands of Hormazd, they were like heaven itself; but the murderous Ahriman interfered with their bliss, by creating various evils within their borders. Some of these evils are said to have been moral, and others, natural. Among those of the former kind, we find the works of burying and burning the dead, which are no doubt ascribed to the devil, because of the imagined sacredness and purity of the earth and fire, to prescriptions for the purification of which a great part of the Vandidád is devoted. Among those of the latter, we find the creation of winter, which is spoken of as 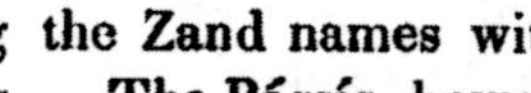 *daêvô-datem*, or "given of the devil," and the formation of numerous ants, flies, and lice, which are supposed to be essentially injurious to man. What kind of being, I would ask the Pársís, is he who can alter the course of the seasons, in opposition to the will of God, by whom it has been established in the exercise of his unerring wisdom and almighty power, and who, but God himself, can form and impart life even to the meanest insect? Is there no sin in robbing the divine Being of his prerogative as the only Creator? Is there no absurdity, for reasons which we have stated in a former chapter, in imagining the winter to be essentially an evil? Can no design in the formation of the detested insects be discovered, without referring them to an imaginary Evil Principle?*

2. The second fargard of the Vandidád introduces to our notice, the alleged intercourse of [Avestan] [Avestan] *Yimó Vívanghanó* † or Jamshid the son of Vivanghão, and his successful endeavours to promote agriculture and diffuse happiness in the districts of Irán. The accounts which are

* Dosabhái, (Tálim-i Zartusht pp. 56-59) with a view to shield the Vandidád from the charge of ascribing divine power to Ahrimán, makes a reference to the fifth chapter of Mark, in which we have an account of the expulsion of two thousand devils from the man who lived among the tombs, their entrance into the herd of swine, and the destruction of those animals by their rushing into the sea. If he had shown that Christ was *baffled* by the devils, he would have got a *parallel* to that against which we object in the Vandidád. As the matter stands, he leaves us with a happy *contrast*, which the Pársí reader will not fail to make, to the disadvantage of his sacred books.

As to the assertion, borrowed by the munshí from Voltaire, that there were no swine kept in the country where the miracle is said to have been performed, the reply is easy. Though the Jews were forbidden to make the sow an article of food, they tolerated its existence for the consumption of refuse and impurities. The swine forming the herd, being intended for food, were probably suffered to be destroyed by Christ, because the Jews ought not to have possessed them for this purpose.

† This is given in the ninth Há of the Izashné as — [Avestan] [Avestan] [Avestan] *Yimó Vívanghaió puthró.* In the same Há, the name of the father, in the nominative case, is given as [Avestan] *Vivanghâo.* A curious anology is thus revealed between *Yimó* of the Vandidád and यम *Yama* of the Hindú Puránas, who is set forth as the son of विवस्वान् Vivasván, or Vivasvat, the Sun. One of the names of Yama is धर्मराज *Dharmarája*, the righteous king. Yama among the Hindús is entirely a mythical personage, the judge of the dead. The identity of the two characters of Yimó and Yama, I have been informed, is about to be exhibited in a treatise by the learned Professor Lassen of Bonn.

given of him, are so exaggerated and absurd, that we cannot for a moment suppose them to be the result of divine revelation.

Zoroaster inquires of Hormazd about the first of mortals who like himself has consulted with this god, on the subject of religion. *Yimó*, it is said in reply, is the person who did so, and to whom he communicated—

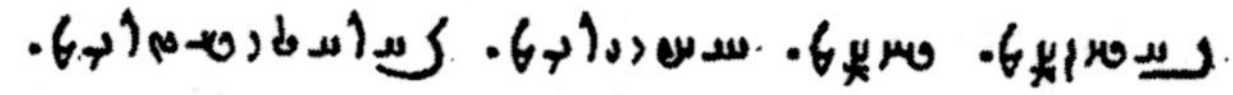

daénãm yãm A'huirím Zarathustrím, the religion which is the Hormazdian and Zoroastrian.* Jamshid, it is stated, was at first modestly disinclined to undertake to deliver the message of Hormazd ; but at last he yielded to a certain extent to the commands of the god,† and promised obedience in ter ms more indicative of pride and foolishness, than of humility and common sense. "In thy world," he said, "I will superintend ; in thy world I will support ; in all thy world, I will provide, and rule, and supervise, so that, in my kingdom, there shall be no damp wind, no heat, and no disease, or death." Jamshíd receives from Hormazd "a golden ring, and a poignard fixed in gold." He advances through different countries, and pressing them with his ring, and striking them with his poig-

* Or the "law of god, and Zoroaster," as I translated the words in my lecture on the Vandidád. Aspandiárjí presumptuously says (Hádí-i-Gum-Rahán p. 8.), that "nothing of this kind is to be found in the second fargard of the Vandidád, except that in the commencement of the same fargard, God is represented having barely stated to Zoroaster, 'I teach you this religion, which I had at first shown to Jamshíd,' yet Padre W., with the view of making it known to the people that Hormazd is not identical with God, has thus put a wrong interpretation on the above passage." The Mobed will find the words which I have quoted, in the 120th page of the lithographed edition of the Vandidád. I repeat the expression of my opinion, that the giving to the Mázdayaçnian religion, the denomination of ZOROASTRIAN, forms a slight presumption that the Vandidád was composed posterior to the days of Zoroaster.

† Edal Dáru says that to Jamshíd were communicated the *kusti* and *sadra*, the sacred badges of the Pársí faith. So highly offended have some of the Pársís been with this asseveration, that Kawasji Manocherjí has thought fit to publish a pamphlet of 72 pages, entitled શરૂઆતે દીન જરતોશ્તી in its negation and refutation.

ward, he fills them with cattle, men, dog, and birds of various colours; and he sometimes addresses his prayers to his own productions. Hormazd, when contrasting before Zoroaster, the happy days of Jamshíd, who is said to have reigned 700 years, grievously laments over winter, and all its ravages. He informs Zoroaster about the formation by Jamshíd of the *Var*, or *Varefsva*, a most blessed region, and of the happiness with which it was pervaded, and in reply to an inquiry about its illumination, he says, that it is enlightened by the *khadátacha raochâo staidhátacha*, by the self-given (or god-given*) light, appointed-also-for-the-world. He also says to him, that a descendant of Zoroaster will be the chief-priest of that region.

The preceding is the most important historical information, which is to be found in the Vandidád. How great, I ask the Pársís, is the value which should be attached to it ?†

* I prefer the rendering "self-given," to "God-given," that of Anquetil. Aspandiarjí, (Hádí-i-Gum-Rahán p. 33,) when trying to dismiss an inference which, in the lecture on the Vandidád, I had made from the expression, that the Vendidád recognizes a God superior to Hormazd, and professing to translate the passage in which it occurs, omits it altogether, and makes Hormazd merely say, "I have illuminated it with the same light with which I have illuminated this world." In connexion with this, he makes a great show of charging me with error!

† Respecting this matter, Professor Stuhr, in his dissertation on the Iranian Fire-Worship, contained in his *Religions-Systeme des Orients*, offers the following explanation:—

"As to the Vandidád, both its contents and its form prove that it was composed at a later period, when the original liveliness of spirit was gone. The traditions of the earlier times which it furnishes, are barren tales of mythic imagination, which had ceased to impress the minds of those to whom we owe the Vandidád in its present lifeless form, with their original spirit and significancy; tales referring to a time which from its remoteness seems to appear to the compositors as almost obsolete.

"The families, living at the eastern frontier of Persia, which, during the dark ages between Darius Codomanus and the Sassanians, were instrumental in keeping up the fire-worship, lived in solitary seclusion under circumstances which necessarily divested many things of their ancient meaning and importance, and obliterated many others altogether from memory. This is the reason why, in the Vandidád, things referring to

3. The third fargard of the Vandidád opens by an account of various matters which render the *zema* earth, or ground,* happy. *How* that which is not possessed of life, can either be pleased or dissatisfied, we are not informed; but it is alleged that it *is* made both happy and miserable. And by what means? Principally by the practice of righteousness, or obedience to the moral commandments of God? No; such an idea seems not to have entered into the mind of the author of the Vandidád. "The first thing which pleases the ground," it is said in the name of Hormazd, "is the pure man who sojourns [upon it], with the *esman* in his hand, the *barsam* in his hand, the *jiván* in his hand, who pronounces the words of the peace-giving religion with a high voice, and who worships Meher Izad, who presides over the jungles." "The second matter which pleases the ground, is when the pure man upon it builds a lofty house, and the cattle, wife, and children of a priest are of a good kind. In consequence of this [state of matters], the cattle of the house will be produced in abundance, the *asoi* will be produced in abundance, the pasturage will be produced in abundance, dogs will be produced in abundance, young women will be produced in abundance, children will be produced in abundance, fire will be produced in abundance, every living thing will be produced in abundance." Various kinds of cultivation are what next please the earth.

The first thing which displeases the earth, is the having deep holes in it, which allow the devils to come and go from

mythic history, are entirely devoid of a close, lively, and intimate connexion with the peculiar historical situation of the population of Irán, as the latter historical documents."— Translation by the Rev. Mr Weigle in the Oriental Christian Spectator for September, 1840.

If I were inclined to hazard a conjecture, I would say that the Pársís have got their ideas of the happy reign of Jamshíd, not so much from *historical* reminiscences, as from the figurative *prophetical* descriptions of the eleventh and other chapters of the prophecies of Isaiah.

* Frámjí Aspandiárjí speaks of the *zema*, as Aspandarmad, who presides over the ground; but he afterwards speaks of "the ground of Asfandarmad" being displeased. Author's MS. vol. i, p. 51.

hell. On these holes, Frámjí Aspandiarjí, in his Gujarátí translation of the Vandidád, thus comments:—"From these places, the devils come and run about, and run back again to hell!" He also speaks of them as the doors of hell.* The second thing which displeases the earth, is the burial within it of dogs and men; the third, is the construction of *dakhmas*, or repositories for the dead; the fourth, the existence upon it of *kharfastars*, or vermin, the production of Ahriman, which make holes in it; and the fifth, the lamentations of those who mourn the departed, throwing dust upon themselves. It is not necessary to enlarge on this nonsense.

Intimation is then given of the pleasure afforded to the earth by the filling up of graves, and the destruction of dakhmas.† The Daruj Naçus is represented as infesting the members which may be mentioned, and those which may not be mentioned, of a person who shall himself carry a dead body, and this for ever.

Directions are laid down about the allotment of a place for the regular disposal of the dead, to the effect that it should be "pure and dry," and "thirty paces distant from fire, thirty paces from water, thirty paces from the bearer of the *barsam*, and three from pure men. The necessity of preserving the purity of the elements, and other objects which the Pársís consider sacred, is thus inculcated.

It is declared that the person who shall partake of food, or wear clothes, which have been near the dead, shall not only be exposed to disease, but shall be visited with the calamity of old age and impotency. Such is his demerit, that the strong and powerful Mazdayaçnas should carry him to a lofty place, where he is to be devoured piece-meal by ravenous birds and brutes, unless he repent and perform the *patit*, through which his offence will be remitted. Surely the propriety of cleanliness in the matter referred to, could be enforced without any exaggerated and false statements respecting the evil consequences of its neglect.

* Author's MS. vol. i, p. 49.

† This, I suppose, is after they have served their purpose.

The cultivation of the soil, is recommended in strong terms; but why should the earth be represented as personally desiring it, and promising blessings to those who treat her with regard? Is there any propriety or dignity in the declaration, that he who sows grain fulfils the law of the Mazdayaçnas, and has as much merit as if he had a hundred children, and one thousand mammæ, and repeated ten thousand izashnés, and that by giving grain he wounds the devils, as if he poured melted iron down their throats? Its wise author, indeed, seems to have felt, that he has thus disparaged the ceremonies and services of the Pársí religion; for he immediately enjoins the recitation of the word, or Avastá.

The gift of land to holy men, or priests, is represented as particularly pleasing to the earth, and very meritorious. "Zoroaster," it is related, "said, O *Dádár aso*, what is the fifth kind of land, which in joy is joyful (or very joyful)?" He [Hormazd] said in reply, "O Çpitama Zoroaster, it is the land presented for the sake of merit to holy men. O çpitama Zoroaster, him who gives not for his good, Spandarmad will cast into darkness, the abode of disease, pain, and every evil." It was certainly a covetous priest who first indited this doctrine.

The fargard returns, in conclusion, to the crime of polluting the earth by the carcases of dead men or dogs. If a carcase be permitted to remain for half a year in the earth, the punishment is 500 stripes; if for a whole year, 1000 stripes, if for two years, everlasting defilement. The excommunication of the offender, to the last mentioned extent, is to follow. Query; is the earth not defiled by the carcases of other animals besides those of men and dogs?

4. In the commencement of the fourth fargard of the Vandidád, — which treats principally of offences between man and man, — borrowing without the intention of restoring, is deservedly condemned.

Six species of crime, denominated in Zand *mithra*, or in Pahlavi *mithra-daruj*, are enumerated, and specific punishments are prescribed for them. Breaking a verbal promise is to be punished by 300 years' torment in hell*; breaking an engagement confirmed by a junction of hands, by 600 years' torment; breaking an engagement to sell small cattle, by 700 years' torment; breaking an engagement to sell large cattle, by 800 years' torment; breaking an engagement to give a son or daughter, by 900 years' torment; and breaking an engagement to sell houses, or lands, by 1000 years' torment. These crimes are to be taken cognizance of by man, as well as God, and 300, 600, 700, 800, 900, and 1000 stripes are respectively to be inflicted on their account. According to these arrangements, the morality and immorality of actions are to be judged of by God and man, by a reference to the value of the articles with which they are connected, or ceremonies observed in bargain-making, and not to the moral advantages and disadvantages of the offender, as connected with his knowledge or ignorance, and the strength of his temptations. The offences of man, the Pársís must surely see, are not equally heinous according to the mercantile view of the article withheld in violation of a promise. In the Christian Scriptures, it is equitably said, "That servant which knew his Lord's will, and prepared not himself, neither did according to his will, shall be beaten with many stripes. But he that knew not, and did commit things worthy of stripes, shall be beaten with few stripes. For unto whomsoever much is given, of him shall much be required: and to whom men have committed much, of him they will ask the more."†

From deeds of untruthfulness, the fargard proceeds to those of violence. Seizing a weapon with an intent to strike, is to be punished with 5 stripes, and repetitions of the crime, by 10, 15, 30, 50, 70, and 80 stripes, till the eighth occasion, when the *Tanafuri*, worthy of 200 stripes, is committed. Pursuing a person, with an intent to strike, is to be punished with 10 stripes, and repetitions of the crime with a number

* Anquetil du Perron (Zand-Avastá, tom. ii, p. 288) interprets the punishment, as consisting of three hundred years confinement in the infernal regions. Frámjí Aspandiárjí, the Gujarátí translator of the Vandidád (Author's MS. vol. i. p. 81) agrees with this interpretation.

† Luke xii. 47, 48.

encreased in the proportion above mentioned, till the seventh occasion, when the Tanafuri is committed. Striking a person to the extent of two inches, is to be punished by 15 stripes, and for repetitions, by an additional number, till the sixth occasion, when the Tanafuri is committed. Striking a person to the extent of two and a half inches, is to be punished by 30 stripes, and repetitions by an encreased number, till the fifth occasion, when the Tanafuri is committed. Wounding a person to the effusion of blood, is to be punished with 50 stripes, and with an encreased number till the fourth occasion, when the Tanafuri is committed. Breaking a bone, is to be visited with 70 stripes, and with an increase, on every repetition, till the third occasion, when the Tanafuri is comitted. For cutting off a member of the body (as a leg or arm), the punishment is 90 stripes, to be encreased on the second occasion to 200 stripes. The equity of these punishments, and that too without any reference to the circumstances of individuals, would not be recognized in the Supreme Court of Bombay. It is evident, that, for general infliction, some of them are most inadequate. In certain states of society, the fear of them would do little to prevent assault.

The practice of the rites of the Mázdayaçní religion is enjoined on the offender. The poor are to be relieved, bachelors to be assisted in getting wives, the ignorant are to be instructed, and cattle are to be fed, and given in presents. Some of the works thus recommended are good ; but the Vandidád, in the conclusion of the fargard, errs when it says, that they will wound the devil of death, as if he who performs them, were to fight against him with an arrow.

The fargard concludes, in very obscure language, with prescribing ceremonies * to the obstinate offender, and ordering

* Among these Anquetil du Perron, in his translation (Zand-Avasta, tom. ii. p. 296) mentions the Barashnom. Aspandiárjí (Hadí-Gum-Rahán p. 72) denies that the reference is to that ceremony. Though in my lecture on the Vandidád, I quoted the passage as bearing the meaning attached to it by the French translator, I do not now repeat it, as an examination of the original has led me to doubt its accuracy; and the Barashnom is mentioned in another part of the Vandidád. What, I would ask Aspan-

his excommunication, if impenitent. A person who breaks his promise of providing water, is to be punished with 700 stripes.

5. The fifth fargard of the Vandidád, is principally occupied with the consideration of diverse kinds of impurities. Other matters, however, are referred to in it, without any particular order or principle of association.

The Mazdayaçna is forbidden to present to the fire of Hormazd any wood, which a bird has defiled by dropping from its bill a portion of a dead body, or by emptying its bowels, or making *pesháb*, after having partaken of a human carcase. A corpse ought to be so disposed of, that no part of it can be removed by a dog, a bird, the wind, a fly, a wolf, or a tiger. There is great sin in permitting water to be defiled by any fragment of it.

Fire and water, which are thus to be preserved in their sacred purity, are represented as incapable of killing a person. We have already quoted the original Zand of the passage, in which an extraordinary declaration is made to this effect, and made it the subject of comment.*

Directions are given about the preparation of a place for the disposal of a corpse, when, owing to any calamity, it cannot be taken to the dakhma. The place ought to be triangular,† and dug so commodiously that neither the head, the hands, nor the feet, should be above ground, while at the same time it should be exposed to the light of the sun.

It will have been observed, that the water found on the earth is to be kept from defilement by a dead body. That water, however, which Hormazd brings by the winds and clouds from the Zere-paránkand sea, and pours down upon the dakhmas in rain, is not defiled by coming in contact with the bodies exposed in them. How can this be, will be the inquiry of some minds.

diárjí, however, is the actual virtue of the Barashnom, if the promise of abundance be withdrawn from it ?

* See p. 157.

† It is to be of this shape, because the hands of the corpse are to be put across the breast, and the legs drawn up.

The moral purity of man is next alluded to. I give the passage referring to it in the original Zand: —

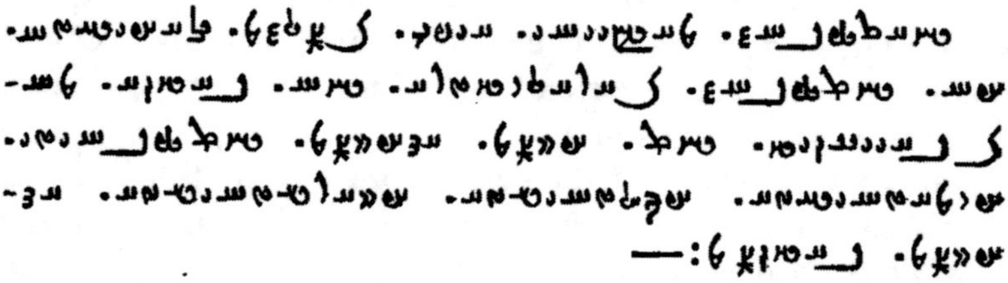

— *Yaojḫdâo mashyâi aipi zãtḫem, vahistáhá, yozhdâo Zarathustra, yá daêna mázdayaçnis. Yo hvãm anghvãm yozhdáiti humatáischa húkḫtaischa hvarstáischa; anghvãm daênãm :* —

— The translation is the following : — "For the man pure upon birth, O pure Zoroaster, [is] this excellent Mázdayaçní religion. Let him preserve his own body in the purity of good thought, good speech, and good conduct." The two last words are elliptical. I suppose *yozḫdáiti* is to be read with each of them thus, "[Let him keep pure his] body; [Let him keep pure] religion." The doctrine here laid down, of the purity of man at his birth, I shall, in the next chapter, expressly make the subject of particular comment. In the meantime, I would here remark, that Aspandiárjí has given me nearly a whole page of abuse* for having formerly referred to this passage as setting forth this doctrine! He translates it: — "O Zoroaster, I reveal to thee the purity which is implied in the Mázdayaçnan religion. Men should abstain from the commission of any sin, and in the (any ?) matter, whether relating to religion, or to the affairs of the world, they must be righteous, speak the truth, and do what is good." I am certain that no Zand scholar will for a single moment sustain this rendering, which violates all grammar, and which introduces what is neither expressed nor implied in the original. Aspandiárjí follows it up by quoting as a Pahlavi comment, rendered in Gujarátí, "It is desirable that all men should strive to preserve their souls in perfect holiness." This comment

* Hádi-i-Gum-Rahán, pp. 66, 67.

implies, I would remark, the very doctrine which Aspandiár-jí disclaims; for a soul cannot be "preserved in holiness," which has not holiness as its attribute. Dosabhái, Aspandiár-jí's fellow controversialist, explicitly *admits* what he denies. He writes, that "it is undoubtedly true that the 7th* fargard says, that man has been created pure, and worthy of going to heaven." He does more than this; he also quotes in English, the words, "*God has created the man's heart pure,*" and falsely says that they occur "in many places of the Bible," and all this with the view of denying the doctrine of original sin!†

Most extravagant praise of the Vandidád, follows the doctrine of man's natural purity:—"O Dádár, how much greater, better, and purer is the Vandidád given to Zoroaster, than other words are exalted, great, good, [and] pure? It was thus replied.— O Çpitama Zoroaster, [here is] an illustration:— The Vandidád, is as much exalted, great, good, and pure beyond other words, as the water of the *Zario-Vauru* (or Zereparankard [Caspian] sea) is more exalted than other waters. Another illustration:—The Vandidád, O Çpitama Zoroaster, is as much more exalted than any other word, as the great water (the ocean) is more exalted than other waters. Another illustration:—The Vandidád, O Çpitama Zoroaster, is as much more exalted, great, good, and pure, than any other word, as the great bird (?) is above little birds. Another illustration:—The Vandidád, O Çpitama Zoroaster, is as much more exalted, great, good, and pure, than any other word, as the land‡ (Alborj, ?) is higher than any other land." This praise, it will be admitted, is sufficiently high. Before we have done with this chapter, it will be apparent, we trust, to the Pársís, that it is altogether unmerited by the book, on which it is so lavishly bestowed. Aspandiárjí, probably from

* This should be the 5th. It is owing probable to a typographical error in my lecture, that the mistake has occurred.

† Tálim-i-Zartusht, p. 184.

‡ Some of the dasturs interpret this as, "the heaven is high above the earth."

a sense of its absurdity, accuses me of falling into "error, by ascribing that excellence, purity, and holiness to the Vandidád, which Hormazd did to the Mázdayaçni religion."* I beg to inform him that it is *he* who has slid into the ditch. In the Zand the word religion (*daêna*) does not once occur in the passage; and the Zand name of the Vandidád,† [illegible], *dátem-vidóyúm*, or given-against-the devils," occurs in every clause; and the comparison throughout is not with *religion*, but with another [illegible] *çravá-is*, or *word.*

In reference to the Vandidád, there is even more praise than that which we have now quoted.‡

The fargard proceeds to tell us how many persons become the habitation of the devil Naçus, when an individual of an assembly sitting together dies. Only one of the number present, it would appear, is exempted from the visits of this fiend. When a dog dies in a company, matters are much in the same state. We have then an allusion to the visits of the two-footed devil Ashmog, with whom we have formed an acquaintance in a former chapter. Lights are to be kept burning for nine days, or a month, near the place where a man has expired.

Untimely births are then treated of. The production must be deposited at the distance of three fathoms from pure

* Hádí-i-Gum-Rahán, pp. 24, 25.

† *Vandidád*, is Pá-Zand. The Pahlavi is *Jud-deva-dád.* Both these words have the same meaning as *Dátem-Vidoyúm.*

‡ It is thus given by Anquetil du Perron. "Que le Destour le récite; que celui qui a péché le récite. S'il ne prend pas sur lui (de faire réciter le Vandidád), qu'on ne s'interesse pas à son sort: s'il est éloigné de donner, (ce qui est prescrit pour cela), qu'on ne lui donne rien (à manger); s'il ne charge pas (le Destour de cet office), qu'on ne prenne pas soin de lui: il est ensuite ordonné au pur Destour de le punire trois fois. Si cet homme avoue le mal qu'il a fait, (cet aveu), ce repentir en sera l'expiation: mais s'il n'avoue pas le mal qu'il a fait, il aura lieu de s'en repentir jusqu'à la résurrection." *Zand-Avastá, vol* ii, *p.* 302. The original is here somewhat obscure; but let not Aspandiárjí grumble at Anquetil's translation of the passage, till he can give us a better.

fire, water, trees, men, etc. The mother's first food is to be the ashes of the Atish Behrám, with three, six, or nine cups of cow's urine.* We should like to know what the Medical Board of Bombay think of this prescription. I would advise the Pársís to take their opinion of its merits, and of those with which it is associated in the Vandidád, before they again follow it.

Hell, is to be the portion of those who may touch a woman's defiled clothes, till they are regularly purified.

6. The subjects treated of in the sixth fargard of the Vandidád, are somewhat similar to those to which the fifth relates.

The cultivation of land upon which there has been the dead body of a man or dog, or the introduction to it of water, before a year has expired from the time of its defilement, is to be held to be equivalent to the crime of the Tanafuri, and to be punished with two hundred stripes. I wonder if the Pársí farmers on the island of *Sáshtí* attend to this ordinance. I should like to know also what they think of that which follows it in the Vandidád?

"Dádár, if it be the wish of the Mazdayaçnas to prepare land, and to make rills to moisten it, that they may cast seed unto it, what ought the Mazdayaçnas to do? It was thus replied, Let the Mazdayaçnas see if there be upon it bones, hair, flesh, urine, fresh blood. If a Mázdayaçna do not examine whether there is in the land, bones, hairs, flesh, urine, and fresh blood, what is their crime. It was thus replied, He will be guilty of the Tanafuri, in thoroughly punishing him with the two hundred, let him be thoroughly punished with two hundred leather cords of the skin of the horse." A substantially correct translation of this passage, which is now literally rendered from the Zand, I gave in my lecture on the Vandidád.† I cannot deny my readers the gratification which they will derive from the persual of the whole of Aspandiárjí's philosophical comment upon it. "To these foregoing lines,"

* Frámji Aspandiárjí expounds this to the effect, that the potion of cow's urine should be repeated for three, six, or nine nights, according to circumstances.

† P. 26.

he says, "it might thus be replied. Whoever would cast a glance over the preceding paragraph, might be fully assured, that the absurdity, of which our friend accuses the Vandidád,— because it enjoins to preserve the brooks or rivulets which the Mazdayaçnas might wish to make, from being mixed with bones, hairs, nails, skin, and newly shed blood, — is quite erroneous, as well as gratuitous. Some such provision must be made, when an aqueduct is constructed for the conveyance of water to a town, or city, otherwise mixed with filth of the nature above described, the water of it might prove productive of numerous evils. Hair, nails, and skins, and such like other animal substances, have almost a poisonous effect on the system, if introduced into the stomach. It has therefore become quite obligatory upon the giver of the law to warn the Mázdyaçnas who might wish to make brooks and rivulets, against their defilement. The Vandidád does not say, that the offender shall be struck two hundred times with the leathern cords of the *skin* of the horse, but with the *horse whip* itself. All of you are aware, that there are many cities and towns, which, from the aridity of their soil, and from their distance from the neighbouring stream or river, have aqueducts conveyed to them, which provide water for the people, and the public authorities who have charge for (of) them, keep a constant watch over the water that it may not be defiled by the populace. If we have such instances of public precaution against the defilement of water, what wrong is there in the Vandidád if it introduces a clause to the very effect? I wonder our friend the Padre should ever think of finding fault with this clause of the Vandidád, while he himself possesses such acute feeling on the subject of wholesome beverage, as to touch no other water but that which has previously undergone the process of distillation."* This is really amusing in no ordinary degree. There is not a single word in the original Zand about conveying water by *aqueducts* to towns or cities. The passage refers solely to the *irrigation of lands for the purposes of husband-*

* Hadí-i-Gum-Raáhn, p. 71, 72.

ry. An intelligent agriculturist will be inclined to consider the articles which are to be so diligently sought for, as not indifferent manure, and helps to vegetation; and were he left to choose between "leather cords of the skin of the horse," and the "horse-whip itself,"* as the instruments of his punishment for leaving them unremoved, he would be at some loss to decide. The notice of my aqueous beverage, is entirely a fiction; and I give Aspandiárjí permission heartily to scourge its author, whenever he can lay hands upon him, with either of those weapons which he is able most effectually to apply.

But we must return to the Vandidád. It next introduces to our notice in a very serious manner, the crime of allowing grease or marrow from the bone of a dead man or dog to make its escape. If the bone be of the size of the little finger to the first joint, 30 stripes are to be inflicted; if of the size of the part extending to the first joint of the finger, between the little and the middle finger, 50 stripes are due; if it be of the size of the part of the large finger extending to the first joint, 70 are due; if it be as long as a finger, and as broad as a rib, 90 are due; if it be of the length and breadth of two fingers, or of the length and breadth of two ribs, 200 stripes are due; if it be of the length and breadth of the side or breast, 400 stripes are due; if it be as large as the part of the head covered with hair, 600 stripes are due; if it be of the size of a whole body of a dead dog or man, 1000 stripes are due. I have no hesitation in saying that such dignified legislation as this is unparalleled. On one occasion I directed to it the attention of a descendant of the Medes and Persians residing in Bombay. "The word of God!" said he, "why, this is not even the word of man. It is the word of stupidity."

The next subject with which the Vandidád has to deal, is that of extracting a dead body from water. The person who discovers it, is to strip himself of his clothes, pull it out, and place it upon dry ground. The water is defiled in all directions for six *gáms*, (paces) round the spot where the dead

* Aspandiárjí, even in a trifling matter of this kind, is not able to preserve consistency.

body was lying; that of a well is altogether defiled; snow is defiled for three *gáms* in all directions; the water of the river for nine *gáms* before, and six behind, and three beneath. How impurities are to be confined within these spaces, and how they are to extend throughout them, we are not informed. The defilement of the Hom tree is in some respects similar to that of water. Dead bodies are to be carried on a bier of iron, stone, or lead, to a high place, where they may be devoured by dogs or birds. If it be impossible to find a place where they may be so devoured, they are to be exposed on a bed to the sun, on a high situation.

7. We have not yet done with the dead bodies of men, and dogs. They form the principal topic of consideration in the seventh fargard.

The Drukhs, or devil Naçus, seems so have a wonderful predilection for them. He enters them from the north as a fly, the second watch after the breath is departed, taking possession, in the first instance, of the knees and hips, and without regard to the manner of their death, whether it be by a dog, a wolf, magic, disease, fear, men, violence, or want. He does not confine his furious visitations to the lifeless carcases; but he pollutes the assemblies in which a death occurs, in the way mentioned in a preceding fargard.

The carpet on which a man or dog has died, must be carefully purified. The parts of it which have been particularly defiled, must either be cut out or thoroughly washed. If it be of leather it is to have three ablutions of cow's urine, to be rubbed three times with ashes, washed three times with water, dried, and laid aside for three months. If it be of cotton, it is to have all these attentions doubled. Water is the great purifier, and it is a vast deal more than this: —

— [illegible] —*

* Lithographed Vandidád, p. 232.

— *Aredvínãm ápa çpitama Zarathustra, há mê ápó yaozhdadháiti há arsnãm khsudhrâo há khsathranãm gerewãm há kshathranãm paêma*: — The water named Areduísur [literally the lofty], O Çpitama Zoroaster, is the-giver-of-purity. It is the strength of young-men; it [is] the fœtus in women; it [is] the milk of women."* This doctrine has no doubt originated in the deification of water. The dasturs themselves seem to be ashamed of it, for Framjí Aspandiarjí, in his Gujarátí version, considerably disguises it.†

The mat, even when purified, is not to be worn by pure men. It is to be reserved for women when they are in a state of separation.

The person who eats of a dead dog or dead man, can never be purified. Hell will undoubtedly be his portion.‡

* The name by which this water is known among the Pársís.

† Author's MS. vol. i, p. 206. Anquetil (Zand-Avasta tom ii, p. 319) translates it thus: — "Elle sera purifiée par l'eau Ardiousour; cette eau qui est à moi, ô Sapetman Zoroaster, qui donne la semence au jeune homme, qui rende la femme féconde, et donne le lait à celle qui a réçu le germe." The Pársís have got such a horrid idea from their books of the water of the firmament, that after expressing it in Greek, I have felt compelled to withdraw what I had written from notice.

‡ In my Lecture on the Vandidád, (p. 31), I referred to the injunctions on this and similar matters, as illustrative of the remark that "ceremonial impurity [according to the Vandidád], is more heinous than moral impurity." Dosabhái, misapprehending or perverting my remark, represents me (Tálím-i-Zartusht pp. 69 — 79) as encouraging the use of dogs for food, and the practice of cannibalism!!. It is only against the doctrine of the *unpardonableness*, of the sin of dog-eating, and corpse-eating, when contrasted with the lenient treatment of other sins of even a deeper die, that my remark was pointed. I know well the injunctions of Moses (Deut. xiv.) forbidding the eating of any abominable thing, to which Dosabhái directs my attention; and I most decidedly admit their propriety. I must declare, however, that Dosabhái is guilty of worse than a logical blunder, when from the words of Christ, "Not that which goeth into the mouth defileth a man; but that which cometh out of the mouth, this defileth a man," he deduces the inference which he makes (p. 80), that Christ has given the order "that man should remain unclean and eat corpses." In the passage to which the Munshi refers, there is no *order* whatever on the subject of bodily impurity, or eating and drinking. There is merely a comparison between bodily defilement and spiritual defilement, according

Directions are given for the purification of the wood, on which a corpse may have been carried, and of the grass on which a corpse may have been deposited. It is much easier, it is said, to purify dry wood and dry grass than that which is moist, because in the latter the sacred juice is affected.

With what has now attracted our notice, the *priest*, I suppose, has most to do. The *physician*, next comes on the stage. He must try his skill in the first instance among the worshippers of the devils; and he must be successful in three attempts to cure them, before he can be warranted to practise among the Mazdayaçnas. If he neglect this rule, and injure a Mazdayaçna, he must be considered as guilty of a capital crime. Take care, O Hindús, of a Pársí doctor, when he first offers you his services, lest he be merely experimenting upon your comparatively useless carcases. With regard to *fees*, a doctor is on the whole to be well treated, except perhaps by the priest, who has merely to give him his blessing.* The master of a house is to give the value of a small animal, such as a sheep or goat; the master of a street, that of an animal such as a cow; the master of a city, that of a large animal; the master of a province, that of four excellent horses. The price of the cure of the wife of a master of a house, is that of a milk-ass; and of the son of the master of a street, who seems to be more valuable than his mother, — that of a large animal, such as a bull. For the cure of a large animal, the price of a middle-sized animal is to be given; for that of a middle-sized animal, that of a small animal, such as a goat; for the cure of a goat, a supply of milk. It is to be hoped

to which the former is represented as utterly insignificant when compared with the latter. "Do not ye yet understand," added Christ, "that whatsoever entereth in at the mouth goeth into the belly, and is cast out into the draught? But those things which proceed out of the mouth, come forth from the heart, and they defile the man. For out of the heart proceed evil thoughts, murders, adulteries, fornications, thefts, false-witness, blasphemies. These are the things which defile a man." See Matthew, chap. xv.

* Framjí Aspandiárjí (Author's MS. vol. i, p. 226,) says that its merit is worth three thousand ordinary fees.

that the doctors of Bombay will henceforth attend to this legislation when they make out their bills. Cures, we are informed, may be effected by the lancet, by drugs, and by the 𐬨𐬄𐬚𐬭𐬀 *mãthra*, or word! Those brought about according to the last mentioned method, are declared to be the most effectual.

On the point now noticed, let us give a hearing to Aspandiárjí. "The *secret* of the fact which he (Dr Wilson) has introduced into his pamphlet," he says, "regarding the most powerful efficacy ascribed to the recitation of the Honover, in driving away evil passions, etc., does not seem to be *fully comprehended* by our learned friend. But before he entered upon the task of imposing a blame upon the Pársí religion, on account, as he imagines, of the absurdity of this circumstance, he should have inquired as to the real signification of the term Honover. But since he has omitted this essential part of his work, I cannot help thinking it, in justice to the subject, as my duty, to supply the deficiency. Honover is the name of that Almighty Being who is the Lord of all things and the possessor of all power. The repetition of this Great Name is described in the Vandidád as being attended with peculiar power and efficacy in expelling the Ahriman, that is, the vicious propensity of the human heart. The manner in which this holy word is to be repeated, and the numerous advantages flowing from such an act, have been described to (at) a considerable length in the Vandidád. What absurdity is there in the repetition of the name of God Almighty? It is the theme of almost all religions now prevalent among the various nations. By the repetition of the holy name of God, wonderful effects have been described in the religious books of the Hindús. Nor is the fact less adverted to, in the Bible itself, for Christ himself has assured his apostles that they might achieve a great many miraculous acts in his name, such as the expulsion of the devils etc. There remain therefore no sufficient grounds for our friend to attack the Vandidád on this ground."* The Mobed is very solicitous, on all

* Hádí-i-Gum-Rahán, p. 73.

occasions, when he cannot upset my arguments, or pervert my statements, to retreat behind "secrets," "mysteries," "parables," and what not; but he is always wonderfully unsuccessful in explaining these occult sayings. In the present instance, he has dug a pit for himself, into which he must tumble head over heels. Hunavar is *not* the name of God, but of the word of Hormazd in general, or of the mãthra, commencing with the words *yatḫá ahú vairyó*. It is not the "vicious propensity of the human heart," that is spoken of in the passage before us; but it is such diseases as may be operated upon by the "lancet," and by "drugs," which are mentioned along with the mãthra, or word, which is declared to be the best remedy. The apostles of Christ performed no miracles by any enchantment following the mere repetition of the name of Christ. They wrought "in the name,"* or by the authority and power vouchsafed to them by the Saviour. The effects said to follow the performance of *námochchárana* by the Hindús, the Mobed knows right well, can never be substantiated.

Leaving the cure of *man*, the fargard before us proceeds again to treat of the cure of defiled *ground*. That on which a corpse has lain, must not be tilled for a year; and that in which a corpse has been buried, must not be tilled till fifty years have expired. That on which a *dakhma*, or repository for the dead, has been constructed, is not to be tilled till all the bones have mingled with the dust. The work of digging up dakhmas, when they are no longer required, is declared to be highly meritorious. He who accomplishes it, has the merit of him who performs the *paitit*, or penitential ceremony, or who is pure in thought, word, and action. The sun, moon, and stars, will be delighted with him, and he shall shine resplendent in the regions of bliss. I gave a translation of the passage, according to Anquetil, in which these statements are made in my lecture on the Vandidád, observing, that according to them, "ceremonies or works approaching to them are more excellent than good moral actions," and adding what

* Acts iii. 6.

follows:—"Moral distinctions, the perception of which is so important for the regulation of human conduct, are hereby entirely lost sight of. Morality is consequently essentially injured. When it is believed, that particular ceremonies are more efficacious than general obedience, the motives to good conduct are sadly weakened, and the eternal claims of the divine Being are lamentably overlooked."* Aspandiárjí has been greatly puzzled to find an answer to my remarks, and that which he has given will surely satisfy no intelligent Pársí. "In the foregoing passage," he says, "the purport is hidden in the *usual mysticism of the Vandidád.* What fault is there to be found with the Vandidád, if it denounces the practice of tilling and cultivating that portion of the ground which had previously been allotted to the reception of the dead bodies? For the production of such ground is, no doubt, injurious to the health of the people. It is also a great mistake on the part of our friend to state that 'They who have destroyed great Dakhmas, where were the bodies of dead men, shall be as if they have made the Paitit of thought, of word, and of action,' for the Vandidád enjoins to disinter, and afterwards to expose to the sun those bodies only, which had previously been buried into [in] the ground; the Dakhmas, which are the sepulchres of the Pársís, are already constructed in such a manner as to be exposed to the perpetual sun; and consequently it is not requisite to remove the dead bodies out of them in order to expose them to the action of the sun. The most reasonable interpretation that can be put upon this mysterious passage of the Vandidád would be, to suppose that by the word 'grave' is meant the body of man, and corpse or dead bodies signify the evil passions. Now to disinter the dead bodies may imply the removal of evil thought from the heart, and to expose them to the sun, may signify to make the heart pure and enlightened by divine knowledge; such a person alone is understood to possess the merit of being pure in thought, in word, and in action. Him the great Dádár Hormazd will reward, and assign a place in

* Lecture on Vandidád, p. 33.

the ninth heaven, the habitation of the souls of holy men. This is the sole mystery of the passage. His other passages such as, — 'He shall have long life, and pure fire shall contribute to his preservation;' 'He shall neither receive blows nor wounds;' are devoid of any authority in the Vandidád. It is also no less a calumny thrown against the scriptures of the Pársís when the Rev. gentleman solemnly declares, — 'moral distinctions, the perception of which is so important for the regulation of human conduct, are hereby entirely lost sight of,' — as if our friend means to insinuate that the Vandidád Sádé enjoins all sorts of evil practices, such as theft, adultery, telling falsehood, the unjust and forcible appropriation of the properties of others, and such like other deeds, quite repugnant to the principles of morality. This unfounded charge of padre Wilson, is therefore quite gratuitous."* — It is not necessary to say much in reply to these lucubrations. The word which the Mobed renders "grave" is *dakhma* 𐬛𐬀𐬑𐬨𐬀 † in the original Zand, as he will see by turning up his Vandidád; and although dead bodies are for sometime exposed to the light of the sun on the margin of the dakhma, it is a fact that the bones and other relics, after the flesh has been torn from them by the vultures, are thrown into the central pit. The disinterment to which, I am sure, the Vandidád alludes, is that of these bones; but even if we take it in the more limited sense of a single grave proposed by the Mobed, it will only give intensity to my charge against the Vandidád, that it prefers an external act to penitence and inward righteousness, and promises eternal happiness as its result. The sentences which the Mobed says are "devoid of any authority in the Vandidád," are not essential to my argument. If he will again inspect that volume, and look at the Zand, instead of his father Framjí Aspandiárjí's comments upon it, he will see substantially a warrant for them, and understand

* The English version here given by Aspandiárjí somewhat differs, as is not unfrequently the case, with his Gujarátí work. As the former, however, may be supposed to have his latest thoughts on the matters in dispute, I prefer it for quotation. Hádí-i-Gum-Rahán, pp. 79, 80.

† Lithographed Vandidád, p. 243.

how Anquetil, from whom I extracted them, has introduced them. The idea of interpreting the word "grave" as "the body of man," "corpse and dead bodies" as the "evil passions," and the "disinterring the dead bodies," the "removal of evil thoughts from the heart," is so absurd, that the priest has been compelled to give it as merely suppositive. "Grave *may* mean," etc. he says; but I ask, what *does* it mean? All that precedes it in the Vandidád, shows that it is neither more nor less than a repository of the dead, for digging up which salvation must be the consequence. If men are thus easily to get rid of their sins, there is certainly *encouragement* given in the Vandidád to transgression. Does the Mobed not understand the difference betwen "weakening the motives to good conduct," and "enjoining all sorts of evil practices?"

That I am correct in taking the passages now referred to in their literal sense, and in repelling Aspandiárji's parabolical interpretation, will further appear from what immediately follows in the fargard before us. "Where", says Zoroaster, "are the male devils and the female devils; where are they that come together and rush together; where are the devils that come in crowds of fifty; of more than fifty — a hundred; of more than a hundred — a thousand; of more than a thousand—ten thousand; of more than ten thousand — an innumerable multitude? It was thus replied, They are in the *dakhmas, O çpitama Zoroaster, which are in the lofty places, in which they place dead men.* In that place are the male devils and the female devils." This must decide the point, as well as evince the absurdity of a *post mortem* diabolical possession. More nonsense of the same kind will be found in the context.

The fargard ends with a repetition of the law about premature births, and other matters mentioned in the fifth fargard. The mother is to have two hundred stripes, if disliking the cow's urine and ashes, she commits a certain offence in reference to her food. Cattle eating of the corpse of a dog or man, are impure for a year. What a silly dictum! Whoever heard of ruminant cattle with the ravenous propensities of the carnivorous?

8. The eighth fargard continues the legislation respecting *impurities.*

The house in which a man or dog has died, is to be purified by incense and certain sweet-smelling odours. It will certainly not be the worse for the use of them even in profusion. The body is to be taken to the dakhma, about the construction of which particular directions are given as in a preceding fargard. The hair and body of the *naçakas,* or bearer of the dead, is to be purified by the urine of cows, etc.

The body is to be conveyed to the dakhma by some other way than that on which cattle, man, woman, or fire, the Son of Hormazd, or the pure *barsam,* are passing. In such a place as Bombay, the observance of this precept must be extremely difficult. A certain yellow dog, is to pass the road three times. He is to have "four eyes,"* and white ears. He must move along the road three times; and he will thus drive away the daruj Naçus to the north. If such a dog be not found, an Athrava, or priest, must first move along the road, "repeating the victorious word, *Yathá ahú vairyó,* etc." A feast is to follow on the fourth day after the interment. No more cloth or leather than is necessary must be used in enveloping a corpse, on the penalty of 400, 600, and 1000 stripes, according to the quantity employed.†

Adultery is to be punished with 800 stripes, and rape is unpardonable till the resurrection. The performance of the *paitit* near a priest and the practice of the rites of the unalterable Mázdayaçní faith, are recommended. The devils are multiplied on the commission of another crime, which I need not mention.

There is no defilement in touching a dead body thoroughly dried; but impurity is contracted by touching one that is fresh. The person to whom it attaches must perform various ablutions. He must first wash from his hands to his shoulders.

* Two of these, as we have already mentioned, are explained by the Dasturs to be merely spots above the eyes.

† In common with Anquetil, I think the Zand forbids the use of a covering altogether. But I here give the Dasturs their own view of the passage.

When the good water has reached the crown of the head, the Drukhs [fiend] Naçus betakes himself to the back of the head. When it has reached the back of the head, the devil Naçus betakes himself to the mouth; when it has reached the mouth, the devil Naçus betakes himself to the right ear; when it has reached the right ear, the devil Naçus retires to the left ear. By a pursuit of this nature, tediously and particularly detailed, the devil is expelled from the toes in the form of a fly, and betakes himself to hell. We have referred to the passage in our third chapter; and we here only advert to it in passing.* There is no difficulty in translating the original, and the narrative, as remarked by Richardson, is quite inconsistent with common sense. "It can easily be solved," says Aspandiárjí, whose sentiments are somewhat similar to those of Dosabháí already noticed, "by reflecting upon what I have already observed, that Ahriman, or the Dews, or Daruj Nesosh are not real beings that might be supposed to have any independent corporeal existence, but are the personifications of the various evil passions which inhere in the breast of man. It is therefore enjoined in the Vandidád to subdue our passions gradually by the purification of our hearts, for it is quite out of the power of a human being to effect their subjugation at once. The washing of the body, which is enjoined in the Vandidád, means, strictly speaking, not only the external washing of the body, but also

* This passage, so absurd in reference to its ceremonial and theological revelations, is not without interest in a philological point of view. The Zand words for the different members of the body, when reduced to their pure form, are easily cognizable in the cognate languages. Thus we have for *dashino gaoso*, the Sanskrit दक्षिण *dakshina* right, and the Persian گوش *gosh* ear; for *hóya*, the S. सव्य *savya* left; for *kasha*, the S. कक्ष *kaksha*, arm-pit; for *parsti*, the S. पृष्ठ *prishtha*, the back; for *fstána*, the S. स्तन *stana*, the breast; for *pereçáva*, the S. पार्श्व *párçva*, the side; for *çraoni*, the S. श्रोणि *çroni*, the loins; for S. the सक्थि *sakthi*, the thigh; for *zhanu*, the S. जानु *jánu* and Greek γόνυ the knee; for *zangha*, ankle, the S. जंघा *janghá*, leg.

the internal purification of the heart. The fire of rage, and the flame of anguish, require to be extinguished by the water of patience. The prohibition which the Vandidád makes in regard to the touching of the dead body, is no doubt, worthy of attention; nothing can be more impure and shocking than the sight of a body from which the pure soul has taken its flight. The frequent contact with corpses is also attended with other contagious évils. The Vandidád is not therefore reprehensible on that account." This solution is such as cannot for one moment prove satisfactory, unless it be admitted, that diabolical possession follows the accidental or deliberate touching of a corpse, and that the simple application of water effects its destruction, which is more absurd than the difficulty it is intended to remove. The ceremony prescribed in the Vandidád, is not said to be symbolical, but to be intrinsically operative. It has primarily to do with the bodies and not with the souls of men. This Aspandiárjí himself cannot deny, for he is forced to speak of the actual defilement of the outward man which accrues to him who comes in contact with the dead. To the removal of *this* defilement, I allow, water will be altogether effectual, if rightly applied. The Vandidád, however, tells us that it frightens away the *devil Naçus.*

The Mazdayaçna, who may observe any person cooking or burning a corpse, is to destroy them, and seize their property. The fire must be put into a hole at a certain distance from the place where it was found, and there fed with wood, and removed, successively to a second, third, fourth, fifth, sixth, seventh, eighth, and ninth, hole, where it is to be fed with odoriferous wood, and other substances, by which 1000 devils, 200 magicians, and a host of Paris,* will be destroyed, and by which, as the fire of Hormazd, it will be duly purified. The person who will then take this fire to the dádgáh, (or fire-temple,) will have as much merit after death, as if he carried ten thousand other fires.

The person who takes to the dádgáh the fire in which excre-

* Fairies, female devils, very attractive in their persons.

ment has been burned, shall have the merit of him who carries 500 other fires. He who takes the fire found in ovens in which bread has been baked, shall have the merit of him who carries 400 fires. He who carries the fire of a potter, shall have the merit of him who is in the habit of carrying other fires. Great merit is in this way obtained by those who carry the fire found by a traveller, or that of a goldsmith, silversmith, ironsmith, steelsmith, coppersmith, that of the desert, of watchmen, shepherds, cowherds, and that which is near a *dádgáh*. Fire, it appears, is thus viewed as sacred, and must not be allowed solitarily to expire.

A person living in the jungle, who may be defiled by a dead body, must either purify himself by ablutions of cow's urine, or betake himself to the towns for the assistance of the priests.

If a man sullied by a corpse enter into water upon a road, his expiation must be 400 stripes. If he come in contact with fire, or pure trees, he is to have the same punishment.

9. The ninth fargard is principally occupied with a long, tedious, and absurd account of the ceremony of the purification denominated the *Barashnom*, to be performed by, and in behalf of, a person who may have been defiled by touching the dead. It informs us how the stones are to be dug out and arranged, and how they should be 54 feet distant from pure water, fire, man, and the barsam; how by ablutions with water and cow's urine the devil Naçus is to be driven from the crown of the head to the toe, fighting every inch of the journey, exactly as narrated in the preceding fargard; how the repetition of the mãthras will stop the devils of Mazanderan and other places; how the person in the course of being purified must be kept separate from the Mazdayaçnas, for a certain number of nights, and for the same time from different purities, as fire, water, etc; how he is to receive a blessing from the priest, worth 4000 treasures; how he is to get presents of camels, horses, cows, goats, and so forth, from other members of the community; and how he is to get heaven as a reward after death. I am certain that no intelligent Pársí can peruse this part of the

Vandidád, without most clearly perceiving the extreme folly which it indicates on the part of its composer.

10. The tenth fargard of the Vandidád informs us what *word* must be repeated twice, thrice, and four times, at the different gáthas, in order that Ahriman and various inferior devils, may be expelled from houses, cities, provinces, and from men and women defiled by touching the dead. If the devils be frightened by mere sound, the Pársís certainly need not be afraid of them.

The fargard, in conclusion, alludes to the choice of a place for the performance of the *Barashnom,* particularly described in the ninth fargard.

11. The eleventh fargard does not much differ from the tenth. It informs us how houses, fire, water, trees, cattle, earth, man, woman, the stars, the moon, and the sun, and all the luminaries, may be purified and hallowed by pronouncing the word. It shows us how fire, water, and the earth, are to be directly addressed in worship, and how a great variety of devils may be exterminated by the repetition of the word.

12. The twelfth, like the other fargards of the Vandidád, exists in the Zand language. It is not, however, as far as I am aware, to be found in the Pahlaví.* This is probably the reason why it has not been translated by Frámjí Aspandíarjí into Gujarátí. The analysis which is given of it by Kaikobád, is more incorrect than that of the other fargards, a circumstance which favours the conclusion that the knowledge of the Zand possessed by the Mobeds is now extremely faint. It is occupied by a description of ceremonies that are to be performed in behalf of the dead, and injunctions about the purifications of the places, clothes, and other articles which have been defiled by lifeless bodies.

When a father and mother die, a son, or daughter, must on their behalf perform [illegible] *thristĕm dáhmanăm,* thirty dáhmans, or religious services addressed to the Izad Dáhman, which are "equal to sixty Tanafurs," or

* Anquetil (Zend-Avastá, vol. ii, p. 371) says "ce fargard ne se trouve dans aucun Vendidád Zend-Pehlvi."

which procure a rémission to this amount of the guilt contracted by the deceased, or the specific merit of the service, if guilt has not to be atoned for.* Thirty dáhmans are prescribed for a deceased child; thirty, for a brother or sister; six, one of which is to be offered each month after the death, for the master or mistress of a house; for a grand-father or grand-mother, twenty-five dáhmans; for a son or daughter, thirty dáhmans; for a grandson or grand-daughter, twenty-five dáhmans; for a cousin, twenty dáhmans; for a great-grand-father, fifteen dáhmans; for a great-grand child, ten dáhmans; for a great-great-grand child, five dáhmans. It will be observed, that a specific merit, in every instance accrues to the departed from the prayers which are presented on his behalf. The custom of praying for the dead among the Pársís, is freely admitted by the controversialists to whom I reply. Aspandiárjí thus expresses himself on the subject. "It is not in the twelfth fargard of the Vendidád, as padre Wilson states, that the directions for offering prayers for the dead are given. It is of little or no consequence in what fargard the order is prescribed. Whatever our learned opponent may say, as to the efficacy of offering prayer for the dead, in relieving the sinners from their just punishment, yet I cannot help believing that the prayers addressed to God in behalf of the deceased, for their relief, are not without an effect in procuring them the remission of their sins. The practice of offering prayers for the dead is observed by all nations; even the Christian clergymen are observed to preach sermons and to make prayers for the dead. Among the Roman Catholics it is, we hear, a common practice to engage priests to say masses and to perform some funeral ceremonies in their churches for the sake of the deceased."†

* Dáhman is the angel, who is supposed to receive departed spirits from the hands of Sarosh, the imaginary guardian of the just, and to conduct them to the regions of bliss. One of the prayers denominated *Afrigáns* is called by his name. The temporal punishment of the *Tanafur*, as we have seen, is 200 stripes. What its *post mortem* punishment is said to be, I do not exactly know.

† Hádí-i-Gum-Rahán, p. 90.

The Mobed, it will be seen, says nothing about the *reasonableness* of prayers for the dead. No Christian, who follows the Bible, ever observes the practice. That divine word thus emphatically speaks of the future state: "He that is unjust, let him be unjust still; and he which is filthy, let him be filthy still; and he that is righteous, let him be righteous still; and he that is holy, let him be holy still."* It *is* in the twelfth fargard, we see, that prayers are prescribed for the dead; and I suspect that it is because there is not a Gujarátí translation of this fargard, and because Aspandiárjí does not understand the original, that he has ventured to deny this fact. This, however, is indeed of little consequence. What merits our particular attention, is the circumstance admitted by him that the Pársís *do* offer up their supplications for their deceased friends. "Prayers and religious services for the dead," I have formerly said to the Pársís, "I must pronounce unavailing. The doctrine that the deceased may be either relieved from their just punishments, or advanced in their bliss, by the conduct of those who survive them, is directly opposed to the fact that men cannot satisfy the claims of the divine justice for themselves as individuals, far less procure a stock of merit which can be available for any of their fellow-creatures. It is calculated to foster daring and dangerous presumption in the minds of the living, inasmuch as it affords them the hope that all that is necessary for their spiritual welfare, may be accomplished after they have been removed from this earthly scene; and it thus conduces to lead them to delay repentance, and to confirm them in their sinful courses."† To this subject, I shall again advert, when, in the next chapter, we come to consider the means of salvation prescribed in the Pársí scriptures.

Directions are given in this fargard for the purification of the places in which the relatives, mentioned above, have died. The cleaning of them is required, not only for the sake of man, but for that of fire, water, and trees! It is to be ac-

* Revelation, xx. 11. † Doctrine of Jehovah, p. 56.

complished not merely by ablution, but by three repetitions of the word and other ceremonies.

The fargard concludes with cautions against the two-footed devil Ashmog.

13. We have much in the preceding fargards about *dead* dogs. The thirteenth is devoted principally to the *living* members of the canine race. It is that which has furnished the principal material of the most pungent satire, addressed by Sir William Jones to Anquetil du Perron. I shall not offend, I hope,the feelings, of the lovers of truth among the Pársís by giving the following translation from the French of a passage contained in a letter by the learned judge.*

" They [the Vandidád, Izashné, and Vispard] contain nothing which corresponds with the character of a philosopher, and of a legislator. We shall cite only the description of the dog ; and if, after this absurd rapsody, the most intelligible, and the most important part of the book, the reader wish to read it entirely, he is indeed a bold spirit. See then how Zoroaster speaks through his *excellent* interpreter.

" *The dog has eight qualities: he is like an Athorné (a priest), he is like a soldier, he is like a labourer, the source of wealth, he is like a bird, he is like a robber, he is like a wild beast, he is like a woman of a bad life, he is like a young person.*† Is not this a beautiful group ! But we must have the details: Oh ! we shall have then really the sublime. List.

" *As the Athorné, the dog eats whatever he finds ; as the Athorné, he is benevolent and happy* ; *as the Athorné, he is content with every thing ; as the Athorné, he puts to a distance those who approach him. He is like the Athorné.* See what a geometrical precision is formally observed. There is only a little want of common sense in the demonstration, but that is well compensated for by the fine and elegant man-

* Sir William Jones addressed Anquetil du Perron in the French language, because it was that in which the translation of the Zand-Avastá appeared.

† The passages given in Italics in this translation, are extracts from the Vandidád.

ner in which Zoroaster has satirized the priests: and these words, *he eats what he finds*, are very emphatic. We must henceforth remember, that long before our day, it has been consistent with a polite style most liberally to bestow the title of a *dog*.

"*The dog advances as a soldier. He attacks pure cattle, when conducting them like a soldier; he roves before and behind places like a soldier: he is like a soldier.* There are many warriors who would not find such a comparison flattering....

"*The dog is active, watchful during the time of sleep, like a labourer the source of wealth; he roves before and behind places, like a labourer the source of wealth: he roves behind and before places, like a labourer, the source of wealth. He is like a labourer.* Before, behind, behind, before. A graceful and emphatic repetition.

"*Like a bird the dog is gay; he approaches man like a bird, he nourishes himself with what he can take like a bird: he is like a bird.*

"In the same way it can be proved that the dog resembles all the animals of Buffon's Natural History. The monkey nourishes himself with what he can take, the cat likewise, the squirrel likewise; and all the animals likewise. Therefore, the dog resembles all the animals. Oh! What a fine thing is the Persian logic! If he who gives us it so eloquently would keep a school, and impregnate the surrounding atmosphere, what an easy tone would not be substituted for the Roman and Greek pedantry!

"*The dog works in the dark, like a robber; he is exposed to hunger like a robber. He often receives some injury like a robber; he is like a robber.* The poor dog is about to be lost in parallels, but notwithstanding the good intention of Zoroaster, in his favour, what has he gained?

"*The dog acts in the dark like a wild beast. His strength is during the night, like a wild beast: sometimes he has nothing to eat, like a wild beast; frequently he receives something bad, like a wild beast; he is like a wild beast.* New and agreeable turnings, at every moment!

Don't laugh reader: respect antiquity; admire all that belongs to Zoroaster.

" *The dog is content like a woman of bad life; he wanders in the streets like a woman of bad life; nourishes himself with what he can find, like a woman of bad life; he is as a woman of bad life.* The philosopher wished to prove that he was acquainted with all conditions! What matter, that it was at the expense of the dog and of reason? But patience! let us have the last comparison, at least as just as the others.

" *The dog sleeps a great deal like a young person; he is lively, and always in action like a young person; he has a long tongue like a young person; he runs in advance like a young person. Such are the two chief dogs which I have caused to move in places, to wit, the dog Pesoschoroun, and the dog Vescheroun.*

" Hormazd, great Hormazd, origin of all good among the Guébres, if thou hast dictated this dog of a description to Zoroaster, I give thee no *yescht*; thou art but a foolish genius; perhaps, with the 'colour of lillies and roses,' but certainly without brain.

" You see, Sir, how the evil encreases; we will in our turn end with these exclamations: will you like better this dilemma? Either Zoroaster had not common sense, or he did not write the book which you attribute to him; if he had not common sense, he ought to have been left in the throng, and in obscurity; if he did not write the book, it was impudent to publish it in his name."*

This we suspect, will be considered by many of our readers a sufficient notice of the twelfth fargard; but, as in the case of its neighbours, we must take a regular, though brief, view of its general contents.

The fargard opens with the following passage:—

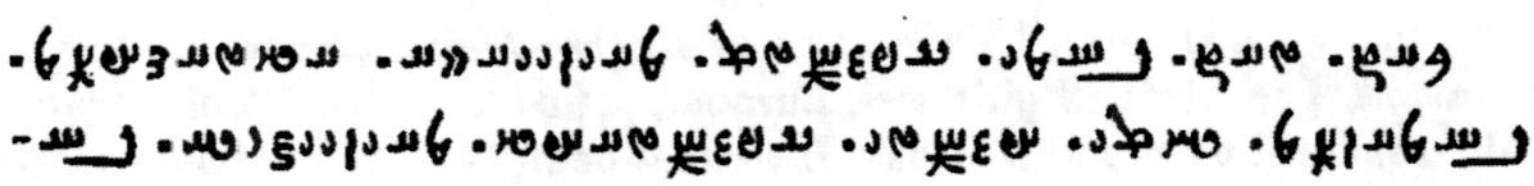

* Sir William Jones' Works, vol. x, pp. 433—437.

[illegible]

*Kaţ taţ dámi çpeñtó mainyava aētanghãm dámanãm yói heñti speñtahē mainyéus dáma dátem víçpem paiti usáonghĕm áhú vakhsáţ hazanghraja angro mainyéus paiti jaçaiti? A'aţ mraoţ Ahuró-Mazdão çpánem sízẖdarem urvíçarem yim vangháparĕm yim maskyáka ava duzẖvachanghó duzẖakem nãm aojaiti aētaţ taţ dáma speñtó mainyava aētanghãm dámanãm yoi heñti speñtahé mainyéus dáma dátem víçpem paiti usãonghem áhú vakẖsáţ hazanghraja angro mainyéus paiti jaçaiti : —**

—"What is that, in the creation, O exalted Spirit, — the creation of him who is the exalted spirit, the crêation, which during the whole of the early Ushen [watch] making a noise [or crying *áhú*], in a thousand ways, assaults the wicked spirit [Ahriman]? † Hormazd replied that it is the sharp small-headed dog Vanghápar to which men speaking evil, give a bad name: —it is this very [dog] which in the creation belonging to the exalted Spirit,— the work of him who is the exalted Spirit, which during the whole of the early Ushen, crying aloud, in a thousand ways, assaults Ahriman." According to this doctrine, dogs defend not only from the thief and robber, but

* Lithographed Vandidád pp. 403, 404.

† This word is derived from *Agro* or *Anghro-Mainyéus* which literally means, The wicked Spirit. See Burnouf, p. 90 &c. The Pársís, generally render it by the Murderous Invisible (being). The Persian *míno* which they render by "invisible," it is evident, is derived from the Zand *mainyu* (noun manó) corresponding with the Sanskrit *manas*, the mind.

from the prince of darkness himself! Valuable protectors, indeed, are they of the human race! Why should we wonder that there should be a Hormazdian legislation for *their* protection? A person who may strike this dog Vanghápar, is to afflict his soul for nine generations! He is one of those who will not pass the bridge of Chinavad. His punishment from men is to be a thousand stripes. Other dogs are mentioned, which assault inferior devils, and for striking of which punishments are also prescribed. The striking of the dog *Wasushuran* is a capital offence. Giving bad food to dogs, is equivalent to giving bad food to the masters of houses, and is to be punished by from 200 to 50 stripes. They should be fed with fresh meat, or fat, and milk. Mad dogs are to be tied up, and kept in confinement. It is a capital offence to kill them. Let this be kept in mind by all the police sepoys of Bombay and the police magistrates also. A mad dog biting a man or beast, is to have his right ear cut off; for the second offence, he is to lose his left ear; for the third, his right foot; for the fourth, his left foot; for the fifth his *tail*!

The beautiful and sublime description of the dog, quoted by Sir William Jones, follows. The fargard concludes with a very impure description of the breeding of water dogs.

14. The fourteenth fargard continues the praises of the canine race.

A person who strikes a water-dog, is to be treated to 10,000 stripes. He must, by way of atonement, carry 10,000 bundles of dry, and the same quantity of soft wood, to the fire of Hormazd. He must furnish 10,000 barsams, 10,000 zors of pure Hom and its juice. He must kill 10,000 reptiles that creep on their bellies,* and 10,000 reptiles of

* Though in these injunctions there is great absurdity, and though the question must occur, How could a sufficient number of reptiles be procured, it is probable that they have a reference to a country, in which noxious animals were very abundant. "Our stay in Mazenderan," says Sir Alexander Burnes, (Travels into Bokhara, vol. iii, p. 108) was soon to close. It is a disagreeable country. It is a land of snakes and frogs; but the snakes are not venemous, being of the water-species. They are to be seen twisting and turning everywhere, and about the thickness of a good

the form of a dog, 10,000 turtles, 10,000 land frogs, 10,000 water frogs, 10,000 ants which drag the grain, and 10,000 stinging ants, 10,000 blood-suckers, 10,000 stinging flies. He must take out 10,000 impure stones from the ground. The fire of the twice-seven kinds (the A'tish-Běhram) is to be honoured by him. He is to present to the priest the instruments of his craft, a knife, the *gostdán*, the *padán*, a whip for killing vermin, the *merkindán*, the *havanim*, the *tasto*, the *hom*, and the *barsam*. He is to present to the soldier the instruments of his craft. He is to present gifts to the agriculturist. He is to present a field and a *virgin of fifteen years of age, with golden ornaments*, fourteen goats, fourteen whelps, etc. etc. to pure men or priests. If he make not these atonements, he must go to the abode of the devils. On this nonsense, I forbear to comment.

15. The fifteenth fargard of the Vandidád commences with the notice of certain crimes which are declared to be [Zend script] *apaititu anuzvarsta*, incapable of being undone by the penitential services, or of being pardoned. The first of them is following out ones' own inclination in reference to religion, and giving even a very little praise to another faith. The second is feeding the dogs Pasushurun, or Veshurun, with hard bones, or too hot food. If the bones stick in their teeth, or throats, and if with the hot food their gums and tongue be burnt, and if they die, the offender has commited a capital *(margzání)* offence. The third is the killing of a dog great with young, or the pursuit or frightening of her by noise, so as to make her fall into a ditch, well, or water, or sewer, to her injury, which is also a capital crime. The fourth is having connexion with a woman, when she should be in a state of separation, which is also a capital crime. The fifth is having connexion with a woman in advanced pregnancy, which is also a capital crime.

Several laws relative to abortions and illegitimate children, are next laid down. One specimen of them we have given in

sized whip. Almost at every pace your horse disturbs some frogs, which scramble in vain for concealment even in a country of bushes and shrubs."

our first chapter. I am greatly mistaken if any intelligent Pársí layman can peruse them without reproaching the memory of their author; and I shall say nothing more respecting them. *Vitanda est rerum et verborum obscœnitas.*

The birth of dogs, and their accommodation, and guardianship, are then treated of at considerable length.

16. The sixteenth fargard is occupied with the treatment of a woman in her separation. The place of her retirement must be dry, fifteen paces from fire, water, and the barsam, and three from pure men; and she must not look upon fire. The persons who convey food to her, must remain three paces distant from her. Her meals must be taken to her in vessels of iron, lead, or other cheap metals. If her infant be taken to her, there must be an instant ablution. She must keep at a distance for three, four, five, six, seven, eight, or nine days, as circumstances may require. Her illness is directly declared to be the work of the devils, and to be removed by performing the Izashné and Níáísh. Three stones are to placed for her, on two of which she has to wash herself with cow's urine, and on the third she has to perform her ablutions with water. She must then set upon the destruction of vermin, to the number of two hundred.

If a man approach a woman in a state of separation, he is guilty of the Tanafur, and is to be treated to 200 stripes. If she come into contact with others, she is to receive 30, 50, 70, 90 stripes, according to the repetition of her offence. If she will not take care of herself, destruction will be her portion.

17. The seventeenth fargard of the Vandidád, I formerly introduced into my lecture, according to the translation of Anquetil du Perron. It ran as follows: —

"Hormazd replied, Behold, O pure Zoroaster! When in the world which exists by my power, men arrange the hair of the head, pull out bad hairs, or cut them off entirely, or when they cut the nails without observing the prescribed ceremonies; — by these two criminal actions, the Dews come upon the earth, by these two criminal actions are produced the

Kharfestars, which men call lice, which go into men, and which run upon their clothes.

"O Zoroaster! when in the world which exists by my power, you pull out the hair or cut it all off, carry it to the distance of ten gáms from men, twenty from pure fire, thirty from water, and thirty from the united Barsam. You must take a hard stone from the uncultivated ground, as large as a veteshto, hard as an almond; you must put it into a hole or pit, leaving the hairs under it, and pronouncing the victorious word, O Zoroaster! Now, O holy Hormazd, cause trees to spring up abundantly in this place. You must trace round the stone, or mark out, three, six, or nine honovers. (It is the desire of Hormazd etc. etc.)

"You must in like manner take another stone of the length of a little finger, which must be placed at the side nearest to Hormazd. You must lay the nails under it, pronouncing the victorious word, O Zoroaster! I invoke thee with purity. Trace round the stone three or nine Keishas with a steel knife, reciting three, six, or nine honovers, and saying, bird Ashoshest, I address my prayer to thee. I invoke thee. I adore thee. Those who address this bird Ashoshest shall be assisted against the Dews of Mazenderan with the lance, the poignard, the bow, the arrow, the pike, and the sling fitted for stones.

"If this bird be not invoked, and addressed, all these weapons will become the prey of the devils of Mazenderan, viz. the lancet, the poignard, etc., with which the Dews of Mazendran can be opposed. The offenders are worthy of hell; they become the possession of the Daruj, without a chief; they receive no assistance from Serosh; they are impure, and are guilty of the Tanafur."

And what are the explanations furnished by the learned dasturs of this trifling and absurd legislation? My quotation, says Aspandiárjí, betrays "the want of sufficient knowledge" of "the *mysterious religion of the Pársís*." It is a pity that he has not made the attempt to unfold the secrets and to remove my ignorance. He says that in my translation, I have, in many places, "misrepresented the facts." But why has he not put them to rights? I have carefully perused the passage in the original, and I find that a more literal version, or even the Gujarátí translation in the hands of the Pársís, will not render it a whit more consistent either with common taste, or common sense. I deny that it is said in it, as Aspandiárjí alleges, that if the hair be not kept clean, it will be infested with *kharfastars*; though a child knows that such will be the result of neglect. I deny that its scope is merely what Aspandiárjí declares it to be:— "Thou shalt keep thy hair clean and comb it; the refuse and the nails which are cut, thou shalt throw aside at some distance from the well or any reservoir of the water. If thou wouldst not take proper precaution for the throwing of the hair or the cut nails, the Dews might crowd there; meaning they will produce stench and animalculæ quite offensive in their nature to the health."* But even though I were to admit, that this is something like the sense of the passage, I would ask, Where is the necessity, or propriety, of making a regular funeral of such trifles as a few cuttings of hair and parings of nails, and reading prayers, or repeating hunavars over the precious relics, as mentioned in the text, and constituting the neglect of these ceremonies a serious offence? It is now upwards of twenty years since the Pársís have had their attention directed to this nonsense; for Mr. W. Erskine in his excellent essay "On the Sacred Books and Religion of the Pársís," says, "Prayers and minute observances, are enjoined on cutting the hair and the nails, the omission of which is a capital offence."† It is not merely on such a slight occasion as this that solemnities are to be resorted to by the Pársís. પેશાબની જગોથી તરણ કદમ દુર ઊભો રહીને પઢે* અને ખડાઊનું ઠેંપુ હાતમાં રાખે* I shall not hurt the polite feelings of any of the Pársís by translating these words, and what follows them in Zand and Gujarátí in the Khurdah-Avastá, the authorized manual of alleged inspired prayers

* Hádí-i-Gum-Rahán, pp. 76, 77.

† Bombay Transactions, vol. ii, p. 323.

which is constantly in their hands,* or by referring to similar services which they are taught to consider incumbent.

18. The eighteenth fargard of the Vandidád opens by bringing before our notice, some of the distinctive characteristics of an *áthrava*,† or priest. He must wear the ***padán***, or mouth-cover, of two fingers-breadth, have an instrument for killing *kharfastars*, be attentive to study during the night, and maintain the brilliancy of the sacred fire, and relieve the distressed.

The agent who spreads death abroad is then introduced. The present dasturs suppose, that it is the person who does not conform to the institutes of the Mázdayaçní faith, who does not wear the kustí for three years, who does not observe the Izashné of water, etc. Anquetil, with more regard to the original, supposes it to apply to the Devil, the author of the evil law, who would not wear the *aiwyâonghãm*, or kustí, at the gahanbárs, or epochs of creation, and submit to any of the other ordinances of Hormazd. The learned Frenchman is correct in his opinion. The agent referred to, there can be no doubt, is denominated *asvagha*, or Ashmog, the Wicked Lord,‡ and he is said to possess certain attributes, which do not belong to a man, however depraved, and is described as *khato-zavañti*, "il vit par lui même,"§ which makes him self-produced, and consequently Ahriman himself.‖

* See Khurdah-Avastá, of Frámjí Sohrábjí pp. 488—491.

† Zand. The name commonly used by the Pársís is *Athorné*.

‡ From *asu* lord, and *agha* wicked.

§ It is somewhat singular to find Anquetil giving this the correct rendering in his text, and adding in his note, "Ces paroles *kheto zeoûentê*, peuvent encore se rendre de cette maniere : *il vit par* (la puissance) *de Dieu* (Zend-Avastá, tom. ii, p. 403). His mistake has arisen from his viewing *kható* as equivalent to the Persian *Khudá*, Lord, while it means *khud*, self, or belonging to one's self. ખુદ જીવનાર is the Gujarátí rendering of the dasturs.

‖ This, I would here remark, forms another proof of the correctness of the doctrine which we have laid down in the third chapter, that, accord-

The bird [illegible] *mereghó Paródars*, said to be vulgarly and improperly called [illegible], *kahrkatáç*, next comes before us. He is said to be the powerful assistant of *Çraos*, or Sarosh; and, flapping his wings and crowing aloud, he awakes men from their sleep at the Ushen *gĕh*, or watch. It is of great importance to attend to his admonitions, for *Búshyañsta*, or Bushyásp, the devil of sloth, is toward morning much inclined to assault men, and should be destroyed by prayer.

Fire is then represented as begging for fuel at the first, second, and third watches, and promising the greatest blessings to its votaries. We have extracted the passage in full in our fourth chapter.

The bird Paródars is a second time brought before us; and it is expressly mentioned, that the person who gives it good food, will be glorified in the mansions of the blest! This way to happiness seems plain and short enough. Whether it is equally sure, is another question.

A conversation between Sarosh, and the Darukhs, (Hashem), his rival, follows. In my lecture on the Vandidád, I have declared it to be so impure that it cannot be quoted; and most certain am I, that I should not be excused were I to introduce its substance into these pages. Aspandiárjí gives me no credit for withholding it; but even he has not ventured to drag it into light.

The fargard concludes by prescribing certain atonements to the man who has intercourse with a woman in certain circumstances. He must present to fire 1,000 goats, the fat of 1,000 other animals, 1,000 bundles of dry and pure wood, and other odoriferous substances, 1,000 barsams, 1,000 zors of hom. He must kill 1,000 reptiles which move on their bellies, and 2,000 other reptiles, 1,000 or 2,000 water frogs, 1000 ants, and 2,000 gnats. He must erect 30 bridges. And, after all, he must submit to the infliction of 1,000 stripes. Will some of the dasturs show us the practicability of these atonements,

ing to the standards of the Pársís, Ahriman is coetaneous with Hormazd, or created independently of the Good Principle.

particularly in India? It is said that if they be performed, heaven will be obtained, and if they be neglected, hell will be the portion of the offender.

19. The nineteenth fargard tells us first of the perils to which Zoroaster, when he had left the earth on his mission, was exposed from the assaults of the murderous Ahriman and his host, who come from the north. As the *Buiti-daêvo*, he ran upon the reputed prophet, who immediately repeated the *ahunavar*, *Yathá ahû vairyó*, etc. and made obeisance to the river Vêhêdáiti. Ahriman anticipates the destruction of *Aka-Manangho*, or Akuman;* and beseeches Zoroaster, the Son of *Póurushaçpa*, or Porusasp, not to destroy his creation, but to forsake the Mázdayaçni religion. Zoroaster is relentless, and says that he will not abandon it, for the sake either of his soul or body. The devil asks by what means his kingdom is to be destroyed, and he is informed that it is to be by the [illegible] *havana*, the [illegible] *tasta*, and the [illegible] *haoma*, and the word, which he declares has been —

[illegible]

dathaṭ çpeñtó-Mainyéus, dathaṭ Zarvánahê-Akaranahê, which means, "given by the exalted Spirit [Hormazd], given by Zarvána-Akarana." We have already alluded to this passage as proving, that Zarvána-Akarana is viewed by the Vandidád, as a personal agent, and not, as Dosabhái would have it, as mere Eternity.

Zoroaster is then represented as asking Hormazd, how Ahriman can be vanquished, and the impurities which proceed from him can be removed. The reply, bringing various objects of worship to his notice, and commanding him to invoke them, I have inserted in the fifth chapter of this work.

Zoroaster then asks how the Izashné for Hormazd and his creation is to be performed. He is directed to pronounce the word near the growing tree [from which the *barsam* is procured]. It is ordered that he should take hold of the barsam

* The rival of the Amsháspand Báhman.

[illegible]
[illegible]

yazemano Ahurem-Mazdãm, yazemano amesé-çpeñta haomaçcha záiris, and "worshipping Hormazd, worshipping the Amsháspands, and the golden coloured hom." To this passage, I referred in my lecture on the Vandidád, as proving that the Pársís recognize multifarious objects of worship. Can the reader imagine how Aspandiárjí has met my statement? He says that the words which I have now quoted are "not to be found in the Vandidád."* He will find them, and the statement with which I introduce them, I beg to inform him, in the 512th page of the lithographed edition of that work; but he will *not* find what he says is there:—"Having performed the ceremonies called Barsam and Hom,† thou shalt worship me abstaining from all worldly enjoyment."‡ Will my respected opponent excuse a joke? The sooner he asks our mutual friend Mullá Rustamjí to apply to his back a couple of hundred stripes, by way of inculcating upon himself a little more regard to accuracy, so much the better. Honest Pársís, I doubt not, will mark his error, whether it be that of knowledge or ignorance. They will also see that as far as the passage which I have quoted goes, it connects the subordinate Amsháspands and the humble *hom*, as objects of reverence with the exalted Hormazd, and that consequently if Hormazd were God, this would be nothing short of blasphemy.

Directions follow for the purification of a defiled person. He must copiously wash himself with cow's urine and water, and repeat a great many *ahunavars*, and so forth.

Zoroaster then proceeds to ask Hormazd whether there will be a resurrection of pure men and pure women, and also of the *darvats*, or darvands, the accursed, and the worshippers

* Hádí-í-Gum-Rahãn, p. 63.

† Ibid.

‡ Barsam is a tree, or its splittings, and *Hom* also a tree, or its juice, and not a "ceremony."

of devils; and he receives a reply in the affirmative.* He then asks when men are to receive the fruit of their works; and he is informed that it will be about the dawn of the morning following the third night [after death], when the splendent Mithra and the brilliant light begin to rise on the mountains. The devil *vizaresó*, or Vizars, at that time having bound the souls of the worshippers of the devils, conveys them away. By the *pathãm Zarvó-dátanãm* "paths given by Time," proceed both the pure, and the accursed. The pure man, when he reaches the *Chinvaṭ-peretúm*, bridge of Chinavad, desires the fruit of his merit acquired in this world. There his righteousness, powerful and beautiful, is present with him. He has the protection of the dog [formerly fed by him], that of his children, [who are praying for him], and various other blessings. The darvand goes into darkness. The pure man proceeds by the way of the lofty *Harãm-berezaitím*†, or Alborz. He passes the bridge of Chinavad, and arrives in the mansions of the Izads. The *Ahú-mano*,‡ or Bahman rises from his golden throne, and asks the holy soul, How hast thou come from the world of death, to that in which there is no evil. The pure soul becomes happy, and receives a golden throne, prepared by Hormazd, and the Amshaspands, in *Garo nmánem*,§ "that high place," the abode of Hormazd, and the abode of the Amshaspands, and of the other pure Spirits.

* If we interpret the Zand aright, Zoroaster himself is to be the instrument of the resurrection. He asks *hakhsáné*, "Shall I raise"? And he receives as a reply the order *hakhsanguha*, "Raise thou," etc.

† Literally "the high mountain." The Zand *hara* resembles the Hebrew הר *har*. From the references which are made to the rising of the sun behind this mountain, it appears to have been to the eastward of the scene of the Vandidád.

‡ Literally, lordly intelligence.

§ From these words have been derived Garothman, the name of the highest heaven.

After the departure of a pure man, the devil in hell knowing only evil is afraid of his flavour. The pure man is with him, — Nariosangh is with him, who is called the friend of Hormazd. Some of this information, if we divest it of its personal references, is consistent with those ideas of a retribution of good and evil, which are universally prevalent among mankind. It forms the whole amount of the revelation which the Pársís profess to have in their possession respecting the future state ; and its poverty must be apparent to the Pársís themselves, who have sought to supplement it by numerous traditions. The resurrection here spoken of, according to the notions of most of their community, is a resurrection not to judgment, which has long preceded it, and takes place at death, but to a deliverance from all suffering.

Toward the conclusion of the fargard, Zoroaster is commanded to engage in religious ceremonies, and he expressly invokes most of the objects to which our attention has been directed in other parts of this work. He also receives the order to feed the fire with dry and odoriferous substances, to do obeisance to Sarosh, and so forth ; and this being done, various devils are seen to be filled with consternation.

20. The twentieth fargard, is devoted to the praise of Jamshíd (according to the interpretations of the Pársís), who is said to have removed disease, death, war, fever, headaches, evil, evil-doers, envy, falsehood, wickedness, and the impurity of Ahriman. Hormazd says of himself that he has created hundreds, thousands, and tens of thousands of trees with healing properties, and particularly the [Avestan script] *gaokerenem*, or *gokard*, from which the Hom is procured. He repeats what he has said, in the commencement of the Vandidád, about the felicity of Jamshíd's reign. The information given is in the language of gross exaggeration. It is worse than what we find in the romance of Firdausí, when he sings the praises of this king.

21. The twenty-first fargard opens with the following salutation. [Avestan script] *Nemeçe-té gaoçpeñta* "Salutation to the exalted Bull," or Taurus, and with a

reference to some of its exalted qualities, and the power of its urine to remove the devil Ashmog. Rain is attributed to the influence of the Bull, and it is represented as effectual to the removal of death and disease, by the abundance which it produces. By the influence of the Bull, the sun, moon, and stars shed their light upon the world from the lofty Alborz.* The bull is declared to be the preserver of Gorothmán, the highest heaven. The reference in this part of the Vandidád is probably to some imaginary effect of one of the constellations associated with the Bull. The passage, however, is so obscure that I shall not attempt to explain its meaning.

The rain produced by the bull is declared to be effectual in removing *istrê*, *agh̦úiri*, *agh̦ara*, *ugh̦ra*, disease, death, pain, fever, headache, the cause of headache, evil, the doer of evil, malice, envy, and other evils, including the magic of the París and the works of the devil! Aspandiárjí admits that this doctrine is in the Vandidád, *istrê*, he says, means "sorrow"; *agh̦úiri*, "indifference;" *agh̦ara* "regret;" and *ugh̦ra*, "oppression or tyranny." In affixing these meanings to these words, he seems wiser than some preceding commentators, who have not ventured to give them any particular signification;† but he ought to have endeavoured to elicit some *sense* at least from the whole passage, as most people will be prone to characterize it as downright nonsense. "Hormazd," he says, "has communicated all the benefits which flow from rain." Will Aspandiárjí explain to those who are dull of understanding, *how* the evils enumerated are removed by it? Will he, in particular, show to us *how* "the rain prevents fornication, and magic, which means all sorts of fraud and deceit," as he declares it does, according to the doctrine of the text of the Vandidád. We have rather a large quantity

* Aspandiárjí has found it more convenient to deny that such a doctrine is to be found in the twenty-first fargard, than to explain its meaning, or evince its reasonableness. It is there stated, however, in express terms. See lithographed Vandidád, pp. 536, 537.

† They are perhaps connected with the Sanskrit ईर्षा, *írshá*, spite; अघोर *aghora*, terrible; अाघ *agha*, sin; and उग्र *ugra*, wrathful.

of it on Mahábaleshwar, where I write this chapter; but I do not find that wickedness is less abundant here than in the parched plains of the Dakhan. But its effects, perhaps, are different in the country of Irán, from which his ancestors have come.

22. In the commencement of the twenty-second fargard, Hormazd speaks of himself as the 𐬛𐬁𐬙𐬀 𐬬𐬀𐬢𐬵𐬬𐬄𐬨 *dáta vanghvãm*, or creator of good, and as having observed from his happy abode, at a distance from himself, Ahriman, or the wicked intelligence, who created 9, 90, 900, 9000, and 90,000, or in all 99,999 Evils.* These evils Zoroaster† is commanded to destroy, through the influence of the word. Hormazd orders him, as *Nairyó-Çanghó*, to establish his worship in the country denominated *Airya-mana* or Irman,‡ for the purpose of rendering it like the abode of Hormazd himself, and removing from it all the works of the devil. A reward of 1,000 horses, 1,000 camels, 1,000 cows, and 1,000 goats are promised to the messenger of Hormazd, who declares that he will prove obedient.

Hormazd now informs Zoroaster that he has replied to the different questions which he had proposed to him upon the mountain in the wilderness, and commands him to take 9 horses, 9 camels, 9 cows and 9 goats, 9 bunches of the barsom, and 9 *kas* to Irman, [with which to commence his worship,] or, as the Pársís interpret it, to perform the great service of the *Nirang-dín*, through which all evil, moral and natural, including evil passions, disease and death will be removed. That the Vandidád, or any ceremonies which it recommends, ever has, or ever can produce such effects as these, no person, in a sound mind, can for a moment believe.§

* I have heard a friend remark that it was almost a pity that an additional evil was not created, to complete the *lákh*.

† Some of the Pársís make Márespand Izad the person addressed.

‡ The same as Irán of the first fargard.

§ One of the most curious and comprehensive supplements to this fargard, and indeed to the whole Vandidád, is that of the *Ulmá-i-Islám*, a translation of which will be found in the Appendix (F.)

Such is a candid analysis of the contents of the Vandidád, faithfully prepared, after a careful examination of the original Zand, with most of the helps to a right understanding of its contents, which both Asia and Europe have provided. It it utterly impossible for a Pársí, of any considerable intelligence, to peruse it with that perception cf its accuracy which inquiry will undoubtedly impart, without coming speedily to the conclusion, that the Vandidád is not only, both in style and in substance, destitute of all claims to be considered as a revelation from God, but that it is from beginning to end most singularly despicable as a human composition. The information which it gives on the most important subjects,—as the character of God, the nature of his providence and law, and the method of his grace, and the responsibility and destiny of man,—is extremely meagre and unsatisfactory, and most frequently unreasonable and erroneous to the greatest extent; and those who make it the rule of their faith and obedience, are not only involved in most distressing doubts, but in insuperable difficulties. Instead of exalting and glorifying the Creator, by declaring the unity of his nature, the perfection and infinity of his attributes of wisdom, power, holiness, justice, goodness, and truth, and extending the universality of his providence to every object and event, it represents him as existing in a state of almost total inactivity, as having both a good and evil offspring, presiding over their respective works of creation, which are endowed with qualities analogous to the opposite characters of their authors, and differing little in their properties from the pure and impure angels and archangels with which they are associated. Many of the works of God himself, it ascribes to the devil. The honours of God, it bestows on the elements of nature, the genii who are supposed to preside over them, and the different forms which they have assumed under the creative energy of him who called them into existence and is supreme in their disposal, arrangement, and combinations. The preservation of their imagined purity, is the principal object of its care and concern, and it is more occupied about the disposal of the carcases of men and dogs, than the guidance of the soul in this life, and its weal or woe in that which is to come. It exalts ceremony far above morality; and the rites which it establishes and recommends, are in general not only devoid of all sober import, but absurd and irrational, both in their own forms and those to which they direct attention. A spirit of suitable and exalted devotion, it neither begets nor directs; while it teaches that sounds, and smells, and ablutions are effectual in the riddance of evil. Its code of human conduct, is not only defective, as entirely silent on the supreme love, and gratitude, and reverence, and service which are due to God, and the affection, like that which we bear to ourselves, which we owe to our fellow-men; but it is inequitable in most of its foundations, and unholy and unjust in many of its special prescriptions. It enters into no historical details, respecting either nations, communities, or individuals, which are calculated to illustrate the ways of God to man; and it affords no virtuous examples deserving of the slightest imitation, or even attention. Its tendency is not to humble the sinner in the sight of God, to convince him of his depravity and guilt, and to lead him to put to himself the solemn and infinitely important question, What must I do be saved? It reveals to him no divine Redeemer, able and willing to save unto the uttermost all that come unto God through him; but it teaches man to depend for deliverance on the paltry atonements which he himself can make, and on the punishments which may be inflicted on him by the priest or magistrate, the ceremonies which may be performed on his behalf by his friends after his removal from this earthly scene, or on the sufferings of hell itself, which are supposed at once to satisfy God, and to purify the offender. It shows not how mercy can be vouchsafed to the transgressor, and yet the authority of the law sustained; how God can be just, and yet the justifier of the ungodly; how the sinner can be delivered from the power of sin, at the same time that he is freed from its curse. It is profitable neither for doctrine, nor reproof, nor correction, nor instruction in righteousness. It neither produces sobriety of thought or feeling; nor affords innocent amusement or occupation. It is only because with most of the Pársís it is in an unknown tongue, that its perusal is tolerated. It is muttered by the priest, but it is not understood by the people; and it is arbitrarily interpreted according to the degree of ignorance or knowledge, of the stupidity or intelligence, of the superstition or reason, of those who may venture to inquire about its meaning. A knowledge of its real contents in the case of every serious reader, as we have already hinted, must be destructive not only of the belief which may have been reposed in it as a supposed revelation from God, but of the respect which may have been felt for it, as a work the composition of man left to the sole guidance of his own faculties.

It is as the friend of truth, and as having already adduced ample reasons for the verdict which I crave, that I write thus respecting its demerits. Learned Europeans of every shade of belief, from that of the wavering sceptic to that of the confirmed Christian, have reprobated it in terms of severity fully as emphatic and expressive as any which I have thought it right to employ. Richardson, to whose Persian and Arabic Dictionary appeals have frequently been made by my opponents, we have seen asking respecting a passage of the Avastá, "Can human credulity suppose this to be the composition of Zoroaster, or of any man who had pretensions to common sense?" Gibbon, who is as prone to palliate that which is questionable, as he is disposed to disparage that which is excellent, in religion, we have found speaking of "that motley composition" (the Zand-Avastá) "as dictated by reason and passion, by enthusiasm and by selfish motives," and as containing only "some useful and sublime truths, disgraced by a mixture of the most abject and dangerous superstition." Sir William Jones, the prince and pioneer of modern orientalists, and who was unrivalled in his day for his scholarship and taste, we have seen declare, that the books of the Avastá "contain nothing which corresponds with the character of a philosopher, and of a legislator," and that "either Zoroaster had not common sense, or he did not write the book which you attribute to him."* Major-General Vans Kennedy, than whom no one is better acquainted with the mythology of the ancient world, says, "That the religion of Zardusht existed nearly in the same state as that in which the Pársís have preserved it to the present day, some centuries before the Christian era, I believe; but I as firmly believe that the Zendavesta is not only a spurious production of comparatively modern times, but that it is also in every respect totally unworthy of attention, for I concur entirely in the justness of this dilemma, proposed by Sir W. Jones to Anquetil du Perron."† The Abbé Foucher, says, "The books of Zoroaster, so barren on the subject of the moral virtues, treat to a fastidious extent of the arbitrary and superstitious ceremonies prescribed by Law; and it is to this they reduce all the religious virtues. Whilst they denounce some gross vices, both opposed to society and to good manners, they denounce with the same severity the most indifferent acts. To strike a dog, or not to feed it, is a crime as great as to kill a man, or to suffer him to die of hunger; to bury, or to throw into water the corpse of man or a brute, is a profanation as great as to practise magic. If we were to judge from the Zand books of the doctrine of the ancient Persians on morality, we could but form a wretched idea of it indeed. But the great philosophers, and especially Xenophon, give us a more favorable picture; and even if we grant the picture to be too bright, we must allow it to retain some resemblance. From this I conclude either that the Persians studied their moral laws in some other books than the Avastá, or that this work of which we have but small extracts in the Zand books, contained other important facts which have not

* Contrast this with what this profound and tasteful scholar says of the *Bible*. "I have regularly and attentively read the Holy Scriptures, and am of opinion, this volume, independently of its divine origin, contains more sublimity and beauty, more pure morality, more important history, and finer strains of poetry and eloquence, than can be collected from all other books, in whatever language they have been composed." See Life of Sir William Jones, prefixed to his works.

† On the Affinity between Ancient and Hindú mythology, p. 401.

reached to our time."* The religion of the Pársís, we have found, the Honorable Mr. Elphinstone, whom they themselves hold in the greatest respect, and who had many opportunities of observing its practical developements, while he was Governor of this presidency, declare to have "nothing inspiring or encouraging," and adding that according to it, "the powers of good and evil are so equally matched, that the constant attention of every man is necessary to defend himself by puerile ceremonies against the malignant spirits from whom his deity is too weak to protect him."† Hundreds of passages of an import similar to those which I have now quoted, it would not be difficult to produce. I conclude by asking the Pársís to seek for a rightful interpretation of the Avastá before they again hire the priests to recite it on their behalf. If, with an earnest desire to discover the truth, they will engage in this pursuit, they will be more disposed to feed the flame of the atishgáhs with their papers and parchments than with the fragrant sandalwood.

* Memoires de Litterature, vol. xxxix, pp. 793—4.

† Hist. of India, vol. i, p. 512.

CHAPTER VII.

THE PA'RSI' NOTIONS OF THE RESPONSIBILITY, DEPRAVITY, AND GUILT OF MAN, AND OF THE MEANS OF HIS SALVATION.

Vandidád and Dosabhái on the purity of man at his birth — Voltaire on Original Sin — Scriptural account of the Primitive State of Man — The Probation of Man — The Fall of Man and its consequences — Reply to Voltaire, quoted by the Pársís — Scriptural account of the Depravity of Man and its Propagation — Opinions on this subject of the Greeks, Romans, and Hindús — Illustrations from natural analogies — Connection of the Posterity of Adam with himself — A want of a due sense of the Responsibility, Depravity, and Guilt of man apparent in the Pársí books — Consequent indifference about a right way of Salvation — Unsuitableness of the Means of Salvation proposed in the Zand-Avastá — The rites of the Mázdayaçní faith, Charity, Repentance, Penances, Intercession of friends — Statement of the Gospel of Christ, and its adaptation to bring glory to God, peace on earth, and good-will to the children of men.

There are some most important matters referred to in the preceding chapter, of which it is necessary to treat with some degree of particularity. I allude to the Pársí notions of the depravity and guilt of man, and the manner of his obtaining salvation, or deliverance, from the punishment and power of sin, and introduction into the regions of glorious bliss. It is especially in connexion with these subjects, that a direct revelation is needed, for to many questions which may be proposed respecting them, our unassisted reason can give no satisfactory reply. It is indispensable to the welfare of man throughout the ages of eternity, that they be seriously and solemnly considered in their various relations.

It will be remembered that the Vandidád inculcates the doctrine of the purity of man at his birth as it actually now takes place; and that Dosabháí, the most accomplished of the controversialists with whom I am called to contend, forgetful of all that he had said about the evil dispositions, and evil nature of man, of which he wishes Ahriman to be a mere personification, cordially supports this doctrine, alleging that it is even in accordance with that of the Christian Scriptures, in which, he erroneously says, it is declared that "God has created the man's heart pure." The same writer endeavours to ridicule the account which is given in the Bible respecting the fall of man; and he introduces a long quotation from Voltaire, in which the doctrine of Original Sin is violently attacked, and in which it is maintained that the "first chapters of Genesis were regarded by all the learned Jews as an allegory, and even as a fable not a little dangerous."* What is the actual state of matters in regard to all these subjects, we shall now particularly enquire. Our appeal shall be first to the Bible, the testimony of which is grossly misrepresented, and to the analogy of nature, and the results of general observation, which, it will be seen, are quite in harmony with that testimony.

To the condition of man, as originally created, however, it is necessary for us to advert for a moment, before we speak of his present depravity. On this subject, the greatest amount of our information is contained in the first book of Moses. After an account is there given of the formation of the material world,—the land and the waters, and the vegetable and animal kingdoms,—the following important statement is given respecting the creation of the human race:—"And God † said, Let us

* Talím-i-Zartusht, pp. 191 — 221

† אלהים *Elohim*, the Hebrew word here used for God, is in the plural number. The Pársí editor of the Rahnamá-i-Zartusht, has devoted ten pages of his work to the endeavour to show that the Bible, by the use of the term, countenances polytheism. He is but a sorry grammarian, else he would have seen that the noun is of the *pluralis excellentiæ*, having a singular verb, as is commonly the case when this form is used, and thus without a plural sense. The pronouns used with Elohim, when the word means the true God, it is also to be observed, are sometimes in the singular, as for example in Genesis v. 13, and 18. "And Elohim said unto Noah..... *I* will destroy them..... with thee will *I* establish *my* covenant." *Elohim* is even sometimes used in reference to an individual

make man in our image, after our likeness; and let them have dominion over the fish of the sea, and over the fowl of the air, and over the cattle, and over all the earth, and over every creeping thing that creepeth upon the earth. So God created man in his own image, in the image of God created he him; male and female created he them. And God blessed them, and God said unto them, Be fruitful, and multiply and replenish the earth, and subdue it; and have dominion over the fish of the sea, and over the fowl of the air, and over every living thing that moveth upon the earth. And God said, Behold I have given you every herb bearing seed, which is upon the face of all the earth, and every tree, in the which is the fruit of a tree yielding seed; to you it shall be for meat; and it was so. And God saw every thing that he had made, and, behold, it was very good. And the evening and the morning were the sixth day...... And the Lord God formed man of the dust of the ground, and breathed into his nostrils the breath of life; and man became a living soul. And the Lord God planted a garden eastward in Eden; and there he put the man whom he had formed. And out of the ground made the Lord God to grow every tree that is pleasant to the sight, and good for food; the tree of life also in the midst of the garden, and the tree of knowledge of good and evil...... And the Lord God took the man, and put him into the gar-

false god, as in I Kings, i. 2. where we read of "Baal-zebub, the Elohim of Ekron." The Persian word *Yazdán*, which, though plural, is rendered by the Pársís as simply "God," when applied to Hormazd, and which in all the Persian dictionaries is given as equivalent to *Khudá*, or Lord," is exactly analogous.

Perhaps the editor of the Rahnamá-i-Zartusht is aware that in different languages the semi-vowels *l*, *m*, *n*, and *r*, are frequently interchangeable; and perhaps, with the aid of the Baron de Sacy, Professor Rask, and other European orientalists, he may be able to see in his own Pahlavi [Pahlavi script] *Anhuma* (instead of *Alhuma*) something very near to, if not identical with, the Hebrew *Elohim*, which, written without the vowel points, is simply *A'lhim.*

To all this, I have merely to add, that the doctrine of a plurality of persons, the Father, Son, and Holy Ghost, in the one Godhead, is actually that of the Bible; and that with reference to this distinction the word Elohim may have *originally* come into use.

den of Eden, to dress it and to keep it. And the Lord God commanded the man, saying, of every tree of the garden thou mayest freely eat. But of the tree of the knowledge of good and evil, thou shalt not eat of it: for in the day that thou eatest thereof thou shalt surely die. And the Lord God said, It is not good that the man should be alone; I will make him an help meet for him. And out of the ground the Lord God formed every beast of the field, and every fowl of the air; and brought them unto Adam to see what he would call them; and whatsoever Adam called every living creature, that was the name thereof. And Adam gave names to all cattle, and to the fowl of the air, and to every beast of the field; but for Adam there was not found an help meet for him. And the Lord God caused a deep sleep to fall upon Adam, and he slept: and he took one of his ribs, and closed up the flesh instead thereof. And the rib which the Lord God had taken from man, made he a woman, and brought her unto the man. And Adam said, This is now bone of my bones, and flesh of my flesh: she shall be called Woman, because she was taken out of man. Therefore shall a man leave his father and his mother, and shall cleave unto his wife; and they shall be one flesh. And they were both naked, the man and his wife, and were not ashamed."*

Man, it will appear from this narrative, was formed in a manner which corresponded with the preparation which was made for his creation as particularly detailed in the opening of the book of Genesis. While his bodily frame, like that of the lower animals which preceded him, was composed of the material substance around him, his soul was immediately called into being by the breath of the divine power. Vitality, and sensation, and instinct, were not the only properties which were conferred upon it; but it was endowed with those moral properties which correspond with the image of God himself, and which, as we learn from Paul's Epistles, consist in "knowledge," and "righteousness and true holiness."† The origi-

* Genesis, i. 26—31, and ii. 7—9, 15—25.

† Col. iii. 10; Ephes. iv. 24. Kalam Kas (Nirang-Há, p. 162.) repre-

nal state of man, therefore, was in the highest degree exalted. He possessed a nature with the most excellent constitution and qualities, and which had no moral blemish, and no moral defect. His soul was illuminated with the light of heaven. He was qualified and inclined to hold communion with God, to contemplate the divine workmanship and providence with an intense and rightly regulated devotion, and to acquiesce in the divine will. He possessed the perfection of purity; and he responded in every respect to the divine law. His desires, affections, and passions were alike free from sin, and rightly regulated by reason, and by the direct intimations made by the Godhead itself. He was a stranger to all doubts, and fears, and misgivings. He enjoyed that holy felicity which only spotless souls can know and appreciate, and with which they only can sympathize. He stood before his Maker, as his noblest work in this world. He was the lord of its creatures. He had "dominion over the fish of the sea, and over the fowl of the air, and over the cattle, and over all the earth, and over every creeping thing that creepeth upon the earth." His nature was immortal; and every circumstance connected with it, stamped it as possessed of infinite value.

The divine goodness which was thus manifested in the creation of man, was signally displayed in the provision which was made for him. God actually "blessed him," and thus pledged his divine wisdom, power, and faithfulness in his behalf, and gave him reason to expect the bestowment of every thing which was good and needful. He provided a residence for him so glorious, that it is ever referred to as emblematical of heaven itself — of that place where God especially displays

sents Moses as attributing to God a corporeal shape, when he says that "God created man in his own image." He will see, from the passages here referred to, that the bible speaks only of a *moral* image of God.

The power of God to manifest himself in any form which he may choose, I may here remark, in reply to objections which I have seen elsewhere stated, is freely admitted by Christians. What they deny is, that a form essentially belongs to the divine nature, and that any form should be worshipped.

his glory. Eastward in Eden,—the land of delight,—he planted a garden, decorated it with every thing which was pleasant to the sight, and filled it with every thing which could gratify the taste, and prove useful for food. In this lovely spot, he appointed him to labour without toil, and to enjoy consummate happiness. In his divine beneficence, he furnished him with a help meet for him, who was bone of his bone and flesh of his flesh, who was thus most strikingly recommended to his affection and regard, and who was to live with him as his most endeared companion and friend. They were commanded to be fruitful, and multiply, and replenish the earth and subdue it, and to exercise that dominion over the lower animals to which their pre-eminence, and the design of their creation entitled them; and they were informed that there were given to them every herb bearing seed, which was upon the face of all the earth, and every tree which is the fruit of a tree yielding seed, that they might be to them for meat. They could, in these circumstances, have no wants which could remain unsupplied. The cup of their bliss was filled too verflowing. They had infinite occasion to praise the Lord for his goodness, and his unmeasured beneficence.

The object for which man was created, endowed, and blessed, was undoubtedly the display of the glory of God. The manifestation of the divine excellence, the complacency and delight which God has in his works, and the enjoyment of himself by the creature, must be considered as the end which God has in view in all his actings. In disposing of man for these objects, it pleased God, in the exercise of his infinite wisdom and sovereign pleasure, to place him in circumstances of peculiar moral probation. He had a perfect right to act in this manner; for it is essential to the nature of the creature, unless it be directly restrained by God, that it should be changeable and fallible; and in the arrangements which he made for the accomplishment of his purposes, we perceive grounds for our highest admiration and praise. He did not alter in the slightest degree the nature which he had originally conferred on our progenitors; he did not deprive that nature of any of the enjoyments which he had provided for it; and he did not place it under any restrictions which in the slightest degree could be injurious. He granted our first parents every thing which their hearts could desire; and he merely interdicted them from eating of the fruit of a single tree which grew in the midst of the garden. He did not deprive them of their free-will and personal agency. He warned them against disobedience, by declaring, in the most express terms, that in the day they should eat of the forbidden fruit, they should surely die. In all these arrangements, we perceive the divine wisdom and goodness. We perceive the display of these attributes even in the peculiar trial to which Adam was subject. It was such as his circumstances permitted; and was calculated to mark the unspotted holiness of God, and to allow an illustration of the dreadful nature of sin. The more insignificant in itself we consider the article interdicted to be, so much the more do we lessen the temptation to touch it, and shut up Adam to obedience; and so much the more do we mark that justice which will not suffer with impunity the violation of the least of the divine commandments. Surely, it might have been expected, we are led to say, that Adam, amidst all the scenes of happiness in which he was placed, and all the abundance with which he was surrounded, would have continued to honour and respect his Creator and bountiful Benefactor, who demanded of him a perpetual test of perfect homage, and humble submission, by requiring him to forbear to eat of the fruit of a particular tree.

Man, then, it will be kept in mind, was placed by a holy, and wise, and just providence, in circumstances of rightful moral probation; and, in the nature of things, he was responsible for the consequences. The information necessary to guide him was communicated to him; and warnings which were calculated to deter him from transgression, were not withheld. The most urgent motives to obedience were before his view.

Let us now take a brief view of the narrative given by Moses of his procedure in the situation in which he appeared. The record of his temptation and fall, is given with great plainness and simplicity by that sacred writer ;* and it is throughout highly instructive. I trust that not a few of my Pársí readers will see and acknowledge that this is its character. For their sake, as I proceed, I shall, draw a few of the inferences to which it plainly points.

Our attention is directed in the first instance, to the "serpent," and of it it is said, that it was "more subtil than any beast of the field which the Lord God had made." We may perhaps conclude from this notice, that the pristine endowments of this animal were very considerable ; and we may infer from other passages of the divine word, that these endowments were under more than their natural direction, even under the direction of "that old Serpent, called the Devil, and Satan which deceiveth the whole world."† This enemy of the human race, we know to have been originally an exalted angel of light. He kept not, however, his first estate, but voluntarily sinned against God, and brought upon himself eternal degradation and misery. Instead of remaining an obedient servant of God, he became a rebel, and like a "roaring lion seeking whom he may devour." He had no doubt assumed the form of the serpent, because of the facilities which it afforded for the accomplishment of his purposes. Perhaps, he chose it on account of its attractiveness, or because he thought that when disguised under it he would least excite suspicion, or because he thought that it would otherwise aid him in giving a colouring to his intended lies. The traditions of most ancient nations accord wonderfully with the statements of Moses respecting it. The Pársís themselves frequently speak of Ahriman under the figure of a reptile.

It was consistent with God's plan of the probation of our first parents, to grant to the serpent the natural permission of access to them. Satan, through the whole of the interview which he had with them, displayed in an eminent degree the

* See Genesis, Chap. iii. † Rev. xii. 9.

cunning which is attributed to him in sacred writ. He directs himself to the woman, naturally the weakest and the most pliable of the two; and he accosts her in a state of solitude, in which she could not enjoy the counsels, and direction, and assistance, of her husband. He does not undisguisedly reveal his foul and base intentions; but he proceeds to the work of delusion in the most reserved and artful manner. From the abrupt way in which the first question respecting the forbidden tree is recorded, it is probable that it was preceded by others of a less suspicious nature. Even *it* is framed so as not to betray the purposes of the tempter. *Information* seems all that is desired, though the mode in which that information is requested is calculated to awaken a silent murmur against the divine sovereignty as displayed in interdicting the forbidden tree. When the terms of the divine prohibition are stated by Eve, the serpent questions only the *sense* in which they were understood, and falsely holds out certain alleged advantages of disobedience. "Ye shall not surely die," was his language, "for God doth know that in the day ye eat thereof, then your eyes shall be opened, and ye shall be as gods, knowing good and evil." His own conversational powers, he perhaps attributed to the unknown virtues of the fruit to which he directed attention. By the falsehood which he practised, he awakened sinful desires; and he appears to have allowed them to take their course, satisfied that they would issue in the accomplishment of his malignant purposes. In the whole proceeding, he manifested that diabolical skill, which, with so much success, he has continued to exercise against our race.

The deceitfulness of the serpent, however, great though it was, was no excuse for the conduct of Eve. The will of God had been made known to her in the most unequivocal terms; and the prohibition which was given, was sanctioned in the most awful manner, by the threatening of certain death. It was her duty to remain at a proper distance from that tree which she was interdicted even from touching. The first attempt of the serpent to inject doubts into her mind about the divine equity and goodness, ought to have been repulsed with the most determined holy indignation which she was capable of exercising. The first perception of falsehood on the part of the serpent, should have ended their communications, and led her to forsake his presence. Instead of repelling his insinuations, however, she allows them to penetrate her soul. Instead of departing from her adversary, she continues to hold with him fellowship and communion. Instead of casting herself on the divine protection, she encreases her own temptations. She gazes at the fruit; she admires it as "good for food," as "pleasant to the eyes," and as promising knowledge; she wishes to be possessed of it; she takes it into her hands; she eats of it; and she gives it unto her husband, and he does eat! She thus practised the grossest and most determined disobedience. She sinned against the divine goodness, exhibited in her creation, her mental and moral endowments, and the rich provision which was made for her; and she thus manifested the vilest ingratitude. She sinned against the best interests of herself and of those who might be connected with her, and thus manifested the greatest folly. Her husband recklessly partook of her sin, even without going through all the stages of her temptation; and he was thus involved in all its guilt, even with aggravations. We are able to form only very inadequate views of his demerit.

Such was the manner in which sin was introduced into the world. We are now called upon to observe its *workings and consequences.* These are of the most lamentable kind, and correspond, of necessity, in every particular, with the divine threatening. Adam and Eve, on the day in which they ate of the forbidden fruit, died spiritually, and became liable to temporal and eternal death. Their *spiritual death* is that which first merits our attention. For an illustration of it, we shall confine ourselves to the narrative of Moses.

We have already alluded to the image of God which was conferred on our first parents, to the holy exercises in which they engaged, and to the consummate happiness in which they rejoiced. Their moral nature was completely changed by their transgression.

The first notice of their depravity represents them as under the influence of *shame.* "The eyes of them both were opened, and they knew that they were naked: and they sewed fig leaves together, and made themselves aprons." The sweet satisfaction which they formerly had with their moral and natural condition is now at an end. They are no longer conscious of innocence and loveliness. Their acquisition of the knowledge of evil, was attended with their loss of the knowledge of good. The blast of the Lord has passed over the trees of his own planting; and they are no longer verdant and fruitful. Our first parents are conscious of their loss, and the efforts which they make to remedy it, have a success so partial that it only serves to exhibit their weakness and wretchedness. They are, in an important sense, "wretched, and miserable, and poor, and blind, and naked."

Ignorance and *fear, and an aversion to that which is good,* are congenite with their shame. "They heard the voice of the Lord God walking (or proceeding) in the garden in the cool of the day." But instead of welcoming that voice, and rejoicing in Him whose manifest presence it intimated, they are filled with dread, forget the divine omnipresence, and vainly endeavour to hide themselves from God among the trees of the garden. They are called from their lurking places; and Adam confesses his terrors. "I heard thy voice in the garden," say she to the Lord God, "and I was afraid, because I was naked, and I hid myself." Can any thing be more humiliating than this declaration, and can any thing speak more emphatically as to the change which Adam had now undergone? The intelligent creature hath ceased to delight in the Creator, and to desire his communion. Poor, base, and sinful man, imagines God, who searcheth the heart and trieth the reins of the children of men, to be like himself in the extent of his knowledge, and God, who filleth heaven and earth, to be like him in the extent of his presence. The fear which he evinced was suited to his circumstances as an offender; but it loudly testified as to his fall, and the extent of his degradation. It proceeded from the consciousness that he had offended God, and that he had not yet reaped the the full effects of his transgressions.

The *direct practice of sin* was superadded to all the shame, ignorance, terror and aversion to good, which our first parents exhibited. They were not ashamed of sin, but ashamed of themselves on account of the state in which sin had placed them. They were not afraid of sin, but afraid of its punishment. They manifest no holy aversion to sin, and no holy contrition on account of sin. In vain we look for a frank and honest confession of their guilt. They prostrate not themselves in the dust before God. God's presence and inspection do not prevent them from sinning; and their experience of its woful consequences does not deter them. Adam exerts all his ingenuity to shift the blame upon God, by attributing it to the arrangement of his own providence. "The man said, The woman whom thou gavest to be with me, she gave me of the tree, and I did eat." Eve practised a similar evasion: — "The woman said, The serpent beguiled me, and I did eat."

We need no stronger proof of the moral death of our first parents, than that which is to be found in the circumstances to which we have now alluded. We have seen the consciousness of innocence leave them; the eyes of their understanding settle in darkness; degradation stamp itself on the powers of their mind; God cease to be the supreme good of their soul; and a proneness to sin, in circumstances of the greatest aggravation, brought into play. And we have seen in them the symptoms of that moral disease which is still committing its ravages among our race. On contemplating these fearful exhibitions, and the pristine glory and happiness of those who make them, we may well exclaim, "Hear, O heavens, and give ear, O earth; The gold has became dim, and the exceeding fine gold is changed; The crown has fallen from off their heads; God made man upright, but they have sought out many inventions." Let none of us imagine, that we should have acted otherwise than our first parents did. They bore our nature in its best estate, and yet they fell. Let us also vindicate in our thoughts the holiness of the divine being. It was displayed in the original endowment of man. It was displayed in the covenant which was made with him, and which must be considered to have involved the bestowment of life in case of obedience, as well as the infliction of death in case of disobedience. It was displayed in the moral death, which we have already seen following the transgression, and the temporal and eternal death, which we shall now notice.

The threatening of God involved *temporal death,* including all the evils of this life, which are connected with it, or which lead to it. How this death was inflicted upon Adam, it is not difficult for us to understand.

There is an intimate connexion between the spiritual and mental and animal constitution of man. A depravity of the spiritual constitution, such as we have already noticed, could not but exercise its malignant influence upon the mental constitution, and lead to such a darkening of the understanding as we have seen exhibited by Adam in his vain attempts to flee and hide himself from the presence and scrutiny of his God. In like manner, a depravity of the spiritual and mental constitution must have been detrimental to his animal and corporeal frame. It is proverbially true, that the ailments of the mind and spirit soon appear in the ailments of the body; and that they are frequently even more destructive to its general health and welfare, than those which are immediately seated in itself. "The spirit of a man," says Solomon, "will sustain his infirmity; but a wounded spirit who can bear?" "The issues of life," he informs us, "are out of the heart." "A merry heart maketh a cheerful countenance: but by sorrow of the heart the spirit is broken."* A great part of his writings is occupied in shewing how folly and sin lead to temporal evils; and the general, nay, the universal, experience of mankind inculcates the lessons which he teaches. This experience instructs not merely in the case of individuals, but in the case of communities even of national extent. We are, in the view of these circumstances, led, when reasoning by analogy, to infer that our first parents must have greatly suffered in their bodily interests in consequence of their moral and intellectual depravity. We are not, however, left to the resources of this reasoning alone. The sacred historian di-

* Proverbs xviii. 14; iv. 23; xv. 13.

rectly informs us that not only such a consequence followed; but that direct misery, and the incipiency of death, were inflicted upon them in consequence of their transgression. The judgment and sentence of the offended majesty of heaven announce the penal arrangements.

Even in the doom of the serpent which beguiled our first parents, they must have read the displeasure which they had incurred, and the woes which they had generated for themselves. "The Lord God said unto the serpent, Because thou hast done this, thou art cursed above all cattle, and above every beast of the field: upon thy belly shalt thou go, and dust shalt thou eat all the days of thy life: and I will put enmity between thee and the woman, and between thy seed and her seed; it shall bruise thy head, and thou shalt bruise his heel." Though Adam and Eve attempted to shift the guilt of their transgression from themselves, they yet laboured under the consciousness of its reality; and on the announcement of the curse of the serpent, their forebodings must have been of a direful nature. Even with the curse itself, they have an intimate connexion. Their enemy who had sought their destruction, and who had artfully deceived them, is still to continue opposed to them. They are to encounter his enmity and hatred, strengthened by the success which he had experienced in his malignant designs, and exasperated by the additional curse and punishment, which, in the exercise of his wickedness, he had brought upon himself. They might with reason, then, anticipate the misery of a continued struggle. They are in fact instructed that a great deliverer is needed by them; and that even when He should appear to bruise the head of the serpent, his own heel was to be bruised.

Their fearful anticipations are directly confirmed by the doom pronounced against themselves. "Unto the woman he said, I will greatly multiply thy sorrow, and thy conception: in sorrow shalt thou bring forth children; and thy desire shall be to thy husband, and he shall rule over thee." Sorrow is declared to be her portion and her possession; and this sorrow, instead of being diminished, is to be greatly encreased. It is to be called forth not merely during the ordinary providences of her existence here below ; but is to be exercised in the peculiar situation in which she stands with regard to her family. Great are to be her sufferings in connexion with her children. Her husband is to rule over her, not as an unfallen, but as a sinful and depraved, being. Her subjection, consequently, while under God it is a duty, cannot but be frequently attended with what is painful and trying.

The curse rests on the man as well as on the woman. "Unto Adam he said, Because thou hast hearkened unto the voice of thy wife, and hast eaten of the tree which I commanded thee, saying, Thou shalt not eat of it : cursed is the ground for thy sake ; in sorrow shalt thou eat of it all the days of thy life : thorns also and thistles shall it bring forth to thee ; and thou shalt eat the herb of the field. In the sweat of thy face shalt thou eat bread, till thou return unto the ground ; for out of it wast thou taken : for dust thou art, and unto dust shalt thou return." There have not been wanting those who have spoken of the curse which was pronounced upon the earth as positively a blessing to Adam ; and who have consequently attempted to palliate his depravity, and to make light of his misery. The curse of the earth, however, is positively declared to have been for Adam's sake, or on Adam's account, and to have originated in his sin. It must therefore, as far as Adam is concerned, be considered penal. The fact that benefits do result from it in the providence of God, does not affect this conclusion; for it is the glory of the working of God, that he brings good out of evil. The fact speaks volumes as to the actual depravity and demerit of Adam, that the welfare of his condition required a change on the face of that earth, which God had pronounced to be " very good " in its primitive state ; that it required to be cultivated with exhausting labour and toil ; that thorns and thistles were to be its most natural produce ; and that the herb of the field, which actually with difficutly was to be procured for the sustenance of man, was to be eaten in sorrow all the days of his life. The curse of the ground, on man's account, is indicative of the intrinsic holiness of God, of his perfect hatred of sin and his determination to punish it. Should any person be sceptical on this subject, let him ask his brethren, who agreeably to the circumstances of their lot, are called to earn their bread by the sweat of their brow, and they will tell him, that necessity alone forces them to make the exertions which they actually do, and that a bettering of their condition would be attended with a change of their pursuits. No discoursing on the miseries of unemployed leisure on the one hand, nor the trials of the exercise of intellect and power on the other, — which trials I may remark in passing, also testify to the depravity and misery of man, — would prevent the formation of the desire for independence on their manual labour for their own sustenance. Adam, whose every prospect in the garden of Eden in his pristine state, and whose every act in its cultivation, must have been attended with enjoyment, must have viewed that curse by which he was subjected to toil as very great. We cannot even sympathize with what his feelings must have been. He had the sense of loss, as well as the sense of an actually degraded condition.

The misery of Adam to which we allude, has a limit; but that limit is nothing else than *death.* Not only does the enjoyment of life pass away; but the possession of it is also transient. He who was created as the chief of God's works below, and to exercise dominion over God's creatures, must return to the ground from which he was taken. That frame which was fearfully and wonderfully made, and which was the tenement of that spirit which was breathed into it by God, and which was fashioned after the divine image, must crumble into dust and be mingled with its kindred ashes. The death which was threatened must be literally endured. The fatal poison was swallowed along with the forbidden fruit; and it will be sure in its operations. It will flow in the veins, obstructing and destroying the functions of the body; and weakened by its agency, the tabernacle shall at last fall, and become its prey, even to dissolution or consumption. That nature which was immortal before it was taken, instantaneously becomes mortal; and in this sense, as well as in that referring to the intellectual and moral nature of man to which we have already alluded, it may be said that Adam, in the day he ate of the forbidden fruit surely died. Voltaire ought to have admitted the fact; and Dosabhái, and all like-minded with himself, ought carefully to mark it, and see the folly of the cavils of which they have approved. It is altogether unphilosophical on their part, to compare the destiny of a rational and responsible creature, with that of unsentient plants and irrational animals.

The appointed time which was to be spent in the world by our first parents, was not to be passed in the garden of Eden. They had forfeited the enjoyment of it as a place of happiness, and they are required to forfeit it even as a place of residence. Adam denominates his wife Eve, or *Haváh*, as the mother of all living. God makes them coats of skin,—in the death of the first owners of which they probably saw both what they were to expect in their last hours, and a symbol of the sacrifice of the seed of the woman,—and he clothes them. The tree of life, which during their obedience existed as a sacramental pledge of their security, is no longer to be within their reach. That they might have no appeal to the fidelity of that God who had declared that while they ate of it they should live, they are sent from their blissful abode to till the ground. They are driven out, and they are debarred from returning. They are now left to the full endurance of their temporal misery, with those mitigations which might originate in the sovereign grace which had been made known to them, or might afterwards be revealed to them.

The liability of our first parents to what has been called *eternal death*, now comes to be noticed. On this awful subject, it is not necessary to say much. It must be apparent from all which we read of Adam's state, that all his intrinsic efforts to remove the curse which he had brought upon himself by his transgressions must be altogether hopeless. He does not receive from God the least hint that he has a remedy in his own possession. The possession of such a remedy would place him morally independent of God, and warrant him to insult the divine majesty, by declaring that he could not only commit sin when he listed, but free himself from its consequences when he listed; that he could proceed not only in opposition to the divine threatenings, but remove the divine curse. His moral depravity, then, which we have seen to be great, must, as far as he is concerned, continue ; and continuing it must influence the life. Under its action, he will continue to dislike communion with God and seek to avoid it; he will fail to recognize the glory of God, and acknowledge his own guilt ; he will indulge carnal pride ; and he will despise his own best interests, and sin according to the circumstances in which he may be placed. Evil, predominating in him will gather strength by its exercise ; and, however much it may be modified, it will mingle with all his thoughts and words and actions. Attaching as it does to the soul, it will continue its fearful operations even after the body is dissolved, — for a future state is to be expected by Adam from the very fact that the temporal death is limited to the destruction of his body,— and in a spiritual state corresponding with that of the devil and his angels, it will so destroy, and so excite the displeasure and call forth the punishment of God, that he on whom it hath settled, may be said to be *eternally dying*. The annihilation of the soul cannot for one moment be expected. It is nowhere revealed in the Bible; and it is the dictate of reason, that the sinner must suffer as long as he stands on his own ground. His annihilation would be nothing else than a relief of him from suffering. God's law, as far as its subjects are intrinsically concerned, must either appear glorious in the obedience of the intelligent creature, or glorious in the penal suffering of the transgressor. The wicked, as we are expressly informed, must go away into everlasting punishment. The fire with which they will be burned is unquenchable; and the smoke of their torment will ascend up forever and ever.

We have now briefly considered the account which is given in Genesis of the fall of man, and its dreadful consequences as connected with those who were its immediate subjects. Let the reader compare our remarks upon it with those of Voltaire, which Dosabhái has introduced into his work, and he will be persuaded that the sophistical scoffer of Ferney has entirely misrepresented that sacred narrative. How feeble and inapt his wit is on the subject, we may see from the following specimen. "The punishment of Adam was never, in any way, introduced into the Jewish law. Adam was no more a Jew than he was a Persian or Chaldean"! The punishment of Adam, it is sufficient for us to know, is *recorded* in the Jewish Scriptures. Nothing can be more reckless, than the assertion, that, "The first chapters of Genesis (at whatever period they were composed), were regarded by all the learned Jews as an allegory, and even as a fable not a little dangerous, since that book was forbidden to be read by any before they had attained the age of twenty-one." The whole narrative of the fall, we have seen to be most profitable and instructive. In the inspired writings, which form the standard of the faith of Jews and Christians, not a single sentence can be found, giving the remotest countenance to the insinuation of an allegory, while much of a directly contrary nature, as will be evident from quotations about to be made, can be produced. Even the Jewish writers, such as Philo, who erroneously teach that the narrative of Moses is somewhat allegorical, admit the *reality* of the fall,* the subject which Voltaire professes principally to discuss. The great majority of learned Jews since his day attach to the account in Genesis a literal sense.† But it is not so much with their interpretation as with the meaning which it naturally bears, and which is indicated in other parts of the sacred oracles, with which we have to deal. Voltaire has found it inconvenient to tell us when, where, and by whom, the restriction as to the perusal of Genesis was made. The use of this most interesting, and invaluable book has from time immemorial been general in the Jewish community. In its twelve *parashioth* or great-

* See the *ΕΞΗΓΗΤΙΚΑ ΣΥΓΓΡΑΜΜΑΤΑ* of Philo, pp. 31—68.

† In this majority, I include Josephus, for though he says that Moses writes "philosophically" in his early chapters, he speaks of the serpent as having had originally *feet*, which he would not have done, had he, like Philo, considered it a figure for ἡδονή, or voluptuousness. (*See Josephus, Antiquities of the Jews, chap. i*). For other notices of the opinions of the Jews respecting the fall, See *Poli Synopsis Criticorum*, tom i, pp. 31—51; and *Caroli Schaaf Opus Aramæum*, pp. 308, 332.

er sections it is regularly read in their synagogues throughout the world. To these synagogues children find access. They are even reckoned members of them, when they arrive at the age of twelve years.

Having said this much on the fall of man, and its consequences as connected with our *progenitors*, it now devolves upon us to refer to the testimony which the sacred Scriptures, and our own observation, and that of our fellow-men, furnish respecting its consequences with regard to their *descendants*. On this subject, we shall find the testimony of Scripture, and the inferences to be made from the general observation of mankind, to be quite accordant.

It is intimated in Genesis v. 3, that Adam " begat a son in his own likeness, after his image." This likeness had a reference not merely to his bodily, but to his spiritual or moral, constitution. It had probably a special reference to the latter because it is with respect to the moral constitution of Adam, as formed after the image of God, that the expression is first used, in a preceding part of the book of Genesis. As Adam's moral constitution, then, had become degraded and debased, previously to the birth of his son, we are led to infer that his son had his sinful likeness. To this propagation of depravity, there can be no doubt that the reference is made when it is asked, in Job, xiv. 4, " Who can bring a clean thing out of an unclean ;" and when it is replied, "Not one ;" and when it is aslo asked, " What is man that he should be clean? and he which is born of a woman that he should be righteous."* This original depravity was confessed by David, when he exclaimed, " Behold, I was shapen in iniquity, and in sin did my mother conceive me ;"† and it is illustrated by him, when he observed, "The wicked are estranged from the womb: they go astray as soon as they be born, speaking lies."‡ It was taught by our Lord, when he declared that, "That which is born of the flesh is flesh,"§ and by his Apostles, who affirm, that man is naturally " dead

* Job, xv. 14. † Psalm, li. 5. ‡ Psalm, lviii. 3.

§ John, iii. 6.

in tresspasses and sins,"* and who use similar language to express that state of sin and misery in which he is found in the world, before the grace of God interferes on his behalf. The comments which have been made by unbelievers on the passages to which I have now referred, cannot weaken their plain import with the candid reader.

A belief in the propagation of moral evil throughout the race of man universally, of the kind brought before our notice in the passages to which I have now alluded, seems to have been very general even among those who have not been favoured by a divine revelation, and who in their speculations have otherwise far departed from its dictates. "The body," says Plato, "is the grave of the soul." "In their present state, men have become weak, unguarded, and thoughtless, hurried away by their own lusts and passions. Hence they are reduced to inextricable miseries. Our present intellectual light is darkness, and knowledge is corrupted at its source." "In man," says Aristotle, "there is something congenite with our frame, which opposes, and is contrary to reason."† "Evil," says Sallust the Cynic, "consists in privation, and arises from the want of a good principle." "A man," says Plutarch, "is ill-disposed from the beginning .... all our evils, and sins, and diseases, proceed from an evil innate principle." "We are born," says Seneca, "liable to no fewer diseases of the mind than of the body." "The seeds of all the vices are in us all; but they do not all unfold themselves in every individual. For a man to acknowledge all this, is as necessary as the beginning of a cure." "As wax to the seal," says Horace, "so we yield to the suggestions of vice, but the monitor to virtue meets with a harsh reception. Fixed and immutable in evil, we naturally recur to the practices we condemn." "I see and approve that which is good,"

* Ephes. ii. 3.

† This passage, I quoted in my lecture on the Vandidád. Dosabháí attempts to destroy its effect by introducing Aristotle as criticising not only the books of Moses, but the epistles of *Paul!* (See Tálim-i-Zartusht, p. 184). Does not the learned Munshí know, that Aristotle was the tutor of Alexander the Great, and lived about four centuries before the writings of Paul were published?

says Ovid, "yet notwithstanding I follow that which is evil."*

* For the original of these and other similar passages, see Cormack on Original Sin, pp. 23 — 26. I have quoted them in my lecture on the Vandidád, and Aspandiárjí, Hádí-i-Gum-Rahán, p. 69, makes them the occasion of the following remarks: — "None of them seems to intimate that man is a creature not fitted for the enjoyment of heavenly bliss. They have only described his *evil nature*. But, if he could render himself free from vice, why should his soul, thus purified from evil, be inadmissible into heaven? If man is made unfit for the blessings of heaven, there seems then to be no necessity whatever of the celestial errands which the angels had from time to time brought to the holy personage." So, after all, man *has* an "evil nature." It is necessary, it must be kept in mind, not only that he should be rendered free from *vice*, but that he should be rendered free from *guilt*. It is because of his own inability to accomplish these deliverances for himself, that the intervention of heaven's messengers, and of the Son of God, by whose merits alone he can be saved, is rendered necessary.

"According to the "Rev. gentleman's doctrine," adds Aspandiárjí, "Moses, David, and several other personages, must be reckoned in the class of the sinful." He is perfectly correct in this inference. The Bible speaks both of their sinful nature, and of its sinful manifestations, and ascribes their salvation entirely to the divine mercy. Kalam Kas (*Nírang-Há*, pp. 10, 11), objects to this sacred volume on this very account. Will both he and his brother controversialist receive a word of explanation on the subject?

The faithfulness of the Christian Scriptures has been frequently appealed to as a proof of their credibility and inspiration. They are impartial in their accounts, both of nations and individuals. They conceal not, and they flatter not. They represent human nature as it actually is, both in its best and worst estates. They exhibit examples of goodness for our encouragement and imitation; and they record examples of evil, that we may avoid it, and be taught watchfulness and humility. They show us the sincerity of repentance, as well as the atrociousness of guilt. Their object is not to exalt man, but to glorify God. It is only because Kalam Kas overlooks their character in this respect that he finds fault with them for bringing before our notice the sins of Lot, Jacob's sons, David, Solomon, and others. Had they approved of the transgressions of these distinguished men, they might have been objected to; but as they uniformly condemn them, their truthfulness and holiness must be respected. The mention which they make of sin is not in a single instance that of palliation, but of marked disapprobation. We find no parallel to it in any of the false systems of religion. Muhammad, it is well known, claims in the Koran, the authority of God for his most marked transgressions, and denounces the most fearful judgments against any one who would venture to apply the principles of moral right to the estimate of

The very Hindús, who have the most indistinct notions of *guilt* which can be imagined, express sentiments similar to these. They tell us that in every human mind from the beginning, there are the six great enemies, काम lust, क्रोध wrath, लोभ avarice, मोह delusion, मद pride, मत्सर malice. The Bráhmans, in their daily ritual Sanskrit prayers, acknowledge that they are conceived in sin, and are altogether sinful.

पापोहं पापकर्म्मोहं पापात्मा पापसंभवः

"I am sin," say they, "I commit sin, my spirit is sinful, I am conceived in sin."

The propagation of moral evil, thus admitted and confessed, though it may not be *proved* by natural analogies, may nevertheless be *illustrated* by them. "Like produces like," is an established axiom. "Men do not gather figs of thorns; nor of a bramble-bush gather they grapes; for every tree is known by its own fruit." "A muddy stream cannot send forth pure waters."

यथा देशस्तथा भाषा, यथा राजा तथा प्रजा,
यथा माता तथा कन्या, यथा बीजं तथांकुरं *

his conduct. The writers of the Hindú shástras relate innumerable transgressions of the heroes of their stories — of the very gods themselves, but in no instance do they describe them as sinful. On the contrary, they expressly declare that this is not their character. For the objects of their veneration, they claim the prerogative of listing wrong, and acting as they list, without challenge. The Pársís, we have seen, ascribe to Jamshíd freedom from all sin; and they attribute to Zoroaster the holiness of God himself. Edal Dáru tells us that Hormazd gave him the title *Asháum* or *Aso*, one of the three great names expressive of divine purity, which he is said to claim for himself. — See *Maujazát-i-Zartusht*, pp. 61, 62.

But Aspandiárjí reminds us that the scripture says that Zacharias and his wife were "both righteous before God, walking in all the commandments and ordinances of the Lord blameless." He requires to be informed that this is not said of them in a natural, but in a renewed, state; not positively, but comparatively. I am happy to find him disposed to go as far as Aristotle and Seneca in the admission of the depravity of human nature. He has thus got considerably beyond the Vandidád.

* This Sanskrit proverb is in the mouth of all the natives of India.

"As is the country so is the speech; as is the prince, so is the people; as is the mother, so is the daughter; as is the seed, so is the shoot." There are many maxims of a similar nature, current in every country, all pointing to the analogy to which I have referred.

That man, along with depravity, inherits the *curse* from his first parents, there cannot be the smallest doubt. The effects of the fall upon Adam are visible among all his children. It is the universal experience, that "man is born unto trouble as the sparks fly upwards." Men either live by the "sweat of their brow," or by the laborious and exhausting exercise of their intellect. Disappointments and trials, beyond number, everywhere present themselves to the anxious desiderants of happiness. Pain, and disease, and death are everywhere committing their fearful ravages. The infant of a span long, and the man of hoary hairs, are alike the unhappy subjects on whom they operate, and whom they destroy. Infidels themselves seem to have been astonished at their operation. "Who can without horror," says even Voltaire, "consider the whole earth as the victim of destruction? It abounds in wonders; it abounds also in victims. In man, there is more wretchedness than in all the other animals put together. He spends the transient moment of his existence in diffusing the miseries which he suffers; in cutting the throats of his fellow-creatures for pay; in cheating and being cheated; in robbing and being robbed; in serving that he may command; and in repenting of all that he does. The bulk of mankind are nothing more than a crowd of wretches, equally criminal and unfortunate; and the globe contains rather carcases than men. I tremble upon a review of this dreadful picture, to find that it contains a complaint against providence, and I wish that I had never been born."* This passage, though written in a daringly impious spirit, contains much truth.

As Scripture and fact alike shew, that we inherit depravity and misery from our first parents, we are naturally led to inquire into the *arrangements* of which this is the consequence.

* Voltaire's Gospel of the day.

Our inquiries are undoubtedly to some degree satisfied by a passage in the fifth chapter of Paul's epistle to the Romans. "Wherefore as by one man sin entered into the world and death by sin; and so death passed upon all men, for that all have sinned: (For until the law, sin was in the world: but sin is not imputed when there is no law. Nevertheless death reigned from Adam to Moses, even over them that had not sinned after the similitude of Adam's transgression, who is the figure of him that was to come: but not as the offence, so also is the free gift. For if through the offence of one many be dead; much more the grace of God, and the gift by grace, which is by one man, Jesus Christ, hath abounded unto many. And not as it was by one that sinned, so is the gift: for the judgment was by one man to condemnation; but the free gift is of many offences unto justification. For if by one man's offence death reigned by one; much more they which receive abundance of grace, and of the gift of righteousness, shall reign in life by one, Jesus Christ.) Therefore as by the offence of one [or by one's offence] judgment came upon all men to condemnation, even so by the righteousness of one *the free gift came* upon all men unto justification of life. For as by one man's disobedience, many were made [or judicially constituted, according to the strict sense of the Greek,] sinners, so by the obedience of one shall many be made righteous." In this passage, and in 1 Cor. xv, 22, "As in Adam all die, even so in Christ shall all be made alive," a comparison is made between Christ and Adam; and it teaches that several striking analogies exist between them. Those of them which are most intimately connected with our subject, are the three following. 1. Sin and death come from Adam; and righteousness and life come from Christ. 2. All that were in Adam were judicially constituted sinners and condemned with him; and all that are in Christ are judicially constituted righteous and justified with him. 3. In the disobedience of Adam, sin and death originate; in the obedience of Christ, righteousness and life originate. It is a fair inference from these analogies, that there was a *representation of mankind in Adam*, in the same manner, that there is a representation of the chosen of God in Christ; and that the posterity of Adam were interested with himself in his obedience or disobedience, and their respective consequences. This inference is set forth in the Catechism most extensively used in my native country, in the following terms: "The covenant being made with Adam, not only for himself, but for his posterity, all mankind sinned in him and fell with him in his first transgression."* Those who admit that sin and death rest on Adam's posterity, directly or indirectly, in consequence of Adam's fall, and refuse to recognize the existence of a representation in Adam, in consequence of its unreasonableness, certainly strain at a gnat, and swallow a camel. They admit the greater difficulty, and refuse to admit what is in some degree an explanation of it, and what seems to be clearly taught on the subject in the Holy Scriptures.† They are not warranted, like Voltaire, to charge those who hold the doctrine of original sin, with the folly of asserting that "God formed all the successive generations of mankind, to deliver them over to eternal tortures, under the pretext of their original ancestor having ate a particular fruit in a garden." God's primary end in the creation of man, was that he might glorify and enjoy him; and if the conduct of man, or the general relations of man, under the probation to which he was subjected, require him to be visited with the wrath of God,

* Assembly's Shorter Catechism.

† That a *covenant* was made with Adam for himself and his posterity, I may remark, is the doctrine of the most pious and learned Protestants. That it was made with Adam, for *himself*, there can be no doubt. All the promises and threatenings addressed to him in the garden of Eden, contained the assurance that the divine treatment of him would be regulated by his own conduct. As a holy being, he could not but acquiesce in them, when proposed by his Creator. The existence of a covenant with Adam is expressly mentioned in Hosea vi, 7. "Like men (or like Adam, as the words כאדם should be translated) they have broken the covenant." The passages which I have quoted from Romans and Corinthians, shew that his *posterity* were connected with him. The *reasons* of the fact, we may not comprehend; but reason warrants no inference contrary to the fact. Revelation is in no degree answerable for the mysteries which remain.

who can complain against the divine justice? Voltaire refuses to admit the equity of the imputation of Adam's sin. But is he or any other man so well informed by the light of nature of all the circumstances of the case, as to declare an unhesitating judgment of the kind which he has expressed? In reference to the objection as expressed by writers of a similar stamp to Voltaire, a respectable divine emphatically remarks: "But it is said, be it [Adam's sin] ever so heinous, why must we be charged with it? Here again, if we consider that union, which, in Scripture, is ever supposed to connect the first parent and the whole human race, it should first be inquired, are you competent to decide upon this union? Know you its real nature and its properties? Till you do, there lies not so much as a presumption against the Almighty's dealings that result from it. Every one must know that men have not this knowledge. The objector knows this very well, and though some may think his conclusions well founded, and perfectly consistent with the union in question, all such conclusions are of no more real weight in the eye of right reason, than the imagination of an infant on the construction of a ship can be."* Out of Voltaire's own mouth, I condemn his sneers. He concludes his article, on original sin with his wonted inconsistency, by saying, "What, my good friends, ought to be said on the subject? Nothing. Accordingly, I do not give any explanation of the difficulty, I say not a single word"† No, *considerate* philosopher, it was enough for your purpose, to shut your eyes to the numerous passages in the Sacred Scriptures in which the doctrine of the original depravity of man is clearly presented, and to present the interpretations made of them by the Jews, and by the ancient and modern Christians, and to deal out the misunderstandings and misrepresentations of heretical Christians, in the lack of courage, on your own part, openly to commit yourself on a point on which the common observation of men are decidedly op-

* Gibbon's Account of Christianity considered, by the Rev. Joseph Milner, pp. 20, 21.

† Quoted in Tálim-i-Zartusht, p. 197.

posed to your speculations.* He can find no enlightened ad-

* The Pársís will bear in mind, that immediately after the days of the apostles of Christ, the inspired teachers of Christianity, many of the ministers and members of the professedly Christian Church, became corrupted both in their doctrines and practice, and this because of their neglect of the testimony of God. Even in reference to the views of the Christians of the ages immediately following the apostles, Voltaire is altogether wrong, when he confidently says, "We admit that St. Augustine was the first who brought this strange notion of original sin into credit." There is a palpable absurdity, indeed, essentially, involved in his statement. "Pelagius, in the beginning of the fifth century," says a late able writer, "opposed the doctrine of original sin; and Augustine, the supposed inventor of it, who is thought to have been born on the same day with Pelagius, wrote against him. According to the above supposition, Pelagius must have held the doctrine of the church, and St. Augustine must have been a single solitary heretic. But if Pelagius held the doctrine of the church, how came it that the terrors of excommunication made him flee from country to country? And how came it that, at last, he and his pupil Celestius actually were excommunicated, and that all the bishops were deprived, who refused to subscribe the condemnation of the PELAGIAN HERESY? Now on the supposition that the doctrine of original sin were an invention of Augustine, the reverse of all this must have taken place . . . . .

"Irenæus, the disciple of Polycarp, who was the disciple of St. John, and who suffered matyrdom in the year 203, says, 'What we lost in Adam, that is, a being after the image of God, this we recovered by Christ.' And in another place, he calls the effect of the Spirit of God on the soul, a 'return to the *ancient* nature of man.'

"Vossius shows that original sin was no new device of Augustine; but 'a doctrine, in which the church of God, in every period, had been unanimous.' 'Who', says Vincentius Lirinensis, 'who before the profane Pelagius, ever presumed to say, that there is such a power in free will, as to supersede the assistance of the grace of God.'

"It will not be disputed, that a name is never invented till there be first a corresponding idea, suggesting the necessity of being distinctly marked. This being admitted, we have satisfactory evidence, that from the times of the apostles to the present day, the Christian Church has always considered original sin, to be an essential doctrine of the gospel. It is mentioned onward from Ignatius, a disciple of the apostle John, (and whom some suppose to have seen Christ,) through every succeeding age of the church. 'Here,' says one [Prideaux], 'the fathers agree with us, so that this doctrine of original sin is called by Ignatius the *ancient iniquity*; by Justin Martyr, *the death derived from Adam*; by Cyprian, *the ancient infection of death*; *the origin of sin*, by Hilary; and *original sin*, by Rufinus." — Cormack on Original Sin, pp. 117—120.

So much for the alleged novelty of the doctrine of original sin in the

vocate of the doctrine of original sin attempting to explain the exact mode of its transmission from generation to generation, and his different suppositions consequently do not apply to the case as stated by those to whose views he is hostile. It is remarkable, that amongst his hypotheses as to the formation of the human soul, he avoids any reference to that of its having any connexion with, or derivation from, the first man, which he must have known those whom he opposes most commonly bring forward.

Dosabháí, it will appear from the preceding remarks, committed a great error, when he introduced Voltaire into his

days of Augustine. It is here clearly proved that it was taught in the Christian church from the very days of the apostles, as it had been formerly taught in the Jewish church. As far as the individual opinions of Clement and Origen of Alexandria are concerned, Voltaire is partly correct. I say only *partly*, for in the works of these writers, I see very many passages which seem to imply, if not express, their belief in the original depravity of man, as he now appears in the world. Thus, for example, Clement says "To sin is to all *innate and common*,— ἔμφυτον καὶ κοινόν. (Paed. iii. 12). Origen, in his comment on the Romans, supposes sin to attach itself to the soul before birth, to be dormant during infancy, but sure to develope itself in mature years. Notwithstanding the influence of these great names at Alexandria, more orthodox doctrines than those they entertained, were not unknown in that famous school. Didymus, A. D. 340—395, for instance, says, "Original Sin is inherent in us; that sin in which all are by succession from Adam." "We are all born in sin." "The first image was lost." — See an interesting paper "On the Catechetical School, or Theological Seminary at Alexandria in Egypt," by Prof. Emerson of America in the Biblical Repository, 1834.

This is a sufficient reply to what Voltaire says, and what Dosabháí adopts, on the origin of the doctrine of original sin. The Pársí munshí will here allow me to propose two plain queries to himself:—

1. Do not you, contradicting both yourself and the Vandidád, admit the doctrine of original sin, when you resolve the Pársí doctrine of the evil Principle into a parabolical representation of "the evil dispositions of man"?

2. Since, like Voltaire, you maintain that the doctrine of original sin is not contained in the Bible, why do you make that sacred volume responsible for it?

I await your reply; and in the mean time I beg to direct the Pársí reader to your glaring inconsistency. They will be able without any hint to distinguish between fair argument, and the wilful perversions, and silly sneers, which you have thought right to adopt.

pages. He has been unable to injure Christianity by what he has done, and he has left the general observation of man, and of the people of his own tribe in particular, to testify against the doctrine of the Vandidád, that man is first noticed by us in a state of original righteousness. It is not necessary for me to retract a single sentence which I have written on the subject in any of my former publications. The evil effects of the erroneous doctrine of the Vandidád, I have frequently witnessed. That dictum, I have found thus expanded and illustrated: — "From the day that his parents bring him from a world replete with light, into this even surpassing it in splendor, a mortal keeps his heart as pure as crystal, yea purer, until the season that he becomes acquainted with the habits of the world"* I have heard a learned dastur declare that it is the general belief of his tribe, that a person does not become a responsible moral agent till such time as he is investted with the kustí, or imaginary sacred girdle, and that all slight transgressions which he may previously have committed, are to be visited upon his parents. In an article on the followers of Zoroaster in the Colonial Magazine, June 1841, written by a Pársí, there is the following statement: — "The Pársís in accordance to commands in their sacred books, wear a white garment and a girdle round their waist, composed of seventy [seventy-two] threads, but not larger than a lady's stay-lace. These they wear as insignia of their religion. Children, after the age of seven, are made to wear it, and they are then considered as confirmed in the faith of Zoroaster; but their parents are held responsible for their moral and religious observances until they arrive at the age of ten, when they are to be responsible for themselves. Should children be taken away from this world before they arrive at the age of ten, they are considered innocent and unthinking — incapable of doing any intentional harm or injury, and that they die happy, free from the temptation and misery of this world, and are received into heaven, to enjoy eternal happiness: such

* Harkárah and Vartamán, 1832.

is the firm belief of the Pársí."* But are *facts*, which should regulate every theory, consistent with the opinions which have now been expressed? Is any man really able to blind himself to the early developement of depravity in every member of the human family who falls under his observation? Can any person be insensible to the original disorder of the human affections, to the manifestations of discontent, peevishness, anger, fretfulness, strife, contention, envy, jealousy, waywardness, and disobedience, which are made in the days of infancy, and long before evil example can lead to imitation? Do we not perceive in the first determinations of the human will, the choice of what is evil, and a strong aversion to what is good? Can we overlook the proneness which is evinced, at the very dawn of intellect, to prefer that which is sensual to that which is spiritual? Can we fail to notice the original alienation of the soul from its Maker, and its innate disinclination to learn the ways of God, and to enter on the paths of righteousness, which parental advice and remonstrance, and authority, however faithfully and diligently plied, find it so difficult to subdue? Do we not see the facility with which an evil example is comprehended and followed, while that of an opposite character is unperceived, or disregarded? On reflecting even on our own early history and experience, is the justness of the confession of the Psalmist, already quoted, not thrust on our attention,—"Behold, I was shapen in iniquity, and in sin did my mother conceive me?"

In the view of what has now been said, we are at perfect

* I am glad to find Aspandiárjí alive to the error which is involved in this opinion. "But I am disposed to believe," he says, (Hádí-i-Gum-Rahan, p. 67,) "no dastur who may possess some (any) degree of common sense would entertain such vain ideas; for, if they ever happen to be founded on any authority, however little, from the Pársí scripture, people may (will) be sure to avail themselves of it as the best reason to refrain themselves from putting on the kustí; for this might render them unanswerable, as our friend alleges, for any wicked acts they may commit during the time."

The "degree of authority" in the Pársí scripture, I have already alluded to. I leave Aspandiárjí, who denies the authority, to settle accounts with Dosabhái who defends it.

liberty to charge the "sacred" writings of the Pársís with giving representations of human nature, in its first developements, utterly opposed to facts which are daily and hourly witnessed. We are also compelled to declare that these writings take only a very partial view of the claims of God on the affections, and reverence, and gratitude, and service of his rational creatures, and of the workings of that disease of depravity under which our whole species labours. They do not exhibit the divine holiness as it is manifested in giving a law which is holy, just, and good in all its requisitions, and which extends these requisitions to the thoughts and intents of the heart. In none of them do we find the high, but reasonable, demand, "Thou shalt love the Lord thy God with all thy heart, and with all thy soul, and with all thy strength, and with all thy mind, and thy neighbour as thyself."* They are more occupied with bodily cleanliness than spiritual purity; with the avoidance of the defilement which occurs from contact with corpses, than that which occurs from contact with sin; with the protection of the elements of nature, than the maintenance and declaration of the honour and glory of God; with unmeaning, and foolish, and absurd ceremony, than enlightened

* Luke x. 27. In the Pársí writings there are frequent references to *hvarsta, humata, húkht,* "good work, good thought, good speech," as the words are to be translated. With reference to this circumstance, the Abbé Foucher (Memoires de Litterature, tom. xxxix, p. 793), adopting the interpretation of Anquetil, *pur de pensée, pur de parole, et pur d'action*, says, "Ce précepte est répété à toutes les pages, sans que l'auteur essaie jamais d'en donner aucun développement; et dès lors c'est une puérilité qui ne fait plus d'impression. Il faudroit donc expliquer ce qui forme la pureté de pensée, de parole, et d'action, et c'est ce que les livres Zends ne font point. Nous disons aux enfans qu'il faut être docile. Ce precepte bien approfondi, renferme tous les devoirs et toutes les vertus; mais si on leur répétoit toujours la même maxime lorsqu'ils avancent en âge, sans leur donner d'autres instructions, ils se moqueroient de leurs instituteurs, et ils auroient raison."

But there is more than the charge of using the expressions quoted above in a cant sense, and without definition and amplification, as stated by the worthy Abbé, to be brought against the Pársí writings. They commonly represent the worshipper as proudly declaring that he possesses the character alluded to, instead of humbly begging for its communication to him by God.

and rational, and solemn devotion; with the disposal of the body, which must infallibly become the prey of corruption, than the final destiny of the soul, which will live throughout the endless ages of eternity. Setting forth an imperfect and erroneous law, they lead those who repose their faith in them to form imperfect views of their transgressions and the guilt which they contract and accumulate. They discover not the sin which mingles itself even in the best thoughts, and words, and actions of men. In none of them do we find the humble, but truthful, acknowledgements and declarations which pervade the sacred page:—"Every imagination of the thought of man's heart is only evil continually."* "Man is abominable and drinketh up iniquity like water."† "The Lord looked down from heaven upon the children of men, to see if there were any that did understand, and seek after God. They are all gone aside, they are altogether become filthy; there is none that doeth good, no, not one."‡ "All we like sheep have gone astray, we have turned every one to his own way."§ "The heart is deceitful above all things and desperately wicked."‖ "Out of the heart of man proceed evil thoughts, adulteries, fornications, murders, thefts, covetousness, wickedness, deceit, lasciviousness, an evil eye, blasphemy, pride, foolishness."¶ "The carnal mind is enmity against God, for it is not subject to the law of God, neither indeed can be."** It is not their object to humble man in the sight of his offended Maker, and so to declare the law, that every mouth may be stopped, and all the world may be held guilty before God.

In these circumstances, we cannot suppose that the Pársí writings will be effectual to convince men of their trespasses, to show them their guilt and demerit, and to awake within the heart the anxious inquiry, "What must I do to be saved." "They that be whole have no need of the physician, but they that are sick;" and they who are left to imagine themselves to be no great sinners in the sight of God, will not with

* Genesis, vi. 5. † Job, xv. 16. ‡ Psalm, xiv. 2, 3.

§ Isaiah, liii. 6. ‖ Jeremiah, xvii. 9. ¶ Mark, vii. 21, 22.

** Romans, iii. 7.

adequate solicitude seek for deliverance from the divine wrath.

But let us now see how the Pársí scriptures would solve the grand inquiry as to a way of salvation, earnestly urged by a soul really convinced of its depravity, guilt, and demerit. Do they extend any reasonable hope of acceptance with God, on terms becoming the divine character and the divine administration of the affairs of the universe? Do they show us how the authority of God can be vindicated, so as to mark the exceeding heinousness of disobedience, even when he passes by transgression, and how he can prove himself to be just, and yet the justifier of the ungodly; how he can exercise his mercy, and yet vindicate his truth; how he can cause righteousness and peace to embrace each other; how he can inflict the threatened punishment for the violation of the demands of his law, and yet vouchsafe deliverance to the offender?

In the preceding chapter, I have given a faithful summary of all the information on these and other matters communicated in the Vandidád, the only professedly authoritative standard of the Pársí faith; and to it I refer the reader for a reply. Salvation, we there see, is represented as wholly dependent on the practice of the rites of the Mázdayaçní faith, and on charity, repentance, penance, and the intercession of friends.* Are these, or any of these, to whatever extent they may be performed, suitable means of purchasing, or procuring this invaluable blessing? In replying to this question, I require to do little more than repeat what I have said to the Pársís on former occasions.

The rites of the Mázdayaçní religion will conduce to the salvation of man! Who that is possessed of any degree of intelligence, who has even a limited view of the claims of God

* "If the numerous means," says Aspandiárjí (Hádi-i-Gum-Rahán p. 85), "which are prescribed in the religion of Zoroaster for the salvation of the soul, had come under the cognizance of the Rev. gentleman, he would never have restricted his observation to the five means [mentioned] above." The means which *he* enumerates, I beg to inform him, are *classed* under the heads which I have given.

and the duty of man, and whose conscience has been even partially enlightened, can imagine for one moment that they will be productive of such a result? Can the most distinguished of them, such as are most frequently thrust on our attention, and to which the greatest importance is attached, be partially described by a Pársí to a European, without his feeling a misgiving of heart, without his clothing himself with the mantle of crimson shame? The religious war with, and relentless slaughter of, kharfastars, or vermin; the mending of holes formed in the earth, through which the devils are supposed to emerge from hell; the feeding of the hungry flame with grease, and fat, and sweet-smelling odours; the muttering and sputtering of prayers and praises in an unknown tongue, to every object which exists, whether intelligent, sentient, or inanimate, and this whether it may be five times a day, or fifty times a day; the disposal of corpses and abortions, so as to pollute the atmosphere which we breathe, rather than the earth on which we tread; the solemn funeral of bones and hair, and nails; the drinking and sipping of cow's urine at morn and eve, as if it were the very elixir of immortality; the scrubbing and rubbing the body with various ablutions for the expulsion of devils; the frightening and driving away of demons by noise; the sagdid or introduction of dogs, to survey the bodies of the deceased, and to prognosticate their fate, and to guard them from the assaults of Satan, and many other practices, said to be enjoined by divine authority, and to be "good and virtuous actions," do not certainly commend themselves to the reason of many of those, with whom "tyrant custom" compels their observance. The most sober exercises of the Pársís, — the invocation, adoration, and supplication of the Amsháspands, Izads, and elements, they must surely see, cannot be resorted to without provoking the righteous indignation of the only living and true God, who demands the supreme regard, and the exclusive worship of his intelligent creatures, and who has solemnly and emphatically declared, that his glory he will not give to another.

We have seen how *charity* to the poor, but more particularly to priests, to dogs, and to birds, is inculcated in the

Vandidád. Some of the objects on which it is there commanded to be lavished, have no special claims upon man for its exercise; but, for the sake of argument, we shall suppose it to be rightly administered, and to the fullest extent of the means enjoyed, and nevertheless ask, how it can conduce to the removal of the sin which has been already committed and registered in the book of God's remembrance, or which man is now daily and hourly perpetrating. Though charity in itself, when proceeding from proper motives, and directed to proper ends, is a duty incumbent upon all according to their ability, the neglect of other duties is not atoned for, the guilt of any one sin committed is not cancelled or removed, and heaven is not purchased as the Pársís are taught to believe, when it is dispensed and exercised.* The liberal man who thinks that he makes amends for his transgressions by his charity, in effect thus addresses the Supreme Being: "O God thou hast endowed me with plenty and riches; and I know how to use them aright. I will make them compensate for some of my transgressions. I will distribute from the stores which thou hast provided for me, for the purpose of blinding thine eyes to the sins which I have committed against thy majesty! I will remove my offences by presenting thee with thine own bounties. By the favours, which thou hast conferred upon me, I shall secure the privilege of putting away my iniquities and offences whenever I please! Thou hast bestowed upon me my possessions, that I may rise superior to thy law! Thou enablest me by my bounty to thee and thy creatures to rise superior to thy authority, and to despise thy

* Aspandiárjí (Hadí-i-Gum-Rahán, p. 86,) says, "I am not perfectly aware whether the Vandidád recommends the act of charity as one of the means of salvation." He will see, in the preceding chapter, specimens of my authorities for the remark which I have made. He himself calls charity a "virtuous deed;" and he says at p. 88. that God "will distribute justice according to the preponderance of the good and bad actions of men," and that "it is a universal belief that good and bad actions counterbalance one another." He will have charity, then, to counterbalance some bad action, which is exactly the idea against which I contend.

judgement." At the impiety of these sentiments, who does not shudder ?

We have already seen that the defective views which the Pársí scriptures take of the depravity and sin of man, are unfavourable to the production of those convictions of guilt in which genuine repentance originates; but even supposing that the case were otherwise, I ask, Can *repentance* remove the guilt of sin ? Let us see the answer of my opponents. "In reference to the remarks of Padre Wilson on the subject of repentance," says Aspandiárjí, "I have to observe, that the arguments which he has brought forward in corroboration of his assertion, that repentance, however rigid and sincere, is still [an] insufficient atonement for sin, — are based solely on [a] comparison which has been founded between God and man. This view of the thing is quite erroneous, and not to be warranted even by common sense. God is omnipotent; his Providence extends from the greatest to the meanest of his creatures. The most prominent feature in his character is mercy; he therefore gives very little heed to the crimes of his creatures. Let it also be observed, that the Vandidád does not enjoin repentance to (on) those who have willingly committed any sinful act . . . . He who breaks through his repentance, is stated in the Vandidád to be destined on (to) the infernal region."* Dosabháí maintains the efficacy of repentance, without even the limitations here stated,† and which, notwithstanding the allegations of Aspandiárjí, have not the support from the Vandidád which he here alleges. But to meet the circumstances of the case, in whatever way it may be put, I have no hesitation in declaring that the repentance of man can neither satisfy the claims of the divine law, nor rightly support the divine authority. Viewed in its most perfect exhibitions, it is neither more nor less than sorrow for sin, hatred of sin, and the turning from sin unto God ; and though considered in this important light, it is an indispensable con-

* Hádi-i-Gum-Rahán, pp. 87, 88.

† Tálím-i-Zartusht, p 108, &c

comitant of our acceptance with God,* it can neither meritoriously, nor providentially, purchase the pardon of sin, nor secure for us a heavenly inheritance. Though God is omnipotent, he cannot act contrary to his own nature, and the established principles of his own moral government. Though he is merciful, his holiness and justice can never be in abeyance; and his divine administration must be so conducted as to support his authority, maintain the honour of his law, and exhibit the evil of transgression. Now, it must be seen by those who keep these facts in view, that the acceptance of repentance by God, as a compensation for past disobedience, would absolutely prevent an adequate demonstration being made of the guilt of sin, which, as contrary to the law of an infinitely glorious God, must be considered, in a most important sense, as an infinite evil. It does not remedy the dishonour done to God by the ingratitude and rebellion which constitute the essence of sin. It is frequently unavailing even in reference to the affairs and occurrences of common life. A man who squanders away his substance and his health in sinful courses, does not recover them on repentance. A man who loses his character, does not regain the confidence of society, when he confesses his guilt. The criminal who is deservedly condemned to death, generally suffers his merited punishment, notwithstanding all his tears, and regrets, and entreaties. No earthly sovereign in announcing his laws to his subjects, would declare to them, that they while they ought to obey these laws, they had only to get sorry for any transgressions into which they might fall, in order to procure pardon. His authority would not be respected, were he to recognize it as a principle of his government, that repentance formed an atonement; and far less would the majesty and authority of the King of kings and Lord of lords be manifested and respected, were *he* to promulgate, that in repentance he can find a satisfaction for his offended justice. It is a fa-

* It is on this account, I beg Aspandiárjí to observe, that it is inculcated in the Christian Scriptures, to which he refers, as absolutely necessary.

tal delusion to imagine with Aspandiárjí, that he gives very little heed to the crimes of his creatures." If man felt at liberty to commit sin, and to remove sin, when he might please, it is evident that he would not continue obedient, but view himself as independent of the control of the Most High ; and that angels, and other intelligent principalities and powers, on witnessing his conduct, and its issue, might be tempted to trifle with the divine holiness, and to rebel against the divine law.

But genuine repentance, it may be said, leads to *amendment of conduct.* This is certainly the case ; but men ought not to allow themselves to be deluded by this view of the matter, important though it be. The obedience of men, however sincere, is never perfect during any period of their life. Though they may hate sin and carry on a perpetual struggle against its power, and though in a great degree they may be successful in their efforts, they do not, till death, become entirely free from its influence, but daily sin against God, in heart, speech, and behaviour. Their obedience, even supposing it were perfect, could have no retrospective effect. God, at every moment of our existence, demands all our affection, and all our reverence, and all our service ; and when we have done our best, when we have satisfied even the fullest demands of the law, we have done only what was imposed upon us by our moral obligations. We have no *overplus* to supply our innumerable past deficiencies ; and as far as our own personal exertions are concerned, they must ever remain. They form, as it were, a debt ; and a debt contracted with a merchant is not cancelled, though every article purchased after it is recorded, is followed by regular and prompt payment. In saying this, I do not " forget," as Aspandiárjí alleges, " that there is a vast difference between the dealings of a man and those of God." I bear in mind that God, upholding the honour of his universal dominion, will not establish it as a principle to accept the future, which is fully demanded for itself, in lieu of the past. " A man if he pleases may *remit* his claim," says the Mobad ;" but remission is not the point of which we are here speaking. I refer to the bare acceptance of equivalents; and I deny that future obedience is an equivalent for past transgressions. God, I allow, is "full of mercy;" but I hold also that he is full of justice; and that he will not permit his mercy to be exercised to the disparagement of his justice. The Pársís, and Musalmáns, who think that in the end the good and bad actions of men will be weighed together as a ground of judgment, err most egregiously. Nothing can be more unreasonable than the following narrative, founded on this idea, contained in the Ardáí Viráf-Námah: "I was conducted back to the bridge of Chinavaḍ by Serosh Izad; where on one side of the bridge, I saw a great multitude, standing in their proper vestments, in an attitude of apathy and in difference. I immediately inquired of Serosh Izad, who they were, and for what purpose they were collected. He answered, the name of this place is the first heaven; and the people you see will there remain until the day of restitution. They are those whose good works exactly counterbalance their evil ones; but if either preponderated, they would go either to a better or worse place."* Nothing can be more erroneous in point of principle than the doctrine of the Saddar, so frequently appealed to by the Pársís, that if a man's righteousness exceed his sin by a single hair, he will obtain salvation.† The imagination that good and bad actions may counterbalance one another, however prevalent it may be, is opposed to every thing like a right understanding of the divine law; for according to it, God does not require us to be perfect, or to have a perfect righteousness, in order to escape punishment, but he requires us to have only a grain of more goodness than we have of evil! This is a most astounding view of God's judgment; for if his final decision is in any degree to be illustrated by the process of weighing, we must suppose a perfect righteousness — the representation of an unerring, and unvarying, and complete obedience, to be in the scale ac-

* Ardáí Viráf-Námah, near the beginning.

† Saddar, 1st Gate. The three following sections dwell on the same idea.

cording to which the trial is to be made. How this weight can be counterbalanced by any thing pertaining to humanity, it is impossible to discover. I am not solitary, as Aspandiárjí alleges, in holding these opinions. They are those of every sound believer in the Christian Scriptures. The Mobad, however, is not far wrong when he says, "Perhaps the Rev. gentleman, when he propagates such tenets, may have an intention of insinuating that unless men place their belief in Christ, how meritorious soever they may be in their actions, they would never obtain the bliss of heaven."* I do more than make an insinuation in this case. I distinctly and solemnly state, that there is salvation in no other but Christ; "for there is none other name under heaven given among men, whereby we must be saved."† But to this infinitely important subject, we shall immediately advert.

What are the *penances* of the Pársís, in this life; and how, and for what purposes, they are to be inflicted, we have seen in the preceding chapter. The culprits, in the case of certain offences are to be subjected to corporeal chastisement, to be inflicted by priests or magistrates, to present expensive fines or offerings, to be doomed to slaughter multitudes of kharfastars and other noxious animals, and to perform various humiliating services. We have seen that there is much absurdity connected with the legislation which refers to those matters; but, even overlooking this circumstance and their bearing on the temporal condition of mankind, I must call upon the Pársís to observe that they can never stand in the room of that punishment which God threatens, and which the transgressions of men demand under the divine administration. The great evil of sin is by no means adequately demonstrated by them. They are neither sufficient to deter from the commission of iniquity; nor to exhibit and vindicate the honour and glory of an offended law-giver. Similar remarks are to be made respecting the temporary pains of hell, which the Pársís think will be endured between the fourth day after death, and the final restitution which they expect.

* Hádí-i-Gum Rahán, p. 89. † Acts, iv. 12.

The hope of deliverance from torment, at any future time, is most delusive, and relaxative of the motives to abstinence from iniquity. Mere suffering, however much it may restrain an offender, in reference to some of the outward manifestations of sin, has never been known to eradicate the love of iniquity from any soul, or to inspire it with the love of God and of holiness. "The same fire that melts and purifies the precious metal, only hardens the clay."

"But the Bible itself," says Aspandiárjí, "enjoins the offering of sacrifices as an atonement for sin."* Sacrifices *were* offered for sin, under the old Testament dispensation; but only to bring sin to remembrance, to show forth emblematically how it entails suffering and death, and to point to the great sacrifice of Christ, the "Lamb of God, who taketh away the sin of the world." The epistle to the Hebrews, to which Aspandiárjí refers, contains the following instructive passage. "For the law [given through Moses] having a shadow of good things to come, and not the very image of the things, can never with those sacrifices which they offered year by year continually make the comers thereunto perfect. For then would they not have ceased to be offered? because that the worshippers once purged should have had no more conscience of sins. But in those sacrifices there is a remembrance again made of sins every year. For it is not possible that the blood of bulls and of goats should take away sins. Wherefore, when he [Christ] cometh into the world, he saith, Sacrifice and offering thou wouldest not, but a body hast thou prepared me: In burnt offerings and sacrifices for sin thou hast had no pleasure. Then said I, Lo, I come (in the volume of the book it is written of me) to do thy will, O God. . . . . . By the which will we are sanctified, through the offering of the body of Jesus Christ once for all."†

On *prayers and other religious services for the dead*, we have seen the Pársís lay the greatest stress, as well as Aspandiárjí zealously plead for their performance.‡ From the affectionate regard which men bear to their relatives, and the

* Hádí-i-Gum-Rahán, p. 89. † Hebrews x. 1—10.

‡ See Chap. vi, p. 323.

tender feelings excited in cases of bereavement, there would be no deficiency of such services whenever they were conceived to be efficacious. The prospect of them as a final resort, however, would be most injurious to the living, who in the hour of trial and temptation would stifle the voice of conscience, and dismiss the apprehension of a fearful doom, in the belief, or expectation, that their friends would free them from the righteous indignation and judgement of God after their removal from the body. That God will remit his claims on the dead, for the sake of the entreaties of the living, is not to be expected. The living do not satisfy the demands of God upon themselves; and far less can they procure a stock of merit available for others. These simple remarks, I am well aware, militate against more religious systems than that of the Pársís.

Now, what is left for me to do, in the view of the principles and facts to which I have now adverted in connexion with the means of salvation prescribed in the Pársí scriptures, and resorted to by the Pársí people? Shall I countenance the delusion which is entertained respecting them, and say, Peace, peace, when there is no peace? To act in this manner were to sacrifice truth at the shrine of a false liberality, and to substitute for the essence and spirit of charity, its veriest semblance. The fear of God, and the love of men,— even of those against whom I thus contend in argument, compel me to say, and to proclaim, that the means of salvation on which the Pársís rely, will be found unavailing before the tribunal of the most High. This is not *my* solitary judgment. It is that of the whole of enlightened and orthodox Christendom, guided by the word of God. It is of the most solemn character which can be imagined; and I pray that its grounds may be duly pondered and considered.

But is the door of hope entirely to be closed against the Pársís, and all other tribes of men, because neither their own religious services, nor repentance, nor obedience, nor penances, nor the intercession of their friends, are available to avert their doom? No; blessed be God, there are still glad tidings to be announced, glad tidings in which there is no delusion, glad tidings proceeding from the throne of God himself, glad tidings which bring "glory to God in the highest, peace on earth, and good will to man." There is the Gospel of Jesus to be proclaimed, which offers pardon to the guilty, sanctification to the impure, and eternal happiness to the miserable, on terms which are not merely compatible with the holiness and justice of God, and the authority of that law in which they are embodied, but which bring to him an inconceivably great revenue of honour and praise; and which demands the admiration of all intelligent creatures, and the cordial and affectionate reception of those to whom it is addressed, as "the wisdom and the power of God unto salvation."

And what *is* the Gospel of Christ, possessed of this high character? As announced by himself, its substance is this:— "God so loved the world, that he gave his only-begotten Son, that whosoever believeth in him should not perish, but have everlasting life:"* Observe what is here said respecting the origin of the plan of human redemption. It devolved on God, and on God alone, to provide a way of salvation: for it is against *his* righteous character, and *his* law, and *his* authority, and *his* government, that sin is directed. HE only can extend forgiveness; and if he withhold it, none else can interfere and none else can dispense it. He determined, however, to magnify his *mercy* in the salvation of a portion of the human race; and he devised a suitable plan for the accomplishment of his purposes, without the violation of any of the essential principles of his moral administration. The righteousness of fallen man, with all its imperfections and impurities, he could not *accept*. The righteousness of the angels and archangels in heaven, who have never known sin, he could not *transfer* from themselves, from whom it is demanded to its furthest extent on their own account. Sin he could not *lightly deal with*, so as to leave the impression, either among the inhabitants of earth below or heaven above, that it is only a trifle, or of little account in the jurisprudence of the Most High. The authority of that law which interdicts all transgression, he could not *lower*; and its dreadful sanc-

* John, iii. 16.

tions he could not *keep in abeyance*. An object in the *appointment* of whom, his *mercy*, his sovereign mercy, to the human race, should be conspicuously displayed, and in the *treatment* of whom his unspotted *holiness* and unswerving *justice* should be most signally manifested, was needed by God, and was found by God. To that infinitely glorious Being, who participates in the unity of his own nature, who stands to him in the relation of an only-begotten Son, as eternally existing in himself, and as being the brightness of his glory, and the express image of his person, and the object of his greatest love, he proposed that he should become the surety, and substitute, and ransom, and Redeemer of fallen man; and that for the accomplishment of this grand and infinitely important object, he should leave the bosom of the Father, assume the nature of man, become subject to, and honour the law, instruct the world, endure unspeakable sufferings in behalf of those whom he should save, and present his unspotted soul as a sacrifice for the redemption of those who were to be constituted the monuments of the divine mercy. "The counsel of peace was between them both." That love to the perishing which led the Father to *propose* to the Son that he should appear in their behalf, led the Son voluntarily and cheerfully to *undertake* their cause. "Lo, I come," he said, "in the volume of the book it is written of me; I delight to do thy will, O God."* The purposes of the divine grace were announced to man, as soon as sin entered into the world; and the mode of their accomplishment, through the sufferings and death of the Saviour, was prefigured and exhibited by the ceremonial sacrifices and burnt-offerings which were prescribed by God himself to our progenitors and their descendants. Many prophets and righteous men saw the day of Christ afar off; and they rejoiced in the prospect of its approach, and prophesied and sang of its unspeakable glories. The "fulness of time" at length arrived; and God was mindful of his promises. He "sent forth his Son, made of a woman, made under the law, to redeem them that were under

* Psalm, xl. 7, 8.

the law, that we might receive the adoption of sons."* "The Desire of all nations," and "the Consolation of Israel" appeared. "The Word" who "was in the beginning with God," and "who was God," "was made flesh," or became incarnate, and "dwelt amongst us;" and those who witnessed this Word have left the testimony, "We beheld his glory, the glory as of the only-begotten of the Father, full of grace and truth."† The humanity of Christ was holy in its origin; and it was preserved by him from all personal evil, for he continued holy, harmless, undefiled, and separated from sinners. When he had sufficiently explained the objects of his mission to the world, and done many mighty and gracious works, in order to make known his own character, and that of his Father by whom he was sent, he came forth to endure the death, and all its unspeakable agonies, through which he was to make an atonement for the sins of his people. He surrendered himself into the hands of sinners; and by them he was nailed to, and suspended on, what was reckoned the "accursed tree." In the visitations of the wrath of God, however, his sufferings principally consisted; and these visitations were inconceivably great. It was under *them*, that he exclaimed "My God, my God, why hast thou forsaken me!" and he shrunk not from them till he could say, "It is finished." They were not laid upon him on his own account, but for the sake of those whom he had covenanted to save. They were not for sin *committed* by himself, for in this sense he knew no sin, but for sin *imputed*. "He was wounded for our transgressions, he was bruised for our iniquities: the chastisement of our peace was upon him; and with his stripes we are healed."‡ "He was made sin for us who knew no sin, that we might be made the righteousness of God in him."§ The evil of sin, which he voluntarily allowed his Father to lay to his account, was awfully displayed at the hour of his crucifixion. In all that he did, and in all that he endured, there was infinite merit, for he was a divine Saviour, whose services and suffer-

* Galatians, iv. 4, 5.

† John, i. 14.

‡ Isaiah, liii. 5.

§ 2 Corinth. v. 21.

ings possessed an infinitely intrinsic value, and on them there rested no legal claim, except that which is to be found in his own voluntary promises and engagements. The merit which he purchased and procured, had men, guilty, undeserving men, as its intended recipients ; and it is this merit which is offered to, and pressed on the acceptance of men, in the Gospel. To every anxious soul, which makes the inquiry, "What must I do to be saved," the reply is given, "Believe in the Lord Jesus Christ, and thou shalt be saved." To those who renounce all confidence in themselves, and exercise faith in his name, and trust in his perfect righteousness, he extends a free and a full pardon of every transgression, and gives a free and a full remission of every demand. He delivers all who take refuge in his grace from their liability to hell, and from the eternal punishment which they have merited, and which is the portion of those who continue impenitent and unbelieving. When they lay hold of his righteousness by faith, he views them as righteous in his sight, receives them into his favour, adopts them into his family, and appoints them to eternal glory in the regions of bliss. God's moral glory, it must be seen, is upheld, nay illustriously displayed, amidst all these transactions, in which *justice* is satisfied, as well as *mercy* magnified. When he pardons sin for the sake of Christ, he acquits the *creditor* only because the *surety* has implemented the demand. When he passes by iniquity, transgression, and sin, it is not without a reference to that overwhelming display of the tremendous consequences of transgression, which was continued throughout the whole humiliation of Christ, but was most remarkable at its termination in his death, when the afflictions of the substitute were unspeakably great. He proclaims to the universe, that since he spared not his own Son when he stood in the room of sinners, he will not spare sinners when they stand on their own footing. He unfolds and follows out a scheme of redemption at once so glorious, and awful, and tremendous in the way in which it has been executed, that it must appear to be his *ultimatum*, such as may not be repeated, if it fail to establish righteousness throughout the unmeasured vastness of his creation. At the same time that he imparts *judicial righteousness* to the believer, he commences the work of imparting *personal righteousness*, or holiness. When he frees men from the *penal consequences* of sin, he also frees them from its *power and pollution*. For the begetting of that simple faith in, and reliance on, Christ, to which he calls men, he is ready to give his Holy Spirit, the third personal subsistence in the Godhead, to them who ask for him. This heavenly teacher, and guide, and renovator, works powerfully within them. Through the word of God, which is quick and powerful, sharper than any two-edged sword, and which is a discerner of the thoughts and intents of the heart, he convinces them of their depravity, guilt, and misery, leads them anxiously to cry for salvation, discovers to them the grace, and power, and suitableness of Christ, renews their wills, enables them to close in with the offers of redemption, fills them with peace and joy in believing, directs them to Christian obedience, upholds them in the discharge of their duties, cleanses them from all their corruptions, and in due time prepares them for the inheritance of the saints in light. Under his influence, and looking to that Saviour whose loveliness and suitableness he discovers, and viewing themselves as heirs of God, and joint heirs with Jesus Christ, they rejoice,—even amidst all their needful trials, with "joy unspeakable and full of glory." They sing the triumphant song, "Who can lay any thing to the charge of God's elect? It is God that justifieth. Who is he that condemneth? It is Christ that died, yea rather that is risen again, who is even at the right hand of God, who also maketh intercession for us. Who shall separate us from the love of Christ? Shall tribulation, or distress, or persecution, or famine, or nakedness, or peril, or sword? . . . . . . Nay, in all these things we are more than conquerors through him that loved us. For I am persuaded that neither death, nor life, nor angels, nor principalities, nor powers, nor things present, nor things to come, nor height, nor depth, nor any other creature, shall be able to separate us from the love of God which is in Christ Jesus our Lord."*

* Romans, viii. 35—39.

These are the glad tidings, which by the authority of God's word itself, I announce to the Pársís, Hindús, Musalmáns, and merely nominal professors of the true faith, in India. To all, I affectionately say, "This is a faithful saying, and worthy of all acceptation, that Christ Jesus came into the world to save sinners." While I call upon them to forsake those vanities which cannot profit, I entreat them to receive the truth of God, and the righteousness of the Son of God from heaven. If they will indeed turn unto the Lord, they will be blessed in time and throughout eternity. To all of them I say, "Turn ye, turn ye, why will ye die." All of them I point to Christ, from whose mouth proceed the gracious words, "Him that cometh unto me, I will in nowise cast out;" "Come unto me, all ye that labour, and are heavy laden, and I will give you rest."

CHAPTER VIII.

THE ALLEGED PROPHETICAL MISSION OF ZOROASTER DISPROVED, AND THE IMPUGNMENT OF THE EXTERNAL AUTHORITY OF THE BOOKS WHICH THE PARSIS RECKON THE STANDARD OF THEIR FAITH AND PRACTICE.

Recapitulation of the internal evidence establishing the fact that the Zand-Avastá has no claim to be considered a divine revelation — Statement of the question as to the Authenticity, Genuineness, and Credibility of the Zand-Avastá — Shirking of this question by the controversialists — Antiquity of the Zand language admitted — Failure of the Pársís to establish the prophetic Mission of Zoroaster — Notices and reviews of all the authorities to which they have appealed on this subject: — The Zinat-at-Tawárikh — The Dabistán — The Shâristán — The Dasátír — The Dín-Kard — The Burhán-i-Kátagh— The Sháhnámah — The Zartusht-Námah — The Rauzat-as-Safá— The Wajar-Kard — The Ardái-Víráf-Námah — The Sháyistah Násháyistah— The Changhraghách-Námah — The Jámásp-Námah — Argument for the divine Mission of Christ, and the divine authority of the Christian Scriptures — Concluding address to the Pársís.

The attentive reader of the preceding chapters will readily preceive, and admit, that a divine confirmation of the books esteemed sacred by the Pársís is not to be expected. God is a God of perfect truth, wisdom, and righteousness; and it is absolutely impossible that he can extend his sanction to that which is either erroneous or absurd. The writers of the Vandidád, and liturgical works which have passed before our notice, have neither his glory in their own view, nor do they exhibit it to the view of others. These works are neither holy nor good; and they are unworthy of God to give, and of man to receive as his gift. From beginning to end, they are characterized by the ignorance, and error, and even the depravity of man. The testimony which they give regarding the divine nature, either falls short of, or contradicts, the testimony which God gives of himself in his own works; and they cannot be viewed with respect even as setting forth a rational system of Natural Theology. They represent the Lord of the Creation as a derivative being, while it must be admitted, that "the invisible things of God from the creation of the world are clearly seen, being understood by the things that are made, even his eternal power and Godhead." They circumscribe the divine power by an imaginary Evil Principle, who is said to create and destroy, not only without the divine permission, but of his own innate and underived energy. They distribute the work of providence among numerous Izads and Amsháspands, who are believed to preside over the different departments of nature; and they permit these imaginary beings to share in, and almost to engross, the honours of the Godhead. They confound the works of God with the nature of God, and treat the lifeless elements and their most conspicuous combinations as if they were sentient, intelligent, and divine. They contain a code of moral conduct, and religious ceremony, frivolous and absurd in a remarkable degree. They prescribe unsuitable plans of salvation, and deceive the soul with fallacious hopes and expectations. The numerous illustrations and proofs which we have given of these and similar propositions, must annihilate, in every considerate mind, the belief, or expectation, that any evidence can be adduced to support thė theory of their possessing divine authority.

Knowing, however, the exceeding proneness of the mind of man to embrace error, notwithstanding its repugnance both to enlightened reason, and natural conscience; and knowing the actual devotedness of the Pársís to serious error connected with the subject to which I now refer, I have more than once challenged them to adduce, for examination and discussion, whatever evidence they may conceive themselves to be in possession of to support the alleged prophetic mission of Zoroaster, and the claims of the Zand-Avastá, attributed to him, to be received as a divine revelation; and I have done this in the plainest and most unequivocal terms. Thus, for example, in my lecture on the Vandidád, I have written as follows:—

"It is ascribed to Zoroaster, who is said to have flourished in the reign of Gushtásp, the son of Lohorasp, or Darius Hystaspes, about 500 years before Christ;* but there is no proof

* Darius Hystaspes ascended the Persian throne about 521 years before Christ.

The testimonies of the ancients respecting the epoch of Zoroaster, the Pársís are probably aware, are very conflicting. The most important of them, as far as I can find them in books to which I have access in this place, are the following. "We have heard of one man Zoroaster," says Pliny, in his work on Natural History, "that he laughed the same day he was born; and that his skull so palpitated that it repelled the hand placed upon it, a presage of his future wisdom" (lib. vii). "Zoroaster considered it the best time to sow, when the sun had passed twelve parts of Scorpio, and the moon was in Taurus" (lib. xii). "Without doubt it [the magic art] originated in Persia with Zoroaster, as it is agreed amongst authors; but whether this was one individual, or another individual at a later period, is not sufficiently evident. Eudoxus who wished it to be reckoned the most distinguished and useful amongst the kinds of wisdom, delivers that this Zoroastres lived 6,000 years before the death of Plato [which took place 384 years before Christ]. So, also, Aristotle. Hermippus, who has written most diligently concerning the whole of this art, and who has expounded the two millions of verses written by Zoroaster, and made indices to his volumes, delivers that Azonaces the teacher, by whom it was established, assuredly existed 5,000 years before the Trojan war...... There is another magical party originating from Moses, Jamne, and Jotape the Jews, but many thousand years after Zoroaster" (lib. xxx). Pliny also mentions another Zoroaster Proconessius who lived a little before Xerxes. Justin, who lived in the first century of the Christian era, and who abridged the celebrated historical work of Trogos Pompeius, born A. C. 46, says (lib. i. cap. 1), that Zoroaster was the contemporary of Ninus king of the Assyrians, by whom he was conquered, and that he was a "king of the Bactrians, who is said first to have invented magical arts, and the elements (principia) of the world, and to have most diligently beheld the motions of the stars." The notice of Zoroaster given by Plutarch, I have already given (see p. 124 of this work). He makes Zoroaster to have lived 500 (or according to some MSS. 5,000) years before the Trojan war, to which the dates of 1184, and 904 years before Christ have been assigned by chronologists. Apuleius, of the first century after Christ (lib. ii), states that Pythagoras was taken prisoner by Cambyses, "and carried into Egypt, where he was instructed by the Magi, and particularly by Zoroaster himself; but the more general opinion is that he went to Egypt voluntarily to study the Egyptian

even of its existence long after his day, far less of the allegation, that it was written by him. While it professes to report the result of an interview of Zoroaster with Hormazd, it speaks of the great Zoroaster as having existed before the time

sciences and from thence set out to consult the Chaldeans and Bráhmans." (Mirkhond translated by Shea p. 277). Apuleius, also mentions (lib. xv.) a Zoroaster after the reign of Cambyses. (Bryant's Mythology, vol. ii. p. 111.) Diogenes Laertius, about the middle of the second century after Christ, in his Lives of the Philosophers, writes, "Hermodorus, the Platonist in his book concerning Discipline, reckons 5,000 years from the Magi, (whose chief, it is handed down to memory, was Zoroaster the Persian) to the destruction of Troy; but Xanthus of Lydia reckons 600 years to the invasion of Xerxes" (Procem. seg. 3). He adds, "Aristotle says in his book on Magic, and Dinon in his fifth book on Histories, that Zoroaster, according to the interpretation of his name, was a star-worshipper... Hermodorus says the same" (Procem. seg. 8.) Clemens of Alexandria (A D. 192) in his Strom. v. p. 255. (ed. Sylburg), says, "Plato, in the tenth book of his Republic, mentions, a certain Eris, son of Armenias, of the family of Pamphylas. This person is Zoroastres; for Zoroastres himself writes thus: this Zoroastres, son of Armenius of the family of Pamphylas, has composed. Killed in battle I learned it in hades from the Gods. Plato mentions also that Zoroaster, on the twelfth day after his death, when he was placed on the pile, did revive." In another place (p. 44) Clemens also mentions Zoroaster the Mede, and that Pythagoras has proved the Magus Zoroaster to have been a Persian (p. 131). Syncellus, in his Chronicon (p. 167) quotes Cephalion as attributing the same date to Zoroastres as to Semiramis (Bryant's Mythology vol ii. p. 111.) Arnobius refers to "Zoroastres the Bactrian," and to "Zoroastres Armenius, the grandson of Zostrianus (Bryant's Ancient Mythology, vol. ii. p. 111). Porphyry (de antr. Nymph.) says, that Zoroaster first consecrated caverns to Mithras, the creator and father of all things. Ammianus Marcellinus, a Latin writer of the fourth century, (Hist. lib. xxiii), states, that "The Bactrian Zoroaster, in remote ages, made many additions to the religion of the Magi, which additions were derived from the mysteries of the Chaldeans; and after him Hystaspes, a most sage monarch, the father of Darius. This prince, in pursuit of knowledge, having penetrated into the remote parts of Northern (Superior) India, reached a secluded place amidst forests, the calm retreats of which were inhabited by Bráhmans of the most exalted order: being counselled by them, he directed his utmost attention to learning the principles of the motions of the universe and the stars, also the pure form of worship. A part of what he had thus acquired, he inculcated on the minds of the Magi; which they handed down to their posterity, in conjunction with the science of foretelling future events." Moses of Chorene, an Armenian of the fifth century, indentifies Zoroas-

at which this interview took place. Near the commencement of the second fargard, or section, Hormazd is represented as saying, 'Jamshíd, ruler of people and of flocks, O holy Zoroaster, is the first man who has consulted Hormazd as you do now, O Zoroaster. I have clearly revealed to him the law of God, and of Zoroaster.' Near the commencement of the nineteenth fargard, Hormazd observes to the person

ter with Zerovan and describes him as the Magian, the king of the Bactrians (Whiston's Translation, p. 16). Agathias, of the sixth century, (lib. ii) has the following passage:—"When Zoroadus, or Zarades (for a double appellation is given to him) first flourished and established laws, it is not clearly manifest. The Persians of this age, however, simply say, that he lived under Hystaspes, but so much without additional information, that it is very doubtful, and cannot be certainly known, whether he was the father of Darius, or some other Hystaspes. But in whatever age he flourished, he was the chief leader of those of the Magian sect; and having changed the first sacred ritual, he introduced certain confused and opposite opinions." Suidas (1087 A. D.) in his Lexicon, has the following sentences: "*Zóroastres* Medo-Persian, excelling all others in his knowledge of Astronomy. He was the first of those called by the name of Magi. He lived 500 years before the Trojan war. He is said to have written about nature, four books; about precious stones, one book; astrological prophecies, five books. *Zóroastres*, an astronomer during the reign of Ninus the Assyrian king. He prayed to be destroyed by the heavenly fire, advising at the same time the Assyrians to preserve his ashes, lest they should lose the supremacy. They preserve it this very day. *Zóromasdres*, a Chaldean philosopher, wrote about mathematical and physical matters." It is not my business to reconcile these authorities. In fact, the attempt, though frequently made, is altogether hopeless. They seem to intimate, either that the epoch of Zoroaster is more remote than the time assigned to it by the Pársís, or that there have been several Zoroasters of the same name.

The Musalmán Arabian writers, and even some of the Persian, confound Zoroaster with Abraham. Firdausí, agrees with the Pársís, in placing him under the reign of Gushtásp. In the *Zand* writings, there are but few data given, to aid us in fixing the time at which he appeared. In the ninth Há of the Yaçna, *Haoma* (identical with the *Som* or Moon of the Vedas) is represented as teaching Zoroaster that the first person who consulted him was *Vivanghão* the father of *Yimó* or Jamshíd; the second, *Athwyó*, the father of *Thrayĕtyaonó*, or Faridun; the third *Sám*, the father of *Urvákhsyó* and *Keresáspó*; and the fourth, *Paourusaçpó*, the father of *Zarathustra*.

Having here mentioned *Haoma*, or Hom, I may allude to the circumstance that the Hom plant and Hom tree of the Pársís, are merely the Som plant and Som juice of the Vedas.

whom he addresses in the Vandidád, that 'Zoroaster was stronger than Ahriman, author of the evil law; he struck the people given by this Dew', etc.

"Whether the Vandidád is the same as when it was originally composed, no man can tell. . . . . There is no history which can associate the reputed miracles of Zoroaster with the book; and there is not the slightest evidence that these miracles ever took place. 'I have asked,' I have observed in one of my controversial letters, 'some persons to state their reasons for believing in the stories about the miracles; and they have been not a little puzzled. Some of them say that they have heard them from their parents; others, that they have read them in books. Are these sufficient reasons for crediting them? Many foolish tales are afloat in the world; and many errors and falsehoods of various kinds are contained in books. An investigation of the strictest kind must be resorted to; and the most diligent search must be made. Who saw these miracles? Who gave testimony respecting them? Who examined the witnesses? Who recorded the evidence? Who can prove that it is uncorrupted? These are inquiries which undoubtedly ought to be made? For a long time I have challenged the Pársís in this place to bring forward information on this subject; but though they have shewed no want of zeal in behalf of their religion, they have as yet done nothing to settle inquiry on the subject.

"The Vandidád Sádé is very defective as a Rule of Faith. It is a mere fragment of a work which is lost; and since this is the case, and since, as I remarked in a former lecture, we have reason to infer, that if God be pleased to grant a revelation of his will, he will be pleased to preserve it either entire, or to such a degree as that it will prove sufficient for the instruction of mankind, it becomes a duty to inquire into the loss of the work to which it is said to have belonged. Why was it permitted to be destroyed, as is alleged, by Sikandar Rúmí, Umar Khálif, or any other individuals? This question requires to be urged, particularly when the professions of the Vandidád are considered."*

* Lecture on the Vandidád, pp. 6—8.

In reply to these observations, the Pársí controversialists now before me, have not been able to present any statements, or authorities, at all calculated to establish the claims which are urged in behalf of Zoroaster, or the Zand-Avastá. The attempts which they have made, in fact, are most conspicuous failures; and to each of them, I would now particularly direct the attention of the speaker.

Dosabháí has favoured us with some remarks on the genuineness and antiquity of the *Zand language.** Connected with this subject, he has introduced a memorandum from a highly respectable quarter, and well entitled to respectful consideration. From Major Rawlinson, whose geographical researches in Persia are already so well known and appreciated, and from whose literary inquiries much has for some time been expected, he gives the following document:—

"It has been asserted by some of our most distinguished British Orientalists, that the language in which the sacred writings of the Pársís are composed, is a fabrication of the Zoroastrian priests subsequent to their expatriation from Persia, and that these writings in consequence are, as far as regards antiquity, entitled to no consideration whatever. Against this assertion I offer the following remark.

"In various parts of Persia are to be found at the present day inscriptions in a character which we denominate Cuneiform, exhibiting historical records of the sixth and fifth centuries before Christ, written in three different languages.

"The inscriptions in the simple literal Cuneiform character invariably occupy the most distinguished place of the three upon the tablets, and exhibit other points of evidence to in-

* Aspandiárjí (Hádí-i-Gum-Rahán, p. 5) very absurdly says, "The Padre must remember that the Vandidád does not exist in the Zand, but in the Avastá language, which is sometimes denominated by the Pársís the celestial language. On this book a Zand Pázand was written, which is no more than a commentary or paraphrase on the original text." One would think, that, after this flourish, he would henceforth refrain from giving the name of the Zand to the language of his sacred books. In the same page, however, in which he has made it, he speaks of the "Zand language," as he afterwards (p. 24) does of a "knowledge of the Zand."

dicate that the language in which they are written must have been the native and vernacular dialect of the sovereigns by whose order they were engraved. To the analysis of this character, and the examination of this language, I have devoted many years of research; and I can now safely assert that the Persian language of the ages of Cyrus and Darius is unquestionably the parent of that tongue which we call the Zand, and which has been so successfully elaborated by continental students, and by none with greater skill and perspicuity than by Monsr. Burnouf in his admirable "Commentaire sur l' Yaçna."

"The Ante-Alexandrian Persian, is in fact to all appearance an intermediate formation between the language of the the Zand-Avastá and some primitive tongue which gave rise to the various cognate derivatives of Sanskrit, Pálí, Pelasgian, Etruscan; and the many branches of the Indo-Teutonic family.

"In the memoir which I am at present writing to illustrate the Cuneiform inscriptions of Persia, I shall have abundant opportunity of establishing the close affinity between this Ante-Alexandrian Persian and the Zand. I may here instance, however, a few points of identity which are most remarkable.

"The Pronouns in the two languages, personal, relative and demonstrative, are nearly the same; the Participles '*fra*, *pati*, *para* and *ha* or *ham*' employed in verbal compositions are precisely similar; the prepositions '*abiga* to, *upa* near, *hadá* with, and *patish* before' have all their Zandic correspondents, as also has the Conjunction '*uta* and.' A very numerous class of verbal formations coincide both in their elements and in their grammatical inflexions; and the same coincidence is observable both in the original themes and in the grammatical declension of the Substantives in the two languages, of which the following paradigma presents an instance.

		Singular.	*Plural.*
Nom.	Zand	Dakhyus..	Daghvo.
	Cun	Dahyaush.	Dahyáwa.

		Singular.	*Plural.*
Gen.	Zand	Dakhyéus..........	Dakhyûnâm.
	Cun	Dahayush..........	Dahyunám.
Dat.	Zand	Dakhyubo.*........	Daghubyó.
	Cun	Dahyuwá..........	Dayushuwa.
Acc.	Zand	Dakhyúm..........	Dagh vó.
	Cun	Dahyáum..........	Dahyawa.

"I must refer to my detailed observations in the memoir for a multitude of similar cases of coincidence, which are amply sufficient to demonstrate the affinity between the two languages; and to establish as incontrovertible, that the dialect in which are composed the Vandidád, Vispered, Izashné, &c. is merely a modification of the true and vernacular tongue, which was used in Persia in the ages of Cyrus and Darius above twelve centuries anterior to the period of the Indian emigration of the Pársís.

"I may also observe that there are several dialects spoken in Persia at the present day, both among the Curdish mountaineers, and by the Gabars of Yezd, Kirman and Séistan, which in a number of their terms for external objects closely approximate to the language of the Zand-Avastá, and that I really believe there is scarcely a single radical of any importance in any of the Pársí sacred books which, under some modification or other, may not be traced to a correspondent term in some living dialect of Persia.

"Passing over, therefore, the difficulty, I may almost say the impossibility, of fabricating a copious, grammatical and richly developed language like that of the Zand-Avastá: these established points of affinity which it possesses with the true native dialects, are certainly sufficient to authenticate the genuineness of the writings as imported from Persia. At what period anterior to that event the precepts of Zoroaster may have been collected and embodied in the language which they now exhibit, it does not enter into my present object to discuss. I am merely desirous, on the grounds which I have

* There is probably a misprint here for Dakhyavê or Dangvê. The cuneiform form of the dative plural given above, has an anomalous appearance.

mentioned, to record my conviction, that the Pársí writings were imported from Persia in their present state during the seventh century of Christ, and are thus entitled to the same degree of consideration among the Pársís of the present day, which they enjoyed among their ancestors at the period of their expatriation. H. C. Rawlinson."

Bombay: Feb. 2d. 1840

From the conclusion respecting the *Zand language* at which Major Rawlinson has here arrived, I am not, on the whole, disposed to dissent. A vocabulary of all the words found in the Cuneiform inscriptions, prepared from Grotefend, Lassen, and Burnouf, by my friend Mr. Weigle of the German Mission of Mangalur, and a few grammatical fragments collected by myself, are now before me. These inscriptions are *not* in the Zand language, though in many words which have been already pointed out, and in others, the coincidence of which is apparent to all, they resemble the Zand in their themes and a few of their grammatical inflexions. But what is the inference to be derived from these facts? *If*, as alleged by Major Rawlinson, the vernacular language of Cyrus and Darius be only the "*parent*" of the Zand, then the Pársí writings cannot be the genuine works of Zoroaster, even supposing him to have appeared at the latest date mentioned in connexion with his name, and that universally set forth by the Pársís, during the reign of Darius Hystaspes. The interval between Cyrus and this latter prince, does not afford a space of time sufficient for the difference in the languages, or dialects, whichever term may be preferred. To these inferences, I am certain, Major Rawlinson himself will not object. In fact, it is an awkward matter for the Pársís, that they have brought him into the witness-box. In his admirable paper on the Atropatenian Ecbatana, he makes the following declarations:—" Since in the numerous Cuneiform inscriptions of Persia, chiefly of a religious nature, which exhibit at the present day the imperishable records of the times of Darius and Xerxes, no trace of the name or character of the prophet Zoroaster is to be found: it is obvious that he either could not have lived in the age which is usually assigned to him, or that we must have most erroneous notions of the influence that he exercised upon the national religion of the country. . . . During the reign of the Arsacidan dynasty in Persia, we know that the religion of Zoroaster gradually fell into disuse; that an idolatrous worship partially usurped its place; that the genuine writings of the prophet were corrupted, or, perhaps, altogether lost; and that the holy fire languished in obscurity on the desecrated altars of the Magi. . . . The fire-worship, however, was at length restored with greater splendour and respect than it had ever previously enjoyed. The priesthood formed a new religious code, which they unblushingly ascribed to Zoroaster; and Ardeshir Bábegán undertook the re-establishment of all the great Pyrœa of the kingdom."* Speaking of the correspondence of the ruins at the Takht-i-Sulimán, with the description of Jamshíd's palace in the Vandidád, he adds, "Indeed, I can only account for the extraordinary accuracy of the description, by supposing the Vandidád to have been written in the reign of Ardeshír Bábegán by Magian priests; who were familiar with the localities, and who had received traditional accounts of the real ancient foundation of the city by the Median king, Dejoces."†

Whether or not the Pársí priests in India, from their traditional reminiscences of the ancient languages, could have fabricated some of the Zand writings, I shall not positively assert. There is a poverty in the expression of some of these writings, particularly of the minor liturgical pieces, which shows that their authors had no ready command of the language in which they wrote. There is an approach to Gujarátí idiom, in some instances, and to a Gujarátí corruption of Sanskrit, which at one time awakened considerable suspicions in my mind. Viewing the matter of the Zand language, however, in its general aspect, I have no hesitation in declaring, that none of the exiled and depressed Pársí priests in India can be supposed to have had the ability to invent that language, with its extensive and minute grammatical forms,

* Journal of the Royal Geographical Society, vol. x, p. 84.

† *Ibid.* p. 131

and with its abundant and regular analogies to the Sanskrit, Persian, Pahlaví, Greek, Latin, and Germanic languages, as so distinctly evinced by Bopp and Burnouf, and evident to the general student, and to write of a state of society altogether different from that in which they themselves were placed, and in many respects dissimilar to that to which the legends of the Sháh-námah and other similar works, to which they attach some importance, refer. Into the mere literary question of the origin and antiquity of the Zand language, however, I am not inclined further to look at present. What I wish the Pársís with whom I am at present engaged in discussion, to bear in mind, is, that they have not brought forward the slightest reasons for impugning my original statement, that "there is no proof of its [the Vandidád's] existence long after his [Zoroaster's] day, far less of its being written by him." They have referred to no ancient works, in which either it, or any other of the writings contained in the Zand-Avastá, is either quoted or described. The authenticity and genuineness of the Christian Scriptures we clearly establish by an appeal to a series of writers beginning with the present day, and extending even to the time of the apostles of Christ, who make innumerable references to them, and produce from them many distinct passages; but the authenticity and genuineness of the Pársí scriptures cannot be established by any such authorities. Thousands of links in the chain are wanting. For hundreds of years, it altogether vanishes. The force of these remarks will be more distinctly understood by my Pársí friends as we advance.

But supposing we were to admit that the Zand-Avastá is the genuine production of Zoroaster, it must be clearly seen that it remains to be proved that Zoroaster was a messenger from God, and that his work is possessed of divine authority. The Pársís think that both Zoroaster and the book have the seal of miracles; but, as has been seen, they have been expressly and directly challenged to bring forward the proof. "There is no history," I have observed, "which can associate the reported miracles of Zoroaster with the book; and there is not the slightest evidence that these miracles ever took place.

Dosabhái says that there *is* such evidence; and, without adducing it, he says that it is to be found in the following works: — 1. The *Zínat-at-Tawáríkh,* written in Persia during the time of Hátím Kadar Fattáh Alí Sháh Kajár. 2. The *Dabistán.* 3. The *Sháristán.* 4. The *Dasátír.* 5. The *Dín-kard,* in Pahlavi, to be found till the present time in the hands of our Dasturs. 6. The *Burhán-i-Kátagh.* 7. The *Sháh-Námah.* 8. The *Zartusht-Námah.*"* Edal Daru refers, in the course of his work, to most of these books, and he gives at length the substance of the last mentioned, which is reckoned by the Pársís the fullest, the most explicit, and the most important. Kalam Kas also quotes several passages from the Zartusht-Námah. Aspandiárjí follows in the train of Dosabhái, enumerating the exact authors he mentions, and adding: — "If the padre be still not satisfied with the number, I beg he would refer to the following others, viz, Rozat-as-Safá, Habíb-al-Assair, Sharah Hikáyat-al-Nur, Zore-Pastán, and the Pahlávi book called Shikun Gomání. Besides these many other authors have adverted to the miraculous deeds of Zoroaster."† Some of the works mentioned, are by Pársís; some, by the Sipásí Sufis; and some, by Musalmáns. They are here referred to without any classification either as to time or authorship. I shall notice, however, the most important of them in the order in which they are here set forth.

The very mention by Dosabhái of the date of the *Zínat-at-Tawáríkh,* ought to have shown to him the absurdity of his bringing forward this work. Fattáh A'lí-Sháh came to the throne in the year of Christ 1797; and the work consequenly is not fifty years old. Is it to *it* that Dosabhái refers me for a reply to the questions, "Who saw the miracles? Who gave testimony respecting them? Who examined the witnesses? Who recorded the evidence? Who can prove that it is uncorrupted?" Dosabhái knew that the reign of Fattáh A'lí-Sháh might appear as ancient to some of his readers as

* Tálim-i-Zartusht, p. 34.

† Hádí-i-Gum-Rahán, p. 17.

that of any of the Kaikobadian Dynasty; and hence, I cannot but suspect, his play on their ignorance. The Zínat-at-Tawáríkh mentions some of the legends current among the Pársís; but it remains to be proved that its author, a Musalmán, attaches any credit to those connected with Zoroaster. The early part of his history is a mere abridgement of the Sháhnámah of Firdausí, to which we shall immediatly advert.

2. The *Dabistán*. The author of this work, to quote the words of Mullá Firuz, the most learned Pársí of his day, "seems to have flourished in the reigns of Jahángír and Sháh Jehán,"* and consequently little more than a couple of centuries ago. It is the most wretched collection of extravagant fables, fictions, and falsehoods which I have ever perused, and of this fact the whole world will soon be able to judge, as an English translation of the work, by the late Mr. Shea and Captain Troyer, is about to be published by the Oriental Translation Fund. Its account of the alleged Mahábádian dynasty, on account of which, on a cursory examination, Sir William Jones appears to have attached some importance to its traditions or inventions, is quite irreconcilable with the mythms of the Vandidád, and the traditions of Firdausí, and the most absurd which can be imagined. It ascribes to the early Iránian sovereigns many of the opinions of the Hindús. The fourteen Mahábáds are neither more nor less than the fourteen Manus of the Shástras. It recognizes the Hindú kalpas. It makes the ancient Iránians supporters of the doctrine of the transmigration of souls, which is quite opposed to the Pársí religion. It declares that they divided the population into four classes, corresponding with the distinctions of Bráhman, Kshattriya, Vaishya, and Shúdra. If speaks of the Dabistán as a revelation to Mahábád himself. It represents Mahábád as succeeded by thirteen prophets and kings, some of whom, it says, reigned millions of years. It tells us that the devils have originated in the use of animal food. It declares that the sacred books of Zoroaster are outwardly opposed to the religion of Mahábád, but not inwardly. It speaks of the Hindú form of wor-

* Preface to the Dasátír, p. vii.

ship of the planets, illustrating them by the figures according to which they are commonly represented among the Bráhmans. It ascribes calamities, and their removal, to the stars. With a view to entrap the Musalmáns into the Sipásí system, it informs them that where their shrines, such as Mecca, Medina, etc. are now to be found, there were formerly fire-temples. It makes the Hindú Tírthas, or places of pilgrimage, places of distinction with the Abádís. It makes all the Devas, Izads, and heroes of the Pársís, including Kai-Khosru and Alexander the Great, mysteries and parables! Of Azar-Kaiwán,* and his followers, who, as Mr Erskine remarks, "have too much the air of conjurors and jugglers,"† it gives us throughout accounts which outrage common sense. Its notices of Zoroaster are expressly from the Sháristán, and Zartusht-Námah; and they must stand or fall with these works. I do not find any passage in it which would lead to the inference that its author had ever perused any of the Zand writings.

3. The *Sháristán* was produced only a few years pre-

* In the following manner it traces the descent of A'zar-Kaiwán.—

1 A'zar-Kaiwán
2 A'zar-Goshasp
3 A'zar-Zartusht
4 A'zar-Burzín
5 A'zar-Ayín
6 A'zar-Behrám
7 A'zar-Nus
8 A'zar-Mehtar or A'zar Sásán, who is called the fifth Sásán!

The fifth Sásán, it makes the fifth in descent from the Lesser Dáráb, son of the Greater Dáráb, the son of Bahman, the son of Aspandiár! The inaccuracy of this chronology must be apparent to every intelligent Pársí. If gives us only thirteen generations for a period of upwards of two thousand years. Azar-Kaiwán, according to Mr. Erskine,* is said to have been born in Persia A. D. 1535 or 1536; to have left it when twenty-eight years of age about 1564; and to have proceeded to India, where he spent the rest of his life; the latter part of it at Patna, in which city he died A. D. 1618, when eighty-five lunar years of age." According to the Dabistán, he began to practise austerities at the age of five years; and he became so successful in his abstemiousness that he was accustomed to live on 48 barley-corns a day. In the Gujaráti translation of the Dabistán (p. 173), it is said that he died at *Pattan in Gujarát* A. H. 1027.

† Bombay Transactions, vol. ii, p. 369.

* Bombay Transactions, vol. ii. p. 368.

vious to the Dabistán, in which it is more than once named and quoted, as the work of Behram Farhád a disciple of Azar-Kaiwán. The author "flourished," says Mullá Firuz in his preface to the Dasátír, "in the reign of Akbár, and about A. D. 1624 in the reign of the emperor Jahángír. This author, who appears to have been a native of Shiráz, though outwardly a Musalmán, was really a Pársí, or rather a disciple of A'zar-Kaiwán, a philosophical ascetic, who founded a new sect on the foundation of the Pársí tenets." I have, in other parts of this work, made several references to it. It is more sober than the Dabistán, but it is not possessed of a whit more authority in a historical point of view. Its testimony to Zoroaster's reputed miracles is not a grain more valuable than that of Dosabhái himself.

5. "The *Dasátír*," says Mullá Firuz, "professes to be a collection of the writings of the different Persian Prophets, who flourished from the time of Mahábád to the time of the fifth Sásán, being fifteen in number; of whom Zerdusht was the thirteenth, and the fifth Sásán the last. The fifth Sásán lived in the time of Khusro Parvez, who was contemporary with the Emperor Heraclius, and died only nine years before the destruction of the ancient Persian monarchy. The writings of these fifteen prophets are in a tongue of which no other vestige appears to remain, and which would have been unintelligible without the assistance of the ancient Persian translation. It is quite a different language from the Zend, the Pahlavi, and the Deri, the most celebrated of the dialects of ancient Persia. The old Persian translation was made by the fifth Sásán who has added a commentary, in which some difficulties of the original text are expounded. The commentary displays a very subtle and refined metaphysics."*

The research and criticism of Mr. Erskine,† and Mr. Norris,‡ have left us little to do in order to evince the unsat-

* Preface of the Dassatír.

† Bombay Transactions, vol. ii, pp. 342—364.

‡ Asiatic Journal, Nov. 1820.—Respecting the language of the work, Mr. Norris observes:—"After the positive assertion of Mullá Firuz, that it is quite a different language from the Zand, the Pahlavi and the Deri,

isfactory nature of this authority. They have proved that the language of the work is an entire fabrication. Mr. Erskine has shown that even its doctrines are not those of the Pársís, and that it is to be attributed to the Sipásí school, which we have now noticed. Let any Pársí turn up "the book of Shet the prophet Zartusht," and he will immediately perceive that its statements are altogether opposed to the Zand writings, which it, in fact, *supercedes* by the alleged command of God to Zartusht, "Do not work but according to the *Dasátír*,"* and of which the Persian commentator, (the fifth Sásán, according to Mullá Firuz!) says, "*That book* is the inspired volume which the prophet of God Zartusht asked of God that he should send down as his book for the purpose of advice"† A reference to the Dasátír, then, it must be seen is altogether vain. Were it even sustained, it would only destroy the authority of the Zand-Avastá. Its historical notices of a general kind are entirely despicable. It makes the Greeks, converts to the religion of Zoroaster in the days of Gushtásp.‡ It brings Vyás, the reputed compiler of the Hindú Vedas and Shástras, and also the Bráhman Changhranghácha to Irán, to do obeisance to Zoroaster. It makes Alexander the Great a convert to the Pársí religion; and its commentator says, that that Grecian prince was the "son of the king of kings Dáráb, the son of the king of kings Bahman, exalted as the first intelligence!"

5. "The Pahlavi *Dín-kard*," says Dosabhái, "is to be found till the present time in the hands of our Das-

you will undoubtedly be surprised at my presumption in asserting with equal positiveness, that excepting in a few instances, the most material of which occur in the prophecies of the two Sásáns, the inflexion of the nouns, pronouns, and verbs, the formation of the derivatives and compounds, and the construction and arrangement of the sentences, are precisely the same as in the Deri; and that though a great part of the language appears to have little or no resemblance to any other that was ever spoken, yet a great part of it likewise, is nothing more than Deri disguised." Of the correctness of these observations, any person may satisfy himself by attending to a single page of the work.

* Dasátír, book of Zartusht, v. 12.

† Dasátír, vol. ii, p. 123.

‡ Dasátír, vol. ii, p. 125.

túrs". Edal Dáru* says that it declares that both Jamshíd and Faridun prophesied of the appearance of Zoroaster. But what personal knowledge could its author have of the proceedings of these heroes? A copy of the work was lately politely shown to me by my friend Mullá Rustamjí, who mentioned that he thought it was composed within the last 700 years, and consequently removed by upwards of sixteen centuries from the days of Zoroaster. It is almost entirely unknown to Europeans; and as, in a literary point of view, it may not be without interest, I have strongly recommended its being made accessible to the orientalist, for particular examination. Mr. Romer says of it, "The late Mullá Firuz, of Bombay, in a controversial work on the Pársí year, called Kitáb-i-Avizhah-Dín, in which he cites many passages from the Dín-kard, quoting the third Daftar of the book, says, 'The translator of the Dín-kard from Greek into Pahlaví himself states, that the original Dín-kard was composed in the time of king Gushtásp, and that the book now extant and known by this name in Pahlaví, is not the original Dín-kard, that book having been burnt by Alexander. That translations of it into Greek, made by order of Alexander, and subsequently also by direction of Ardashír Bábágán, were preserved and remained in Persia until the Arabian conquest. That the reliques of these ancient and mutilated translations falling into the hands of a learned man, named Adarbád, he put them together to the best of his ability, compiling, from what remained intelligible to him of such materials, a new book in the Pahlaví language. That it is nevertheless doubtful, whether the Dín-kard extant, is the work of Adarbád, or of some other person: but, be this as it may, it is certain the book was brought to India from Persia. In the text the author is named Máwandád son of Bahrám Mihrbán, the date of writing the book, the year 369 of Yazdijírd, A. D. 999. In A. Y. 865, A. D. 1496, it was transcribed by Shaharyár Ardashír, and another copy appears to have been made by Máwandád Bahrám Ardashír, of Túr-

* Maujazát-i-Zartusht, p. 31.

kábád, in A. Y. 1009, A. D. 1639." There are admissions here, which, I suspect, the Rasamís of Bombay, will by no means relish. All the extracts from the Dín-kard which I have read, convince me that it is a modern work disagreeing on many points with the Vandidád. Its legends respecting Zoroaster are equally absurd with those of the Zartusht-Námah, to which we shall immediately advert.*

6. The *Barhán-i-Kátagh* is certainly a valuable Persian dictionary; but it too is quite a modern work. Its author, Hákim-bin-Khalif-at-Tabrizí Muhammed Husain, lived in the reign of Sháh Jahán; and as a decided Musalmán, he was quite averse to the Pársí faith. I do not much admire the *honesty* of the references made to him, and the other authors whom we here notice, by the Pársí controversialists. I suspect that they have no great relish for his account of Zoroaster, which is simply this: — "And they also call him Zardusht, who was the leader and guide of the sect of the fire-worshippers, and who brought in the religion of worshipping fire, and who composed the book called Zand."†

* Journal of the Royal Asiatic Society, vol. iv, p. 348, 349.—In the work from which Mr. Romer quotes, which is on the whole very creditable to the candour, as it undoubtedly is to the learning, of Mullá Firuz, there is a vast deal of very curious information. At p. 306, he exposes the ignorance of Pahlavi evinced by the Pársí priests (as in the context he acknowledges the comparative modernness of the Pahlavi books) by observing:

જે પેહેલવીમાં હાલમાં થોડાએક બોલ છે તેહેને દસ્તુર લોકો જેમ જેહેને ગમેચ તે વાંચેછે* પેહેલવીમાં દાહાનો બોલ છે તેહેને કેટલાએક [જવમ] કરીને વાંચેછે અને કેહેછે જે પેહેલવી મધે દાહાડને જવમ કરીને કેહેછે અને કેટલાએક દસ્તુરો દાહાડના બોલને [જોમ] કરીને વાંચેછે*

"The Pahlavi, of which there are now a few words, the Dasturs read as they list. There is a Pahlaví word for 'a day' which some read *jawam*, and which they say is *jawam* in Pahlavi; but some Dasturs read the word *jom*." The word here referred to, expressed by [Pahlavi] in Pahlavi, is neither more nor less than the Hebrew *iom*, or *yom* a day. Alleged translations by the priests from Pahlaví, it will be apparent, are to be received *cum grano*.

† Barhán-i-Kátagh, under Zardusht.

7. The *Sháhnámah* of Firdausi, we have already particularly noticed. It is at least thirteen centuries posterior to the time of Zoroaster. As the Pársís lay very great stress upon it, I shall here introduce the account which it gives of Zoroaster.

The passage translated, with every advantage, into verse imitative of the original, is the following :—

Fulfil we the rules that should govern a king,
When back to God's service the sinner we bring.
From the daughter of Kaisár's imperial line,
(Nahid was the name of the princess divine)
Two brothers—twin children of beauty were born,
Like the moon at her full or the smiles of the morn.
And call we the eldest famed Asfandiyár
The leader of battles, the monarch of war.
When years had rolled on there up sprung from the earth,
A tree of strange produce, of marvellous birth,
High surmounting the palace of Gushtásp it grew,
And boundless the shadow its thick branches threw,
Its branches sage counsel, and wisdom its fruit,
The eater wes changed to a man from a brute.
Thrice holy that tree — its blessed name Zardasht,
And Ahriman's power before it was crushed.
  In me, O king, the prophet said, behold
Him who the way of wisdom shall unfold,
Observe the starry heavens and wide-spread earth,
And own the Almighty hand that gave them birth,
Ere matter was, ere yet was heat, they heard,
And rose rejoicing at their Maker's word.
Could any thus have done but I alone?
In me then know thy God, thy Maker own;
By this instructed, the Eternal learn,
And in his works creation's God discern;
Believe his prophet, in his faith abide,
And take his laws and statutes for thy guide,
In all thy actions own him for thy Lord,
And in creation trace his heavenly word;
Tread thou obedient in his faith, for they
Alone rule well who own a mightier sway.
  Warmed by the words of truth the monarch heard,
And gave obedience to the prophet's word.
Straight to all climes his warrior hosts repair,
To all the mandate of Gushtásp declare:
The rites of fire commence ; the faithful few,

Dismayed the Gabar's impious altars view.
Ere yet the worship through the world had spread,
A'zar bar-zín first rears its stately head.
Before the fane a plant of wonderous power,
Confessed the prophet's care — and in the hour
It gained its utmost height ; the sacred flame
A convert found in Lohorásp's royal name.
'Tis Irán's glory that to her was given
To spread though listening lands the faith of heaven.
In Irán first arose the man divine
Who claimed the apostle's name, the prophet's line.
From heaven, he cried, I come, my place of birth,
Sent from the glory of the skies to earth ;
In Heaven I saw the Highest, and he gave
The Zandavastá fraught with power to save.
In hell, I saw the evil one, beheld
The realms of Ahriman to light revealed.
And now I come, O King of men, to thee,
And bring the passport of eternity.
He spake and at his word the son of Lohorásp
Leader of Irán's host the royal Gushtásp,
For so the men of Irán named their chief,
Bound on the Gabar's belt in token of belief;
The faith of fire-diffusing fills the land,
And Irán worships at her king's command.
Enshrined 'mid prophets sits the priest of guile
*Fills falsehood's cup and spreads the ready wile."**

The faith of Zoroaster, though poetically described, is here represented as a system of delusion. I call upon the Pársís to mark the fact.

* E. B. Eastwick.—The original Persian of this passage, rendered into verse by my friend, I extracted from a copy of the Sháhnámah, shown to me last year by Habib Khán, the minister of the Nawáb of Junágad in Kátiáwád. I mention this circumstance, because in the MSS., for reasons already mentioned, there may be some variations. The following is part of what is given by Mr. Atkinson in his Abridgement of the Sháhnámah, published by the Oriental Translation Fund. "In those days lived Zardusht, the Gaber, who was highly accomplished in the knowledge of divine things ; and having waited upon Gushtásp, the king became greatly pleased with his learning and piety, and took him into his confidence. The philosopher explained to him the doctrines of the fire-worshippers, and by his art he reared a tree before the house of Gushtásp, beautiful in its foliage and branches, and whoever ate of the leaves of that tree became learned and accomplished in the mys

8. The *Zartusht* or *Zartasht-Námah* is a work in Persian, composed by a Pársí named Zartusht-Bĕhrám, and bearing the date of A. D. 1277. It is very highly valued by the Pársís, as containing the alleged history of their prophet Zoroaster. It forms the basis and substance of the *Maujazát-i-Zartusht* of Edal Dáru, and it is frequently referred to and quoted by the other controversialists who have lately appeared. The titles of its chapters are given by Dr. Hyde; and it is copiously quoted by Anquetil du Perron in his Life of Zoroaster. A brief view of its contents, and a few words respecting its merits, are here necessary. A translation of the whole work by E. B. Eastwick, Esq. appears in the Appendix, A.

The author of the Zartusht-Námah informs us, as we have already seen, that the work was hastily composed by him, and that too in suspicious circumstances. "In this day of A'zár," he says, "I took [this work] in hand. In A'bán was the feast, [and] we were intoxicated (*mast*). During the night of Khur I wrote it to the end. In this very day, I completed it."

It is at once apparent from the date of the work, upwards of sixteen hundred years posterior to Zoroaster, that it does not contain a personal testimony to the life of that individual.

teries of the future world, and those who ate of the fruit thereof became perfect in wisdom and holiness.

"In consequence of the illness of Lohorásp, who was nearly at the point of death, Zardusht went to Balkh for the purpose of administering relief to him, and he happily succeeded in restoring him to health. On his return he was received with additional favour by Gushtásp, who immediately afterwards became his disciple. Zardusht then told him that he was the prophet of God, and promised to shew him miracles. He said he had been to heaven and to hell. He could send any one, by prayer to heaven; and whomsoever he was angry with he could send to hell. He had seen the seven mansions of the celestial regions, and the thrones of sapphires; and all the secrets of heaven were made known to him by his attendant angel. He said that the sacred book, called Zandavastá, descended from above expressly for him, and that if Gushtásp followed the precepts in that blessed volume, he would attain celestial felicity Gushtásp readily became a convert to his *doctrines, forsaking the pure adoration of God for the religion of the fire-worshippers*."—Atkinson's Sháhnámah, pp. 385, 386.

It is not the narrative of a contemporary well acquainted with the facts of the case, and challenging the observation and corrections, if such were needed, of those as well acquainted with them as himself. It is not even a digest of information published by others, and to which reference can now be made to ascertain its accuracy. Not the slightest dependence can be placed upon it as a historical authority.

It opens with an invocation similar to what is commonly used by Musalmán writers, and which does not require any particular notice. It then makes us acquainted with an interview which the author had with an old priest, who showed to him a dusty volume in the Pahliví language, of which neither the name nor the source was known.* The contents of this book, he promised to set forth in Persian verse; and after a dream about the importance of his undertaking, he returned to the Mobed, who is said to have related to him the legends which he has recorded.

With regard to the ancestry of Zartusht, it is declared, that he was descended from Faridun, his grandfather being Patarasp, and his father Purshasp, and his mother Daghdú.

The early dreams of his mother, were certainly of a fearful character. There is no dignity connected with the narrative of them. From a portentous cloud, there issues a shower of lions, tigers, wolves, dragons, crocodiles, and panthers, and other horrible and ravenous creatures and imaginings. One of the monsters rushes upon Daghdú, threatening prematurely to tear her child from her side. She is terribly afraid; but her fears are at length calmed by the infant, who makes his appearance in this extremity. A hill descends from the firmament, and forth from it there rushes a blast which puts the monstrous crew to flight, with the exception of a wolf, a lion, and a pard, which retired, however, before the rod of Zartusht, who ultimately returns to his resting-place without injury to

* Zartusht Béhrám himself acknowledges that this is the case. Edal Dáru (Maujazát-i-Zartusht, p. 33) hints that it was the *Wajar-Kard*, written by Mediomáh the son of A'rásp, the paternal uncle of Zoroaster, who was born about twenty-three years before the "prophet." This work we afterwards notice.

his parent, and there conducts a conversation for her special instruction. The whole Daghdú ascertains to have been a dream; and she applies to a sage for its interpretation. In order to satisfy her inquiries, he has recourse to Astrology, a science, falsely so called, which every educated Pársí youth in Bombay acknowledges to be exploded.

> With quadrant viewing, then, he marks with care
> What signs and changes in the sun appear,
> And next the stars observing he discerns
> The horoscope, and slow surveys by turns
> Bahrám and Nahid, Tír, and Kaiwán old,
> Each planet circling in its path of gold.

The sage interprets the dream as indicative of Zoroaster's greatness and his triumph over his enemies; and he attributes his success to his computation of the stars, from which he learns that Daghdú was in her fifth month, and twenty-third day. It must be admitted, if this were the case, that the science of astrography is now on the decline. Are we to look for its revival to Mr Assistant Professor Naurojí Fardunjí, or any of his enlightened pupils?

The birth of Zoroaster is said to have bee nattended with a notable miracle. The moment he appeared in the regions of day, he "laughed" outright, and thus, in a suitable manner, intimated the importance and solemnity of his mission to this sinful world. "Great and small heard his laugh." "The women were envious of his laughter." "All who were unclean and evil, were stung to the heart at that laughter." The "magicians said, this is a calamity to us. We must remove this child from the world."

How they came to know of the infant's appointed destiny we are not informed, unless we suppose it was revealed to them by magic, more famous for its deceptions than its prophetical discoveries. They are represented, however, as bent on the destruction of the infant. Dúránsarún, the chief of the magicians, and the ruler at the place of the nativity of Zartusht, repairs to the house of his parents, demands a sight of him, raises a dagger for his destruction, is struck with anguish, and has his hand withered up. His followers, however, at his request, bore off the infant; and, instead of simply endeavouring to retain possession of his person, they threw him into an immense fire of blazing timber, naphtha, and brimstone. He was able to fall asleep in the midst of the horrible conflagration; and his mother who had been alarmed on receiving accounts of his death, had no sooner found him than she "kissed his eyebrows and his forehead" neither more nor less than "*two hundred times.*" "Again the magicians, fiends, and París, displayed their fierceness." They endeavoured to drive oxen upon him when exposed in a narrow defile; but one of them stood over him, defending him, till the others passed. They exposed him in a similar way to wild horses; and he was protected in a like manner by "a mare that was the chief of mares." His mother was overjoyed on the occasion of his deliverance; but as "God was his protector," it is asked, "what could Dews or París do to harm him?" "If a hundred thousand accursed Dews come to work you ill, if they hear from you the name of God, they will one and all take to flight." The "prophet" is next exposed to the attacks of wolves, exasperated by the destruction of their young; but "the instant he placed his hand on the foremost wolf, its mouth was closed," and the fury of its companions was calmed. Two cows then came, and placed their teats in the mouth of the infant; and consequently "the breath (spirit) of the wolf will be with that of the cow, if it be the merciful will of God." Bartarúsh, a chief magician, now ascertained that he could not be destroyed by the counsels of his companions; and sets upon prophesying about his future greatness, and reads the stars on his behalf to Zoroaster's father. Burzin-Karús, an old man, asks permission to bring up the child, and it is granted. He reached his seventh year in safety, during which "no hot wind breathed from the devices of the Dews working magic."

Bartarúsh and Dúránsarún now vainly set upon Zartusht with their magic. After this he became sick. Bartarúsh, under the pretence of administering medicine, attempts to poison him; but his prescriptions are detected, and he is sternly rebuked by the boy. "Every thing," it is said, "was magic in those days, and nothing was done without the magic art. The inpure fiends consulted with the magicians. They walked and sat with them on the earth." Even Purshasp, the father of Zoroaster, walked in their ways; and he was consequently rebuked by his child, who also so discoursed with Bartarúsh that "through grief he was sick with fever," and "he lay afflicted with that illness, also his wife and children." Zoroaster was now fifteen years of age.

And now for his doings in his youth. He is said to have been particularly attentive to what he conceived to have been the duties of religion. "His heart was directed to Irán;" and he and his companions seem to have arrived at a sea on the road, which is no more to be found, and which was then destitute of ships. He wept from the difficulty of getting the women conveyed across, as it was improper to take them into the water, and expose their persons. He at length found, however, that they could walk through on dry land, and they followed him as their leader. They travelled for a month, and at length reached the confines of Irán, where Zoroaster was highly honoured at a feast. Zoroaster here had an extraordinary dream, which, though he was a "prophet" required to be expounded to him by an interpreter. It was explained as intimating that he was to be removed to the presence of God, where the mysteries of the divine will were to be unfolded to him through the Zand-Avastá, which when "read with a loud voice," should put the fiends to flight. He proceeds on his journey, and reaches the waters of Dáetí, "a deep sea without bottom"! His courage enabled him to look to it without dismay. Zartusht's "heart was not afraid." "The first stream reached the middle of his leg; the second flowed above his knee; the third reached his waist; and the fourth came up to his neck." The waters, it was explained, were emblematical of four endeavours to spread and purify the faith by Zoroaster, Hushidár, Máh-Hushidár, and the Sásánish.

The angel Bahman now came to Zoroaster, and said, "Arise and appear before God;" "close thine eyes," and "proceed swiftly." "When Zartusht opened his eyes, he found himself in heaven." Two brilliant assemblies presented themselves to his view; and the angels were joyed to see him. They pointed with their fingers, and Zartusht went into the presence of God. He asked first "Who of God's creatures on earth is best?" He is informed "That God who was and is, is [best];" and that "He of all men is best who is true of heart;" "also he who is merciful to all things in the world, to *fires*, *waters*, and *animals*, whether *sheep*, *cows*, or *apes*." In reply to inquiries about the angels and the divine mysteries, he is said to have been thus addressed: — "I have no foreknowledge of evil acts.... Think not that evil comes except from Ahriman, and from the accursed and impure fiend," etc. "Then in all the sublime sciences, both from the beginning and from the end, in all these severally, God made Zartusht wise." "He acquainted him with the revolution of the heavens, and with the good and bad influences of the stars, with the Hauris also of paradise, whose spirits are formed of pure light, also with the forms and stature of the angels adorned like lofty cypress trees." "He showed him also the face of Ahriman the evil one," who "raised a cry from the pit of hell." Most extraordinary signs and wonders then followed. Zartusht passes through a mountain of fire; and his body felt no harm. Vast quantities of melted brass were poured upon his breast; and "not a hair of his body was lost." "Again, they opened his belly, and dragged forth the inside, and returned it to its place." "Afterwards," he is informed by God in explanation of these marvels, "when the true faith throughout the world shall be diffused and the Dews dispersed, then to fight against them a high-priest shall gird up his loins." "A′darbád Máraspand shall come and shall overthrow all their devices; he shall pour over himself that molten brass." "All shall learn the right way." More, it must be allowed, is A′darbád needed at the present time than in the days of the Sassanides. Zoroaster's conversation with God is continued. "Whatsoever is bright and full of light," says the Divine Being, "let them know that this is the *brightness of my glory*." "Nothing in the world is better than light, both among small and great." "Of light we created the angels and paradise, afterwards hell was formed from darkness." "Then God taught the Zand-Avastá to Zartusht," and commanded him to make known his statutes to king Gustásp.

After his interview with God, Zoroaster was visited by the Amsháspands. *Bahman* delivers to him the care of cattle. "Acquaint," he said, "every man of understanding to take great care of sheep." "Let no one kill a calf, or a sheep which is a lamb." "I am the guardian of sheep. All the sheep that are in the world, I have received from God." And where had some of them, at this time, not strayed? *Ardebehísht* commits the fire-temples to the "prophet's" care; and adds, "when they have erected the abodes of fire-worship, let them bequeath vast possessions for their support," "since that light is from the light of God." "All it asks of men is wood; it asks neither more nor less. Its body is powerful like wood. Every moment it becomes younger." *Sháhríwar* orders the edges of warlike instruments to be kept clean, and is so particular in his instructions about them, that he scarcely takes it for granted that Zoroaster is possessed of common sense. *Asfandármad* orders the face of the earth to be "kept clean from blood, and filth, and carrion;" and declares that "he is the best of kings who encourages the cultivation of the soil." *Khurdád* lays down injunctions about streams of water, which are ordered to be preserved in purity. *Amardád* discourses of the care of trees and vegetation, and with reference to the Mobeds, says, "Let them *exert subtlety in every way, that they may be able to give an answer to all men*," even I suppose to ——.

Zoroaster returned from heaven "glad of heart;" but the magicians were filled with sorrow. On seeing the predicament in which they were, his "heart was filled with laughter." "Then he recited one passage from the Zand-Avastá, and raised his voice aloud;" and "when the Dews heard his words, they all fled from the battle!" And, "if you place your reliance on God, you may break your own neck without harm."

Zoroaster next bends his footsteps towards Balkh, the

court of Sháh Gushtásp,* where he is received with high honours. He is invited to enter upon the discourses of wisdom and the sages of the day were compelled to yield to him the victory, and the Sháh is greatly interested in his discussions and shows him favour. On a second occasion, he terrifies the sages with a display of learning. A great assembly of the mighty men of the court, and of the wise, is called to witness his powers. He states his own pretensions as a prophet, and flatters the prince, saying, "your sway is over all people." He then recites the Avastá and the Zand; and counsels the king about its use. When asked for proofs of its divine origin, he said, being witness in his own cause, "*My* proof is sufficient ;-it is the commandment I have brought." "By means of this book which I have brought, all fiends and magicians shall be banished from the earth." A chapter of it is read, but it did not at first give satisfaction. At length, however, the Sháh praises Zoroaster, and promises inquiry, and thus satisfies his instructor. The sages again take counsel for the destruction of the prophet, and "search for all that is most impure in the world, such as blood, and filth, and things impure, and the divided heads of a cat and dog, also the bones of carrion!" "They placed them on his pillow, and in his robes." On their return from their adventure, they warn Gushtásp against the wiles of Zartusht, and the king sends to examine his furniture and apparel, which were produced in court. "When they had turned these things over, the heads of the cat and dog were found, the nails and the hair, and the bones which had dropped from the bodies of the dead." Gushtásp "bit his finger with his teeth." Zoroaster's "two eyes were blind at the carrion." In vain he protested his innocence. The king "cast from him the Zand-Avastá, and ordered Zartusht into confinement." Zartusht "remained seven days in that doleful state." But, now, hear the story of his chief miracle, that of the ***black horse***. When this favorite brute of the king was one morning examined by his keeper, it was found that his four feet

* Darius Hystaspes.

had disappeared in his belly! The wise men could neither account for the phenomenon, nor provide a remedy. "Every one" in the city, "was bereft of his senses." Zoroaster, when informed of the circumstance, offers his services; and "the king of the world having removed his bands," he promised to effect a cure on four conditions. The first of these was, that he should be accepted as a prophet, and the duties of religion observed; and as soon as compliance with it was promised, he placed his hand on the horse, and the right fore-leg came out. The second condition was, that Aspandiár, the son of Gushtásp, should fight for religion: and when it was accepted, "the right hind-leg of the steed came out." The third condition was, that he should find access to the queen and convert her to his own faith; and when it was, granted, another foot appeared. The fourth condition was, that the keeper of the king's gate should be compelled to disclose the names of the persons who had carried the filth into Zartusht's chamber; and when it was complied with, and the "wise men were carried forth and impaled alive," the fourth leg made its appearance, and the Sháh honoured and praised the prophet. The Sháh wished four additional favours to be conferred upon him; but, on receiving a hint from Zoroaster, he limits his request to one favour,—that he should see his place in paradise, which was granted. Bahman, Ardebehísht, A'zar Khurdád, and A'zar Gushásp approach him on steeds; and "from dread he fell down from his throne." When he arose, he begged the intercession of Zartusht, who gave him a draught which put him to sleep. During his slumbers, he saw paradise, and all that he wished to be revealed. When he awoke, he gave his courtiers some trifles. He gave some perfumes to Jámásp, who "immediately knew all knowledge." He gave a seed of a pomegranate to Aspandiár, whose body became like a stone, absolutely invulnerable. He called for Zoroaster, and asked him to read the whole of the Zand-Avastá. "The Dews fled from the rehearsal of the Zand. They all concealed themselves under the earth." The Mobeds are ordered forward, and the command is given that there should be a universal erection of fire-temples.

Zoroaster is now represented as expounding, in several articles, his faith to Gushtásp. We find no such summary as is attributed to him in the Zand-Avastá. The author of the Zartusht-Námah himself engages in the praise of God; and then proceeds with his marvellous narrative.

Zoroaster, it tells us in continuation, received one drop of a draught from the Creator; and "he immediately saw the world and every thing it. As one who slumbers and beholds in sleep, he saw good and evil without concealment. He saw the blood and brains of the bodies of men, and the good and evil thoughts of every one," and something scarcely short of all existences, celestial, terrestrial and infernal. He then describes his visions; and the manner in which they were interpreted, as intimating his own mission, the devastations of the Ashkanians, and the prosperous reign of A'rdeshir Bábegán, and subsequent occurrences, including the decline of the Zoroastrian faith, and the infliction of great and awful judgments. He continues his inquiries of God; and other signs of the latter days are unfolded. He asks, "*when will the wearers of dark garments be discomfited*,"and shows great anxiety for different kinds of information. The army of the enemies of the faith, he is told, is to come from Rúm, or Constantinople, — a direction from which it did *not* come when the Persian faith was overthrown in Irán; and various pretended predictions are delivered, with serious blunders in chronology, history, and geography, too tedious to mention.

The author of the work concludes with the praise of Zoroaster, approaching to blasphemy, and tells us of his intoxication, — either from the fumes of his belly or his brains, — during the day intervening between the two days which he devoted to its composition.

Such is a summary of the contents of the Zartusht-Námah, the most important testimony, as the Pársís reckon it, to the alleged divine mission of Zoroaster, and which the high-priest of the Rasamís has thought to be of such importance, that he has anew given an expansion of it in Gujarátí, for the sake of the Běhdíns of Bombay. Alas! for the common sense of mankind. If it had the sway, the work would be seen by all to be a tissue of fables and falsehoods. It is void of sobriety, rationality, and credibility. I do not wonder that the editor of the Chábuk reprobated the republication of its substance, in the most unmeasured terms, when the work Maujazát-i-Zartusht was given to the world.

So much, then, for the testimony expressly brought forward by the Pársí controversialists in favour of the alleged divine mission of Zoroaster. How insignificant, unsatisfactory, and absurd, it is, from beginning to end, must be apparent to every reader. The appeal which has been made to it, indeed, is calculated to overthrow the cause which it is intended to support. I am convinced that some of my opponents themselves more than suspected that this would be the result. Aspandiárjí says, "If the Padre be not satisfied with the number of authorities, I beg he would refer to the following others, viz. Rauzat-as-Safá, Habib-al-Assair, &c."* Authorities, he must bear in mind, are to be examined as well as named, to be weighed as well as numbered. Those already mentioned by him have been found wanting, or hostile to his own cause; and those now mentioned are exactly similar. The arrow, which he has shot at a venture, lights in the Pársí camp.

9. See, for example, how the author of the *Rauzat-as-Safá* writes of Zoroaster. "Gushtásp was reckoned a prince exalted in power, abundant in justice, sublime in energy: he however engaged in one criminal undertaking, namely, his adopting the faith of Zerdusht. The Táríkh Bina Gítí, and the Táríkh Maajem, state, that Zerdusht, the sage, appeared at this time: he was at first instructed by one of the disciples of Jeremiah the prophet, until he had learned the sciences of the Arabians: he is said to have devoted himself particularly to astrology, and to have ascertained, from the positions of the stars, that some one resembling Moses was to appear, to whom the reflection of the Creator of light and darkness would manifest itself, through the brilliancy of fire and his search of it; which afterwards gave rise to his pretensions. Satan, after this, suggested to his mind, 'The promised person is a type

* Hádí-i-Gum-Rahán, p. 87.

of thyself'; on which, Zerdusht gave himself up to retirement, seclusion, and holy meditation, to such a degree, that a glory shone round him, through the multitude of his austerities: from the want of some spiritual guide to make him surmount the obstacles of presumption and idle vanities, Satan exhibited to him that splendor under the form of fire, and began to converse with him from the midst of it. Zerdusht collected all his conversations with Iblis, in a book called by him Zend-pázend; and reckoning himself a prophet, exhorted the people to embrace the faith of the Magi and the worship of fire. It is to be observed, that the name of Zindík is given to the heretics who believe in this book. The people always so prone to sedition, that even while the grapes of events were still unripe, they commenced their fanatic proceedings: in Azarbaij'án, particularly, great multitudes, deluded by Zerdusht, laid their heads at his feet, and the seducer spoke to them after this manner: — 'I am a prophet: the Holy Spirit aids me to reveal the secrets of futurity; he has brought me a communication from the Almighty, the Holy One.' When this declaration was made public, the fame of Zerdusht was circulated by every tongue, and the Zand-pázend had become the topic of general conversation: his praises were at last repeated in the court of Gushtásp, so that this prince testified a desire to see him. As the king attached great importance to an interview with Zerdusht, he set out from the confines of Balkh with a numerous retinue and great pomp to meet him; so that matters were finally brought from the mystery of concealment to the certainty of demonstration. Gushtásp afterwards, through the exertion of his son Aspandiár, came over to the religion of the Magi, and erected fire-temples in all parts of his dominions. He also commanded twelve thousands cow-hides to be tanned, and made into sheets as fine as the skins of the gazel, on the pages of which, illumined with gold and silver, were inscribed things which ought to have been committed to the flames, namely, the subtle delusions which proceeded from the corrupt nature of Zerdusht. Gushtásp, on his arrival at Istakhár, ordered a vault to be made, in which the Zand-pázend was deposited with great solemnity, and also appointed a considerable force to guard it: at the same time that he prohibited the common people from being instructed in it, he exhorted the nobility to guard and peruse it. He next put to death a great many who were opposed to the religion of the Magi, so that all people embraced the worship of fire: being convinced how necessary it was to abandon the path of opposition and hostility, therefore they all exclaimed with one accord,

'Internally and externally we are branded with the character of conformity:
'Internally we are as you; and outwardly also we are the same."

The Guebres (on whom be the curses of the Almighty!) relate strange things of Zerdusht; among which is the following:—God had originally created the soul of Zerdusht in a tree, which was placed in the highest firmament: after which his essence was removed into a cow; of whose milk Zerdusht's father having partaken, the influence of it was communicated to his mother. Satan, however, being determined to destroy the child, breathed on his mother with a pestilential blast, so that she became sick; but the same instant a voice from Heaven said to her, 'Thou shalt find relief from these pains'; after which her affliction was changed into health. At the moment of Zerdusht's birth, he laughed so loud, that all present heard the sound distinctly. As soon as he was grown up, he retired to one of the mountains of Ardebíl,* on his descent from which he held a book in his hand, and said, 'This volume has descended to me from the roof of the house which is on that mountain.' This volume he called the Zend; but as its meaning was not intelligible to all men, he gave the name of Pázend to a Commentary written to explain it. The following is another of those traditions: — Zerdusht had a kind of fire, which he could handle without injury to himself; and when Gushtásp came to see him, he put some of it

* "Ardebil, a city of Azarbai'ján, part of the Ancient Media: here are the tombs of the Shaikhs Seffi and Haidar, ancestors to the royal family of Persia. These two holy personages are highly venerated by the followers of Ali, and have procured for Ardebíl the title of Holy."

into the king's hands, who was also unhurt by it: and the same result followed when put it into the hands of others. Ibn A-thur records, that the fire at present worshipped by the Magi is derived from this; which, according to their belief, has never been extinguished. It is also said, that Zerdusht lay down on the threshold of the fire-temple, and ordered ten rotoli of brass to be put into four crucibles, which, when melted, was poured on his breast: whatever part of the metal touched his breast was instantly turned into small globules, nor was there a visible trace of any injury sustained by him. Some writers assure us, that Gushtásp, in the beginning of his reign, not only opposed the tenets of Zerdusht, but even detained him in prison during seven years: it however happened, that one day the royal train came to the same place, where suddenly his horse's feet were so drawn into his belly, that not a trace of them was discernible, so that all the people exclaimed with wonder, 'What can be the cause of this?' Gushtásp, sending for Zerdusht out of prison, asked him to explain this extraordinary, event: to whom Zerdusht thus answered; 'This has been caused by you unbelief: you are not obedient to me, who am a prophet: now, therefore, if you will obey me, I shall pray to the Almighty to restore your horse's feet.' To this proposal Gushtásp having agreed, Zerdusht prayed to God; upon which the horse was straight restored to his former state, and the king immediately professed his belief in the prophetic mission of Zerdusht. In short, there are many things recorded of this personage, which, if repeated at full length, would be the cause of too great prolixity. Háfiz A'brú relates, in his Táríkh, that Gushtásp sent an annual tribute to Turkestán; but this was now prevented by Zerdusht, who said to him: 'It does not become a sovereign, adorned with the collar of true faith, to send tribute to an idol-worshipper':—

'Thus spoke the aged Zerdusht to the youthful monarch:
'It is not in conformity with my tenets,
'That you pay tribute to the sovereign of Chín;
'Such conduct is unworthy of those who profess my faith.'

On this, Gushtásp kept back the tribute: and as all the people of Irán had now embraced his belief, Zerdusht, besides, thus addressed the king : — 'Now is the time to give battle to the Turks ; for it is not permitted to those who adopt my faith to maintain communion with infidels : they are assisted by Satan, but our support and aid come from the Great and Glorious God.'"*

Here is the establishment of Zoroaster's divine mission with a witness! I must now be excused from following Aspandiárjí farther, till he give some visibility, or form, to himself, by producing ***actual quotations*** from the works he mentions and showing their ***applicability*** to the matters which he professes to discuss.

Beside the works now mentioned, occasional references are made by the Pársí controversialists to some other works, of which it may be proper for us to take a brief notice.

10. The *Wajar-Kard*, is said by Edal Dáru † to have been written by Mediomáh the son of A'rásp, the paternal uncle of Zoroaster, who was born about twenty-three years ‡ before the "prophet," and who afterwards became his disciple. The very name of this work, the Distinguisher or Teacher, awakens suspicions as to its antiquity. Edal Dáru himself very innocently and unconsciously reveals its novelty. At the tenth page of his work, he makes it explain the meaning of the Sadra, or sacred vestment of the Pársís, not only in Zand, but Páhlivi, or Pázand, and Persian ! The able and intelligent editor of the Chábuk thus writes respecting it, on the occasion of an appeal being made to it in a small Pársí periodical. "What is written in the Rah-Namá-i-Zartusht about the

* Rauzat-as-Safá. Part translated by Mr. Shea ; under the title of the History of the early Kings of Persia, pp. 283 — 288.

† Maujazát-i Zartusht, p. 33.

‡ Acording to an extract from the Wajar-Kard, given in the third number of the Rahnamá-i-Zartusht (p. 75), Mediomáh modestly speaks of himself as "possessed of all wisdom, observation, and intelligence, etc." He says that Zoroaster was born in the 110th year of the reign of Gushtásp and on Khurdád the 6th day of the month, and in the month Farvardin, of that year.

book called the Wajar-Kard being written in the time of king Gushtásp by Mediomáh, a disciple of the exalted Zartusht, is altogether erroneous. The book was neither made by Mediomáh, nor made at the time of king Gushtásp, ; but it is certain that it was made after the time of Yazdejard. Many Persian copies of this Wajar-Kard are found with the Dasturs and Mobeds ; and it manifestly appears from them that the material of this history did not exist at the time of Gushtásp. The Pahliví which is contained in it, is contrary to rule and regulation. By the foregoing reasons, it is proved, that this book was made after Alexander the Great, and the Arabs had destroyed our libraries. Another consideration is this, that matters which took place after the time of Yazdejard are written in the book ; and if the book were written in the days of Gushtásp, how, and in what manner, *could* the events which happened 1,200 years after it find admission into it ? It is proverbial, that a child cannot be born before its father. Our dasturs have made extracts from some religious books, and written them according to question and answer in Pahliví, and given the work the name of the *Wajar-Kard.* We have no time at present fully to expose this matter ; but if it be the wish of any Zoroastrian that we should compose a pamphlet against the Rah-Namá-i-Zartusht for gratuitous distribution among our subscribers, we shall afterward make a complete exposure." The learned Mullá Firuz, in his work entitled *Avizah-Din*, candidly admits that this work and the Sháyist-Náshâyist, also attributed to Mediomáh, are not genuine and authentic. "The two or five Pahliví books, which now exist," he says, "were made by our own people after the destruction of our government..... They did not exist at the time of the holy Zoroaster."*

I have had only a casual inspection of the work, granted to me through his grandson by Edal Dáru, in the presence of Mr. Westergaard; but we have found it to be identical with the *Vad-*

* Avizhah-Dín, p. 303, etc. The remarks which follow in this work are well worthy of the attention of the Pársís.

jerguerd briefly described by Anquetil du Perron.* From the specimens of it with which Edal Daru has furnished us,† however, we are forced to come to the conclusion, that it is entirely destitute of authority. Its narratives are equally absurd with those of the Zartusht-Námah, of which it is said by some to be the foundation. I here insert a translation of such of them as are given at greatest length by the chief-priest of the Rasamís, the highest Pársí authority in Bombay. They present specimens of folly and credulity seldom surpassed.

"Another wonder of the holy Zand-Avastá is this. It is written in the book called the Wajar-Kard-Dín, that through the favour of God the distinguished (*khorhé*) glory, and grandeur, and marvel of the *Ahunavad Gáthá*, the seventh Háh of the Izashné, is so great that when it is read over a departed soul [body],—that is to say, after he is placed on the bier and carried to the Dakhma, — no bad odour arises from the body of that follower of the good-faith. And it is certain that from the blessing of reading the Avastá, on placing the body on the bier as above said, there is ease of the body of the departed; and from the blessing of the Avastá this inestimable blessing is derived. And another wonder of the Avastá is this:—Of its twenty-one glorious Núsks brought by the exalted Zoroaster from the presence of Yazdán, there is one named the Vandidád or Jud-Dew-Dád, [given against the devils], of which this is a miracle and wonder: — When our Mobeds re-

* Zand-Avastá, tom. ii. p. xxxix. After mentioning that the work is in Persian, and alleged to be a translation from the original Pahliví, and that it is in 82 pages 12mo., Anquetil says, "Le nom du *Vadjerguerd* signifie, *qui explique, Docteur.* Cet Ouvrage parle d'abord des *Darouns* (p. 1). Il donne ensuite les Prieres & les Cérémonies prescrites lorsque l'on cueille le *Barsom* (p. 9), le *Hom* (p. 13), lorsque l'on fait le *Zour* (p. 18), & plusieurs décisions qui regardent la Morale & les cérémonies de la Loi (p. 20-82).

Le volume commence par ces mots :

Pavan schamé Djatoun. Daroun aschoan...

Il finit par ceux-ci : *Khodae maaf darad vassalam.*

† Edal Darú's references to it may be seen in the Maujazát-i-Zartusht pp. 9, 26, 30, 32, 33, 40, 54, 55, 58, 79—82, 98.

solve to make the *Nirang-Dín*, and two of the pure Mobeds with holy carefulness take the *barasnúm*,—that is to say, when having drank the pure consecrated urine, for the purpose of cleansing their internal person from the filth and pollution of the world, and when having cleansed their outward person with *nirang* and *ava*, that it is to say, the consecrated urine and water, they sit in a pure place night and day serving God and reading the Zand-Avastá, the two Mobeds remain engaged, and according to the law of religion they carefully complete nine nights,and during these nine nights,—after each third night,—on the fourth day, and on the seventh day, and on the tenth day, they cleanse their body with pure *nirang* and water, and when after the completion of the nine nights, on the tenth day, preserving their souls in a good intention, they read the Izashné for six days according to the laws of religion, —then there is a consecrated white bull called by us *warsio*, which has not like others been castrated, and which is not shameless and diseased, which they keep healthy and in readiness for some time. Afterwards, those two careful Mobeds, having cleansed and consecrated and dried according to the laws of religion, two brazen pots, collect together into the first the urine of the white bullock, and into the other the *ava* or pure water, and keep the mouth of the vessels covered. Afterwards, these two Mobeds, having taken them to the place for performing the Izashné, the half of the night having passed, they commence the recitation of the Vandidád, Izashné, and Visparad. At the dawn, when these two Mobeds cease from the consecration of the nirang, they tie the mouth of the vessels with a clean cloth, and keep them separately in a pure place. Afterward, if we keep this pure urine and pure water in a bottle or in a clean vessel for the space of ten years, then they will remain as they are without smell, and without injury, while if a Jud-dín were to keep the same urine in a vessel, it would be injured in ten or fifteen days, and an evil odour would proceed from it, and if water were kept for many days, then insects would be produced in it. Wherefore, observe with the eye of wisdom, that as water in ten or twelve days becomes bad, so the urine and water from the blessing of the ceremonies of our religion, are not injured for the space of ten years, but remain in their original state. Wherefore, it ought to be certainly known, that all this goodness is owing to our holy Zand-Avastá. It ought to be known that this circumstance is mentioned in the first book of the Wajar-Kard."* And it ought also to be known, and is known, that all this is downright nonsense. My Pársí readers, I dare say, are now satisfied with the Wajar-Kard. I call upon Edal Darú to *prove* that it was written in the days of Gushtásp ; and I call upon him to translate the whole of it for the perusal of his countrymen. The appeal, which he has made to it is indeed worthy of the cause which it is intended to support.

11. To the *Ardai-Viráf-Námah,* Aspandiárjí has made a reference also very unfortunate. "It can never be denied," he says, "that the Vandidád made its appearance *immediately after the death of Zoroaster,* † and that the same book has been transmitted down to our days. If it had not then been in existence, what other authority was possessed by Ardai-bin-Viráf, and other wise men in the days of Ardeshir Bábagán,‡ and also by several other kings and dasturs both about and subsequent to the days of Nausherawán, for the propagation of their religion, an act in which Mazdak was slain." Now, be it observed, it was the very *want* of authorities on the Zoroastrian faith, which was the alleged cause of Ardai-Viráf's reputed miracles and visions. To make good

* Maujazát-i-Zartusht, pp. 79—82.

† This in the Gujarátí copy of Aspandiárj'is book is વંદીદાદ જર તોશ્ત પછી લાંમબી મુદત ગીઆ શુધી હતો, "The Vandidád existed a long time after the days of Zoroaster." There is no dispute about this point. The book exists even in the present day.

By what singular infatuation does the Mobed say in his English text, "The Vandidád made its appearance immediately *after the death of Zoroaster*"? It will be observed that he himself abandons the authenticity, and genuineness of the work. Perhaps, he is guilty of a mere *lapsus pennæ.*

‡ Ardeshir Bábagan ascended the throne about the year 223, A. D.

this assertion ; to show how easily some of the occurrences alleged, in the Námah, to have taken place, could be accounted for by a combination of the king and the priests, and consequent trickery and deception ; and to point out the utter worthlessness of the work as an authority, on which Edal Dáru, as well as Aspandiárjí, lays great stress,* let us look to the book itself.

In the commencement, we find this passage. "Ardeshír Bábegán, having settled the Persian Monarchy by the conquering of the provinces, and the putting to death of ninety kings, who refused to acknowledge his authority : and being also desirous to establish the national religion in its wonted purity, collected together all the priests, doctors, etc. of the Magian religion, to the amount of forty thousand, and addressed them as follows :

"'The revolution caused by the invasion of Alexander having destroyed the evidences of our holy religion, it is my wish that proper persons be selected from out of your number to collate and collect the laws left us by our prophet Zarátush, that we may follow these laws, and get rid of the heresies that have been from time to time introduced, and of the schisms that exist amongst us ; for this purpose let a selection be made out of your number, that this desirable object may be in the end obtained.' According to the king's order, four thousand were selected out of the forty thousand, which being reported to him, he ordered another selection to be made, and out of the four thousand four hundred were chosen, men of the most approved abilities, all of them being conversant with the mysteries of the Zand-Avastá.

"The king being farther intent on having the most able and clever men appointed to this business, ordered another selection to be made, and out of the four hundred, forty only were selected. A still farther selection being made, seven only remained out of the forty, who were men of the most holy lives, without blemish, and who had never wilfully com-

* Maujazát-i Zartusht, pp. 86, 110, 118.

mitted the least crime or sin against God or man.* These seven were taken before the king, who explained to them his wishes with respect to the laws, and the restoring the true religion of Zarátush to its ancient purity; but having himself also many doubts, he expressed a hope that these holy men would be able to convince not only himself, but the population of his empire, of the truth and sanctity of the Magian faith by some miracle. The seven holy men assented, and having pitched on one of their number, the six addressed the king as follows:—'Ardái Viráf, O king, is ready to convince you of the truth of our holy religion by a miracle, and we beg leave to recommend him to your Majesty as the most holy man in your vast empire; he has been devoted to the study of divine things since the age of seven years, and is infinitely our superior in every thing; we shall assist him to the best of our power in the grand undertaking; and for the better understanding of this, the soul of Ardái Viráf will take its flight to the presence of God, and will return with proofs that will convince the nation of the truth and sanctity of the Magian religion'. Ardái Viráf assented to this, and explained his belief in the goodness of God, who would permit this miracle to be performed, to retrieve so many people from the sin of heresy and schism.

"The king being well pleased at this determination, accompanied these holy men and the forty thousand priests, with his whole court, to the temple of fire, and joined with them devoutly in prayer; and Ardái Viráf having performed the usual ablutions, and attired himself in garments of the purest white; also put on the Panam, and, perfumed himself according to the rites of the Magian religion, again presented himself in an attitude of prayer and humility before the sacred fire.

"After this the king, with his suite, and the forty thousand priests, formed a circle round the temple, (which was given up entirely to Ardái Viráf and his six associates), for the bet-

* Extraordinary saints indeed, they must have been!

ter preventing of any kind of disturbance or molestation being given to these holy men.*

"Ardái Viráf having finished his prayers, reposed himself on a couch prepared for him, and his associates brought him some consecrated wine in a golden cup, and besought him to drink one portion out of three in faith and truth; and the second portion with the same fear and respect for truth; and the third portion with the promise of performing only good actions. After having drunk the wine, he composed himself to rest,† and continued in this state of repose and abstraction for seven days and seven nights, during which time his six associates continued watching and in prayer, as well as the forty thousand of the priesthood, who, with the king and his court, had formed a circle on the outside of the temple, to prevent any person approaching to disturb the holy persons in the inside.

"At the expiration of the seven days and nights, Ardái Viráf gave some signs of animation, and after some time sat up on the couch, to the great joy of his associates, who saluted him with great pleasure; and the king having been made acquainted with the circumstance, came also to make his congratulations, and desired that he would lose no time in informing them of what he had seen, that they might also understand. Ardái Viráf replied, 'I am quite exhausted, O king, with long fasting, but after that I have refreshed myself with food, and returned thanks to God for his goodness, I will relate to you what I have seen and heard.' Refreshments having been brought, of which he partook, he ordered that a writer should be brought, who might write down what he should relate both of Heaven and Hell, that all people might know the rewards for the good and the punishments that awaited the wicked doer.

"The writer being seated near Ardái Viráf, prepared to

* Rather, for the purpose of more securely effecting fraud, by the exclusion of the public?

† Query: Was he not intoxicated like the author of the Zartusht-Námah?

write down what he should relate. Ardái Viráf commenced his relation."

"The king" it is added at the close, "being much pleased with the narration of Ardái Viráf, and placing implicit confidence in it,* ordered it to be promulgated throughout the empire, and having rewarded the good priest, by showering on him all kinds of favours, and giving him a place of honour, he ordered the relation to be written in letters of gold, and placed in the archives of the empire.

"The king further directed the observance of these precepts, and made known, that in the failure of their non-observance, punishment awaited: and for their more speedy promulgation, the king ordered the priests to disperse themselves throughout the empire, to instruct the people in the ways of holiness, and in the laws of the prophet Zarátush, and in their confirmation as brought down by the holy man Ardái Viráf. By these means heresy and schism were banished, the empire was restored to tranquillity, and remained so for many years."

Let us have a few specimens of the discoveries which were thus honoured, and had these wonderful results. It will be seen by all, that they are nonsensical, and not prophetical.

When Ardái Viráf, and his reputed guide Sarosh Izad, approached the bridge of Chinavad, they "heard a strong and extraordinary voice." "I perceived", says Ardái, "that it came from a *dog*, that was chained with a collar and chain of gold, near the right side of the bridge. I was at first afraid of his barking, and of the huge teeth he displayed, and said to myself, this monster may devour me." He was comforted by his guide, and after he had recovered himself a little from his terror, he asked, "Why is this dog here? for what purpose is he here placed? and why does he make so great a noise?" Sarosh Izad replied, "He makes this noise

* It was perhaps not expedient for him to inquire into the *authority* of the dreams and visions. "*Methought*", said Ardái Viráf, "my soul took its flight towards the holy regions." — Pope's Translation, p, 9. — *Methinks*, it never left the earth, except perhaps borne up by the fumes of the "consecrated wine."

to frighten Ahriman, and keeps watch here to prevent his approach; his name is Zeriag Goash, and the devils shake at his voice; and any soul that has during its residence in the lower world, hurt, or ill-used, or destroyed any of those animals, is prevented by Zeriag Goash, from any farther proceeding across the bridge."

A dog again frightening the devil! A chained dog the protector of souls, and the guardian of heaven! A dog performing the work of judgment in behalf of its species! Let all tremble at his "barking, and the huge teeth he displays." And let every one say, "perhaps he may devour *me*."

The travellers find their way into the Hamistán Behísht, or the first heaven. "The people you see there," says Sarosh, "will remain until the day of judgment. They are those whose good works exactly counterbalance their evil ones; but if either preponderated, they would go to either a better or worse place." On this statement, we have already commented. If it be true, we have only to perform one good action for every evil one, and finally have one good action in excess, and yet be saved!

In Máh Pia Behisht, the third heaven, or the heaven of the moon, are found, says Sarosh, the souls of "the good and well intentioned; but who from indolence performed the worship of the true God in a careless or negligent manner." Happy, indolent, careless, and negligent fellows! You are tolerably well elevated and dignified in the third heaven. No great mishap will occur, if *we* "perform the worship of the true God in a careless or negligent manner." Will not many hasten to this inference?

When the company were about to see the punishments inflicted on the wicked, "they came to a river that emitted the most pestilential vapours, and on it floated a vast number of souls, in all the agony of drowning, many of them sinking, and all of them in the greatest agitation, calling on God, and complaining of their lot; but all was lost in the winds, no body heard them, or paid attention to their complaints; no person came to their assistance, all their cries were unavailing. All kinds of noxious reptiles, with which the river abounded, gave them no respite, and they were carried down the stream notwithstanding their cries and lamentations. I felt astonished and humbled by this sight, and pity for their sufferings entered into my heart, and I inquired of my conductors, who they were who merited such punishment, and what was the name of the river; to which Sarosh Izad replied, 'The river that you see before you is *composed of the tears of mankind*, shed (against the express command of the Almighty) *for the departed;* therefore when you return again to the earth, inculcate this to mankind — that to grieve immoderately for the departed is in the sight of God a most heinous sin; and the river is constantly encreased by this folly, every tear making the poor wretches who float on it more distant from ease and relief." This narrative opposes all justice. It represents the sufferings of the departed as originating in, and encreased by, the sins of the living.*

In connection with the above information, it is stated that "To pray for the souls of the deceased, is a duty we owe them, and is pleasing to God." According to this view of matters, as we have already remarked, the deceased may either be relieved from their just punishment or difficulties, or advanced in their bliss, by the conduct of those who survive them. It is not only unreasonable, but appears to be in direct opposition to what is mentioned in another place, "Let us not believe that punishment will be remitted at the intercession of those they leave behind; nor will the prayers of priests avail them; as they sow, so will they reap; neither reward nor punishment will be remitted."† It is required of a revelation that it be consistent with itself.

The neglect of wearing the Sadra and the Kustí, is characterized as the most heinous sin. "We then proceeded forward, and came to a place where a vast multitude of souls were collected, in the midst of whom were all kinds of reptiles and noxious animals, who constantly assailed them with their teeth and their stings, and gave them not a moment's respite. They were uttering the most dreadful and appalling

* Ardái-Viráf-Námah, Pope's Translation, p. 51. † Ibid. p, 91.

cries. I enquired of Sarosh Izad, 'What sins have been committed by this multitude?' To which he replied, 'Those people neglected in the lower world to wear the Sadra and the Kustí, as prescribed by the law of the Magi; and also wearing covering for the feet; and they performed the natural evacuations without regard to cleanliness, or covering the head and body; for the neglect of their duties, you see, O Ardái Viráf! how they are punished; and, *above all*, inculcate the strict observance of these duties." Is not ceremony here preferred to morality?

The following exemption from punishment is truly ridiculous. "I saw a man, the whole of whose body, except one of his feet, was plunged into hell,and was tortured by every species of loathsome reptiles; his foot was, however, exempted from the punishment. Witnessing this extraordinary exemption of the foot, I inquired of my conductors as to the cause; to which they replied, 'This man is so punished for his total negligence in performing the moral duties; an idle, indolent sluggard, who found trouble in the most common and necessary duties of life, and never performed any of them without repining, and ill temper; his foot is exempted (from the general punishment inflicted on the other parts of the body) for having once in his life performed a good action with it. Sarosh Izad then related to me as follows: 'As this man was one day walking in the fields, he perceived a sheep tied to a tree, bleating in a piteous manner; he approached, and found that its cries were because its food was placed out of its reach; impelled by a sentiment of pity, he kicked the straw within its reach. For this good action his foot is exempted from the tortures inflicted on the other parts of the body.'"* This man, I must observe, made a very fortunate blow with his foot. Had he given another kick with his other foot, according to the spirit of this story, it would also have been exempted. Had he employed all the other members of his body aright on any one occasion, they would likewise have escaped all torment.

* Ardái Viráf-Námah, p. 72, 73.

The following piece of information is sufficiently curious :— "Dogs are the best friends of man, and to protect them is of all things the most pleasing in the sight of God. How happy would men be, if they would remember this." Dogs should be kindly treated ; but reason teaches us that a proper regard to them is certainly not the highest of the moral duties, as here stated.

Men's eternal destiny is represented as dependent on a circumstance, over which they may frequently have no control. At the bridge of Chinavad, many souls thus addressed the professed prophet. "O Ardaí Viráf, remember this our advice — let no one die without heirs; in default of natural ones, it is a good action to adopt them; for want of heirs, to hand our name to posterity, we cannot pass the bridge, but wander up and down in an uncomfortable manner, without enjoyment. Let this be known, that men may err no more in this matter. We are in sight of heaven, a river flows before us, yet we die of thirst, for the obtaining of these things is denied us. Report to our families, O Ardái Viráf, our miserable situation, that sons may be adopted in our names, that we may be enabled to pass the bridge, and let it be known that to hand our names to posterity is one of the highest duties."* Surely the Pársís can see that a man may be suddenly cut off without the appointment of an heir, and without any impeachment of his conduct.

In the following narrative the forgiveness of God, is made to depend on the forgiveness of men. "We are doomed to wander near the bridge," say certain souls, "until the arrival of those against whom we have sinned. If they admit our pleadings, and forgive us, God will also extend his mercy, and admit us into his holy place; but if those against whom we have offended do not forgive us, here we must continue to wander, and linger on in this state of shame and anguish forever and ever."†

* The opinions of the Hindús on the subject of the appointment of an heir, are somewhat similar to those of the Pársís. The Sanskrit word पुत्र *putra* is stated in the Brahmanical writings to be composed of पुत् *put* the hell, and त्रा *tra* to preserve, from the idea that a son saves from hell.

† Ardái-Viráf, by Pope, pp. 95, 96.

The persons who can believe this statement, have a most melancholy prospect before them. Their redemption may depend on the will of a fellow-mortal, who, even in the exercise of the vilest revenge, may wish to detain them.

The instances to which I have directed attention are surely sufficient to lead the Pársís to consider the Ardái-Viráf-Namah to be only a poor unworthy fabrication. I have been happy for some time to observe a decrease of confidence in it among many members of their community.

12. Edal Dáru* refers to the ***Farhang Jahángírí***, a Persian dictionary made during the reign of the emperor Jahángír, for the corroboration of a legend which he repeats at length, respecting the bringing of the *sarva,* or cypress tree, from heaven by Zoroaster, and which he says was planted in the city of Kashmir. The testimony of the author of this work as to the doings or non-doings of Zoroaster, is of not the slightest value. To suppose that the cypress tree, which is so extensively dispersed over the world, was brought from heaven by Zoroaster is altogether absurd. That some of his disciples, on seeing some magnificent and aged specimen of the tree, in an age of ignorance, may have claimed for it a heavenly origin, is not at all unlikely. Groves have been favorite places of worship from the earliest ages; and superstition has not only appropriated them for convenience; but made large demands on the credulity of man, in the attempt to establish their sacredness.

13. From a Pahliví book called the *Sháyist-Náshâyist*, and the Narimán-Hoshang Rawáyat, Edal Dáru professes to give the following as the names of the twenty-one *Núsks* of the Avastá, which Zoroaster is said to have brought from heaven. They are arranged according to the words of the most frequently repeated prayer of the Pársís.

1	"*Yathá*	Satud-yast	5	*ratus*	Duwazdah-hámást
2	*ahú*	Satudgar			
3	*vairyó*	Bahist-mántrah	6	*asháṭ*	Nádar
4	*athá*	Bagh	7	*chíṭ*	Pájam

* Maujazát i-Zartusht, p. 74.

8 *hachá*	Ratushtái	15 *khasathr-emchái*	Baghán-yast
9 *vanghéus*	Barash		
10 *dazdá*	Kashasrub	16 *ahurái*	Níáram
11 *manangkó*	Vistáspa	17 *á* ·	Aspáram
12 *skyasthe-nanãm*	Khashat	18 *yim*	Duásarwajd
		19 *dareghubyó*	Ashkáram
13 *anghéus*	Safand	20 *dathat*	Vandídád*
14 *mazdái*	Jarshat	21 *vastárem* †	Hadokht"‡

This list, I have not noticed in the Sháyist-Násháyist; but I have seen it in several of the Rawáyats. It determines nothing however, about the divine origin of these Núsks, or even their existence in early times, or about the divine mission of Zoroaster. That the Sháyist-Násháyist, had a being before the days of the Sásánians, I defy the Pársís to prove. It does not appear that any of the Núsks were forth-coming at the time that this work was written, except the Vandidád. If they are now to be found, it seems strange that the Pársís should be content to remain without their possession.

14. Edal Dáru makes one allusion to the *Changhraghách-Námah*, in which it is said that the Bráhman Chinghraghách, from India, visited the court of Gushtásp, and became convinced of the claims of Zoroaster, with whom he conversed.§ Mr. Erskine says, that this work was written about three hundred years ago.|| Edal Dáru himself must see that it is quite a modern work, for he attributes it to "Zartusht Behrám," whom we have noticed as the author of the Zartusht-Námah, and of whose absurd legends the reader has already had an abundance of specimens.

15. The *Jámásp-Námah* has been alluded to, in connex-

* Or Jud-dew-dád.

† The words given in Italics compose the prayer alluded to above. I have represented them according to the correct orthography of the Zand. The others I represent according to the Persian of the Narimán Hoshang, as given in my own Collection of Rawáyats (Traditions) fol. 150. In the transferences into Gujarátí, little accuracy is observed.

‡ Maujazát-i-Zartusht, p. 77.

§ Maujazát-i-Zartusht, p. 105.

|| Bombay Transactions, vol. ii, p. 358.

ion with the preceding work, by Dosabhái.* It is a Persian tract, professing to be translated from the Pahliví, which, with other matters, particularly records the prophecies said to have been delivered to Gushtásp, by the sage Jámásp. These prophecies professedly extend to the time of the resurrection; but they become very general and indefinite, after the Sásánian dynasty is brought to an end; and for this obvious reason:—The writer had an outline of history to guide him as to the mention of the different kings who preceded the overthrow of the Persian monarchy; while he was left to his own resources in reference to the events which were to follow his own day. He evidently lived after the destruction of the Pársí government. If the Zoroastrians will insist on setting him forth as a prophet contemporary with Zoroaster, I hold myself ready to prove the inaccuracy of the predictions ascribed to him, as well as of the historical notices which are recorded in his name. From authentic history, I am prepared to establish the existence of many essential errors in his chronology. For saying this, I hope that I shall not be beaten with "the black ice," and battered with the "red hail," which he mentions as about to fall "four times;"† and that all connected with me will escape the curses which are thus written, and to be literally accomplished:—"It shall rain reptiles, and cattle shall bear young less frequently, and shall dwindle in size, and shall give milk and flesh, and wool in less quantities, and fowls shall lay fewer eggs."‡

Such, then, is a sufficiently comprehensive notice of all the authorities, Indian and Persian, to which the Pársí controversialists have referred, in the hope of establishing the divine mission of Zoroaster. How miserably they have failed in all the attempts which they have made to make good their point, must be apparent to every person in the slightest degree accustomed to look at historical evidence, or that by which the authenticity, genuineness, and credibility of ancient books are

* Tálim-i-Zartusht, p. 19.

† Jámásp-Námah, Author's MS. p. 13. ‡ *Ibid.* p. 10.

ascertained. Every impartial Pársí, even, must arrive at the decisions which I have already intimated,—that it has not been proved that Zoroaster is the author of the Zand-avastá, —that there is no authoritative document which can be appealed to which associates the reported miracles of Zoroaster, or his disciples, with the book,—that there is no evidence that Zoroaster ever uttered a single prophecy, or performed a single miracle. He will also see and admit, that the legends about Zoroaster and his followers, which are now current among the Pársís, are a mere tissue of comparatively modern fables and fictions. And, for the reasons we have brought forward in the preceding chapters, he will acknowledge, that the Vandidád, and the liturgical works in the Zand language, are productions so wretched as to have really no claim to a philosophical, much less to a divine, origin.

As far as the exposure of error is concerned, then, I have now brought my task, for the present, nearly to a close. While I have sought to weaken and destroy the confidence of my Pársí friends in the gross delusions which they have received by tradition from their fathers, I have directed their attention to the truth of God, as we have proceeded. This truth I again press on their attention; and I rejoice to think, that it is within the reach of all. It is recorded in the Bible, comprised in the Old and New Testaments, the grand topic of which is the mission and death of the Incarnate Son of God for the redemption and salvation of the world, and the divine authority of which is established by proofs both numerous and irrefragable. On the principal subject of its revelation, and on some of the evidence that the apostles of Christ did not follow cunningly devised fables, when they made known the power and coming of our Lord Jesus Christ, I must be permitted to say a few words, before I conclude.

The existence before the days of Christ of the books comprised in the *Old Testament*, is indisputable. Josephus, who was almost a contemporary of Christ, admits their reception by the Jews, and declares the care with which they were guarded, and the sacred esteem in which they were held, by that people. "For we have not," he says, "an innumerable multitude of books among us, disagreeing from and contradicting one another [as the Greeks have], but only twenty-two books, which contain the records of all the past times, which are justly believed to be divine. And of them five belong to Moses, which contain his laws, and the traditions of the origin of mankind till his death. This interval of time was little short of three thousand years. But as to the time from the death of Moses till the reign of Artaxerxes king of Persia, who reigned after Xerxes, the prophets who were after Moses wrote down what was done in their times in thirteen books. The remaining four books contain hymns to God, and precepts for the conduct of human life. It is true, our history hath been written since Artaxerxes very particularly, but hath not been esteemed of like authority with the former by our forefathers, because there hath not been an exact succession of prophets since that time: and how firmly we have given credit to these books of our own nation is evident by what we do; for during so many ages as have already passed, no one hath been so bold as either to add any thing to them, to take any thing from them, or to make any change in them; but it is become natural to all Jews, immediately and from their very birth, to esteem these books to contain divine doctrines, and to persist in them, and, if occasion be, willingly to die for them. For it is no new thing for our captives, many of them in number, and frequently in time, to be seen to endure racks and deaths of all kinds upon the theatres, that they may not be obliged to say one word against our laws and the records that contain them."* About fifty years before the time of Christ, were written the Targums, or Interpretations, of Onkelos, of the books of Moses; and of Jonathan ben Uzziel, of the prophets from Joshua to Ezekiel. In the book of Ecclesiasticus, written about 232 years before Christ, there is a brief abstract of Jewish history, evidently founded on the Bible; Isaiah is spoken of as "the prophet who was great and faithful in his vision;" the "prophecy of Jeremiah" is alluded to; Ezekiel is spoken of as having "seen the glorious vision which was shewed

* Josephus against Apion, book, i. par. 8.

him;" the twelve minor prophets are referred to; many sentences are expressed in language similar to that used by Solomon, to whom "songs, and proverbs, and parables, and interpretations" are ascribed; Samuel is spoken of as a prophet beloved of God's heart; and the "Law and the Prophets" are declared to be extant.* About 280 years before Christ, a Greek version of the whole collection of books was commenced at Alexandria in Egypt, in the reign of Ptolemy Philadelphus, and ultimately concluded not much posterior to his day. They were at that time celebrated as containing the authoritative records and laws of the Jewish people; and regularly read and expounded in the synagogues. The Hebrew language ceased to be spoken in its purity, after the return of the Jews from their captivity in Babylon, an event which occurred nearly five hundred years before the time of Christ, and those of them which are written in that language in its purity and simplicity, must have been composed before that era. The five books of Moses, which have both external and internal evidence that they possess the highest antiquity, were received as a divine law by the Samaritans, who were at enmity with the Jews, most probably from the days of Jeroboam, about 970 years before Christ. The scenes and events which are said to have been witnessed by Moses, are described with a particularity and liveliness, which show that the writer had a personal familiarity with the subjects of his narrative. The existence of these books, is clearly indicated in all the Jewish writings which were posterior to them. The books of the Old Testament, then, were not called into existence either by Christ, or his apostles. They were received as divine by the Jewish nation long before he appeared in the world.

On examining these books, we find many passages which refer to a great personage who was to be the Saviour of the world. This personage was revealed to our first parents as the seed of the woman who should bruise the head of the serpent,† or the devil, by whom they were first tempted to the

* Ecclesiasticus, prologue, and chapters, xlvii — l.

† Genesis, iii. 15.

commission of transgression. The sacrifice of animals was appointed as typical of his blessed work, when he should present himself as a sacrifice for the sins of his people. To Abraham, Isaac, and Jacob, to whom he appeared as Jehovah, it was declared, that as pertaining to the flesh he should be of their seed; and that in him all "families of the earth should be blessed." According to the laws and ordinances communicated by him to Moses, the tabernacle and temple services of the Jews were regulated so as to prefigure the nature and economy of his work, and the blessings of his salvation. "He died [typically] in every sacrifice; he ascended in every cloud of incense; his name was in every jubilee shout; his majesty in the awfulness of the holy of Holies."* Moses directly represented him as a prophet who should reveal the will of God, and a prince whose laws should be obeyed under the most awful sanctions. "The Lord your God," said he, "will raise up unto thee a prophet, from the midst of thee, of thy brethren, like unto me; unto him ye shall hearken ..... and it shall come to pass, that whosever will not hearken unto my words, which he shall speak in my name, I will require it of him."† Many prophets and righteous men wrote of his coming advent, the circumstances of his birth, his work as an instructor, the miracles which he should perform, the sufferings and death which he should endure, the blessings of pardon and sanctification which he should purchase, his resurrection from the grave, his ascension to heaven, and the establishment of his kingdom upon earth. They characterized him as the "*Lord-our-Righteousness*;"‡ and on his suretiship they rested their hopes of acceptance before God. The predictions which they delivered respecting him are to be found particularly in the Psalms and the books of the Prophets. The Jews who do not yet believe in Christianity are among the faithful keepers of these books; and they admit that the passages to which I refer are to be found in them. Aspandiárjí is entirely mistaken when he speaks of these pas-

* Melville's Sermons, vol. ii, p. 54. † Deut. xviii. 15, 19.

‡ Jeremiah, xxxiii. 16.

sages "as interlocations introduced into the Old Testament by the Christian priests."* The Jews themselves will most indignantly repel his insinuation. Though they unreasonably deny that the prophecies have yet been fulfilled, they most readily admit their existence, and regulate by them their own hopes and expectations.

We now pass on to the books of the *New Testament*. They profess to have been written by the disciples of Christ a short time after his ascension to heaven. That they have actually existed since the first age of Christianity, we have the most satisfactory proofs. Innumerable quotations and references are made to them as authorities, by a series of authors belonging to different nations, and of different creeds, and extending to the very age at which they are said to have appeared.† They were attacked by the early adversaries of Christianity as containing the accounts on which the religion is founded; and their genuineness, as the works of the immediate disciples of Christ, was universally admitted. Let us glance at the information which we receive from them respecting the person who set himself forth as the Messiah promised unto the fathers. When we have thus looked at the information which they deliver, we shall be prepared to appreciate the evidence which they bear, the tests to which they have been, and may now be, subjected.

Christ, they inform us, had become the "desire of all nations;" and his advent was eagerly expected, especially by the people of the Lord. To prepare the way for this event, God had providentially effected the greatest changes in human society, and the governments of the nations of the earth. The empires of the East,—of Assyria, Babylon and Persia,—and of Greece, had arisen, run their course, and perished. Rome had become the mistress of the world; and in the strength of the power which was given to her, she maintained

* Hádí-i-Gum-Rahán, p. 15.

† On these and similar matters, the Pársís will find ample and most satisfactory information, in a work deservedly celebrated in the Christian community, entitled, The Credibility of the Gospel History, by Nathaniel Lardner, D. D.

universal peace in her vast dominions, extending throughout the greater part of Europe, the north of Africa, the Lesser Asia, and the countries between the Mediterranean and the Euphrates. Preparation was thus made to procure attention to Christianity, and to grant facilities for its promulgation. The spirit of prophetic discernment which had been extinct for about four centuries previous, was again given to the Church. The great and mighty angel Gabriel who stands in the presence of God, was sent to speak unto Zacharias, a Jewish priest officiating at Jerusalem, and to shew him glad tidings. He announced the approaching birth of a son, John the Baptist, who endowed with the power and spirit of Elias, a distinguished prophet of antiquity, should announce the immediate approach of the Messiah, and preach repentance in the view of the nearness of his reign, — in the wilderness of Judah, lift up the voice, "Prepare ye the way of the Lord, make straight in the desert a high way for our God,—" come for a witness, to bear witness of the Light, — and, with fidelity and humility, deliver the testimony, "He that cometh after me is preferred before me, for he was before me," "whose shoes latchet I am not worthy to unloose."* Simeon, and Anna, remarkable saints, prophesied, and, along with others, waited for the "Consolation of Israel."

The archangel Gabriel was a second time commissioned to leave the abode of God's glorious presence, and to travel to this lower world, destined to be the theatre of the most wonderful events which the universe has been called to witness. He bends his flight to Nazareth, a city of Galilee, in the land of Israel; and to a virgin named Mary, of royal descent, but espoused to an humble carpenter, he reveals his message. "Hail thou that art highly favoured, blessed art thou among women," was his salutation. "Behold thou shalt conceive in in thy womb, and bring forth a son, and shalt call his name Jesus. He shall be great, and shall be called the Son of the Highest; and the Lord shall give unto him the throne of his father David; and he shall reign over the house of Jacob for

* John i. 15, 27.

ever; and of his kingdom there shall be no end," was his announcement. "The Holy Ghost shall come upon thee, and the power of the Highest shall overshadow thee," was the explanation which her anxious enquiries received. "Behold the handmaid of the Lord; Be it unto me according to thy word," was the response of her faith and love. Well might she break forth, as she actually did after the interview with her cousin, the mother of John the Baptist, in the song, "My soul doth magnify the Lord, and my spirit hath rejoiced in God my Saviour. For he hath regarded the low estate of his handmaiden: for, behold, from henceforth all generations shall call me blessed. For he that is mighty hath done me great things and holy is his name. And his mercy is on them that fear him from generation to generation. He hath shewed strength with his arm: he hath scattered the proud in the imagination of their hearts. He hath put down the mighty from their seats, and exalted them of low degree. He hath filled the hungry with good things; and the rich he hath sent empty away. He hath holpen his servant Israel in remembrance of his mercy; as he spake to our fathers, to Abraham, and to his seed forever."* In this her devotion, we have nothing but dignity, humility, gratitude, and praise, becoming the unspeakable mercy which was to be revealed to the human race.

The "fulness of time," speedily arrived. "The days were accomplished that Mary should be delivered; and she brought forth her first-born son, and wrapped him in swaddling clothes, and laid him in a manger, because there was no room for him in the inn.†" It was the will of God that his Son should

* See the second Chapter of Luke.

† Luke ii. 7. Aspandiárjí (Hádi-i-Gum-Rahán p. 14), asks, "Would God permit his own child to be thrown into a manger?" Joseph and Mary, the narrative informs us, "laid" the child in a manger; and we are left to admire the wonderful condescension of God, not only in dwelling with man,—becoming manifest in the flesh,—but appearing in the world in the lowest condition. Moral glory often shines most conspicuously through worldly humiliation.

"How wondrous it is to suppose," adds Aspandiárjí, "that there was no room in the inn for the little babe, while the parents could stay in it." He here makes a false interpretation of the sacred narrative.

appear in this lowly state; and it was the will of his Son to enter into it. "Though he was rich yet for your sakes he became poor, that ye through his poverty might be rich."* His humiliation, however, was not unattended with unequivocal intimations of his divine greatness. A wondrous star arose in the heavens, to mark the birth of Jesus, and to guide the wise men of a distant land to his abode, that they might do him reverence.† In the plains of Bethlehem, the angel of the Lord appeared to the shepherds watching their flock by night; "and the glory of the Lord shone round about them and they were sore afraid. And the angel said unto them, Fear not, for behold I bring you good things of great joy which shall be to all people. For unto you is born this day in the city of David, the Saviour who is Christ the Lord.... And suddenly there was with the angel a multitude of the heavenly host, praising God, and saying, GLORY TO GOD IN THE HIGHEST, ON EARTH PEACE, GOOD WILL TOWARD MEN."‡ Their song embraced the great objects of the Incarnation. That event, the greatest in creation's history, shall redound throughout the endless ages of eternity to the praise of Jehovah, and the promotion of the best interests of man.§

* 2 Cor. viii. 9. † Matthew, ii. 1—10. ‡ Luke, ii. 9—14.

§ The association of the divine glory with the birth of Christ, as related in the Gospels, has attracted the attention of some of the Pársí controversialists. Aspandiárjí, after quoting the narratives of both Matthew and Luke, says, that they "do not agree with each other in all essential points."* A single point of *disagreement*, however, he does not point out. He only accuses Luke of observing "silence" with regard to some of the matters mentioned by Matthew. For this silence, there may have been the best of reasons; and it is the combined testimony of witnesses, which it is usual to regard, when they are free of contradiction. It is not necessary that every thing mentioned in one Gospel, should be repeated in another; particularly when it was designed that all the Gospels should be together in the hands of Christians. Aspandiárjí complains that more particulars are not mentioned about the appearance of the star; but it was obviously the object of the Evangelist to direct special attention to Christ, and not to the star. If the star pointed to Christ, he continues, there was no room to the wise men to "inquire of the inhabitants of Je-

* Hádí-i-Gum-Rahán, p. 12.

The moral beauty and excellency of Christ, while he sojourned in the world, was infinitely great, every way worthy of the supreme divinity, and spotless humanity, which were united in his person. His bodily and mental powers as man, were developed according to the usual course of divine providence. "The child grew, and waxed strong in spirit, filled

rusalem, about the place where this new-born king of Israel was kept." If they had minutely regarded the pointing of the star, their inquiries might perhaps have been unnecessary; but arriving in the neighbourhood of the place to which it did point, it was most natural for them to inquire of those whom they met, if such a birth was known to have occurred below as that which was indicated above. "If the miracle of the star had actually taken place, as is asserted in the Bible, all the Israelites would have placed their full confidence at that very moment in the divine nature of Christ; and the lives of thousands of children might have been spared." The miracle might not have been understood by all the Israelites; and, as was frequently the case with them in more ancient times, they might have had no great readiness to yield to the claims of truth. With regard to the massacre of the children, I beg to direct his attention to an explanation which I have already given to the Hindús. "In regard to the murder of the Bethlehemitish children, it must be observed, that Christ was not the guilty cause of this murder, but the innocent occasion of it. It was not he who sinned, but Herod the king who sinned. He neither encouraged that wicked tyrant to commit murder, nor excused him after he had accomplished his atrocious purposes. It is in the highest degree absurd to blame Christ for not preventing the murder, because it must appear to every one who will reflect with any degree of attention on the course of God's providence in this world, that while God testifies against sin, and punishes it, he yet permits it to exist. For the permission, on the part of God, of the murder of the infants, blame can no more be attached to him, than for the permission of murder in our own day. He is the sovereign of life; and he can remove it whenever it may seem fit to his sovereign pleasure. He had no doubt the best of reasons for permitting Herod to destroy the children. Considering the temptations to which they might have been exposed, and the trials to which they might have been subjected had they lived, he may have wished to remove them from an evil world, and introduce them into a state of happy existence in another world. He may have wished to punish their parents by their bereavement, for the sins which they had committed, and for their ingratitude for the mercies which they had received. The infants, moreover, had been conceived in sin, and brought forth in iniquity, and possessed a depraved nature."—See Second Exposure of Hindúism, pp. 106, 107. To the observations in the same work (pp. 114—116) on the star which indicated the birth of Christ, I direct the attention of the Pársís.

with wisdom ; and the grace of God was upon him."* Every candid reader of the Gospels of his disciples, must admit, that by the simple narrative of his actings among the children of men, they exhibit him as possessed of every grace and every virtue. There was no act performed by him, and no circumstance connected with him, as he is represented by these simple writers, which was inconsistent with his lofty character, his holy nature, and the grand object for which he had been sent into the world.

During his infancy, or when he was only twelve years of age, he attracted the attention of the principal doctors of Jerusalem, and so discoursed with them that those who heard him were "astonished."† His entrance upon his public ministry, however, was delayed till he was about thirty years of age. It was marked by the utmost propriety, and the meekest condescension. Though he had no sins to confess, no repentance to avow, and no forgiveness to implore, he nevertheless,—with a view to fulfil all righteousness, and to mark his entire consecration to his heavenly work, and to have a typical representation to himself of the salvation of those whom he had come to accomplish, — solicited, and obtained, baptism from his forerunner John, who had confessed that he was unworthy to stoop down and unloose the latchet of his shoes.‡ He was shortly afterwards called to encounter the assaults of Satan, the enemy of holiness.§ These assaults were not of a physical, but a moral, kind; and their object was not to impart to him casual external pollution, but to lead him to the actual commission of personal sin. They found in him no corruption, however, which could be excited or inflamed, and they could impart to him no depravity, or defilement. The incarnate Son of God held himself at the disposal of his Father ; and in every respect he proved obedient to the divine will. As man he was willing to suffer, and he

* Luke ii. 40. † Luke ii. 47.

‡ Matthew, iii, 13—17. Luke iii, 21.

§ See Matthew iv. 1—11. Luke iv. 1—13.

actually suffered according to the infirmities of the nature which he had assumed. Though he had been long a hungered in the wilderness, he trusted in the providence of God, and refused to satisfy his wants, on the suggestion of Satan, by converting, as he could have done, the stones into bread. While he knew that he enjoyed the divine protection and support, he would not wantonly expose himself to danger, or tempt the Lord God, and needlessly and heedlessly cast himself from the pinnacle of the temple, to obtain a miraculous preservation. Though he was in a lowly state, having come not to be ministered unto, but to minister and to give his life a ransom for many, he was undazzled by the splendour and power of the world, when it was presented to his view. All the temptations to impiety, impatience, discontentment, vanity, and ambition, which were addressed to him, were ineffectual. Even to *contrast* the moral dignity which he thus displayed, with the position in which the Pársí legends have placed Zoroaster, would be a degradation.

"The Sun of Righteousness" had now arisen on the darkened world with "healing under his wings;" and he proved himself emphatically the "light of the world." Christ commenced his work as the preacher of righteousness in the midst of the "great congregation;" and surely never man spake as he spake. The simple fishermen of Galilee, whom he called to be his apostles,—that in them the power and truth of God might be manifested,—were so attracted by his personal demeanour and gracious invitations, that they left all and followed him.* Thousands crowded around him to listen to the words which proceeded out of his mouth.† They assembled together from all the different provinces of the land of Israel; and, frequently labouring under hunger and want, they continued to hang upon his lips. His popularity was thus great; but it was neither begotten nor cherished by any compromise or flattery. Most faithfully did he declare the message of God! He showed no partiality with regard to his instructions; but he addressed them to all classes of the

* Matthew, iv. 18—22. † Matthew, iv. 25.

community with whom he came into contact, to high and low, rich and poor, young and old, learned and unlearned. He did not embrace merely occasional and regularly returning opportunities of delivering them ; but he daily and hourly continued in his work, and advanced it in season and out of season. Wherever the objects of his ministry presented themselves, he was prepared to fulfil it with regard to them. The temple, the synagogue, and the private apartment ; the narrow street, and the public high-way ; the open plain, and the lofty mount ; the garden, and the wilderness ; the bank of the river, and the margin of the sea, were equally consecrated and hallowed by the heavenly teacher. His aspect, his voice, and his action, manifested his sincerity, earnestness and love. He viewed the people around him in the light of eternity ; and he never trifled with their immortal interests. His doctrines were in the highest degree important. They referred to the character, and will, and providence, and grace, of God, and the salvation of man, and all their solemn and important relations. He made known the divine law in all its extent ; and he exhibited it with all its sanctions. He exposed and rebuked sin as arising in the heart ; and he revealed it in all its forms, with all its danger and odiousness. He warned impenitent and careless sinners to flee from the wrath to come ; and he exhibited himself as the Lamb of God, — the sacrifice appointed by God, — who taketh away the sin of the world ; as the good Shepherd who giveth his life for the sheep, and as the only Saviour and Redeemer. The song of the angelic host at his birth, " GLORY TO GOD IN THE HIGHEST, ON EARTH PEACE, GOOD WILL TO MEN, was the very substance and burden of his own ministry. With inimitable simplicity and grace, he made known his connexion with his Father, and declared that " God so loved the world, that he gave his only-begotten Son, that whosover believeth in him should not perish but have everlasting life."* Nothing could be more affecting than the references which he made to his heavenly origin, to his appointed sufferings, and to the in-

* John iii. 16.

appreciable blessings which were to flow through him to the human race. He conveyed, with infinite love, the overtures of mercy and of peace to those whose nature he bore; and he appeared with the charter of salvation in his hands and ready to seal it with his blood. How unspeakably gracious were his invitations, and how tender and overpowering his entreaties! "The Spirit of the Lord is upon me," he announced, "because he hath anointed me to preach the Gospel to the poor, he hath sent me to heal the broken-hearted, to preach deliverance to the captives, and recovering of sight to the blind, to set at liberty them that are bruised, to preach the acceptable year of the Lord."* All were astonished at the words, which proceeded out of his mouth; and well they might, for they were alike the words of truth, of wisdom, of righteousness, and of mercy.

Christ's doctrines clearly showed that he was a teacher come from God; but in order to strengthen this impression, to awaken still further attention, to manifest his power as the incarnate Son of God, to display the divine glory, and to reveal his own character, he publicly wrought a great number of indubitable miracles, — works surpassing the power of man, surpassing the power of the creature, as involving the control, or suspension, of the powers and laws of nature. When occasion required his interference, he multiplied the means of human support and comfort, changing water into wine, and feeding several thousand individuals with the extended products of a few loaves and fishes. He dealt with the bodily frame of man according to his will, removing imperfections, weaknesses, and distempers, — when he instantaneously gave sight to the blind, hearing to the deaf, speech to the dumb, and soundness to the lame, — and when he purified lepers, cast out devils, restored paralytics, stopped bloody issues, renovated withered hands, allayed fevers, and cured dropsies, infirmities, and a great multitude of diseases. He proved his supremacy over the spirit of man, recalling the departed soul to its earthly tenement, and raising the dead, and restoring them

* Luke iv. 18, 19.

to their joyful friends and associates. He arrested the course of vegetation by his word,—when he doomed a fig-tree, and it immediately withered. He controlled the elements of nature, restrained the winds, changed the storm into a calm, and walked upon the sea. All these, and all his other miracles, were of a benevolent, and instructive, and useful, and sober, and important nature; and they were performed in the most interesting circumstances. There was no ostentation, or trifling, or amusement, connected with any of them; and the power of God was manifested in every one of them. They were generally accompanied with the communication of spiritual blessings to those who were the objects of them; and with benefit to those who beheld them. They were accomplished within the reach of the observation of friend and foe. They were such as men could judge of by their senses, and respecting which, as matters of fact, they could make no mistake. They were not evanescent but permanent in their effects. The enemies of Christ themselves admitted their occurrence, ascribing them to the devil, whose power, every reflecting person must see, they greatly transcend.*

* Connected with some of the miracles of Christ, the Pársí controversialists have brought forward very frivolous objections. To those of them which I have not already noticed, I shall here briefly advert.

"Perhaps Christ," says Aspandiárjí, (Hádí-i-Gum-Rahán, p. 18) "was acquainted with the practice of medicine, which may have enabled him to cure the blind and the lame." The cures were not gradual but instantaneous, immediately following the volition of Christ, or his word, or his touch, or some application, which, in itself, did *not form an adequate natural instrumentality.* The cure of the blind man, noticed by Aspandiárjí, was performed through such an application as is here alluded to. But there was still room for a miraculous cause and effect. Aspandiárjí's suppositions are entirely gratuitous.

Aspandiárjí says that Christ's riding into Jersualem on an ass has been "dignified to (by) the title of a miracle." Here he is guilty of a gross misrepresentation. "All this was done," it is stated by Matthew (Chap. xxi. 4—5), "that it might be fulfilled which was spoken by the prophet, saying; Tell ye the daughter of Sion, Behold thy king cometh unto thee, *meek*, and sitting upon an ass, and a colt the foal of an ass." These words Aspandiárjí has found it convenient to omit in his quotation.

Christ's refusal to give the Pharisees a "sign from heaven," originated in their neglect of the signs already given, and the great sign of his

The Saviour who was thus distinguished in his public ministry, was no less glorious in the private walks of life and the abodes of domestic friendship; and blessed were those who enjoyed his society and his special regard. All his intercourse with them was calculated to promote their improvement. It was marked by the deepest sensibility and tenderness, and by true and unaffected sympathy. His attachments were founded in love; and they knew no capricious change. His presence communicated spiritual joy; and the hearts of those who beheld him glowed with delight.

On the ground of the circumstances to which we have now adverted, we must admit that in his moral character and public and private labours, Christ enjoyed a distinction far surpassing that of the children of men. Our personal admiration of him must be greatly enhanced, however, when we advert to the situation in which he was placed during the course of his ministry. "He came unto his own, and his own received him not."* The scenes which were presented to his view were frequently of the most melancholy and repulsive kind. He observed wonder; but this wonder did not settle down in holy impression. He heard the shout of praise; but he also heard the sound of the scoffer, and experienced the bitter reproach of the profane. He was followed; but he was also forsaken and perscuted. His love was repaid by enmity; and the movements of his compassion were met by

rising from the dead, which remained to be given. Compare Matthew xvi. 1—4, with Mark viii. 11—12. Christ wrought miracles sufficient to convince the candid observer. He refused to meet the demands of the obstinate scoffer.

Aspandiárjí, p. 23, writes of the feeding of the hungry with bread and fish, &c., as "ridiculous." In this estimate of the gracious miracle, he will get few to agree with him.

The Pársís are not sincere in objecting to the miraculous production of wine by Christ; for they know, that wine, of a right quality, when not abused, proves a blessing.

It was for the sake of the moral instruction to be conveyed by the blasting of the fig-tree that it was cursed by Christ. Christ was man, it must be remembered, by those who object to his seeking figs, as well as God.

* John i. 11.

the repulses of exasperated pride. Many of his disciples, offended on account of the strict and uncomprising nature of his doctrines, went back and walked no more with him. The foulest accusations were wickedly brought against him; his purposes and pursuits misrepresented; and his doctrines abused. He lived in circumstances of the deepest poverty. "The foxes had holes, and the birds of the air had nests; but the Son of man had not where to lay his head."* He was despised and rejected of men, a man of sorrows and acquainted with griefs; and his life was eagerly desired and sought after, by those whom he came to save. Notwithstanding all this opposition and unjust and cruel treatment, he continued, undeterred, and even unrestrained, in his great work. His fortitude never forsook him in the most appalling circumstances; his patience never failed him; his faithfulness was never moved, and his love was never diminished. He never abandoned the conflict, grew weary in well-doing, relaxed his exertions, or diminished his instructions.

The wonder of wonders still remains. Christ is exhibited to us, not merely as possessed of a super-excellent personal character; as speaking with an authority and power such as that with which never man spake; as sealing his doctrines by great, numerous, and unequivocal miracles; and as persecuted by those whom he sought to bless by his ministry; but he is revealed to us as the voluntary substitute of his people in the endurance of the curse merited by their sins, as visited with the rage of man, — infuriated by Satan, — and above all, by the wrath of God unspeakably, inconceivably, great. He allows himself, of his own free will, and moved by the infinity of his love to man, and his fidelity to that covenant into which he had entered with his father in behalf of his people, — circumstances which form the explanation of all that humiliation against which the Pársís complain, — to be apprehended, to be falsely accused, to be treated with indignity and cruelty, and to be unjustly condemned. He endured the "contradiction of sinners against himself;" and he breathes forgiveness towards

* Matthew, viii. 20.

his enemies. He is nailed to the cross; and though able to descend from it, and to free himself from the hands of his adversaries, he willingly endured those sufferings and death through which the atonement for the sins of his people was to be effected. He experienced the hidings of his Father's countenance; and during the time that they continued, he exclaimed in the anguish of his soul "My God, my God, why hast thou forsaken me." When he had "finished transgression and made an end of sin," he "bowed his head and gave up the ghost, saying, "Father into thy hands, I commit my spirit." His love to man was stronger than death; and "for the joy" of the salvation of his people, which was "set before him, he endured the cross, and despised its shame." God himself gave the most solemn and awful testimony to the importance of the unparalleled transaction in which he was engaged. "The sun was darkened, and the veil of the temple was rent in the midst." "When the centurion," who attended the crucifixion, "saw what was done, he glorified God," saying, "Certainly this was a righteous man." "Truly this was the Son of God." And all the people that came together to that sight, beholding the things which were done, smote their breasts and returned." The reality of Christ's death was certified to those who were instrumental in effecting it. Though they saw that he was dead, they pierced his side with a spear. They observed the interment of his body in the new tomb, allotted to it by Joseph of Arimathea. "Pilate," the Roman governor, "said unto them, ye have a watch, go your way, make it as sure as you can. So they went, and made the sepulchre sure, sealing the stone, and setting a watch."*

Christ thus died for our sins according to the Scriptures, and entered the silent grave; and with this event his voluntary humiliation was completed. On the third day after his crucifixion, agreeably to his own prophetical declaration, he

* For an account of the last sufferings and death of Christ, see the conclusion of the Gospels. The object of these sufferings and death, is more particularly stated in the apostolical epistles. What is greatly to be desired of the Pársís, is a perusal of the whole New Testament.

burst the bonds of death asunder, and rose again for our justification. The soldiers who were appointed to watch his sepulchre, declared that while they were asleep, his disciples came and stole away his body; but their conspiracy with the authorities to propagate this falsehood was manifested to all by the fact that they were allowed to escape death, the wonted punishment, under the Roman government, of such a neglect of duty as that which they laid to their own charge. To the apostles whom Christ had chosen, "he shewed himself alive after his passion by many infallible proofs, being seen of them forty days, and speaking of the things pertaining to the kingdom of God." In the view of his disciples, he ascended to heaven, and "a cloud received him out of their sight." His followers soon enjoyed the most marvellous proofs of his exaltation at the right hand of God, to give repentance unto Israel and forgiveness of sins. They were miraculously endowed by the Holy Ghost, enabled to speak in various tongues, as the Spirit gave them utterance, and so declared the word of God, that thousands in Jerusalem, who must have been acquainted with the truth or falsehood of all that was averred respecting the public transactions of Christ, believed in his name, ranked themselves amongst his followers, and publicly professed their attachment to his cause, notwithstanding all the opposition and persecution which could be brought against them. "They" also "went forth and preached everywhere, the Lord working with them, and confirming the word with signs following."*

At present, I merely ask the Pársís to admit that in the New Testament, there are accounts of Christ corresponding with the statements which I have now made; and no person who will peruse the Gospels and the Acts of the Apostles, will hesitate to grant this my request. To the following plain and legitimate inferences, I request attention.

1. The character of Christ, as described in the New Testament, is such as is evidently real, and not supposititious. The account of the life of Christ, from its commencement to its

* See the Acts of the Apostles for particulars as to their movements.

conclusion, is so minute, full, and circumstantial, in its references to times, places, persons, and events, both public, and private, and so consistent with all that is known of the situation of the people and country of the Jews, that it cannot be imagined to be the product of fiction even the most ingenious and laborious. It is evidently the plain, simple, straight-forward, sober, unvarnished, narrative of truth.

2. The character of Christ is altogether, and in all its particulars, so wonderful and glorious, in the descriptions which are given of it, and the practical and manifest developements which are made of it, that it could not have been originally set forth by the apostles of Christ, or any other writers, without their enjoying supernatural assistance. Every natural and spiritual excellence centres within that character; and the more it is contemplated, the more must it be seen to demand both admiration and praise. It is such as has been unexampled in the world, for it is revealed in connexion both with the nature of God and the nature of man, united in one person; and the conception of it, and the description of it, particularly in all the incidents of the ministry of Christ, his doctrines, miracles, sufferings, and resurrection, are alike beyond the unaided power of the most philosophical and accomplished, and particularly of the humble companions of Christ. "We know what description of men," says Aspandiárjí, "were the apostles of Christ. They were mere fishermen or peasants."* Surely, if this were the case, we must admit that God was on their side, when we perceive that the record with which they have furnished us, surpasses the endeavours of the greatest sages and philosophers who have yet appeared.

3. The apostles and disciples of Christ were both competent and tried and trust-worthy witnesses of all the facts connected with his life, which they have set forth in their writings. There was not, says Aspandiárjí, "a single man of letters among them," "on whose word we might fairly rely."† I have yet to learn that a man of letters is necessary to give a faithful testimony. All who have eyes to see, and ears to hear, and hands to handle, and tongues to speak, and the un-

* Hadi-i-Gum-Rahán, p. 21. † Ibid.

derstanding of the lowest rational men, can give a creditable testimony respecting palpable occurrences. The less talent and ingenuity, and learning, and power, they may have, the less likely is it that they will be able successfully to combine together for the propagation of falsehood. The apostles of Christ come undauntedly forward as honest men to treat "of all that Jesus began both to do and to teach;" and in particular to charge the authorities and people of Jerusalem with having "killed the Prince of life, whom God had raised from the dead, whereof" they were "witnesses." They give a clear and satisfactory account of reputed events, with which they must have known thousands upon thousands were familiar. They repeat their testimony before Jews and Gentiles, their countrymen and strangers; before irritated and inquisitive, governors and law-officers; and before interested priests and philosophers. In consequence of the opinions which they held, and sought to propagate, they change their habits of life and official pursuits, encounter the most serious difficulties, and expose themselves to the greatest trials and dangers. They continue unmoved by promises, and unawed by threatenings. They travel through many provinces and countries, encountering the greatest perils. They are tortured; but they accept not deliverance. They submit to death; and the last act of their lives, is the expression of reliance on the risen and exalted Saviour. They give, in short, the most abundant and satisfactory confirmations to their testimony.

4. It was utterly impossible for the apostles of Christ to obtain credit to their statements respecting his life, had not well-known facts corresponded with these statements. The people of Jersusalem and of all the different provinces of Judea, must have known whether or not the actions of Christ corresponded with the descriptions which are given of them; whether or not he performed the miracles attributed to him; whether or not he had actually risen from the dead. Christ was not unobserved by his countrymen, and what was done by him, was not done in a corner, or before a few interested partisans. He had attracted the attention of a hostile government, a hostile people, and a hostile priesthood; and his ac-

tions, as well as the reports given of them by his disciples and the multitude, were most diligently scrutinized. There was no inducement for the inhabitants of the land to favour a system of deception. They had every thing of a temporal kind to lose, and nothing to gain, by professing their attachment to the Christian cause; and nothing but the overwhelming force of truth could have induced them to yield to the claims of Jesus as the Messiah. Even those, who in spite of all the demonstrations of truth and grace which were made to them, continued unbelieving and impenitent, admitted the performance of the miracles of Christ, ascribing them to the devil, whose power,—as they involve a control of the laws of nature established by God,— we must admit they surpass.

5. A comparison of the New Testament accounts of Christ, which we have seen to be veritable, with the Old Testament accounts of the Messiah, which we have shown to exist long before his day, reveals a most extensive, and striking fulfilment of prophecy, — a miracle of knowledge, the foretelling of future events, which could be foreseen and declared only by God himself. How powerful this argument is for the divine origin of the Christian Scriptures, Aspandiárjí himself would appear to perceive, for he attempts to assail its very foundations. In reference to the prophecies of the Old Testament, he says, as we have already seen, that "the Jews mantain that they are but interlocations newly introduced into the Old Testament by the Christian priests, and it is on this account that the parties are so conflicting enemies of one another!"* The Jews, he will find on inquiry, neither have made, nor do make, any such allegation. They strenuously maintain the purity and integrity of the text of the Old Testament Scriptures, which it is admitted on all hands, they have most sedulously and successfully guarded. The application of the prophecies to Christ, they deny; and it is just this manifest application to which we Christians point in all our reasonings against their unbelief. How direct and conclusive it is in all its parts, we call upon both Jew and Gentile to mark. For the sake of my Pársí readers, whom, as well as others, it most

* Hadí-i-Gum-Rahán, p. 15.

intimately concerns, I insert, in the appendix (G), a brief summary of its most important particulars. A due attention to the subject will discover not only a body of evidence for the divine authority of Christianity, but an explanation of the nature and genius of Christianity itself. It may be proper to remark in passing, that it forms only a portion of the evidence of Christianity derived from prophecy. There are numerous unequivocal predictions in the Bible respecting countries, cities, nations, families, churches, individuals, and events, and trains of events, which it can most clearly be shown have been already fulfilled, and are now fulfilling.*

6. The scheme of salvation propounded by the prophets of old, and by Christ and his apostles, is so glorious, that it must be admitted that it transcends all human device. I request the reader to recall to his remembrance what I have said on this subject in the preceding chapter, and incidentally throughout this work. It brings, as we have seen, glory to God in the highest, on earth peace, and good will to men. It is emphatically the *wisdom* and the *power* of God unto salvation, sustaining as it does the authority and majesty of the divine law, and securing the deliverance and everlasting welfare of man. If we inquire for a demonstration of the *love* of God, it reveals its infinity, by showing us that God so loved the world that he gave his only-begotten Son, that whosoever believeth in him should not perish, but have everlasting life. It we seek for a vindication of the *holiness* and *justice* of God, it shows us in the sufferings inflicted on Christ, and voluntarily endured by him, as the substitute of man, a display of the exceeding evil of sin, and its direful consequences, the most overwhelming. If we ask for a manifestation of the *mercy* and *goodness* of God, it shows it to us in his sparing the guilty who take refuge in his grace as made known, in promoting their regeneration and sanctification, restoring to

* Let the Pársís attentively peruse the admirable work on this subject of the Rev. Dr. Keith, entitled, "Evidence of the Truth of the Christian Religion, derived from the literal Fulfilment of Prophecy; particularly as illustrated by the History of the Jews, and by the Discoveries of recent Travellers.

them the image of God, and making them blessed in the full enjoyment and uninterrupted praise and service of God throughout the endless ages of eternity. When the Pársís see the exceeding breadth and the reasonableness, in all its demands, of the law of God; when they see how far they have positively offended and dishonoured God, by their disobedience and rebellion, and how far they have fallen short of the claims which he has to their reverence and affection and obedience, by their forgetfulness and ingratitude; and when they see the danger of their circumstances, and their exposure to the awful and righteous indignation of their Creator and Preserver, then they will contemplate the Gospel scheme with interest and admiration, and joyfully betake themselves to that Saviour, able and willing to save unto the uttermost, whom it reveals. The whole of the system of faith to which they have hitherto been devoted, they will perceive and acknowledge to be but a compound of vanities and lies, and things which do not and cannot profit.

7. The general doctrines and precepts of Christ, as recorded in the New Testament, are unexampled for their purity, suitableness, dignity, importance, and sublimity, such as well became Him who is said to have spoken as never man spake. They exhibit the glory of God, in all the natural and moral perfections and attributes of his character; in the universality, righteousness, and goodness of his providence, as it embraces every being and event existing and occurring throughout eternity; in the majesty, and holiness of his law, interdicting all sin of heart, speech, and behaviour, and requiring perfect and constant conformity to the divine will; and in the infinity of his grace, exercised in harmony with that justice, which is the immovable foundation of his government. They are divinely suited to all the circumstances of man, as the creature of time, and the aspirant after immortal bliss. They meet all the capacities of his nature as a rational and spiritual being, and all his necessities as a sinner seeking for the removal of his condemnation, and the restoration of his soul to the image of God. They are never adverse to an enlightened Natural Theology; while they far transcend its highest discoveries. Their wondrous adaptations, and exalted revela-

tions, are marked by the knowledge and wisdom of God himself. The discourses of the sages and philosophers of antiquity, are seen to be the merest vanity, when beheld in their light.

8. The actual effects of Christianity in the world, whenever it is received in its purity and simplicity, demonstrate its divine origin. Wherever it is unknown and unacknowledged, there is ignorance, superstition, cruelty, oppression, and immorality. Where it exercises its benignant sway, there is knowledge, faith, benevolence, liberty, and righteousness. It ameliorates and exalts the condition of individuals, families, and communities. The nations of the earth have sunk or risen in moral dignity, and even in solid and substantial power, according as they have imbibed its principles and respected its precepts, and institutions. It has proved the parent and nurse of intellectual culture, and moral refinement, throughout the world. It has supported and upheld its disciples amidst all the sufferings and trials of humanity; and it has given them, by its hopes and joys, a victory, a glorious victory, over death and the grave. It is almost degrading to contrast it,—not to speak of comparing it,—in these respects, with the Pársí religion, a religion of which its own votaries are now ashamed, and which is a mere compound of foolish speculation, outrageous legendry, and frivolous, puerile, and degrading ceremony.

But I must conclude. Such is the copiousness of the evidence of the divine authority of the Christian faith, that, from the contracted limits by which I am now restricted, I feel that I have failed to afford my readers anything more than a mere glimpse of some of its more prominent, and conspicuous points. Many of them, however, know that on more than one occasion, I have made the attempt in this place to secure their attention to a lengthened statement of its details, continued weekly for many months. To those who wish to examine the subject in all its parts, the missionaries of Bombay are ever ready to lend their assistance. I refer inquirers to the books, a list of which I add to this work,* which will more than abundantly satisfy every candid mind.

* See Appendix, H.

Their successful refutation by the Pársís of India, or the infidels of Europe, I have no hesitation in declaring to be an absolute impossibility. Let not the attempt be made to accomplish it, without much serious consideration, lest those connected with it should expose themselves to confusion and shame.

In taking leave of my native readers, I beg to assure them that it is the desire of promoting their best interests,—the welfare of their own immortal souls in time and eternity,—which has been the animating principle of the endeavour which I have now made to expose the errors into which they have fallen from the vain traditions received from their fathers, and to set forth and defend the truth of God. It is Christian love, let me tell them, in language which I have already used at a meeting of natives,—including some of the most enlightened members of their community,—which is also the animating principle of the patrons and supporters of the different Christian Missions which have been established throughout the world. This sacred principle, breathing the most fervent desires for the welfare of India, inhabits the breasts and animates the exertions of hundreds of our countrymen scattered throughout the length and breadth of this land, and of hundreds, — indeed I may say, millions, — sojourning in the more highly favoured land of Britain, and other countries of Europe. Some of the blessings which this love offers to you, you can understand, and even appreciate. You attach a high value to the knowledge of literature, science, and philosophy, which we seek to diffuse. You delight to have unfolded to your view, and submitted to your inspection, the mysteries of of nature, so multifarious and glorious; the essays and productions of human genius and learning; the records of the history of our race connected with the different countries of the world; and the application of art to the promotion of the economic well-being of man. But you do not yet fully understand and appreciate the magnitude of the other blessings of which we seek to put you in possession, and which are of of infinite, eternal, consequence; those blessings which have respect to God, our responsibility to his law, our access to his grace, and our own final destiny. Would that you were acquainted with their true nature, and could place upon them their true value, and were disposed to give us credit for that benevolence, in the exercise of which we offer them to you and press them on your acceptance! With reference to this last matter, I would bespeak from you all a moment's consideration, by putting to you a very plain and intelligible case. Suppose a dreadful disease to exist in this country, and to commit its ravages among all classes of society, high and low, rich and poor, young and old, arresting them in their enjoyments and occupations, and consigning them to a fearful and untimely grave; suppose that in the providence of God, we were to discover a remedy, an unfailing specific, for this disease; and suppose that we were to come forward to declare our discovery to you, and our readiness to explain its efficacy, and to give you the advantage of its application, — would you not, in these circumstances, give us your anxious attention, and deliberately consider the claims which we might advance, and earnestly desire to see them established? And would you not, on the other hand, visit us with your most decided disapprobation, were we to conceal from you our discovery, or withhold from you its advantages? Now, what, let me ask, is the state of the case with regard to the moral situation in which we find you to be placed? We see that, like ourselves, you are sinners, the workers of iniquity, and those who have withheld from God the love, and reverence, and service, which are his due; and that consequently his displeasure rests upon you, and that if his divine justice be alone that attribute with which you have to deal, you must be doomed to unspeakable suffering, to an eternal dying, to a perpetual residence in that place where God has forgotten to be gracious, and where his mercy is clean gone forever. We believe that you imperiously need salvation; and we believe that we know where salvation is to be found. We have heard with our ears, and have received the report into our souls, that "God so loved the world as to give his only-begotten Son, that whosoever believeth in him should not perish, but have everlasting life." We believe that an actual incarnation of the Godhead has occurred for the salvation of man, in the person of the Lord Jesus Christ, who, when he graciously stood in the room of sinners, allowed the demonstration of the evil of sin, and the exhibition of its punishment, to alight on his own devoted head, and thus gave satisfaction to the offended justice of his Father. We have experienced the preciousness of his grace; and, in his holy Gospel, we find him saying to ourselves, and to all, "Him that cometh unto me I will in no wise cast out," and commanding his disciples to go and teach all nations, baptizing them in the name of the Father, and of the Son, and of the Holy Ghost. We have found the Gospel of Christ efficacious for the regeneration and salvation of man in all the diversity of circumstances in which he can be placed. We have seen its powerful workings among yourselves, and others of your countrymen. We offer it to you, and we press it on your acceptance. Our desire to discharge our duty, and to promote your salvation, urges us to the course which we pursue. Will you respect our motives, and avail yourselves of the unspeakably precious blessings which we hold forth? The wonder, my friends, is not that we do something on your behalf, not that we do that which is considerable in the eyes of our fellows; but that we do not feel constrained to devote all our energies, and all our faculties, and all our influence to the sacred work in which we are engaged, that we are not constrained by the mercies of God to present ourselves, on your behalf, a living sacrifice, holy, and acceptable unto God, through Jesus Christ! What we do imperfectly accomplish, I beseech you, do not ye despise. Consider, I entreat you, the testimony of which we are the bearers. Christianity comes before you recommended by the judgment, as well as offered by the benevolence, of Britain, of Europe, and of America. Imagine not that its high and exclusive claims, and self-denying demands, have been accepted without inquiry,—without the most careful and profound investigation. Those mighty minds, which have penetrated the innermost recesses of their own being; which have analyzed the most secret springs of human thought and feeling and action; which have so sagaciously philosophized on the changes of society, and the advancement and decline of the nations of the earth; which have surveyed the whole face of the world on which we dwell, and the countless diversities of beings which inhabit its wide domains; which have dived into the recesses of the deep, and explored the caverns of the earth; and which have measured and weighed the masses of the worlds which roll in the heaven above, and observed and developed the laws which regulate their mighty movements,—those great minds, I say, which have engaged in all this research, and achieved all these wonders, have not vainly and inconsiderately surrendered their faith to the religion of the Bible. No; they have considered and weighed its claims, before they have pronounced their judgment. Its authority has been established in their view by irrefragable evidence. They acknowledge it to be the source of all the hopes of salvation which they are permitted to cherish, and of all that national greatness and majesty which you yourselves cannot but admire. The Bible, in the providence of God, comes before you with their united, their strong, recommendation; and it becomes you seriously to entertain the question of its divine origin, to see whether or not it is fitted to allay the fears of your conscience, to satisfy your desires for happiness, and to confer upon you all the spiritual blessings of which you stand in need. There is such a thing as heavenly truth, and there is such an agent as the Spirit of truth; and it becomes you to consider what homage and obedience you are prepared to render to them, while they address your fears and hopes, and offer to direct you to an abundant supply of all your necessities. There is such an hour as death, and such a transaction as judgment; and it becomes you to think of your preparation to encounter their solemnities, and to meet your doom. I could not resist this opportunity of giving you one word of affectionate warning, of inviting you to look to Him, who now says to you, "Turn you at my reproof; behold, I will pour out my Spirit upon you, I will make known my words unto you;" but who may afterwards address to you the sentence of condemnation, for mercies despised, and privileges abused, and deliverance rejected, and declare to you the loss, the eternal loss, of your own souls.

APPENDIX.

APPENDIX.

A.— TRANSLATION OF THE ZARTUSHT-NA'MAH *

BY E. B. EASTWICK, ESQ.

Invocation.

In all thy actions secret or displayed,
Be it first thy care to seek thy Maker's aid.
Through Him alone each work attains its end,
And things opposed in just concordance blend.
Omniscient Maker and Support of all,
Creator, Ruler of this earthly ball!
Lord of the seven skies and earths, for thee,
Are spread the highest heavens, thy canopy,
O God of wisdom, Lord of life, thy hand,
Lit up the starry hosts, heaven's glittering band.
Bright sun and moon, and Náhíd † queen of night,
Tír and Kaiwán, Bahrám, and Ormazd's light.
All giving Lord! Creator, wise and just,
How great thy bounties on the sons of dust!
Reason and knowledge are thy gifts — to know
The evil from the good and weal from woe.
Let reason be his guide, and man shall gain,
In each estate, a sure escape from pain.
For those who strive to learn the faith of heaven,
Be first their thoughts to God's existence given.
And let them know this truth,—that God is one,
Exists nought like Him, He is God alone.
From man his Maker asks humility,
Of prayer the accents and the suppliant's knee.
Seek ye the truth ? from me the truth receive,
And thus instructed listen and believe.

Beginning of the Book.

I saw a book in Khúsrau's royal hall,
Writ in the Pahlaví, for so they call

* For a brief review of the Zartusht-Námah. See pp. 417—427, of this work.

† Náhíd is the planet Venus ; Tír is Mercury ; Bahrám, Mars ; Kaiwán, Saturn ; Ormazd, Jupiter.

That ancient tongue—the great arch-priest of fire,
Had placed it there — chief of the learned choir.
Within the book in varied tale were told
The deeds of ancient kings and heroes old.
There too the Zandavastá's sacred line,
Was traced, holy Zartusht's book divine;
And there the story of his wondrous birth,
And all that marked the sage's stay on earth.
Time-worn the volume and the mystic page,
Was veiled in doubt, and dim with mists of age.
Said, then, the priest, "This sacred volume see!
By this in heaven's pure faith instructed be."
Then to my listening ear a part he read,
And strong emotion through his bosom spread.
"Learning," he cried, "herein would much avail,
For mark this long-forgotten lore—this tale
Of whom none knows the source—this ancient creed
May perish, since but few this page can read.
'Tis best that you this tale in verse should dress,
And in fair Persia's tongue its words express,
With wisdom ornament this faith divine,
Renew its canvas in your living line.
If thus the faith you celebrate, of thee
A fair memorial shall established be.
And thus renewed from thee, all men shall learn,
The faith of old—to it for guidance turn.
All will acknowledge that to us is given,
The purest faith and truest road to Heaven.
List to my words, for I too,—late have come,
Among my fellowmen—not here my home.
Bound on my waist the sacred belt, behold.
I too the sacred volumes can unfold.
Then hearken, for on thee no loved one smiles,
Nor wife, or child, from wisdom's path beguiles."
He said, and as his counsel sage I heard,
My heart was guided by the old man's word.
"My name," I said, "will live to future years,
And hope of Heaven's reward the labour cheers.
May God for this, the All-wise, Almighty Sire,
Release my soul from dread of penal fire."
Home I returned, and pleasing visions steep
My eyes in soft forgetfulness and sleep.
I dreamed a Darwísh stood beside my bed;
And, "sleepest thou idly?" thus the phantom said.
"Awake, bethink thee of thy vow, nor pause,
Till Zartusht sees renewed his sacred laws:

'Tis thine to gladden thus the prophet's soul,
And reach thyself intact the heavenly gaol.
His intercession shall avail thee best,
Before thy God — on him securely rest."
Scared by the vision, sleep my eyelids flies,
I wake and bursting tear-drops fill my eyes.
All night, revolving in my anxious mind
These thoughts, I lay, nor rest nor slumber find.
Soon as the sun from out his turret high,
Cast the first links of gold adown the sky,
To Kai-Khúsrau my sire's most honoured ear,
The strange relation of my dream I bear.
(Know ye who would my place of birth inquire,
'Twas Kujápúr* the city of my sire.
The house of Kujá is an ancient name,
The children now, not first, approved to fame).
"Beware," he said, "no vain resistance raise,
He pleases Heaven who at once obeys.
No worldly cares disturb thy tranquil mind,
In this behest thy only labour find."
Thus when I heard his answer, I prepared
To execute my task and back repaired
To the old priest who first aroused my zeal.
"Begin," I cried, "the work, for now I feel
My heart with ardor filled."— Thus then began
The history of the past that ancient man.

Tale of the old Priest.

When earth beneath the weight of evil groaned,
No teacher, guide, or chief her children owned.
Reckless of God, they felt no righteous awe,
And cast aside the dictates of his law.
The fiend accursed his banner wide unfurl'd,
And shook his pinions joyous o'er the world.
Exulting laughed haughty Ahriman,
And marked creation struggling in his chain.
'Twas in that dark despairing hour, that God,
To helpless man his saving mercy shewed.
To save that rebel race his prophet rose,
Salvation's portal opened to his foes.
From the unconquered race of Ferídún,
From royal sires arose the inspired son.
As shoots the tender offspring of the vine,

* Literally, 'Where-town'! The writer seems to have been unwilling to mention the real place of his abode.

So sprung Zartusht from the prophet line.
(Save God alone none knows or good or ill.
Learn this ye wise—ye children of his will.)
From Feridún descended Petarasp
The wise and good, his son was named Púrshasp.
Born of his loins the great Zarátusht came,
To free the imprisoned world from sin and shame.
A sapling he of that same noble race,
Lords of bright lineage, dignity and grace.
They called him Zartusht, and his mother's name
Was the chaste Daghdú, fair, unspotted dame.
Said then the priest, "now hear the legend true,
When Daghdú pregnant of her Zartusht grew,
Five slow revolving moons had passed; again
The sixth pale moon was hastening to her wane.

Dream of the Mother of Zartusht.

She dreamed she wondering marked in heaven's clear skies
A cloud like to an eagle's pinion rise.
So thick a gloom its gathering shadow spread,
The sun is veiled, the day grows dark and dread.
And from that cloud no rain, but, strange to tell,
Lions and tigers, wolves and dragons fell,
The crocodile and panther of the waste,
All that is horrible, misshapen, vast,
The writhing serpent and the bird obscene,
All things detested that the eye has seen,
Or fancy feigned, and still with gathering storm,
Fast falls each savage shape, and grisly form.
Sudden from forth that phantom train appears,
One who than all a ghastlier semblance wears.
On Daghdú rushing, in her tender side
The direful monster tore an opening wide,
And thence the infant Zartusht in his grasp
Dragged forth to light—death seemed in every gasp,
But on their prey ere yet those jaws could close,
Loud threatening shouts as those of men arose.
And in that hour of seeming misery
While hapless Daghdú strove for aid to cry,
"Wail not," her infant said, "for not from these
Shall harm approach me or destruction seize.
God is my guardian and protection. He
From every evil thing shall keep me free;
Then dread not, though you view assembled here,
These monsters grim and loathsome forms of fears."
Cheered with these words, the mother calms her care,

When lo! a hill descends from upper air,
And from its side, beams forth refulgent light,
Dispels the clouds and breaks the gloom of night.
Then comes a hurrying blast, before whose breadth
Fast fly those grim aspects and shapes of death.
When nearer came that holy light, was seen
An angel form, a youth of heavenly mien.
Fair as the morn, a shepherd youth he seems,
And Jamshíd's lustrous glory round him beams.
In his right hand he holds a dazzling wand,
Hell shrinks aghast before the vengeful brand.
His left supports the oracles of heaven,
The written word for man's instruction given,
These when they see, back quail the demon crew,
And hid in air, are lost to human view.
Three shapes alone of all the monster train,
A wolf, a lion, and a pard remain.
The youth advancing in their savage gaze,
Rears his bright wand and darts its dazzling blaze.
Vainly before his steps the fiends retire,
And wrapped in fierce consuming flames expire.
The infant Zartusht, rescued from the tomb,
Again is sheltered in his mother's womb.
Her wound is healed, by mercy from above,
And Hell's fierce rage is foiled by heavenly love.
To Daghdú, then, the heavenly stripling said;—
"Arise, nor let thy heart grow faint with dread,
Comfort thee, for from thee a child shall spring,
On whom shall rest the favour of heaven's king.
The world beholds the glad event with joy,
And future ages hail the promised boy.
A prophet of the truth his pen shall trace
To a lost world the mysteries of grace.
Glad earth rejoices at his coming feet,
The wolf and lamb in peace and union meet.
Then let no anxious cares thy breast alarm;
Whom God protects is safe from every harm."
Thus spake the youth, and vanished from her sight,
And with him fled the vision of the night.
Daghdú is left alone, and busy thought
Recalls the dreams with strange forebodings fraught.
A neighbouring sage there was, well skilled to read
The circling stars and tell the fates decreed.
Nor of less worth, to him fair Daghdú speaks
Her fears, and pity and instruction seeks.
And asks what destiny prepares? and how
The sure event of future years to know?

Said then the man of age,—"but few I ween
Such dream, such marvels of the night have seen.
First be thy infant born, ere I relate
To thy glad ear the oracles of fate.
All that thy heart desires thy child shall give;
Through him to distant lands thy name shall live.
His glory shall o'ershadow earth — his foes
Shall quail before him and in vain oppose.
Go, then, and when three days are past, return,
And the bright tidings of the future learn."
He said and Daghdú seeks her home — her breast
Is filled with care, nor food nor needful rest
She takes, till fail three suns and the fourth day
Casts o'er the earth its joy-inspiring ray.
Again the seer she seeks; glad smiled the sage,
And rising thoughts his labouring mind engage.
With quadrant viewing, then, he marks with care
What signs and changes in the sun appear,
And next the stars observing he discerns
The horoscope, and slow surveys by turns
Bahrám and Náhíd, Tír, and Kaiwán old,
Each planet circling in its path of gold.
He sees the moment of conjunction bright
With fortunes fair and joy's unfading light,
And thus he speaks; "I view a destiny
Of hope sublime and wondrous augury,
Know, that thy son, great, virtuous and wise,
High o'er his sires in glory's path shall rise."

*Interpretation of the dream.**

"This night that thou hast seen this dream, and beheld this suffering and woe, thou wert five months gone with child and twenty days and three. When thou art delivered of that holy thing, he shall grow up in righteousness and mercy; his name shall be the glorious Zarátusht; all his actions shall be fulfilled in goodness. Every faith and sect opposed to him shall be brought low, through the excellence of his fortune. At the first they shall struggle with him for the mastery, and shall endeavour much against him. Thou shalt experience much evil from the tyranny of the wicked, as thou didst dream of sustaining from the wild beasts. At the end thou shalt be prosperous and happy, and shalt rejoice in this child which is yet unborn. And what thou sawest in the

* It was the intention of my friend to have translated the whole of the Zartusht-Námah into verse. Its gross absurdity, however, and the almost total want in it of poetical conception forced him at this stage to resort to plain prose.— W.

latter part of thy dream, for that let thy spirit be raised above the sixth heaven: the bright branch thou sawest which brought the gladness, is the glory of God manifested against the oppressors, which shall keep back from thy child every evil thing. And that writing which the youth held in his hand, with that he shall sow the seed of righteousness. That is the token of the prophethood, with which the wicked and the fiends shall be blinded. His name shall be perpetual in the world, and all his desire shall be accomplished. The three beasts which remained and were destroyed by that flaming brand, are three foes, the deadliest and worst. They shall endeavour but shall not succeed; and at the last they shall be overthrown. He shall separate the truth and the right way from vanity. The bright sun is not hid by particles of dust, and those only shall doubt of thy son who are void of faith and understanding. In those days shall arise a king who shall make known the true faith; he shall aid in celebrating the faith of Zartusht, and shall establish it in the sight of all. Blessed is the tree that God shall cause to bear such fruit; you shall be blessed in this unblemished pearl, and by this holy child shall rise above the stars. Paradise shall reward those who obey him; the souls of his enemies shall descend to Hell; would that I might live to behold his day — my life and all I possess should be his sacrifice." When Daghdû heard these precious words, she said, "O Prophet of wisdom! How knowest thou that this was my fifth month?" The seer replied, "let the days be reckoned, thou shalt know that I have spoken right; thy computation is by the stars' ordination, and thus it is written with dates of the past. Behold what God will bring to thee by thy son; the world shall be filled with his praise, and the righteous shall rejoice in him." When Daghdû heard the interpretation of her dream, she prepared to return to her home. She told the prediction to Pûrshasp, the son of Petarasp. When the ninth month arrived the chaste matron prepared all things for the event.

The Miracles which attended the birth of Zartusht.

When the time of his birth drew near, his relations were filled with lamentation. His mother called for the wise women and also for those who were dear to her, in order that they might minister to her, and might support her in her travail. The women who were her neighbours, and men evil-enchanters, surrounded the door of her house, and were, you would say, her watchers. When the moon breathed light on the world, the holy Zartusht was born. As he left the womb he laughed; the house was enlightened by that laughter; his father was astonished at him, at his laughter and beauty and loveliness. He said in his heart, "This is the glory of God." Save this child, every infant born into the world has wept. They named the child Zartusht; great and small heard thereof; the word of the seer was fulfilled, as he had foretold the birth of the child. The women were envious of his laughter, and of the brightness of his destiny; they remained covetous of him, since the like of him had not been seen; they said, "We know not how this will be, or what will be the event." Child like this, saw they never; in beauty the world could shew no equal to him: the city was filled with the news of the beauty and laughter of the infant; all who were unclean and evil were stung to the heart at that laughter. In those days were many magicians who filled every place with their art; among them was spread anxiety; their souls were consumed as a torch; they said, "This is a calamity to us, we must remove this child from the world."

Miracle II. Escape of Zartusht from Dúránsarún.

There was a king in those days; his name was Dúránsarún; he was the chief of the magicians, and an alien from God. He discovered the birth of Zartusht; he knew that when Zartusht appeared, the art of magic would be lost and forgotten, and that he would establish a pure faith, and would bring to disgrace all magicians. The pure would receive their faith from him, his glory would reach the sun; the evil he would utterly destroy, and would reveal the pure faith. When the Sháh heard of his birth, his face became pale as hay. Instantly he mounted his steed, and departed to the house of Púrshasp. He came to the bed of the child, and behold a face like the early spring, beaming with the glory of God. The Sháh discerned the mystery revealed in him; at sight of him the Sháh grew pale. He said, "Take him from the cradle." They raised the child, and the wicked king drew forth a dagger of brightness; he thought to dissever the child, that his heart might be relieved from fear and bodings. In that moment he was struck with anguish; you would say it was the agony of death. The hands of the Sháh were dried up by the command of God the merciful. When the Sháh was disappointed of his hopes, that instant he withdrew from the bed of the child, since God, he saw, protected the infant and defended his life from every evil thing. All the magicians were sad and faint of heart; they were troubled and became like grass. They obeyed the order of the Sháh and departed. They were cut to the soul for the anguish of the king; when dismay fell among them, they bore off the infant Zartusht from his father.

Miracle III. Escape of Zartusht from the Fire.

They conveyed the child to the desert, and raised a vast heap of timber; they made it like Lájaward, with white naphtha and yellow brimstone. They quickly kindled one immense fire and cast Zartusht therein. By the command of God the cherisher, no evil reached Zartusht. That blazing fire became as water. In it Zartusht fell asleep. When that thing was done in the desert by those evil men, they departed. They carried the glad tidings to Dúránsarún, and told him their enemy had perished. "We kindled a fierce flame, we burned Zartusht therein." When his mother heard thereof, she wandered forth for grief for her loss, like a maniac; she reached the desert and the place where the fire of the magicians was kindled; she saw in the flames the figure of her child, and her breast rejoiced at the sight of her offspring. Pearls were scattered by him in his prophethood, like the starry light of Náhíd and Mushtarí. Instantly she snatched him to her bosom, and kissed his eyebrows and his forehead two hundred times, thence she bore him secretly to her house. Such was this event in the world. Thus says the Priest of priests; "The world was never free from evil doers, but God the Protector gives victory to the pure and good; the Author of righteousness will protect the right; it is therefore best that you follow the right way."

Miracle IV. Escape of Zartusht from the feet of the Oxen.

Short time elapsed when the miracles of Zartusht became known. The fire had had no effect upon him, and his mother bore him home free of pain and hurt. Again the magicians, fiends and París displayed their fierceness and bad intention; again they consulted and devised, in order to contrive a way to put him to death. They secretly carried forth Zartusht by order of that Sháh the leader of the aliens. They placed him in the narrow way, where the oxen were accustomed to pass; they threw down that unweaned babe in that narrow way, hopeless and forlorn, that when the oxen came by that way they might trample on him and destroy him. When the herd began to move, one advanced before the rest, mightier than the rest in strength and size, like him who presides among an assembly of men. It came forward to the beautiful child, like a mother seeking her offspring; it protected the child between its forefeet with care in the name of God. It was not possible for the rest of the herd to pass on it, or to trample the child under their feet. When one endeavoured to pass that way it stooped down its ears and shielded the child; until they all had passed, it moved not from the place. Then it resought the herd as the hawk its prey. The mother of Zartusht was filled with frenzy; every where she thought to behold her child. When she heard the story of the oxen, she hasted till she reached the spot. Thence she raised up the beloved babe, and returned with thanks to her home: she called down a little curse with wailing and tears on that evil people of wrong doers.—"May the great God do even so to them as they would have done to the child had he not saved it; may they not find a hearing before God, and may their hopes fail in this world and the next."

Miracle V. Escape of Zartusht from the feet of Horses.

And when that news reached the wicked Dúránsarún, that Zartusht had escaped the feet of the bulls and not a hair of his body had been injured, this news stung him to the heart, and he prepared another device. He sought for a narrow way, where wild horses used to pass. He ordered them to carry forth Zartusht, and cast him without food in that perilous way, that when the horses passed that way they might trample on his body. When the Sháh gave this order they obeyed, but were disappointed in their hopes. They threw him where the herd used to pass;

they left him there friendless and destitute. In that terrible place, the heart of the mighty, through the burning heat, waxed afraid. When the wild horses began to enter the defile, a single mare advanced before the rest. By the command of God the cherisher, it came and stood by the pillow of the babe; it stood forward in defence of the noble child. The horses were unable to bite it. You would say that was the queen of mares, which both sheltered the child and befriended it. Again when the mother of Zartusht heard the news, she wandered everywhere as one distracted. She at length drew near her child, and her heart was afflicted at his danger. Many thanksgivings gave she to God, that her infant had met no harm from the horses. Again she bore him to her house; day and night her heart trembled on account of him; but while God was his Protector, what could Dews or París do to harm him? If a hundred thousand accursed Dews came to work you ill, if they hear from you the name of God, they will one and all take to flight. Such is the name of the holy God; from it destruction shall reach the wicked.

Miracle VI. Escapes of Zartusht from the Wolves.

When the wicked king Dúránsarún saw no success from the wild bulls and horses, he perceived that God protected the child and was unable to discover any expedient. Again he set about contriving, and hardened his heart like steel. Then he ordered that search should be made for a place the abode of wolves, a place where the wolves harboured, that there they might seize and destroy their young, and then place there the infant Zartusht, and see if their cause of anxiety would thus be removed, that when the savage wolves descended from the mountains, they would find their young ones slain and be seized with fury; then certainly, they would tear Zartusht in pieces, and when hungry would devour his body. They carried out Zartusht as the evil Sháh directed. They slew the young wolves, and cast them there, and hastened back from the place. See now the providence of God, and always select the path of righteousness. When the old wolves came to the spot, they saw a painful sight—all their young slain. They beheld a single infant weeping there; and at once they rushed upon him, they prepared to tear him in pieces, and satiate their fury for the loss of their young. The holy Zartusht by the will of God, in that danger moved nor head nor foot. He placed not his hand on the foremost wolf, yet in that instant its mouth was closed. And the life of Zartusht was uninjured. The other wolves became tame, the fury of the savage wolves was calmed. Behold when the leader's heart waxes faint, the army trembles with fear. It was the will of God that the pack of wolves should become friendly, and injure not the child; they sat down besides his pillow, and forgot their resentment for the loss of their young. Such is the power of God, that he makes the savage wolf feel pity; therefore it is right that at all times, you should cause your lips to utter his name. When the jaws of the wolf were closed, and it had taken its watch near the child's pillow, two cows descended from the mountain and came to that wonder of the age; they placed their teats filled with milk without deceit or evil purpose in his mouth. Who till that moment had seen the cow and the wolf together, and the jaws of the wolf closed from doing harm? The breath of the wolf will be with that of the cow, if it be the merciful will of God. God was merciful to that holy child; his body sustained no hurt from the wolves. By turns the cows gave him milk, until eventide was passed. When the bright sun lit up its crown of light, and the tree of ivory rose up from the wave,* the mother of Zartusht was weeping for her child, and was hastening through the deserts and mountains; she was crying out and making search, and endeavouring to find the road to her child; she knew not herself where her beloved one was, nor did any one shew her the right path. When she saw that wolf on the summit of the mountain, fearless she hastened towards it. She imagined the wolf had torn her child and had rent his limbs. When she found her child, that chaste mother threw herself before God on her knees. She said, "O God, giver of mercies, thou gavest me this dear son, thou savedst him from the wild beasts and evil men. I testify that thou art one; neither in this world, nor in the next, is any like thee; it behoveth all things to praise thee, both the visible and invisible world. She then took up her child. She wondered at the circumstance of the cow and wolf which she had seen near her child. The news became known to the magicians, that the lamb had escaped from the wolves, that Zartusht was brought back in safety and gladness from that peril. Again they assembled together and prepared every art and contrivance. They said, "This our danger is lengthened out, we see no remedy for this; it is better for us to look into this matter, and obtain some fruit of our labour." There was a chief of the magicians, whose name was Bartarúsh; he was a powerful wizard, and he said to the magicians, "Why raise you this outcry? I know respecting Zartusht, since I have examined regarding him with diligence, that he will not be destroyed by our counsels, since God protects him from every evil. The glory of God has been revealed in him; we shall not find a key to this closed door. Bahman took him before God, and acquainted him with the secrets of the two worlds, of the prophets of the God of the world. He alone is the guide of the world:—the world shall receive its laws from him; his faith shall be established among men; there shall be a righteous king who shall render him good assistance;—he shall break every enchantment, and shall destroy every work of the Dews." Then the father of Zar-

* We must confess our inability to follow the poet through these heights and depths. The words in the original are —

چو خورشید رخشان بر افراخت تاج پدید آمد از چشمه ساج عاج

"when the splendent sun lifted up his crown, and there appeared the ivory from the fountain of ebony." Query. Does not Zartusht Béhrám here improve upon the Muhammadan idea of the sun rising from a fountain of black mud?—W.

tusht asked him to tell him that which he knew. "What good, or ill, see you in his destiny? What have his stars in store for him? What meant that laughter at his birth? Tell it, whether betokening evil or good." Bartarúsh gave him this answer:—"Be thou wary of heart and discerning; your child shall be the leader of the world, since his equal has never appeared. All the propitious powers of heaven watch over him; all goodness is present with him; he shall guide all people in righteousness according to the will of God the cherisher. He shall make known the Zandavastá; he shall spread his name through the wide world; he shall drive out the wicked from the world; enchantment shall not remain, nor the doers thereof. The Sháh Gushtásp shall receive the faith from him, he shall bless him in the joy of his heart." When the father heard these things of him he rejoiced thereat in his heart. There was an old man in those days, wise, pure, and intelligent; his name was Barzinkarús. He came in the early morn to the house of Púrshasp, and said to him, "O holy man, I must bring up Zartusht with affection, like the sun in heaven. I shall esteem him as a beloved son, I shall keep him from evil as a flower. Take me to that dear son, and entrust his valued person to me." The father accordingly gave him to his care, and rested for a while from conversing with him. Zartusht attained his seventh year; the glorious God protected him; no hot wind breathed on him from the devices of the Dews, working magic.

Miracle VII. In the seventh year of Zartusht.

When his seventh year was fulfilled, God arranged all his affairs. Bartarúsh and Dúránsarún at that time went to him together, to work magic arts upon him and afflict and disgrace his soul. They made many magic rites there, but none of them succeeded. They increased fear and caused dread; the hearts of people were rent in twain, the heart of Zartusht quailed not, and he was not moved thereat; from that house men fled away, and became like dead men from fear. His clear soul in his body knew that he was protected from that magic. The great God was his protection, from the terrible devices of the magicians. When the evil enchanters saw, that their arts availed them not, they left the house disappointed, and their hearts were filled with blood from that woe.

Miracle VIII. During the sickness of Zartusht.

After this Zartusht became sick; the hearts of his friends were filled with grief; the filthy magicians heard thereof that sickness had fallen upon him. Bartarúsh, the chief of enchanters, secretly contrived a device:—He collected drugs from all quarters, and mixed therewith the vilest abomination. He brought thereof to the Sháh and desired to kill Zartusht therewith; he told him to take that medicine, that he might be freed from pain and sickness. By the command of the glorious God the holy Zartusht knew the fraud—that it was a drug destructive of life, which should not be given to God's creatures. He took the medicine from that infidel wizard, and poured it instantly on the ground. He said to him,—"Vile sorcerer! thy drugs are not efficacious with me; this medicine thou hast brought, thou hast mixed with filthy water. Practise all thy magic arts, they are of no force with me. If you should put on other apparel, what will it avail before one who knows the heart? And should you clothe yourself differently, I should know thee, O thou full of deceit! God has shewn me how to recognize thee—that God who rules the universe, who gives subsistence and life and takes them back at his will." Again, when the evil magicians were grieved on account of Zartusht, although they contrived many things they returned disappointed in all. Every thing was magic in those days, and nothing was done without the magic art. The fiends impure consorted with the magicians. They walked and sat with them on the earth. They gained all their magic from the fiends, and knew not God, the King of kings. They worshipped the unclean devil, as the pure God is now worshipped. Even Púrshasp, in those days, walked in the way that was known to all. One day several of those magicians who were the chief in that assembly,—Búrántarúsh and Dúránsarún,—whoever was chief in stratagem and deceit, all he took to his own house and made a splendid banquet. He had collected stores of dainties, and expended much labour on that feast. After they had finished eating, Púrshasp made an assembly at that entertainment. He then said to Búrántarúsh, "You are of all most skilled in magic; make you a good and becoming device, that we may be delighted and exalted. You know magic best this day, since you are chief of the sorcerers of the world." When Zartusht heard what his father said, he said, "Speak not improperly, have you nothing to do with magic or sorcery How long will you wander in the evil way? If you follow any way but that of righteousness, in the end you will convey yourself to hell; and if your heart is turned to any but God, certainly your place shall be in hell. Follow in that way which God your creator has made manifest to all people. From the deceits of magic you remain in ignorance, and are neglectful of your duty to the God of the world. The end of magic is hell, and all that is gained by it is lamentation." Then Bartarúsh said to Zartusht,—"Why speak you vain words, and why are you not silent? What are you before me, or your father, that you always speak in this manner? And know you not my power, that you thus reveal my secrets to all the mighty on the face of the earth. No one should venture to speak thus in my presence. This is what you require, that in this city I should bring your name to disgrace, and make you abased before all people, and spread falsehoods regarding you among all. You have taken away all the lustre of my power and have brought ruin into my affairs. May your name be forgotten among all people, and may your end be disappointed of every hope." Zartusht said to him,—"You vile one! your falsehoods will not injure me; if you speak falsely of me, your estimation among men will be lessened, but in every thing I say to you, I will use nothing but truth. By my arguments, I will break your head and hands, and will overthrow you with this hand of mine. I will place you on the ass of impotency, and, however much you contend, you shall be compelled to fly by the order of God, the giver of all things. I will overthrow your power by my arguments, I will cause your destruction, I will break and humble your body." All the magicians were awe-struck at him, at his manner, and his words. When Búrántarúsh heard his words, you would say his reason and senses had left him. He went to his own house. That night through grief he was sick with fever, he lay afflicted with that illness, and also his children and wife; when the holy Zartusht was fifteen years old, he rested not a moment from fear and dread.

The doings of Zartusht in his youth.

Day and night before the giver of justice, he bowed down his head to the ground; his heart was not in this world; his body from fear of God was in pain and affliction; he did much good in the world, both in the sight of all and secretly. Every where that there was any poor man who obtruded not his wants, till he was called for, he sent for him and treated him kindly and gave him every thing. Whenever there was any person afflicted, he sympathized with that affliction; he gave him clothes, and cared for him and arranged all his affairs. He held the world in no estimation, neither regarded silver or gold, except in the worship and mention of God. His body was not employed at any time; he spread a good name through the world among both great and small. He whose habits and customs are such as these, be assured that he is pure and truly religious. Every one whose heart is in the fear of God, will be saved from hell. When Zartusht attained his thirtieth year, he was relieved from danger and his works bare fruit.

Departure of Zartusht to Irán.

His heart was directed to Irán. He left his place in company with some others. Of those, some who were his relations, accompanied him in this journey. When with his companions he reached the sea, no ship was to be found. Then Zartusht, desirous of a vessel, remained there like one in grief. He wished to return back from thence. He could not take the women by that road, for he was jealous of the men. Inasmuch as it behoved not to take women into the water, it was not right for women to be naked especially in sight of a strange company. He wept to the Almighty God, and prayed for a passage across that sea. Since he prayed with truth and devotion, he was accepted by the holy God.

Passage of Zartusht across the Sea.

Zartusht arose and entered the water, and ordered the people to make haste. They all hastened to enter that sea, and removed not their clothes from their limbs. As a vessel moves with the stream, so moved they in the water of the sea; you would say a bridge had been formed there and that Zartusht crossed quickly thereon. The whole month of Sipandármad, they went on till the day which is called Anirán.* On that day the holy Zartusht reached the confines of Irán. There was a feast there in those days; the mighty of that clime in countless numbers, had come to that festal place, and were met together in joy and mirth. Zartusht desired to join that feast. Night came and extinguished the lights of the world; he slept alone that dark night by the way side, but understanding was the companion of his soul.

What Zartusht saw in a dream.

He dreamed he saw, that from the east a countless army was collected; and they came upon him in the way he was going, and drew near him with hostile purpose. They encompassed him on every side, and stopped his passage in all directions. When Zartusht looked that way another army became visible. They came up from the direction of the south, all warlike and fierce men; they joined swords together, the eastern army fled. Since God shewed him this dream, attend to the interpretation thereof.

Interpretation of the dream of Zartusht.

The exposition of the dream is on this wise, — for so the interpreter expounded it,—that Zartusht should go before God, and should hear all secrets from him. His heart should be informed of the faith, and should learn the mysteries of the true religion; and on his return from God, from that bright place to this dark world, he should make manifest the true faith and clear the rose-tree of truth from thorns. When the Dews and magicians should hear thereof, they would gird up their loins to do him battle, and would draw near him, preparing fight, seeking the battle like lions, and Mediomáh having heard thereof would be converted to the true faith, (though grief be ordained in this world) with willing soul and cheerfulness, and would receive from him the true faith, and learn the ordinances of religion. And after that he would read the Zandávestá with a loud voice to those fiends and magicians. The fierce fiends would fly and all the accursed magicians. When he had heard the exposition of his dream and had come to that banquet, his heart was glad at that festivity, and joy returned as to its source. After some time, pleased and joyous, he departed from that feast which resembled paradise.

The Passage of Zartusht by the water of Dáetí.

When he had returned from that feast, he came near waters, when half the month of Ardebehisht had passed, and the earth become like paradise. On the day you call Dêp-Meher, when the sun showed his face, on that day he reached the waters, a deep sea without bottom. The name of it in the Vastá is Dáetí, and never has its depth been fathomed. It is a tradition among men, that the waters of this sea are divided in four. The holy Zartusht entered the waters, and his heart was not afraid. The

* The last day of the month.—W.

first stream reached the middle of his leg, the second flowed above his knee, the third reached his waist, and the fourth came up to his neck. Be not astonished at whatever I tell you as having been done by God the cherisher.

Explanation of the above.

There are nine thousand proofs of the above, that the true faith will be four times renewed. First Zartusht Asfantamán without doubt introduced the true faith; next Hushídar accepts the faith; and then the prophet Máh Hushídar; the fourth the good Sásánish. I shall purify the earth, like paradise. The glorious God shewed him a passage over the waters, as I have said. His body was cleansed by that water, and was not afflicted or fatigued by it. Like gold cleansed by the fire, so value is increased by purifying. His head and his body he washed, and his head was clean, for his loins were girded to obey the will of God.

The coming to Zartusht of the Amsháspand Bahman, who conveys him to God.

Then came to the holy Zartusht on that same day Bahman, by the order of God. Refulgent from afar, like the sun and clothed in raiment of light, he said to Zartusht; "Name the thing which you desire in this world? What is your wish?" Zartusht said to him, "O good spirit, I seek nothing but God's pleasure; all wishes are directed to his will, since both worlds are his. My heart seeks nought but truth; my soul follows not after vanity. If I fulfil the commands of God, I accomplish all the desires of my heart. But I think, O holy spirit, that you are my guide in the right way." When the angel Bahman heard his words, he spoke to him suitably, and said, "Arise and appear before God, and hear from him all you desire." Immediately Zartusht stood on his feet. When Bahman shewed him the path, he said to Zartusht, "Close thine eyes an instant, and proceed swiftly." You would say a bird bore him from that place, and took him before God. When Zartusht opened his eyes, he found himself in heaven. First he looked on an assembly, so bright that he saw his shadow in their light. Between him and that assembly was a space of twenty-four steps. Hear and attend! There was another body of pure light and heavenly spirits attended it. Many angels in that instant came to him and one by one were joyed to see him. Each asked of Zartusht, and pointed with his fingers. He went into the presence of the holy God, with glad heart, but trembling body. When he came into the divine presence, he performed the fitting worship. And after he had glorified God, he began to inquire certain things.

Zartusht inquires of God.

He asked first; — "Who of God's creatures on earth is best?" God gave him this answer; — that God who was and is, — "He of all men is best who is true of heart, also he who is really generous—by whose charity the hearts of all are made glad—who inclines not save to the way of truth, and turns not his eyes upon vanity; also he who is merciful on all things in the world, on fire, water,* and animals, whether sheep, cows or asses. Whose heart obtains a portion of their gratitude, he shall escape from hell forever. Whatever thing is useful to you, if you afflict it, you displease God. And every one who in the world inflicts pain and vexes God's creatures, such a one has transgressed his statutes. Tell these words to that people. Hell shall be his perpetual abode who steps aside from this law."

The second question asked of God.

Again, Zartusht inquired of God, the supporter of the just. "Of the angels, who is most devout and most approved by God?" He asked to know their names and appearance, and that he might hear their discourses—also to know of the wicked Ahriman,† who would never consent to goodness, also regarding the good and bad deeds done in the world, what is ordained regarding them at the end, and other things of a fleeting nature that always appear under a new shape, and other secret things he had stored up:— All these he laid before God.

God's answer to Zartusht.

Thus he found answer from his God, the answer of the questions he had put;—"My desire is to exhibit goodness, the seeking of evil is the act of Ahriman; I am not pleased with any worker of evil; I have no foreknowledge of evil acts; I desire not grief, nor trouble, nor pain, nor injury, that it should happen to the inhabitants of earth. Think not that evil arises except from Ahriman and from the accursed and impure fiends. The same evil beings are the tribe of Ahriman, their recompense is hell. Behold the folly of those who speak falsely of me and testify that I work evil; I will give up their souls and bodies to hell who ascribe evil unto me." Then in all the sublime sciences, both from the beginning and from the end, in all these severally, God made Zartusht wise, from Adam to the last resurrection, from the first creation of the world to the destruction of all things at the end. He acquainted him with the revolution of the heavens, and with the good and bad influence of the stars, with the Hauris also of paradise whose spirits are formed of pure light, also with the forms and stature of the Angels, adorned like lofty cypress trees, also with the Hauris of light, created by God, of whom he has given us hope. All of them are exactly alike, for so God the Creator made them, walking gracefully like cypress trees in the beautiful paradise of the Jins. He shewed him also the face of Ahriman the evil one, revealed to him in the dark and narrow pit of hell, and also the recompense awarded to each person according to their deeds. When Ahriman beheld him from his

* Here, it will be observed, the elements are represented as sentient.—W.

† Here Ahriman is represented as the active Principle of evil.—W.

abode he raised a cry from the pit of hell and said to Zartusht, "from this pure faith be separated, and cast it away from thee — that in this world you may gain your desire; therefore consider in this your own interest."

The signs shown to Zartusht.

When Zartusht the wise and pure in faith was made thus informed of the things which pertain to God, returning from thence, as he cast down his eyes, he saw a mountain burning with fire. The order was given that the wise Zartusht should pass through that flaming fire. Through that heap of fire, lofty as a mountain, he passed and his body felt no harm, and after that, by the order of God, behold what happened to him and give ear. Again they melted down vast quantities of brass, and with the lava made his breast like silver. A hair of his body was not lost, nor was his delicate body injured. Again they opened his belly, and dragged forth the inside. Again they returned it to its place and it became as before, by the order of God. Whoso is protected by God, iron in his hand is like wax. Why should he fear fire or water, if his guardian is the holy God? Then God said to Zartusht, — "With regard to that mountain of fire you passed, and the belly you saw torn, from which flowed a stream of blood, with reference to that, tell all men, that you are their shepherd and they are your flock. Say, that whoever comes not to the true faith, but seeks the way of error, by the order of the evil Ahriman, his blood shall be thus poured forth. His body shall burn,* and shall not enter paradise, his soul shall not rejoice therein. When his heart is turned from the pure faith, his body shall be destroyed. And that brass which was three times melted and which poured on thy breast became like ice, no injury came on thee therefrom, not a hair was lost on thy body. One tribe shall turn from the faith, by the order of the deceitful Ahriman. Afterwards when the true faith throughout the world shall be diffused and the Dews dispersed, then to fight against them, a high priest shall gird up his loins. Men's hearts shall be in doubt, then this molten brass shall be a miracle to point out their leader. Azarbád Márasfand shall come, and shall overthrow all their devices; he shall pour over himself that molten brass, yet no harm shall reach his body. When men shall behold his deeds, doubt and hesitation shall be removed from their hearts. They shall draw back from crooked paths, and all shall learn the right way.

Another interrogation regarding the praise of God.

Again Zartusht inquired from the Creator, the knower of mysteries, regarding those who worship and priests and Mobeds of wakeful hearts. "Whoever worships before thee, what shall he say, and wherewithal shall he praise thee? When any desire to celebrate thy praise what form of worship shall they observe? To what Kiblah is it right to turn? Answer once more thus thy servant."

* Query: — Will not the pure fire thus be defiled?—W.

Answer of God to Zartusht.

God, the giver of subsistence who alone is without wants, thus answered Zartusht: — "Inform the people of the world, that so they may see things, both hidden and revealed. *Whatever is bright and full of light, let them know that that is the brightness of my glory.** They will not err in their worship of me, if they turn their faces to that which is bright. If they observe my commandments, Ahriman shall fly from them; nothing in the world is better than light, both among small and great. Of light we created angels and paradise, afterwards hell was formed from darkness. Wherever you may be in the two worlds you will find no place void of my light.

Then God taught the Zandávasta to Zartusht — a sublime work. Wherever pure light is produced there it is not proper to bring darkness. God said to Zartusht, "Go and before Sháh Gushtásp read this book, that he may come into the faith. Exhort him to goodness, that he may know me, and that none may impute injustice to me. Day and night, I am bountiful and gracious. From God is whatever you behold in creation. Keep all my counsel and repeat it word by word to Sháh Gushtásp. Inform all the Mobeds regarding me, that they may cast aside the way of Ahriman. Inform also, all the people of the world, that Dews and magicians may fly from them." When all this converse with God was ended, the good Zartusht remained astonished. He multiplied the praises of God, and magnified his bounties.

Return of Zartusht from Yazdán and the coming of the Amshíspand to him, and the trust committed to Zartusht, and the words spoken to him by the Amsháspand Bahman.

When Zartusht had returned from before Yazdán the God, with the wish of his heart accomplished, the Angel Bahman came to his dwelling, that angel namely who presides over sheep. He said to him, — "Behold all these sheep I commit to your care, wherever the flocks may be. Tell all the Mobeds and learned priests (*Rads*) to acquaint every man of understanding to take great care of sheep, that they may be useful in the world. Let no one kill a calf, or a sheep which is a lamb, nor any sheep that is young; for it will be useful in the world. He will not be acceptable to God who shall thus kill any animal, nor is it right to kill them idly. Tell this commandment, which is a strict one, aright. You must take good care of animals, and thence reap benefit. You have heard from me these words of advice, for I am the guardian of sheep. All the sheep that are in the world, I have received from God the merciful.† As I have spoken, do you receive, and tell these words to old and young. Take care

* Here light and the essence of God are confounded together.—W.

† Query: — May not Bahman be running after his sheep, when the Pársis are praying to him.—W.

you give them not over to the evil, and think not this commandment a small matter. I have told you all my desire, now do you know therest." Then Zartusht received these words from the angel who exerts himself in favor of sheep.

Coming of the Angel Ardebihisht and his discourse regarding fire-temples.

The noble angel Ardebihisht came forward, as the former angel withdrew. He said to Zartusht; — "O holy one, accepted of God the beneficent! take my message to the Sháh Gushtásp; say, 'O king of earth and majesty, I have committed to thy care every fire-temple, that you may gain renown on earth. Command that they be carefully preserved, and proper support be granted for them, that none venture to extinguish their fires with light water or heavy earth. Command that the Mobeds and priests and the Herbuds, pure and clean of heart, gird up their loins and be diligent and worship at every fire-temple. That they build fire-temples in every city, and increase the rites of the Sadah.* When they have erected the abodes of fire-worship, let them bequeath vast possessions for their support. And until their acts bear fruit abundantly, let them not consider this my injunction fulfilled, since that *light is from the light of God, which makes it so resplendent in your view.* What see you in the world better than this, which is ready to fulfil the desires of all. Whoever has uncontrolable want, is in want of its aid— both old and young. All it asks of men is wood, it asks neither more nor less. Its body is powerful like wood. Every moment it becomes younger. Its body fears neither death nor old age, if you place wood around it. If you pour perfumes on it which are really sweet, it will instantly give forth a pleasing odour. If you give it bad smelling things, it gives forth a bad smell; you will at once discover the difference. It removes from you the pain of cold. It lights up your darkness. Therefore, since its merits are so great, it is right that you should know its value. As God has committed it to my care, so I commit it to you, O chief of men! Whoever despises in his heart this my counsel, his body shall be seized in hell. Whoever fulfils my ordinance, shall find acceptance with God. When the holy Zartusht received from Ardebihisht these words, the angel departed from him.

Coming of the Angel Shahriwar and what he says regarding the weapons of war.

He saw the Angel Shahríwar come forward with his mind full of counsel. He said, "O wise and holy one! you who spend day and night in praising, since you have descended to earth from high heaven, bear a message from me to men. Tell every one who possesses arms, swords, javelin, mace, or spear, to keep its edge keen and always free from stain,

* This is a festival in honor of the killing of a Dragon by king Hoshang. It is celebrated by the kindling of many fires.—E.

that when his enemy is before him he may tear his flesh therewith, causing pain. His object will be attained by his weapons, and in battle they will resemble the sun. Let him keep them at his own abode, let him not entrust them to his enemy, nor give them to his foe, for they will effect many things. Tell the people of earth this message—the whole of it from beginning to end."*

Coming of the Angel Asfandármad and her † instruction regarding the Earth.

When the former angel had finished his discourse, Asfandármad came forward. When she had surveyed Zartusht well, she blessed him and his family. She said to him;—"O holy man; hear a message from me. Such is the command of God,—that the face of the earth be kept clean from blood and filth and carrion. It is not right that the earth be defiled with these. Wherever there is no cultivation, do not direct flowing water thereon. Let filth and that which is impure, be conveyed to a place by which men do not pass. When the earth is brought under cultivation, men derive countless benefits therefrom. He is the best of kings who encourages the cultivation of the soil." When he heard this advice of good meaning, he found it wholesome and advantageous.

Coming of the Angel Khúrdád and his directions regarding the care of Water.

When Zartusht had turned his face, the Angel Khúrdád advanced before him. He said to Zartusht, "O holy one; I commit to your care streams of water, both the water of canals and that of rivers, which descend from above and spring from below, and the rivulet which flows in the plain; also the canals and waters, which irrigate fields and gardens. Say to the people of earth that their bodies are strengthened and nourished by water. Animal life exists thereby, and earth and fruits are freshened therefrom. Keep carrion apart therefrom. Do not trifle in this business; pollute not water with blood or filthiness, that God may be pleased with thee. If your reason is willingly polluted by yourself, your pain in both worlds shall be increased. Every eatable thing which is defiled, pleasure and wholesomeness is removed therefrom, every one cooks his food with water, and when thirsty, drinks thereof. When the way thereof is clean, there is no danger in the passage. Keep pure such an incomparable blessing above all, since such is the command of God."

Coming of the Angel Amardád and his direction regarding Vegetation.

When Khúrdád had finished his discourse, instantly Amardád advanced. He spoke regarding vegetable existence to Zartusht. "The holy

* Are these counsels worthy of a supernatural revelation?—W.

† This Amsháspand is a female.

and undefiled, it is not right to destroy it uselessly, or to remove it without a purpose, for men and animals are gladdened thereby. God is its protector." He then gave every sort of advice to Zartusht, regarding religion and justice. "Order," he said, "the Mobeds, that they travel in the world. They will thus diffuse the faith among men, in doing which they will reveal truth. Let them exert subtilty in every way that they may be able to give an answer to all men. When religion and justice become known, no injustice will be left in the world. Let them know the Vastá and praise God and extol the God of creation. Let them keep fast their girdle in holiness, that your good name may remain on earth. Let every one bind his waist with the sacred girdle, since the Kustí is the sign of the pure faith. Let them be diligent, that the four elements be kept pure and free from blemish, the light air and flowing water, bright fire, and heavy earth, the animal body of these four elements was composed by the will of God. It is good that they be kept pure and be considered as the blessings of God." When Zartusht had heard all the mysteries of God he returned back, glad of heart.

Return of Zartusht to this earth and his battle with the Dews.

Having obtained his desire from the bounty of God, he returned to earth rejoicing. All the magicians heard thereof, they hastened to fight with Zartusht. With them were all the impure fiends—an army dreadful and without number. When they beheld the wise Zartusht, they bit the finger of astonishment. Then the leaders of the accursed magicians and the princes of the impure fiends said to Zartusht, — " O noble Sir, keep concealed the Zandavastá, for we approve not of your device, nor the dazzling show of your contrivance. If you know and are acquainted with us, you will not strive to practise magic on magicians." When from those wicked ones, the holy Zartusht heard these words, his heart wa filled with laughter. Then he recited one passage of the Zandavastá and raised his voice aloud. When the Dews heard his words they all fled from the battle; they all hid themselves under the earth; all the magicians were afraid and dispirited. A part of them died on that very spot, and a part were dejected and cast down by the power of God the Protector. He vanquished those Dews and magicians. He whom Yazdán protects and aids will be fortunate all his days. In every thing put your trust in God, for you will find no better guide than Him. If you place your reliance on God you may break your own neck without harm.

Zartusht visits Balkh and the court of the Sháh Gushtásp.

When the holy and pure Zartusht had won the victory over the army of Ahriman—had overthrown all the magicians and cast down the impure fiends, he took his way towards Balkh to the court of Sháh Gushtásp. He arrived there in a fortunate moment, and reposed for a while at his own dwelling. First, however, he praised God exceedingly and then took his way to the Sháh. He came with stately step to the palace, and cast his eyes on the king of earth. First he beheld two rows of Princes, standing on their feet, with girded loins, the great men of Irán and of every clime—every where that there was a chief or leader. You would say, that in that palace appeared the splendor of Venus and the moon and sun; and that from their brightness, two ranks were formed; all the wise men dignified with honor and rank. There were two ranks of men in that palace surrounding the throne of Sháh Gushtásp. The rank of each was marked according to the degree of his wisdom. All were humbled before him — the king of kings — of noble attributes — but those who excelled in wisdom, were ranked nearest the Sháh. The Sháh was seated on a throne of ivory. On his head was a brilliant crown. The holy Zartusht came forward and called down a blessing on the Sháh. When Gushtásp heard his words, he was in some degree aware of his dignity; he asked him of his health and received him honorably, and desired to place him with the wise men. They first brought forward a chair and placed it before him between the two ranks, and said to Zartusht, — " Sit thereon, and bring forth the minute wisdom, you possess." When Zartusht took his seat before those two ranks, he brought forth the rich pearl from its shell. Successfully none could argue with him. Each was cast down when he questioned him. They began to contend with each other, but Zartusht won the victory and succeeded.

The Contest of Zartusht with the wise men of Sháh Gushtásp.—The first day.

One man from the right hand of the Sháh contended with Zartusht and sought to vanquish him. He and the one who first contended threw away their shield, and were compelled to yield the victory to Zartusht. Then another succeeded them, and unfolded the secrets of ancient learning. He said much, but found not success. At last he was defeated. Zartusht followed the order of their sitting, and called on each for a display of their learning. Every one who exalted his neck was disappointed and cast away his shield. Three others and a fourth retired. From the fifth he carried off, as you might say, his senses. When all the assembly were reduced to silence, they gave precedence to Zartusht. Gushtásp cast his eyes upon him and was astonished at his discourse. In this manner, from thirty persons who sat on the right, he carried off the palm, and succeeded. In the same way from thirty on the left he bore off the palm and left them silent. All the wise men were astonished and their hearts were secretly cast down. Each devoured his own grief. When they were ashamed in the contest, the king of kings called forward Zartusht and seated him beside him. He asked him many questions relative to ancient learning and former history. He found all his answers right. The king of kings was mightily delighted. The monarch gave him a house of strength near his own palace. All the philosophers were cut to the heart and were ashamed before the king of kings. They went away until the morning, when they would return to the king of kings. They said to each other, — "If thou art a faithful man, thou will contend and disgrace Zartusht. They knew not regarding him, that God supported him in all things. They went home and slept not at all that night but were each engaged in preparation. Zartusht the pure of heart and holy, went to his house from the assembly. Much thanksgiving he made to God that he had enabled him to vanquish his foes.

The Contest of Zartusht with the wise men of Sháh Gushtásp. — Day the second.

The next day, when the azure vault drew forth its sharp sword from the scabbard, the wise men came to the throne of the Sháh and formed their ranks according to custom. The holy Zartusht came forth, sent from God as a guide. They contended with one another, but at the last Zartusht was victorious. When the contest of the wise was over, they were cut to the heart. Through grief and regret every one said;— "What voice is this!" Each was certain that this was the power of God. Zartusht was like a lion of the forest that leaps from ambush on the herd. The wise men, like the herd, were filled with fear. Zartusht was like the male lion, he drew forth his tongue like a sharp sword, and raised commotion in that assembly; and to the wisdom which that man of God expounded, he brought forward a hundred proofs. The king of kings exalted the rank of Zartusht and brought him near himself. He asked him regarding his name and race — of his city, and family, and descent. Zartusht told him his name and family — the city of his birth, and his family, and parentage. He told the Sháh, that, "on the morrow, which was the day of Hormazd, as soon as the lamp of day was kindled, —he should order the captains of his host to assemble together at his palace; also, that the wise men should be collected and should learn to abandon their hopes of exaltation. In the same way as the others contended with me, and strove with me for the mastery in learning, in like manner will I answer them all in every kind of wisdom. I will reply to them aright. After that I will speak of my own pretensions, and will convey to you the message entrusted to me." When Gushtásp Sháh heard these words, he surveyed Zartusht well. He ordered that at the dawn of morning, every one should be present at the palace. On that condition the holy Zartusht departed, and came forth to his own dwelling. Much thanksgiving he made to God before whom mysteries are revealed. All night he placed not his head on his pillow, but remained stedfastly praising God. And in another direction, the wise men of Sháh Gushtásp went away dispirited and downcast. Their tongues were full of murmuring and strife. Their souls full of fire and contention, that a strange man had come among them and had in suchwise overthrown them. Their honour before the Sháh was lost, and such a reproach was cast upon them. It was not right that Zartusht should thus impair their credit and cast their reputation in the dust. Two divisions of them were refuted and confused, and had at once fallen from their dignity. "Tomorrow," they said, "when Zartusht arrives, his place will be near our own. Therefore it behoves us, with one tongue and one mind, to seat ourselves before the Sháh of the world. We will refute all his words and will break down his prosperity." With this agreement, each sought his home, and from anxiety remained sleepless.

Contest of Zartusht with the wise men of Gushtásp Sháh. — The third day.

The third day, as soon as the sun appeared, that king of the lights of heaven, Gushtásp Sháh came forth from his palace; and every one who possessed place or learning, the wise men, came to the palace, all of one mind and full of envy. The captains of the host drew nigh and formed their ranks before the Sháh. The blessed Zartusht came forward in the palace of the king of kings. He gave an answer to the wise men of the Sháh. In the hour of contest he gave them full measure. Though for a short time they struggled, at last, disappointed they yielded their position. Again, they buckled on their armour; again Zartusht broke it in pieces, and its fastenings. Again, they framed various devices; but they were compelled to abandon their post.

Zartusht claims the office of Prophet.

What avails injustice, for when right is not on one's side, he, who possesses right, will overcome his enemies. When not one of the wise men remained who could utter a word before Zartusht, he took his seat next the Sháh, above all the rest in dignity and rank. He said to Gushtásp, "O master of the world! I am a prophet sent from God to thee — that God before whom the seven skies and earth are held in perfect obedience. He created the heavenly bodies in the manner you see, and as men behold. The God who gave life and gives our daily support and who confers benefits on his creatures. The God who has given thee the lands— the throne and crown of the whole world. Who brought thee forth from non-existence and by whose command you have reached this dignity, that your sway is over all people, and the princes of the earth obey thee."

Zartusht recites the Zandavastá before Sháh Gushtásp.

Thus he spoke and drew forth from his robe the Zandavastá in the presence of the noble king, and said to him, — "God has given me this and has sent me to his creatures. Know that according to this should be your acts, for it is the commandment of God the cherisher. Its name is the Vastá and Zand. Learn its statutes and walk therein. If your desire is towards its laws, your abode shall be in the paradise of heaven. But if you turn away from its commandments, you shall bring down your crowned head to the dust. Your God will be displeased with you, and will overthrow your prosperous condition. At the last you shall descend into hell, if you hear not the counsel of the Almighty. Act in nothing by the instigation of the Dews, but hereafter lend attention to my words." To him replied Gushtásp, king of the world, "What proof have you of this? At once produce it. If your proof appears conclusive, it will be right for me to act accordingly. We will acquaint the world with your ordinances, and will keep back the hand of oppression from you." Zartusht replied, "My proof is sufficient, it is the commandment I have brought. God said to me, O free from necessity! This shall be thy warrant to the proud king. After the manifestation of this book, you shall not see one accursed fiend on the face of the earth. By means of this book which I have brought all fiends and magicians shall be banished from the earth. If you learn well the Zandavastá, you will require no argument and advice from me. This book is sufficient argument and advice, which I have brought thee thus openly. By this learn the secrets of the two worlds. Behold in it the revolution of the stars. Discover by it the door of truth and turn not your head to wrong. You know that, like this, in the world no one has spoken things concealed and known." That holy Sháh said to Zartusht, — "Read some of this Zandavastá to me." Zartusht read to him one entire chapter, and explained to him its meaning. When Gushtásp heard the Zandavastá he was not at first pleased therewith. He approved it not, and he was excusable therein, since he was far from that holiness. See ye not the child without understanding? Jewels are valueless before him. When he grows up and becomes wise he learns that which before he despised. In the same way, the ignorant man values not the wisdom which is delivered by learned men. One day when the Sháh had become acquainted with that knowledge, and was desirous of those words, the affair of Zartusht was then esteemed by the Sháh, that he did not value him in his court, the Sháh praised him — the Sháh of the world and of majesty! He said to Zartusht, "The claim you have advanced is right; but it cannot be decided hastily nor until I examine it well, and revolve every thing connected with it. I will read the Zand for some days. I will know of its contents whether they be good. First of all, I will read what you advance, and see whether it agrees with reason. I will not take up this affair inconsiderately. I will accept it when I have seen well into it. You, according to your custom, each morning attend my palace and be content of heart. You are at liberty to come, whenever you please. Whatever you desire make it known." Zartusht said, "The king is right, let him do what his heart desires. If you wish to consider the proof for a while, I consent until you accept my message." He spoke and rose from his place and retired to the house appointed by the Sháh. The wise men of Gushtásp went forth. Their hearts were filled with grief and dismay. They remained astonished at the success of Zartusht; they bit their lips and fingers with their teeth; they yielded not to his endeavours or to those of the Sháh presiding over the world. When they saw the proof of his prophethood, they gave up in despair the arts of magic.

The devices of the wise men against Zartusht.

When they heard the words of Zartusht, they hastened to plot his death. They formed every sort of contrivance and consulted variously thereon. When they had agreed with each other in the stratagem to be employed, and had fixed on a contrivance, they resolved to convey secretly to his house things which should involve his life in danger. And by which they might disgrace him, and that would give them a reason for clamour. The holy Zartusht was ignorant of the arts of that wicked and impure tribe. When he left his house and came to Sháh Gushtásp, he gave the key of his apartment to the porter of the Sháh. The wise men learnt thereof and went to the porter of the Sháh; they gave a bribe to that traitor, who delivered the key to them secretly. The wise men made secret search for all that is most impure in the world, such as blood and filth and things impure, and the divided heads of a cat and a dog, also the bones of carrion, and much they were, at that moment, able to find. They carried these things to the house of Zartusht. When they had thus arranged a plot against him, they placed them on his pillow and in his robes, and executed this fraud against him. Again they made fast the door, and gave back the key to the porter. They returned it and charged him straitly never to reveal this matter.

The clamour raised by the wise men against Zartusht, who is cast into prison.

Thence they went to the Sháh; they drew near to his throne. Zartusht was sitting with the Sháh Gushtásp, and they were examining the Zandavastá. The Sháh was amazed at the writing thereof; in reality he approved not thereof. The wise men said, "O prince, vex not thy delicate body, for this Zandavastá is nought but magic. You know not, O king, who this man is. This magician intends in any way he can, to bring thee under his power. He has softened you by his magic art, and has inflamed your soul with his words. All night he practises sorcery, and endeavours to destroy your fame. When he shall succeed in bringing you under his power, he will spread wickedness in the earth. You are the Sháh, and we are your servants, we are the foremost of your subjects. Be not proud of the words of this man, and display not the power of magic through the world. Be not, as far as you are able, his supporter, for you are not acquainted with his secret, tomorrow you will repent thereof. Pain and grief will increase in your heart. The world is governed by your justice, and from thy endeavours has received peace. At the word of this impure person, cast not the world into trouble and disorder. We have said what we know to be true; as to the rest, you are the Sháh and t'is thine to command." When Gushtásp heard their words, he bethought him of the affair. He ordered that search should be made in the house of Zartusht for whatever might be discovered there, — that they should bring it before the Sháh and that it should be well examined. Zartusht knew not of his danger, and therefore felt no anxiety. He said his key was with the porter. They went and brought that which they found in his apartment, whatever there was found of food, or whatever apparel, or carpet, there was. The robes and books and apparel, they brought before the king of the world.

The false speaking of the wise men before the Sháh and the casting of Zartusht into prison.

When they had turned those things over, the heads of the cat and dog were found. The nails, and the hair, and the bones, which had dropped from the bodies of the dead. They placed them together before the Sháh, and Gushtásp examined them. The king of kings was wroth thereat, he called forward his wise men. He shewed them those things, and his regard for them was mightily increased. He bit his finger with his teeth, and he uttered abuse against Zartusht. He said, "O sorcerer! O wicked magician, evil in act and thought, and vile in purpose! what is this vile carrion of thine? This thy action is not void of magic. These are clearly the instruments of sorcery. Thou hast not the pure fear of God." Zartusht was amazed at the circumstance; his two eyes were blinded at the carrion. He said to Gushtásp, "O great king! I know nothing of this affair. I brought it not, nor ordered it, and I have not engaged in it at all." He sent for the porter of the king, that perhaps he might inform the Sháh of the matter. Gushtásp sent and inquired of him saying, — "Tell me truly of this matter. Who has gone into his house?" The keeper of the gate gave him this answer,—"Who could go into the house of Zartusht? The wind could not pass by that way!" When the keeper of the gate spoke thus, the anger of the Sháh increased mightily. He said to Zartusht, "Vile dog! You are worthy of the javelin and of impalement. Do you behold the doom which is before you? You are now among the disgraced. No one will have brought such things from heaven, and concealed them in his bed and garments." That instant he cast from him the Zandavastá and ordered Zartusht into confinement. He commanded that they should bear him to prison and should no more listen to his words, since he was none but a chief of sorcerers, who desired to overturn the world. At once, at the order of the Sháh, they carried forth Zartusht to prison. They gave order that the keeper of the prison should carry him his daily pittance. A keeper was appointed over him, lest he should suddenly escape. Three days and nights, that holy man abode there and the keeper brought him his food. One loaf and one vessel of water the keeper brought him for his ablutions. Zartusht remained seven days in that doleful state in prison, but he abode in holiness.

History of the black Horse.

I have heard of the relater of traditions, that Gushtásp, the just Sháh, possessed among his steeds one that was called the Black Horse. He prized that steed above all. When he sat thereon, his heart was lifted up. In the plain, that steed was like a moving mountain.* In speed, it equalled the breeze. Its elephant-like body beneath the saddle resembled a bride in its graceful motion. It raised its crest like a lion when it rushes forward on its prey. When it leaped forth to the race, you would have thought it moved like the wind. When Sháh Gushtásp went out to battle, he always mounted his black steed. Moon and sun, when they beheld that steed, shed good fortune on the Sháh. Whoever went forth to battle on its back, returned back prosperous. It happened that one day in the morning, when the bright sun breathed forth light, when the master of the horse surveyed the steeds, he examined the feet of the black horse. At last he became full of grief and became motionless with sorrow, for the four feet of the horse entered his belly. The master of the horse was filled with fear; he came running to the throne of the Sháh and told him what had befallen the black steed. The king of earth was displeased thereat, he said this is a wondrous thing!

The Miracle shewn by Zartusht.

The Sháh sent for his wise men, and seated them beside him, in order that they might seek a remedy for the horse, and examine into the mystery, and say whence arose this matter, and what would be the result of these wonders. All of them assembled together and discussed the good and bad appearance of the case, — " This thing has never befallen any one, that we should derive counsel in it from experience. Each of them argued differently, and repeated many magic spells. They devised every kind of counsel, but could not discover a remedy. When the Sháh saw they were impotent in this matter, although they were wise and crafty from affliction, he ate nothing that day, but continually bethought him of his steed. All his host, from the grief of their prince, remained lamenting on the ground. From the crowds of men that pressed to the palace, you could not have inserted there the point of a needle. The city was in commotion the whole day. At last, night came, and the sun veiled his face. In the prison, the innocent Zartusht remained the entire day, until evening. He ate nothing and knew not the calamity which had befallen Sháh Gushtásp; he knew not, that, from the grief of the king, every one was bereft of his senses. In the evening, the keeper came to him, and brought his food. Zartusht said, " What has happened that you have this day forgotten me ?" He told him the tale of the black horse and the manner in which it was lying in the stable. All its limbs had entered its belly, and the Sháh remained grieving thereat. The whole day we have been afflicted, nor has any drank water, or eaten bread. When Zartusht heard his story, he was pleased at heart and glad of countenance. He said " O keeper! if you are desirous of honor, tomorrow approach the Sháh and say, that if Zartusht is brought out of his dungeon, he will bring out the limbs of the steed. He will remove this grief from your

* What a wonderful brute!

mind, and will restore to its former state the steed. When you leave this (said Zartusht to the keeper) at early morn, repeat all I have told you to the Sháh." The next day when the glittering sun put on his crown of twisted rubies, and adorned with light the face of earth, so that door and terrace was clad in gold, the noble keeper came in haste, and told what he had heard, to the king, that "Zartusht speaks in this wise and will wash the Sháh's heart from grief. He says, let me behold the horse, I will bring forth its limbs." The Sháh instantly ordered the keeper to bring him from his place of confinement. The keeper returned to Zartusht with the tidings that the king of the world had removed his bonds. Zartusht went from the prison to a bath, and washed his head, and beard and body and feet; and thence he came to the king. They were two roses in a garden of cucumbers. He knew not what reception he should meet with from the king, and marvelled much thereat in his heart. You would have said, his reception was honorable; for the Sháh called a blessing on him with an affable countenance. Then Zartusht, in favor of the king, invoked countless blessings. The king of kings seated him there, and told him the story of the steed. He asked him his opinion thereof. "How will the limbs of the horse be freed? Before me you have raised a high claim, but have not established the truth of it. If you are in truth a prophet, bring back the steed to health. Zartusht said, "O fortunate Sháh! I think not this a contemptible thing. Whenever you shall perform four things according to compact with successful endeavour, — having made the compact without subterfuge and having fulfilled it without duplicity, —then shall be displayed to you the steed's two fore-feet and two hind-feet, all four of them." The Sháh said to Zartusht, "Tell me what are the four things? For I will make a compact with you and a promise which I will never break." Zartusht said, — "I will tell the Sháh each of the four things beside the horse." They went to the stable and all the army followed them.

The reception of the four promises and the confirmation of what Zartusht had said.

When Zartusht saw the horse, he was astonished, and bit his lip with his teeth. He said to Gushtásp, "O wise king! hear one of the four conditions." At the command of the Sháh he spake, "Believe really in your heart the truth, that I certainly am a prophet sent from our Creator, — that God who formed your body and placed your soul therein. The moment that your heart is right, instantly your desire will be accomplished. And if your tongue and heart are at variance, all my labor will be unprofitable." The king of kings accepted the word, and promised that he would never draw back from religion and justice. "I am content to accept this condition from thee. As you direct, so will I obey."

The first Prayer and Miracle of the Prophet Zartusht.

Then Zartusht prayed unto God, and wept before him mightily, when he heard the words of the Sháh and saw the whole world spectators of the scene. After lamentation to God, he praised him and placed his hand on the horse. The right fore-leg of the horse came out, since the word of the Sháh was true. The king of kings rejoiced thereat, and his heart was filled with gratitude. All the host of the Sháh were glad, and that grief was at once removed from them. They heaped praises on the man of God. And every one joined in extolling him. The situation of Zartusht became prosperous. Such was the commotion, that you would have said it was the day of the resurrection.

The second condition and coming down of the second leg.

When one of the four conditions was fulfilled, Zartusht said, "O famous king, give the injunction to Asfandiár, the glorious hero and patron of the age, that he conclude an agreement with me in your presence, to the effect that he will support the true religion. That he will gird up his loins for the faith of heaven, and will not turn back therefrom. Whoever shews himself the enemy of God, he will destroy his life and body." The hero Asfandiár came before his sire, and accepted from Zartusht the labour imposed on him. He gave him his hand in assurance and swore to him on oath, — to be the friend and support of Zartusht with heart and hand, with sword and speech. Whoever should disobey him, he would remove his soul from his body. When in the presence of the Sháh, the hero Asfandiár and Zartusht had thus concluded a compact, Zartusht prayed again and besought God. The right hind-leg of the steed came out by the commandment of God. All the religious men who feared God, repeated the praises of Zartusht. When one fore-leg and one hind-leg had come out, they congratulated the Sháh much.

The third condition and descent of the third leg.

Again Zartusht said, "O incomparable Sháh, worthy of dominion and the throne! It is necessary that you direct some one to accompany me to your palace,—that your royal consort may hear my words and become acquainted with the faith." The king of kings commanded an attendant who conveyed him into the retired apartments, and thence conveyed him to the women's room which were opened to him in the name of God. Zartusht said to the mother of Asfandiár, "O ornament of the crown and throne! God has preferred you before all women, and has given you every blessing since you were found deserving. He gave you a husband such as is the king, and such a son as Asfandiár. In this world all thy wishes have been fulfilled, and thy condition in the next world will be blessed. God the Creator has sent me to the Sháh, and has pointed out every path to me. Know that I will purify the world of wickedness by the command of God. I will make manifest the true faith; I will display the statutes of holiness. Now that the king of kings and Asfandiár have embraced the faith with their whole hearts, they have accepted fully my arguments, my commandments have been received. It now behoves you,

O queen of women! to believe implicitly on me. Let your clear heart accept the true faith, since good morals follow the faith." The chaste queen returned him answer, "Your word I have accepted. I will not turn back from the command of God. And I will hereafter walk only in the way of righteousness. I have heard of all your actions, and have not received your words lightly." When Zartusht heard this answer, he praised the princess exceedingly. He then rose and left the apartment and returned to the black horse. Again he prayed, and lamented vehemently, before the Almighty Creator of the world. Out came the left leg; and the king of kings was turned from his trouble and sorrow.

The fourth condition and descent of the fourth leg, and disgrace of the wise men.

Again the holy Zartusht said to Gushtásp, "O sovereign Sháh! It is now necessary that the keeper of your gate should come before me. By your order, you must inflict punishment on him, that he disclose who entered my apartment, and who conveyed this calumny to your ear, by which I fell into disgrace. If he will speak the truth, all will be well; but, if he lies, your steed is remediless." Then came forward the keeper of the gate of the Sháh in that assembly, by order of the Sháh. He said, "Tell me the truth, and what was that deceitful fraud? Who went into the apartment of the man of God? Who was it who brought this affliction on him? Who has ventured to do such things? Who conveyed the carrion into his chamber? If you speak the truth you escape pain, if you adhere scrupulously to what is true. Otherwise this instant thy head from its trunk I will strike off, before this assembly." The Sháh gave him such a fright that he trembled like a willow trembling in the wind. When the keeper of the gate heard the words of the Sháh, he saw no remedy but to speak the truth. He fell on his face, and cried for mercy. When it was granted, he stood up. He said, "The affair was on this wise. The thing was done by the pitiless wise men. They corrupted me and gave me a bribe, and engaged me in their undertaking. I have not extenuated their case, although they were high in your confidence. For now that I have received a pardon from the Sháh, what should I fear, even if I am in bad repute with them." When the king of kings heard his words, he believed in the faith of Zartusht. He ordered that the wise men should be carried forth and impaled alive. Zartusht returned thanks to God publicly and in his own heart. Again he repeated another prayer which he had learned from God. The horse drew forth its fourth leg, and leaped up like a lion! When the four legs of the horse were restored, and the Sháh was freed from that grief, the wise king stood on his feet, near Zartusht the high priest. He kissed often his eyebrows and head. So did also the hero of the age, Asfandiár. All praised Zartusht thereat, and offered him congratulation. After this the Sháh exalted Zartusht. He led him to his throne and seated him by himself. He begged pardon for the pain he had caused. He accepted Zartusht, whose fortunes thus prospered. He restored to him his property. The heart of Zartusht rejoiced thereat; he knew that God had done this,—who was his guide of infinite power. Truth alone is pleasing to him; falsehood is not acceptable to him. He does as he will, for He is king. No one can ask him the reason of his actions. He raises one from below the ground to the starry host of heaven. Him who possesses an infinite army and has reached the seventh heaven—him he casts down from thence; his head and neck and back he casts down. Then no one is able to deliver him, since he is King and we are his slaves. Whatever he does is just and right; you ought to rejoice therein.

Calling for additional proof from Zartusht.

When Zartusht had thus gained the Sháh, his dignity and rank were exalted. The Shah received all his statutes and transgressed not the promise he had made; he gave ear to the counsel of Zartusht; he heard with attention all his words. One day when the sun arose and heaven and earth were bright therewith, Zartusht went forth in the morning, and the countenances of the envious grew pale. He asked the Sháh after various matters and considered divers expedients. When one hour of the day was passed he engaged in various consultations. The king of the earth, Gushtásp, said to him "O Prophet of the world, observer of truth! I have four wishes to prefer to God, and the demonstration of your power lies therein. Ask thou of God the bountiful, that he may give me herein the victory by your intercession; the difficult will become easy and there will be seen a proof of the true faith." Zartusht said, "Tell them all four that I may know them openly. These four desires of thine are easy. I will ask them of God." The Sháh said to him, "O man of power, listen to my words. Of these four requests which I make to you, and of these four wishes which I seek, one is that I should know what will be my final doom; the second, that my body should become such that I shall not have cause to fear my enemies, and no weapon shall be able to injure it in the hour of battle, since when I make known the faith, I shall be compelled to many battles; the third is, that I should know every thing good and evil, concealed and manifest, that I should be informed of all that will happen, every thing that will befall in the world; the fourth, that to the day of resurrection my soul shall not leave my body." When Zartusht heard the word of the Sháh, he said, "O sovereign king, I will make these four requests from Him to whom all is easy. But it is necessary that, of those four requests you should seek one for yourself, and leave the other three for other people, that I may ask them of God. He will however grant them all, since He alone is God." The king of kings said, "I consent hereto and desire to see paradise that I may know my place therein, and what shall be my condition." Zartusht accepted this request, and consented to ask of God to shew him paradise. When the sun was relieved by the stars and the earth changed its colour, Zartusht went thence to his house and commenced the praise of God. He desired of God the giver of wishes, the petition which the Sháh had made. He praised God and retired to sleep, when God showed him all his desire.

Story of the coming of Azar Khúrdád and Azar Kashásp, and the Amshá-spands Bahman and Ardebihisht, to the Sháh Gushtásp.

When the lamp which lights up the world was kindled, and the face of day was disclosed from the east, the king of kings took his seat on a throne of gold, a crown being on his head of gold and jewels. Zartusht came before the Sháh; he offered praise and went into the court. When the tribunal of the Sháh had sat a short time, the keeper of the gate came in with haste. He said, "At the door, are four horsemen, armed as from the battle. Each resembles a moving mountain clothed in mail, and their horses buckled with steel. Horsemen like these, saw I never—with the glory of God and the weapons of war. Through fear of them, I fled; with difficulty I escaped into the palace." The king of kings said, "What may this be!" He said to Zartusht, "What means this! He had scarcely finished the word, when four horsemen came in, clothed in green, and in full armour, raising their spears before the king. Terrible and dreadful were they in pomp and majesty — like four mountains they advanced to the throne. One was Bahman and another Ardebihisht, sent by God from paradise. And with them Azar Khúrdád and Azar Kashásp, each of them mounted on a steed. They said to Gushtásp, "O Prince, we four are messengers to you. God says, 'Have you care of Zartusht; support and do not desent him. Since you have received from him the true faith and, from his commandment, the law of the statutes. Remember all his words, and keep your soul from the breath of hell. Never afflict Zartusht, and cast not your own body in peril. Since you have received from Zartusht the wish of your heart, turn not the rein from his government. Since it is I who I have sent Zartusht, and have given the world to be subject to him." When the Sháh observed their words, from dread he fell down from his throne. His understanding left his body, and his senses deserted his heart. He became dumb, and his eyes and ears became void. When his senses returned to him a little, he cried, "Have mercy, O God of mercies! I am the least of all thy servants; my loins are girded to observe thy commandments." When they heard his answer, in one moment the horsemen departed like an arrow from a bow. All the host of the Sháh collected, and formed ranks round his bed; his body shook with fear like a willow; he wondered at that matter and remained astonished. When Gushtásp rose from his seat, he went before Zartusht to beg his intercession. He said, "Your commandment is on my life; thy life is to me like the command of God. My body, life and possessions are thy sacrifice, by the command of God, the Lord of Majesty." Zartusht said, "Fear not, since your affairs are prosperous. I have asked your desire of God, you shall see presently how I have managed it."

Zartusht performs the Dárun and shews four more Miracles, and the Sháh Gushtásp sees his place in Paradise.

Zartusht prepared to perform the *Dárun.* Since he was about to prove the faith by miracles, they placed four things within — wine, and perfumes, and milk, and a pomegranate. Then he read prayers to them from the Zandavastá, — the noble Prophet Zartusht. After that prayer he told the Sháh to drink wine. After drinking, the Sháh suddenly slept. In the sleep, he saw the heaven of God ; his soul saw all these blessings obviously. He saw his own place in paradise ; he saw the mansions of the good and blessed ; he saw therein the rank of every one. Moreover, he saw many wonders. He gave Bashútan the milk for his share ; he ate and forgot death. He gave the perfumes of that feast to Jámásp ; immediately he knew all knowledge. He knew every thing that was in the future—all that would happen till the day of the resurrection. After that he gave to Asfandiár of that feast one grain of a pomegranate. He ate and his body waxed like stone ; no wound could be inflicted upon him. From this learn the meaning of the saying that Asfandiár was brazen-bodied. After that the king of kings awoke and recovered his senses from that dream of forgetfulness ; he rubbed his face on the earth and paid thanksgivings to God. He said, "O God, guide of my path, hear those my prayers in this world and the next ; thou art worthy to be king, since thou art without equal, and thy sovereignty never declines." The king of kings called Zartusht forward, and told him all that he had seen. He told all people to receive from him the true faith, and the statutes of righteousness. When Zartusht was seated on a lofty throne, the Sháh desired of him the Zandavastá. He said to him, "Repeat to me the whole of it, since it is free of doubt or of error." Zartusht was pleased thereat, and he instantly opened the volume; after he had commenced in the name of God, he read the beginning of the Zand. To Gushtásp, the noble Zartusht read some chapters of that volume. When the Dews beheld his actions, they remained astonished thereat. They fled from the rehearsal of the Zand ; they all concealed themselves under the earth.* He then ordered that the Mobads and the Hérbads, pure of heart, should advance. He spoke regarding the fire-temples in the presence of the Sháh of the mighty ;— that they should see that their works brought fourth fruit every where without hinderance ; that they should erect towers in all places, and that to each a Hérbad should be appointed ;— that they should kindle a fire in each tower and erect a lofty seat therein. He gave them much silver and gold that they should bequeath much property for its support, and should regard the fire-temples with reverence. The man who worships God will rejoice at the escape from dangers from the Dews.

* Dosabhái, what think you of these Dews ?— W.

Zartusht admonishes the Sháh regarding all holiness.

First regarding the name of the great God and the chief guide, he commenced to speak. That God who created the world and makes the end of the wicked destruction, the creator of the lofty heavens, the kindler of the stars which give light, — his eternal reign finds no decay, since he is king and the giver of benefits. Thus spoke Zartusht from the volume to Gustásp the king of the earth, "If you believe truly in the existence of God, your abode will be in the paradise of heaven." He told him that "the wicked Ahriman is the enemy of God the Creator. He turns back the hearts of men from the right way, and thus continually seduces them aside, that he may convey them down to hell, whereat he rejoices greatly. When he beholds the bodies of men in torment, he openly rejoices in hell. He scoffs at them and says,—O void of understanding, why did you foolishly commit evil actions. Now that you have turned from the holy God you have bought for yourself the terrors of hell. God had compassion on his creatures and said to me, —'Zartusht hear thou my message, and since thou goest to them as a prophet, take care that thou dost not treat this office lightly. Tell the people of the world strictly, that they turn back from the way of crookedness. Whoever turns his heart from evil, his place will always be in Paradise.' Every one who is iniquitous, in spite of his wickedness, desires thee O God! He approves not his own iniquity; he guides others to the right way. The Lord of the world sent me to thee, O lion-like Sháh! He said to me, 'Go and tell my servants, let them not turn away their faces from my commandments. Let them receive my faith and the right way, then the paradise of heaven will be their reward. Whoever disobeys my statutes shall be a companion of Ahriman in hell. And to the orders also of Zartusht the holy, give ear and listen submissively. He alone has not valued, or esteemed, the world, since he knew that the world passes away. He has neither son nor relation, but has embraced the way of salvation. What is the Sháh or servant before him? He regards not their circumstances in any wise. Thirdly, he never declared to men that in the resurrection he would intercede for them. I do not desire your crimes but I lessen your grief and pain. He said,—"Your hopes must rest on your actions; reap the harvest you have sown. Whoever has sown righteousness in this world, his reward also shall be paradise. And if you have acted iniquitously, Ahriman shall receive you in hell." Zartusht told every one near him the same, saying neither more nor less — that whosoever commits crime, his rewards shall be in hell. In the fifth place, he said to the wise and to the Mobeds of enlightened hearts,— "Who in the world has spoken words like these, both regarding things concealed and known? You would say he resembled pure water truly, for in him was neither excess nor defect. If you can bring any parallel to this, then my words are entirely vain. But if no parallel to this can be brought, then let them look on these words with humility; let them know certainly that this is the word of God and not the word of impure Dews.

since the Dews would not speak thus of themselves, nor would they utter the praises of God. Sixthly, Whoever has come as a prophet to bring mankind to the faith, has never told what was within the earth or what will occur hereafter. Zartusht alone has acquired this glory, since, in the Zandavastá, he has narrated these things; he has told whatever will take place in the world, good or evil, concealed or known, from the time that God created the world till the day of the resurrection. Zartusht has declared all things; he has told every thing in the Zandavastá, and the time and manner of its occurrence — of the king's remarkable propriety or justice he has recited the history, as you could wish — all their names have been mentioned by him — their words and actions, just or unjust, he has marked the signs of them good or bad, so that an understanding man will recognize them. Seventhly, Be assured that the prophet never flattered the powerful or warlike; whoever was, in his heart and faith, truly with him, his end never failed in affection for him. Such was the holy Zartusht who was permitted to offer his praise near God. He was wont to say to pious men — O ye faithful, whoever acts righteously shall reap a good reward. Eighthly, thus said Zartusht, — O people of earth, ye who commit sin shall abide perpetually in Hell. The soul of each shall be recompensed in the proportion of the sin he has committed; they shall confess that they are sinners and acknowledge themselves to be the creatures of God. Zartusht also said, "Whatever ye desire not yourselves, do it not to another. Whoever has committed sin in the world, is subject to the retribution thereof." Since I consider his words a proof of the truth of his mission, I have recited them to you from the beginning; I have repeated one chapter, attend well thereto and consider carefully what has been said.

A Recital of the Praise of God.

In the name of the God of the seven heavens, the powerful and the merciful towards his creatures, the God of beneficence and truth, who will not be pleased with my iniquity. Who always was and is! To him alone the hearts of the wise are turned; to him belong empire and sovereignty; to him alone is it right to pay homage. Why gird up your loins to obey him, who in weakness resembles thyself? Fix your heart on God in both worlds and ask pardon of him, O ye wise! Whatsoever ye may say contrary to this, be assured that your words are without foundation; he is our God and we are his creatures, abject, weak, and helpless. How shall a God such as he is, be praised by the words of such creatures as we are; know this in what ye undertake, and call on the name of God for help. Begin with the name of God, and then commence your history; see what manner of belief Zartusht obtained when he inquired of his Creator. Compare the manner of his relation with that of other narrators. If I obtain any strength at all, I shall obtain my desire from the composition of this story. My hope from the God of mercy is this, that he will have compassion on this weak body, that he will grant me my life by his grace, and will save my soul from Hell.*

Zartusht asks Immortality of God.

Hear attentively this noble story, from the relation of God the cherisher. I have written the story in the Persian language, that it might be easy for your perusal. Thus said Zartusht, the pure in heart, at the time of inquiring of God, at the season when with the angel Bahman he ascended towards high heaven, — "Close the door of death to me, and let the hearts of the wicked be bound, that the faithful may rejoice and may not remember the crooked path." To him said God the cherisher, "O thou who hast embraced the faith, the skilful, I will close the door of death for thee, but you will a second time ask death of me." Zartusht was silent in his request. Then he prayed to his God; God the Creator gave him something which resembled honey. He said to Zartusht, "Drink one drop of this, and tell me what you behold. When the man of holiness drank thereof he saw the world and every thing in it. As one who slumbers and beholds in sleep, he saw good and evil without concealment; he saw the blood and brains of the bodies of men, and the good and evil thoughts of every one. The words and actions of all were beheld by that good and virtuous person. He saw the number of flocks of sheep — their fleece and every circumstance regarding them. The leaves and roots of trees and of grass were beheld by that undaunted and fortunate person. He saw them exactly as they were by the order of God, neither more nor less. Again he beheld paradise and also hell, dark and frightful. He who believed thus, thought that he beheld these things in a dream. When he recovered his senses by the order of the God of the two worlds, God said to him, "O faithful servant, tell me what you have beheld." That man of holiness replied, "O thou who hast spread out the heavens and the earth. I have beheld many rich men their souls being in hell and torment, since thy were not thankful for the blessings of God, and were supplicants of Ahriman. I beheld many persons rich in silver and gold, who were day and night in the service of God, and were pleased with all they received and never rested from the praises of God. Their souls were in the paradise of heaven. I saw them in the place of the blest. I saw many rich persons who were afflicted, as being childless. When I beheld their abode in hell, my heart was sorry for them. I saw many persons of the common people who were happy in their children; when I behold their souls in paradise, my heart was glad at their happiness. I saw a tree on which were seven branches whose shades extended every where. One branch was of gold and one of silver, the third was of costly pearl; the fourth was entirely of brass; the fifth of lead, the sixth branch was of hard steel, and the seventh

* It is difficult to see the connection of this paragraph with the story. It seems like the preface to some other book. — W.

was of mixed iron." God said to Zartusht, "O man of wisdom and understanding! The tree which you saw with seven branches and which overshadowed the world is this, there shall be seven times a stir in the world by the good and bad revolution of the heavens. That golden branch which you beheld is yourself my messenger. My faith and message you have received, which you will deliver to the people of the world. That branch of silver is the Sháh of the earth, who will receive from you the right faith. The skin of the impure Dews will be broken, and they will be compelled to hide under the earth. When they behold their own bodies destitute of strength, they will conceal their evil actions. When Ahriman beholds the condition of his army, he shall utter cries of fury. According to the faith, men shall give due sanctity to (or take due care of) water, fire, earth and air. The copper branch you saw is the king of the Ashkánians. Whoever at that time owns not the faith, that holy tribe will abhor him. They will not remain long after this, but will be dispersed in wretchedness throughout the world. The branch which had the appearance of brass, represents the prosperous reign of that king whose name is Ardeshér, the son of Sásán. Listen to my relation. He shall adorn the world and shall free the righteous from pain. He shall renovate the true faith, and shall renew its statutes. Every one shall accept from him the right faith. Since by him the proof of the faith shall be established, all people shall behold his wonders. They shall pour on his breast melted brass, but no injury shall reach his body, since he shall derive strength from me. The fifth branch you beheld of lead is the king named Bahrám. His name shall be known as Bahrám, and his people shall rejoice at his reign. He shall he prosperous and happy. The world shall be well governed by him. When the people of the earth shall rejoice, Ahriman shall be grieved thereat; he shall remain in hell in grief and pain, and shall weep in deep tones of sorrow. The sixth branch of steel, O man of wisdom, which you saw ornamenting the tree, that is the time of Nosherwan, by whose justice youth will be restored to the earth. In his reign the wicked Mazdak shall appear, but there shall be no danger from him. He shall be a heretic from the true faith, and shall be acquainted with every kind of deceit. But when he begins to oppress the faithful, while they fly from him fate shall seize him. Leave the wicked to his evil doing, since the evil he does shall return upon him. The seventh branch you saw is of mixed iron. During that time, fly from the world. Many shall be converted to you during the season, but the aspect of the world shall be changed. That man of malice will be a monarch, who shall cast down the true faith to the earth. The Darwíshes shall wear black garments; the honor of the world shall be lost. Whoever lives in the time of that king, his end shall be evil. One virtue shall not be possessed by that generation, nought but malice and sedition and strife and evil. They shall be dealers in deceit and hypocrisy; and fraud and bitterness shall be in their hearts, but honey on their tongues. They shall not respect the bread and salt they have eaten, nor shall they honor their old men. And those whose hearts shall have accepted the faith, shall be afflicted by their enemies. Neither wisdom nor prudence shall be seen among them, nor shall reliance be placed on their words. Those who are faithful shall have no power or strength, nor shall the good be reverenced or respected. Whoever is pure in principle and faith, they shall cast down his name to the ground. Whoever is certainly wickedly disposed, whose tongue is filled with lying and deceit, all his affairs shall succeed and he shall prosper and the world shall be thrown into commotion. The face of the world shall be covered with impunity, nor shall they keep their food separate from it. All kinds of food shall they eat in common, and no one shall be aware of any distinction. They shall have no statutes or Herbads or instructors, nor shall these have any authority with them. Wherever they go, they shall fail of their object. You shall find nothing on earth, save covetousness and impotence and anger and strife; they shall choose the path to hell, and none shall answer according to the faith. Whoever is well affected to the faith, his affairs shall fall into indigence. They shall be shameless and without modesty, and day and night confusion shall prevail. Thus shall the faith become weak, and true believers wax few in number. The prayers of evil men shall be listened to since their condition shall be of indigence. The worship of the fire-temples shall be neglected. A hundred fires shall be reduced to one. Neither wood nor perfumes shall be supplied to them, and the enemies of the faith shall oppose. None shall sympathize or care for them, nor shall any leader for those dispersed persons be found. That sect of impure persons shall bring much riches from out of the earth. The high priests who dwell in Irán shall acknowledge their sway. This sect shall take in marriage many well-born daughters of the true faith. All the sons of the freemen and priests shall remain afflicted in the service of the wicked, day and night. They shall toil in their service — in the service of those unjust and evil persons. Since they will be faithless and void of mercy— they will not fear to break their promises. In the country of Irán a king shall fall from the hands of the mighty into the power of the wicked. They shall at once work out iniquity and shall know nought save oppression. Whoever is guiltless and true of heart, they shall believe his words to be deceitful; then, whoever is worse than his fellows, his affairs shall prosper more and more. They shall bear witness falsely; that from that falsehood, advantage may accrue to them. They shall have no shame for such crimes, nor shall they have any honesty or faith. When the Hazárahs shall appear, * the appearance of the world shall be changed. Many clouds shall appear in the sky but rain shall not descend. From the intense heat and bitter cold many a tree shall lose leaves and branches. The waters of the rivulets shall fail; all things shall become difficult;

* This word hazárah is of doubtful meaning. The passage is very obscure. The word may allude to the thousands of believers. — E.

from the scarcity of rain on the earth, the channels of the rivers shall be disclosed, flocks and herds shall decrease in number, and the stature of mankind shall dwindle; the strength of men shall wax weak and inferior, the speed of the horse and the strength of his rider shall grow less, the cow shall lose its valuable qualities. Whoever has bound on the Kustí shall be in fear and shall flee away. The pain and hardships which he will undergo, will make him desire death. They shall forget their prayers to God and their habits shall become opposed thereto. They shall neither recognize the *Nauroz* * nor the *Mehergán*† nor feast nor entertainment, nor the *Farwardagán*.‡ Whoever asks a question of the High Priest shall find no wisdom in the answer. Of what has been ordained for the departed soul, every one will be ashamed, and withdraw disappointed. Many a man of the true faith, and of holy mind, shall then go over to the opposite religion — many noble men and many honorable men shall wander destitute through the world! From poverty, and pain, and dishonor, the hearts of men shall be afflicted and their hands shortened. From the men of that evil generation, you shall not see one in a hundred possessed of understanding. Sifandármád (the angel of the earth) shall open his mouth and shall cast forth secret treasures. The Turks of Baykand,§ and of Khattán‖ and of Chín shall lead their armies into Persia. When the princes shall lose throne and fortune, their slaves shall possess the crown and empire. They shall collect much wealth and riches, but they shall scatter it on the ground. They shall be guilty of evil actions, but they shall feel no shame for what they do. From hardships, and difficulty, and pain, and weakness, men shall be ready to meet death and pain. Then thus spake God to Zartusht the prophet of the age,—"Tell these things to Mobeds and Ráds, and desire them to repeat the same to the wise. Let each know his own advantage and let them not take up iniquity. When they behold misery on the earth, then will be rejoicing and happiness in heaven. If your body is afflicted with pain, your soul from that pain shall find a rich reward. If you indulge your body in luxury, your soul shall therefrom fall into fire. In truth, know this mystery, that according to thy state of mind so will thou suffer or enjoy. From good, thou wilt find a good result, and none ever

* Literally the "new day," the first day of the year, which, with the five which follow, is observed as a festival, now most regarded at its close.—W.

† A festival in honour of Meher (Mithra) which commences on Meher the 15th day of the month Meher, and is observed for six days, the last as, in the former case, being the greatest.—W.

‡ The five last days of the year, to be observed as holidays.—W.

§ Name of a city, built by Jamshíd.

‖ Name of a district in Chinese Tartary. A Muhammadan pilgrim lately created a great sensation among the Pársis of Bombay by asserting that a colony of Gabars exists in this region.—W.

reaped honor from evil actions." Again Zártusht inquired of God the holy and free from infirmity. "In that evil time—that season of danger—what calamity will befall the faith from evil men? Whoever has the Wastá in his mind, or the Kustí bound on his waist, how shall such a one mingle with the people of that generation, his soul being in misery and his body in torment? How shall they pray, privately as directed, or how shall they read the Zandavastá?"—Thus the Creator of the world gave answer to Zartusht the good and holy,—"Great affliction shall befall true believers in that evil and disturbed season. He who shall pray then aright, may be accounted twelve phoenixes. A man who prays shall then be as rare as one who observes the whole law at another time; for one word of the Vastá and Zand in that time, shall be equal to the Vandíd and Hádokht.* Again, when the Hazárahs make head, pain and grief shall be multiplied without end. From the hardships which the bodies of the faithful shall endure they shall resemble iron. Such affliction and pain has never been experienced, not even in the days of Zohák and Afrásiáb, for even in those days the believers of the Zand were more numerous, and more abundant in wealth and blessings. Then, when the Hazárahs shall grow powerful, none of the faithful shall remain. From every side they shall press towards Irán and shall desolate it beneath the feet of their camels. And when they shall turn back to the mountains, they shall carry off both religion and empire. The affairs of those evil people shall grow desperate, and they shall wander, destitute of house and food. Thus will it be a mingled scene of good and bad, of prosperity and the reverse. The state of the world shall not remain one, like the wind which is now good and now injurious."

Zartusht inquires the third time of God, respecting the latter times.

Zartusht asked three things farther of Hormazd, the Creator and Lord. "After these troublous times, will there be any believers in the true faith? Shall these statutes and laws be restored? Will any one support the true faith? When will the wearers of dark garments be discomfited? And how will the impure fiend be cast down? When life is thus shortened, and toil increased, how will their affairs be conducted? How will their object be accomplished? And how will virtue succeed? O Creator and merciful God! inform thy creatures of this, for my soul is disquieted on account (of the people of those times), my heart is burnt up from pain and affliction." God the cherisher said to him, "O faithful man, be not sorrowful! For no one remains perpetually in woe, nor does any one suffer in both worlds; whoever has been afflicted in this world shall likewise be pardoned in paradise. And as to what you have inquired respecting those times, whether any one will seek the true faith,— When the mark of blackness comes upon the world, the restoration of the faith shall be prepared in another way. All the desire of the angry Dews shall be fulfilled

* The Vandidád, and Hádokht, two of the Nusks of the Avastá.

by the merciless Turk of narrow sight. At that time an army shall come from Rúm, of evil thoughts, and acts impure and ill-omened, with red garments and their horse trappings of red, their actions resembling those of impure Dews. When the season for their appearance in the world shall arrive, various signs shall be manifested. The land of Khúrásán, from wet and heat, shall become dark and gloomy as the gloom of might. The world shall grow dark with tempests, and the brightness of water shall be obscured. Many earthquakes shall happen, and ill-omened birds be seen. Every city and land shall be made desolate; desire and want shall wax strong upon people; trouble and pain and woe shall increase in that time. Hormazd gathers strength and casts down Náhíd; the Turk and the men of Rúm shall meet and shall join battle, like the wind Samúm. At the same time shall come the tribe of Arabs, raising strife and battle and violence. From each tribe men shall be slain in every land; the slain shall be in heaps. From the mingling tints of the blood shed, the world shall be red, yellow, and violet. The whole land of Irán shall be desolate from the armies of Turks, and Arabs, and Hindús. All the fire-temples shall be removed thence to the mountains in those troublous times. They shall remove them with difficulty from their places; but they shall bring them into the hill country. They shall bring A'zar Gushtásp with care to the faithful, in the land of Karmán. The spoiler shall fall on the land of Irán. Flight and dispersion to another country! They shall hide in caves and hollows of mountains, and no outlet to the mountains shall remain. The father shall have no thought for his son, from the pain and affliction which shall befall himself." Then said Zartusht of enlightened heart, after he had wept before God, — "Since the life of this people is shortened, let them not finally fall into misery and torment — let them not, in the end, choose evil, nor fill up the catalogue of their crimes." "From the shortness of their lives there is no fear, since death and life are but the same."* Again Zartusht said, — "O holy God! how will their destruction ensue? When their period has elapsed, what sign of evil will they first discover? What will be the termination of their history and how will their prosperity be destroyed."† God returned the following answer to Zartusht, the prophet of the age, "A black sign shall come forth from Khúrásán when the period of empire shall arrive; when Hushidar is born, this is the period. I have told you when he is thirty years old and has wisdom, he shall choose the faith and way of the faithful. There shall be a Sháh in Hindustán and Chín, of the seed of the ‡ Kaián in that evil time. He shall have a son of becoming worth; the name of thatson shall be Bahrám. His title shall be Hamáwand, by parentage and race of the kings of the

* This appears to be the answer of God to the first question put by Zartusht.— E.

† This second question of Zartusht seems to refer to the enemies of the faith, as the former did to the remnant of believers. — E.

‡ The second Persian dynasty.

world. They shall call his tribe Sháhpur; he shall win much honor and delight in the world. The sign of the period of his coming shall be the falling of stars from heaven. His father shall die of old age in the month of Abán and the day of Bád. And when twenty-one years shall have expired, he shall assemble a vast army. He shall invade every quarter of the globe, and shall win his desire of his enemies. He shall lead his armies to Balkh and Bokhárá, and shall survey the world on every side. He shall lead a countless host from Hindústán and Chín, that noble king shall lead them against I'rán. He shall lead them forth in glittering array. The faithful shall rejoice at the sight of him. And then, when Hormazd is in the ascendant and has brought beneath him Náhíd, then you shall see a man of the true faith gird up his loins from the hill country. From the countries of Khúrásán and Seistán, he shall lead a wondrous and countless army. It shall gleam with triple colors, and shall go forth to the succour of I'rán. The army of the impure leader shall many of them be cast down and slain in the battle from the ships of Dawal* and from Rúm and Farang, from the dark-clothed devils, the bicolor wolves. Then shall be three fierce battles in I'rán, and many famous men shall be killed. All Fárs of Shiráz shall be filled with woe. Grief and mourning shall take the place of joy. Then shall the noble Sháh come thither and shall join battle with the foes of I'rán; he shall read the heavens and shall draw out his enemy from the lowest depth. By the will of God the cherisher, he shall destroy those evil people. Such shall be the events of those times, and thousands of women shall wander forth; they shall wander through the bázárs and streets. From the want of husbands, they shall seek men; wherever they behold a man, they shall remain gazing on him with wonder. From desire they shall approach him, and shall seek a remedy of their pain. When their period shall truly arrive it shall resemble a tree full of leaves, and fruit on which at night a cold wind blows. Its leaves and fruit shall fall down. I will send tidings to Kangadas. I will send a good angel to Bashútan.† He shall gird up his loins for the Sháh, and the faith, and he shall come to the land of I'rán. Bashútan shall come at my bidding and shallcleanse the world from those who speak against me. With him shall come thrice fifty heroes, and they shall perform the whole Yasht to God. Ahriman shall desire battle, and the strife-loving Dews. From Ahriman a countless host shall approach Bashútan, breathing fury. When they heard the Hádokht from the Zandavastá, from those Mobeds and Ráds— the Dews shall fly from I'rán, they shall be dispersed and afflicted. Then shall come that Sháh of fortunate name, called by all people, Bahrám. He shall take the throne, and the imperial crown, and shall free the world from those aliens from God. The Mobed of Mobeds

* I know not if this word be a proper name or merely the name signifying rich.— E.

† The brother of Asfandiár, who, as before mentioned, was gifted with immortality.— E.

shall sit with him in presence of the wise, and the learned priests. He shall quickly restore the fire-temples and shall gather those which were long dispersed. They shall place him like a Sháh on his throne, and the savage wolf shall resemble a cow. He shall remove the wicked from the earth, and shall sit down with the wise according to his desire. Bashútan shall heap countless praises on that country, people, and king. He shall go to his own principality and palaces when he finds all things obedient to him. Such, O my son, is the history of the world; that, in the world no one has cause to fear. Neither good nor evil endure perpetually, nor remain fixed unchangeably."

I have made this good relation according to the words of Mobeds, the chief of true believers. Who can relate good tales like milk and wine to you except Kaús Kai? When you see this writing, my story, give me the applause due to me. When you read the whole history of Zartusht in your heart repeat perfect praise. Every heart in which dwells love for him, the face of that man shall be bright as the sun. Praise be to God the cherisher, that I am acquainted with Zartusht and the faith. I am not a heretic or a demon, nor are my principles or habits such as these. What could I have done, O man of wisdom! had I been born of a wicked father, if I had been brought into the world as a heretic and had prostrated myself before I'blis; if I had abode in hell till the resurrection, and the juggling fiends had accomplished their wish through me. I am unable to utter the praises of God who made me acquainted with wisdom and the faith. Thanks to God the cherisher, that I was able to complete this memorial; he gave me aid and brought me success. I have written this history; from me be hundreds of blessings on that noble child of heaven, and may his holiness be perfected from the Creator, God the Almighty. Praise and prayer to Zartusht the prophet of the faithful—more numerous than the sands, or leaves of trees.* May my blessings rest on that auspicious person. I have written this admirable history, by the advice of the wise and prudent person, the excellent and faithful Kaús Kaí, whose father was Kai-Khosrau and whose city is Rai. A thousand blessings on Zartusht from me, and on Noshírvan! By the will and command of God, I have written this history of His people, in order that when the faithful read it they may pronounce blessings on me. Whoever blesses Anusharawán, (Zoroaster) may his fortune always prosper. A thousand blessings upon him whoever blesses our Anusharawán. Praise be upon that noble person who desires to intercede for me with God. It was the six hundred, and forty-seventh year of Yazdejard, the month of Abán, which is the *month of* (?), I commenced the work on the day of A'zár. On the feast of Abán I was intoxicated; I finished it on the night of Khur, on this day I completed it.† I ask praise and prayer from the reader, I also

* This expression is little less then blasphemy.—E.

† The days of A'zar, A'bán, and Khúr, are the ninth, tenth, and eleventh of the month. During one of these the author of the Zartusht-Námah, ac-

ask pardon of God. Heaven be the abode of the soul of Anusharawán, which Hoshah Rawán sends from his heart. If you should not know my name, if you will hear or read this story, you will find that my name is Zartusht Bahrám bin Pazdawám, a history of both of them, since I have related this history of them. I have interpreted it aright. I have repeated many blessings and praise, so that no one will compose similar.

The end of the ZARTUSHT-NAMAH, [the copying of] which was completed on the day of Arshasang, in the month of A'zar, in the year of Izad, 1005 of the prince Yazdejard.

The writer of this history and I that am of God, and of the faith of Zartusht the Mazdayasnan, the son of a Hérbad—the Hérbad Barzu Bin Kawám-ud-Dín, bin Kaikobád, bin Hormazdiár, bearing the title of Sanjánán, worshipper of fire and of Bahrám. Whoever reads let him applaud!

B. — COMMENT ON THE ANTI-CONVERSION MEMORIAL.*

The duty devolves upon us of laying before our readers, an extraordinary document, lately presented by some of the natives to the Governor in Council of this place. Though it has been disguised by European supervision, — *not* that we are happy to say, connected with the honorable bar of our Supreme Court—its features are too marked to escape observation, and its demands are too astounding, and directly opposed to the principles of eternal right, to meet with the slightest compliance. We have no wrathful feeling towards its originators; but we do regret to see them follow a course, which in our calmest judgment, appears to us to be directed by intolerance and injustice, opposed to the interests of truth, injurious to their fellow-men, destructive of the salutary influence which it is desirable they should exercise in the native community, and calculated to impair the respect which is accorded to them by their European friends. We have for months pursued a most conciliatory course towards them, under unexampled provocation; and it is a regard to our own legitimate defence, and the cause of Christian philanthropy, in the eyes of those whose information is limited, which now compels us publicly to ex-

cording to his own confession, was "intoxicated." He had consequently only two days left for the composition of the poem, a work of about 3200 lines! — W.

* The origin and fate of the document here commented upon, I have explained in the opening chapter of this work. In making extracts from the critique upon it, which, after insertion in a Bombay periodical, I laid before Government for its information, I select merely those passages which bear upon statements made by Dosabhái, and some of the other Pársí controversialists. The complete comment, as well as the Memorial to which it refers, may be seen in the Oriental Christian Spectator, January, 1840.

amine their complaints, and to discuss the merits of the petition which they have addressed to the authorities. While we do this, we are more anxious to awaken their consciences, than to arouse their anger; and more desirous to see them brought to an acknowledgement of their errors, and an amendment of their ways, than to inflict upon them the slightest injury.....

We regret that in our remarks, we cannot altogether be guided by the sequence of the paragraphs of the petition, which are remarkably confused in their order, and declamatory in composition. We shall not overlook, however, any of the topics to which it adverts.

1. The account which the petitioners give of the feelings entertained in the native community relative to the subject of their address, is most erroneous. The "alarm and distrust" of which they speak, has been far from being general, and where it does exist, it has arisen principally from the *refusal* of the people to re-echo the cry of persecution raised by the illiberal and tyrannical few, rather than from any sense of injury inflicted on the many by the friends of the Christian cause. Of the correctness of what we now aver, every candid person in Bombay, who has eyes to see and ears to hear, must be well aware. Little stress is to be laid on what the petitioners state in support of their averment, that on the occasion of the conversion of the Pársí youth "several hundred boys, Hindoos, Mahommedans, and Parsees were immediately withdrawn from the Mission Schools." The number of pupils removed from the General Assembly's Institution, was exactly 234; and they were rather *driven away* than *withdrawn*. Many of their parents and guardians have respectfully apologized for the step which the rage and threats of their superiors compelled them to take; and not a few have restored their wards to the enjoyment of the privilege of Christian and general instruction, which they formerly enjoyed. The loss sustained by the seminary has already been repaired to the amount of 85 scholars; and it now contains 135 pupils, while there is the reasonable prospect of a gradual increase.* What is worthy of particular notice, is, that the attendance at the vernacular schools of the General Assembly's Mission, which are under the same superintendence as the English Institution, has *considerably encreased* since the prosecution of Dr. Wilson in the Supereme Court, and this notwithstanding that several warnings and remonstrances were printed and circulated throughout the city, in which it was declared that "doubtless calamities happened to the Hindú religion from the sword of the Musalmáns, but greater calamities than these will occur from the books and schools of the Padres," and in which the promise was given that schools in abundance should be erected in which the native religions should be taught. Were more liberal funds at the disposal of the Missionaries, for the support of teachers, there would be no limit to the scholars. The people know that the Missionaries deal with them fairly

* The hope here expressed has long ere this been realized.

and honestly, and not a few of them consider them to be their best friends. Dr. Wilson was hailed by many of them, in different parts of the city, because the decision of the Court was in favour of religious liberty; and his ministrations, and those of his fellow-labourers of all denominations, however cordially they may be hated by the petitioners, are not less highly valued by the *community* at this moment than they have ever been since their commencement. It is notorious that the demand for bibles and tracts has lately encreased both in Bombay, and other towns of the Presidency; and that the natives continue to come forward to profess their faith in Christ, and to solicit admission into the Christian church. Of these facts, the petitioners seem to be well aware. What is "the picture of misery," in their view, they say more truthfully than elegantly, to the Governor in Council, is in "daily *progress* before you, and one which will have no *end*, unless you in your goodness step forward to obtain relief."

2. "To the great cry of late years, Educate the Natives," say the petitioners, "we have responded with heart and hand, little dreaming that under the cloak of education, the work of conversion was insidiously to be carried on." "Missionary schools," they add, "are now extending themselves in all directions, having for their ostensible object the education of the natives, but for their real object the conversion of the native youth, whom the poor and the ignorant may commit to their charge." What their "*dreams*" may have been we cannot, of course, divine; but most certainly, the principal complainants, when they were in the Supreme Court in May last completely failed to establish the truth of what they now aver. "That defendant," said the Judge, "if not by advertisements, yet by the course of public examination, and many other things conclusively proved to-day, is cleared from the imputation of clandestine proceedings, is most clear; but I think, to use Mr. Advocate General's words, that the respectable Parsee gentlemen have been *sleeping** over the intimations given." According to their own account, their countrymen are not yet *awake*. If they are really still in their slumbers, we believe that something more than missionary reports, speeches, and sermons, which are full of professions respecting endeavours to lead the natives to embrace Christianity,—and more than conversions through the instrumentality of missionaries,—and more than the intimations of the editors of native newspapers, and the thundering warnings of Pancháyats, are necessary to arouse them. We suppose that when they do become awake, some of them may be more formidable to our opponents than when they were in an attitude of repose. The following are extracts from a note by an educated native of respectability, which was brought to us by three pupils who were this day received under our own charge. "I am very glad to embrace the opportunity to place my nephew, and two other boys un-

* The Italics are our own.

der your most fostering Christian care and tuition; so that you will be pleased to issue special instructions for their being admitted in the Assembly's Institution...... Pray let the youthful mind have only as much knowledge of English as will enable it to comprehend every word of *the Word*, in comparison with which every scientific acquirement is as insignificant as the child's whims. I leave these forlorn souls to you in the most earnest hope the Infinite Goodness will be most graciously pleased to regenerate them, and guide them in the *narrow passage*. By and bye, I shall also place ——— under your religious instruction, which I feel assured is the only efficient remedy to mitigate, if not to heal, the poor afflicted hearts." We have other documents in our possession not less precise and definite than that from which we now quote.

3. The petitioners have ventured to say, that they have "but too great reason for believing that temporal rewards have been held forth as inducements, and that even the passions of these young children have been tampered with to effect the end in view" [conversion]. We defy one and all of them to the proof. A fouler and more disgraceful libel than that of which they are here guilty was never penned.

4. The accusation brought against the Missionaries at Násik, of "reviling in most unmeasured terms all that the natives hold dear and most sacred in their religion and observances," is one which from our distance from the scene of their operations, we cannot rebut from our personal knowledge. It is one, however, to which, from our acquaintance with the high Christian character of our brethren at that place, we cannot attach the slightest weight. Conviction, it is admitted by them, as by every other Missionary in the country, must be the result of a consistent announcement of the truth and legitimate reasoning, accompained by the divine blessing, and not of violent reproach, and unmeaning invective. They all acknowledge that "the wrath of man worketh not the righteousness of God." That no redress would be afforded to persons who might have their feelings wantonly injured in the manner alleged by the petitioners, is most untrue. The Bombay Regulations make ample provision for the punishment of religious insults; and this we are persuaded most of the petitioners know right well. Among their number there are individuals who should have been *ashamed* to complain, who were not only the quondam patrons of the Gujaráti AGE OF REASON, but its active translators, and who, in the native newspapers, have nearly exhausted, within these few months, the vocabulary of abuse, in their raillery against Christianity and its professors.

5. That divisions and ruptures in families may follow conversions, we cannot and do not deny. It is with reference to them, and those which occur in larger communities, that our blessed Lord himself said, "Think not that I am come to send peace on earth: I came not to send peace, but a sword. For I am come to set a man at variance against his father, and the daughter against her mother, and the daughter-in-law against her

mother-in-law. And a man's foes shall be those of his own household. He that loveth father or mother more than me is not worthy of me; and he that loveth son or daughter more than me is not worthy of me." Christianity, however, though it may be the *occasion* of these separations and variances, is most certainly not their *cause*. It fills the breast of those who embrace it with *love to man*, as well as *love to God*. It is its holiness and purity which stirs up the enmity of the carnal mind, and which begets a spirit of persecution in those who resist its claims. Its converts lose none of their affection for their kindred according to the flesh; but the love of Christ, the sovereign principle of their mind, compels them to forego their friendship when it cannot be retained without their denying the Lord who bought them, and without their abandoning his holy worship. In leaving all for Christ's sake, in these circumstances, they evince the purity of their principles,— the power of that grace which is vouchsafed to them by the Holy Spirit. In a moral point of view, they stand infinitely higher than those, who restrained by the fear of man, suppress the workings of their consciences, conceal their actual belief, and pursue the course of hypocrites and deceivers. In the instances in which they find their civil and religious liberty, and their personal safety, respected in their families, they forsake them not; and it is only the actual or threatened violence of their relatives, or the experience of restraints, or the harsh and cruel discipline of caste, and its sinful demands, which constitutes them aliens in a social point of view,— in a religious point, they must be aliens,— from the communities with which they were formerly connected, and which forces them to seek for shelter and protection among their Christian brethren from the West. They abandon not the civil right to the custody of their own offspring during the years of infancy and childhood; and though their children may sometimes be surreptitiously removed from them, they fail not to reclaim them when opportunities offer, and hesitate not most faithfully and tenderly to discharge the parental duties. When their partners are willing to stay with them after their conversion, they still cleave to them, for the institute of the Christian faith on this subject is most precise: —"If any brother hath a wife that believeth not, and she be pleased to dwell with him, let him not put her away. And the woman which hath an husband that believeth not, and if he be pleased to dwell with her, let her not leave him." Christianity is not answerable for any separations which take place. It is only the intolerance prevalent in the land, which cuts asunder the ties of nature; and the unconverted natives on this account ought to remember that *they* have the remedy in their own hands. If they will agree to treat their converted friends with kindness, they may have much of their society, and as, in some cases which are before our view, find them dearer to themselves than ever. Instances are known to us in which after a few years the most violent opposition has subsided into cordial support; and in which those who at one time have been persecutors, have become the humble disciples of those whom they sought to injure.

The conduct of the Pársí youth, to whom the petitioners refer, in connexion with the divisions in families to which we have now alluded, has from first to last appeared to us to be of the most exemplary character. When it is pourtrayed by the pen of truth, it will call forth on their behalf the highest admiration, or rather induce the exalted praise of God for the abundant grace conferred upon them in the hour of trial and temptation. Necessity alone, not merely supposed, but most fully *proved,* to exist, in the highest court of this Presidency, compelled them to leave their homes, and to solicit protection from the missionaries. The attempt which is made to bring home the charge of untruthfulness against the younger of them, Dhunjeebhoy Nowrojee, in reference to one of his parents, as far as those who know the real state of the case, as some of the petitioners do, is most disgraceful. It was not as alleged with the view of "defeating the endeavours of his family to obtain through the aid of the Supreme Court possession of his person," that he characterized his father's widow "Sobhoy," as only his step-mother; for the nature of Sobhoy's relation to him, as every lawyer knows, had nothing to do with the question of his personal liberty which was tried before the Court; but it was with the view of merely correcting *en passant* what he considered to be the error of his opponent. His own explanation of the matter, in his second affidavit, is simple and natural:—"Dhunjeebhoy Nowrojee of Bombay, Christian inhabitant, maketh oath and saith, that this information about his family has been principally derived from his uncle Heerjeebhoy Dadabhoy mentioned in this deponent's former affidavit in this matter, and from his other relatives, and that up to this present month, the said Heerjeebhoy Dadabhoy has uniformly stated to this deponent, that the name of the mother of this deponent was Manickbhoy, and that the said Manickbhoy was not such a troublesome woman as Sobhoy mentioned in this deponent's affidavit, as this deponent's step-mother. And this deponent saith, that when this deponent resided at Arow near to Broach, he was informed by his oldest paternal uncle Hormusjee Dadabhoy, mentioned in this deponent's former affidavit, in this matter, that the name of his, this deponent's mother, was Manickbhoy." Dr. Wilson swore that he had no personal knowledge of the parentage of the young man; but that long previous to his special inquiries on the subject of Christianity, he heard him speak of himself as having no mother alive. Mr. Campbell's reasoning on the matter in the Court was most appropriate. "We say all our information had been gathered from Heerjeebhoy himself. We also give the subject of former conversations with Heerjeebhoy about Sobhoy, and unless you believe that Dhunjeebhoy has invented all this, it is imposible to believe Heerjeebhoy. Dr. Wilson affirms on oath, that he had always been informed by Dhunjeebhoy that Sobhoy was not his mother. Dunjeebhoy does not now come forward to make this statement for the first time." Here the matter stood in the Supreme Court. Since the trial, we have obtained a variety of positive evidence that Dhunjeebhoy was correct, and which we are prepared to adduce, should the Pársís again bring the matter into any tribunal competent to examine it. We mention a simple fact. Sobhoy, when asked by Mr. Warden of the Civil Service, late one of the Magistrates of Police, if Dhunjeebhoy was really her *pet ka beta*, (her *own* son), was *silent*, at the very moment too at which, at the instigation of some Pársís, she had applied to Mr. Warden to get a new writ of habeas corpus on her own behalf! But enough of this matter for the present. Let some of the Pársís be cautious about their affidavits, and let them remember that those which we printed in June last, have long ere this had the verdict of the public pronounced upon them.

6. In order to impede as far as possible, the work of the conversion of the natives of India, and to awaken sympathy on their own behalf, the petitioners strive to blacken the character of the native Christians. The alleged examples of depravity to which they specially refer, are those, it is remarkable, with which Protestant Missionaries have no connexion, the native Christians of Salsette, Goa, Travancore, and elsewhere, and whom we are under no particular obligations to defend. It so happens, however, that the character of these Christians, though not so high as those which are really the greatest eye-sore in the view of the petitioners, will stand an honorable comparison with that of their heathen and Muhammadan neighbours. The authorities at Tanna have been long accustoned to speak, on the whole, in a favourable manner of the Christian population placed under their charge. The native Christians at Goa conduct themselves better, to say the least, than their European masters. The Christians in Travancore and Cochin were declared by Mr. Baber, in his examination before a Committee of Parliament, to be "the best subjects the Travancore and Cochin Rajahs have." "They are," he added, "the most industrious, moral, and obedient, and many of them, I believe, opulent." Messrs Conner and Ward, the Company's surveyors, in the official report which we quoted in our October number, say of them:—"Partially at least free from the prevarications that characterize the Nairs, they have an infinitely franker deportment, and seem capable of a more lasting attachment than they. If they have less capacity, their greater integrity might argue the possession of superior virtues. Peaceable and valuable subjects they return obedience for toleration and protection." Though individual nominal Christians, in India, as in every country of the world, may be found to equal, or even exceed some of the heathen in their depravity, it is because they break through greater restraints, and have their sin characterized by greater aggravations. This is quite in accordance with the analogy of nature; for "the richest soil breeds the rankest weeds." Christianity itself is holy in its motives, holy in its precepts, holy in its examples, and holy in its sanctions; and to the degree in which its glorious truths are taught and received by faith, it is the parent of morality. It is *pure* Christianity, which the Missionaries, against whom the petitioners complain, seek to propagate in India.

7. In one part of the document on which we comment, the petition-

ers make a great show of liberality. "If attempts to make converts," say they, "were confined to men of full age and understanding, whilst we might deplore, we could not complain of, the labours of the Missionaries, and if any of our adult population capable of sound reflection embraced the Christian faith, we could only lament their infatuation and pray, that their desertion from their own religion might be forgiven to them." We were scarcely prepared for this advance of profession, as only a few months have intervened between the present hour, and that in which some of the principal petitioners put themselves to the trouble of swearing in the Supreme Court, "that it is an universal and inflexible rule of domestic government among Pársís, that the father has until his death, the entire control of his male-children of whatever age, and of their male descendants." Now that it is before us, we are sorry to be compelled by the petitioners themselves to give it to the winds. In the second prayer with which they conclude their memorial, and to which we shall again advert, they entreat that adult converts may be grievously persecuted, robbed of their wives and children, fined in a reasonable sum for their maintenance even when they are deprived of them, and forfeit all right and title to inherit the family or ancestorial property of their parents! This is "only lamenting the infatuation of," and "praying for forgiveness" for converts with a vengeance!!

8. The tone and expressions of the petitioners would lead a stranger to believe that the late Pársí converts to Christianity were mere children in the proper sense of the term, and incompetent to form any judgment on the subject of religion. This is not, however, a true statement of the case. The parties who prosecuted Dr. Wilson in May last, failed to prove that the younger was then below the age of sixteen years and a half. The elder is now in his twentieth year, and was himself a parent upwards of two years ago. "As to their education, and competency to judge for themselves in matters of religion," it was remarked by Dr. Wilson on a former occasion, "the Pársís have not the slightest right to complain. It is long since they were both constituted disciples of Zoroaster on their own responsibility and according to the forms of the Pársí faith. As far as their knowledge of the essential principles of Christianity is concerned, I believe that they would gain admittance into the strictest communion in Europe. The younger of them is not inferior in point of *general education* to any of the Pársí gentlemen who bear Her Majesty's commission of the Peace. *Should any of them doubt the correctness of my statement on this subject, I shall be happy to submit the matter to the judgment of any umpires who may be equitably selected by both parties, and who will permit a public examination to be conducted, before judgment is pronounced.*" This challenge has not yet been accepted. It should silence those to whom it was addressed."

While we distinctly mention the facts of the case connected with the case of the Pársí converts, and we do not object, on civil grounds, to heathen parents having the guardianship of their children during absolute non-age, we would not be understood as insinuating, that we should not in any case rejoice to see faith in Christ exhibited in the earliest years of life. The claims of God for the heart of man, are not morally suspended while responsibility exists. He can espouse to himself the affections of a child with the first dawnings of discernment and reflection. "Out of the mouths of babes and sucklings, hast thou ordained strength because of thine enemies, that thou mightest still the enemy and the avenger." Let the natives around us rest satisfied by attempts to regulate the creeds of their offspring by moral suasion, and let them remember the account which they themselves must render to God for all the instruction which they impart to them.

9. We are not called upon to defend the proceedings either of the Supreme Court or the Government of Bombay, but for the sake of the petitioners, and the natives whom they seek to inflame, we shall say a few words respecting their complaints against these Honorable bodies. The Pársís suffered no detriment to their cause from the application to it of English law, for the Hindú law, the only other system of jurisprudence by which it could have been tried, would have found Dhunjeebhoy Nowrojee to have been "of age," on the completion of his sixteenth year. When they venture to say, "that the judge never gave one moment's consideration to the circumstances of the case," they use language which by some may be interpreted as a punishable contempt of Court. The question before the judge was simply one in which the interest of natives were concerned; and the youth, in whose behalf the writ of Habeas Corpus was issued, was left to choose his own abode. Parliament has not sanctioned the recommendation of the report of the Select Committee, quoted by the petitioners; and on questions of *absolute right*, native and Europeans must of necessity stand on the same footing, while equity is allowed to rule in our legislation. Nothing indecorous occurred on the part of the defendant during the whole legal proceedings. The assistance of the Government was neither asked nor received by him on that occasion; and in calling out the troops, it acted solely in its capacity of supreme conservator of the peace. It is the height of presumption in any body of men, however respectable they may be, to seek to supplant it in the exercise of this function. Those who denominate themselves "the most respectable persons of all castes," saw the mob at the Court, on the first day of the hearing of the case, and they did not cause it to disperse. Where was the assurance to be found, except in their own declaration, that they were either willing or able to disperse it, should it have collected on the second day? The proclamation which was circulated among the Pársís had not a single signature attached to it; and though it forbad all Zoroastrians to attend the Court with the exception of those connected with the prosecution, a considerable number were present in spite of it, while many had congregated in a neighbouring street. However offensive the arms of the soldiers might be to the pride of a few, they inspired a salutary fear in the minds of many; and

the display of them was more merciful than their concealment, which might have encouraged a disturbance, similar to that which formerly occurred, and which might ultimately have led to a loss of life. Nothing can be more absurd than the complaint of the petitioners that the members of the Government gave their "good wishes" to the missionaries, during the late trial; for "good wishes" for the righteous spread of Christianity, essentially exist in all its disciples who are worthy of the name. Of these "good wishes," no expression was made, and no expression was sought. Dr. Wilson had no support, but in the reasonableness of his cause, and the law of the realm. *The prosecuting Pársis, and some of their friends, were the only parties who communicated with Government during the pending of the trial.* How improper their conduct was in this matter will appear from the following document......

13. We now find ourselves at the prayer of the memorial; but as there is not the slightest reason to believe, that it can for one moment be entertained, we shall not extend our observations. Nothing can be more absurd than to call for the passing of laws for impeding the conversion of the natives to our holy faith.

(1). There is no such impression either in the European or native community, as will beget or foster the belief, that, on the part of the missionaries, any thing of an improper character was done in the "case which recently happened." It would not be difficult for us to procure an expression of sympathy of an entirely opposite character. Missionary schools in the interior are everywhere acceptable to the people, who avail themselves of their advantages, else they could not exist. There are thousands of parents, who are perfectly willing that their children should receive Christian instruction, but who would hesitate to give any "sanction in writing" in reference to this subject, from the apprehension that in consequence they might be persecuted nearly to death by tyrannical Pancháyats, and the heroes of caste. It is sufficient that they themselves send their children to the schools, or willingly permit them to attend. The Hindú Rishis, have fixed the age at which a youth arrives at his majority at sixteen years;* and these far-seeing sages, did they still retain their olden spirit, if they again visited the world, would propose at least the banishment of the petitioners for imagining the propriety of a more extended age. Muhammad would not be more indulgent to the folks of his

* We could adduce many Sanskrit distichs in which *fifteen* years is given as the date at which a youth arrives at his majority. "The distinction may be thus recapitulated," says Colebrooke, in his digest of Hindú Law; "a minor (bála) is in early infancy to the end of his fourth year, and called *kumara;* in law he is an infant to the end of his seventh year, and in this period of his life is called *shishya;* he is called a boy *(pogenda)* from his fifth to the end of his ninth year; and his adolescence as *kisora* continues from the tenth to the end of the fifteenth year." Sir Thomas Strange thinks that the weight of authority is in favour of a majority at the completion of the sixteenth year.

family. Even in England, personal liberty is secure for a youth at fourteen, though he does not obtain control over his property till he is twenty-one; and the precocity of the human constitution in India must never be overlooked.

(2.) The insolence and injustice which call upon Christian men to pass an act legally to deprive converts to their own faith of their wives and children,— to bind them to support them when in a state of alienation from their authority,— and to deprive them of "all right and title to inherit family, or ancestorial property," except what may be bequeathed by will, are unparalleled. From the display which has been made of them, we learn how little disposed some persons are calmly to reason and reflect on any question connected with the economy of public Government, and how weak the native religions are in themselves when called to conflict with Christianity. Some of the petitioners, we are happy to state, are startled at the infatuation which has led them to commit themselves in a case so evidently connected with the natural and inalienable rights of their fellow-creatures. Most of them, we have learnt, dread the publication of their names.

(3.) We object not to the multiplication of Government schools throughout the length and breadth of the land, though we wish them conducted on somewhat different principles from those of the Native Education Society, and established, in the first instance, in those places in which they are most needed. Even their own working may not be exactly what the petitioners expect. The sooner they make up their minds to a solemn consideration of the claims of the Bible, so much the better. Their best friends are those who tell them the whole truth on this subject. Upwards of five years ago, we expressed ourselves as follows:— "There is great inconsistency in the practice of the principal supporters of the educational institutions from which Christianity is excluded. They refrain, they say, from interfering with the religious belief of the natives, and yet they deliberately teach the elements of Geography and Astronomy, which will inevitably prove its destruction. They will not present to the scholar any system of truth on which the soul may repose, by which it may be delivered from sin, and by which it may be prepared for the duties of life, and the services of heaven; but they will congratulate themselves, like the 'General Committee of Public Instruction in Bengal' [a strictly Government body], 'when an impatience of Hindúism, and a disregard of its ceremonies, are openly avowed by many young men of respectable birth and talents, and entertained by many more, who outwardly conform to the practices of their countrymen.'* The eyes of the principal natives, we trust, will soon be open to their best interests. The question, they should perceive, is not, whether religion shall be destroyed by education, but whether for it they are to receive any substitute."

14. Had it been our object to indulge in personalities, and to direct the scorn and mockery of the public, against the individuals who have ri-

* Report for 1832.

sen up against us, we could have now shown that, with regard to some of them, we are not destitute of the opportunity. A more hallowed purpose, however, has guided our endeavours; and we trust that our opponents will see that we have acted merely in defence of ourselves, and the cause of truth and holiness. In taking leave of them, we beg again to disclaim the slightest wish on our part to be accessory to their injury, and to express the hope, and the prayer, that the day may not be far distant, when they will give us the fullest credit for the sincerity of the profession which we now make. We supplicate for their welfare in time and eternity; and for the promotion of it we are ready, through divine grace, to perform any amount of labour, and to undergo any amount of suffering which may be required at our hand. We wish not to be execrated even by the few last men of the passing generation; but should this be our lot, we shall be content humbly to seek the approbation of that God whom we desire to serve in the Gospel of his Son, and to indulge the hope, founded on his own infallible word, that his cause will soon triumph, in spite of the errors of its friends, and the opposition of its enemies. Many will still run to and fro, and knowledge will be encreased. Christ has been lifted up, and he will draw all men unto him. Men shall be blessed in him: all nations shall call him blessed.

As the writer of this article, has no objection to assume the personal responsiblility which it involves, he subscribes his name.

JOHN WILSON.

Bombay, January, 1840.

C.—MISCELLANEOUS REMARKS ON CERTAIN PASSAGES OF THE PA'RSI' CONTROVERSIALISTS.

At p. 105 of this work, I have intimated, that it was my intention to notice under this head any parts of the publications of my opponents, deserving of the least attention, which might not come in my way in the course of argument which I might be called to pursue in consistency with the plan which I had laid down for my guidance. Such passages, I now find, are few in number, and of no great significance.

I. Turning to the *Tálím-i-Zartusht*, and adverting to matters in the order observed by Dosabhâí, I make the following notes.

1. I have already produced many of the passages of Scripture in which the divine Sonship and the divine nature of Christ are set forth. Christ was the Son of *Mary*, because of her he was born according to the flesh; he was the son of *Joseph*, as born and residing in his family, and "supposed" by those unacquainted with the miraculous conception of his mother, to be of his parentage; and he was the Son of *David*, as descended, in his human nature, from that monarch, and the appointed and rightful, king of his people. The apparent discrepancies in the genealogies of

Matthew and Luke, are perfectly explicable on the supposition that they represent the descent of Christ by different lines, according to the public registers of which they are probably extracts. The actual father of Joseph, as stated by Matthew, was Jacob. Heli is mentioned by Luke as also his father,—according to the reckoning of the Jews, who did not allow the names of females to stand in their genealogical tables,— because he was the father of Mary his wife, and because he may have adopted him as his son. The number of forty-two generations referred to by Matthew will be complete, if we read with many MSS, "Josias begat Jakim, and Jakim begat Jechonias." There is scarcely a commentary on the Bible in which Dosabhái will not find his objections from the genealogies satisfactorily solved.

2. Circumcision was a suitable sign, or seal, of the covenant of grace before the shedding of the atoning blood of Christ; but not being *necessary* as an ordinance, it was permitted to be laid aside, by the same authority by which it was enjoined. The reasons of the baptism of Christ, which is distinctly testified to in the New Testament, I have already incidentally mentioned in connexion with the notice taken of Christ's entrance on his public ministry.

3. Dosabhái's sneers at the miraculous conception of the Virgin Mary, will be seen to be uncalled for, when the explanation of the angel (Luke ii. 35) is adverted to:— "The Holy Ghost shall come upon thee, and the power of the Highest shall overshadow thee." There is here nothing inconsistent with the spirituality of God.

4. When Christ said, "Why callest thou me good? There is none good but one that is God," he did not disclaim his divinity, but called upon the person who had addressed him to reflect on the meaning of his own words.

5. Dosabhái accuses certain "Christians" of the practice of idolatry. Those who are guilty of this sin, are not Bible Christians; and I shall be thankful to see Dosabhái successful in aiding us in convincing them of their error. Idolatrous Christians are not a beam in our eye, while we neither learn nor observe their ways.

6. Christians either do observe, or ought to observe, the first day of the week as holy to God, because it is expressly said in the New Testament to be the "Lord's Day," and was observed as such by the apostles and early disciples of Christ. Dosabhái is clearly beyond his depth when he adverts to the Sabbath.

7. I am glad to find Dosabhái condemn that faith which is without works. It is verily an insincere faith, a lifeless faith. "Faith," says the apostle James, (ii. 26), "is *dead* without works."

8. There is a passage in Josephus (Antiq. xviii, 33) relative to Christ to this effect:—"At this time lived Jesus, a wise man; if indeed it be proper to call him a man. For he was a doer of wonderful works, a teacher of such men as receive the truth with pleasure. He drew over to him both many of the Jews, and many of the Gentiles. He was Christ.

And when Pilate at the suggestion of the principal men among us, had condemned him to the cross, those that loved him at the first did not forsake him; for he appeared to them alive again the third day; as the divine prophets had foretold these and ten thousand other wonderful things concerning him. And even to the present day the class of persons who were called Christians from him, have not become extinct." Dosabháí must have better authority than that of Voltaire for holding "that *all men of true learning* are now *agreed*," that this passage "has been *interpolated*." The passage is found in all the ancient MSS. which have been consulted; and it is quoted, or referred to, by many ancient writers from the time of Eusebius, about A. D. 324. If Dosabháí will examine a tract by Bretschneider, a German author,—a translation of which I shall be happy to show to him in the Biblical Repository (vol. iv),—or the appendix to Whiston's Translation of Josephus, he will probably admit that much more can be said in favour of the passage than he is at all aware of. In the superabundance of proof of the divine mission of Christ, however, we can easily dispense with it without any injury to our cause. If Josephus really said nothing respecting Christ, we must see in his silence an admission of the excellence of the character of Christ.

"Josephus," says a late able writer on the Evidences of Christianity,* "was born about four years after the crucifixion of Christ, of a noble and priestly family, and brought up in Jerusalem, where even in boyhood he was celebrated for his knowledge of the law. He fully acquainted himself with the principles of the Jewish sects, and became a Pharisee. In his twenty-sixth year (about the seventh year of Nero), he made a voyage to Rome, where he was well received at court.† During his years of study and inquiry, the Christian sect must undeniably have excited much attention in Judæa, and he was in the very focus of all those parties and traditions by which the character of its founder and his followers would be aspersed. In his first visit to Rome the growth of Christianity *there* must have been an object of notice, for it was only three years before that violent persecution by Nero, which Tacitus records.‡ After the destruction of Jerusalem, Josephus accompanied Titus to Rome, received from Vespasian a court-residence and a pension, and was afterwards in favour with the emperors Titus and Domitian, and with the empress Domitia.§ In this abode at Rome, if not sooner, he must have heard of the cruel and extraordinary punishments inflicted on the Christians by Nero a few years before; and must have been acquainted with the existing persecution under Domitian. His Jewish Antiquities, or History of the Jews down to the twelfth year of Nero, was finished in the reign of Domitian, and that of the Jewish war in the reign of Vespasian.‖ We cannot there-

* John Sheppard, Esquire.

† These particulars we learn from his Life, written by himself; and see Lar. iii. 488—9.

‡ Ibid. 611. § Ibid. 490. ‖ Lar. iii. p. 491.

fore explain the silence of Josephus with regard to Christ and his religion by supposing that he overlooked it, or deemed it too inconsiderable to be noticed. It had excited the strongest feelings, and occasioned the strongest measures, not only in Judæa, but through great part of the Roman empire. Even Tacitus and Suetonius, who were much less qualified, less called on, and less interested, to treat of its origin and character, and wrote much more concisely, a few years after him both thought it important enough to be expressly named. But it becomes still less reasonable to ascribe the silence of Josephus to neglect, when we observe that in his Antiquities he treats particularly of the Jewish sects; and that he moreover distinctly treats of the seditious impostors who arose in Judæa from the time of Augustus. Six of these leaders, and the issue of their respective enterprises, are severally named by him.* He also relates the preaching and death of John the Baptist, but not referring to him as the forerunner of the Christ.† Yet all these leaders of parties had failed. They had had no followers except in Judæa, and these had been soon dispersed; while the sect formed by Jesus had spread through the provinces, and even through the metropolis.

"The silence, then, of this historian (if he was silent) concerning Christ, cannot but have been *purposed* and *deliberate*. To what motive *can* we ascribe it but to this,—that he believed the character of Jesus and his apostles to be excellent, and their pretensions, in some sense, genuine; that he had on the one hand too much of honesty, of modesty, or of conviction, to state the contrary, and become the propagator of atrocious calumnies; but on the other hand, too much of a national, and at the same time of a courtly and interested spirit, to attest openly what would be so unwelcome both to the Jewish and Roman people, and to his imperial patrons? To a similar kind of feelings Augustine has expressly attributed the silence of Seneca. It is not credible that Josephus, so favoured by, and dependent on a heathen and persecuting court, if he could have alleged any thing without *utter* violence to his honour and conscience, *against* the founders of the 'new superstition,' or even have brought himself to *insinuate* immorality, deceit, sedition, or imposture, would have omitted to do so. Is it not manifest that every such assertion or intimation would have had the highest value and the warmest welcome both in the minds of Jew and Gentile, as coming from a person of note, brought up on the very spot where Christianity originated? If he *did* write the passage which is doubted of, it may be justly called 'a noble testimony,' not only for its explicitness as to the character and claims of Christ and his disciples, but as indicating fearless disinterested honesty in a pensioner at Rome. If he did *not* write it, but observed silence, *this* kind of testimony, though *less* noble, is in a measure creditable to him; and is

* The particulars are given in B. Pr. pp. 173—4, quoted in Appendix x. to Lardner's life, prefixed to his works, vol. i. p. xlvii.

† Lar. iii. p. 534—6.

equally conclusive as to the fact that there was no *evil* which could be truly and without deep criminality alleged concerning Christ and his companions."*

The munshí, with Voltaire, is unable to account for the silence of Josephus respecting the star which intimated the birth of Christ, the murder of the Bethlehemitish children, the darkness which accompanied the crucifixion, and the resurrection of Christ. These phenomena and events, remarkable though they were, did not fall within the scope of his history, in the same way that the origin of the Christian community, embracing multitudes of Jews and Gentiles throughout the Roman world, may be supposed to have done. While he was not a *follower* of Jesus, he would be shy in adverting to the circumstances which established his claims to be esteemed the Messiah, even though he could speak of him as called the Christ, or even actually indolently believe that he was the Christ.

9. The wise men were in the east when they saw the star which appeared on the occasion of the birth of Christ; but it does not follow that they must have got to the west of it as they proceeded to Jerusalem. All Dosabhái's objections I have long ago anticipated. "On the supposition that a meteor, or any luminous body of a like nature, appeared to the wise men who came from the east to see Christ, no difficulty is experienced in the consideration of the narrative which is given in the New Testament. On the supposition that a new fixed star appeared in the heavens to the Magi, at the time at which the Messiah was born, it is not difficult to see, that when they discovered that the star went before them, they merely ascertained that they had not arrived at its precise zenith point in the heavens, till 'they came to the house where the young child was.' The use of figurative language, according to which the star is viewed as moving, is popularly correct, and is similar to what we employ when we speak of the sun rising and setting. The birth of Christ, the Saviour of men, was such a grand event that it might well be signalized by the creation of a new star. In its appearance,—supposing it no longer to exist,—there is nothing inconsistent with the power of God, and nothing even inconsistent with the experience of astronomers. 'Several new stars,' says Mr. Barlow, one of the Professors of Mathematics at the Royal Military Academy at Woolwich, 'have appeared for a time, and then vanished; some that are given in the ancient catalogues, are no longer to be found; while others are constantly and distinctly visible, which have not been described by the ancients; some stars like *beta* in the whale, have gradually increased in brilliancy; others like *delta* in the great bear, have been constantly diminishing in brightness; and a great number sustain a periodical variation in their brilliancy. The new star which was seen by Tycho in 1572, in the constellation Cassiopeia, suffered very remarkable changes. On a sudden it became so brilliant that it surpass-

* Sheppard on the Evidences of Christianity, vol. i. pp. 107—109.

ed in brightness even Venus and Mercury, and was visible on the meridian in the day time. Its light then began to diminish, till it disappeared about sixteen months after it had been observed. The new star which appeared in 1603 (1604.) in the constellation Serpentarius, exhibited similar phenomena, and disappeared after being visible for some months.'*"

10. Dosabhái objects to the expression, "the heavens were opened" (Matthew, iii.16); but how could he better describe the *appearance* of the firmament on the occasion of the descent of the Spirit like a dove. It is not said in the New Testament that none saw this miracle but Christ. The *reality* of a miracle, however, does not depend on its publicity; though when miracles are designed to be signs, publicity is to be desired. The voice which said "This is my beloved Son, in whom I am well pleased," is declared by Matthew, a better authority than Dosabhái, to have proceeded "from heaven."

11. The feeding of the five thousand with the five loaves and two fishes, is represented in the Gospels as *miraculous;* and hence there is no room for an objection as to its *possibility*, on the ground of *power* to effect it. Neither is there room for objection to the miracle on the ground of *impropriety*. To the question, "Who saw the miracle," I reply, "The multitudes who were present on the occasion of its performance." Accounts of the miracle were published by the evangelists shortly after it occurred; and had these accounts been false, there would have been found many to disprove them. Will Dosabhái direct my attention to any creditable account of Zoroaster's reputed miracles, which he can prove to have been published by his immediate disciples, and which he can show were tested aright at the time of their publication? Azar Kaiwán's reputed miracles are recorded in the Dabistán, a work pregnant with absurdities; and they were neither more nor less than the tricks and deceptions of a juggler and impostor.

12. The laws and institutes of Moses prefigured Christ, and the predictions of the prophets foretold Christ. The appearance of Christ was consequently their "fulfilment." A prefigurement is not needed after an accomplishment; and hence the ceremonial precepts of the law are not now viewed as obligatory. They are perused by us for historical purposes, and for the doctrinal and practical information which they convey.

13. Dosabhái expresses his astonishment that God should have had any intercourse with Solomon after his idolatrous declension. The Lord, however, did not countenance Solomon in his sinful and pernicious ways. "The Lord," it is said, "was *angry* with Solomon" (II Kings xi. 9), and

* *Mathematical Dictionary*. For an account of "temporary stars," see also *Sir John F. W. Herschell's Treatise on Astronomy*, pp. 383-384. This is a work, which, being written in a popular style, and illustrating the mechanism of the heavenly bodies by an appeal to familiar analogies, may be circulated with great advantage among the native youth acquainted with the English language.— See Second Exposure of Hinduism, pp. 115—116.

threatened to rend the kingdom from his posterity on the ground of his defection. It was unjust, says Dosabhái, to prolong the kingdom for David's sake ; and to take it from Solomon's son for Solomon's sake. But is it not generally the case that particular persons occupy their thrones on account of their descent ? And was it not a *gracious*, and not an unjust, act on the part of God, to defer the effects of a merited forfeiture even for a single generation ? Rehoboam, the son of Solomon, could not equitably demand from God the continuance of that sovereignty which his father deserved to lose, and which by his own deeds he showed himself so unworthy to retain.

14. Christ, says Dosabhái, "cursed and blasted the fig-tree, for not having borne figs when it was not the fig season." The tree referred to had "*leaves*" (Mark xi. 13), which it is well known follow the fruit on fig-trees ; and according to this indication it was to be expected that fruit should have been found upon it, whatever may have been the season of the year with regard to fig trees in general. "The time of figs was not yet," is a clause probably intimating the reason why Christ *went* to this tree, which he saw "afar off." It is not to be connected with the *blasting* of the tree, which had a reference to its vain display. Instead of objecting to the miracle because there was something "allegorical" in its application, Dosabhái should have discovered its propriety in this very circumstance. The display of leaves without fruit, was emblematic of fair professions, without a corresponding faith, and love, and obedience. Mark emphatically says, that the disciples "heard" the doom of the tree ; and they could scarcely fail to make of it a suitable improvement.

15. There is no where ground for the inference that the "guests were already too much heated," when Christ changed the water into wine for their use.

16. Dosabhái (p. 110) speaks of "Christians" receiving Christ, who are nevertheless guilty of murder, adultery, theft, and so forth. Their receiving of Christ, he may learn from this circumstance, is not that of the heart, and such as is acceptable to God, and will be attended with salvation.

17. Though what is called the Apostle's Creed contains nothing but apostolical truth, it is not generally believed to have been composed by the apostles. The creed of the Abbé de St. Pierre, which Dosabhái translates (p. 140) for the information of his countrymen, is very defective.

18. Dosabhái says, that the ceremonies enjoined in the first chapters of Leviticus are more ridiculous than those contained in the Vandidád. In what respects they are ridiculous, however, he has not told us. The directions there given for the burnt-offerings are minute and specific, for the guidance of the priesthood ; but they suggest nothing offensive to reason, or unbecoming a right symbolical interpretation.

19. It is not simply because the Pársí religion attaches ceremonial impurity to the touching of a dead body, or any other thing that has

been defiled that I condemn it; but because it dwells more on this ceremonial impurity, than on moral impurity.

II. On Edal Dárú's work, no further remarks appear to be here called for.

III. A considerable number of the questions and remarks of Kalam Kas, find an answer in what has now been said in reply to Dosabhái. I add, for his consideration, the following notanda.

1. He complains (p. 13) of the circumstance that the New Testament was not written by Christ, but by his apostles. This, however, he ought to see, does not militate against the position that the New Testament is the word of God, while we claim for the apostles divine inspiration. Had Christ been an impostor, he would probably have himself written, or caused to be written, something in support of his own claims.

2. There are some men who are harmlessly possessed *of* riches, and there are others who are injuriously possessed *by* riches. It is of those who are "rich" in the latter sense, that it is said, that it is "impossible" for them to enter into heaven. Not till a man's heart is detached from the world by God can he be saved.

3. Christ prophesied not, says Kalam Kas, before those who smote him. And why should he? They who treated him so cruelly and unjustly, and who were blind to all the evidence of his divine mission, deserved no additional signs from heaven. Christ was ready to suffer for men, because for this very purpose he had come into the world.

4. Kalam Kas says, that my attacks on the Pársí religion are like smiting the Pársís} on the cheek, while I should meekly give my cheek to them to be smitten. When he proves that I injure the Pársís,— whose benefit I seek,— by attacking their religion, and when a suitable occasion of showing my meekness by giving my cheek to be smitten occurs, it may not be turned away.

5. The following remarks explain the statement of the Bible that God rested on the seventh day from all his work. "In the world around us, we perceive the works of God, and we constantly acknowledge them to be his, even though they are not completed at once, but carried on by degrees. We allow that trees flourish, and that men grow, by the divine power, while we perceive that they do not attain to their full stature and perfection at the first moment at which God begins to act upon them. We see, in fact, a progression in every work throughout the universe with which we are acquainted; and we constantly refer it to the sovereign will of God. We can even discern in it the proofs of supreme wisdom. God acts in order that he may display his own glory; and he acts in such manner as is suitable to the nature of the intelligent beings who are called to witness that glory, and in such a manner as is calculated to shew the importance of his work, and to encourge reflection upon it. Before he commenced the work of forming the world, he had called into being numerous exalted angels, who could watch its progress, rejoice over its manifestations, and praise him on its accomplishment. He

created the world particularly for the sake of man; and it is evident, that we, on reflecting on the display of his power connected with it, can survey it with more interest, than we could do, were we merely informed, that God accomplished his work in the twinkling of an eye. We cannot imagine for a moment that it was a want of power which led God to employ six days in the work of creation. We have in the narrative of Moses itself, the most striking illustrations of the divine omnipotence. We find God saying 'Let there be light, and there was light;' and in every instance commanding and all things standing fast. When we read that God *rested* from his work on the seventh day, we only learn that he *ceased* from his work, and that he was in that state which we denominate rest, when contrasted with his previous engagement. The Hebrew word for rest denotes mere cessation from work, or those feelings which are experienced when work is completed, without any reference to the feelings of the agent as wearied. God, without doubt, after the completion of his glorious work, must have viewed it, as he actually did, as 'very good,' and manifested in connexion with it divine complacency. That he was *tired* is an inference which is not warranted by any of the statements in *Genesis*."

6. Mistakes in calculations about the date of the birth of Christ have nothing to do with the religion of Christ.

7. Some kinds of impurity are removed by washing, and some by melting. The human heart is so impure that it requires an agency like that of *fire*, even of the Holy Spirit himself, to cleanse it. Kalam Kas may now, if he choose, understand what is meant by Christ baptizing with the Holy Spirit, as with fire.

IV. And now for a few words to Aspandiárjí.

1. In his introduction he draws a presumption in favour of Zoroastrianism from the fact that it was not *expressly condemned* by Christ. How utterly opposed to the Christian Scriptures that system is, will appear from the whole of this work. It was the command of Christ to his disciples that they should "Go and teach (or disciple) *all* nations." The countries over which the faith of Zoroaster prevailed, were thus included in those *to be converted*.

2. In the following passage which I transcribe verbatim from Aspandiárjí (p. 8), we have a mysterious comment on a mysterious text. "The Padre in alluding to the 19th fargard [of the Vandidád] observes, that 'Zoroaster was stronger than Ahriman, author of the evil law; he struck the people given by this dew, &c.' It must be borne in mind, that this is one of those *mysterious passages which distinguish the writings of Zoroaster*, but its insertion in this place argues the intention of the Padre to insinuate to his readers, how could Ahriman, who is represented as being the most irreconcilable enemy and rival of Hormazd or God, be superior to Zoroaster in power and strength; and if so he could neither disturb the good works of God, much less undo them. But I have observed that this is *one of those mysteries or enigmas ascribed to Zoroaster*, who on ac-

count of his *mysterious sayings,* is also denominated Pegumbare Simbari, that is to say a *mysterious prophet.*"

3. The following (p. 16) is a curious specimen of logic. "The assertion regarding the earthquake is also a forged work of the priests, for if this had been a real fact, the houses of the persons who were concerned in the murder of Christ might have been swallowed up in the earth." According to this, accounts of earthquakes must be esteemed fabulous, when they allow murderers to escape destruction.

4. When it is said in Romans i. 28, that "even as they did not like to retain God in their knowledge, God *gave them over* to a reprobate mind, to do those things which are not convenient," it is not said, as Aspandiárjí affirms, that God "*inspired* them with such bad and sinful thoughts, that they might be urged the more to commit various enormities." It is said only, that God left them to the influence of their own depravities, to reap the fruit of their own evil doings.

5. The Parables of Christ, when rightly viewed, by those to whom they were addressed, were found to *illustrate*, and not to *obscure* divine *truth.*

6. Of the mantras addressed to fire, Aspandiárjí will find a specimen in the A'tish-Níáísh.

D. — ESNIK ON ZARVA'NA-AKARANA AND THE TWO PRINCIPLES.

TRANSLATED FROM THE ARMENIAN BY AVIET AGANOOR, ESQ.*

It is said that before there was any thing existing either in the heavens or the earth, or any other creation that is in the heavens or in the earth, there was one by name Zerwan, which signifies fortune or glory. He offered sacrifice for a thousand years that a son, Ormizd, might be born unto him, who should create the heavens and earth and all that are in them; and after offering sacrifice for a thousand years he began to reflect, saying "Is the sacrifice that I make of any benefit?" And shall I get the son Ormizd, or do I toil in vain? And whilst he spoke thus, Ormizd and Arhiman were conceived in the womb of their mother. — Ormizd through the sacrifice, and Arhiman through the doubt. Then Zerwan having discovered this, said, "There are two sons conceived, whichever will come to me first, I shall make him king." And Ormizd perceiving his father's intention, revealed it to Arhiman saying, "Our father Zerwan has resolved, that whichever of us shall first go to him, he will make him

* To my excellent friend Mr. Aganur, I am indebted for a translation of the whole article of Esnik on the Pársí Religion. Though some of it is irrelevant to the present notions of the Zoroastrians, it is not without interest in a historical point of view. The portion which I here insert refers to legends which are known to the Pársís only in an obscure form. They bear some resemblance, it will be observed, to those of the I'lmá-i-Islám.

king." On hearing this, Arhiman pierced the womb, and came out and stood before his father. Zerwan on seeing him, knew not who he was, and asked him, "Who art thou?" And he replied, "I am thy son." Zarwan told him, "My son is odoriferous and of light, and thou art of darkness and of disagreeable scent." And whilst they were talking thus together, Ormizd, having been born in due time, bright and odoriferous, came and stood before Zerwan. On seeing him Zerwan knew that it was his son Ormizd, for whom he offered the sacrifice, and taking the sceptre which he held in his hand and that with which he offered the sacrifice, he gave them to Ormizd, and said, "Hitherto I have offered sacrifice for thee, henceforward thou shouldst offer for me." And when Zerwan had given the sceptre to Ormizd and blessed him, Arhiman, presenting himself before Zerwan, said unto him, "Didst thou not vow that whichever of my two sons should first come to me, I shall make him king?" And Zerwan, in order not to break the vow, said to Arhiman, "O thou false and wicked one, let the sovereignty of nine thousand years be given to thee, and Ormizd be placed king over thee; and after nine thousand years Ormizd shall reign and do whatsoever he shall choose." Then began Ormizd and Arhiman to make creations; and all that Ormizd made was good and right, and what Arhiman did was evil and wrong.

II. To such incredulous and delirious-like sayings patched together by the fancy of the ignorant, there would have been no necessity of making any reply at all, for it is sufficient for their own ignorance to reproach them out of their own words, which contest with, and are contrary to, each other. Yet since the priests of their religion thus appear estimable to their followers, and having put a rope round their necks drag them into a gulph, it is necessary to answer them, and to prove that they say nothing more than Mání (whom they flayed) had said.

For he spoke of two origins, of good and of evil, and that, not by conception and birth, but self-existing, and contrary to each other; and they (the Pársís) say the same, by the desire of Zerwan, by conception and birth. And if it is the same religion which both hold, wherefore do the Magi hate the Zandiks, * unless they differ from each other in conduct, although in appearance and not in reality? But in their faith they are both the same; the former of lengthened roll and the latter the same; they are worshippers of the sun, and these servants to the same; — the former consider all inanimate objects as animate, and the latter regard the same in the same manner.

But since Mání pretended to show a conduct superior to theirs, that is, that he was entirely free from all lustful desires, and not only superior to theirs but to that of all other religions, he was exposed to the irritation of maidens and was flayed to death. Hence it is evident that by conduct alone they are separate; for the former are pretenders and the latter debauchees and open lechers; but in faith they are one and the same.

* Perhaps the followers of Mání. — A.

III. Now leaving the former, we would ask the latter, whether Zerwan, who is said to have existed before every thing, was a perfect being or an imperfect one. If they say he was perfect, it should be asked, of whom could a perfect being stand in need when asking for a son, that should come and create the heavens and the earth; for if he were perfect, he would have created them himself. But if he was imperfect, it is evident that there was one above him who could consummate his imperfections; and if there was one above him, *he* ought to have created the heavens and the earth and all that are in them, in order to manifest his goodness and power, and to have bestowed a son on Zerwan for the purpose of making the heavens and the earth and all that are in them.

But they affirm that the sacrifice was made to the glory. We would ask, whether glory was conferred on him by any one, or that because he was eternal, he was glorified. If the glory was bestowed on him by some one, it should be admitted that there was one above him more powerful and glorious, whose glory came to him. But if there was no one above him, the offering of the sacrifice for a thousand years, was of no avail; for glory is not a personal being, but only so named from the good fortune of some one, as from the misfortunes of any one is derived the name of misery; both of which are the effects of chance and not proofs of personality.

Moreover, if the sun and the moon had not been in existence, whereby the hours and the day, the months and the years, are fixed, whence was the thousand years known; for there were not luminaries which could regulate the number of days, months and years; but it is evident that their vain talk is full of ignorance.

Furthermore, if the heavens and the earth and all that are in them had not been in existence, where did he make the sacrifice and in what manner. When there was no earth and plant whatever the produce thereof, whence did he get the sceptre which he held in his hand, or what did he offer up as a sacrifice; for animals had not then been created. And what is still more foolish, for a thousand years he offered sacrifice and after the thousand years he began to doubt, saying, whether I shall get the son Ormizd or not, and whether or not do I toil in vain? Hence, it is proved that Zerwan was weak and dependent and without wisdom; and is the cause of evil and not Arhiman; for if he had not doubted, as they say he did, there would not have been Arhiman, whom they proclaim as the cause of all evils; but he (Zerwan) distrusted, which (statement) is incredible and full of disorder.

For out of one spring two rivers can never flow, the one sweet and the other bitter; neither can one tree produce two fruits, one sweet and the other disagreeable. Now if they think Zerwan sweet, they should not attribute to him Arhiman, the bitter fruit; but if they consider him bitter, it is not just to impute to him the sweet fruit Ormizd. And well do the divine words suit them, which say, "Either make the tree good and its fruit good, or make the tree corrupt and its fruit corrupt; for the tree is known by its fruit."

And if all creations are firm in their regular bounds, and never step beyond the limits assigned to them, how much more Zerwan, if he were eternal and sought means of making creations, whether personally, or through his son (as they say), should have shown order, and not disorder and confusion. For it is never known of cows having brought forth asses; and asses, oxen; nor wolves, ewes; neither ewes, foxes; nor lionesses, horses; nor horses, serpents; but there is only one breed which men have contrived against the order of nature, and that is to produce mules out of horses and asses, and they are fruitless and barren for they were not the creation of God but the contrivance of men. Now if Zerwan was an ox, how did he give birth to the scorpion Arhiman; and if he was a wolf, how did he bring forth the lamb Ormizd: — is this not a foolish production of the human mind?

For Zerwan himself was a man, a brave one at the time of the Titanians; and as it is customary with the Greeks and Ariks * and the heathen nations in general, to number the brave among the gods, the inventor of the Pársí religion observed that since men number him among the gods, he should also attribute the creation of the heavens and of the earth and of all things unto him.

And this is known to be the case from the fact that in a human manner he patches their faith, and by the conception and birth conjoins the same. For at first, he proclaims the birth of two creations, those of good and of evil from the same father, and then by maternal and sisterly exposure he introduces the creations of the luminaries. And that on no other account but that of sensuality and concupiscence. For observing the Ari people to have been addicted to women, according to his loose conduct, he invented laws to him (Zerwan); for when they hear of their gods having meditated unworthy connections, they follow their example, and pursue, without scruple, the same disorderly life; from which the divine laws are very remote. For it is not fit that God should have a son by marriage but by eternity, as mind produces reasoning, aspring the river, and fire the heat, and the sun the light. And not, as they pretend, that he longed that a son should be born unto him whose name should be Ormizd.

Alas! for their ignorance; before there had been a son, he named him

* Ari in the Armenian language signifies brave. The word Arik is in the plural number and is said to be the name of a people in the East who were good archers and great warriors. They were also called Ariakank or Ambostakak, and by other nations Kŭsty Khorasan or Cŭshank. Their country therefore is called Arik, also the country of Kushan, which is a large province of Asia Major, and has for its boundaries, on the north Scythia, on the west the Caspian sea and the country of Mars, and on the south Persia, and extends along from the Caspian sea to the frontiers of Hindustan. Formerly this was a great and famous kingdom, but it is now under Persia, and the greatest part of it is called Khorasan. — A.

who was not conceived and born. To all children names are given after their birth; how did he give him the name Ormizd before he was born, unless he believed firmly that he should get a son? And if he believed, wherefore did he doubt, and by doubting become the cause of the birth of Arhiman whereby evil has entered into the world? But the wonder is that the one could scarcely come by the sacrifice of a thousand years, and the other did so instantly by the doubt.

Besides, he who perceived that there were two sons in the womb, why did he not discover that the one was good and the other evil? And if he did so, but did not destroy the evil one, he is the cause of evil. But if he did not discover it, how is it possible that he could know the other one? And if he did not discover them, did he not do so when he beheld him obscene and of nauseous scent? But since he knew and saw and made the obscene one king, he is the cause of evil inasmuch as he did not destroy the evil, but on the contrary, gave him even the sovereignty of nine thousand years. And over whom did he appoint him king but over the good creations of Ormizd, in order to torment them, by mixing with them his evil creations?

Moreover, they say that he appointed Ormizd king over him.

If Ormizd be his king, how would he give up his good creation to be tormented? If the father did not spare the creation of his son, inasmuch as he delivered it up to the evil one, yet how could the son refrain from sparing his own? Is it from weakness, (that he did so) or from malevolence? If from weakness he does not restrain, then he neither reigns now; nor can he conquer, as they say he will, in the end. But if it is from malevolence, it is proved that not only the father, who made the evil one reign, is the cause of the evil, but also the son who became an accomplice with the father and encourager of the evil one.

Moreover, if he gave the sovereignty to his sons, to the one for nine thousand years and to the other for eternity, what is he himself to be reckoned? For whilst there was nothing in existence, he was consequently a being of nothing, for he was not even the creator of any thing. And when his sons were born they became creators, one of good works and the other of evil ones, and they were kings, one temporarily and the other for eternity, and nothing was left to Zerwan either of creation or of sovereignty. That he is not creator, it is evident from the fact that he created nothing; and not a king, for over what could he have reigned! It is, therefore, evident that there never was Zerwan, nor can he be. For a being is either a creator or creation. Now since he is neither a creator nor a creation, he never was, nor is, nor can be a God.

IV. But when Zerwan, they say, resolved thus in his mind, that the one of my two sons who shall first come to me, I shall make him king, Ormizd discovered his design and revealed it to Arhiman.

If Ormizd discovered the intention of the father, why did he not discover the intention of his malignant brother, viz. that he would pierce the womb and come out, and, preceding him, receive the sovereignty, which was to prove to him and his creations atrocious; for at the very beginning he (Arhiman) having taken the start of him, would weaken him, and then cause nine thousand years to be regretful and contritious on account of his corrupting and deviating from the good creation.

Moreover, how could he, who knew already his son Ormizd to have been light and odoriferous in the womb, not perceive the other son to have been of bad odour and of darkness? Is it not evident, that truth is not related by them, but fictitious tales?

And that which is least of all credible, is, that the one could hardly come by the sacrifice of a thousand years, and the other did so instantly by the doubt. And if Arhiman was conceived by the doubt, he should not have called him his son; for if he were his son, he should have been like him; had he been good, he should have been good, if evil, he should have been evil. Was Zerwan, the father, indeed, good and evil at the same time; and out of his good vein he got his good son, and from his evil vein, he got the evil son? And if it had not been so, he would not have, in that case, called the evil his son; nor would he have given him the sovereignty. But on the contrary, if he were good, he would have destroyed the evil one and given the sovereignty to the good one, whereby he would have become renowned, and not have caused the feelings of his good son, Ormizd, to be hurt. But it is plain from these facts, that Zerwan was neither the father of gods, nor the disposer of kingdoms.

V. Further, they pretend that he gave the sceptres which he held in his hand to his son, Ormizd, and said, "Hitherto I have been offering sacrifice for thee, henceforward thou shouldst do so for me."

Now, if be offered sacrifice on his own account, that a son should be born to him, on what account did Ormizd do the same for him? Was it that he had any apprehension from any quarters, and that on that account he enjoined Ormizd to make the sacrifice for him? Was it possible that he, of whom he had asked the son, should, on granting the son, take him away as tribute? If such had been his fears, the sceptres could have been of no avail. And on presenting the sceptres he did not say, that you should offer sacrifice to me; because he showed that there was one to whom he offered sacrifice for his son; and enjoined his son to offer sacrifice to the same, for himself.

And if there was one above him and his son, to whom they both offered sacrifice, *he* should have been looked upon as their origin, and the creator of all and not Zerwan, as the cause of Ormizd and Arhiman, and these again as the creators of the good and of the evil. He who was greater than Zerwan, gave him a son creator above him; but he could not himself create the heavens and the earth and all that are in them, (as we have before observed) and thereby manifest his power and goodness. Or, if he had any apprehensions from his son Arihman, and therefore he gave the sceptres to Ormizd, that by offering therewith sacrifice to the higher one, he should be free from apprehension, then there ought to have been some one to whom he made the sacrifice. And if there were some one to whom it was lawful to make the sacrifice, then Zerwan was not eternal; but derived from some one. It is necessary, therefore, to inquire from whom did he rise, and to whom it was he offered the sacrifice, and who that was to whom he enjoined his son to offer sacrifice for himself. For it is impossible for any one to begin his own existence, unless he receives it from another; and God alone can make what he pleases, out of nothing. Now, then, who was it that made Zerwan, unless it was God, to whom he offered the sacrifice, and who gave him such a son as should make the heavens and the earth and all that are in them? But the wonder is, that he did not create them himself; and yet he can give the son of Zerwan the power of creating them.

But there was no one, they say, to whom Zerwan offered sacrifice; if so, then neither was Zerwan; and it is very ridiculous to say, that he that did not exist, offered sacrifice to him that did not exist, on account of him who had no existence also.

VI. Further, if Zerwan was fortune, as they pretend he was, then he was, indeed, the fortune of some one; and who was it, forsooth, whose fortune he was? For, fortune is not a thing personal, but merely the issue of prosperity; as for example, from justice the just is named, and from courage the brave; in the same manner from prosperity is named, the fortunate. Now if Zerwan were fortune, he was not a personal being; whence it is evident that there never was Zerwan.

And if, as they pretend, Ahriman was conceived through the doubt, he (Zerwan) should have doubted sooner, and immediately got a son, instead of suffering for a thousand years and offering sacrifice that a son might be born. But he obtained both evil and good, and the evil was of its own nature and not from the birth; for it was not possible for the same womb to receive in itself at the same time the maker of the evil and the creator of the good. For if it were evil, it should only have sheltered the evil; and if good, the good. Because good and evil could not have been united together, even as wolves and lambs are not born of the same womb. And they give the good part, such as the oxen, the sheep and other useful (animals) to Ormizd, and the evil, such as the wolves, wild beasts, and destructive vermin to Ahriman. But they know not that as the hurtful cannot abide with the harmless, so it was not possible for the good to have been conceived in the same womb with the evil, since, for example, it is not possible to bring fire and water together, lest the greater side should prove destructive to its neighbour. In the same manner it is not possible for the good and the evil to combine together, else either the former would destroy the latter, or the latter would destroy the former.*

Further, why did not the offspring that was of the sacrifice, vanquish the one that was of the doubt, and become an obstacle to him? Instead of this, these two personal enemies reclined together peaceably and quietly in the same womb. Also, if the father perceived two sons in the

* Here we have omitted two sentences.— W.

womb, the one good and the other evil, he should not have promised the sovereignty in so confused a manner, but assigned it to him alone for whom he made the sacrifice.

But in fact, Ormizd was imperfect until he was born, and how did the imperfect discover the intention of his father? For he who can discover the design of any one, is above him. Therefore Ormizd is superior to his father and more powerful and wiser than he. For whilst he was in the womb, he discovered the intention of his father, and when he left it, he was able to make the heavens and the earth, which the father was unable to make.

Now he who was so much more powerful and wiser than the father, is proved to be more contemptible than he; for he was deceived by the wicked one, inasmuch as he revealed the intention of the father to him, to whom he should have borne an implacable enmity and not an intimate friendship.

Moreover, if it were necessary to pierce the womb and come out of it, he who knew the intention of the father should have done so himself. For he ought to have gone to him first, and received the sovereignty, instead of Ahriman, who neither knew the intention of the father, nor was fit for the sovereignty. But if he pierced the womb, he killed, perchance, the mother besides:—and it is necessary to inquire, whether, in fact, they had a mother.

But whence is it evident that there was a mother, especially since they even affirm, that before there ever was any thing, whether the heaven or the earth, Zerwan was alone? And it is deserving of great ridicule, if he is said to be both father and mother, and the sower and the receiver. And what is worse, when Ahriman pierced, they say, the womb and came and stood before the father, the latter did not know him. Now why was he at a loss to know him; for there had been no one any where whilst he was alone? Was it not, therefore, clear that he who came to him, must have been one of his sons. He is, therefore, proved to be worse than the evil (Ahriman), for the latter knew him, but he did not know the latter. And he disowned the son, saying that my son is odoriferous and light, and thou art of darkness and of bad smell. And how was he not his son who had been conceived along with the good son in the same womb? And he disowned him saying that thou art not my son, and acknowledge the other, that he was his son. Now if he disowned the evil, he should not have granted him the conception; but, on the contrary, he ought to have avoided the wicked and destroyed him, and not only him but Ormizd also, who had revealed his secret.

VII. But the other thing is still more absurd, which they say, that he also gave him the sceptres for the purpose of making sacrifice for him, as if the virtue was not either in Ormizd or in the sacrifice, but in the rods. For if he were confident of being heard, it was superfluous to have the rods in his hand; and if he was unworthy, not even the rods could have been sufficient to make the unworthy deserving the sacrifice: nay, to hold sceptres and offer sacrifice are deeds of men and not of God! But if he (Ormizd) were God and could make the heavens and the earth, what need had he of the sceptre and of the sacrifice for saving his father from apprehension. He who could make the heavens and the earth without the sceptres, could not repose confidence in the father, without them. It is therefore plain, that the father also was unwise and weak and looked on another for protection; and the son was likewise weak and unwise; for as he could not give birth to the son without sacrifice, so the son was unable, without holding the rods in his hands, to free him from apprehension.

VIII. Nay, they both are the cause of the vexation occasioned by the evil one (Ahriman) in his harrassing the good* creations of Ormizd, who is said to have made all that was good, as well as the just and pious men, and Ahriman evil creations and the devils.

Now, if the devils were the works of the evil (Ahriman) and they themselves evil by nature, not even one of them could ever comprehend a good deed, nay not Ahriman himself. But we are told that that which is the most excellent in the creation, was discovered by Ahriman. When he saw, they say, that Ormizd made a good creation, but could not make the light, he (Ahriman) consulted with the devils, and said, what credit

* In the Hormazd Yast, Hormazd is expressly called the "Creator of Good." The publisher of the Rahnamá-i-Zartusht, with a view to convince me, as he supposes, of the Supreme Divinity of Hormazd, has sent me a translation, roughly made by one of his friends, of part of the Hormazd Yast, in which one of the names of Hormazd, said to be mentioned by himself, is rendered by him "Creator, in my good sense and wisdom, of every good thing that is well known in the world for its purity." This rendering shows how careful, even in the present day, are the Pársís not to attribute to Hormazd the creation of animals and objects believed to be impure. Its author seems to imagine that it would be troublesome to Hormazd actually to know all things, for after mentioning that he is "Omniscient," he adds, "That is All-knowing, or possesses as much knowledge as is necessary for knowing all things." Afterwards, however, without limitation, he speaks of Hormazd, as the "Creator of all things (i. e. the universe)," and as the "Beholder of all things," and "Omniscient." The fact is that many of the Pársís know not what to make of Hormazd, to escape the reproach which their sacred books suggest. Yet in the repetition of his name, would appear to be their safety from "the dangers and injuries of evil genii, wicked men, sorcerers, fairies, tyrants, blind men, who are misled and regard the perfections of the Almighty with an evil eye, persons who do not believe in the pure faith (and in the revelation), daring high-way men, instigators of quarrels (i. e. cheats or knaves misinterpreters of the Avastá), ravenous quadrupeds, such as tigers or wolves, numerous armies of enemies, persons who keep offensive instruments and banners, and sharp instruments, and persons who carry with them weapons of destruction." (Translation of the Hormazd Yast forwarded to me by Pestanjí Manakjí). — W.

is it to Ormizd to have so many fine creations, whilst they are all in darkness, for the could not make the light. Now, if he had been wise he would have gone to his mother, and the sun would have been born a son to him, and known his sister, and he would beget the moon : at the same time he enjoined that no one should reveal the secret. But this having come to the knowledge of the devil Mahmi, he immediately repairs to Ormizd and discovers the secret to him. What ignorance and absurd stupidity ! He who could find the way of creating the heavens and the earth and all things, could not discover the slender means of certain inventions, on which they not only represent Ormizd as unwise and ignorant, but Ahriman as the inventor of good works.

As they further allege that Ahriman said, that I am not unable to make good works, but I am unwilling; and to prove which, he created the peacock. It is seen therefore, that he is evil by will and not by nature.

Now, what is there more magnificent than light, which Ahriman found means of inventing,* and what more beautiful than the peacock which he created in order to show its beauty? Whereby it is clear, that if Ahriman were evil by nature he would neither have been the inventor of the light nor the maker of any beautiful creations. Also, if the devils had been wicked by nature, it was impossible for Mahmi to have been the revealer of the means of creating the light; to whom (Mahmi) the priests of that religion to this day offer sacrifice three times in the year; wherefore they are reproachfully condemned as worshippers of the devil; and, the devils are not wicked by nature but by will. And worshippers if they offer sacrifice to the devil, with what face did they persecute the of the devil! It is clearly seen, therefore, that all that is said by them is fabulous, and idle stories.

E.—TRANSLATION OF THE SIFAT-I-SIROZAH OF THE PARSIS.†

BY JOHN WILSON, D.D.

In the third volume of Anquetil du Perron's translation of the *Zand-Avástá*, there are versions of two small liturgical works of the Pársís, entitled by him the "Lesser *Sí-rozé*,"‡ and the "Greater *Sirozé*." There is, another *Sirozé* [of a very different kind], however, possessed by the Pársís which he does not translate. It treats of the qualities of the thirty days of the month, as auspicious or inauspicious. Though its intimations are absurd in the highest degree, it exercises great influence over the whole body of Zoroastrians. It is so much regarded by them, that there is scarce-

* This idea is foreign to the Pársí faith. — W.

† This article, to which reference is made in the 128th page of this work is reprinted from the Journal of the Royal Asiatic Society, No. VIII.

‡ From *si* thirty, and *roz* day.

ly a family without a copy, and there are few individuals who have not its precepts written on the tablet of their hearts. On this account, as well as because of the brief information which it gives respecting the *Amsháspands* and *Izads*, to whom the days of the month are sacred, it is not unworthy of the attention of Europeans. It exists in the Persian language; but there are several Gujarátí versions, which are generally used.* The translation which I give is very literal, and is formed from a collation of these versions, and a careful comparison with the original. I have added a few explanatory notes. The only general remark which I would make on the Precepts of Fate which this *Sirozah* contains, is, that its framers seem to have made such a distribution of good and evil throughout the month, and its different days, as is calculated to render those who credit it, neither much elated, nor much cast down, on account of any of its portions. Blessings and curses are made to go hand in hand during the whole journey of the moon.

The following is a list of the names of Celestial Beings who preside over the days of the month, as given in the *Pahlavi Farhang*:

1 *Anhumá*, 2 *Vahuman*, 3 *Antavahisht*, 4 *Shatnavín*, 5 *Sapandomad*,
6 *Khundad*, 7 *Amandad*, 8 *Díni pavan Atún*, 9 *Atún*, 10 *Aván*,
11 *Khur*, 12 *Máha*, 13 *Tír*, 14 *Gosh*, 15 *Díni pavan Mátún*, 16 *Matún*,
17 *Sarush*, 18 *Rashan*, 19 *Farvardín*, 20 *Varahrám*, 21 *Rám*,
22 *Wád*, 23 *Díni pavan Dín*, 24 *Dín*, 25 *Ard*, 26 *Ashtád*,
27 *Asmán*, 28 *Zamiád*, 29 *Mánsaraspand*, 30 *Anírán*.†

1. Let it be known to all that the first day of the month of the Behedín, is that of the good Hormazd. This day is reckoned auspicious for all good undertakings, especially such as commencing new buildings, sending children to school (for the first time), and commencing the cultivation of a field or garden. It is auspicious for all kinds of consultation, for selling and for buying, for uniting together, and for marrying; for dressing in new clothes, and for cutting nails. Shaving, going to the bath, and perjury, on this day, meet with instantaneous punishment from God. If a person be taken ill, he will soon be restored to health. The day is well adapted for

* I am indebted to Mánackji, Kharshedji, M.R.A.S., for aiding me in procuring some of the copies which I have used.

† The Pahlavi letters are not given in the Journal of the Asiatic Society.

a short journey. If a person may have mislaid any thing, he will recover it. Should a child be born, it becomes very fortunate, and enjoys long life. Dreaming is attended with good; and the dream ought not to be revealed to any person, till its result be known. The signification of a dream will be manifest, and not occult. What has now been stated accords with experience, through the divine power. We have not divine authority for our statements.

2. The second day is that of Bahman, the angel who presides over the increase of mankind, and protects horses and goats. It is a fortunate day, and well suited to sensual indulgences, to the performance of marriage ceremonies, to the drinking of wine,* to putting on new clothes, to scraping nails, to forming new hopes, to contracting friendly alliances, and to giving instruction. Taking medicine and riding on horseback are on this day detrimental. It is fortunate for visiting a king, and for holding consultations. The child born this day is of a comely figure, but is possessed of neither good talents nor sense. The illness of a person who is attacked this day, will be long in duration, though he may recover. If any thing be lost or missing, it will be found. Should a tree be planted, it will wither, or its fruit will not be good. Events dreamt of, will occur in four days, but the hopes which may be cherished will be disappointed.

3. The third day is that of Ardebehisht, the angel who is the guardian of fire.† This day is inauspicious; we should desist on it from doing any work. Fire must be worshipped. Nothing else must be done, lest its issue should prove unfortunate. It is to be maintained that whoever shall work this day, will repent it at the end. The day is certainly not good for selling and buying. The child born this day will be miserable, stupid, and deceitful, during a long life. Good reports are neither to be approved nor credited. The visions of dreams will not be realized. Should a person fall ill, his life is in danger. If any thing be lost, it will never be recovered, unless by a special interposition of Providence.

4. The fourth day is that of Shárivar, the angel who presides over hills and mountains, and over mines, gold, and silver. This is a good day; and it is suitable for diversion, for marriage-ceremonies, and for contracts. It is auspicious for erecting buildings, for cultivating land, for selling, buying and laying new foundations, for going to the court of a magistrate, for treating an enemy with hatred, for going to the court of a king, and forming hopes, and for purchasing a horse. But proceeding to a foreign country, putting on new clothes, and going to a bath, are forbidden. The child born this day becomes very virtuous, and speaks but little; and on any person exacting obedience from it, he will be respected. The person who gets indisposed on this day will speedily recover. The visions of dreams will be speedily realized. An article lost or missing will soon be found. There will be truth in reports heard.

5. The fifth day of the month is that of Sipandármad, the protector of

* On the day of Bahman, as likewise on three other days afterwards mentioned, the Pársis eat no flesh. They are not forbidden, however, the use of flesh.

† This is one of the four days of the month on which the more "devout" of the Pársis repair to the fire-temples.

animated beings. This day is unfortunate; and consequently we must refrain from doing any work. Prayers may be made in private; and, by all means, we must keep ourselves quiet. The day, however, is well adapted to commencing the perusal of a book. On this day we may sail across a river,* and make the earth joyful. Nothing else ought to be done. If a person happen to fall ill this day, he will not soon recover, and if he does not improve within five days, he will probably die. The child born will be fortunate and courageous. The visions of dreams will have a speedy realization. Things which are missing or mislaid, will never be recovered. Reports heard on this day will prove insignificant, or be afterwards contradicted.

6. The sixth day of the month is that of Khurdád, the angel who presides over water and vegetation. It is a fortunate day and auspicious for sowing seeds, and planting trees, for drinking wine, and opening veins; for setting out on a long journey, and marrying. But no new hope should be entertained. The day is suitable for shaving, for scraping nails, and for going to a bath. The child born this day will prove of bad character and qualities. Those who fall sick will soon be restored. The visions of dreams will be realized before the close of a day. Whatever may be lost or mislaid, will never be recovered. Rumours will not be contradicted, but prove true.

7. The seventh day of the month is that of the Amsháspand (archangel) Amardád, who presides over trees and grass. This is not a good day; and during it no work should be performed. But the worshipping God (by offerings) and praying to him publicly, and any thing of a like nature may be done. Great men must not be visited this day. The child born will either speedily die, or if it live, will prove a bad one. The day is auspicious for forming unions, for learning science, and casting a malicious look at an enemy. The person taken ill will be in danger of his life; and the good or bad result of a dream will be known within twenty days. Any thing lost or mislaid will not be recovered. Rumours will not prove false.†

8. The eighth day is denominated from Dépádar Izad. It is a lucky day. Selling and buying, laying new foundations, dressing in new clothes, and bathing, and drinking wine, are proper. It is also good for eating and drinking, and marrying, when music is laid aside. It is good in like manner for travelling. But planting young trees, and commencing new works are forbidden. No war or negotiations ought to be made this day. The child that is born will prove honest, and expert in reading and writing and other kinds of learning. He will be the instrument of good to others. If a person be taken ill this day, he will probably soon recover; but if he continue ill for twenty days, he will certainly die. Should any thing be lost or mislaid, it will be found. The visions of dreams will be realized within ten days. The intelligence which may be heard, will be partly false, and partly true.

* Or take a short voyage.

† The preceding seven days are sacred, it will be observed, to the seven Amsháspands, viz, Hormazd, Bahman, Ardebehisht, Shárivar, Sipandármad, Khurdád, and Amardád. The days which follow are sacred to the Izads.

9. The ninth day of the month is denominated from A'dar, the angel who presides over fire.* This day is inauspicious and unlucky. There should be cessation from labour during its continuance. The child born this day will be dishonest and mischievous, cowardly and guilty of manslaughter, and of a malevolent disposition. If any thing be mislaid or lost, it will not be found. Should any person get ill, he will continue indisposed for a long time. The visions of dreams will be realized within a fortnight. The intelligence received this day will prove false.

10. The tenth day of the month is denominated from A'wán Izad,† who presides over water. The day is lucky, and may be used for all good works. Commencing cultivation, laying the foundations of buildings, purchasing cattle,‡ putting on new clothes, cutting out new clothes, and discharging debts, are proper. Should a person start on a journey this day, he will get possessed of immense property and wealth. But the day is not good for fighting battles, or holding negotiations; for depositing money, bathing, scraping nails, and sitting in water. The child born this day will be wealthy, and prove a blessing to its parents; and it will enjoy long life. If any thing be mislaid or lost this day, it will be recovered. Should any person get unwell, he will either recover within eighteen days, or will die after that time. The visions of dreams will be realized within ten days. The news heard will prove true.

11. The eleventh day is that of Khúrshíd, the angel who presides over the sun. This day is auspicious, and proper for all good works. Whatever work is required may be performed; but marriage, sensual pleasures, and setting out on a journey, are to be avoided. Should any person pray to God, he will obtain his desires. The child born this day, will be possessed of good talents, and will become learned, and enjoy many comforts. He who steals any thing this day, will soon be punished. He who falls sick, will soon recover. If any thing be lost or mislaid, it will be found again. The news heard will prove true.

12. The twelfth day of the month, is that of the angel Máha,§ who takes care of cattle. This is an excellent day. All sorts of amusement, and diversion, and enjoyment, visits to ministers, and consultations with them, and the maltreatment of enemies, are lawful. The visions of dreams will be realized within three days. This day is favourable for the cultivation of land, and the prosecution of learning. But it is not good for depositing money, and for killing and eating cattle.|| Should any one wish to recommence a work which was discontinued, he should twice pray and practise genuflexion; and after his morning prayer is finished, the sun, the illuminator of the universe, must be invoked. But the prayer should be offered from the terrace of a house or from the summit of a mountain; the prayer is then immediately granted. The child born this day becomes very enterprising and fortunate. Should the public send any person on

* On this day the fire temples are frequented.

† Or Abán.

‡ Or quadrupeds.

§ Or Máh.

|| This day is on the same footing with regard to animal food as that of Bahman, already noticed. Mr. Erskine, I may here remark, is not strictly correct, when he says that the Pársis have no fasts.

deputation, the day will prove lucky. If a person fall sick, he will soon recover his health, though he may suffer great distress. What is lost will be recovered. The visions of dreams will be immediately realized. The news heard will prove true.

13. The thirteenth day of the month is that of Tír, the angel who presides over clouds and rain. This day is inauspicious; no work ought to be performed during its continuance; but it is suitable for worship, prayer, and sacrifice. Should any one form new desires, they will be successful Should any one contract a friendship or effect a reconciliation, he will be injured. There ought to be no shaving, or scraping of nails. It is not probable that a birth will occur this day; but should a child be born, it will prove wicked and debauched. If any one becomes unwell this day, he will recover. If one be attacked with fever, he will be better within twenty-eight days. Articles lost will not be again found. Dreams will be realized within forty days, and news will prove false.

14. The fourteenth day is that of Gosh, the angel who presides over animals.* This is a good day, and suitable for selling and buying, for conferring benedictions, opening veins, dressing in new suits, taking medicine, and making the earth flourishing, for sport and amusement, for giving in marriage, and for making private negotiation. The child that is born will be a poet and an astronomer, and fortunate and wealthy. Should any thing be lost or mislaid this day, it will be recovered. If a person fall sick, he will soon be restored. The visions of dreams will be realized within twenty days. The news heard will prove true.

15. The fifteenth day of the month is called Depméhér, the Izad who presides over all the languages of the world. These languages are seventy-two in number, as known to the glorious God, and to ourselves. This is an auspicious day, and is suitable for all kinds of good undertakings. This day should be devoted to charity and prayer. Reconciliation may be made with friends; estates may be purchased; baths may be attended; heads may be shaved; children may be sent to school; and hopes may be entertained. But none should set out on a journey, or deposit any article with others. The child born this day, will be universally beloved, and expert in the use of bows and arrows. His death will occur in the first month of a year. The visions of dreams will be realized the same day. Should any one pray twice this day, and supplicate for any thing, he will readily obtain it. He who is ill will soon get well. If a person be imprisoned, it will be long before he will be set free. He will be frightened. Evil deeds should be refrained from. News will prove true.

16. The sixteenth day is that of Meher Izad (Mithra), the angel who resides with the sun and presides over the blossoming of trees. It is a lucky day. Selling and buying, planting trees, and cultivating fields, purchasing land, giving entertainments, travelling, opposing an enemy, indulging in amusement, drinking wine, entertaining new hopes, and, in a word, all pure works, are on this day auspicious. But shaving, going to a bath, anointing the body, sensual enjoyments, and putting on a new jámah,† are prohibited,

* Hence no flesh is eaten on this day.

† The upper vest, as distinguished from the Sadar, or perhaps, a complete suit.

lest great evils should accrue. The child born this day will become a notorious liar, and daring blasphemer. Marriage is on this day auspicious. If any one become unwell, he will be restored within five days. If any thing be lost or mislaid, it will be recovered. The visions of dreams will be realized before the close of the day. The news heard will mostly be true.

17. The seventeenth day is that of Serosh, the angel who presides over learning.* This is an inauspicious day; all work should be laid aside. Worshipping, praying, entertaining hopes, visiting kings and great men, and returning home from a foreign country, are good. The child born will enjoy long life, and become a drunkard and debauchee. Should any one contract a friendship this day, the friend will prove a foe. Should any one be attacked with illness, or fever, he will not live, but at the end of seventeen days he will die. If any one be committed to prison, he will either come out within ten days, or meet death. All the visions of dreams will prove false. If any thing be lost or mislaid, it will be recovered. The news heard will prove true.

18. The eighteenth day of the month is that of Rashné, the angel who presides over truth and righteousness.† It is an auspicious day. For recreation and amusement, for selling and purchasing, for aspiring at something new, and for taking medicine, for bathing, and for shaving the head, it is particularly suitable; but for scraping and cutting nails, putting on new clothes, drawing blood, or drinking wine, it is unsuitable. Should any person take medicine on this day, he will experience a speedy cure, and continue well for a year. The child born this day will become a good man, and be endowed with a calm and modest disposition. Should any person get unwell, he will soon recover. The visions of dreams will be fulfilled within sixteen days. If any thing be lost or mislaid, it will be recovered. The news heard will prove true.

19. The nineteenth day is that of Farvardín, the angel who presides over Paradise,‡ and over the souls of men. This day is very auspicious. A journey may be commenced, deposits may be made. Illuminations and marriages are proper. Presents may be given, consultations may be held. The fire temple of Behrám ought to be attended,§ but not that of Adarán.

* This day is sacred to the worship of fire.

† He is generally spoken of as Rashne-rast.

‡ Behisht.

§ The A'tish Behrám is said to be composed of 1001 kinds of fire. The temples in which it is deposited are six in number, and their locations, &c. are as follows:

1. Udhwádá. The temple at this place was erected by Anjumán of Sanján, in Samvat 777, or A. D. 720.

2. Nausári. The temple here was erected by Desai Kharshedji in Samvat 1822, *i. e.*, A. D. 1765, and concecrated by Dastur Sohorabji Rustamji.

3. Mumbai, (Bombay). The first temple was erected by Dádábhái Nassarwánji, in Samvat 1838, or A. D. 1781, and consecrated by Dastur Mullá Káwas, the father, I suppose, of Mullá Firuz.

4. Surat. The first temple was erected by Dádábhái Nassarwánji, and Shet Hormazdji Bahmanji, in Samvat 1880, or A. D. 1823, and consecrated by Dastur Edalji Dárabji Rustamji Sanjána.

5. Surat. The second temple was erected by Pestanji Kálábhái Wakil, and consecrated by Dastur Sohorábji Jamshedji, the famous Zand scholar, in Samvat 1880, or A. D. 1823.

Blood may be drawn; all kinds of bargains are auspicious. But the foundations of buildings ought not to be laid, lest they should soon be injured. New clothes should not be put on, and nails should not be cut. The child born will be of a beautiful form, and excellent disposition. If a person fall ill, he will long suffer, but he will eventually be restored. The visions of dreams will be realized in eight days. The things lost or mislaid will be recovered. News will prove false.

20. The twentieth day is that of Behrám,* the angel who presides over travellers. It is a good day; worship ought to be performed, and alms dispensed. Consultation may be held with an enemy. Good things may be desired. Should a person start on a journey, he will acquire considerable wealth, and will return in safety. New clothes should not be put on, and no marriage or amusement should take place. The child born will prove a poet and an astrologer. The visions of dreams will be realized within ten days. If any thing be lost, it will be recovered; and if a person elopes with any article, he will be seized and punished. News heard will prove true. If a person gets unwell, he will be in danger of his life. All this is agreeable to our experience, as God knows.

21. The twenty-first day is that of Rám,† the angel who presides over destiny.‡ This is a good day. Worship may be performed, hopes entertained, blood drawn, and cattle purchased; but shaving, bathing, and cutting nails, are forbidden. The child born will be miserable and ill-looking. If a person get unwell, his life will be in danger. The visions of dreams will prove delusive. Whatever may be stolen or mislaid will be recovered. News heard will prove false.

22. The twenty-second day of the month is that of Guvád (Vád),§ the angel who presides over the winds. It is a good day. The purchase and ornamenting of cattle are proper. Work should be deliberately done this day; for if it be rashly done, the issue will be bad. Should any person start on a journey, he will encounter many difficulties, but at the end he will accomplish his objects. News heard will prove true. The child born will be circumspect. In the first stage of life he will experience misery, but in the last he will possess riches. If any person get unwell, he will soon be restored. The visions of dreams will be realized. If any thing be lost or mislaid, it will be recovered.

23. The twenty-third day of the month is that of Dep-Dín, who is God himself. This is an inauspicious day. All works should be suspended; but God should be worshipped and adored. Selling and purchasing, dressing in new clothes, starting on a journey, taking amusement, and marrying,

6. Mumbai (Bombay). The second temple, which is more frequented than any in Bombay, was erected by Wádiáji Shet Hormazdji Bahmanji, in Samvat 1887, or A. D. 1830, and consecrated by Dastur Edal Daru Sanjáná, the highpriest of the Sheheresáhis, the larger of the two sects into which the Kabisah controversy has divided the Pársis of India.

* The temple of Behrám is much frequented on this day.

† No animal food is used on this day.

‡ Kismat, incorrectly written Khalwat, in some copies.

§ Or Bád.

are proper. A person guilty of perjury to-day, will be immediately punished and disgraced by God. If a child be born it will enjoy long life. A person who may get unwell will arrive at the point of death, yet God will eventually restore his health. Whatever may be dreamt of, ought to be kept secret. If any thing be lost or mislaid, it will be recovered. Reports heard will prove true, as God knows

24. The twenty-fourth day of the month is that of Dín, the angel who presides over the Mázdayasnan religion. It is an auspicious day, and suitable for approving works. During it amusements, marriages, and the laying the foundation of new houses, are proper; no other kind of work should be done. The child born will be a blessing to its parents, and become possessed of great property. Should any person be taken ill, he will soon be restored. The vision of dreams will be realized before the close of the day. Should any person run away he will get into difficulties, and will speedily return. Reports heard will prove true, as God knows.

25. The twenty-fifth day of the month is that of Ashasang, the angel who presides over religious mendicants. It is an inauspicious day, and during its continuance all works should be laid aside. But hopes may be entertained, because they will soon be fulfilled. The child born will suffer illness and pain, or will meet with a violent death. If a man fall ill, it will go hard with him. The visions of dreams will be bad, and their issue unpleasant. They will be realized within five days. The news heard will prove false.

26. The twenty-sixth day is that of Ashtád, the angel who presides over the seeds of the earth. This is a good day, and proper for all good works. New works may be commenced this day, buildings may be begun, wine may be drunk, journeys may be entered upon, and there may be selling and buying. The child born will live in poverty, though called to labour hard. The person who becomes unwell will soon be restored. Whatever may be lost, or missing, will be recovered before the day close. The visions of dreams will be realized within ten days. News heard will prove true. Weddings which take place to-day, will end in future divorces.

27. The twenty-seventh day is that of A'smán, the angel who presides over heaven. It is an excellent day, and is suitable for work. It is suitable for despatching a messenger or a letter, for drinking wine, for putting on new clothes, for shaving, for forming new desires, for marrying, and for forming connexions. But it is inauspicious for drawing blood. The child born will prove correct in morals, and fortunate. Whoever may be taken ill will soon be restored. Whatever may be lost or stolen, will soon be recovered. The visions of dreams will be realized within ten days. News heard will prove false.

28. The twenty-eighth day of the month is that of Zamiád, the angel who presides over fruit-bearing trees. This is an indifferent day. All work should be desisted from. A journey is not good No deposit should be made. Few children will be born this day; and such as are born, will speedily die. The visions of dreams will soon be realized. Should a person elope, he will be apprehended. Should a person be taken ill, he will speedily recover. News heard will prove false.

29. The twenty-ninth day of the month is that of Máharaspand, the angel

who presides over paradise. It is a good day, and suitable for labour. Setting out on a journey, forming new projects, reading the Zand-Avastá, are becoming. But no will should be written. The child born will prove upright. If a person be taken ill, he will shortly be restored. The things lost will not be recovered. The man who elopes will not be apprehended. The news heard will prove true.

30. The thirtieth day is that of Anírán, the angel who presides over marriage among mankind. It is a good day. For drinking wine, for sensual pleasures, for maltreating enemies, for purchasing cattle, the day is well adapted. And it is also good for drawing blood, for taking medicine for worshipping God, for forming new projects, and for marrying. The child born will be a speaker of truth and prove honest. The person who gets unwell this day will be in danger of death. The visions of dreams will soon be realized. Whatever be taken away or lost will be restored. The news heard will prove false.

F.—VIEWS OF THE PARSI RELIGION FROM THE I'LMA-I-ISLAM.*

The wise men of Islám have compiled certain examples relative to the faith, and have discussed the subject and have made a book thereon; and they have named the book, The circumstances of the world and the soul of man, from the beginning to the end of eternity. In this it is asked, 'What do you call the raising of the dead, and do you believe therein or not?' The Mobed of Mobeds said 'We believe in the raising of the dead that is the resurrection.' Then the wise men of Islám inquire, 'When the world existed, God created man and destroyed him, and about God's causing man to die and then restoring him to life, what is your opinion and belief?' And the Dastur of that age replied, 'With regard to our inquiries relative to the resurrection, one must first know what creation means, and what causing to die means, and wherefore life is again restored. And then it is necessary to say whether the world has existed from eternity, or has been created. If they say it has been created, we say that is impossible, because in the world new things are constantly produced and as constantly decay. And since they decay, and increase, and decrease, and again increase; and since whatever admits decay and increase is imperfect and imperfection cannot be ascribed to God, it is clear that the world has not existed from eternity but been created. And that which is created must have had a Creator. Now it is to be observed, that in the Pahlaví faith, of which sect are the followers of Zartusht, they say the world is created. Again as we say that the world was created, we ought to say, who created it, when was it created, how it was created,

* For notice of the I'lmá-i-Islám, see page 135 of this work. As I have already hinted, (p. 341), it throws considerable light on the twenty-second fargard of the Vandidád.

and why it was created. In the religion of Zartusht it is written, that in former ages all things were created, and the Creator is Time, and Time has no bound, and its height or depth is not discoverable, and it has always existed; and whoever possesses understanding, is unable to say whence Time was produced; and great as it is, there exists no one, who can be said to have produced it. Why? because it was not created. And then fire and water were produced, and when they came together, Ormazd was produced, and Time also may be called the Creator and also master of what he created. Now Ormazd was bright and pure and of a pleasing smell and the performer of good actions, and powerful with regard to all good. And when he looked down, at the distance of 96000 Farsangs, he saw Ahriman black and of bad smell and filthy and doing evil; and Ormazd was astonished and reflected that this was a terrible enemy. And Ormazd, when he saw his enemy, considered that it was requisite to remove this foe, and he reflected on the means and manner. And then he commenced. And whatever Ormazd does is by the assistance of Time, and all good is to be ascribed to Ormazd, and Long Time created the God Ormazd, and this may be reckoned at about 12,000 years; and he created heaven and the ornaments thereof. And these 12 signs, which are fixed in the heavens, each of these superintends during a 1000 years and for three thousand years this spiritual task had been accomplished. Aries, Taurus, and Gemini had performed their work of superintendence, each a thousand years, according to their station. And then Ahriman lifted up his countenance to fight with Ormazd, and drew together an army of Dews and formed them in battle array, and rushed forth with Hell and the filth and darkness and evil smell which was in him. Of these qualities he formed an army; and there is much to be related on this head. However he did not succeed, although he came forth with the powers of Hell. And because of what he saw in Ormazd, he did not cease causing trouble for 3000 years; and in this time the creation took place and the superintendence of the world devolved on Cancer and Leo and Virgo, and there is much to be said on this subject. However we will relate somewhat concerning it. And with regard to the creation, heaven was first created, and to the distance of 24,000 Farsangs it reaches upward as far as the heaven Karûsmán; and after 45 days water was created on the face of heaven; and after 60 days water and earth were produced, and after 75 days vegetation small and great, and after 30 days the Bull and Kiámurs; and after 80 days man and air; and after 75 days all was completed.* And when the superintendence of the world devolved on Cancer, man and air were produced, and when the 3000 years I have mentioned had elapsed, men and the earth and the rest of creation which I have mentioned began to exist. And again the evil Ahriman began to cause trouble, and made holes in heaven and in the

* These days respectively form the amount of the Gahambárs or periods of creation.—W.

mountains, and in earth, and ran through creation and polluted with his evil and filth whatever was in creation, and when he possessed no power over the heavenly spirits, he warred with them 90 days and nights, and broke through heaven; and the inhabitants of heaven came to the assistance of creation and seized the seven worst Dews and carried them above the sky and bound them in heaven. And Ahriman inflicted a thousand pains on the body of Káyúmars until he died and several things were produced by him; and with regard to this too there is much to be related; and from the Bull also several things and animals were produced. And then they seized Ahriman and carried him down to hell by that very hole, which had been made in the world, and they bound him with the chains of the sky and two angels Ardibihisht and Warahrám Izad were appointed to guard him. And if any one should say that as all this trouble was caused by him, why did they not kill him when they seized him, it must be observed, that if any one kills an animal, he says, I killed a certain animal; and when he has killed the animal, its fire mingles with fire, and its water with water, and its earth with earth, and its wind with wind, and at the resurrection it will be raised up in the body of the killer. If they say that as we have stated that Ormazd and Ahriman are both produced from Time; so every sect makes a different assertion.* One says, that Ahriman possessed the same knowledge as Ormazd, and that Time is Almighty. And another sect says, one should not be given and Ahriman said to Ormazd, I can do even as you, and Ormazd ought not thus to inflict pain on me. And another says, what pain or pleasure has time from the evil of Ahriman or the good of Ormazd. And another says, that Ormazd gave permission to Ahriman to mix evil with good, and thus different kinds of things are produced. And another sect says, that Ahriman was an angel of those nearest to God and was accursed for disobedience, so is there much to be said on this subject. And now we return to our story. When the heavenly powers had bound Ahriman in hell they burnt up the Dews that were with men, and the body of man was formed from paradise and hell; first of all from heaven they mix fire with fire, and water with water, and earth with earth, and wind with wind, and then the soul comes into the body, and the evil which is in the body of man, then enters. And at the resurrection evil will cease and men will be free from death, and old age, and want, and will thus live for ever. And quadrupeds, and birds, and fish, have no soul, and heaven forms them of the four elements, and therefore they are not reckoned or counted, since they possess no soul, (Farohar), and the proof of this is that men possess reason; and reason and understanding and truth and upright stature and speech and action all proceed from the soul; but animals share in the four elements which compose the body, but men possess this in excess on account of the soul, and by reason thereof men are reckoned, and animals are not. And with regard to what has been said as to what creation

* Here follows a sentence which is wholly unintelligible.

is and what causing to die is, and wherefore the hope of another life exists, it is to be observed, that creating and causing to die is for this reason;

> "If you died not, and Ahriman had no power among us,
> His filth and evil smell would ever remain,
> He afflicts us and pains us and torment us."

He rejoices in the evil which occurs. This is the cause of death. And the restoration of life is ordained by God, because we have suffered much as well in this world as in heaven. Therefore it is ordained by God by his mercy that we should rise again. Although nothing perishes, but the particles of our body are dispersed by death, these he collects, and raises up man and gives him the reward of his good actions. And they name 21 Núsks of the Vastá. The Vastá is the language of Ormazd, and the Zand is our language, and the Pázand is what every one knows what it says. And those 21 volumes, and Zand and Pázand are what we acquire, and seven volumes in Zand and Pázand are what we learn by heart; and seven volumes relate to what ought and ought not to be done, and do and do not, and say and say not, and take and take not, and eat and eat not, and clean and unclean, and put on for clothing and do not put on, and the like; all of which if we were to repeat, there would be no end to the book.

G.—PROPHECIES RESPECTING CHRIST WITH THEIR FULFILMENT.*

We learn from the first book of Moses, iii. 15, that God, in addressing the serpent by whom our first parents were deceived, spoke thus, "And I will put enmity between thee and the woman, and between thy seed and her seed; it shall bruise thy head, and thou shalt bruise his heel." In the first epistle of John, iii. 8, it is stated, that "the Son of God was manifested that he might destroy the works of the devil," or in other words bruise his head.

The deliverer promised to our first parents appears from the first book of Moses, xxii. 18, to have been necessarily connected with *Abraham*, for of this patriarch it is said, "In thy seed shall all the nations of the earth be blessed." The deliverer, according to the same authority, xxvi. 4, was necessarily connected with *Isaac*, because the promise was addressed to him, exactly in the same words, "In thy seed shall all the nations of the earth be blessed." The deliverer according to the same authority, xxviii. 14, was connected with *Jacob*, for with regard to him it is likewise said, "In thee and in thy seed shall all the families of the earth be blessed." That Christ was a descendant of Abraham, Isaac, and Jacob, it cannot, and will not be denied.

* This, I reprint, from my reply to Hájí Muhammad Háshím, entitled *Raddi-i-Din Musalmani*, published in Hindustání and Persian.

When Jacob was dying, he thus addressed his son Judah, "The sceptre shall not depart from Judah, nor a lawgiver from between his feet, until Shiloh come, and unto him shall the gathering of the people be." The word Shiloh is equivalent to Messiah; and it was just when the tribe or country of Judah was about to lose its civil power, that Christ appeared, and introduced that Spiritual Kingdom which will continue forever.

Moses, in his fifth book, xviii. 15—20, gives the following important prophecy:—"The Lord thy God will raise up unto thee a Prophet from the midst of thee of thy brethren, like unto me; unto him ye shall hearken; according to all that thou desirest of the Lord thy God in Horeb in the day of the assembly saying, Let me not hear again the voice of the Lord my God, neither let me see this great fire any more that I die not. And the Lord said unto me they have well spoken that which they have spoken. I will raise them up a prophet, from among their brethren like unto thee, and will put my words in his mouth; and he shall speak unto them all that I shall command him. And it shall come to pass, that whosoever will not hearken unto my words which he shall speak in my name, I will require it of him. But the prophet who shall presume to speak a word in my name which I have not commanded him to speak, or that shall speak in the name of other gods, even that prophet shall die."

The words of Moses clearly point to the *Israelites*, as the people from whom the great prophet was to spring. "The Lord thy God," he says, "will raise up unto thee a prophet *from the midst of thee*, of thy brethren." The speciality of his language sets the matter at rest.

The Apostle Peter, in Acts, iii. 22, and Stephen the first Martyr of Christ, in Acts vii. 37, apply the prophecy to Christ....

Christ was a prophet like unto Moses, as is evident from his intimacy with his Father, the doctrines which he taught, the miracles which he performed, the prophecies he delivered, the change which he introduced in the dispensation of the covenant of grace, and other circumstances. He was in fact a prophet greater than Moses.

We have numerous prophecies connected with the Messiah, in the Psalms of David, and the writings of the Prophets. I shall select some of the most important of them, which refer to his Divine Dignity; his human descent; the circumstances of his birth; the places of his residence; the condition of his life; the nature of his work; the extent of his sufferings; his resurrection from the grave; his ascension into heaven; the consequences of his advent; and the danger of neglecting his Salvation; I shall subjoin to them an account of their fulfilment as stated in the New Testament, and certified by history.

1. *The* DIVINE DIGNITY *of the Messiah is alluded to in the following passages, in some of which it is certified that he should be both God and Man.*

Prophecies. "Thy throne O God, is forever and ever; the sceptre of thy kingdom is a right sceptre:

Fulfilment. "God who at sundry times and in divers manners spake in time past unto the fathers by the

Thou lovest righteousness,and hatest wickedness, therefore God, thy God, hath anointed thee with the oil of gladness above thy fellows." Psalms, xlv. 6, 1. "I will declare the decree; the Lord hath said unto me, Thou art my Son, this day have I begotten thee." Psalm ii. 7. "Then thou spakest in vision to thy holy one, and saidst, I have laid help upon one that is mighty : I have exalted one chosen out of the people. I will make him my first born higher than the kings of the earth." Psalms, lxxxix. 18. "Unto us a child is born, unto us a Son is given, and the government shall be upon his shoulder ; and his name shall be called Wonderful, Counseller, The mighty God, The everlasting Father, The Prince of Peace." Isaiah, ix. 6.

prophets, hath in these last days spoken unto us by his Son, whom he hath appointed heir of all things, by whom also he made the worlds. ... For unto which of the angels said he at any time, Thou art my Son,this day have I begotten thee? And again I will be to him a Father and he will be to me a son? And again, when he bringeth the first begotten into the world, he saith, And let all the angels of God worship him. And of the angels he saith, who maketh his angels spirits,and his ministers a flame of fire. But unto the Son he saith, Thy throne, O God, is for ever and ever, a sceptre of righteousness is the sceptre of thy kingdom, &c. Hebrews, i. 1—9. "They shall call his name Emmanuel,which being interpreted is, God with us." Matth. i. 23. "In the beginning was the Word and the Word was with God, and the Word was God. And the Word was made flesh and dwelt among us, and we beheld his glory, the glory as of the only begotten of the Father, full of grace and truth." John, i. 14. Whose [the Israelites] are the fathers, and of whom as concerning the flesh, Christ came, who is over all, God blessed for ever, Amen." Romans, ix. 5.

II. *The* HUMAN DESCENT *of Christ, as connected with the Jews, and the families of Jesse and David, is distinctly marked in the following passages.*

Prophecies. "And there shall come forth a rod out of the stem of Jesse, and a branch shall grow out of his roots. And the spirit of the Lord shall rest upon him. And he shall set up an ensign for the nations, and shall assemble the outcasts of Israel." Isaiah, xi. 1, 2, 12. "My covenant will I not break, nor alter the thing which is gone out of my lips. Once have I sworn by my holiness

Fulfilment. " Jesse begat David the king. The book of the generation of Jesus Christ, the Son of David. Matthew, i. 6, 1. "The Lord God shall give to him the throne of his Father David.' Luke. i. 32.

that I will not lie unto David. His seed shall endure for ever, and his throne as the sun before me." Psalm, lxxxix. 34—36.

III. *Several circumstances connected with the* BIRTH *of the Messiah are mentioned.*

I. *The Messiah was to be born of a* VIRGIN.

Prophecies. "Behold a virgin shall conceive, and bear a son, and shall his call name Emmanuel." Isaiah vii, 14. "The Lord hath created a new thing in the earth, a woman shall compass a man. Jeremiah, xxxi. 22.

Fulfilment. "Now the birth of Jesus Christ was on this wise: When as his mother Mary was espoused to Joseph, before they came together she was found with child of the Holy Ghost. Then Joseph her husband being a just man, and not willing to make her a public example, was minded to put her away privily. But while he thought on these things, behold the angel of the Lord appeared unto him in a dream, saying, Joseph thou son of David, fear not to take unto thee Mary thy wife: for that which is conceived of her is of the Holy Ghost, and she shall bring forth a son, and thou shalt call his name Jesus, for he shall save his people from their sins. Matthew, i. 21. See also the first chapter of Luke.

2. *The Messiah was to be born at* BETHLEHEM.

Prophecy. "But thou Bethlehem Ephratah, though thou be little among the thousands of Judah, yet out of thee shall he come forth unto me, that is to be ruler in Israel; whose goings forth have been from of old from everlasting." Micah, v. 2.

Fulfilment. "Jesus was born in Bethlehem of Judea, in the days of Herod the King." Matthew, ii. 1. Read to the twelfth verse.

3. *The Messiah was to come before the* DESTRUCTION OF THE SECOND TEMPLE OF JERUSALEM, *and at a time when there should be a general* EXPECTATION *of him.*

Prophecy. "And I will shake all nations, and the desire of all nations shall come, and I will fill this house [the second temple] with glory, saith the Lord of hosts." Haggai, ii. 7.

Fulfilment. When Christ was born, wise men from the East, as stated in the second chapter of Matthew, came to inquire about him. He often preached in the temple of Jerusalem, as appears from many passages of the gospels; and it was destroyed about forty years after his death.

4. *The Messiah was to be preceded by a* MESSENGER *who should prepare the people for his advent, and preach in the wilderness.*

Prophecies. "Behold I will send my messenger, and he shall prepare the way before me: and the Lord whom ye seek shall suddenly come to his temple." Malachi, iii, 1. "The voice of him that crieth in the wilderness, Prepare ye the way of the Lord, make straight in the desert a highway for our God." Isaiah xl, 3.

Fulfilment. "There was a man sent from God whose name was John. The same came for a witness to bear witness of the light, that all men through him might believe. And this is the record of John, when the Jews sent Priests and Levites from Jerusalem to ask him, who art thou? He said I am the voice of one crying in the wilderness, make straight the way of the Lord, as said the prophet Isaiah. John, i. 19, 23.

IV. *Several of the* PLACES *which the Messiah was to visit, or in which he was to reside, are mentioned.*

1. EGYPT.

Prophecy. "I loved him and called my Son out of Egypt." Hosea, i. 1.

Fulfilment. "He (Joseph) arose and took the young child, and his mother by night, and departed into Egypt, and was there until the death of Herod; that it might be fulfilled which was spoken of the Lord by the prophet, saying, Out of Egypt have I called my son," Matth. ii. 14, 15.

2. ZEBULON *and* NAPHTALI, *and other places of* GALILEE.

Prophecy. "The people [of Zebulon and Naphtali and Galilee] that walked in darkness have seen a great light: they that dwell in the land of the shadow of death, upon them hath the light shined." Isaiah, ix. 1, 2.

Fulfilment. "When Jesus had heard that John was cast into prison, he departed into Galilee, and leaving Nazareth, he came and dwelt in Capernaum, which is upon the sea coast, in the borders of Zebulon and Naphtalim; that it might be fulfilled which was spoken by Isaiah the prophet, saying, The land of Zebulon, and the land of Naphtalim by the way of the sea beyond Jordan, Galilee of the Gentiles; The people who sat in darkness have seen a great light; and to them who sat in the region and shadow of death, light is sprung up." Matthew, iv. 12—16.

3. *The* TEMPLE OF JERUSALEM.

For the illustration of this point, I refer to what I have said respecting the circumstances connected with the Messiah's birth.

V. *The Condition of the* MESSIAH'S LIFE *is mentioned and described.*

Prophecy. It is delared in the following passage that the Messiah should have no worldly grandeur, nor riches. "For He shall grow up before him as a tender plant, and as a root out of a dry ground: he hath no form nor comeliness: and when we shall see him, there is no beauty that we should desire him." Isaiah, liii. 2.

Fulfilment. Christ, as is testified in many passages of the Gospels, was born and lived in a state of poverty, and he declared respecting himself that, "The foxes have holes and the birds of the air have nests: but the Son of man hath not where to lay his head." Luke, ix. 58.

VI. *The Nature of the* MESSIAH'S WORK *is mentioned, and described.*

1. *The Messiah was to be a* PROPHET AND TEACHER.

Prophecies. "The Lord whom ye seek shall suddenly come to his temple, even the messenger of the covenant whom ye delight in. Malachi, iii. 1. "The Spirit of the Lord shall rest upon him, the spirit of wisdom and understanding, the spirit of counsel and might, the spirit of knowledge, and of the fear of the Lord; and shall make him of quick understanding in the fear of the Lord." Isaiah, xi. 2, 3. "The spirit of the Lord God is upon me, because the Lord hath anointed me to preach good tidings to the meek; he hath sent me to bind up the broken-hearted, to proclaim liberty to the captives, and opening of the prison to them that are bound; to proclaim the acceptable year of the Lord, and the day of vengeance of our God; to comfort all that mourn; to appoint unto them that mourn in Zion, to give unto them beauty for ashes, the oil of joy for mourning,

Fulfilment. Most of the Gospels are filled with the record of Christ's doctrines and prophecies. John the Baptist testified respecting him saying, "He whom God hath sent speaketh the words of God; for God giveth not the spirit by measure unto him." Jesus, after discoursing on the words which I have quoted from Isaiah, said "This day is this scripture fulfilled in your ears. And all bare him witness and wondered at the gracious words which proceeded out of his mouth." Read the 4th Chapter of Luke.

the garment of praise for the spirit of heaviness; that they might be called Trees of Righteousness, the planting of the Lord that he may be glorified." Isaiah lxi. 1, 3. Many passages of a similar nature might be quoted from the Old Testament.

2. *The Messiah was to confirm his doctrines by his* MIRACLES.

Prophecies. "Then the eyes of the blind shall be opened, and the ears of the deaf shall be unstopped; then shall the lame man leap as an hart, and the tongue of the dumb sing." Isaiah xxxiv. 5, 6. "I the Lord have called thee in righteousness, and will hold thine hand, and will keep thee, and give thee for a covenant of the people, for a light to the Gentiles; to open the blind eyes, to bring out the prisoner from the prison, and them that sit in darkness out of the prison house. Isaiah xlii. 6, 7.

Fulfilment. "When John had heard in the prison the works of Christ, he sent two of his disciples, and said unto him, Art thou he that should come, or do we look for another? Jesus answered and said unto them, Go and shew John again those things which ye do hear and see; the blind receive their sight, the lame walk, the lepers are cleansed, and the deaf hear; the dead are raised up and the poor have the Gospel preached unto them." Matthew xi. 2, 5. "Nicodemus a ruler of the Jews came unto Jesus by night, and said unto him, Rabbi, we know that thou art a teacher come from God; for no man can do these miracles which thou doest except God be with him." John iii. 1, 2. The miracles which Christ performed were numerous and unequivocal.

3. *The Messiah was to be a* SAVIOUR FROM SIN.

Prophecies. "Behold a King shall reign in righteousness, and princes shall rule in judgment. And a man shall be as an hiding place from the wind, and a covert from the tempest; as rivers of water in a dry place, as the shadow of a great rock in a weary land." Isaiah xxxii. 1, 2. "Say to them that are of a fearful heart, Be strong, fear not: behold your God will come with vengeance, even God with a recompense, he will come and save

Fulfilment. "Thou shalt call his name Jesus, for he shall save his people from their sins." Mathew i. 21. "The son of man is come to save that which was lost." Mathew xviii. 11. God so loved the world, as to give his only begotten Son, that whosoever believeth in him should not perish, but have everlasting life. For God sent not his Son into the world to condemn the world; but that the world through him might be saved." John iii. 16,

you." Isaiah xxxv. 4. And the Redeemer shall come to Zion, and unto them that turn from transgression in Jacob, saith the Lord." Isaiah l. 20. "Behold the Lord hath proclaimed to the end of the world, say ye to the daughter of Zion, Behold, thy salvation cometh, behold his reward is with him and his work before him." Isaiah lxii. 11. "This is the name whereby he shall be called, the Lord our righteousness." Jeremiah xxiii. 6.

17. "There is none other name given under heaven among men whereby we must be saved." Acts iv. 12. "This is a faithful saying and worthy of all acceptation, that Christ Jesus came into the world to save sinners." Tim. i. 16. "Righteousness is through the faith of Christ." Philippians iii. 9.

VI. *The extent of the Messiah's* SUFFERINGS *is mentioned.*

Prophecies. "Trouble is near, for there is none to help, I am poured out like water and all my bones are out of joint, my heart is like wax, it is melted in the midst of my bowels. My strength is dried up like a potsherd: and my tongue cleaveth to my jaws; and thou hast brought me into the dust of death." Ps. xxii. 11, 14, 15. "He is despised and rejected of men, a man of sorrows and acquainted with grief." Isaiah liii, 3. Many similar prophecies could be quoted on this subject.

Fulfilment. In many passages of the Gospels, we have an account of Christ's sufferings. He was frequently assaulted by the devil and wicked men, and from his birth till his death he lived in a state of suffering. His agony during his last moments was indescribable.

VIII. *Many circumstances connected with Christ's* DEATH *are mentioned.*

1. *The Messiah was to be betrayed into the hands of his enemies by an intimate friend.*

Prophecy. "Mine own familiar friend in whom I trusted, who did eat of my bread hath lifted up his heel against me." Psalm xlii. 9. See also Psalm lv. 12, 13.

Fulfilment. "While he yet spake, lo, Judas, one of the twelve, came, and with him a great multitude, with swords and staves, from the chief priests and elders of the people. Now he that betrayed him gave him a sign, saying, whomsoever I shall kiss, that same is he, hold him fast. And forthwith he came to Jesus, and said, Hail, Master: and kissed him. And Jesus said unto him, Friend, wherefore art thou come?" Matthew xxvi. 47—50.

2. *The Messiah was to be sold for thirty pieces of silver.*

Prophecy. "They weighed for my price thirty pieces of silver." Zechariah xi. 12.

Fulfilment. "They [the chief priests] covenanted with him [Judas] for thirty pieces of silver." Matthew xxvi. 15.

3. *Messiah's price was to be cast to the potter in the house of the Lord.*

Prophecy. "And I took the thirty pieces of silver, and cast them to the potter in the house of the Lord." Zechariah xi. 13.

Fulfilment. "Judas. . . repented and brought again the thirty pieces of silver to the chief priests. . . and they took counsel, and bought with them the potter's field to bury strangers in." Matthew xxvii. 37.

4. *The Messiah was to be taken from prison and from judgment.*

Prophecy. "He was taken from prison and judgment." Isaiah liii. 8.

Fulfilment. "Jesus stood before the governor, &c." Read the 27th Chapter of Matthew.

5. *The followers of the Messiah were to abandon him in the season of his greatest trial.*

Prophecy. "Smite the shepherd, and the sheep shall be scattered." Zechariah xiii. 7.

Fulfilment. "All the disciples forsook him and fled." Matthew xxvi. 56.

6. *The Messiah was to be scourged, buffetted, and spit upon.*

Prophecy. "I gave my back to the smiters and my cheeks to them that plucked off the hair: I hid not my face from shame and spitting." Isaiah l. 7.

Fulfilment. "When Pilate had scourged Jesus he delivered him to be crucified. Then the soldiers of the Governor took Jesus into the common hall, and gathered unto him the whole band of soldiers. And they stripped him, and put on him a scarlet robe. And when they had platted a crown of thorns, they put it on his head, and a reed in his right hand; and they bowed the knee before him, and mocked him, saying, Hail, King of the Jews. And they spit upon him, and took the reed and smote him on the head." Matthew xxvii. 26—30.

7. *The Messiah was to be wounded in his hands and his feet.*

Prophecy. "They pierced my hands and my feet." Psalm xxii. 17.

Fulfilment. When Jesus was crucified, his hands and feet were nailed to the cross. After his resurrection he showed the wounds in his hands to Thomas. John xx. 27.

8. *The Messiah was to suffer with the greatest meekness and resignation.*

Prophecy. "He was oppressed and he was afflicted, yet he opened not his mouth: he is brought as a lamb to the slaughter, and as a sheep before her shearers is dumb, so he openeth not his mouth. Isaiah liii. 7.

Fulfilment. When he [Jesus] was accused of the chief priests and elders, he answered nothing." Matthew xxvii. 12. See the context.

9. *The Messiah was to be numbered with the transgressors.*

Prophecy. "He was numbered with the transgressors." Isaiah liii. 12.

Fulfilment. "Then were two thieves crucified with him; one on the right and another on the left." Matthew xxvii. 38.

10. *The Messiah was to be presented with vinegar and gall.*

Prophecy. "They gave me also gall to my meat, and in my thirst they gave me vinegar to drink." Psalm lxix. 21.

Fulfilment. "They gave him vinegar to drink mixed with gall." Matthew xxvii. 34.

11. *The Messiah was to be derided during the continuance of his agonies.*

Prophecy. "All they that see me, laugh me to scorn; they shoot out the lip, they shake the head saying, He trusted on the Lord: let him deliver him seeing he delighted in him." Psalm xxii. 7, 8.

Fulfilment. "And they that passed by, reviled him wagging their heads," &c. See Matthew xxvii. 39—44.

12. *Lots were to be cast for the Messiah's raiment.*

Prophecy. "They part my garments among them, and cast lots upon my vesture." Psalm xxii. 18.

Fulfilment. They parted his garments casting lots." Matth. xxvii. 35.

13. *The Messiah was to be pierced.*

Prophecy. "They shall look upon me whom they have pierced." Zechariah xii. 10.

Fulfilment. "One of the soldiers with a spear pierced his side." John xix. 34.

14. *The Messiah's grave was to be with the rich.*

Prophecy. "And he was to have made his grave with the wicked, but he was with the rich in his death. Isaiah. liii. 9.

Fulfilment. "There came a rich man of Arimathea, named Joseph . . . . he went to Pilate, and begged the body of Jesus . . . . and laid it in his own new tomb." Matthew xxvii. 57, 60.

15. *The Messiah was to be cut off about* 490 *years, from the time when the commandment should go forth from the King of Persia, to restore and build Jerusalem.*

Prophecy. Daniel ix. 24 — 26, compared with Ezra vii, 8.

Fulfilment. The death of the Messiah took place at the time specified, as proved by the best writers on chronology.

16. *The Messiah was to die as a sacrifice and atonement for the sins of mankind.*

Prophecy. "He was wounded for our transgressions, he was bruised for our iniquities, the chastisement of our peace was upon him, and with his stripes we are healed. All we like sheep have gone astray: we have turned every one to his own way, and the Lord hath laid on him the iniquity of us all....He was cut off out of the land of the living; for the transgression of my people was he striken .... Yet it pleased the Lord to bruise him, he hath put him to grief: when thou shalt make his soul an offering for sin, he shall see his seed .... He bare the sins of many and made intercession for the transgressors." Isaiah liii. 5 — 12. "The Messiah shall be cut off, but not for himself." Daniel ix. 26.

Fulfilment. "He (the Son) by himself purged our sins." Hebrews i. 3. "This man after he had offered one sacrifice for sin forever sat down at the right hand of God." Hebrews x. 12. In the epistle to the Hebrews, many passages of a like nature are to be found. "Ye know that ye were not redeemed with corruptible things such as silver and gold; but with the precious blood of Christ, as of a lamb without blemish and without spot." 1 Peter i. 18, 19. "Christ, who his own self bare our sins in his own body on the tree." 1 Peter ii. 24. Many texts of a similar nature occur in the New Testament.

VIII. *The* RESURRECTION *of the Messiah from the* GRAVE *is mentioned.*

Prophecy. "My flesh also shall rest in hope. For thou wilt not leave my soul in *Sheol*, [that is, in the state of the dead,] neither wilt thou suffer thine holy one to see corruption. Thou wilt shew me the path of life." Psalm xvi. 9, 11.

Fulfilment. "Men and brethren, let me freely speak unto you of the Patriarch David, that he is both dead and buried, and his sepulchre is with us unto this day, therefore being a prophet, and knowing that God had sworn with an oath to him that of the fruit of this loins according to the flesh, he would raise up Christ to sit on his throne. He seeing this before spake of the resurrection of Christ that his soul was not left in [*Sheol*, or] Hades, neither his flesh did see corruption. This Jesus hath God raised up, whereof we are all witnesses." Acts ii. 29, 32.

There are other passages of a nature similar to the preceding.

IX. *The* ASCENSION *of the Messiah into heaven is mentioned.*

Prophecy. "Thou hast ascended on high. Thou hast led captivity captive." Psalm lxviii. 18.

Fulfilment. "And he [Christ] led them [his disciples] out as far as to Bethany. And it came to pass while he blessed them, he was parted from them, and carried up into heaven." Luke xxiv. 50 — 51.

X. *The* CONSEQUENCES *of the Messiah's advent are mentioned.*

Prophecies. It is declared respecting him, that he should be a King and exalted to great glory; that his gospel should be preached first at Jerusalem, and afterwards among all nations; that though he was generally to be rejected in his lifetime, he was to be believed on by great numbers of the human race; that the kings of the earth, though in the first instance they were to oppose him, were to acknowledge his spiritual dominion, and devote themselves to the service of his church; that he is to reign till he has made his enemies his footstool; that at the end of the world he is to appear to raise the dead, and to act as the universal Judge. The prophecies on these subjects are so numerous that my space will not permit their quotation. I merely make a reference to a few of them. Psalms, ii. xxii. lxxii. lxxxix. cx. Isaiah, ix. 7, 11, 52, 61. Job. xix. 23, 27. Isaiah. ii. 58. Hosea, xiii. 14. Daniel, xii. 1 — 3. Micah. ii. 13.

Fulfilment. The New Testament is filled with similar declarations. Though it represents the personal ministry of Christ as confined to the Jews, yet it represents him as saying, "Other sheep I have which are not of this fold; them also I must bring and they shall hear my voice, and there shall be one fold and one shepherd." John x, 16; as informing his disciples that all power is given to him in heaven and on earth," as commanding them to "go and teach all nations, baptizing them in the name of the Father, and of the Son and of the Holy Ghost," and as promising to be with them to "the end of the world." Matthew xxviii. 18 — 20. It represents his apostles as proclaiming with success his Gospel in Jerusalem, and other towns in Judea, and throughout the whole Roman empire; as teaching every where that in him were fulfilled the promises given to the Fathers; as exhibiting him as the only Saviour; as ascribing the blessings of pardon, sanctification, and glory entirely to his merits;

and as representing him as highly exalted at the right hand of God as a Prince and Saviour, and as the Judge of the world, to which he will come at the last day. [Acts and Epistles throughout.] The reader of the New Testament will find that God has given Christ a name which is above every name, that at the name of Jesus every knee should bow of things in heaven, and things in earth, and things under the earth; and that every tongue should confess that Jesus Christ is Lord to the glory of God the Father. Philip. ii. 11.

XII. *The* DANGER OF NEGLECTING THE SALVATION *of the Messiah is mentioned.*

Prophecies. "Kiss the Son lest he be angry, and ye perish from the way, when his wrath is kindled but a little: blessed are all they that put their trust in him." Psalm, ii. 12. "Let them (the enemies of the Messiah) be blotted out of the book of the living, and not be written with the righteous." Psalm, lxviii. 28. "I will beat down his foes before his face and plague them that hate him." Psalm. lxxxix. 28. "He shall judge among the heathen, he shall fill the places with the dead bodies: he shall wound the heads over many countries. Psalm, cx. 6. "For he put on righteousness as a breastplate, and an helmet of salvation upon his head; and he put on the garments of vengeance for clothing, and was clad with zeal as a cloak. According to their deeds, accordingly he will repay, fury to his adversaries, recompense to his enemies; to the islands he will repay recompense. Isaiah lix. 17, 18.

Fulfilment. "He that believeth on the Son hath everlasting life, and he that believeth not on the Son shall not see life; but the wrath of God abideth on him." John iii. 36. "He that believeth and is baptized shall be saved; but he that believeth not shall be damned." Matthew xvi. 16. "How shall we escape if we neglect so great salvation, which at the first began to be spoken by the Lord, and was confirmed unto us by them that heard him." Hebrews ii. 3. "But there were false prophets also among the people, even as there shall be false teachers among you, who privily shall bring in damnable heresies, even denying the Lord that bought them, and bring upon themselves swift destruction. And many shall follow their pernicious ways, by reason of whom the way of truth shall be evil spoken of .....These shall receive the reward of unrighteousness." 2 Peter ii. 1, 2, 13. "The fearful and unbelieving, and the abominable, and murderers, and whoremongers, and sorcerers, and idolators, and all liars, shall have their part in the lake which burneth with fire and brimstone. Revelation xxi. 8.

The prophetical testimony which is given to the Messiah, it will appear from the preceding passages, is ample and precise. They could easily be multiplied; but those which I have adduced are sufficient for the object for which I have brought them forward.

H.—SELECT LIST OF WORKS ON THE EVIDENCES OF CHRISTIANITY, AND COLLATERAL SUBJECTS, RECOMMENDED TO THE ATTENTION OF THE PA'RSI'S.

Addison. The Evidences of the Christian Religion. By Joseph Addison, Esq. Editor of the Spectator.

Alexander. Brief Outline of the Evidences of the Christian Religion. By Archibald Alexander, D.D., Princeton, America.

Beattie. Evidences of the Christian Religion; briefly and plainly stated. By James Beattie, LL.D., Professor of Moral Philosophy, Marischal College, Aberdeen.

——— Essay on the Nature and Immutability of Truth. By James Beattie, LL.D.

Benson. Two Courses of Hulsean Lectures. By the Rev. C. Benson, D.D.

Blunt. The Veracity of the Gospels and Acts, argued from the undesigned coincidences found in them. By the Rev. J. J. Blunt.

Bryant. Treatise upon the Authenticity of the Scriptures, and the Truth of the Christian Religion. By Jacob Bryant.

Butler. The Analogy of Religion, Natural and Revealed, to the Constitution and Course of Nature. By Bishop Butler.

Campbell. A Dissertation on Miracles. By George Campbell, D.D.

Carpenter. An Examination of Scripture Difficulties; elucidating nearly seven hundred passages of the Old and New Testament. By William Carpenter.

Cecil. Reasons for Repose. By the Rev. Richard Cecil.

Chalmers. On the Miraculous and Internal Evidences of the Christian Revelation and the Authority of its Records. By Thomas Chalmers, D.D., LL.D.

Clarke. The Truth and Certainty of the Christian Religion. By Samuel Clarke.

Collyer. Lectures on the Evidences of Christianity. By W. B. Collyer, LL.D.

Doddridge. The Evidences of Christianity briefly stated. By Philip Doddridge, D.D.

Douglas. The Criterion of Miracles. By Bishop Douglas.

Dwight. Lectures in Theology. By T. Dwight, D.D.

Edwards. History of Redemption. By Jonathan Edwards.

Ellis. The Knowledge of Divine Things from Revelation, not from Nature. By John Ellis.

Erskine. Remarks on the Internal Evidence for the truth of Revealed Religion. By Thomas Erskine, Esq., Advocate, Edinburgh.

Faber. The Difficulties of Infidelity. By the Rev. G. S. Faber, A.M.

Fuller. The Gospel its own Witness. By Andrew Fuller.

Gregory. Letters to a Friend on the Evidences, Doctrines, and Duties of the Christian Religion. By Olinthus Gregory, LL.D.

Grotius. The Truth of the Christian Religion, with Notes by LeClerc, translated by Clarke.

Haldane. The Evidence and Authority of Divine Revelation, being a view of the testimony of the Law and the Prophets to the Messiah, with the subsequent testimonies. By Robert Haldane, Esq.

Hales. Analyses of Chronology, History, &c. By William Hales.

Halyburton. Natural Religion Insufficient and Revelation Necessary. By Thomas Halyburton.

Hill. Lectures in Divinity. By Alex. Hill, D.D.

Horne. Introduction to the Critical Study and Knowledge of the Scriptures. By T. Hartwell Horne, A.M.

Horne. Letter to Adam Smith, on the Life, Death, and Philosophy of his friend David Hume. By Bishop Horne.

Hurd. An Introduction to the Study of the Prophecies, concerning the Christian Church; and, in particular, concerning the Church of Papal Rome. By Richard Hurd, D.D.

Inglis. A Vindication of the Christian Faith, addressed to those who believing in God, yet refuse or hesitate to believe in Jesus Christ whom he hath sent. By John Inglis, D.D.

Ireland. Paganism and Christianity compared. By John Ireland, D.D.

Jenyns. A View of the Internal Evidence of the Christian Religion. By Soame Jenyns.

Jortin. Discourses concerning the Truth of the Christian Religion. By John Jortin, D.D.

Keith. A Demonstration of the Truth of Christianity. By Alexander Keith, D.D.

Keith. Evidence of the Christian Religion derived from the literal Fulfilment of Prophecy. By A. Keith, D.D.

Lardner. The Credibility of the Gospel History. By Nathaniel Lardner, D.D.

Leland. View of the Principal Deistical Writers, By John Leland. D.D.

——— The Advantage and Necessity of the Christian Revelation, shewn from the state of Religion in the Ancient Heathen World: especially with respect to the knowledge and worship of the One True

God: A Rule of Moral Duty, and a State of Future Rewards and Punishments. By John Leland, D.D.

Lesslie. Short and Easy Method with the Deists, and the Truth of Christianity Demonstrated.* By Charles Lesslie.

Lyttleton. Observations on the Conversion and Apostleship of St. Paul. By George Lord Lyttleton.

Milner. Gibbon's Account of Christianity considered; together with some Strictures on Hume's Dialogues on Natural Religion. By the Rev. Joseph Milner, A.M.

Munter. Narrative of the Conversion and Death of Count Struensee, formerly Prime Minister of Denmark. By Dr. Munter. Translated from the German, by Wendsom.

Newton. Dissertations on the Prophecies which have been remarkably fulfilled, and at this time are fulfilling in the world. By Bishop Newton.

Paley. The Evidences of Christianity. By William Paley, D.D.

Pascal. Thoughts on Religion. By B. Pascal.

Porteus. The Evidences of the Christian Religion. By Bishop Porteus.

Scott. Essays on various Subjects, (the first). By Thomas Scott.

Smith. Answer to the Works of Robert Taylor. By J.P. Smith.

Sumner. The Evidence of Christianity, derived from its Nature and Reception. By Bishop Sumner.

Sumner. A Treatise on the Records of Creation. By Bishop Sumner.

Watson. Two Apologies, one for Christianity addressed to Edward Gibbon, Esq. the other, for the Bible, in answer to Thomas Paine. By Bishop Watson.

West. Observations on the History and Evidence of the Resurrection of Jesus Christ. By Gilbert West, Esq.

Wilson. The Evidences of Christianity stated in a popular and practical manner. By Daniel Wilson, D.D. Metropolitan of India.

I. — HISTORICAL LEGENDS OF PERSIA FROM KAYOMARS TO THE MUHAMMADAN CONQUEST.

ABRIDGED AND SLIGHTLY ALTERED FROM SIR WILLIAM JONES.

The Peshdádián Family.

*KAYOMARS**, (before CHRIST, 890,) founded the Persian empire, and fixed the seat of it in the province of *Azarbaiján.* He was opposed in his noble enterprizes by the inhabitants of the mountains and forests, who, like the wild *Tartars* and *Arabs*, dwelled in tents or caverns, and led a rambling life among rocks and in deserts. The rude appearance of these savages, compared with the more polished manners of those, who first

* كيومرث

began to be civilized, gave rise to *the fiction of Dæmons and Giants* among the *Persians*, who call them *Dews** and represent them as declared enemies to Man.

HOSHANG,† grandson of *Kayomars*, was, probably, contemporary with *Minos*, and, like him, was eminent for his justice and excellent laws, which gained him the surname of *Peshdád*,‡ or *The Legislator*, whence the first race of *Persian* Kings took the name of *Peshdádiáns*. He taught agriculture to his subjects, and made great improvoments in the art; he advised them to water their fields with artificial canals, a custom still frequent in *Persia*, where the soil is uncommonly dry. He also discovered, mines of iron in his kingdom, which metal he wrought into weapons, and tools for husbandry. He was the first, who bred dogs and leopards for hunting, and introduced the fashion of wearing the furs of wild beasts in winter. He is also said to have built the city of *Shustar* or *Susa*, to have extended the bounds of his empire, and to have penetrated as far as the coast of the *Indian* Sea.

TAHMURS,§ (B. C. 835) succeeded his father *Hoshang*; he built several cities in the two provinces of *Irak*, and among them *Babel* or Babylon, and *Nineveh*. He assigned the government of these cities, with large territories annexed to them, to his most illustrious ministers, who are known to us by the names of *Assyrian* and *Babylonian* monarchs, though, most probably, they paid homage to the sovereign lords of Irán.

This prince encouraged arts and manufactures, and particularly *the planting of rice, and the breeding of silk-worms*; he first used a complete suit of armour, and civilized many barbarous nations, whence he was called *Dewband*||, or, *The Tamer of Giants*.

JAMSHID ¶ (B. C. 809) finished the city of *Istakhar*, or, as the *Greeks* called it, *Persepolis*, which his uncle *Tahmurs* had begun, and the ruins of which are still shown, by the name of *Chahlminár*** or, *The Forty Pillars*. He introduced the use of the Solar Year among the *Persians*, and ordered the first day of it, called *Nauroz* ††, when the Sun enters the Ram, to be solemnized by a splendid festival. *Jamshid*, or *Jam*, for he is known by both names, was a wise and magnificent prince: he was the first, who instituted public baths, and encouraged his subjects to dive for pearls in the *Green Sea*, or *Persian Gulf*; he invented tents and pavilions, and discovered the use of lime in building: he built a strong bridge over the *Tigris*, which according to the *Asiatic* writers, was demolished by the *Greeks*. Yet this illustrious monarch was unfortunate in war: he was driven from his throne by *Zohák*, a native of *Arabia*, and spent the remainder of his life in travel. The queen, his wife, saved her son *Fari-*

* دیو † هوشنگ ‡ پیشداد

§ طهمورث || دیوبند ¶ جمشید

** چهل منار †† نوروز

dun from the usurper, and educated him in a distant retreat. The Persians say, that *musical instruments* were invented in the reign of *Jamshid*; and they add, that *Pythagoras* and *Thales* were his contemporaries.

*ZOHA'K**, (B. C. 780) the Usurper, was a detestable tyrant: his cruelty forced the Persians to revolt, and a general (blacksmith), named *Gáo*, having defeated him, drew the young *Faridun* from his retirement, and placed him upon the throne.

FARIDUN† (B. C. 750) is considered by the Persians as a model of every virtue: he gave the province of *Irak* or *Parthia* to his deliverer *Gáo*, as a principality for life; and having sent for the standard, which that officer used in his battle against *Zohak*, he adorned it with precious stones, and preserved it in his treasury.‡

Faridun, wishing to spend the last years of his life in a studious retirement, divided his vast dominions between his three sons: he allotted *Syria* and the western provinces to *Salm*, who was, perhaps, the *Salmanasser* of the *Jews*; he gave the country beyond the *Oxus* to *Túr*, whence the *Transoxan* regions were called *Turan*, and assigned the kingdom of *Khorásán* and all the heart of his empire to *Iraj*, his youngest son, whose share took the name of *Irán*, which it still retains. The two elder brothers thinking this division partial, made war against *Iraj*, and slew him in a cruel manner; they would even have dethroned *Faridun*, had not *Manuchahar*, son of *Iraj*, a youth of great hopes, led a powerful army against them, and avenged the death of his father. This division of the Persian empire into *Irán* and *Turán* has been a source of perpetual dissensions between the Persians and Tartars, as the latter have taken every opportunity of passing the Oxus, and laying waste the districts of *Khorásán*; they have even pushed their conquests so far, as to overturn the power of the *khalifs*, and afterwards to raise a mighty empire on the banks of the *Ganges*.

MANUCHAHAR § (B. C. 720) made great improvements in the government of *Persia*, and was the first who began to fortify his cities with ramparts and ditches. He was fond of improving gardens, and of cultivating curious plants. He was not fortunate in war, though his general and vazír, the son of *Nariman*, was the bravest hero of his age. In his reign the celebrated *Rustam* is said to have been born of *Rudaba*, an Indian princess, by Zálzer or *The golden-haired*, a youth of exquisite beauty

* ضحاک . † فریدون

‡ This Standard, which bore for many ages the name of *Gaváni*, کاوانی is said to have been brought into the field by the last king of the *Sassanian* race, when his army engaged the *Arabs* at *Cadessa*, in the year 636 of our era; but it was taken by *Saad*, *Omar's* general, who distributed the jewels, which adorned it, among his officers.

§ منوچهر

and eminent virtues: but, as *Rustam* was, certainly, a commander under Cyrus, he must, if we place him under *Manuchahar*, have lived above an hundred and fifty years; which is scarce credible, though such a fiction may be allowed in the poems of *Firdausi*.

*NUZAR** (B. C. 695.) son of *Manuchahar*, succeeded to the diadem, but not to the glory of his father. While his court was torn in pieces by a number of factions, *Afrasiáb*, King of *Turan*, a lineal descendant from *Tur*, son of *Faridun*, passed the *Oxus* with a formidable army, and, having defeated the *Persian* monarch, slew him with his own hand. This invader reigned twelve years in *Persia*, but was forced by *Zálzer*, or *The Prince with golden Hair*, to repass the *Oxus*, and return to his own dominions. It is more than probable, that *Afrasiáb* was a common name for the Kings of *Asiatic Tartary*, since the grandfather of *Cyrus*, whom we commonly call *Astyages*, bore the same name, and we cannot suppose him to have been the first invader of *Persia*†.

It was not long before the *Turanians* invaded *Iran* a second time, and, by forcing the great commanders of *Persia* to defend their own principalities, reduced the power of the *Persian* kings to a shadow. *Afrasiáb* either the monarch above-mentioned, or another of his name, is reckoned the ninth king of *Persia*.

ZAW ‡ was a prince of the Royal line, and was placed on the throne by *Zálzer*, but enjoyed only *the title of King*, as the *Turánián*s had overrun great part of his empire, and kept him in continual alarm. These are the *Scythians* of our Ancient Histories, who are said about this time to have invaded the kingdom of the *Medes*; but our best historians are apt to confound them with *the Scythians of the North*.

GARSHÁ'SP§, son of *Zaw*, or *KISHTÁ'SP*, as some writers call him, reigned but a few years, if it could be called reigning, to have the *name* of *king*, and to be more helpless than his subjects: he was the last prince of the *Peshdádiáns*.

The Kaiánian Family.

WHILE Zálzer, (B. C. 610.) the most powerful prince of *Persia*, was encamped in his province of *Saistan*, the Drangiana of the Greeks, *Afrasiáb*, who had subdued all *Media*, considered himself as Sovereign of the empire. By this time, another son of *Zaw*, named *Kobad*, began to distinguish himself in his engagements against the *Turanians*, and, being assisted by *Zálzer*, whose son *Rustam* was very young at this time, he was enabled to drive the invaders from *Irán*, and to place himself upon

* نوذر

† The family *Othman*, who now reign at *Constantinople*, are willing to be reputed descendants from this King of *Turan*, and are flattered with the Epithet of *Afra'sia'b Jah*, or افرا سیاب جاه *Powerful as Afrasiab*.

‡ زو   § گرشاسب

the throne of his ancestors. *Æschylus,* who flourished but an hundred years after this event, rightly attributes the recovery of the empire to this prince, whom he calls *a Mede, in his Tragedy of the Persians:* "The first Leader of the army, says he, was a *Mede*; the next, his son, completed (or rather promoted) this work, for wisdom guided his mind: the third was *Cyrus,* a fortunate man." It is evident that these three kings are *Kai Kobad* *, *Kai Kaus,* and *Kai Kosru* or *Khosru*; whom the Greeks call *Cyaxeres, Darius* the *Mede,* and *Cyrus.* The first syllable of *Cyaxeres* is apparently the *Kai* of the *Persians,* which signifies *a Great King,* and was prefixed to the names of those three princes, whence the whole race were named *Kaiánians.* The ancients tell us, that *Cyaxeres* slew the *Scythian* chiefs at a feast, to which he had invited them; but the *Easterns* are silent on this head, and it seems more probable, that the *Tartars* were compelled by force to repass the *Oxus;* our authors make them retire beyond *Cholcos* and *Iberia,* confounding, as usual, the *Oriental* with the *Northern* Scythians. *Kai Kobad* made several wise regulations in his kingdom, and ordered the public roads to be divided into *farsangs* or spaces of about four miles.

KAI KAUS † (B. C. 600.) is called by our writers *Darius the Mede,* and it may here be observed, that *Dara,* or *the Sovereign,* was rather an epithet than a proper name of the *Persian* Kings; so that the *Daricks,* or pieces of money, which were known at *Athens,* might have been coined by any *Persian* Monarch, and have born that name without the least impropriety. We must also remember, that the *Asiatic* princes *had several different names or titles,* which circumstance has been the source of great confusion in our histories of the East. The *Persian* writers mention nothing of the *Lydian* war; they only say, that *Kai Kaus carried his arms into the Lower Asia, and was very successful in his enterprize.* The *Turanians,* led by another *Afrásiáb,* invaded *Persia* a third time, and laid waste the province of Media. *Siavash,* son of Kai Káus, being unjustly accused by *Sudábá,* his father's concubine, of an attempt to violate her, went over to *Afràsiáb,* who received him with open arms, and gave him his daughter in marriage. This princess was called *Firenkis* by the *Persians,* and *Mandane* by the *Greeks,* who had a singular fondness for soft and melodious names, and neglected truth itself for a pleasing sound. A few months after her nuptials, *Siavash,* who deserved a longer life, was killed by a brother of *Afràsiáb,* and the princess, of whom *Khosru* was soon after born, was obliged to fly with her infant. The young *Khosru* was, some years after, seen by a Persian general, who guessed by his features that he was the son of *Siavash,* and, his conjecture being confirmed by the Princess his mother, he brought them both into *Persia,* where *Kai Káus* embraced his grandson with the highest joy imaginable, and, after a short interval, resigned his throne to him.

* کی قباد

† کي کاوس

*KAI KHOSRU**, or *CYRUS*, (B. C. 568.) whom the Persians consider almost as a demi-god, determined to avenge the death of his father, and to deliver his kingdom from the tyranny of *Afràsiáb*. He, therefore, assembled all his forces and gave battle to the usurper, who, on the other side, was supported by the kings of *Khatai* and *India*: but the valour of *Cyrus*, and of his general *Rustam*, prevailed against the united powers of so many sovereigns, and Afrásiáb lost his life in the mountains of *Media*. This war is celebrated in a noble poem, by the illustrious *Firdausi*, who may well be called the *Homer* of *Persia*.

LOHORA'SP † (B. C. 530) was placed on the throne before the death of *Cyrus*, who lived some years after his resignation. One would think at first, that he was the *Cambyses* of the *Greeks*; but nothing can be more different than the characters of *Cambyses* and of *Lohorásp*, the first being described as a cruel tyrant, the second as a virtuous and amiable prince. He had a general named *Gudarz*‡, who, according to the Oriental writers, pushed his conquests very far into the west.

GUSHTA'SP§, (B. C. 500) whom the Greeks call *Darius*, the son of *Hystaspes*, transferred the seat of empire from Balkh in *Khorásán* to *Istakhar*, for which reason he was better known to the *European* than *Lohoràsp*, who led a retired life in the most eastern province of his kingdom. In his reign *Zardusht* or *Zarátusht*, whom we know by the name of *Zoroaster*, is said to have published his moral work, which inculcated the doctrine of *two principles*, and recommended the worship of the good principle under the allegory of *Light*, which he opposed to the bad, whose emblem was *Darkness*. The king was much inclined to this doctrine, and raised a number of temples to *the Sun*, *the fountain of Light*; which the people, as usual, conceiving in a gross and literal sense, began to adore, the effect instead of the cause, and the figure instead of the archetype: the priests took the hint, and *the Sun* or *Mithra*, became really to them, as our alchymists absurdly consider it, *a powerful elixir, which transformed their base metals into gold*. The chief of *Zaratusht's* scholars was *Jámásp*||, who is said to have published a strange work upon Astrology.

ARDESHIR,¶ or *BAHAMAN*, surnamed *Dirázdast***, or *The Long-handed*, (B. C. 464.) is no doubt, the *Artaxerxes* of the *Greeks* who called him *Makrokheir*, a name literally translated from the *Persian*, and implying only a very extensive power.

HOMAI††, a name which signifies *The Bird of Paradise*, was the

* کي خسرو کيخسرو † لهراسب ‡ کودرز

§ کشتاسب || In Persian جاماسب

¶ ارد شير *Ardeshir* signifies in Persian *a strong lion*.

** درازدست †† هماي

daughter of *Ardeshir*, and sat on the throne during the infancy of her son *Dáráb*. She raised a sumptuous palace in the city of *Istakhar*, some pillars of which remain to this day; she built also a city called *Samram*, whence the learned M. *d'Herbelot* supposes her to be *Semiramis*; but our chronologers place the reign of that princess three hundred years earlier.

DA'RA'B, or *D'A'RA'**, whom the *Greeks* call *The Bastard*, succeeded to *Homai* (B. C. 424.) Here the *Persian* histories begin to be full of absurd fables, for we may suppose that the records of these times were lost or neglected during the *Grecian* wars. The Eastern writers tell a story of *Dáráb*, which has quite the air of a romance; "that he was exposed by his mother, like the *Hebrew* Lawgiver, on a river, which by its rapid current carried him to the habitation of a dyer who knew him to be a child of high birth by the trinkets, which adorned his cradle; that he was educated by this honest man, who sent him to the wars, where he distinguished himself in fighting against the *Greeks*; that, being introduced to the queen as a brave youth, she knew him by the jewels which he wore, and which his reputed father had restored to him." So far we may indulge these writers in the liberty of embellishing their Chronicles with lively tales; but we cannot so easily excuse them, when they make *Alexander*, the son of *Da'ra'b*, and tell us of a daughter of *Philip*, whom the king of *Persia* married, but sent back to *Macedon* after his nuptials, because he found her less agreeable than he supposed her to be. These are stories, which would be unworthy of *The Thousand and one Days*.

There seems in this place to be a chasm of many years in the annals of the *Persians*; for they say nothing of *Ardeshir*, son of *Da'ra'*, by *Parizádah*, or *Parysatis*†, whose brother *Cyrus* led the *Greeks* to *Babylon* in that memorable expedition which *Xenophon* so elegantly relates; nor of the third *Ardeshir*, whom our historians call *Ochus*; nor of *Arogus*, whose true name it has not been in my power to discover. Now if we suppose, as we reasonably may, that these three kings reigned about twenty-one years each, we shall bring the reign of *Dàra'* the younger to the year 337 before Christ, which will agree tolerably well with the chronologers both of *Asia* and *Europe*.

DA'RA' the younger is better known to *us*, than *to the natives of Persia*; we may, however, be deceived in his character, for we represent him as a mild and benevolent prince, while they assert that he was severe, cruel, and implacable. The *Persians* cannot comprehend the motives that induced *Alexander* to invade the dominions of *Dàrà*; and they assign a number of ridiculous reasons for it, which are too absurd to be related: in many points, however, they agree with our historians. The success of *Alexan-*

* داراب دارا

† پریزاده 'born of an Angel, or *Fairy*.

der, and the battle of *Arbel* *, or *Arbela*, are too well known to need any further description. *Dara* was assassinated about *three hundred and thirty years* before our epoch, and the monarchy of the *Kaianians* was transferred to the *Greeks*.

How long the *Greeks* were able to hold the *Persian* empire in their own hands, or whether they ever intended to exclude the princes of *Persia* from all share in the government, are points not easy to be settled with any certainty; but, if we suppose that *the fifteen kings of the Ashkanians*, who reigned before the birth of *Christ*, sat on the throne twenty years each one with another, we shall place the rise of that family three hundred years before our epoch; which calculation will not seem much amiss, if we believe, what the *Persians* assure us, that the successors of *Alexander* reserved for themselves only *Irak* or *Parthia* and *Persia*, properly so called, but *resigned the more Eastern provinces to the princes of the royal family*; while the descendants of *Seleucus* reigned in *Syria*. The founder of this race was *Ashak* or *Arshak*,† whom the *Greeks* call *Arsaces*: his successors, who were styled *Kings of Parthia* by our historians, reigned till about two hundred years after *Christ*, and are famous for nothing but *their wars against the Romans*, in which they were always valiant, and often successful. The last prince of the *Ashkanians*, or *Parthians*, was *Ardaván* ‡ known to us by the name of *Artabanus*, against whom *Ardeshir* revolted, and transferred the empire to the *Sassanians*.

The Sassanian Family.

ARDESHIR BABEGAN§, A. D. 202. whom our writers call *Artaxares*, was the son of *Sassan*, a man originally in a low station of life, but descended from a son of *Ardeshir the Long-handed*, who was disinherited in favour of *Homái*. He was surnamed *Bábegán* from *Bábeg* his grandfather, who was a *Persian* prince of eminent rank, and was so pleased with the amiable qualities of *Sassan*, his shepherd, that he gave him his daughter in marriage. *Ardeshir* was bold and warlike, yet a wise and learned prince, and is said to have composed two excellent books, the first, a *Kárnámah*‖, or *a Commentary of his life and actions*; the second, a moral work, of which *Naushirván the Great*, some ages after, published a second edition. These were employments truly worthy of great Princes; but the Kings of *Europe* have not written many *Kárnámahs*, nor given many *lessons of morality*.

SHAPUR¶, son of *Ardeshir*, whom we call *Sapores*, built many cities in *Persia*, and rebuilt that of *Nishápur***, which the *Macedonians* had de-

* In *Persian* اربل Lat. 35° Long, 77° 20′.

† اشک ‡ اردوان § اردشیر بابگان

‖ کارنامه ¶ شاپور ** نیشا پور

stroyed. This Prince was very successful in his wars against the *Roman* emperors: he reduced all *Syria* and *Cilicia*, and took *Valerian* prisoner, but was checked in his career by the more fortunate arms of *Odenatus*. In his reign *Máni* *, a Painter, having learned by the conversation of some Christians, *that the Redeemer had promised to send a Comforter after him*, formed the wild design of passing for the *Paraclete*; and, as no opinions are so absurd, which many will not embrace, he soon drew together a multitude of proselytes. *Shápur* was enraged at this imposture, and wished to punish the author of it; but *Mani* found means to escape, and fled into *Eastern Tartary*, as far as the borders of *China*, having first told his followers, that he was going to heaven, and promised to meet them in a certain grot, at the end of the year. In his retreat he amused himself with painting a number of strange figures and views, which, at the year's end, he shewed to his disciples, as a work given to him by angels: he was a very ingenious artist, and had a lively fancy, so that his pictures which were finely coloured, easily persuaded the credulous multitude, in the infancy of the art in *Asia*, that they were really divine; they were bound together, in a book called *Artang*†, which is often alluded to by the *Persian* poets, one of whom, addressing himself to a great painter, says, *The point of thy pencil draws a line over the leaves of Artang*, that is *effaces them* ‡. *Mani*, by a whimsical mixture, blended in his doctrine the Metempsychosis of *Brahma* and *Vishnu* §, and the *two Principles* of *Zaratusht*, together with several tenets of the *Gospel*; yet this motley religion, ridiculous as it may seem, was followed even by bishops and patriarchs. Our writers call the professors of this sect *Manicheans*, but they should, by analogy, be called *Manians*. The impostor was put to death in the reign of *Baharám*, grandson of *Shapur*: had he been, like *Muhammad*, a successful warrior, instead of an obscure artist, his religion would, perhaps, have been spread over all *Asia*; for it was the miraculous privilege of *the true faith* alone, to make its way, in defiance of persecution, by the force of its indisputable truth, and the sanctity of its precepts.

HORMAZD‖, or *Hormizdas*, as our historians call him, had the advantage of a graceful person, and an agreeable air; but he was neither active nor warlike. He was much addicted to study, and strongly inclined to favour *Mani*, whom his son, as it was said above, afterwards destroyed.

BAHARAM,¶ son of *Hormazd*, after the death of *Mani*, led a peaceful and studious life. He was surnamed *The Beneficent*, and used to say, that *Good-nature and Benevolence could not be defined separately, because they were the aggregate of all Virtues*. His adopted son, who succeeded

* ماني

† ارتنگ or ارژنگ

‡ زنوک کلک تو در خط صحیفهٔ ارژنگ *Kemal Isfabani*

§ برهمه and بشنو

‖ هرمزد

¶ بهرام

him, paid little regard to this maxim, and his violence procured him the name of *Khálef*, or *The Unjust** ; but it is said that he changed his temper and conduct upon the remonstrances of his nobles.

There was nothing memorable in the reign of his successor *Narsi*†, whom we call *Narses : Hormazd* II. his son, was a just and magnificent prince; he raised *a Court of Judicature* in his metropolis, in which he sometimes presided in person; and he built, it is thought, the city of *Hormaz* in *Carmania*, the name of which was afterwards given to the island in the *Persian* Gulf, which our travellers call *Ormus*.

SHAPUR, whom the *Arabians* name *DHU LACTAF*‡, or *The Round-Shouldered*, was taken prisoner by the *Greek* Emperor, and, during his captivity, many of his finest provinces were laid waste; but having recovered his liberty by the help of the Emperor's mistress, he returned to *Azarbáiján*, where he made himself known to his people, and soon after totally defeated the *Greeks:* in memory of this action he built the city of *Kazvin* §, which, for its singular beauty, was also named *Jamálábád*.‖ His grandson *Bahrám* had but a short reign, which was disturbed by frequent rebellions. It was usual for the *Persian* kings to give their sons some considerable government with the title of *Shah* ; that of *Carmania* was allotted to *Bahrám*, who assumed, in consequence of it, the surname of *Karmánsháh*¶, which our writers have corrupted into *Carmasat*.

The reign of his son *Yazdejard* had nothing in it, that deserves to be related.

BAHRAM the Fourth**, or the sixth, (A. D.351,) as some authors reckon him, was educated in *Arabia*, and had some difficulty to recover the throne of *Persia*, which the nobles of his father's court had, in his absence, given to a prince named *Kasri*. His favourite prey was a beast called *Gur*, which seems to be the *Onagros*, or, *Wild Ass* ; and it is said that he was killed in a chase. The word *Gur*, which signifies *a tomb*, as well as *a wild ass*, gave occasion to a pun of some *Persian* wit, which circulated after *Bahrám*'s death : *See*, says he, *how* Bahrám, *who chased the* Gúr, *or* wild ass *all his life, was at length chased and taken by* Gúr, *or* the tomb.

The successor of *Bahrám* was *Yazdejard* II. a wise and resolute prince, whose soldiers were so fond of him, that they gave him the surname of *Sipáhdóst*, or, *Beloved by the army*. He left his throne to his younger son *Hormuz*, surnamed *Firzánah*††, or, *The Prudent*; but that prince was dethroned, in less than a year, by his elder brother *Firuz*.

* خالف † نرسي ‡ In *Arabic* ذو الاكتاف

§ قزوين ‖ جمال اباد *The Region of Beauty.*

¶ كرمانشاه ** بهرام گور †† فرزانه

*FIRUZ**, having deposed his brother by the help of *Khosnavaz*, a king of the *Indoscythians*, soon forgot his obligation to him, and turned his arms against his protector; but he was constantly defeated by that prince, and was at last obliged to conclude a dishonourable peace. The people whom the *Greeks* call *Indoscythians*, and the *Persians Haiatelis*, inhabited the mountains between *Kandahar* and *India*, and were, perhaps, nearly the same with the *Afghans*, who ruined the *Persian* monarchy in the present age (i. e. last century).

Belash and *Cobad* succeeded *Firúz*; the second of them was the father of *Naushervan the Great*, before whom *Jamasp*, or, as we call him, *Zamaspes*, reigned one year.

NAUSHERWAN†, better known in *Europe* by the name of *Cosroes*, reigned till near the close of the sixth century; he was a prince of eminent virtues, fortunate in war, and illustrious in peace.

KHOSRU PARVIZ ‡ was a magnificent and amiable monarch: he fought against the *Greek* emperors with great success, but was at length defeated by *Heraclius*. He is said to have married a daughter of the Emperor *Maurice*, named *Irene*: the *Persians* call this princess *Shírín*, or *Sweet*, and the progress of her love for *Parviz* furnished *Nezami*, and other poets, with the subject of an entertaining romance; they tell us that a certain statuary, named *Farhád*, was in love with the same lady, and pierced through the heart of a large mountain, either to gratify his mistress, or to employ his melancholy hours. There is an elegant couplet of *Jami* on this celebrated beauty and her lovers: *When* Shírín, says he, *opened her lips, that shed sweetness around, she stole the heart of* Parviz, *and the soul of* Farhád.

لب شیرین بشکر ریز بکشاد
دل از پرویز برد وجان ز فرهاد

Parviz, if we believe the Easterns, was a lover of music, and a patron of those who professed that art.

After the death of *Parviz*, A. D. 628, the empire began to decline: the five Princes, and the two Queens who succeeded to *Shirúieh*, or *Siroes*, *as they were eminent neither in peace nor in war*, are not worthy of a place in history.

The *Arabs*, under the command of *Omar*, were perpetually making inroads upon the *Persian* empire, and finally overthrew it by the defeat of *YAZDEJARD*§, who was killed *in the middle of the seventh century*; and by his death the famliy of *Sassan* became extinct.||

* فیروز † نوشیروان ‡ خسرو پرویز

§ یزد جرد

|| The subsequent history of the Zoroastrians may be briefly told. Such of them as did not succumb to the Muhammadan religion, are said to have

retreated to the deserts, or the mountains of Khorásán. Several scores of years after this retreat, a considerable emigration of the Pársis took place. Those who preferred exile to slavery proceeded, in the first instance, to the island of Hormuz, where they remained fifteen years. The island of Diva was subsequently their resting-place, and abode for nineteen years. They landed at Sanján in Gujarát, in the circumstances mentioned in other parts of this work, about A. D. 717.

The settlement of the Pársís at Sanján, is said to have remained in a consolidated state for about three hundred years, at the expiry of which it sent forth some colonists to Khambháyat, Baroch, Akaleshwar, Variáo, Nausárí, and other places to the northward. Its history is a complete blank, from this date, till the attempt made against the part of the country in which it is situated, by Sultan Mahmud Begada, about the year 1507, when it greatly aided the Hindú prince in his defence, and consequently suffered much from the troops of the Muhammadans. At this time, the sacred fire was carried into the jungles of Wasandá, and when the danger was past, it was removed to Nausárí, at the expense of two opulent Zoroastrians.

The Pársis in Western India now amount to about 50,000 souls. Of these, according to a census made about five years ago, 20,184 are resident in Bombay. In the collectorate of the Northern Konkan there are 1451. There are about 200 in Daman. About fifteen years ago, 10,507 dwelt in the town of Surat; but the number there is now understood to be very considerably reduced. Most of the remainder, are to be found in the northern, and southern parts of the Surat collectorate, and particularly in Baroch, * and its neighbourhood, and Balsár and Nausárí. There are some in the Ahmadábád collectorate, and a few families at most of the different military stations, both in the Company's territories in the Bombay Presidency, and in those of the native princes. A few adventurers are more widely scattered. Though not a numerous body, the Pársís of India have great influence wherever they reside.

The Pársís of Persia are to be found chiefly at Karmán and Yazd. Their numbers there may be stated at from ten to twenty thousand. W.

* The Parsi population of Baroch, amounted, in 1834, to 2063, according to a table presented to me by Mr. Kirkland.

J.—COMPARISON OF THE ZAND, WITH THE PERSIAN, PAHLIVI, DEVA-NAGARI AND GUJARATI, ALPHABETS.

Gujarátí	Nágarí	Persian	Pahliví	Roman	Zand
અ	अ	ا	[illegible]	a	𐬀
આ	आ	آ	[illegible]	á	𐬁
	इ			i	𐬌
ઈ	ई	ي	[illegible]	í	𐬍
	उ			u	𐬎 *or* 𐬎
ઊ	ऊ	و	[illegible]	ú	𐬏
		*		e	𐬈
એ	ए	ِ		é	𐬉
				ê	𐬆
		†		ŏ	𐬊
ઓ	ओ	او		ó	𐬋
				âo	𐬃
આં	आं	آن	[illegible]	ã	𐬄
ક	क	ک	[illegible]	k	𐬐
ખ	ख	خ ‡	[illegible]	kh̠	𐬑
	´		[illegible]	q *or* kh̠	𐬓
ગ	ग	گ	[illegible]	g	𐬔
ઘ	घ		[illegible]	gh̠	𐬖
ઙ	ङ			ng, g̃	𐬢
ચ	च	چ	[illegible]	ch	𐬗

* As an initial this sound seldom occurs in Persian or Arabic. It is exemplified in به *beh* or *bah* good.

† Exemplified in دختر *dokhtar*, daughter.

‡ Sound somewhat modified.

Gujarátí	Nágarí	Persian	Pahliví	Roman	Zand
જ	ज	ج	𐬘	j	𐬘
		ز	𐬰	z	𐬰
*		ژ		zh	𐬲
ણ	ण			ñ	𐬦
ત	त	ت	𐬙	t	𐬙
†		ط		ṭ	𐬝
થ	थ	ث ‡		th	𐬚
દ	द	د	[illegible] *or* 𐬙§	d	𐬛
ધ	ध	ذ ‡		dh	𐬜
ન	न	ن	𐬥	n	𐬥
પ	प	پ	𐬞	p	𐬞
		ف	𐬞	f	𐬟
બ	ब	ب	𐬠	b	𐬠
મ	म	م	𐬨	m	𐬨
	य	ي	𐬫	y *init.*	𐬫
	य	ي ¶		y *med.*	𐬌𐬌
ર	र	ر	𐬭	r	𐬭
લ	ल	ل	𐬭	l	-

* Here the Dasturs use the Gujarátí જ *j*, which does not, however, correspond with the sound of the Zand 𐬰 z.

† The Dasturs here always use the 𐬝 ; but the appearance of the letter, as well as the grammar, shows that the Zand letter is merely the final form of the preceding *t*. Rask considers it equivalent to the Arabic ط or the Hebrew ט.

‡ Approximation.

§ This is evidently the *t*.

¶ When considered a consonant.

Gujarátí	Nágarí	Persian	Pahliví	Roman	Zand
વ	व	و	[illegible]	v *init*	[illegible]
વ	व			v *med.*	»
વ		و *	[illegible]	w	[illegible]
શ	श			ç	[illegible]
શ	स	س	[illegible]	s	[illegible]
શ	ष	ش	[illegible] †	sh	[illegible]
હ	ह	ه	[illegible]	h	[illegible]
અહ	अह			ah	[illegible]
શ્ક	स्क			sk	[illegible]
શ્ત	स्त			st	[illegible]
હ્મ	ह्म			hm	[illegible]

* Quiescent, preceded by a heterogeneous vowel, or when it opens upon a vowel.

† The three dots of the Persian letter are generally used abo[illegible]his sign.

This table has been formed after a comparison of the researches of Rask, Burnouf, and Bopp, with the transferences observed in the Pársí MSS. in my own possessions.

For the letters which are wanting in the Gujarátí, the Dasturs use those with proximate sounds.

Some of the Pahliví forms of the letters are not here given, it not having been found necessary at present, to add to the complete fount of the Zand more than the Pahliví forms which essentially differ from the Zand.

Pahliví groups of letters in use are [illegible] *an*, [illegible] *ai*, [illegible] hú *or* khú.

INDEX.

INDEX.

B.

C.

G.

H.

I.

P.

*** The author of this work is extremely sorry, that, owing to his departure from India, at the time of its appearance, he has been unable to reperuse it with a view to the preparation of a table of errata. He hopes, however, that no serious inconvenience will arise from this omission. The work, it must be borne in mind, has been put in type by natives possessed of an extremely limited acquaintance with English, and who have consequently greatly multiplied the demands of editorial labour.

The Zand » *v*, it will be observed, is sometimes, erroneously rendered by 6.